THE OXFORD HANDBOOK OF

PERSONNEL

PSYCHOLOGY

THE OXFORD HANDBOOK OF

PERSONNEL PSYCHOLOGY

Edited by

SUSAN CARTWRIGHT

and

CARY L. COOPER

OXFORD
UNIVERSITY PRESS

OXFORD

UNIVERSITY PRESS

Great Clarendon Street, Oxford OX2 6DP
United Kingdom

Oxford University Press is a department of the University of Oxford.
It furthers the University's objective of excellence in research, scholarship,
and education by publishing worldwide. Oxford is a registered trade mark of
Oxford University Press in the UK and in certain other countries

First published 2008
First published in paperback 2012
Reprinted 2013

British Library Cataloguing in Publication Data
Data available

Library of Congress Cataloging in Publication Data
Data available

ISBN 978-0-19-965581-6

Contents

PART VI   FUTURE CHALLENGES   543

LIST OF FIGURES

LIST OF TABLES

About the Editors

Susan Cartwright is a Chartered Psychologist, a Fellow of the British Psychological Society, and an Academician of the Academy of Social Sciences. She is currently Professor of Organizational Psychology and Well-Being and the Director of the Centre for Organizational Health and Well-Being at Lancaster University. Susan is also a Fellow and Past President of the British Academy of Management. She is a past editor of the *Leadership and Organization Development Journal* and former Associate Editor of the *British Journal of Management*. Susan has authored fourteen books, over forty-five scholarly articles, and thirty-two book chapters.

Cary L. Cooper, CBE, is Distinguished Professor of Organizational Psychology and Health at Lancaster University Management School. He is also Chair of the Academy of Social Sciences, President of the British Association of Counselling and Psychotherapy, and President of RELATE. Cary was founding Editor of the *Journal of Organizational Behavior* and is currently Editor of *Stress and Health*. In 2001 he was awarded the CBE by the Queen for his contribution to organizational health. He is the author of over 150 books on occupational stress, well-being, engagement, and organizational psychology, and has written over 400 scholarly articles.

List of Contributors

Neal M. Ashkanasy, UQ Business School, University of Queensland, Brisbane, Queensland 4072, Australia

Carolyn Axtell, Institute of Work Psychology, University of Sheffield, Sheffield S10 2TN, UK

Dave Bartram, SHL Group Ltd., The Pavilion, 1 Atwell Place, Thames Ditton, Surrey KT7 0NE, UK

Melinda Blackman, Department of Psychology, California State University, Fullerton, California CA 92834–9480, USA

Kevin Daniels, Loughborough Business School, Loughborough, Leicestershire LE11 3TU, UK

Catherine S. Daus, Psychology Department, Southern Illinois University at Edwardsville, Edwardsville, IL 62026–1121, USA

Liesbet De Koster, Ghent University, Henri Dunantlaan 2, 9000 Ghent, Belgium

Silvia Della Russo, University of Rome, Italy

Iain L. Densten, Department of Management and Security, Cranfield University, Defence Academy of the United Kingdom, Shrivenham, Swindon, SN6 8LA, UK

Staale Einarsen, Department of Psychological Sciences, University of Bergen, Christiesgt 12, N-5015 Bergen, Norway

Arne Evers, Work and Organizational Psychology Group, University of Amsterdam, Roetersstraat 15, 1018 WB Amsterdam, The Netherlands

Jessica Fandre, Department of Psychology, Michigan State University, East Lansing, MI 48824–1116, USA

J. Kevin Ford, Department of Psychology, Michigan State University, East Lansing, MI 48824–1117, USA

Lori Francis, St. Mary's University, Halifax, Nova Scotia B3H 3C3, Canada

Michael Frese, Department of Work Psychology, Geissen University, Fachbereich 06 Psychologie, Otto-Behaghel-Strasse 10/F, D-35394 Giessen, Germany

Yitzhak Fried, Whitman School of Management, Syracuse University, Syracuse, NY 13244, USA

Adrian Furnham, Department of Psychology, University College London, 26 Bedford Way, London WC1H 0AP, UK

Laura M. Graves, Graduate School of Management, Clark University, 950 Main Street, Worcester, MA 01610, USA

Barbara Griffin, University of Western Sydney, Parramatta North Campus, Locked Bag 1797, Penrith South DC New South Wales 1797, Australia

Lars Johan Hauge, Department of Psychological Sciences, University of Bergen, Christiesgt 12, N-5015 Bergen, Norway

C. Gail Hepburn, University of Lethbridge, Lethbridge, Alberta, Canada

Beryl Hesketh, College of Health and Science, University of Western Sydney, New South Wales 2006, Australia

Sarah A. Hezlett, Personnel Decisions Research Institutes, 650 Third Avenue South, Suite 1350, Minneapolis, MN SS4 02, USA

Donald Hislop, Business School, Loughborough University, Leicestershire LE11 3TU, UK

Kerr Inkson, University of Waikato, Private Bag 3105, Hamilton 3240, New Zealand

Jeff W. Johnson, Personnel Decisions Research Institutes, 650 Third Avenue South, Suite 1350, Minneapolis, MN SS4 02, USA

Peter J. Jordan, Griffith Business School, Nathan, Queensland 4111, Australia

E. Kevin Kelloway, St Mary's University, Halifax, Nova Scotia B3H 3C3, Canada

Gary P. Latham, University of Toronto, 105 St George Street, Toronto, Ontario M5S 3E6, Canada

Gregory Laurence, Whitman School of Management, Syracuse University, Syracuse, NY 13244, USA

Ariel S. Levi, School of Business, Wayne State University, Detroit, MI 48202, USA

Suzan Lewis, Middlesex University Business School, Hendon Campus, The Burroughs, Hendon, London NW4 4BT, UK

Filip Lievens, Department of Personnel Management, Work and Organizational Psychology, Ghent University, Henri Dunantlaan 2, 9000 Ghent, Belgium

Stig Berge Matthiesen, Department of Psychological Sciences, University of Bergen, Christiesgt 12, N-5015 Bergen, Norway

Kevin R. Murphy, Department of Psychology, Pennsylvania State University, 417 Moore Building, University Park, Pennsylvania, PA 16802, USA

Gary N. Powell, School of Business, University of Connecticut, 2100 Hillside Road, Unit 1041, Storrs, CT 06269–1041, USA

Andreas Rauch, RSM Erasmus University Rotterdam, Burg. Oudlaan 50, 3062 PA Rotterdam, The Netherlands

Ann Marie Ryan, Department of Psychology, Michigan State University, East Lansing, MI 48824–1117, USA

Ian Roper, Middlesex University Business School, Hendon Campus, The Burroughs Hendon, London NW4 4BT, UK

Neal Schmitt, Department of Psychology, Michigan State University, 316 Psychology Building, East Lansing, MI 48824–1116, USA

Eveline Schollaert, Ghent University, Henri Dunantlaan 2, 9000 Ghent, Belgium

Ruchi Sinha, Department of Psychology, Michigan State University, East Lansing, MI 48824–1117, USA

Peter B. Smith, Department of Psychology, University of Sussex, Falmer BN1 9QG, UK

Olga F. Voskuijl, Work and Organizational Psychology Group, University of Amsterdam, Roetersstraat 15, 1018 WB Amsterdam, The Netherlands

Jennifer Wessel, Department of Psychology, Michigan Sate University, East Lansing, MI 48824–1117, USA

Stephen A. Woods, Aston Business School, Aston University, Birmingham B4 7ET, UK

INTRODUCTION

SUSAN CARTWRIGHT
CARY L. COOPER

FOR most organizations, human resource costs continue to be the single largest operating cost, accounting for between 50 and 80 percent of annual expenditure (Saratoga Institute 1994; Becker and Gerhart 1996). The term "human capital" is used to describe people within an organization and the value they create (Rodgers 2003). Whilst the debate as to the most effective way to measure human capital continues to capture the interest of both academics and practitioners (Sparrow and West 2002), there is a shared belief that individual employee performance contributes to organizational outcomes (Huselid 1995). Consequently, achieving optional performance from individual employees is of paramount importance to the sustained growth development and financial performance of any organization.

The field of Personnel Psychology is broadly concerned with the study of individual differences and their consequences for the organization. It is about providing a comprehensive understanding of a range of factors which influence and enhance individual performance.

The purpose of this volume is to bring together the contributions of leading international scholars within the field to present state-of-the-art reviews on topical and emergent issues, constructs, and research in personnel psychology.

The book is divided into six parts. We begin the volume by exploring (Part I) individual differences and work performance. The sources of individual differences covered in this part include traditional topics such as IQ, cognitive abilities, personality and leadership, as well as the emergent and more controversial topic of emotional intelligence.

The following part (Part II) is concerned with the extent to which organizations can improve their effectiveness through the process of personnel selection. The chapters within this part consider a range of topics from job analysis and competency modeling, the validity of selection procedures, the effective interview, and the practice of assessment centers. In addition, the part includes a chapter debating the advantages and disadvantages of on-line testing.

The effectiveness of any personnel selection system is dependent upon the reliability and validity of any tests and structured assessments used to inform selection decisions. Therefore, the focus of the following part (Part III) is on methodological issues. The first three chapters in this part consider models for evaluating the reliability and validity of measures, recent advances in the evaluation of training, and the relationship between job attitudes and job performance. The fourth and final chapter in this part challenges and debates the extent to which personnel practices honed in monocultural setting can be applied to a more diverse workforce.

The chapters in the next part (Part IV) consider topics relating to training and development. Policies and practices then form the focus of the following part (Part V). This part includes traditional topics such as discrimination and fairness as well as emergent issues like workplace bullying.

Finally, we close with a part devoted to examining changes in the work environment and the future challenges in the new world of work.

In total, the book is composed of twenty-four chapters compiled by forty-three contributors from ten different countries. We are most grateful for their contribution. In addition, we would like to thank Cath Hearne and Gerry Wood for their help and efforts in putting the volume together, as well as the production team at Oxford University Press.

Susan Cartwright
Cary L. Cooper

References

BECKER, B., and GERHART, B. 1996. The impact of Human Resource Management on organizational performance: progress and prospects. *Academy of Management Journal*, 39 (4): 779–801.

HUSELID, M. A. 1995. The impact of Human Resource Management practices on turnover, productivity and corporate financial performance. *Academy of Management Journal*, 38 (3): 635–72.

RODGERS, W. 2003. Measurement and reporting of knowledge-based assets. *Journal of Intellectual Capital*, 4 (2): 181–90.

SARATOGA INSTITUTE. 1994. *1993 Human Resource Effectiveness Reports.* Saratoga, CA: Saratoga Institute.

SPARROW, P., and WEST, M. 2002. Psychology and organizational effectiveness. In *Organizational Effectiveness: The Role of Psychology,* ed. D. Bartram, I. T. Robertson, and M. Callinan. Chichester: John Wiley.

PART I

INDIVIDUAL DIFFERENCES AND WORK PERFORMANCE

INTELLIGENCE AND COGNITIVE ABILITIES AT WORK

ADRIAN FURNHAM

1. INTRODUCTION

THE definition, measurement, and validation of intelligence tests remain, at least among lay people, among the most controversial subjects in psychology. University lecturers have been sacked and suspended for stating their views on the subject. Among themselves, however, there is surprisingly little dispute, as can be witnessed when fifty of the world's experts responded to the *Bell Curve* Controversy (Herrnstein and Murray 1994) by writing the *Wall Street Journal* stating what they agreed upon regarding issues like the meaning and measurement of intelligence, group differences, and the like.

As an example of their work they made five points under the heading of Practical Importance. Their points were as followed:

- IQ is strongly related, probably more so than any other single measurable human trait, to many important educational, occupational, economic and social outcomes. Its relation to the welfare and performance of individuals is very strong in some arenas in life (education, military training), moderate but robust in others (social competence), and modest but consistent in others (law-abidingness). Whatever IQ tests measure, it is of great practical and social importance.

- A high IQ is an advantage in life because virtually all activities require some reasoning and decision making. Conversely, a low IQ is often a disadvantage, especially in disorganized environments. Of course, a high IQ no more guarantees success than a low IQ guarantees failure in life. There are many exceptions, but the odds for success in our society greatly favour individuals with higher IQs.
- The practical advantages of having a higher IQ increase as life settings become more complex (novel, ambiguous, changing, unpredictable or multifaceted). For example, a high IQ is generally necessary to perform well in highly complex or fluid jobs (the professions, management); it is a considerable advantage in moderately complex jobs (crafts, clerical and police work); but it provides less advantage in settings that require only routine decision-making or simple problem solving (unskilled work).
- Differences in intelligence certainly are not the only factor affecting performance in education, training and highly complex jobs (no one claims they are), but intelligence is often the most important. When individuals have already been selected for high (or low) intelligence and so do not differ as much in IQ, as in graduate school (or special education), other influences on performance loom larger in comparison.
- Certain personality traits, special talents, aptitudes, physical capabilities, experience and the like are important (sometimes essential) for successful performance in many jobs, but they have narrower (or unknown) applicability or "transferability" across tasks and settings compared with general intelligence. Some scholars choose to refer to these other human traits as other "intelligences".

Since the turn of the millennium there have been some excellent reviews on the subject of intelligence at work. Better and bigger data sets, sophisticated multi-variate statistics, and theory-driven research questions have meant there are now enough good studies on cognitive ability predictors of work-related behavior to do meta-analysis. The "bottom line" conclusion for many of those working in the field is essentially this: for complex, senior management level jobs in particular, intelligence is the single best individual difference predictor of work success however that is measured. Below are three quotes from those leading researchers in reviews:

There is abundant evidence that general cognitive ability is highly relevant in a wide range of jobs and settings that measures of general cognitive ability represent perhaps the best predictors of performance. Ability–performance relations are essentially linear and the correlation between general cognitive ability and performance appears similar across jobs that differ considerably in content. There is some evidence that ability–performance correlations tend to increase as jobs become more complex but few other consistent moderators of the ability–performance correlation have been reported. Finally, the incremental contribution of specific abilities (defined as ability factors unrelated to the general factor) to the prediction of performance or training outcomes may very well be minimal. (Murphy 2002, 175)

Given the overwhelming research evidence showing the strong link between general cognitive ability (GCA) and job performance, it is not logically possible for industrial–organisational (I/O) psychologists to have a serious debate over whether GCA is important for job performance. However, even if none of this evidence existed in I/O psychology, research findings in differential psychology on the nature and correlates of GCA provide a sufficient basis for the conclusion that GCA is strongly related to job performance. From the viewpoint of the kind of world we would like to live in—and would like to believe we live in—the research findings on GCA are not what most people would hope for and are not welcome. However, if we want to remain a science-based field, we cannot reject what we know to be true in favour of what we would like to be true. (Schmidt 2002, 187)

… the utility of "g," is that g (i.e., possessing a higher level of g) has value across all kinds of work and levels of job-specific experience, but that its value rises with a) the complexity of work, b) the more "core" the performance criterion being considered (good performance of technical duties rather than "citizenship"), c) the more objectively performance is measured (e.g. job samples rather than supervisor ratings). Predictive validities, when corrected for various statistical artifacts, range from about .2 to .8 in civilian jobs, with an average near .5. In mid-level military jobs, uncorrected validities tend to range between .3 and .6. These are substantial. To illustrate, tests with these levels of predictive validity would provide 30% to 60% of the gain in aggregate levels of worker performance that would be realised from using tests with perfect validity (there is not rush thing) rather than hiring randomly. (Gottfredson 2003a, 309).

Over the last five years there has been a plethora of excellent meta-analyses, studies, and discussion on the role of intelligence testing at work (Kuncel, Hezlett, and Ones 2004; Lubinski 2004; Murphy 2002; Schmidt and Hunter 2004; Tenoypr 2002; Viswesvaran and Ones 2002).

Those investigating the relationship between cognitive ability and job performance have agreed on the basis of the data numerous times. *First*, validities are around the .3 to .5 mark and higher for training, than job performance. *Second*, validity increases with job complexity but also the validity generalizes well across countries, criteria, jobs, settings, and industries. *Third*, intelligence is quite simply the best predictor of overall job and training (and specific task) performance. *Fourth*, the predictive validity of tests increases as job complexity increases. *Fifth*, measuring very specific abilities (like verbal or numerical) ability do not give much incremental advantage over general IQ or mental ability scores.

Gottfredson (2003a) argues that *life is a mental test battery*, because the business of living involves solving various problems and completing various tasks. Jobs like good psychometric IQ tests have a variety of performance tasks which are judged against an accepted standard. The more demanding the job, the brighter people have to be. Jobs operate like "differentially g loaded mental tests" because workers' differences in job performance simultaneously measure their differences in intelligence. Being more intelligent gives one a competitive edge for performing the job's core technical duties. Superior knowledge and extensive job experience, she argues, may sometimes hide a lower intelligence level, but never nullify or compensate for them. Brighter workers apply past knowledge more effectively and deal with novel problems more effectively and efficiently.

In a series of extremely important, critical, and comprehensive papers Gottfredson (1997; 1998; 2002; 2003a; 2003b) has made an overwhelming case to measure general (g) intelligence and to take it into consideration in everyday management decisions. "Intelligence turns out to be more important in predicting job performance than even personnel psychologists thought just two decades ago" (Gottfredson 1997, 81). Interestingly it was civil rights laws and regulations aimed at reducing discrimination that encouraged researchers to look very closely at this area. Looking at this research she came to various very important conclusions:

1. The predictive validity of intelligence is ubiquitous. Across all jobs and all ratings of success intelligence is very important.
2. The predictive power of intelligence rises with job complexity. The more intellectually and technically demanding the job, the more important is intelligence for success.
3. The validity of intelligence is high compared to other factors like personality, particular aptitudes, or vocational interests.
4. Intelligence is important in a casual sense. More surprising differences between individuals do not decrease with training (the less good become better and the good remain much the same) but can increase. Intelligence is a major source of enduring, consequential differences in job performance.
5. Higher levels of intelligence are required as people rise up the occupational ladder. Occupations both attract and accommodate individuals from a wide range of IQ levels but job incumbents are more homogeneous than applicants. But there does appear to be minimum IQ thresholds that rise steadily with job level.
6. Higher intelligence reflects higher trainability. That is, intelligence predicts a person's capacity to learn, i.e. trainability.
7. The essence of intelligence at work is the ability to deal with complexity which is an individual ability to acquire, apply, organize, recognize, select, and update on salient work-related information. In other words to mentally manipulate information.
8. Complexity is the key feature in the workplace. It is the major distinguishing factor between jobs. It is all about information processing.
9. As social, cultural, and work life becomes more complex the role of intelligence inevitably increases.
10. Where people have little time and ability to learn and be trained it is best to focus on specific training for specific skills.

Gottfredson (2002) believes it is vitally important for personnel psychologists and managers to understand the role of intelligence at work. In a wonderfully clear and important synthesis, she outlines the real importance of g at work (Gottfredson 2002, 44–6). She argues that higher levels of g lead to higher levels of performance in all jobs and on dimensions of performance. The average correlation of IQ scores with overall rated job performance is around .5 (corrected for statistical artifacts).

Further the effects of g are linear: successive increments in g lead to successive increments of job performance. Of equal importance is the fact that the value of higher levels of g does not fade with longer experience on the job. It is quite clear that g predicts job performance better in more complex jobs. It also predicts the core technical dimensions of performance better than it does the non-core "citizenship" dimension of performance.

Further, g predicts objectively measured performance (either job knowledge or job sample performance) better than it does subjectively rated performance (such as supervisor ratings).

Despite many people believing otherwise, specific mental abilities (such as spatial, mechanical, or verbal ability) add very little, beyond g, to the prediction of job performance. Yet we know that specific mental abilities (such as clerical ability) sometimes add usefully to prediction, net of g, but only in certain classes of jobs.

At work g predicts core performance much better than do "non-cognitive" (less g-loaded) traits, such as vocational interests and different personality traits. Similarly, g predicts most dimensions of non-core performance (such as personal discipline and soldier bearing) much less well than do "non-cognitive" traits of personality and temperament. Different non-cognitive traits appear to usefully supplement g in different jobs, like the personality trait of Conscientiousness/integrity.

We know g affects job performance primarily indirectly through its effect on job-specific knowledge. Further it seems that g's direct effects on job performance increase when jobs are less routinized, training is less complete, and workers retain more discretion. Job-specific knowledge generally predicts job performance as well as does g among experienced workers.

Experience predicts performance less well as all workers become more experienced. In contrast, higher levels of g remain an asset regardless of length of experience. Finally, experience predicts job performance less well as job complexity rises, which is opposite to the trend for g. Like general psychomotor ability, experience matters least where g matters most to individuals and their organisations.

Quite simply for Gottfredson (2004) all of life is a mental test battery. In this sense a higher intelligence is related to most advantages in life. The better paid, more demanding, more socially desirable jobs recruit workers from the higher reaches of the IQ distribution. Intelligence provides the competitive edge for a job performance particularly in high-level, more technically demanding jobs. Being intelligent provides a big, but not decisive advantage. Intelligence has a large causal effect on one's career.

Gottfredson (2004) believes that jobs act as a template for understanding the role of intelligence in all daily life. Intelligence relates to functional literacy which has many educational, health, and social relationship concomitants. Indeed Gottfredson and Deary (2004) showed that intelligence is a good predictor of health and longevity. The central question of course is why this is true. It seems that less intelligent people adhere less often to treatment regimens; learn and understand less about how to protect their health; seek less preventive care, even when free; and less often practice healthy behaviors for slowing and preventing chronic disease.

2. DIFFERENTIATION AND DISCRIMINATION

Those favorable to the idea of using cognitive ability/intelligence tests at work in assessment, promotion, and selection note test scores are the *best single predictor* of job performance (efficiency, productivity, profit), along with personality and motivational variables. Those unfavorable stress racial/ethnic minority discrimination, inequity, and unfairness. This represents a severe and perhaps irreconcilable clash of values (Murphy 2002).

Cognitive ability tests do show adverse race and sometimes gender impact. But racial differences in test scores are larger than in measures of job performance. Thus, a workforce based on actual performance would be less racially segregated than one based on ability tests. Yet there remains a powerful applied quandary:

If you emphasize efficiency criteria, and are willing to live with adverse impact, your choice is easy—that is, rely heavily on cognitive ability tests. If you emphasize equity criteria and are willing to live with lower levels of performance, longer training time, more errors, and so forth, your choice is also easy—that is, remove cognitive tests and other selection devices that have strong cognitive components (e.g. scores on cognitive ability test are correlated with scores on structured interviews and on assessment centers). Many decision makers care about both efficiency and equity, and the choice faced by these decision makers is necessarily more complex. (Murphy 2002, 178)

One solution is to try to find non-cognitive, non-discriminatory tests that predict work performance as well as intelligence tests. Indeed the problem seems so intractable that, Murphy (2002) argues, one cannot avoid *value tradeoffs* but one has to learn how to make value-based, tradeoff decisions. He cautions against values distorting the evidence and suggests that when organizations choose either to or not to use tests they should make the values underlying this decision explicit and public.

It is indeed these applied and practical quandaries rather than the science behind intelligence testing that have led it to be such a controversial topic in organizational psychology. There is a scientific argument and an ethical argument. They are based on different assumptions. The temptation of those favoring the ethical it-is-wrong-to-discriminate argument is that they are tempted to distort, ignore, or misreport the "scientific" evidence, so as to strengthen their case. Equally those favoring the scientific this-is-simply-what-the-data-show argument need to be sensitive to the socio-political consequence of selection by cognitive tests. Passions run high. It is indeed for this reason that the whole issue has become "too hot to handle" for human resource and research professionals alike.

3. Distinctions, Differences, and Disagreements

There are very different approaches to intelligence. Sternberg (1990) identified seven academic metaphors of intelligence, their central questions, and typical theorists taking each position. He argued that specific models or metaphors generate specific questions about intelligence which theories and research seek to address. Scientists may be unaware of these metaphors which can both limit but also expand views on intelligence. The metaphors are:

1. *Geographic*, which seeks to map the mind and understand the structure of intelligence.
2. *Computational*, which seeks to understand information-processing programs and processes underlying intelligence.
3. *Biological*, which attempts to understand how the anatomy, physiology, and chemistry of the brain and CNS accounts for intelligence through hemispheric localization and neural transmission.
4. *Epistemological*, which attempts to answer the fundamental question of what are the structures of the mind through which all knowledge and mental processes are organized.
5. *Anthropological*, which asks what form intelligence takes as a cultural invention and may be comparative and relativistic.
6. *Sociological*, which examines how social pressure (mediated learning experiences) in development are internalized.
7. *Systems*, which is concerned with how we understand the mind as a system which cross-cuts metaphors.

According to Sternberg, researchers in the controversial field of intelligence tend either to be *lumpers* or *splitters*. The former emphasizes that people who tend to do well on one sort of IQ test do well on practically all others. They talk of general intelligence (g) and see the IQ score (derived, of course, from a good test) as highly predictive of educational, business, and life success.

Splitters on the other hand are advocates of multiple intelligence. Gardner's (1999) theory of multiple intelligence is best known and of the multiple intelligences it is *emotional intelligence* (a combination of inter- and intra-personal intelligence) which has excited most popular interest as well as recent academic interest. As Brody (2004) has noted emotional intelligence is not strictly speaking on intelligence and there is little correlation between self-report trait measures of emotional intelligence or performance measure.

Sternberg himself is a splitter and a well-known advocate of practical or successful intelligence (Sternberg 1997). Claims and evidence for the theory, however, have been exhaustively and analytically investigated and found wanting (Gottfredson 2003a).

However, a more important and widely accepted distinction has been made between *fluid* and *crystallized* intelligence by Cattell (1987). The analogy is to water—fluid water can take any shape, whereas ice crystals are rigid. Fluid intelligence is effectively the power of reasoning, and processing information. It includes the ability to perceive relationships, deal with unfamiliar problems, and gain new types of knowledge. Crystallized intelligence consists of acquired skills and specific knowledge in a person's experience. Crystallized intelligence thus includes the skills of an accountant, lawyer, as well as mechanic and salesperson.

Fluid intelligence peaks before the age of 20 and remains constant, with some decline in later years. Crystallized intelligence, on the other hand, continues to increase as long as the person remains active. Thus, a schoolchild is quicker than an old-age pensioner at solving a problem that is unfamiliar to both of them, but even the most average older person will excel at solving problems in his/her previous area of occupational specialization.

In some cases, people try to solve problems by thinking about them in familiar terms—that is by using crystallized intelligence. Most intelligence tests use both types of intelligence, though there is a clear preference for fluid intelligence tests. Thus, consider the following:

(a) Underline which of these numbers does not belong with the others: 625, 361, 256, 193, 144
(b) Underline which of the following towns is the odd one out: Oslo, London, New York, Cairo, Bombay, Caracas, Madrid.

The former is a measure of fluid, the latter of crystallized intelligence.

These two types of intelligence are highly correlated, although they are conceptually different. Usually *what* you have learned (crystallized intelligence) is determined by *how well* you learn (fluid intelligence). Other factors, like personality, do play a part—introverts like to read, study, and learn, while equally bright extroverts like to socialize, have fun, and experiment. Introverts who like learning thus often do better at tests of crystallized intelligence. Self-evidently, motivation is important—a highly motivated adult will learn more efficiently and effectively than an adult less interested in learning.

Thus, one good reason to have a measure of crystallized ability is that a tendency to work hard is a good measure of scholastic and business success—and hard work results in better scores in tests of crystallized ability. Another reason is that even short *vocabulary tests* give very reliable scores, though one has to be careful to check the mother tongue of testees.

With changing technology, the value of crystallized intelligence may be dropping. Crystallized intelligence comes with age and experience. It is a repository of general and specific knowledge. Yet, if that knowledge can be cheaply, accurately, and efficiently stored and accessed by computers whence the usefulness of the years of experience? Sceptics may argue that computers could also assist in fluid intelligence problems thus making that sort of intelligence equally less valuable. Yet, in the business world, it seems to be less and less the case. However, the argument is not about the usefulness of computers but what individual differences in intelligence indicate.

Furnham (2001) has argued that it is business CEOs' fluid intelligence, personality, and motivation that appear to be the key to success. In a different age, when education came through the apprenticeship system, the value of crystallized intelligence was particularly great. It still is in some sectors. Crystallized intelligence is of less use, save, of course, a good memory for how things did not work out in the past.

In an attempt to understand the relationship between related concepts Ackerman and colleagues have tried to map out and explain the relationship between concepts like intelligence, interests, knowledge, and personality. In a very important historical and conceptual overview Ackerman and Heggestad (1997) found evidence of what they called *trait complexes*. These are clusters of personality, and ability traits and interests that have striking overlap or commonalities. These were labeled social, clerical, conventional, science/maths, and intellectual/cultural. They argue that it is possible that abilities, interests, and personality develop *in tandem* because ability and personality predict success (and failure) in a particular task domain and interests determine the motivation to attempt the task. Success thus leads to increased motivation and interest and vice versa.

Ackerman and colleagues (Ackerman and Rolfhus 1999; Beier and Ackerman 2001; Rolfhus and Ackerman 1999) have looked at academic and occupational knowledge as conceptually a way of understanding how ability and non-ability traits interact. They proposed PPIK theory which sees intelligence as process, personality, interests, and knowledge. Knowledge is accumulated only through expanded effort over time. Personality traits influence the process of acquiring knowledge. Ackerman and Rolfhus (1999) found knowledge in twenty areas (from astronomy and biology through to physics and world literature) was predicted by a combination of general intelligence, crystallized abilities, personality, interests, and self-concept. Rolfhus and Ackerman (1999) found further evidence for PPIK theory. Domain knowledge (i.e., of biology or business management; music or physics) is logically and statistically related to general intelligence, verbal abilities, trait Openness, Typical Intellectual Engagement, and specific vocational interests.

Beier and Ackerman (2001) add further evidence to the call for expanding the type of knowledge included in adult intelligence assessment especially the type of knowledge important for success in work and adult life. It is essentially as *investment theory* that suggests knowledge represents an individual's choice to invest cognitive resources, effort, and time in acquiring knowledge about the world.

In one sense controversy has been good for intelligence researchers because it has given them an opportunity to articulate in straightforward language what the research data reveal. Whilst intelligence as a research area has seen a recent rise of interest there remain few journals in the area. However, what has attracted a good deal of attention is the relationship between intelligence and personality which are acknowledged as the two great pillars of differential psychology (Chamorro-Premuzic and Furnham 2005). Indeed the question for those interested in organizational behavior is how these two sets of variables interact to influence all aspects of work behavior from job selection to productivity.

4. INTELLIGENCE RESEARCH AND TESTING AT WORK

Intelligence is about learning, adaptation, and problem solving. It is about being good at abstract reasoning, decision making, and speed of information processing. It is about cognitive and behavioral efficiency. Fundamental differences in definitions revolve around how wide or inclusive it should be. Thus some researchers want social competence, creativity, practical solving all to be included in the definition.

Lay people use the term to describe people, though they do not always understand the mechanism or process by which it is possible to deduce or measure that one person is significantly more intelligent than another. A lot of focus has been on the use of tests and the meaning of the scores. However, it is difficult to deny the accumulated evidence that intelligence scores do have predicted significance: that is that tests administered and scored at time 1 predict the predictable behavior, educational, and work achievement at time 2 (Mackintosh 1998; Deary 2000; 2001).

There are at least half-a-dozen hotly debated issues in the area, many of which have been around since tests were first constructed 100 years ago. Harrell and Harrell (1945) showed that individuals with low IQs were unlikely to be found in higher status, "white collar" jobs that appeared to require high levels of education as a condition of entry to that occupation. They found more variability at the bottom than the top: that is, there is a greater range in the IQs of people in less prestigious skilled and unskilled professions than those in higher professions. However, studies and reviews by Ghiselli (1966) suggested that IQ scores were modest (even mediocre) predictors of job performance over time in a particular occupation.

The armed services have always been a good source of data on intelligence and job performance. Indeed many have developed their own intelligence tests like the American Armed Services Vocational Aptitude Battery (ASVAB). Because of the number of recruits into the army and because of the necessity of technical training it has been relatively easy for psychologists to relate test to job performance on large numbers of recruits (Campbell, McHenry, and Wise 1990).

Thus Jones (1988) looked at an overall g score and training outcomes for various courses (Mechanical, Administrative, Technical, and Electronics) for nearly 25,000 soldiers. The correlation was $r = .75$. Ree and Earles (1994) did a similar analysis across 89 military jobs with big samples (between 274 and 3,939) and found a correlation of $r = .76$. McHenry et al. (1990) looked at nine army jobs and found correlations of around $r = .64$, between IQ test scores and "core technical proficiency" and "general soldiering proficiency."

Ree, Earles, and Teachout (1994) looked at seven army jobs: air traffic controller, laboratory scientist, armories communication specialist, ground equipment mechanic, jet engine mechanic, radio operator, and personnel specialist. In each case they were given the IQ subtest ASVAB. When the overall g score was correlated with good criteria measure, the r varied between .21 (air traffic) to .72 with an average of .44. In accordance with previous research the study showed quite simply that general (rather than specific) intelligence was the best predictor of all the work outcomes.

Yet various reviews published in the 1960s and 1970s suggested that intelligence (and personality) tests did *not predict* organizational outcomes very well. Further the socio-political zeitgeist of these times discouraged many business people from trying to measure intelligence. Major controversies about intelligence and race suggested that tests were significantly biased as well as lacking in predictive validity.

However, things were to change dramatically with the paper by Hunter and Hunter (1984), who presented a re-analysis of earlier plus other databases. In their analysis they took into account various statistical factors that impact on the size of correlations: size of sample, restriction of range, and reliability of data. Based on data from 30,000 people and 425 correlations their "bottom-line" figure for the correlation between supervisor-rated job performance and IQ was $r = .53$. They broke this down for various job families. The highest correlation was for salespeople ($r = .62$) and nearly all were over $r = .40$. Thus for service workers it was $r = .49$, trades and crafts workers $r = .50$ and vehicle operators $r = .46$.

As Brody (1992) noted that despite some criticisms of their methods Hunter and Hunter (1984) demonstrated quite clearly that IQ scores related logically and consistently with many kinds of job performance. By the end of the century reviewers like Ree and Carretta (1998) felt able to conclude: "Occupational performance begins with learning the knowledge and skills required for the job and continues into on-the-job performance and beyond. We and other investigators have demonstrated that g predicts training performance, job performance, lifetime productivity, and finally, early mortality" (p. 179). More recent reviews are even more positive about the role of intelligence in all aspects of life.

However, as noted earlier, the use and the usefulness of using intelligence tests at work is both a commercial *and* an ethical decision. If tests are believed to be unfair in that they discriminate against certain groups and do not predict work productivity organizations which choose to use them could suffer serious negative publicity. On the other hand, if as nearly all intelligence researchers conclude that tests are quick, cheap, and accurate measures that predict work outcomes, it could be that shareholders might object to organizations that did not use tests in selection, training, and assessment.

Ultimately the two fundamental questions are what is the size of the correlation between test scores and work output (that is, how much variance is accounted for) and how does one explain that relationship.

5. INTELLIGENCE AND OCCUPATIONAL PERFORMANCE

There is a very long and important literature on IQ and education which of course informs the concept of training at work. The efficiency, speed, and generalizability of learning via training is indeed related to intelligence. Estimates differ from about $r = .30$ to $r = .60$ (Ree and Carretta 1998).

Researchers have been interested in this question of intelligence and work outcomes since at least World War I. A central, often unanswered question is how intelligence predicts overall or specific job performance. This, in the first instance, can best be done via path analysis. Hunter (1986) showed that intelligence strongly predicted Job Knowledge, which predicted both "objective" job performance and supervisors ratings.

Borman et al. (1993) tested a model which went thus: IQ (ability) results in a person having an opportunity to acquire job experience as a supervisor. It also predicts an increase in job knowledge. Experience in turn leads to a further increase in job knowledge. Experience, ability, and knowledge predict proficiency. Thus intelligence predicts job performance. Ree, Carretta, and Teachout (1995) also argued that intelligence predicts job knowledge prior to training as well as job knowledge acquired during training.

Thus it seems that intelligence predicts learning, knowledge, and proficiency which in turn usually predicts learning from experience. Bright people learn faster, demonstrate salient skills, and get promoted. This adds to their knowledge and experience, all of which influence supervisor ratings or any other measure of job performance.

Ree and Carretta (1998) noted that intelligence predicts performance and promotion. That is, longitudinal studies have shown that brighter individuals attain higher occupational status. Thus intelligence predicts job knowledge which predicts job performance.

After some important early work which, because of both poor measurement and poor meta-analytic techniques, seemed to suggest both personality and intelligence tests had poor predictive validity in predicting behavior at work, the situation has changed. Over the last twenty years there have been around a dozen good large meta-analyses looking at the validity of cognitive ability tests.

Whilst these analyses used different tests they were all reliable and highly intercorrelated. However, it is possible to divide the tests essentially into those that measure general mental ability compared to specific cognitive abilities.

The best-known meta-analyses from the 1980s were those by Hunter and Hunter (1984) and Hunter (1986), though there were others before. Although there were some trends, what was noticeable was the variability in the correlations between IQ test scores and job performance: some very high, others very low. This led to the "doctrine of situational specificity" which argued that the relationship was dependent on the particular job, job performance criteria, and IQ test itself. However, this, in turn, led to the development of meta-analysis which through various statistical and "corrective" techniques aims to show the true operational validity between GMA (general mental ability) and work outcomes (Hunter 1986; Hunter and Hunter 1984; Hunter and Schmidt 1976; 1990; Schmidt and Hunter 1977; 1984; 1998).

Ones, Viswesvaran, and Dilchert (2006) in a comprehensive and up-to-date review of the meta-analysis were concerned with cognitive ability, selection decisions, and success at work. In doing so they examined many different areas and came to clear conclusions:

- Based on data of well over a million students they note GMA is a strong, valid predictor of exam success, learning, and outcome at school and university regardless of the speciality or subject considered.
- Training success at work, as measured by such things as supervisor ratings or job knowledge acquired, is predicted by GMA and the more complex the job, the more powerfully it predicts.

- Regarding job performance cognitive ability tests predict outcomes across jobs, situations, and outcomes—i.e., validity is transportable across occupational group and is cross-culturally generalizable.
- Tests of specific ability do *not* have incremental validity over general measures and although they may be more acceptable to job applicants the relative importance of these abilities alters over time.
- Intelligence predicts job performance well because it is linked to the speed and quality of learning, adaptability, and problem-solving ability.
- Cognitive ability tests are predictively fair to minority groups but can have an adverse impact which is a sensitive political issue.
- In short, GMA is one of the best, if not the best predictor of success in applied settings.

Various meta-analyses have been done over the last five years that have attempted a critical, comprehensive overview of the role of intelligence (often called general mental ability or cognitive ability test results) in predicting work related outcomes (see Tables 1.1–1.3).

Some reviewers have tended to concentrate on data from one country, like America (Schmidt and Hunter 2004) or Britain (Bertua, Anderson, and Salgado 2005) or from wider areas like the European Community (Salgado et al. 2003). Despite these differences the results were essentially the same and all reviewers argued for *the practical use of cognitive ability tests which are quite clearly good predictors of both overall job performance as well as training success.*

Salgado et al. (2003) looked at the predictive validity of GMA as well as specific cognitive abilities like verbal, numerical, spatial-mechanical, perceptual, and memory to predict measurable job performance and training success. Different selection and personnel practices could, they argue, lead to difference when comparing American and European data. Over 250 studies that tested over 25,000 Europeans they found an operational validity of .62 which they note "means GMA is an excellent predictor of job performance" (p. 585) and that "GMA is the best predictor of job performance" (p. 585). The validity of the five specific measures

Table1.1 The validities of overall and specific abilities for job performance and training

	Performance	Training
GMA	.62	.54
Verbal	.35	.44
Numerical	.52	.48
Spatial/Mech.	.51	.40
Perceptual	.52	.25
Memory	.56	.43

varied from .35 for verbal to .56 for memory. The data on training ratings was broadly similar if slightly lower (.54 for GMA; .44 for verbal; and .34 for memory).

Intelligence test scores are therefore seen as *best predictors* of work performance. That is, despite differences in tests used—measures/conceptualizations of job performance and training; differences in unemployment rates, cultural values, demographics—GMA still wins out as the best individual difference psychometric measure. Indeed the results are strikingly similar to earlier data coming out of America (Hunter 1986; Hunter and Hunter 1984; Viswesvaran, Ones, and Schmidt 1996; Kuncel, Hezlett, and Ones 2001). They conclude that because of the predictive validity of GMA at work across cultures one can easily conceive of a scientifically feasible general theory of personnel selection. They also point out: "tests of specific abilities such as verbal, numerical, spatial-mechanical, perceptual and memory failed to demonstrate higher validity than GMA measures. It is thus prudent to reiterate the main practical implications of this finding that GMA tests predicted these two criteria most successfully" (p. 594).

Another meta-analysis focused exclusively on British data. This had 283 samples of in total over 13,000 people (Bertua, Anderson, and Salgado 2005). This analysis looked at the predictive validity of specific abilities (i.e., verbal, numerical, etc.) as well as GMA over seven main groups (clerical, engineer, professional, driver, operator, manager, sales). As in all meta-analyses they found GMA and abilities valid predictors of job performance and training success (performance rho = .48; training rho = .50). They also found, as one may predict, the greater the job complexity, the higher the operational validities between the different cognitive tests and job performance and training success.

Thus these results were broadly in line with those from both Europe and America. Once again the conclusion is that GMA measures may be the best single predictor for personnel selection for all occupations. They recommended the use of psychometrically proven measures of GMA for use in selection "regardless of job type, hierarchical seniority, potential future changes in job role composition or whether the tests are principally for general or specific cognitive ability" (p. 403).

Table 1.2 **Correlations between overall and specific IQ measures and job performance and training**

	Performance	Training
GMA	.48	.50
Verbal	.39	.49
Numerical	.42	.54
Perceptual	.50	.50
Spatial	.35	.42
Average	.42	.49

Table 1.3 **The meta-analytic results for GMA over the eight occupational groups**

	Performance	Training
Clerical	.32	.55
Engineer	.70	.64
Professional	.74	.59
Driver	.37	.47
Operator	.53	.34
Manager	.69	
Sales	.55	
Miscellaneous	.40	.55

Over the past twenty-five years there is a "large and compelling literature" showing that intelligence is a good predictor of both job performance and training proficiency at work (Dragow 2003). Reviews have shown that intelligence was a good predictor of job performance but particularly in complex jobs. Although debated, researchers suggest the correlation between intelligence and job performance is around $r = .50$ (Schmidt and Hunter 1998). The central question is what other factors like personality or social/ emotional intelligence (sometimes called "social skills") accounts for the rest of the variance. But referring to g or general intelligence Dragow (2003) is forced to conclude, "for understanding performance in the workplace, and especially task performance and training performance, g is the key. . . . g accounts for an overwhelming proportion of the explained variance when predicting training and job performance" (p. 126).

Ree and Carretta (1998) in another careful review of their own and others work, as well as criticisms of it, concluded thus: "Occupational performance begins with learning the knowledge and skills required for the job and continues into on-the-job performance and beyond. We and other investigators have demonstrated that g predicts training performance, job performance, lifetime productivity, and finally, early mortality" (p. 179).

One hundred years after Spearman (1904) published his paper "General Intelligence: objectively determined and measured" in the *Journal of Applied Psychology* there were various celebrations, conferences and special issues to celebrate the fact. One paper entitled "Academic performance, career potential, creativity and job performance: can one construct predict them all?" concluded, *yes!* (Kuncel, Hezlett, and Ones 2004). Further, as Lubinski (2004) notes it is no surprise that intelligence test scores have such predictive validity over so many areas like education, health, interpersonal relationships, and job performance. He concluded:

As modern societies move to create more information and to make this information readily available, more opportunities become available for differential development. In addition, tasks important at school, at work, and in life are becoming less concrete and less well defined. The dimensions of educational, occupational and social niches are becoming more abstract and fluid. An examination of phrases used to characterise skills needed in today's most complex learning and work environments quickly reveals that the current need is for abilities for "coping with change," "dealing with novelty," "quickly grasping" the relevance of innovative ideas for staying "ahead of the curve" and "anticipating change." The skills needed in modern society require dealing with complexity and with change and more than ever before, these changes are relatively content free. At work as in life in general, people are required to respond to situations for which they have not practiced.

The specific content is not fundamental, because the specific content of life is ever changing. Coping with life requires the continuous development of new skills, so abilities useful for mastering new content—and new relationships—are what is needed.

Assessment designed to index individual differences in pre-specified domains (e.g., mastery of prescribed content in educational and occupational contexts) will always be important, but, increasingly, skills in coping with novelty, generalising and discriminating dynamic relationships, and making inferences that anticipate distal events are what modern society demands. (p. 108)

Schmidt and Hunter (2004, 162) also came to a clear conclusion based on 100 years of work. Their conclusion was this:

The research evidence shows that GMA predicts both occupational level attained and performance within one's chosen occupation and does so better than any other ability, trait, or disposition and better than job experience. The sizes of these relationships with GMA are also larger than most found in psychological research. Evidence is presented that weighted combination of specific aptitudes tailored to individual jobs do not predict job performance better than GMA along, disconfirming specific aptitude theory. A theory of job performance is described that explicates the central role of GMA in the world of work. These findings support Spearman's proposition that GMA is of critical importance in human affairs.

Thus for complex, senior jobs the correlation between GMA and job performance is around .50. Intelligence seems always to be a more powerful predictor than personality, because people with higher GMA acquire job knowledge more efficiently (faster and more) that it is such a good marker of career success. Job experience does relate to job performance but it declines over time, unlike the intelligence–performance relationship which increases.

6. APPLICATIONS AND IMPLICATIONS OF TESTING AT WORK

Is it advisable to use cognitive tests to make selection, training, and promotion decisions? If so, what tests should be administered to whom for what purpose? Are the potential negative consequences greater than the benefits? Could one make a good economic, as opposed to legal, argument for testing in the workplace?

Viswesvaran and Ones (2002) examined in detail eight issues surrounding the use of ability testing in the workplace. It was a summary of eleven articles published in *Human Performance*, 2002, Vol. 15, including many important papers (i.e., Murphy 2002; Schmidt 2002; Reeve and Hakel 2002; Tenopyr 2002). They were even-handed in their approach, happy to point out areas of agreement and disagreement.

A. *What is the predictive value of intelligence (general mental ability) tests for real life outcomes and work behavior?*

Results show consistently that intelligence is positively related to educational level, income, positive health behaviors and negatively related to delinquency, disciplinary problems and health issues. People need a level of ability to thrive in a particular work environment: more cognitive demands, more ability required. To many this is self-evident.

But there are three criticisms. The *first* is the size of correlation between intelligence and job outcome—in other words the strength of that relationship and the amount of variance being accounted for. Some argue that the relationship is too weak or two small and may only account for 25 percent of the variance. Thus hard work, honesty, and training could all easily compensate for relatively low intelligence in a competitive working environment.

A *second* criticism is which relationship to look at. If you examine the relationship between intelligence and work outcomes of job incumbents and find them small, that should be no surprise, because if they have been well selected there should be little variance. That is, they should all be within the appropriate intelligence range. On the other hand, if all job applicants are tested that would yield a far better index. Equally we need to consider how reliable the measurement of the criterion work outcome/variable is. Critics argue then, that if we correct for range restriction (of those in the job) and the unreliability of the outcome measure we will see a much stronger relationship between IQ and work. The *third* critique, quickly dismissed by Viswesvaran and Ones (2002), is that intelligent behavior at work is the result of more than just what intelligence tests measure.

B. *Do overall IQ test scores predict better than measures of specific abilities?*

This question is whether very specific tests of verbal, or mathematical or spatial ability will relate to work outcomes, more strongly and logically than general IQ test results. It is agreed that there are non-cognitive factors that do predict job performance in addition to GMA. But are there very specific abilities that predict success in all jobs (rather than very specific jobs).

Whilst there maybe good reason to use very specific ability measures like those of verbal reasoning or mathematical ability (for face validity, legal reasons) give incremental validity over a GMA the evidence suggests that it is small. This could be for many reasons: restriction of range in certain occupational samples; a limited number of criteria. Nevertheless, based on the current data, it is fairly difficult to provide evidence to justify the tests of tests of specific ability above that of GMA.

C. *How good is the criteria (job/training performance)?*
The central question here is how reliable, representative and parsimonious are the traditional outcome measures? There have always been doubts about the narrowness of these measures that neglect, for instance, both team and organizational effectiveness. Few researchers are completely happy with the criteria but find it difficult finding better ones.

D. *Is the utility evidence for GMA convincing?*
Is it possible to place monetary values on the consequence for an organization choosing people of high, average or low intelligence based on the provided predictive validity of IQ test/job performance links. This is not a methodological issue but one of focusing only on organizational productivity as opposed to health or harmony. Utility evidence is therefore a value statement. However it is frequently done and yields some startling results usually showing the great economic benefits of testing.

E. *Are the negative reactions to GMA tests a result of group differences?*
That is, is the debate about black/white differences and the association of such concepts as "adverse impact," bias, discrimination and fairness the real cause of public cynicism, and scepticism about tests? In other words, would the controversies about intelligence be less intense and passionate if there were no evidence of group differences?

The problem is of logic: GMA predicts work performance better than specific ability measures but there are recognized, replicable group differences in IQ not due (solely) to measurement bias. Yet it seems that negative attitudes to testing go beyond the race (and sex) issue. They may be caused by historically recorded abuses of testing as well as the philosophy of equality and equal opportunity that eschew selection on ability. Another reason is that most people believe that IQ is not the only important predictor of educational, job, and life success. Indeed it is not even the most important predictor.

F. *Is the theoretical knowledge of GMA adequate?*
At the heart of the problem is the very meaning of the concept of GMA. That is researchers seem not to understand the process or mechanism that leads to GMA or indeed its association with job success. There may be interesting statistical evidence of behavioral and biological correlates of GMA scores but

how it operates remains unclear. Defenders say we know as much about the construct as many others in psychology while critics detect a theoretical dark hole at the center of all this research.

G. *Is there promise in various new methods of testing for GMA?*

That is, using different technologies—biological, computational, video-based—will we be able to measure intelligence more reliably, and presumably understand, GMA? The question is whether changing the measurement changes what is measured? Some have hoped that tests using different media would reduce group differences; however, some believe all they have done is increase measurement error. However, as Viswesvaran and Ones (2002) have noted, "Whether these potentially more invasive assessments are developed and become available for use depended on how society decides to balance the privacy rights of individuals against the needs of organisations" (p. 224).

H. *What is the current status of non-GMA predictors and substitutes or supplements to GMA?*

The search for other good predictors has been long and hard. Thus can personality variables, work samples, or some measured motivational variable act as a substitute or supplement to GMA as an accurate predictor? Can we find factors that both increase predictive validity but reduce group differences? Many have been suggested from tacit knowledge, through working memory capacity to psychomotor ability. The problem is that few (good) studies attempt to compare the predictive validity of alternative tests with GMA. Two issues are important here according to Viswesvaran and Ones (2002); first not to confuse constructs and methods and second to examine predictor intercorrelations. Further there are important consequences of choosing people on the basis of the supplementary predictor. Thus, Conscientiousness is thought to be a better predictor of GMA than one would have in an organization full of ambitious, hard-working, persistent, dutiful and perhaps dependent people rather than fast, accurate, effective problem solvers.

7. Controversies in Intelligence Research

Using psychometrically valid intelligence tests in selection and promotion may seem a logical consequence of reading the academic literature. However, this is far from the case as there are numerous controversies around the fair use of tests in selection. Controversies revolve around group differences (especially sex and race) and the Flynn effect. Group differences refer to the collective property of a group as distinct from the individual property of an individual.

The issue regarding group differences refers to possible illegal as well as unwise discrimination at work. If there are sex and race differences in test scores, and if it is illegal to discriminate (i.e., choose or reject applicants) on the basis of group differences tests may lead organizations to, in effect, break the law. What then is the evidence for these differences?

8. Sex Differences

Few dispute that there are consistent, replicable and significant differences in cognitive test scores (Halpern 1997). Females do better at tasks that require rapid access to, and use of, phonological, semantic, and other information in long-term memory. Females are better at speed articulation, production, and comprehension of complex prose and tend to get higher grades in school (for most subjects). Males do better on tasks that require transformations in visual working memory: i.e. those involving moving objects and aiming. These differences are small and reviewers tend to argue five things. *First*, gender differences in general intellectual ability are small and virtually non-existent. *Next*, secular changes in society have diminished gender differences in special ability scores. *Third*, mean differences in verbal ability and mathematical ability in the general population have virtually disappeared. Though this is not true of spatial ability. *Fourth*, males appeared to be more variable in a number of ability measures and this differences in variability, particularly at the high end of the distribution of ability, may contribute to an excess number of males above relatively high cutting scores. *Finally*, there are gender differences on tests of spatial ability. The magnitude of the difference appears to vary with the type of test and may be as high as .75 standard deviation units in favour of males over females for tests of mental rotation.

Brody (1992) notes that meta-analyses point to the smallest effect sizes (.10 to .20) relating gender differences in IQ scores. Sex differences in IQ scores appear to be declining due to a reduction in sex stereotyping of activities, interests, and curricular choices. Sex differences are more likely to be present in samples that are above average in abilities.

Mackintosh (1998) argued that it is not true that tests were designed and defined to show sex differences. Most early test constructions were not very interested in sex differences and tended not to find much evidence for them. There are sex differences on particular WAIS tests that are robust and reliable but small (2 IQ points). The sexes do not differ on measures of general reasoning ability. There are various biological (sex-linked recessive gene hypothesis) and environmental (early socialization) explanations for sex differences but they remain unclear.

However, Lynn and colleagues (Lynn 1999; Lynn and Irwing 2004) have argued and demonstrated the small (around .3 of a SD) sex differences in favor of males. Through a developmental theory they argued after the age of 16 the male advantage is most noticeable. This may be more particularly true of spatial tasks. The argument is logical: it is known, brain size is correlated with intelligence; males have bigger brains than females; therefore males are more intelligent. Females mature more rapidly than males in terms of neurological development and brain size up to the age of 15 years. This "compensates" for their smaller brain size with the result that there are negligible differences, but from the age of 16 years the growth rate of girls decelerates relative to that of boys. Thus, by (early) adulthood, there is a discernible 4 IQ point difference (almost one-third of a SD) in favour of males that is consistent with their brain size difference.

The theory was confirmed in a fifty-seven-study meta-analysis of sex differences in the general population using Raven's Progressive Matrices (Lynn and Irwing 2004). It showed that after the age of 15, but not before, the male advantage occurred. Interestingly they found little cross-cultural variation in sex differences, despite some marked cultural differences in adult sex roles. Further they found no evidence of generational change i.e. the reduction is sex differences over time. However, they felt obliged to try to explain the anomalous finding that (at least in Great Britain) data suggest that in secondary schools and at universities females tend to perform as well as or better than males. Their suggestion is that females' greater achievement motivation is the primary explanation for these findings.

Asserting sex differences causes considerable debate in the popular press based more on ideology than a cool and disinterested evaluation of the evidence. However, if indeed there are sex differences in intelligence, they are very small. There may well be gender differences in self-estimated intelligence (Furnham 2001) or indeed the way males and females attempt intelligence tests but there is very little evidence to suggest that testing at work would be advantageous or disadvantageous to either males or females.

9. RACE DIFFERENCES

Since he published a paper in 1969 Jensen has continued to argue for there being systematic and replicable differences in IQ between different racial (and national) groups. He has been supported by many working in the area Herrnstein and

Murray (1994) and Rushton (1995). Few who have done research on the topic of IQ believe that there are not race differences but they do argue, quite passionately, about the cause of race differences in IQ scores.

The predictive validity of IQ (for education and job) is comparable for black and white samples. Tests, even subtests of knowledge, are not particularly race biased in favour of WASP Culture. That is, there is little difference between culture bound and non-culture bound tests. Further, test administration (i.e., race of examiner) is a small and not very important source of difference. Class and status of examiner have a little effect and English dialect of test or tester has little effect.

Brody (1992) argues:

More generally, one can conclude from this review of research on bias in mental testing that the black–white difference in performance on tests of intelligence is not substantially attributable to differences in the construct validity of the tests for black and white samples. The factor analytic studies, item analysis research, and research on the predictive validity of tests suggests that the black–white difference in test scores is substantial attributable to differences in the construct that is assessed by the test.

Mackintosh (1998), however, is less impressed by the universal validity of IQ tests. He notes: "We need to remember that standard IQ tests were designed to measure the knowledge, intellectual skills, and cognitive abilities valued in Western indus-trial societies, especially by the education systems of these societies. They may do a reasonable job of that. But there is no reason to assume that other cultures and societies share the same values. Administering such tests to people of other cultures may tell us whether they do or do not share the same values. But it will not necessarily tell us much about their 'intelligence'" (p. 221).

Despite some doubt as to the culture fairness of some tests, the real argument lies between the genetic vs. environment camps. Certainly while everybody accepts the role of certain environmental factors, even singly, or together they cannot account for the observable, empirically derived differences in IQ. Mackintosh (1998) makes the following points: The established black–white difference debate/research has a major social and political impact. There are three strong positions: Genetic; Environmental; Test Bias. Interbreeding means geneticists/anthropologists do not find "race" a useful concept. There are no clear single markers; adoptive studies (of black children by white parents) are problematic and yield contradictory evidence. The acid test of the environment argument is to manipulate (enrich) the environ-ment and see its effects on IQ. But enriched and compensatory environments have limited and short-term effects. Poverty and discrimination cannot be sufficient explanations; so the environmental factors that do affect IQ remain unclear. Chinese/Japanese superiority also remains a challenging issue. All IQ tests are imperfect measures aimed to provide a true (unbiased, valid) measure of intellec-tual functioning. But valid tests should predict/correlate with educational and occupational attainment.

The debate continues and is likely to do so. A whole issue of the journal *Psychology, Public Policy and Law* (June 2005, Vol. 11, No. 2) was dedicated to the thorny issue of race differences in cognitive ability with those on all sides of the argument making their case (Gottfredson 2005; Rushton and Jensen 2005; Sternberg 2005).

There are, it seems, three types of explanations. *First*, there is evidence of biological, genetic differences between the races. *Second*, there is evidence of socio-cultural, economic, and political forces, that are quite distinct from racial characteristics though confounded with them. *Third*, race differences are essentially artifacts of test design, administration, or measurement. In other words, there are no real differences.

Brody has noted that the study of race differences in intelligence goes back to the beginning of research. Substantial research shows black Americans score 15 points (1 SD) lower than white Americans. It is clear variations *within* race are larger than variations *between* races. This means 16 percent of the black population have scores above the white mean; at a cutoff 70 points for special education there will be 1 white for every 7 blacks. Black–white differences appear to be constant over time and over the life span. Further, racial differences are present prior to school entry. Racial differences are however not constant for different types of measures of intelligence.

He argues that those who reject race differences as a function of test measurement are wrong:

Research on black–white differences in intelligence fails to provide answers to three critical questions. 1) what are the reasons for the difference? 2) Can we eliminate it? 3) If we cannot eliminate the difference, can we design an environment in which the effects of individual differences in intelligence are mitigated such that they are not determinative to the extent they are now of racial differences in performance in the schools and in other socially relevant contexts? If we could make progress on the third question, the answers to the first two questions would appear to be less pressing. It is possible that the answer to the first question might enable us to eliminate the difference or to design ways to mitigate the difference. If so, the study of the reasons for black–white differences would be socially useful. (Brody 1992, 310)

Gottfredson (2002, 41) provides a clear example from America:

To take some more specific examples, about 22% of Whites and 59% of Blacks have IQs below 90, which makes considerably fewer Blacks competitive for mid-level jobs, such as firefighting, the skilled trades and many clerical jobs. The average IQ of incumbents in such jobs is nearer IQ 100, one standard deviation above the Black average of roughly IQ 85. IQ 80 seems to be the threshold for competitiveness in even the lowest level jobs, and four times as many Blacks (30%) as Whites (7%) fall below that threshold. Looking toward the other tail of the IQ distribution, IQ 125 is about average for professionals (e.g. lawyers, physicians, engineers, professors) and high level executives. The Black–White ratio of availability is only 1:30 at this level.

Disparate impact, and therefore political and legal tension, is thus particularly acute in the most complex, most socially desirable jobs.

Gottfredson notes that many hoped psychologists would "invent" better tests that reduce the racial disparity. This did not happen and tests were blamed for the problem: that is, for some, if tests showed a race difference, they did not want or expect this and blamed the test. Some turned away from testing. She concludes cautiously thus:

Reducing disparate impact is a worthy goal to which probably all selection professionals subscribe. What is troubling are the new means being promulgated: minimising or eliminating the best overall predictor of job performance. They amount to a call for reducing test validity and thereby violating personnel psychology's primary testing standard. Reducing the role of g in selection may be legally and politically expedient in the short term, but it delays more effective responses to the huge racial gaps in job-relevant skills, abilities and knowledge (p. 43)

10. GENERATIONAL EFFECTS

For over twenty years since the papers of Flynn (1984; 1987), psychologists have debated the possible causes of the established phenomenon concerning the rise of intelligence over each generation. Looking at twenty countries over a fifty-year period there has been an increase of 2.9 points per decade on non-verbal IQ (specifically abstract problem-solving ability) and 3.7 points on verbal IQ. This rapid increase cannot be due to genetic factors. The likely causes are: increases in the number of years of education; greater access to information (e.g., television, internet); the increased cognitive complexity of the average person's job now compared to several decades ago; more generally, a large increase in the number of middle-class families.

Flynn's data have been replicated but still have no clear explanation. Various ideas have been put forward: improved nutrition, educational innovation, television, experience of speeded tests. Yet he had received stern and cogent criticism for his methods and conclusions. Most reviews have inferred longitudinal explanation from cross-sectional data. Rodgers (1999) points out that population IQ gains do not operate within the individual. In fact IQ declines with age. Similarly the Flynn effect does not operate within the family. IQ declines with birth order. It is not clear whether the Flynn effect is a period effect (i.e., changes over time because of improved education) or a cohort effect (i.e., changes over time in that one generation would carry with it).

Further, Rodgers (1999) points out that it is unclear whether the Flynn effect operates across all races and ability distributions or whether it operates on only certain abilities (like problem solving or vocabulary). Rodgers (1999) has noted that the Flynn effect is an inference from data. He proposed an alternative model based on the variability of scores. Thus if over the population as a whole changes (better diet, education, etc.) reduced variability of scores (fewer people scored low) this would result very clearly in the Flynn effect.

What remains clear is that the Flynn effect is a phenomenon still in search of a cogent explanation. It certainly has important implications for everyone interested in age and group differences in intelligence.

11. Conclusion

Few areas of psychology attract as much discussion and debate as the topic of intelligence more particularly the use of intelligence tests in selection at work. More academic researchers have been attacked (physically), hounded, sacked, and vilified by what they have written about intelligence than any other topic (even evolutionary psychology). The area that inevitably causes most passion is that of sex and race differences. There is also still considerable debate about the role of intelligence testing in educational settings.

There are essentially two issues: an empirical and a social policy issue. Most of the debate is about the latter not the former though there remains still considerable controversy about the predictive power of intelligence tests.

The data on general intelligence as a predictor of work-related behaviors is, however, very clear. There are very few researchers who have inspected recent meta-analyses who could not be impressed by the fact that, without doubt, the best single predictor of success at work (particularly in senior complex jobs) is intelligence. This is not to deny that there are not other important factors nor that it is patently obvious that not all intelligent people do particularly well in the workplace.

Intelligence is relatively easy to measure reliably and accurately. Intelligence test scores are influenced by other factors (like personality) but not to any great extent. Intelligence is cognitive capacity and refers to both efficient problem solving but also accumulated knowledge.

However, the science and the practice of intelligence testing remain far apart because of the history of misunderstanding, misapplications, and political differences. It remains difficult even with supposedly disinterested scientists to have an evidence-based debate about the origin of individual differences in intelligence, the measurement of intelligence, and the application of tests in commercial and educational settings. The signs are hopeful for the future where differential psychologists and people at work could benefit from some of the most valid and predictive of all measures in the workplace.

Cook (2002, 131) concluded his review succinctly thus:

Mental ability tests are the focus of much controversy. There are various types of ability test, some of which are more specialised while others are more general. There are various ways of presenting and interpreting test scores. Test scores are not perfectly reliable, and there are various ways of estimating reliability. Validation research has methodological limits, including small samples, unreliable work performance measures and restricted ranges, that create the impression of low validity. Research therefore needs to be analysed carefully. Validity generalisation analysis is intended to generate an accurate estimate of test validity. Validity generalisation analysis also suggests that validity of mental ability tests may be fairly constant, and that the true relationship between mental ability and work performance is stronger than it seems. Mental ability tests predict work performance fairly well—as well as any other method available. The relationship between mental ability and work performance is continuous and linear—the brighter someone is, the more likely their work performance is to be good. Research on mental ability and team (rather than individual) performance suggests the existence of more complex relationships. Low scorers may hold the whole team back. Research on why mental ability tests predict work performance is less well developed, but suggests that mental ability leads to improved job knowledge, which in turn leads to better work performance. Mental ability tests create a large adverse impact on some ethnic minorities in the USA. There is a dearth of information on this issue elsewhere. Attempts to solve the adverse impact problem in the USA include trying to identify features of mental ability testing that will reduce adverse impact. Attempts to deal with the adverse impact problem in the USA include score banding, which defines a range of scores as equivalent, thus allowing selection within the band to be based on achieving diversity.

References

ACKERMAN, P., and GOFF, M. 1994. Typical intellectual engagement and personality. *Journal of Educational Psychology*, 86: 150–3.

—— and HEGGESTAD, E. 1997. Intelligence, personality and interests. *Psychological Bulletin*, 121: 219–45.

—— and ROLFHUS, E. 1999. The locus of adult intelligence. *Psychology and Aging*, 14: 314–30.

BEIER, M., and ACKERMAN, P. 2001. Current-events knowledge in adults. *Psychology and Aging*, 16: 615–28.

—— —— 2003. Determinants of health knowledge. *Journal of Personality and Social Psychology*, 84: 439–41.

BERTUA, C., ANDERSON, N., and SALGADO, J. 2005. The predictive validity of cognitive ability tests: a UK meta-analysis. *Journal of Occupational and Organisational Psychology*, 78: 387.

BORMAN, W., HANSON, M., OPPLER, S., PULAKIS, E., and WHITE, L. 1993. Role of early supervisory experience in supervisor performance. *Journal of Applied Psychology*, 78: 443–9.

BRODY, N. 1992. *Intelligence*. London: Academic Press.

CAMPBELL, P., McHENRY, J., and WISE, L. 1990. Modeling job performance in a population of jobs. *Personnel Psychology*, 43: 313–33.

CARROLL, J. 1993. *Human Cognitive Abilities*. Cambridge: Cambridge University Press.

CATTELL, R. 1987. *Intelligence: Its Structure, Growth and Action*. New York: North Holland.

CHAMORRO-PREMUZIC, T., and FURNHAM, A. 2005. *Personality and Intellectual Competence*. Mahwah, NY: LEA.

——— ——— 2006. The intelligent personality. *Review of General Psychology*.

COOK, M. 2003. *Personnel Selection*. Chichester: Wiley.

DEARY, I. 2000. *Looking down on Human Intelligence*. Oxford: Oxford University Press.

——— 2001. *Intelligence: A Very Short Introduction*. Oxford: Oxford University Press.

DRAGOW, F. 2002. Intelligence and the workplace. Pp. 107–30 in *Handbook of Psychology*, vol. xii, ed. W. Borman, D. Ilgen, and R. Klimozki. New York: Wiley.

EYSENCK, H. 1990. *Know your own IQ*. Harmondsworth: Penguin.

——— 1994. *Test your own IQ*. Harmondsworth: Penguin.

——— 1998. *Intelligence: A New Look*. London: Transaction Publishers.

FLYNN, J. 1984. The mean IQ of Americans: massive gains 1932 to 1978. *Psychological Bulletin*, 95: 29–51.

——— 1987. Massive IQ gains in 14 nations: what IQ tests really measure. *Psychological Bulletin*, 101: 171–91.

FURNHAM, A. 2001. *The 3D Manager*. London: Whurr.

GARDNER, H. 1999. Intelligence reframed. New York: Basic Books.

GHISELLI, E. 1966. *The Validity of Occupational Aptitude Tests*. New York: Wiley.

GOTTFREDSON, L. 1997. Why g matters: the complexity of everyday life. *Intelligence*, 24: 79–132.

——— 1998. The general intelligence factor. *Scientific American*, 24–9.

——— 2002. Where and why g matters: not a mystery. *Human Performance*, 15: 25–46.

——— 2003a. g jobs and life. In *The Science of Mental Ability*, ed. J. Nyborg. Oxford: Pergamon.

——— 2003b. Dissecting practical intelligence theory: its claims and evidence. *Intelligence*, 31: 343–97.

——— 2004. What if the hereditarians' hypothesis is true? *Psychology, Public Policy and Law*.

——— and DEARY, I. 2004. Intelligence predicts health and longevity, but why? *Current Direction in Psychological Science*, 13: 1–4.

HALPERN, D. 1997. *Sex Differences in Cognitive Abilities*. Hillsdale, NJ: Erlbaum.

HARRELL, T., and HARRELL, M. 1945. Army general classification test scores for civilian occupations. *Educational and Psychological Measurement*, 5: 229–39.

HERRNSTEIN, R., and MURRAY, C. 1994. *The Bell Curve*. New York: Free Press.

HUNTER, J. 1986. Cognitive ability, cognitive aptitudes, job knowledge and job performance. *Intelligence*, 29: 340–62.

——— and HUNTER, R. 1984. Validity and utility of alternative predictors of job performance. *Psychological Bulletin*, 96: 72–98.

HUNTER, J. E., and SCHMIDT, F. L. 1976. A critical analysis of the statistical and ethical implications of various definitions of test fairness. *Psychological Bulletin*, 83: 1053–71.

—— —— 1990. *Methods of Meta-analysis: Correcting for Error and Bias in Research Findings*. Newbury Park, CA: Sage.

JENSEN, A. 1969. How much can we boost IQ and scholastic achievement? *Harvard Educational Review*, 39: 1–123.

JONES, G. 1988. Investigation of the efficacy of general ability versus specific abilities as predictors of occupational success. Unpublished thesis: St Mary's University of Texas.

KUNCEL, N., HEZLETT, S., and ONES, D. 2001. A comprehensive meta-analysis of the predictive validity of the Graduate Record Examinations. *Psychological Bulletin*, 127: 162–81.

—— —— —— 2004. Academic performance, career potential, creativity and job performance. *Journal of Personality and Social Psychology*, 86: 148–61.

LUBINSKI, D. 2004. Introduction to the special section on cognitive abilities. *Journal of Personality and Social Psychology*, 86: 96–111.

LYNN, R. 1999. Sex differences in intelligence and brain size. *Intelligence*, 27: 1–12.

—— and IRWING, P. 2004. Sex differences on the progressive matrices: a meta analysis. *Intelligence*, 32: 481–98.

McHENRY, J., HOUGH, L., TOQUAM, J., HANSEN, M., and ASHWORTH, S. 1990. Project A validity results. *Personnel Psychology*, 43: 335–54.

MACKINTOSH, N. 1998. *IQ and Human Intelligence*. Oxford: Oxford University Press.

MIKLEWSKA, A., KACZMAREK, A., and STRELAU, J. 2005. The relationship between temperament and intelligence. *Personality and Individual Differences*.

MURPHY, K. 2002. Can conflicting perspectives on the role of g in personnel selection be resolved? *Human Performance*, 15: 173–86.

NEISSER, U. 1967. *Cognitive Psychology*. New York: Appleton Century Crofts.

—— BOODOO, G., BOUCHARD, T., BOYKIN, A., BRODY, N., and CECI, A. 1996. Intelligence: knowns and unknowns. *American Psychologist*, 51: 77–101.

NETTLEBECK, T., and WILSON, C. 2005. Intelligence and IQ: what teachers should know? *Educational Psychology*, 25: 609–30.

ONES, D., VISWESVARAN, C., and DILCHERT, A. 2006. Cognitive ability in selection decisions. In *Understanding and Measuring Intelligence*, ed. D. Wilheml and R. Engle. London: Sage.

REE, M., and CARRETTA, T. 1998. General cognitive ability and occupational performance. *International Review of Industrial and Organisational Psychology*, 13: 161–89.

—— —— and TEACHOUT, M. 1995. The role of ability and prior job knowledge in complex training performance. *Journal of Applied Psychology*, 80: 721–30.

—— and EARLES, J. 1994. The ubiquitous predictiveness of g. Pp. 127–35 in *Personnel Selection and Classification*, ed. M. Rumsey, C. Walker, and J. Harris. Hillsdale, NJ: Lawrence Erlbaum.

—— —— and TEACHOUT, M. 1994. Predicting job performance. *Journal of Applied Psychology*, 79: 518–24.

REEVE, C., and HAKEL, M. 2002. Asking the right questions about g. *Human Performance*, 15: 47–74.

ROCKLIN, T. 1994. Relation between typical intellectual engagement and openness. *Journal of Educational Psychology*, 86: 145–9.

RODGERS, J. 1999. A critique of the Flynn effect. *Intelligence*, 26: 337–56.

ROLFHUS, E., and ACKERMAN, P. 1999. Assessing individual differences in knowledge. *Journal of Educational Psychology*, 91: 511–26.

RUSHTON, J. 1995. *Race, Evolution and Behaviour.* New Brunswick, NJ: Transaction.

—— and JENSEN, A. R. 2005. Thirty years of research on race differences in cognitive ability. *Psychology, Public Policy and Law,* 11: 235–94.

SALGADO, J., ANDERSON, N., MOSCOSO, S., BERTUA, C., and DE FRUYT, F. 2003. International validity generalisation of GMA and cognitive abilities. *Personnel Psychology,* 56: 573–605.

SCHMIDT, F. 2002. The role of general cognitive ability and job performance. *Human Performance,* 15: 187–210.

SPEARMAN, C. 1904. "General intelligence" objectively determined and measured. *American Journal of Psychology,* 15: 201–93.

—— and HUNTER, J. E. 1977. Development of a general solution to the problem of validity generalisation. *Journal of Applied Psychology,* 62 (5): 529–40.

—— —— 1984. A within setting empirical test of the situational specificity hypothesis in personnel selection. *Personnel Psychology,* 37: 317–26.

—— —— 1998. The validity and utility of selection methods in personnel psychology: practical and theoretical implications of 85 years of research findings. *Psychological Bulletin,* 124: 262–74.

—— —— 2004. General mental ability in the world of work. *Journal of Personality and Social Psychology,* 86: 162–73.

STERNBERG, R. 1990. *Metaphors of Mind.* Cambridge: Cambridge University Press.

—— 1997. *Successful Intelligence.* New York: Plume.

—— 2005. There are no public-policy implications. *Psychology, Public Policy and Law,* 11: 295–301.

TENOPYR, M. 2002. Theory versus reality: evaluation of g in the workplace. *Human Performance,* 15: 107–22.

VISWEVARAN, C., and ONES, D. 2002. Agreements and disagreements on the role of General mental Ability (GMA) in Industrial work and organisational psychology. *Human Performance,* 15: 211–31.

—— ONES, D., and SCHMIDT, F. 1996. Comparative analysis of the reliability of job performance ratings. *Journal of Applied Psychology,* 81: 557–74.

WICHERTS, J., DOLAN, C., HESSEN, D., OOSTERVELD, P., VAN BAAL, G., BOOMSMA, D., and SPAN, M. 2004. Are intelligence tests measurement invariant over time? *Intelligence,* 32: 509–31.

2

EMOTIONAL INTELLIGENCE: RHETORIC OR REALITY?

PETER J. JORDAN

NEAL M. ASHKANASY

CATHERINE S. DAUS

1. INTRODUCTION

THERE is little doubt that, to some, the construct of emotional intelligence is confusing, and emotional intelligence researchers must "seem mad" to be embroiled in (sometimes bitter) debate. To be sure, emotional intelligence has been one of the more controversial constructs to be considered in personnel psychology. There have been varying opinions as to the efficacy of emotional intelligence for predicting workplace behaviors and performance. On one hand, respected researchers like Murphy (2006) argue that the popularity of the emotional intelligence construct is faddish and is little more than low-grade personality research. On the other hand, equally respected researchers such as Daus and Ashkanasy (2005) mount a strong case for further examination of the emotional intelligence construct as a useful framework for assessing the emotional side of organizational behavior and workplace performance.

What is not contested is that emotional intelligence research, initiated in 1990 by Salovey and Mayer, is still young in comparison to research into areas such as personality and intelligence.[1] On the positive side, there are a broad (but steadily decreasing) number of construct definitions, and finally, some valid and reliable measures of emotional intelligence are emerging (see Jordan, Ashkanasy, and Ascough 2007 for a review). Emotional intelligence research has been applied to a number of fields such as education (Salovey and Sluyter 1997), adolescent development (Lopes, Salovey, and Straus 2003), family relationships (Zeidner et al. 2003), criminology (Moriarty et al. 2001), psychology (Parker, Taylor, and Bagby 2001), and business (Cherniss and Adler 2001). In a business setting, most researchers in emotional intelligence have looked at it as an individual difference variable, and examined the relationship between emotional intelligence and attitudinal variables such as job satisfaction and commitment and, in some cases, performance. Yet, to us, what is missing from this research is an overarching framework for emotional intelligence research; to organize current research and guide future research.

There have been wide-ranging and substantial claims about the potential of emotional intelligence in predicting a broad range of workplace behavior. Previous reviews of the emotional intelligence construct have tested the links between emotional intelligence and workplace performance, emotional intelligence and career success, and emotional intelligence and leadership (Jordan, Ashkanasy, and Ashton-James, 2006). Van Rooy and Viswesvaran (2004) conducted a meta-analysis of emotional intelligence to performance, finding that there was indeed some basis for a link, but that the evidence was equivocal.[2] Reviews have also found evidence of the links between emotional intelligence and the ability to work productively with customers and clients, the ability to deal with conflict in the workplace, and positive organizational behaviors such as affective commitment (see Jordan, Ashkanasy, and Ascough 2007).

Most of these reviews, however, have examined the impact of emotional intelligence at the individual level or, on rare occasions, in teams. For this chapter, we have also chosen to assess the efficacy of the emotional intelligence construct by examining variables that have an impact at the organizational level. In particular, we will examine impact of emotional intelligence on prosocial behaviors, antisocial

---

[1] Payne (1985) in fact coined the term "emotional intelligence" in his doctoral dissertation, but did not pursue the topic. Salovey and Mayer (1990) subsequently and independently published what is regarded now as the first peer reviewed article in the field.

[2] Yet this review did not distinguish between *ability* models of emotional intelligence (e.g., Mayer, Salovey, and Caruso 2000) and personality-based models or mixed models (see Ashkanasy and Daus 2005; Mayer, Salovey, and Caruso 2000), and therefore, results of this review should be interpreted with caution.

behaviors, and leadership. We have chosen these areas as each of these variables has an impact on the ambience of the organization, and in particular emotional ambience (Ashkanasy 2003). In this chapter, we will conclude with some recommendations for advancing research into emotional intelligence in the area of personnel psychology, and in particular, we will comment on the need for emotional intelligence research to be extended to cover macro-organizational variables such as culture and climate.

2. EMOTIONAL INTELLIGENCE RESEARCH PERSPECTIVES

Although, as we noted earlier, substantial debate continues about the nature and content of emotional intelligence (e.g., see Daus and Ashkanasy 2003), we believe that a consensus is now firming about a framework for the construct. In the seventeen years since Salovey and Mayer (1990) proposed the initial model of emotional intelligence, authors such as Cherniss (in press) and Mayer, Salovey, and Caruso (2000) have identified divergent models of emotional intelligence: an ability model, which conceptualizes emotional intelligence as the ability to balance emotion and cognition; and mixed or competencies models of emotional intelligence that consider emotional intelligence to be akin to personality (see Cherniss in press). Of these models, the ability model outlined by Mayer and Salovey (1997) is the one that most academic researchers have focused on as providing prima-facie incremental validity over existing constructs of personality and intelligence (Ashkanasy and Daus 2005).

The model of emotional intelligence as outlined by Mayer and Salovey (1997) comprises four basic abilities: (a) emotional awareness; (b) emotional facilitation; (c) emotional knowledge; and (d) emotional management. This model emphasizes that emotional intelligence is a multidimensional construct, and that the four "branches" of emotional intelligence are iterative, in that all four abilities interact to shape the manifestation of the construct. For instance, in reflecting on reactions (emotional management) during a crisis situation, an individual's emotional self-awareness can contribute to a better understanding of the emotions involved (emotional knowledge).

Emotional awareness refers to the ability of individuals to be aware of their own emotional experiences and to express emotions and emotional needs accurately to others. This ability also includes awareness of others' emotions and the ability to distinguish between accurate and inaccurate, or honest and dishonest expressions of emotions (Mayer and Salovey 1997). The second ability identified by Mayer and

Salovey (1997) is emotional facilitation. This refers to an individual's ability to use emotions to prioritize thinking by focusing on important information that explains why feelings are being experienced. This factor also includes the ability to adopt multiple perspectives to assess a problem from all sides, including pessimistic and optimistic perspectives. Emotional knowledge, the third emotional intelligence ability, refers to an ability to understand emotional progressions (e.g., from less intense to more intense) and cycles (e.g., a grief cycle), and to interpret complex emotions (e.g., envy). The final ability is referred to by Mayer and Salovey (1997) as "emotional management." This ability revolves around the management of emotions; an individual's ability to connect or disconnect from an emotion depending on its usefulness in any given situation. For example, feelings of fear may contribute to either prosocial or antisocial behaviors within an organization. An individual with high emotional intelligence, for example, may become aware of a feeling of fear (emotional awareness). She or he should therefore be able to analyze the source of that fear (emotional understanding), and then to regulate that fear (emotional management) to activate the social support that prosocial behavior can produce during times of stress (emotional facilitation). The resulting positive coping approach that high emotional intelligence engenders may be helpful in dealing with the fear (Ashkanasy, Ashton-James, and Jordan 2004). Alternatively, individuals with low emotional intelligence may allow fear to consume their thoughts (low emotional understanding), which may result in impulsive acts of an antisocial nature (low emotional management) that reduces their ability to deal with the fear, and also reduces their performance in an organization (Ashkanasy, Ashton-James, and Jordan 2004).

We concede, however, that empirical data on the generic (ability and mixed) concept of emotional intelligence, some of which is inconsistent with the construct of emotional intelligence described by Mayer and Salovey (1997), continues to accumulate. In this respect, Ashkanasy and Daus (2005) identified three "streams" of emotional Intelligence research. *Stream 1* refers to research that is based on the Mayer and Salovey model, and also uses the Mayer–Salovey–Caruso Emotional Intelligence Test (MSCEIT: Mayer, Salovey, and Caruso 2002). *Stream 2* refers to research, still based on the Mayer and Salovey model, but which uses other (mostly self-report) measures of the construct (e.g., Brackett et al. 2006; Jordan et al. 2002; Palmer and Stough 2001; Schutte et al. 1998; Wong and Law 2002). *Stream 3* research refers to research that departs radically from the Mayer and Salovey definition and includes research that uses instruments such as the Emotional Intelligence Quotient (EQi: Bar-On 1997), the Emotional Competency Index (ECI; Sala 2002), the Emotional Intelligence Questionnaire (EIQ: Dulewicz, Higgs, and Slaski 2003), and the Swinburne University Emotional Intelligence Test (SUEIT: Palmer and Stough 2001).

In assessing the claims in this chapter, we will focus primarily on the results of Stream 1 or 2 research, specifically noting when findings are derived from a Stream

3 perspective. We also examine prima-facie theoretical arguments that link each claim to the emotional intelligence construct. For this assessment therefore, we draw on Mayer and Salovey's (1997) theoretical model of emotional intelligence as the appropriate framework for conceptualizing emotional intelligence. In particular, this is the only framework that is defensibly distinguishable from existing individual difference variables (Jordan, Ashkanasy, and Härtel 2003). Finally, we examine existing related research evaluating the validity of each claim according to whether or not it can be logically deduced from data, theory, and relevant research.

3. EMOTIONAL INTELLIGENCE AND ORGANIZATIONAL EFFECTIVENESS

Cherniss (2001), in an overview chapter on the nexus of emotional intelligence and organizational effectiveness, argues that emotional intelligence underlies almost all factors responsible for organizational success: including (among others) recruitment, selection, training and development, retention, motivation, and leadership. Cherniss argues further that leadership, human resource management functions, organizational climate, and culture all collectively influence the quality of relationships in organizations that are, in turn, affected by group and individual emotional intelligence.

This idea of relationships providing a foundation for organizations also resonates with Mumby and Putnam's (1992) concept of "bounded emotionality," a concept akin to emotional labor. According to Martin, Knopoff, and Beckman (1998), bounded emotionality "encourages the constrained expression of emotions at work in order to encourage community building and personal well-being" (p. 429). Martin and her colleagues suggest further that managing both the surface and the undercurrent of emotions present in an organization serves to enhance relationships, and that these relationships ultimately impact productivity. Within this framework, it is reasonable to expect that the abilities involved in building, managing, and maintaining relationships, which are inherently emotional activities, are determinants of organizational effectiveness. We agree that managing relationships vis-à-vis emotional intelligence is critical but consistent with Ashkanasy (2003), and we contend further that this can also be interpreted as a by-product of an emotionally intelligent culture, reflecting a deep and pervasive influence of emotions and emotional intelligence in the organization. In other words, behaviors that manifest through emotional intelligence are modeled as organizational norms that then influence employee behavior.

This is consistent with Schein's (1985; 1990; 1996) idea that, at its deepest levels, an organization and its leaders hold to certain deeply held assumptions (e.g., excellent customer service leads to profitability). Also, certain values are held in high esteem (e.g., the customer is worthy of respect) and serve to guide the organization, including inculcation of these values in employees. Further, these assumptions and values impact organizational goals and indicate where an organization is likely to concentrate energy. Organizational mission, value, and goal statements merely are supposed to reflect these deeply held assumptions and values. Schein (1996) emphasizes that it is organizational culture as a whole that provides evidence as to what these assumptions, values, and goals are.

We posit in this chapter, therefore, that an emotionally intelligent organization would assume the following characteristics: (1) emotions are seen by organizational members to be a form of capital (Cherniss 2001); (2) perceiving emotions accurately is therefore critical at all levels in an organization, from managers and leaders accurately perceiving employees' emotions, to front-line employees accurately perceiving customers and clients' emotions (Ashkanasy 2003); (3) understanding the basis of emotions, both positive and negative will provide important input and data to help make effective decisions (Ashton-James and Ashkanasy in press; Jordan, Ashkanasy and Härtel 2002); and that managing emotions (of self and others) effectively will lead to improved organizational effectiveness and profitability (Cherniss 2001). Related values may be such things as valuing emotionally expressivity that is a balance between extreme suppression or expression of emotions, valuing training and development opportunities for employees that stretch and hone their emotional skills and abilities, and valuing employees' use of alternative emotional ways of coping with stress such as seeking social support (Lawrence, Gardner, and Callan 2007).

Based on these arguments, we contend that emotional intelligence could have far reaching consequences for organizational effectiveness and performance. In the following sections, we flesh out this idea in an examination of the impact of emotional intelligence on three important dimensions of organizational effectiveness: (1) prosocial behaviors; (2) antisocial behaviors; and (3) leadership.

4. PROSOCIAL BEHAVIORS

Goleman (1998) proposed that altruism and empathy are components of emotional intelligence. Cherniss and Adler (2001) have more recently commented that altruism is better seen as a derivative of emotional intelligence. Similarly, Mayer and Salovey (1997) posit that empathy is better regarded as an outcome of emotional intelligence. Either way, however, all agree that altruism and empathy are closely tied to emotional intelligence. Eisenberg (1986) defined altruism as self-sacrifice or the act of engaging in behavior designed to keep others happy; and empathy as a feeling of concern and understanding for another's situation or feelings. While altruism and empathy encourage people to work collaboratively, from a personnel psychology perspective what managers are hoping for is *prosocial behavior*. In this respect, Eisenberg and Fabes (1990) describe empathy and altruism as facets of prosocial behavior that, in organizations, are linked to a positive organizational climate.

Organizational research in prosocial behavior has traditionally been in the form of studies of organizational citizenship behaviors (OCBs: Organ 1988; Organ and Ryan 1995) and affective commitment (Allen and Meyer 1990). Both of these research streams consider the extent to which employees take on work above and beyond their stipulated roles. The question that then follows is: To what extent are prosocial behaviors linked to emotional intelligence?

4.1 Linking Prosocial Behaviors to Emotional Intelligence

Eisenberg (1986; 2000) argues that emotion underlies the development of empathic attitudes and altruistic values. Assertions that emotionally intelligent people are more likely to exhibit prosocial behaviors are based on theoretical frameworks that propose that altruism and empathy underlie prosocial acts (e.g., see Cherniss and Adler 2001). Based on these models, it becomes axiomatic that emotionally intelligent people are going to be more prosocial, since empathy and altruism flow from emotional intelligence. This view is also consistent with Mayer and Salovey (1995), who argue that positive emotional management leads to both pro-individual and prosocial behaviors.

Still, a question remains as to whether prosocial behaviors also can emerge from other emotional abilities such as emotional awareness, emotional knowledge, or emotional understanding. In this respect, Salovey, Hsee, and Mayer (1993) suggest that helping others may be usefully viewed as a *mood-regulation strategy*. In essence, Salovey et al. (1993) and others (e.g., Erber and Erber 2001) argue that people engage in prosocial behavior in order to improve their negative mood (mood repair) or to maintain their positive mood (mood maintenance). It could be hypothesized that whether or not people engage in mood repair or maintenance behaviors depends on their emotional understanding and emotion management ability. According to this perspective, people who engage in prosocial behavior to maintain or repair their mood (a) have an understanding of how emotions are affected by prosocial acts; and (b) are motivated to instigate prosocial behavior in order to regulate their mood. Thus, someone with high emotional intelligence would be more likely to engage in prosocial behavior, even when she or he is in a negative mood, than someone who is low in emotional intelligence.

A corollary to the foregoing arguments is that emotion underlies many of the determinants of prosocial behavior. It is therefore reasonable to conclude that prosocial behaviors in organizations should lead to more positive relationships in organizations and a more positive culture within that organization. To create this positive environment, therefore, managing the emotional aspects of people working together is essential. Thus, in the following section, we examine the emotional intelligence perspective on prosocial behaviors.

4.2 Linking Emotional Intelligence to Prosocial Behaviors

To date, there is no research that confirms a direct link between emotional intelligence and prosocial behavior. There is, however, research into organizational citizenship behaviors that might give us some insight to this relationship. In a now classic reference on the topic of job performance, Borman and Motowidlo (1997) discuss the distinction between core task performance and performance that is outside core job responsibilities and is viewed as more discretionary—contextual performance. In this view, employees who perform extra-role behaviors that go beyond formal role requirements are seen to be contributing positively to an organization; they are demonstrating good citizenship to that organization. Thus, the term, *organizational citizenship behaviors* (Organ 1988) captures the flavor of behaviors that employees perform, that are not mandated by the job, but are things that go "above-and-beyond." In a recent comprehensive review of this literature, Podsakoff, et al. (2000) discuss seven distinct dimensions that literature has captured regarding types of organizational citizenship behaviors: (1) helping behaviors (a.k.a. altruism)—"voluntarily helping others and preventing...work-related problems" (p. 516); (2) sportsmanship or not complaining about the organization; (3) organizational loyalty—"promoting the organization to outsiders, protecting and defending it against external threats, and remaining committed to it even under adverse conditions" (p. 517); (4) organizational compliance which involves accepting and following company policy and rules, even when not being observed; (5) individual initiative, conscientiousness; (6) civic virtue, which "represents a macro-level interest in, or commitment to, the organization as a whole" (p. 525), and is manifested by a willingness to be involved in the organization, to show concern, and to voice opinions; and (7) self-development. Some of these have received quite a bit of research attention (e.g., altruism, conscientiousness), while others have received little to none (e.g., sportsmanship, self-development) (Podsakoff et al. 2000). Although some of these attributes are linked to personality traits, others such as loyalty and civic virtue clearly have an emotional basis.

Day and Carroll (2004) found a relationship between emotional intelligence and group civic virtue (the extent to which the individual contributes to the group) and group sportsmanship (the extent to which the individual is supportive of the group). Other research, while not specifically in the field of emotional intelligence, also points to a link between emotional management and organizational citizenship behaviors. Lee and Allen (2002) identified the important role of emotions in developing organizational citizenship behaviors. Charbonneau and Nicol (2002) also found that emotional intelligence was linked to prosocial behavior. Charbonneau and Nicol (2002) examined the relationship between self-reported emotional intelligence and peer-reports of OCBs with a sample of adolescents attending a military training camp. Self-report emotional intelligence (Schutte et al.'s 1998 Stream 2 measure) was positively correlated with other reported altruism and civic virtue. In another study using the Schutte et al. (1998) self-report measure, Carmeli and Josman (2006) also showed that emotional intelligence predicted supervisor-rated altruism and compliance. Specifically, appraisal and expression of emotions was positively associated with altruism, whereas both recognition and utilization of emotions were significantly associated with both altruism and compliance.

In a more recent Stream 1 study, Lopes et al. (2006) found that high emotional intelligence employees (based on the MSCEIT) were rated by their colleagues as contributing to a positive work environment. At the same time, supervisors rated the high emotional intelligence employees as more sociable and better able to deal with others. Again all of these attributes are indicative of prosocial behaviors.

Based on the foregoing review, a consensus based on empirical studies is emerging that emotions contribute to the development of prosocial behaviors. The research evidence also suggests that specific emotional abilities contribute to prosocial behaviors. Emotional awareness and emotional regulation are important factors that predict positive behaviors in organizations. More research is required, however, to clarify which particular emotional intelligence abilities are integral in creating prosocial behaviors, and to separate the incremental contribution from other factors such as personality and attitudinal variables.

5. ANTISOCIAL BEHAVIOR

Research has identified two broad types of antisocial behavior: antisocial behavior directed at individuals and antisocial behavior directed at the organization (Bennett and Robinson 2000). According to Bennett and Robinson, antisocial behavior directed at individuals includes playing pranks and hurtful comments made to co-workers, while behaviors directed at the organization include falsification of records and dragging out work. Broadly, antisocial actions in organizations can result in harm to individuals within the organization or to the organization as a whole. This can be physical, economic, psychological, or emotional harm (Robinson and O'Leary-Kelly 1998). Antisocial acts thus have the potential to influence the ambience of an organization in a negative way.

In addition, antisocial behavior such as aggression, withdrawal or avoidance, risk taking, rule violations, dishonesty, deviance, and absenteeism are often the product of emotional episodes such as expressions of anger (Granic and Butler 1998) or depressed moods (Sareen et al. 2004). Spector (1997) argues that events and conditions at work can induce anger and frustration that are accompanied by antisocial acts such as aggression, sabotage, theft, and the intentional withholding of output. Weiss and Cropanzano (1996) view antisocial behavior as a form of impulsive emotional reaction to negative work events.

In a meta-analysis examining the effect of negative affect on job-related outcomes, Thoresen et al. (2003) found that negative affect positively correlated with emotional exhaustion, depersonalization, turnover intentions; and negatively correlated with job satisfaction, organizational commitment, and personal accomplishment. These findings held for both state and trait negative affect. In a more recent study into the experience of emotions in the workplace, Jordan and Murray (2006) found that negative emotions were twice as likely to be experienced as positive emotions using a workplace sample. In their study, they found that negative emotions were also experienced at a greater intensity than positive emotions. The most reported negative emotion was frustration. Consistent with previous research that reported negative emotions (Keenan and Newton 1985; Narayanan, Menon, and Spector 1999), the other common negative emotions discussed by participants were anger and annoyance, frustration, and loathing. Given this prevalence of negative emotions in organizations and the link between negative emotions and antisocial behavior, the question that therefore needs to be addressed is to what extent low emotional intelligence predicts antisocial behavior.

5.1 Linking Antisocial Behavior to Emotional Intelligence

Ability to manage or to regulate behavioral expression of emotions (the fourth component of Mayer and Salovey's 1997 model of emotional intelligence) may also be related to individual differences in antisocial behavior at work. That is, people who have poor emotion management ability would, by definition, be more likely to manifest antisocial workplace behavior in response to emotional triggers. Individuals with high emotional intelligence, or more specifically those who are able to understand and to manage their emotions, are less likely to engage in these behaviors as they will risk damaging working relationships with their peers, and so reduce the quality of their work environment. This idea that poor self-regulation and antisocial behavior are related is also supported by the research of Eisenberg (2000), Krueger, Hicks, and McGue (2001), and Scarpa and Raine (1997).

A further example of antisocial behavior can be found in bullying (Sheehan 1999). Sheehan argues that bullying in organizations can be addressed, in part, by applying emotional intelligence abilities. He further suggests that a significant amount of bullying emerges from poor communication and inability of managers to deal with negative experiences in the workplace. Even though not specific about how emotional abilities address antisocial behavior, one process that Sheehan emphasizes is the ability to deal with negative emotions that emerge during organizational change.

Consistent with this line of reasoning, and our emphasis on emotional intelligence as an organizational cultural phenomenon, we argue further that there is likely to be a relationship between negative emotions, antisocial behaviors, and a poor work climate resulting from a negative organizational culture (Denison 1996). Fox and Spector (1999), for example, found that negative emotions were significantly negatively correlated with job satisfaction and significantly positively correlated with the counter-productive behaviors of abuse, production deviance, and behavioral withdrawal. Spector and his colleagues (Chen and Spector 1991; Fox and Spector 1999) also reported positive correlations between negative emotions such as frustration, anger, and anxiety and a variety of counter-productive workplace behaviors including sabotage, interpersonal aggression, absenteeism, and theft.

5.2 Linking Emotional Intelligence to Antisocial Behavior

Unfortunately, there is also a dearth of research examining the link between emotional intelligence and antisocial behaviors in organizations. There has, however, been some research into emotional intelligence and antisocial behavior among adolescents. For instance, Petrides, Frederickson, and Furnham (2004) looked at emotional intelligence (measured using Stream 2 measure of emotional intelligence) and found, controlling for personality, that emotional intelligence predicted students being excluded from school. Since exclusion in schools is usually for rule breaking, it is reasonable to assume it is a proxy for antisocial behavior.

Brackett, Mayer, and Warner (2004), in a Stream 1 study of university students, found that high emotional intelligence was negatively associated with male deviant behavior including using illegal drugs, drinking alcohol excessively, and engaging in fighting and vandalism (after controlling for personality and intellectual intelligence). Male students with low emotional intelligence also reported greater difficult in creating meaningful friendships than those with high emotional intelligence.

Further evidence of the link between emotional intelligence and antisocial behavior emerges from a review by Vardi and Weitz (2003). These authors concluded that attitudes and subjective norms explain significant amounts of variance in the intention to misbehave in organizations. They are supported by Lewicki et al. (1997) who, in a related review on workplace dishonesty, found that organizational, rather than personality factors were the best predictors of dishonesty and deviance. On the basis that perceived unfair treatment, poor organizational culture, and poor supervision motivate employees to engage in deviant behavior (Greenberg 1987), it is reasonable to conclude that these results can be interpreted as supporting our position that low emotional intelligence is a precursor to antisocial behavior.

We conclude therefore that, despite the lack of direct empirical evidence in organizational settings, there is a sound rationale to expect that low emotional intelligence should be related to manifestations of antisocial behavior in organizations. Much evidence to date regards the effect of negative emotions and adolescent samples; thus there is clearly a need for organizational research. Also, research needs to establish the specific emotional intelligence abilities that are linked to antisocial behaviors in organizations.

6. LEADERSHIP

Leaders of organizations have arguably the most pervasive and long-lasting influence on shaping their organizations' cultures (Cherniss 2001; Schein 1990). Ways they do this include through assumptions, both directly stated and implicitly held, and public and private organizational goals. In Cherniss's model of emotional intelligence and organizational effectiveness (2001), he places leadership alongside organizational culture and HR functions as being critical precursors to having a fully developed emotionally intelligent organization. Thus, the importance of leadership in shaping an emotionally intelligent organization cannot be overstated. In this respect, Schein (1985) argued that founding leaders provide long-term vision and corporate values around which they build their organization's culture; and that contemporary leaders continue to shape and, at times, redirect the organizational culture to reflect current organizational values and goals. Moreover, in view of today's massive organizational changes, including mergers, acquisitions, and downsizing, "to be effective in helping their organizations manage change, leaders first need to be aware of and to manage their own feelings of anxiety and uncertainty" (Bunker 1997, 135). Bunker (1997) also notes that leaders have an essential role in modeling emotional vulnerability and responsiveness with their employees during such major change.

Persons in lower-level positions of leadership such as middle managers also have a primary role in shaping culture and influencing employees. The influence of a boss is so critical that it is a primary determinant of whether and how long employees stay with an organization. Zipkin (2000) reported on a 1999 Gallup poll that found 40 percent of employees who felt their boss was poor were likely to begin searching for a job, compared to only 11 percent of employees who felt their bosses were excellent. Many authors have suggested the critical nature of leaders/ bosses being able to sense employees' emotions and manage them effectively, as well as to understand and manage their own effectively (Ashkanasy and Tse 2000; Ashkanasy, Härtel and Daus 2002; Cherniss 2001; George 2000).

6.1 Linking Leadership to Emotional Intelligence

Bass (1990) was one of the first scholars to note the importance of emotional maturity in leadership. This view is reflected in more recent literature on emotional intelligence (e.g., Cooper and Sawaf 1997), where it is assumed that the ability of leaders to understand and manage emotions is central to the leader's effectiveness (see also Dasborough 2006). Goleman, Boyatzis, and McKee (2002) argue in particular that a leader's ability to manage the emotions of others is the key to supporting and motivating employees. Kellett, Humphrey, and Sleeth (2006) emphasize the leader's ability to display and to manage her or his own emotions, and the followers' perception of the leader's displayed emotions. This is consistent with Dasborough and Ashkanasy (2002), who argue that the leader's emotional displays are critical for maintaining relationships with followers.

These ideas were translated into a theory of emotional intelligence and leadership by George (2000), who based her ideas on the Mayer and Salovey (1997) ability model. In George's theory, emotional intelligence helps followers to develop group goals and objectives. This is achieved through the leader motivating followers to perform well in their work tasks, and to do so in an atmosphere of cooperation, confidence, trust, and optimism. Zhou and George (2003) subsequently extended this model to suggest that emotionally intelligent leaders also foster group creativity.

Despite these claims, there are some who feel strongly that the role of emotional intelligence in leadership has been overstated. Antonakis (2004), for example, maintains that emotional intelligence cannot add any predictive power to leadership effectiveness beyond personality and cognitive intelligence. These claims seem to be driven in the main, however, by a misunderstanding of the role of emotional intelligence abilities in leadership. As we have already argued in this chapter, emotional intelligence abilities are largely concerned with managing interpersonal relationships. Since leadership is inherently a process of social interaction, it would seem to follow that emotional intelligence has some role to play, especially in social situations where emotional feelings and displays are important. Clearly, when the leader does not have close social contact with followers, the role of emotional intelligence is likely to be diminished. We argue, however, that this is the exception, rather than the norm.

6.2 Evidence Linking Leadership to Emotional Intelligence

Despite some of the exaggerated and largely unsubstantiated claims made by Goleman and his colleagues (2002), serious and rigorous research into this topic is really only just beginning. Daus and Ashkanasy (2005) argue that research based in the Stream 1 approach to emotional intelligence is likely to be the most productive, and describe several unpublished (at that stage) empirical studies of this genre that show an association between transformational leadership and emotional intelligence. Two studies of this genre that have been published, however, and that have found positive relationships, are by Rosete and Ciarrochi (2005) and Kerr et al. (2006). Rosete and Ciarrochi found that MSCEIT scores were correlated with administrative ratings of leader effectiveness, while Kerr and his colleagues found similar effects for follower ratings of leader effectiveness.

Nonetheless, the majority of published research lies in the Stream 2 and 3 approaches. For example, Palmer et al. (2000) using a Stream 3 approach, found support for a hypothesized effect of emotional intelligence on effective leadership. More recently, Moss, Ritossa, and Ngu (2006), using the same emotional intelligence measure in a field setting, found only mixed support for emotional intelligence and its effect on leadership effectiveness. Wong and Law (2002) employed a Stream 2 approach, again in a field study, and reported that leader emotional intelligence predicted follower job satisfaction and extra-role behavior. They did not, however, find that leader emotional intelligence was related to group performance.

More positive results, however, have been found in studies that have looked specifically at leadership emergence in groups and follower perceptions of leaders. Here, several researchers (Pescosolido 2002; Wolff, Pescosolido, and Druskat 2002; Pirola-Merlo et al. 2002) have found support for the idea that emotional intelligence predicts leader emergence although, of course, this does not necessarily mean that the leader will be effective in this role. Regarding follower perceptions of leader effectiveness, Kellett and colleagues (2006), using a Stream 2 approach, found that a leader's emotional intelligence predicted follower perceptions of leadership effectiveness.

The link between emotional intelligence and leadership is intuitively appealing, and this has been capitalized on by popular authors such as Goleman (1998). At the same time, the propensity of these authors to make unsubstantiated grand claims (see Jordan, Ashkanasy, and Ascough 2007 for more details of these claims) has muddied the waters, and critics such as Antonakis (2004) have been quick to respond. Nonetheless, recent research is beginning to paint a more positive picture. Studies by Rosete and Ciarrochi (2005) and Kerr and colleagues (2006) are starting to find effects in field studies of organizational leadership, and Daus and Ashkanasy (2005) describe several unpublished Stream 1 research projects that point in the same direction. Thus, while there is still a need for additional research into emotional intelligence and leadership, results to date are encouraging.

7. Behaviors in an Emotionally Intelligent Organization

The behavior of individuals in organizations is the most visible manifestation of organizational culture (Ott 1989). In particular, behaviors convey a particular message or "feel" of the organization. In a healthy organizational environment, behaviors are consistent with the organization's basic values, where employees consistently "walk the talk" of its organizational culture. We argue that, in the case of an "emotionally intelligent organization," employee behaviors are predominantly prosocial and positive in nature.

Clearly for us, emotionally intelligent organizations that have employees with a strong person-environment fit will perform better. Note that in this case we focus on the emotional aspects of person environment fit (Kristof 1996). We therefore argue that employees who exhibit emotional intelligence will seek out emotionally intelligent cultures, and organizations that are emotionally intelligent will seek to employ emotionally intelligent employees. Schneider's attraction-selection-attrition model (1987) suggests this process: strong organizations attract individuals who match their culture, and the individuals who fit best stay and prosper in the organizational environment, while those who don't either select themselves out or get "forced" out. Emotionally intelligent employees are much more likely to exhibit OCBs, often characterized by emotion recognition, understanding, and management. For example, helping others voluntarily is predicated on: (1) *recognizing the need* expressed (likely emotionally) by a colleague; (2) *being willing to help* (which is related to empathy, a core aspect of emotional intelligence); and (3) *understanding what emotions* (e.g., empathy; compassion; confidence) and behaviors *to convey* as best fits the situation. Clearly sportsmanship heavily involves emotional intelligence—the ability to convey a positive emotional state about the organization and to refrain from being infected with negative emotional states.

8. IMPLICATIONS FOR THEORY, PRACTICE, AND RESEARCH

The inevitable conclusion from the evidence we have presented in this chapter is that emotional intelligence as a positive influence on organizational behavior is most likely more than mere rhetoric. We have shown in this review that research evidence is mounting that emotional intelligence can and does have an impact in terms of building a positive organizational culture. In particular, emotional intelligence contributes to more positive relationships in organizations through the promotion of prosocial behaviors between employees and between managers and employees. Based on Ashkanasy's (2003) call for multi-level research on emotions in organizations, we note that there is a lack of theory that clearly links emotional intelligence to organizational level variables. In this chapter, therefore, we have suggested some forward directions in testing this relationship, but a comprehensive theory of what constitutes an emotionally intelligent organization is still required.

From a practical point of view, the implications of this chapter are clear: behavior in organizations has a direct and reciprocal impact on organizational culture. More specifically, emotional abilities have an impact on leadership in organizations, and on how employees relate to each other. It follows therefore that promoting emotional intelligence as a core competency with organizations must be accompanied by an equal emphasis on how these competencies are manifested in organizational practices and policies. We believe we have demonstrated the impact of emotional intelligence on prosocial behaviors and antisocial behaviors in organizational contexts, as well as organizational leadership. In this case, managers trying to develop a positive organizational culture or climate need to be keenly aware of this evidence.

Finally, from a research perspective, and as we have already emphasized, future research needs to focus on the specific emotional intelligence abilities that contribute to encouragement of prosocial behaviors, discouragement of antisocial behaviors, and better leadership in organizations.

REFERENCES

ALLEN, N. J., and MEYER, J. P. 1990. The measurement and antecedents of affective, continuance, and normative commitment to the organization. *Journal of Occupational Psychology*, 63: 1–18.

ANTONAKIS, J. 2004. On why "emotional intelligence" will not predict leadership effectiveness beyond IQ or the "big five": an extension and rejoinder. *Organizational Analysis*, 12: 171–82.

ASHKANASY, N. M. 2003. Emotions in organizations: a multilevel perspective. Pp. 9–54 in *Research in Multi-Level Issues* vol. ii: *Multi-Level Issues in Organizational Behavior and Strategy*, ed. F. Dansereau. Oxford: Elsevier Science.

—— and DAUS, C. S. 2005. Rumors of the death of emotional intelligence in organizational behavior are vastly exaggerated. *Journal of Organizational Behavior*, 26: 441–52.

—— and TSE, B. 2000. Transformational leadership as management of emotion. Pp. 221–35 in *Emotions in the Workplace: Research, Theory, and Practice*, ed. N. M. Ashkanasy, C. E. J. Hartel, and W. Zerbe Westport, CT: Quorum Books.

—— ASHTON-JAMES, C. E., and JORDAN, P. J. 2004. Performance impacts of appraisal and coping with stress in workplace settings: the role of affect and emotional intelligence. Pp. 1–43 in *Research in Occupational Stress and Wellbeing*, vol. iii: *Emotional and Psychological Processes and Positive Intervention Strategies*, ed. P. Perrewé and D. Ganster. Oxford: Elsevier/JAI Press.

—— HÄRTEL, C. E. J., and DAUS, C. S. 2002. Diversity and emotion: the new frontiers in organizational behavior research. *Journal of Management*, 28 (3): 307–38.

ASHTON-JAMES, C. E., and ASHKANASY, N. M. (in press). Affective events theory: a strategic perspective. In *Research on Emotion in Organizations*, vol. iv: *Emotions, Ethics, and Decision-Making*, ed. W. J. Zerbe, C. E. J. Härtel, and N. M. Ashkanasy. Oxford: Elsevier/JAI Press.

BAR-ON, R. (1997). *Bar-On Emotional Quotient Inventory: A Measure of Emotional Intelligence*. Toronto: Multi-Health Systems, Inc.

BASS, B. M. 1990. *Bass and Stogdill's Handbook of Leadership: A Survey of Theory and Research*. New York: Free Press.

BENNETT, R. J. and ROBINSON, S. L. 2000. The development of a measure of workplace deviance. *Journal of Applied Psychology*, 85: 349–60.

BORMAN, W. C., and MOTOWIDLO, S. J. 1997. Task performance and contextual performance: the meaning for personnel selection research. *Human Performance*, 10: 99–109.

BRACKETT, M. A., MAYER, J. D., and WARNER, R. M. 2004. Emotional intelligence and the prediction of behavior. *Personality and Individual Differences*, 36: 1387–402.

—— RIVERS, S. E, SHIFFMAN, S., LERNER N., and SALOVEY P. 2006. Relating emotional abilities to social functioning: a comparison of self-report and performance measures of emotional intelligence. *Journal of Personality and Social Psychology*, 91: 780–95.

BUNKER, K. A. 1997. The power of vulnerability in contemporary leadership. *Consulting Psychology Journal: Practice and Research*, 49 (2): 122–36.

CARMELI, A., and JOSMAN, Z. E. 2006. The relationship among emotional intelligence, task performance, and organizational citizenship behaviors. *Human Performance*, 19 (4): 403–19.

CHARBONNEAU, D., and NICOL, A. A. M. 2002. Emotional intelligence and prosocial behavior in adolescents. *Psychological Reports*, 90: 361–70.

CHEN, P. Y., and SPECTOR, P. E. 1991. Negative affectivity as the underlying cause of correlations between stressors and strains. *Journal of Applied Psychology*, 76: 398–407.

CHERNISS, C. 2001. Emotional intelligence and organizational effectiveness. Pp. 4–12 in *The Emotionally Intelligent Workplace: How to Select for, Measure, and Improve Emotional Intelligence in Individuals, Groups, and Organizations*, ed. C. Cherniss and D. Goleman. San Francisco: Jossey-Bass.

—— In press. Emotional intelligence: towards clarification of a concept. Working paper.

CHERNISS, C. and ADLER, M. 2001. *Promoting Emotional Intelligence in Organizations.* Alexandria, VA: American Society for Training and Development (ASTD).

COOPER, R. K. and SAWAF, A. 1997. *Executive EQ: Emotional Intelligence in Leadership and Organizations.* New York: Grosset/Putman.

DASBOROUGH, M. T. 2006. Cognitive asymmetry in employee emotional reactions to leadership behaviours. *Leadership Quarterly,* 17: 163–78.

—— and ASHKANASY, N. M. 2002. Emotion and attribution of intentionality in leader-follower relationships. *Leadership Quarterly,* 13: 615–34.

DAUS, C. S., and ASHKANASY, N. M. 2003. Will the real emotional intelligence please stand up? On deconstructing the emotional intelligence "debate". *The Industrial and Organizational Psychologist,* 41 (2): 69–72.

—— —— 2005. The case for the ability based model of emotional intelligence in organizational behavior. *Journal of Organizational Behavior,* 26: 453–66.

DAY, A. L., and CARROLL, S. A. 2004. Using an ability-based measure of emotional intelligence to predict individual performance, group performance, and group citizenship behaviours. *Personality and Individual Differences,* 36: 1443–58.

DENISON, D. R. 1996. What IS the difference between organizational culture and organizational climate? A native's point of view on a decade of paradigm wars. *Academy of Management Review,* 21: 1–36.

DULEWICZ, V., HIGGS, M., and SLASKI, M. 2003. Measuring emotional intelligence: content, construct and criterion-related validity. *Journal of Managerial Psychology,* 18: 405.

EISENBERG, N. 1986. *Altruistic Emotion, Cognition, and Behavior.* Hillsdale, NJ: Lawrence Erlbaum.

—— 2000. Emotion regulation and moral development. *Annual Review of Psychology,* 51: 665–97.

—— and FABES, R. A. 1990. Empathy: conceptualization, assessment, and relation to prosocial behavior. *Motivation and Emotion,* 14: 131–49.

ERBER, R., and ERBER, M. W. 2001. Mood and processing: a view from a self-regulation perspective. Pp. 63–84 in *Theories of Mood and Cognition: A User's Guidebook,* ed. L. L. Martin and G. L. Clore. Mahwah, NJ: Erlbaum.

FOX, S., and SPECTOR, P. E. 1999. A model of work frustration-aggression. *Journal of Organizational Behaviour,* 20: 915–31.

GEORGE, J. M. 2000. Emotions and leadership: the role of emotional intelligence. *Human Relations,* 53: 1027–55.

GOLEMAN, D. 1998. *Working with Emotional Intelligence.* New York: Bantam Books.

—— BOYATZIS. R., and McKEE, A. 2002. *Primal Leadership: Realizing the Power of Emotional Intelligence.* Cambridge, MA: Harvard Business School Press.

GRANIC, I., and BUTLER, S. 1998. The Relationship between Anger and Anti-social Beliefs in Young Offenders. *Personality and Individual Differences,* 24: 759–65.

GREENBERG, J. 1987. A taxonomy of organizational justice theories. *Academy of Management Review,* 12: 9–22.

JORDAN, P. J., and MURRAY, J. P. 2006. *Memory of Emotions at Work.* A poster presented at the Annual Meeting of the Society of Australasian Social Psychologists (SASP), Canberra.

—— ASHKANASY, N. M., and ASCOUGH K. 2007. Emotional intelligence in organizational behavior and industrial-organizational psychology. In *Science of Emotional Intelligence: Knowns and Unknowns,* ed. G. Matthews, M. Zeidner, and R. D. Roberts. New York: Oxford University Press.

—— and ASHTON-JAMES, C. E. 2006. Evaluating the claims: emotional intelligence in the workplace. Pp. 189–210 in *A Critique of Emotional Intelligence: What are the Problems and How can They be Fixed?*, ed. K. R. Murphy. Mahwah, NJ: Lawrence Erlbaum.

—— —— and HÄRTEL, C. E. J. 2002. Emotional intelligence as a moderator of emotional and behavioral reactions to job insecurity. *Academy of Management Review*, 27: 361–72.

—— —— —— 2003. The case for emotional intelligence in organizational research. *Academy of Management Review*, 28 (2): 195–7.

—— —— —— and HOOPER, G. S. (2002). Workgroup emotional intelligence: scale development and relationship to team process effectiveness and goal focus. *Human Resource Management Review*, 12: 195–214.

KEENAN, A., and NEWTON, T. J. 1985. Stressful events, stressors and psychological strains in young professional engineers. *Journal of Occupational Behaviour*, 6: 151–6.

KELLETT, J. B., HUMPHREY, R. H., and SLEETH, R. G. 2006. Empathy and the emergence of task and relations leaders. *Leadership Quarterly*, 17: 146–62.

KERR, R., GARVIN, J., HEATON, N., and BOYLE, E. 2006. Emotional intelligence and leadership effectiveness. *Leadership and Organization Development Journal*, 27: 265–79.

KRISTOF, A. L. 1996. Person-organization fit: an integrative review of its conceptualizations, measurement and implications. *Personnel Psychology*, 49: 1–49.

KRUEGER, R. F., HICKS, B. M., and McGUE, M. 2001. Altruism and antisocial behavior: Independent tendencies, unique personality correlates, distinct etiologies. *Psychological Science*, 12: 397–402.

LAWRENCE S.A., GARDNER J., and CALLAN V. J. 2007. The support appraisal for work stressors inventory: construction and initial validation. *Journal of Vocational Behavior*, 70: 172–204.

LEE, K., and ALLEN, N. J. 2002. Organizational citizenship and workplace deviance: the role of affect and cognitions. *Journal of Applied Psychology*, 87: 131–42.

LEWICKI, R. J., POLAND, T., MINTON, J. W., and SHEPPARD, B. H. 1997. Dishonesty as deviance: a typology of workplace dishonesty and contributing factors. In Pp. 53–86 in *Research on Negotiations in Organizations*, ed. R. J. Lewicki, R. J. Bies and B. H. Sheppard. Greenwich, CT.: JAI Press Inc.

LOPES, P. N., GREWAL, D., KADIS, J., GALL, M., and SALOVEY, P. 2006. Evidence that emotional intelligence is related to job performance and affect and attitudes at work. *Psicothema*, 18: Suppl: 132–8.

—— SALOVEY, P., and STRAUS, R. 2003. Emotional intelligence, personality, and the perceived quality of social relationships. *Personality and Individual Differences*, 35: 641–58.

MARTIN, J., KNOPOFF, K., and BECKMAN, C. 1998. An alternative to bureaucratic impersonality and emotional labor: bounded emotionality at The Body Shop. *Administrative Science Quarterly*, 43: 429–69.

MAYER, J., and SALOVEY, P. 1995. Emotional intelligence and the construction and regulation of feelings. *Applied and Preventative Psychology*, 4: 197–208.

—— —— 1997. What is emotional intelligence? Pp. 3–31 in *Emotional Development and Emotional Intelligence: Educational Implications*, ed. P. Salovey and D. J. Sluyter. New York: Basic Books.

—— —— and CARUSO, D. R. 2000. Models of emotional intelligence. Pp. 396–420 in *Handbook of Human Intelligence*, 2nd edn., ed. R. J. Sternberg. New York: Cambridge University Press.

MAYER, J., and SALOVEY, P. 2002. *Mayer–Salovey–Caruso Emotional Intelligence Test (MSCEIT) Users Manual.* Toronto: MHS Test Publishers.

MORIARTY, N., STOUGH, C., TIDMARSH, P., EGER, D., and DENNISON, S. 2001. Deficits in emotional intelligence underlying adolescent sex offending. *Journal of Adolescence,* 24: 1–9.

MOSS, S., RITOSSA, D., and NGU, S. 2006. The effect of follower regulatory focus and extraversion on leadership behavior. *Journal of Individual Differences,* 27: 93–107.

MUMBY, D. K., and PUTNAM, L. A. 1992. The politics of emotion: a feminist reading of bounded rationality. *Academy of Management Review,* 17: 465–86.

MURPHY, K. R., ed. 2006. *A Critique of Emotional Intelligence: What are the Problems and how can they be Fixed?* Mahwah, NJ: Lawrence Erlbaum.

NARAYANAN, L., MENON, S., and SPECTOR, P. E. 1999. Stress in the workplace: a comparison of gender and occupations. *Journal of Organizational Behavior,* 20: 63–73.

ORGAN, D. W. 1988. *Organizational Citizenship Behavior,* Lexington, MA: Lexington Books.

—— and RYAN, K. 1995. A meta-analytic review of attitudinal and dispositional predictors of organizational citizenship behavior. *Personnel Psychology,* 48: 775–802.

OTT, J. S. 1989. *The Organizational Culture Perspective.* New York: Brooks/Cole.

PALMER, B., and STOUGH, C. 2001. *Workplace SUEIT: Swinburne University Emotional Intelligence Test—Descriptive Report.* Organisational Psychology Research Unit, Swinburne University.

—— WALLS, M., BURGESS, Z., and STOUGH, C. 2001. Emotional intelligence and effective leadership. *Leadership and Organization Development Journal,* 22: 5–10.

PARKER, J. D. A., TAYLOR, G. J., and BAGBY, R. M. 2001. The relationship between emotional intelligence and alexithymia. *Personality and Individual Differences,* 30: 107–15.

PAYNE, W. L. 1985. A study of emotion: developing emotional intelligence; self-integration; relating to fear, pain and desire (theory, structure of reality, problem-solving, contraction/expansion, tuning in/coming out/letting go). Unpublished Doctoral Dissertation. Cincinnati, OH: The Union for Experimenting Colleges and Universities (now The Union Institute).

PESCOSOLIDO, A. T. 2002. Emergent leaders as managers of group emotion. *Leadership Quarterly,* 13: 583–99.

PETRIDES, K. V., FREDERICKSON, N., and FURNHAM, A. 2004. The role of trait emotional intelligence in academic performance and deviant behavior at school. *Personality and Individual Difference,* 36: 277–93.

PIROLA-MERLO, A., HÄRTEL, C., MANN, L., and HIRST, G. 2002. How leaders influence the impact of affective events on team climate and performance in R and D teams. *Leadership Quarterly,* 13: 561–81.

PODSAKOFF, P. M., MACKENZIE, S. B., PAINE, J. B., and BACHRACH, D. G. 2000. Organizational citizenship behaviors: a critical review of the theoretical and empirical literature and suggestions for future research. *Journal of Management,* 2: 513–63.

ROBINSON, S. L., and O'LEARY-KELLY, A. 1998. Monkey see, monkey do: the influence of work groups on the antisocial behavior of employees. *Academy of Management Journal,* 41: 658–72.

ROSETE, D., and CIARROCHI, J. 2005. Emotional intelligence and its relationship to workplace performance outcomes of leadership effectiveness. *Leadership and Organization Development Journal,* 26: 388–99.

SALA, F. 2002. *Emotional Competence Inventory: Technical Manual*. McClelland Center For Research: Hay Group.

SALOVEY, P., and MAYER, J. D. 1990. Emotional intelligence. *Imagination, Cognition and Personality*, 9: 185–211.

—— and SLUYTER D. J. (1997). *Emotional Development and Emotional Intelligence: Educational Implications*. New York: Basic Books.

—— HSEE, C. K., and MAYER, J. D. 1993. Emotional intelligence and the self-regulation of affect. Pp. 258–77 in *Handbook of Mental Control*, ed. D. M. Wegner and J. W. Pennebaker. Englewood Cliffs, NJ: Prentice Hall.

SAREEN, J., STEIN, M. B., COX, B. J., and HASSARD, S. T. 2004. Understanding comorbidity of anxiety disorders with antisocial behavior. *Journal of Nervous and Mental Disease*, 192: 178–86.

SCARPA, A., and RAINE, A. 1997. Psychophysiology of anger and violent behavior. *Psychiatric Clinics of North America*, 20: 375–94.

SCHEIN, E. H. 1985. *Organizational Culture and Leadership: A Dynamic View*. San Fransisco: Jossey-Bass Inc.

—— 1990. Organizational culture: the changing face and place of work. *American Psychologist*, 45 (2): 109–19.

—— 1996. Culture: the missing concept in organization studies. *Administrative Science Quarterly*, 41: 229–40.

SCHNEIDER, B. (1987). *Organization Climate and Culture*. San Francisco: Jossey-Bass.

SCHUTTE, N. S., MALOUFF, J. M., HALL, L. E., HAGGERTY, D. J., COOPER, J. T., GOLDEN, C. J., and DORNHEIM, L. 1998. Development and validation of a measure of emotional intelligence. *Personality and Individual Differences*, 25: 167–77.

SHEEHAN, M. 1999. Workplace bullying: responding with some emotional intelligence. *International Journal of Manpower*, 20 (1/2): 57–69.

SPECTOR, P. E. 1997. *Job satisfaction: application, assessment, causes, and consequences*. Thousand Oaks, CA: Sage.

THORESEN, C. J., KAPLAN, S. A., BARSKY, A. P., WARREN, C. R., and DE CHERMONT, K. 2003. The affective underpinnings of job perceptions and attitudes: a meta-analytic review and integration. *Psychological Bulletin*, 129 (6): 914–45.

VAN ROOY, D. L. and VISWESVARAN, C. 2004. Emotional intelligence: a meta-analytic investigation of predictive validity and nomological net. *Journal of Vocational Behavior*, 65: 71–95.

VARDI, Y. and WEITZ E. 2004. *Misbehavior in Organizations: Theory, Research, and Management*. Mahwah, NJ: Lawrence Erlbaum.

WEISS, H. M., and CROPANZANO, R. 1996. Affective events theory: a theoretical discussion of the structure, causes and consequences of affective experiences at work. Pp. 1–74 in *Research in Organizational Behavior*, vol. xix, ed. B. M. Staw and L. L. Cummings. Greenwich, CT: JAI Press.

WOLFF, S. B., PESCOSOLIDO, A. T., and DRUSKAT, V. U. 2002. Emotional intelligence as the basis of leadership emergence in self-managing teams. *Leadership Quarterly*, 13: 505–22.

WONG, C. S., and LAW, K. S. 2002. The effect of leader and follower emotional intelligence on performance and attitude: an exploratory study. *Leadership Quarterly*, 13: 243–74.

ZEIDNER, M., MATTHEWS, G., ROBERTS, R. D., and MacCANN, C. 2003. Development of emotional intelligence: towards a multi-level investment model. *Human Development*, 46 (2–3): 69–96.

ZHOU, J., and GEORGE, J. M. 2003. Awakening employee creativity: the role of leader emotional intelligence. *The Leadership Quarterly*, 14: 545–68.

ZIPKIN, A. 2000. Kinder, gentler workplace replaces era of tough boss. *New York Times News Service*, 1.

3

MODELING THE INFLUENCE OF PERSONALITY ON INDIVIDUALS AT WORK: A REVIEW AND RESEARCH AGENDA

JEFF W. JOHNSON

SARAH A. HEZLETT

1. INTRODUCTION

FUNDER (2001) defined personality as "an individual's characteristic patterns of thought, emotion, and behavior, together with the psychological mechanisms—hidden or not—behind those patterns" (p. 2). Thus, personality characteristics are stable individual differences (i.e., traits) that are psychological in nature, although it may be difficult to isolate and measure the psychological mechanisms underlying these traits (Saucier and Goldberg 2003). It is hard to imagine an individual work outcome that would not be influenced by the individual's characteristic patterns of thought, emotion, and behavior. The challenge for researchers interested in describing, explaining, and predicting the behavior of individuals at work is to accurately identify and measure the personality traits that influence the outcomes of interest.

Mount, Barrick, and Ryan (2003) classified individual-level work outcomes that are influenced by personality into two classes: (1) attitudes (i.e., satisfaction, or "are you happy doing it?"); and (2) performance (i.e., satisfactoriness, or "are you able to do it?"). Attitudes have both affective (level of positive or negative feelings about a target) and cognitive (beliefs or thoughts about a target) components (Weiss 2002). Examples of work attitudes include job satisfaction, organizational commitment, and career satisfaction. Attitudes are not only of interest as work outcomes themselves. They also are related to other outcomes that more directly affect the success of the organization, including job performance, turnover, and productivity.

Performance is defined as behavior that is relevant to the goals of the organization and that can be measured in terms of the level of the individual's contribution to those goals (Campbell 1990). Performance can be distinguished from effectiveness, which is some aggregate of the outcomes of performance that can be influenced to some extent by factors other than the individual's performance (e.g., dollar volume of sales). The performance outcomes focused on in this chapter are aspects of individual job performance (e.g., task performance, citizenship performance, adaptive performance) and counter-productive work behaviors (e.g., theft, poor attendance, drug or alcohol abuse).

The purpose of this chapter is to review research relevant to understanding the processes through which personality influences work outcomes. We first provide an overview of personality constructs prominent in the literature on personality at work. Next, we review recent research on personality measurement, including: (a) issues associated with different measurement methods; and (b) how the level of measurement and alternative personality taxonomies influence relationships between personality and work outcomes. Then, we summarize models describing the processes underlying observed correlations between personality traits and both attitudes and performance. We then present an integrated model of the relationship between personality and performance that pulls together aspects of each model reviewed. This integrated model highlights the mediating role attitudes play in the path from personality to performance. Finally, we close with a research agenda suggested by our model.

2. PERSONALITY CONSTRUCTS

Advances in delineating the construct space of personality have significantly enhanced research on personality in work settings over the past two decades. The emergence of the Big Five model of personality as a means of categorizing the thousands of extant personality traits is one of the major reasons for the renewal of interest in personality in the workplace. The Big Five was utilized in key meta-analyses (e.g., Barrick and Mount 1991) that changed many psychologists' views of the validity of personality tests and facilitated the subsequent explosion of research on personality in the workplace (Morgeson et al. 2007). Other personality taxonomies, as well as research on individual traits, have also proved valuable in identifying and measuring personality traits that are associated with work outcomes (Ones et al. 2007).

To provide a foundation for discussing the roles personality plays in influencing work outcomes, two approaches to organizing the domain of personality traits are briefly reviewed: (a) models derived from the lexical approaches; and (b) the nomological web clustering approach. In addition, two individual personality traits that have been the focus of recent research on work behaviors and attitudes are briefly described.

2.1 Lexical Personality Models

The Big Five is currently the most widely known and utilized personality taxonomy (Walsh and Eggerth 2005). Although its critics have argued the Big Five is insufficiently comprehensive and excessively heterogeneous (Hough and Schneider 1996), it is widely accepted as a meaningful description of the structure of personality (Mount, Ilies, and Johnson 2006). The Big Five was identified through factor analyses of diverse personality inventories, including measures using adjective descriptors (Goldberg 1992) and questionnaires for which survey items were developed from the same lexical tradition (Costa and McCrae 1992). The popularity of the Big Five as a comprehensive model of personality is greatly owed to a series of studies conducted by Costa and McRae in the 1980s and 1990s that demonstrated the Big Five factors accommodated most of the personality traits assessed by existing personality inventories (Ashton and Lee 2005).

Personality theorists have differed in how they characterize the Big Five. There continues to be little agreement on the number and organization of their lower-order facets (Mount et al. 2006) and historically there have been differences in naming the Big Five factors. There now appears to be a trend towards labeling them Extroversion, Agreeableness, Conscientiousness, Emotional Stability, and Openness to Experience (Walsh and Eggerth 2005).

In a number of languages, recent research in the lexical tradition has suggested the existence of six, rather than five, replicable personality dimensions. Ashton and Lee's (2005) HEXACO model includes three factors analogous to the Big Five's Extroversion (X), Conscientiousness (C), and Openness to Experience (O). The HEXACO factors of Emotionality (E) and Agreeableness (A) are rotated versions of the Big Five's Emotional Stability and Agreeableness. The sixth HEXACO factor is

Honesty-Humility, which is defined as sincere, fair, and unassuming versus sly, greedy, and pretentious. The HEXACO model has proved useful in understanding the validity of integrity tests (Marcus, Lee, and Ashton 2007), indicating it may be valuable to incorporate in future research on personality at work.

2.2 Nomological Web Clustering Approach

Lexical taxonomies are based on the interrelationships of personality traits with one another. In contrast, the nomological web clustering approach also takes into consideration the relationship of personality traits with other variables. Hough and her colleagues have argued that correlated personality traits should only be grouped in the same construct when they have similar patterns of relationships with other variables (Hough 1992; Hough, et al., 1990; Hough and Schneider 1996). For example, Hough (1992) demonstrated that dependability and achievement, which are often conceived of as facets of Conscientiousness, are differentially correlated with a variety of criteria. Based on this empirical evidence, she concluded that the Big Five factor, Conscientiousness, is too heterogeneous and too broad. Applying the nomological web clustering approach in a review of the literature, Hough and Ones (2001) developed a working taxonomy of personality variables.

2.3 Other Traits

Other research advancing understanding of personality in the workplace has focused on traits that appear to be related to, but distinct from, traits featured in other personality taxonomies. For example, core self-evaluations are "fundamental assessments that individuals make about themselves and their self-worth" (Judge, Bono, and Locke 2000, 237). Four traits, which meta-analyses have shown to be highly related (Judge et al. 2002), are incorporated into this construct: (a) self-esteem; (b) generalized self-efficacy; (c) locus of control; and (d) emotional stability. Research suggests that these four traits are related to, but distinct from, the Big Five (Bono and Judge 2003). Although additional research is needed to fully understand the nature of core self-evaluations (Bono and Judge 2003), this trait has proved to be a valuable construct for predicting and understanding organizational outcomes.

Similarly, several researchers have used the concept of proactive personality in research on work outcomes. Proactive personality reflects individual differences in the propensity to take action to change one's environment (Bateman and Crant 1993; Seibert, Crant, and Kraimer 1999). Research on core self-evaluations and proactive personality highlight the valuable insights that may be gained through studying traits in addition to the Big Five.

3. MEASURING PERSONALITY

Much research and practice on personality at work relies on self-report measures of personality. A major criticism leveled at their use in selection situations is that they may be susceptible to faking. Faking occurs when individuals intentionally present misleading or deceptive information about themselves in order to influence others' perceptions or actions (Kuncel and Borneman 2007). A growing body of research has been devoted to assessing the extent to which faking occurs and its impact on criterion-related validities, indicating faking is seen as an important problem in personality testing (Morgeson et al. 2007). The interpretation of this work remains hotly debated.

3.1 Faking

One point of contention is the extent to which faking affects the validity of personality tests. Underlying this debate is the question of whether faking primarily causes upward shifts across the entire distribution of personality test scores—increasing mean scores, but leaving the rank order of applicants intact—or tends to generate marked changes in the rank order of applicants. Mean score changes would not affect criterion-related validities; changes in rank order would. The two most common approaches to evaluating whether faking affects personality test validities have involved the use of social desirability scales to correct for faking or the comparison of validities across groups with different motivations to fake (Tett and Christiansen 2007). Both approaches have significant flaws that limit their ability to provide meaningful information about the impact of faking on validity.

First, even among scholars who diverge in their views on the extent to which criterion-related validities are affected by faking, there appears to be consensus that social desirability scales do a poor job capturing faking (Morgeson et al. 2007; Tett and Christiansen in press). Even if better measures of social desirability are developed, mathematical constraints limit the ability of partialing techniques to correct for faking (Ones et al. 2007; Tett and Christiansen 2007). Therefore, this line of inquiry provides little insight into whether or not faking affects the validity of personality tests (Tett and Christiansen 2007).

Second, directed faking studies have been criticized as having poor external validity. It has been argued that laboratory studies in which research participants are directed to fake represent maximal attempts to distort responses, reflecting different phenomena than the faking of job applicants on personality tests (Ones et al. 2007). This limits the relevance of studies that have found that manipulating motivation to fake by providing incentives or asking individuals to respond as if they are applying for jobs reduces the validity of personality tests (Tett and Christiansen 2007).

The implications of research on faking by job applicants are disputed. Although job applicants tend to have higher scores on personality inventories than job incumbents (Tett and Christiansen 2007), it is not clear if faking causes significant rank order differences between applicants. Some personality researchers, highlighting noteworthy criterion-related validities observed in predictive studies of job applicants and the replication of factor structures in job applicant samples, conclude that faking has little adverse effect on the criterion-related or construct validity of personality tests (Ones et al. 2007). Others, after examining mean validity coefficients for applicant samples compared to incumbent samples, conclude that faking attenuates personality test validities somewhat but they are still useful for predicting job performance (Tett and Christiansen 2007). To the extent that attenuation is the result of changes in individuals' rank order on personality inventories, there is the possibility that faking may change which individuals are hired. Some psychologists consequently are troubled by the use of personality tests in selection situations because individual job applicants who do not fake may be displaced by those who do (Morgeson et al. 2007). Others have argued that the ability to fake may be job related; failure to fake may indicate an inability to behave in a socially adaptive way (Morgeson et al. 2007). However, it has not been demonstrated that faking is linked to social competence or improved job performance (Tett and Christiansen 2007). Meta-analyses and large-scale studies have yielded negligibly small correlations between measures of faking (e.g., social desirability, impression management) and assessments of job performance (Ones et al. 2007).

One area of agreement is that robust, thoroughly researched, and established methods for detecting and correcting for faking are not currently available (Morgeson et al. 2007; Ones et al. 2007; Tett and Christiansen 2007). Views diverge somewhat on the potential value of emerging approaches to detecting faking (e.g., the use of bogus statements to identify careless or random responding, response latency; Morgeson et al. 2007). Innovative methods of assessing faking are being developed (e.g., Kuncel and Borneman 2007), however, and may prove useful in future research focused on understanding faking and its impact.

3.2 Other Assessment Methods

The controversy over the potential for faking self-report measures has fueled interest in other methods of assessing personality. One method of addressing the potential problems associated with self-report personality measures is to ask other individuals, such as peers and spouses, to rate a target person's personality. Compared to self-report data, observer ratings yield acceptable reliabilities, comparable factor structures, higher criterion-related validities, and incremental validity (Ones et al. 2007). It would be difficult to use other ratings for selection purposes, however, because motivation to distort may still be significant when the observer is close to the target person (Ones et al. 2007).

Another alternative is conditional reasoning tests, which are based on the premise that an individual's trait level is related to the justification offered for a behavior (James 1998). Because they look like tests of inductive reasoning, conditional reasoning tests are similar to traditional projective measures of personality in that they offer a covert method of assessing traits. Proponents of conditional reasoning tests argue they may be less susceptible to faking than are self-report personality inventories (Morgeson et al. 2007). Additional research on these tests appears warranted. Although they are challenging and costly to develop, the cumulative evidence to date suggests their criterion-related validity may be comparable to self-report personality measures (Ones et al. 2007). Recent research suggests that combining self-report and conditional reasoning methodologies to measure both explicit and implicit components of a personality trait provides the best prediction (Bing et al. 2007).

Forced choice personality items also have been recommended as a means of reducing faking. These items require individuals to endorse one of a set of equally desirable responses that measure different traits. The resulting ipsative data suffer from psychometric limitations, including forced multicollinearity, difficulties in evaluating reliability, and threats to construct validity (Ones et al. 2007). Recent advances with Item Response Theory (IRT) approaches offer the promise of overcoming these problems by deriving normative scores from the ipsative data, but additional research is needed to evaluate the predictive validity of these approaches (Ones et al. 2007). Some studies have reported higher criterion-related validities for forced choice measures of personality, but evidence on whether forced choice formats are less susceptible to response distortion has been mixed (Ones et al. 2007; Tett and Christiansen 2007).

4. Personality and Work Attitudes

Work attitudes are central to I/O (industrial-organizational) psychology (Judge, Parker, et al. 2001). Not only has there been a long tradition of attempting to predict and understand work attitudes as outcomes of interest by themselves, work attitudes also have been utilized to explain other work outcomes, such as job performance and turnover. The following sections provide a brief overview of two key work attitudes, summarize their associations with personality traits, and review models linking personality and work attitudes. We focus on job satisfaction and work commitment because of their prominence in industrial-organizational (I/O) psychology, but note that valuable research has examined links between personality and many other work attitudes, such as career satisfaction and perceived organizational support.

4.1 Commonly Studied Work Attitudes

Job satisfaction refers to the psychological responses resulting from an employee's evaluation of his or her job, job experiences, and working conditions (Judge, Parker, et al. 2001). Job satisfaction is multidimensional, comprised of facets such as satisfaction with pay, promotions, co-workers, supervision, and work itself (Judge, Parker, et al. 2001). Job satisfaction is one of the most studied topics in I/O psychology, but the role played by personality in job satisfaction is not yet well understood. Although dispositional influences on job satisfaction have been recognized since the 1930s, systematic research on the connections between personality and job satisfaction was not initiated until the mid-1980s (Judge, Parker, et al. 2001; Walsh and Eggerth 2005).

Commitment is another attitude that has received considerable attention in the research literature. Numerous forms of organizational commitment have been proposed and studied, but the positive manifold observed across most of these constructs suggests there may be a common underlying construct of work commitment, with some notable exceptions (Cooper-Hakim and Viswesvaran 2005). One of the most studied models of organizational commitment has three components: (a) affective; (b) continuance; and (c) normative (Meyer and Allen 1997). Affective commitment reflects an employee's emotional attachment to the organization. Continuance commitment involves an employee's perceptions of the costs associated with leaving the organization. Normative commitment refers to an employee's perceived obligation to stay with the organization. Meta-analytic results suggest that although affective and normative commitment overlap considerably, these three dimensions of commitment are distinguishable by their distinctive correlations with other outcome variables (Cooper-Hakim and Viswesvaran 2005; Meyer et al. 2002). Evidence indicates that the idea that continuance commitment has two sub-components—perceived sacrifice and lack of alternatives— warrants additional investigation (Meyer et al. 2002).

4.2 Correlations between Personality and Work Attitudes

Personality traits have been linked to a variety of job attitudes. Although many relationships between personality traits and work attitudes have not been fully explored, there already is considerable evidence that personality accounts for meaningful variance in job satisfaction and organizational commitment.

4.2.1 *Job satisfaction*

Several early streams of research on dispositional approaches to job satisfaction focused on positive and negative affectivity, which may be rotated variants of Extroversion and Emotional Stability (Judge, Heller, and Mount 2002). In a meta-analysis of this literature, Connolly and Viswesvaran (2000) reported that the corrected mean correlations of job satisfaction with positive and negative affectivity were .49 and −.33, respectively. In a meta-analysis summarizing the relationship between the Big Five and job satisfaction, Judge et al. (2002) found support for hypotheses linking job satisfaction to all of the Big Five except Openness to Experience. Emotional Stability, Extroversion, Conscientiousness, and Agreeableness had corrected mean correlations of .29, .25, .26, and .17 with job satisfaction. Regression analyses indicated that Emotional Stability, Conscientiousness, and Extroversion were significant predictors of job satisfaction, accounting for at least 40 percent of its variance.

Meta-analytic evidence also indicates that there are moderately strong correlations between the four core self-evaluation traits and job satisfaction (Judge and Bono 2001). Estimated true score correlations ranged from .24 for Emotional Stability to .45 for generalized self-efficacy, leading Judge and Bono to suggest, "these traits may be the principle dispositional correlates of job satisfaction" (p. 84). Dormann et al. (2006) estimated that 24 percent of the variance in job satisfaction may be considered stable or due to trait factors, with a substantial proportion of this stable variance (84 percent) being accounted for by core self-evaluations.

4.2.2 *Organizational commitment*

In comparison, relatively little research has examined the relationship between personality and organizational commitment. One groundbreaking study used correlation coefficients and hierarchical regression analyses to test five hypotheses about the relationship between specific Big Five factors and the three major components of organizational commitment (Erdheim, Wang, and Zickar 2006). Relationships between all Big Five factors and one or more components of organizational commitment were observed, although not all relationships were hypothesized. Extroversion was the personality trait most consistently related to organizational commitment. It positively predicted affective commitment and normative commitment and negatively predicted continuance commitment, while accounting for incremental validity beyond several control variables and the other four Big Five factors. Although the cross-sectional nature of the data prevented definitive causal conclusions from being drawn, these results suggest that personality may play an important role in the development of organizational commitment. This conclusion is supported by a meta-analysis of the antecedents and outcomes of organizational commitment that included a limited number of studies examining two of the four defining core self-evaluation traits—locus of control and self-efficacy. The corrected mean correlation between locus of control and affective commitment was −.29, indicating those with a more external locus of control had less emotional attachment to their organizations. The corrected mean correlation between self-efficacy and affective commitment was .11. In both cases, the credibility intervals excluded zero, suggesting the results may generalize across situations and settings (Meyer et al. 2002). Finally, pro-active personality also has been positively linked to affective commitment (Allen, Weeks, and Moffitt 2005).

4.3 Models Explaining the Personality–Work Attitudes Link

Attempts to explain the processes through which personality influences job satis-faction have identified three explanatory variables: (a) job characteristics; (b) work stress; and (c) mood.

Integrating diverse streams of research on factors influencing job satisfaction, several researchers have investigated the relationships between personality traits, job characteristics, and job satisfaction. Direct, indirect, and moderating effects have been examined. Research has suggested that perceived job characteristics may partially or fully mediate the relationship between personality traits and job satisfaction. For example, Van den Berg and Feij (2003) found support for a model in which feedback (a perceived job characteristic) mediated the relationship between achievement motivation and job satisfaction.

Additional evidence for the mediating effect of job characteristics comes from a series of studies on core-self evaluations. Integrating the construct of core self-evaluations with job characteristics theory, Judge et al. (1998) used three samples to test a model in which core self-evaluations directly influenced job and life satis-faction, as well as indirectly affected job satisfaction by influencing perceptions of job characteristics. Consistent with their hypotheses, perceived job characteristics partially mediated the relationship between core self-evaluations and job satisfac-tion in all three samples.

Judge, Bono, and Locke (2000) extended this research, incorporating objective job features and demonstrating the previous findings were not just due to percep-tual processes. Based on person by situation theories, self-regulation theory, and the literature on self-esteem and goals, the authors argued that individuals who have high core self-evaluations should be more likely to (a) seek out and take on complex jobs; (b) have better skills for coping and thus, succeeding, in complex jobs; (c) set more difficult goals; and (d) be less likely to withdraw if they experience failure. Consistent with these arguments, significant, positive, direct relationships were observed between core self-evaluations and job complexity in two studies. In one study, perceived job characteristics mediated the relationship between job complexity and job satisfaction. In a second study, core self-evaluations measured earlier in life predicted later job complexity. Thus, research suggests that personality influences job satisfaction not only through perceived job characteristics but in the choice of jobs that feature certain job characteristics. In contrast, several studies have found little evidence for the interaction of job characteristics and personality traits in predicting job satisfaction (Judge et al. 1998; Van den Berg and Feij 2003).

Several studies have found support for the idea that stress may help explain the link between personality and job satisfaction. In their research modeling the relationship between personality traits and job satisfaction, Van den Berg and Feij (2003) found that work stress (job-induced tension) mediated the relationship between Neuroticism and job satisfaction. Using a different set of measures and constructs, Day, Bedeian, and Conte (1998) found support for a model in which role stress (role conflict and role ambiguity) mediated the relationship between the trait of Control and job satisfaction. Control was assessed with scales from the California Personality Inventory with elements similar to the Big Five's Conscientiousness (e.g., self-control, responsibility) and Neuroticism (e.g., well-being) factors. The model also included direct paths between Extroversion and Control and job satisfaction which were significant, negative, and small. A direct path between Flexibility and role stress was non-significant. These initial studies suggest one process through which personality may influence job satisfaction is through stress partially mediating the relationship between Emotional Stability and job satisfaction.

Mood also has been examined as a variable influencing the relationship between personality and job satisfaction. Ilies and Judge (2002) investigated the role played by Extroversion and Neuroticism in moderating the relationship between mood and job satisfaction. Ilies and Judge found support for their hypotheses that mood was related to job satisfaction both across and within individuals, and that Extroversion was significantly related to the average level of positive mood at work. Neuroticism was positively associated with average levels of negative mood, but this relationship was not significant. Neuroticism was significantly related to within-individual variability in negative affect and job satisfaction. Partial support was obtained for the hypothesis that Neuroticism would moderate the strength of the relationship between mood and satisfaction. There was a stronger relationship between positive affect and job satisfaction for individuals higher on Neuroticism. Extroversion did not moderate the relationship between mood and satisfaction. Based on results of exploratory analyses, the authors recommended that future research examine mood as a mediator of the personality–job satisfaction relationship.

5. PERSONALITY AND JOB PERFORMANCE

5.1 Taxonomy of Job Performance Dimensions

A priority for research on personality at work is the development of a nomological net of personality–performance relationships for use in building prediction equations for specific situations (Barrick, Mount, and Judge 2001; Hough 2003; Hough and Ones 2001). This kind of a matrix requires comprehensive taxonomies of the predictor and criterion domains. As we noted in our overview of personality constructs, there have been significant advances in the development of personality taxonomies. Research on the criterion side has lagged behind in this area, with most meta-analyses of personality–performance relationships being limited to whatever assortment of criteria were available in the primary studies analyzed.

Johnson (2003) proposed a taxonomy of job performance dimensions for linking specific predictor constructs to specific performance constructs and cumulating results across studies for meta-analyses. This taxonomy includes task performance, citizenship performance, and adaptive performance at the highest level, with second and third levels of more specific dimensions. Examples of second-level task performance dimensions are Campbell's (1990) job-specific task proficiency, non-job-specific task proficiency, written and oral communication, and management/administration tasks. Second-level citizenship performance dimensions identified by Borman et al. (2001) are (a) personal support (behaviors benefiting individuals, such as helping and cooperating); (b) organizational support (behaviors benefiting the organization, such as showing loyalty and complying with rules); and (c) conscientious initiative (behaviors benefiting the job or task, such as persisting with extra effort and showing initiative).

Adaptive performance is the proficiency with which a person alters his or her behavior to meet the demands of the environment, an event, or a new situation (Pulakos et al. 2000). Pulakos et al. (2000) developed and found support for a taxonomy of adaptive performance consisting of eight dimensions, many of which can also be considered aspects of task performance, citizenship performance, or both. Johnson (2003) considered the dimension of dealing with uncertain and unpredictable work situations as the only component of Pulakos et al.'s taxonomy that was distinct from task and citizenship performance. Elements of this dimension include taking action when necessary without having all the facts at hand; adjusting plans, actions, or priorities to deal with changing situations; and imposing structure to provide focus in dynamic situations.

A fourth broad category of performance that is predicted by personality is counter-productive work behavior (CWB). CWB is any intentional behavior on the part of an employee that is contrary to the legitimate interests of the organization (Sackett and DeVore 2001). Examples of CWBs include theft; property destruction; misuse of information, time, or resources; drug or alcohol use; unsafe behavior; poor attendance; intentionally slow or sloppy work; and inappropriate verbal or physical actions (Gruys 2000). CWB is synonymous with Maintaining Personal Discipline in Campbell's (1990) comprehensive taxonomy of major performance components.

5.2 Correlations between Personality and Performance

In early personality research, correlations were computed between all personality variables and all criteria. Most of these correlations were near zero, creating the impression that personality was generally unrelated to performance (Guion and Gottier 1965). This view continues to be perpetuated (Morgeson et al. 2007; Murphy and Dzieweczynski 2005), based on mean or median validity coefficients from meta-analyses that are generally quite low (e.g., Barrick and Mount 1991; Barrick, Mount, and Judge 2001; Hough et al. 1990; Hurtz and Donovan 2000). This interpretation of personality validities overlooks several factors that obscure the true potential of personality variables to predict performance.

First, most researchers now understand that predictors and criteria should be conceptualized as constructs and that the trait being investigated must be relevant to the criterion (Hough and Oswald 2005; Hough and Schneider 1996; Tett and Christiansen 2007). When personality research involves the specification of a personality taxonomy, a job performance taxonomy, and hypothesized relationships between them, very meaningful validity coefficients can be obtained. Tett et al. (1999) found that studies using a confirmatory validation approach had much higher mean validity coefficients than did studies using an exploratory, "fishing expedition," approach (.20 vs. .10, uncorrected; .26 vs. .14, corrected). Hogan and Holland (2003) showed that mean correlations between Hogan Personality Inventory scales and conceptually aligned performance criteria (.20 uncorrected, .29 corrected) were higher than mean correlations between those scales and other criteria that were not conceptually aligned (.07 uncorrected, .10 corrected). Bartram (2005) created personality scale composites based on hypothesized relationships with each of eight criterion variables. The average uncorrected correlation for hypothesized relationships was .16 and the average uncorrected correlation for non-hypothesized relationships was .02.

Second, measures of broad higher-order traits often do not predict as well as more narrow trait measures (Rothstein and Goffin 2006; Schneider, Hough, and Dunnette 1996). This is related to the first point because specificity promotes more precise conceptual linkages. Although the Big Five is a ubiquitous way of organizing personality variables for meta-analyses, lower-level facets of the same Big Five factor often have very different correlations with job performance criteria, revealing meaningful relationships that are masked if broader measures are used (Hough

1992). For example, Hurtz and Donovan's (2000) meta-analysis found a mean corrected correlation between Conscientiousness and job dedication of .18, but a meta-analysis by Dudley et al. (2006) found that two facets of Conscientiousness—achievement and dependability—had corrected correlations with job dedication of .34 and .40, respectively.

Third, data from personality meta-analyses suggest that substantive moderators may affect the size of personality–performance relationships. In other words, situational specificity may be the rule for personality measure validity, as opposed to the highly generalizable validities seen with cognitive ability tests. In their summary of meta-analytic results for Big Five validities, Tett and Christiansen (2007) found an average 80 percent credibility interval of .30, indicating a great deal of variability in ρ across studies is not accounted for by sampling error. Tett et al. (1994) showed that negative correlations occur 2.5 times more often than expected as a result of sampling error and that significant negative correlations occur 28 times more often than expected by chance. Thus, personality scales that are positively related to a performance dimension in some situations may have legitimately negative correlations with the same performance dimension in other situations. For example, a person high in agreeableness may do well in an organization that has a team-based, cooperative culture but may have a lot of difficulty in an organization with a culture that is highly competitive and adversarial. Some of the breadth of the credibility intervals may be due to combining lower-level facets with differential correlations with a particular criterion into a single analysis. Nevertheless, research aimed at determining in what situations the validity of a particular measure of personality will be maximized would likely be very valuable. Some of the moderators that have been found to influence the extent to which personality predicts performance are situational strength (Beaty, Cleveland, and Murphy 2001), occupation (Barrick, Mount, and Judge 2001; Ones et al. 2007), time on job (Helmreich, Sawin, and Carsrud 1986), autonomy (Gellatly and Irving 2001), and typical vs. maximum performance measurement (Marcus et al. 2007). Personality and ability have been found to interact when predicting performance (Wright et al. 1995), although most recent studies have shown no interaction (Mount, Barrick, and Strauss 1999; Sackett, Gruys, and Ellingson 1998).

Finally, examining the validity of a single personality variable is misleading because personality is a multidimensional construct. Few organizations would try to predict performance with a single trait scale, so it makes sense to examine validity from the standpoint of combinations of personality variables. Personality variables can be combined to enhance prediction in three ways: (a) creating compound traits; (b) creating multiple-trait composites; and (c) exploring configural scoring possibilities.

Compound traits are combinations of basic personality traits that do not necessarily covary but are put together in a single scale to maximize the prediction of a specific criterion construct (Hough and Schneider 1996). Some examples of compound personality traits that have been found to be valid for predicting their intended criterion construct are integrity, customer service orientation, employee reliability, and managerial potential (Hough and Ones 2001). Ones, Viswesvaran, and Dilchert (2005) summarized meta-analytic validities for compound trait scales and reported corrected mean validities for predicting overall job performance of .19 for drug and alcohol abuse, .39 for customer service orientation, .41 for integrity, .41 for violence and aggression, .41 for stress tolerance, and .42 for managerial potential.

A typical practice in employee selection is to administer several personality scales and create a composite by adding the scores from each scale, perhaps with differential weights. Ones et al. (2007) computed multiple correlations of regression-weighted composites of Big Five scales based on meta-analytic corrected validities. The mean multiple correlation across different types of job performance criteria was .31, including .27 for overall job performance and .45 for CWB: Organizational deviance. The mean validity for unit-weighted composites was .26, including .23 for overall performance and .36 for CWB: Organizational deviance.

Multiple personality traits may interact to influence performance. For example, the impact of dominance on leadership performance may depend on the leader's level of emotional stability (Tett and Christiansen 2007). Witt et al. (2002) found a significant interaction between Conscientiousness and Agreeableness in five samples of employees in occupations characterized by cooperative interactions with others. When the job was high in interpersonal demands, Conscientiousness was negatively related to performance in employees who were low on Agreeableness. Configural scoring may enhance prediction by taking into account such interactions between personality traits.

5.3 Process Models

The previous section makes clear that measures of personality have complex patterns of validity results. To account for a substantial proportion of the variance in the criterion space requires theories and models that reflect the complexity of the determinants of personality-relevant work performance (Hough and Oswald 2005). A number of process models of how personality influences performance have been proposed in recent years, both for individual job performance and for CWB.

5.3.1 *Individual job performance models*

Several theories of how personality and other individual differences influence job performance have been proposed. Johnson (2003) built on and expanded earlier performance prediction models developed by Campbell (1990) and Motowidlo, Borman, and Schmit (1997) to explain the process by which specific personality traits influence performance on specific dimensions. As in the Campbell model, performance is determined directly by a combination of three determinants: (a) knowledge; (b) skill; and (c) motivation. The direct determinants are distinguished from indirect performance determinants, which can only influence performance via the direct determinants. Personality is an indirect determinant, along with variables such as abilities, education, experience, organizational reward systems, training, and management practices.

Motowidlo et al. (1997) rolled motivation into work habits, which they defined as stylistic ways people handle different kinds of situations that occur on the job, learned as their basic tendencies (personality traits) interact with their environments over time. Johnson (2003) included work habits in addition to motivation, however, because (a) habits may interfere with performance despite motivation to perform in a certain way; and (b) motivational choices may go against one's habitual tendencies. To implement an intention that goes against habitual tendencies and other intentions competing for one's attention, one must engage self-regulatory or volitional mechanisms. Self-regulation refers to the higher-level cognitive processes that guide the allocation of attention, time, and effort across activities directed toward attaining a goal (Kanfer 1990) and protect an intention from being replaced by a competing action tendency before the intended action is completed (Kuhl 1985).

In outlining key motivational processes, Johnson (2003) incorporated Mitchell and Daniels's (2003) distinction between proactive and on-line cognitive processes. Proactive cognitive processes occur before a task is commenced, and reflect cognitions about expectations for achieving a goal or the value of outcomes resulting from achieving a goal. During this phase, people determine what course of action to take, resulting in the formation of an intention. Expectancy, self-efficacy, and goal setting are in the proactive category of motivation theories. On-line cognitive processes occur while the person is working on a task, and are characterized by self-regulatory processes that are necessary to maintain goal-directed action. This phase refers to the process of implementing an intention to achieve a goal. Control theory, action theory, and self-regulation are on-line theories of motivation (Mitchell and Daniels 2003).

Johnson (2003) added psychological motives as a third component of motivation. A motive is a reason (e.g., value, interest, preference, attitude) for choosing to exert effort in a particular direction. Motive-based theories recognize that people may have very different purposes for exhibiting the same behavior (Borman and Penner 2001). Motives are expected to directly influence proactive cognitive processes (Johnson 2003; Kanfer 1992). Job attitudes such as job satisfaction, organizational commitment, and fairness perceptions are examples of motives that may mediate the relationship between personality and proactive cognitive processes.

To sum up Johnson's (2003) model, performance on a given dimension is a direct function of knowledge, skill, motivation, and work habits. Work habits also influence performance indirectly by influencing the need for and choice of self-regulatory strategies. The primary indirect determinants are personality and ability, but the model can accommodate other classes of indirect performance determinants. The model also recognizes the numerous potential moderators (e.g., occupation, tenure) that can influence the extent to which personality predicts performance. The relative strength of each path from one construct to another depends on the predictor variables included and the performance dimension that is the criterion. The strength of the relationship between a personality trait and a performance dimension depends on (a) the number of direct determinants of the performance dimension to which the trait is related; (b) the strength of the relationship between the trait and each direct determinant; (c) the strength of the relationship between each direct determinant and the performance dimension; and (d) the presence of relevant moderators.

Johnson et al. (2007) found partial support for the Johnson (2003) model for five different performance dimensions. With the exception of work habits, each hypothesized direct determinant was directly related to at least two performance dimensions. The lack of support for work habits as a direct determinant may have been due to the nature of the behaviors defining each performance dimension, which may not have been amenable to automatic processing. Another difference from the Johnson model was that it was possible for each element of the motivation component to be a direct determinant of performance, rather than proactive cognitions and self-regulation always mediating the relationship between motives and performance. For each of the three citizenship performance dimensions studied, a motive construct including job satisfaction, affective commitment, and military values was a direct determinant of performance. The model was supported in that personality, ability, and experience influenced performance through the hypothesized mediating variables. There was also support for the notion that personality variables have differential relationships with different components of motivation, as suggested by Heckhausen and Kuhl (1985). This, along with direct paths to performance from each component, supports the need for splitting motivation into its components in order to truly understand how personality influences performance.

Barrick, Mitchell, and Stewart's (2003) model of the personality-performance relationship is consistent with Johnson's (2003) model, but focuses on motivation as a more central feature while ignoring the influence of knowledge, skill, and habits. In their model, the relationship between personality and performance is mediated by three primary types of motivation, which they labeled Accomplishment Striving, Status Striving, and Communion Striving. These constructs incorporate both the motives and proactive cognitive processes aspects of motivation, and exclude on-line cognitive processes. Conscientiousness and Emotional Stability are expected to influence Accomplishment Striving, Extroversion is expected to influence Status Striving, and Agreeableness is expected to influence Communion Striving.

The Barrick et al. model also recognizes the importance of situational demands on the expression of personality. A personality trait will be most highly related to behavior when the situation is relevant to the trait's expression and is not so strong that there is little opportunity for variance in behavior. Barrick et al. focus on competitive and cooperative social demands as aspects of the situation that influence trait expression. The relationship between Accomplishment Striving and performance is mediated by Status Striving in situations in which competitive demands operate and by Communion Striving in situations in which cooperative demands operate. The relationship between personality and each motivational construct is moderated by the amount of autonomy in the situation. Autonomy is the extent to which the environment allows an individual to behave in idiosyncratic ways. The more autonomy in a situation, the greater the relationship between personality traits, motivational variables, and performance.

This model would predict that Conscientiousness and Emotional Stability would be relatively predictive in all jobs because Accomplishment Striving is relevant to all jobs. Extroversion will be related to job performance only in situations in which competitive demands operate (e.g., people work independently and are rewarded for personal accomplishments). Agreeableness will be related to job performance only in situations in which cooperative demands operate (e.g., people work together and are rewarded for team accomplishments). Support for the model was provided by Barrick, Stewart, and Piotrowski (2002), who found that Status Striving mediated the relationship between Accomplishment Striving and performance in a sample of sales representatives who worked in a competitive sales setting.

Tett and Burnett (2003) went into more detail to describe the influence of the situation on trait expression. Their trait activation theory asserts that traits are activated by situations that provide trait expression opportunities, or "cues." These cues operate at three levels: (a) task (e.g., a tight deadline); (b) social (e.g., a co-worker who needs help); and (c) organizational (e.g., a competitive organizational culture). Behavior consistent with the trait is considered job performance when that behavior is valued by the organization. The behavior is reinforced as employees gain intrinsic satisfaction from expressing their traits and gain extrinsic satisfaction from being rewarded for good performance.

Like Barrick et al. (2003), Tett and Burnett (2003) refer to cues that are valued positively as *demands*. Cues that are valued negatively when acted upon are called *distracters*. Two other situational features identified are *constraints*, which eliminate or restrict cues (e.g., dispersing co-workers over a wide geographic area), and *releasers*, which counteract constraints (e.g., co-workers come together for a face-to-face meeting). Imposing constraints on distracters will improve trait-based performance, while imposing constraints on demands will weaken trait-based performance, unless those constraints are released.

Trait activation theory predicts that relationships between personality traits and performance will be stronger to the extent that a given work situation provides cues for trait expression that are valued by those who judge performance. Correlations are positive when trait expression is judged to meet work demands and negative when trait expression is judged to interfere with meeting work demands, or as responding to distracters. Because cues operate at multiple levels, potential complications can come up when cues at different levels operate in different directions. For example, an organizational culture that stresses team decision making might clash with a task that requires quick decisions with no time to consult with others.

5.3.2 *Counter-productive work behavior models*

Cullen and Sackett (2003) proposed a model of the influence of personality traits on CWBs. They distinguish between initiated CWBs, which are initiated by the individual to satisfy some need or motive, and reactive CWBs, which occur in response to an actual or perceived organizational event. Personality traits may initiate CWBs directly on rare occasions through impulsive behavior that by-passes any cognitive assessment of appropriateness. Personality traits indirectly influence CWBs through their impact on (a) perceptual variables such as job satisfaction, mood, stress, and workplace injustice; and (b) attitudes toward CWBs. An important feature of the Cullen and Sackett model is the incorporation of Fishbein and Ajzen's (1975) theory of reasoned action. In this theory, intention to perform a behavior is a function of a person's attitude toward the behavior and subjective norms about what relevant others think about the behavior. An attitude toward a behavior is a combination of an individual's beliefs about the consequences of the behavior and the desirability of those consequences. Subjective norms are a combination of a normative belief about whether others think the individual should perform the behavior and the individual's motivation to comply with what others think. Cullen and Sackett discussed how personality traits can influence each of the components of attitudes and subjective norms.

Personality traits may also moderate relationships between organizational events and CWBs in two ways. First, personality may moderate how organizational events are perceived. For example, a suspicious person may perceive an event as unjust whereas a trusting person may perceive it as just. Second, personality may moderate the cognitive, affective, and emotional reactions to perceived environmental events. For example, an aggressive person is more likely to engage in reactive CWB as a response to perceived injustice than is a passive person.

Mount et al. (2006) distinguished between interpersonal CWBs, which are behaviors directed at individuals in the organization with the intent to produce emotional or physical discomfort or harm, and organizational CWBs, which are behaviors directed toward harming the interests of the organization. Mount et al.

found support for a model in which job satisfaction partially mediated the relationships between personality traits and CWB. Job satisfaction was related to both types of CWB. Agreeableness had a direct effect on interpersonal CWB as well as an indirect effect on both types of CWB through job satisfaction. Conscientiousness had a direct path to organizational CWB, but the mediating effect through job satisfaction was weaker.

This model is consistent with what Johnson et al. (2007) found for the performance dimensions of organizational commitment and maintaining good working relationships. Although not the same as CWB, maintaining good working relationships and organizational commitment should be highly negatively correlated with interpersonal CWB and organizational CWB, respectively. Johnson et al. found that Agreeableness had an indirect effect on maintaining good working relationships through both military motives (which includes job satisfaction) and knowledge. In the organizational commitment model, the Agreeableness facet of trust had an indirect influence through military motives. Conscientiousness also had an indirect influence through military motives and self-regulation.

6. AN INTEGRATED MODEL OF THE INFLUENCE OF PERSONALITY TRAITS ON PERFORMANCE

The individual job performance and CWB models reviewed are generally consistent with each other, with each model emphasizing different aspects of the personality–performance process. Figure 3.1 presents a general model of the processes through which personality influences job performance (including CWB) that attempts to integrate these different models. All variables are expressed as broad construct domains. This is a high-level model that incorporates all of the major potential influences of personality on performance. The purpose of the general model is to provide a guide for constructing separate models for specific performance components. The most useful level of specificity for performance components is probably one level below the task, citizenship, adaptive, and CWB distinction (i.e., Level 2 dimensions; Johnson 2003). It is unlikely that every path specified in the model would operate for any given performance component. The idea is to identify the potential paths through which personality and other variables influence performance. In the following sections, each aspect of Figure 3.1 is described and explained.

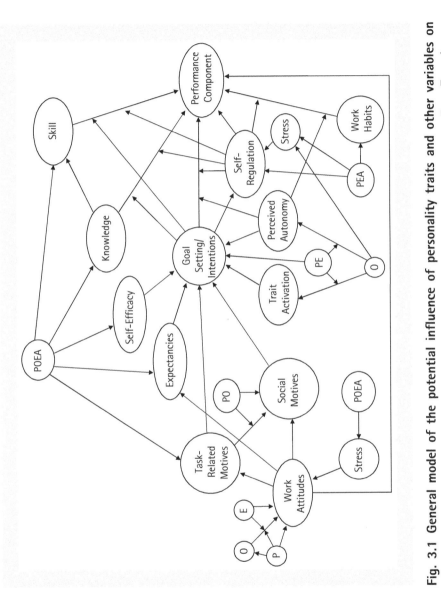

Fig. 3.1 General model of the potential influence of personality traits and other variables on determinants of performance. P = Personality. O = Organizational context. E = Experience. A = Ability.

6.1 Indirect Performance Determinants

The indirect performance determinants are broad predictor domains, which are represented throughout the model by the initials *P* (Personality), *O* (Organizational context), *E* (Experience), and *A* (Ability). When predicting a given performance component, variables from each domain are specified that are theoretically related to each of the more proximal performance determinants. The specific variables should be based on previous research and theories focusing on each aspect of the general model. A great deal of research has been conducted documenting relationships between personality traits, abilities, and aspects of the general model. Personality traits are expected to directly influence each aspect of the model, as well as moderating some relationships. Abilities have their strongest relationships with knowledge and skill, but may have weaker relationships with many other aspects of the model.

Experience can be operationalized as the amount of time on the job or the number of times a task has been performed in the past (Lance and Bennett 2000). Like cognitive ability, experience has been shown to be a meaningful indirect determinant in process models of job performance. Schmidt, Hunter, and Outerbridge (1986) and Lance and Bennett (2000) found that the relationships between supervisory performance ratings and both cognitive ability and experience were mediated by job knowledge and work sample performance (a measure of procedural knowledge or skill). Johnson et al. (2007) found that the relationship between experience and performance was mediated by knowledge, skill, and each component of motivation, depending on the specific performance dimension in question. Experience is also expected to moderate the relationships between certain variables.

Organizational context includes a wide variety of variables. Tett and Burnett's (2003) task, social, and organizational cues (demands, distracters, constraints, and releasers) are part of the organizational context. The job itself is an important part of the organizational context that influences the relationship between personality and performance (Ones et al. 2007). Other aspects of the organizational context are supervision, procedural fairness, training, reward systems, and stressors.

6.2 Motives

To integrate the performance models that we reviewed, it was necessary to further expand the motivation component of the model from what was introduced in Johnson (2003). First, we separated task-related motives from social motives, based on Barrick, Mitchell, and Stewart's (2003) model.[1] Task-related motives are similar to Barrick et al.'s Accomplishment Striving,

---

[1] Although Barrick et al.'s (2003) motivational constructs include the entire process from motive to intention, we separate all components to more completely describe the influence of personality on motivation.

which is a generalized intention to exert effort and work hard. This is determined jointly by personality (e.g., need for achievement, emotional stability), organizational context (e.g., incentives to perform well, difficulty or meaningfulness of the task; Barrick et al. 2003), experience, ability, and work attitudes. Social motives include Barrick et al.'s Communion Striving and Status Striving, which they proposed mediate the relationship between Accomplishment Striving and performance. In our model, social motives mediate the relationship between task-related motives and intentions, but we also allow for a direct path from task-related motives to intentions. The relationship between each type of motive is moderated by personality and organizational context. For example, Barrick et al.'s (2003) model predicts that the path from Accomplishment Striving to Status Striving is moderated by Extroversion and competitive demands in the situation. Social motives are determined primarily by personality, as well as by organizational context and work attitudes.

6.3 Work Attitudes and Stress

Although work attitudes can be a motive for performing a behavior (e.g., commitment to the organization could be a reason for working late to complete a task; Penner, Midili, and Kegelmeyer 1997), they can also have a direct effect on both task-related and social motives. For example, satisfaction with the work group may cause Communion Striving to be a more salient motive, whereas dissatisfaction with the work group may increase the salience of Status Striving so that the individual can get ahead of the rest of the members of the group. Johnson et al. (2007) showed that work attitudes are directly related to expectancies, probably because employees who are more satisfied are more likely to see or have experienced the link between good performance and valued rewards.

Figure 3.1 also includes a direct path from work attitudes to performance. We expect this path to be present for dimensions of citizenship performance, based on the results of Johnson et al. (2007). Given that citizenship performance often involves behaviors that are not formally required and do not directly benefit the individual, it is not surprising that work attitudes can directly determine citizenship performance. Someone who is dissatisfied with the job, does not have an affective attachment to the organization, and does not share the values of the organization would be very unlikely to engage in behaviors like participating in social activities, exceeding standards when carrying out assignments, or performing extra work without being asked.

For simplicity, perceived job characteristics, specific attitudes (e.g., supervisor support), and general attitudes (e.g., job satisfaction) are included in a single work attitudes component, although we do expect a hierarchical structure leading from specific perceptions to general attitudes. Personality has a direct influence on work attitudes (e.g., positive or negative affectivity may lead people to form more positive or negative perceptions of their environment, independent of their actual situation). We also expect personality to sometimes moderate the relationship between organizational context and attitudes (e.g., a lack of feedback would likely be evaluated more negatively by someone lower on tolerance for ambiguity), although research has not yet supported this kind of effect (Judge et al. 1998; Van den Berg and Feij 2003).

We included stress as a direct influence on work attitudes based on research showing that work stress mediated the relationship between personality and attitudes (Day, Bedeian, and Conte 1998; van den Berg and Feij 2003). Organizational context, experience, and ability also influence the experience of stress. Stress also contributes directly to self-regulation. This is based on Sinclair and Tucker's (2006) model of individual differences in Soldier performance under stress, in which stress constrains the amount of motivational resources that can be allocated to performance.

6.4 Goal Setting/Intentions

Cullen and Sackett (2003) incorporated Fishbein and Ajzen's (1975) theory of reasoned action into their model of CWB determinants because intentions are the best predictor of behavior and this theory explains how an intention is formed. A later version of this theory is Ajzen's (1985) theory of planned behavior, which adds perceived behavioral control to attitudes and subjective norms as the determinants of intention formation.[2] The components of the theory of planned behavior overlap considerably with concepts in motivation and personality theories that we have reviewed in this chapter. For example, goal-setting theory is based on the idea that most behaviors are the result of one's consciously chosen goals and intentions (Mitchell and Daniels 2003). When someone sets a goal and is committed to that goal, they are by definition forming an intention to engage in behavior aimed at goal attainment. Thus, we combine goal setting and intentions in our model.

An attitude toward a behavior is a function of the individual's beliefs about the consequences of performing the behavior and the desirability of those consequences. These components of an attitude are similar to the components of expectancy theories of motivation (expectancy, instrumentality, valence; Mitchell and Daniels 2003). The expectancy and instrumentality components combined refer to an individual's belief that a certain level of effort will result in a certain level of performance and that that level of performance will result in certain consequences (e.g., personal recognition, work unit success, career advancement). The

---

[2] Cullen and Sackett (2003) did not include perceived behavioral control because most CWBs (e.g., unsafe behavior, poor attendance, alcohol use) are under the complete control of the individual.

valence component refers to the value placed on those potential consequences. Thus, in our model, expectancies influence goal setting/intentions in the same way that attitudes influence intentions in the theory of planned behavior.

Subjective norms are a combination of a normative belief about whether others think the individual should perform the behavior and the individual's motivation to comply with what others think. Tett and Burnett's (2003) trait activation theory provides an explanation for how people in organizations arrive at these subjective norms. Task, social, and organizational cues indicate what kind of behavior is valued positively and what kind of behavior is valued negatively. When people express their traits through their behavior, the behavior is considered job performance when it is valued by relevant others. As the individual continues to experience trait-relevant cues and the value placed on certain behavior is communicated, normative beliefs about what others in the organization think the individual should do are formed. Motivation to comply with what others think depends on the intrinsic and extrinsic satisfaction gained by engaging in behaviors. Individuals gain extrinsic satisfaction when rewarded for good performance, and they gain intrinsic satisfaction by expressing their traits in an environment that values such trait expression (e.g., nurturant people like expressing nurturance; Tett and Christiansen 2007). Therefore, the subjective norms component is represented in our model by trait activation, which includes perceptions of trait-relevant cues and motivation to perform behaviors that are valued by others in the organization. These things are determined by the organizational context, personality, and experience. Personality and experience also moderate perceptions of the organizational context. For example, more ambiguous cues are likely to be interpreted as calling for behavior relevant to a trait the individual possesses, especially if the individual has less experience with interpreting these types of cues.

Perceived behavioral control refers to an individual's perception of the relative difficulty associated with performing a behavior, which takes into account situations in which behavior is not under the complete volitional control of the individual. We represent perceived behavioral control by two constructs in our model. First, self-efficacy is the belief in one's own capabilities to successfully accomplish a task or perform a behavior at a given level of proficiency. A person who is high in self-efficacy should have a stronger perception that the behavior is under his or her control. Second, autonomy should contribute to perceived behavioral control. Autonomy is the extent to which the situation allows a person freedom to behave in an idiosyncratic manner, and is an important part of trait activation theory (Tett and Burnett 2003) and the Barrick et al. (2003) motivational model of personality-performance relationships. In strong situations, the constraints of the environment allow very little autonomy in deciding what behaviors to display (e.g., working on an assembly line). In weak situations, the individual determines the behaviors in which to engage because there is very little environmental pressure to conform. Personality is more highly related to performance in weak situations, because people are free to perform their jobs in idiosyncratic ways (Barrick et al. 2003). Several studies have found that the degree of autonomy in the situation moderates the relationship between personality and performance (e.g., Barrick and Mount 1993; Beaty, Cleveland, and Murphy 2001). Thus, the amount of autonomy the individual perceives in a situation will contribute to the amount of perceived behavioral control, so there is a direct path from autonomy to goal setting/intentions. In addition, autonomy can moderate the relationship between an intention and performance if the individual sets a goal without realizing the constraints of the situation.

Support for this conceptualization of the proactive cognitive processes aspect of motivation comes from a review of the antecedents of goal setting (Wofford, Goodwin, and Premack 1992). They found that the best predictors of an individual's goal commitment were self-efficacy, expectancy of goal attainment, and task difficulty. In addition, the major determinants of an individual's goal level were past performance and ability. In a meta-analysis of the personality correlates of motivation, all the Big Five traits had significant relationships with goal level (Judge and Ilies 2002). We have therefore included direct paths from personality, organizational context, experience, and ability to goal setting/intentions, as well as indirect paths through self-efficacy and expectancies.

6.5 Knowledge, Skill, and Work Habits

As in the Johnson (2003) model, knowledge, skill, and work habits are direct determinants of performance. Knowledge and skill are determined primarily by ability and experience (Lance and Bennett 2000), but organizational context variables such as the availability of training will also influence knowledge and skill acquisition. Personality influences knowledge and skill acquisition in different ways depending on the type of performance. For task performance, Colquitt, LePine, and Noe (2000) found that personality variables predicted declarative knowledge and skill acquisition both directly and indirectly through motivation to learn. For citizenship performance, Motowidlo, Borman, and Schmit (1997) suggested that citizenship knowledge and skill are primarily determined by personality because people possessing certain personality characteristics may be more likely to notice the relative effectiveness of certain behaviors in relevant situations and be more likely to master that knowledge or skill. Johnson et al. (2007) demonstrated this mediating effect of citizenship knowledge and skill empirically. They found that knowledge mediated the relationship between Agreeableness and maintaining good working relationships, and skill mediated the relationship between Extroversion and showing initiative.

We include a path from knowledge to skill to recognize situations in which skill depends on possessing declarative knowledge. This mediating effect of skill between knowledge and performance has been demonstrated in several studies (e.g., Borman, White, and Dorsey 1995; Lance and Bennett 2000; Schmidt, Hunter, and Outerbridge 1986). For CWB, knowledge and skill are probably not a factor because most CWBs only require motivation to engage in the behavior.

Work habits are expected to influence performance directly when job-relevant behavior occurs automatically despite motivation to behave otherwise. Autonomy moderates this direct relationship because habits will have less of an influence on performance in stronger situations. Habitual tendencies develop through a combination of personality, experience, and ability.

6.6 Self-Regulation

Johnson's (2003) model included on-line cognitive processes (i.e., self-regulation) as a mediator between proactive cognitive processes and performance. Johnson et al. (2007) demonstrated that both self-regulation and proactive cognitions have direct effects on performance. They did find that goal commitment was related to self-regulation, but never in a model in which self-regulation was a determinant of performance. We maintained this path in Figure 3.1 because those who are more committed to a goal are likely to work harder at maintaining goal-directed action. It is probably also appropriate to think of self-regulation as a moderator of the relationship between other direct determinants and performance. If two people have similar knowledge, skill, habits, and desire to perform but different levels of performance, this would be explained by differing levels of ability to self-regulate.

Self-regulation moderates the relationship between intentions and performance because this relationship is stronger the greater one's ability to protect the intention from competing action tendencies (Kuhl 1985). Self-regulatory ability is also expected to enable people to more effectively use their knowledge, skill, and abilities, especially in reaction to stress (Sinclair and Tucker 2006). Work habits that detract from good performance can be overcome through self-regulatory strategies so these habits will have less of an influence for people who are better at self-regulating. Self-regulation has been found to be related to personality (Kanfer and Heggestad 1997) and ability (Kanfer and Ackerman 1989). Experience should also influence the acquisition of self-regulatory strategies because as more situations are encountered in which self-regulation is necessary, effective strategies are learned and refined while ineffective strategies are dropped. Johnson et al. (2007) found support for this relationship.

7. RESEARCH AGENDA

The integrated model of the personality–performance process suggests a number of avenues for research. Because this is a general model of potential influences on performance, the model for any specific performance dimension will not include all of the paths specified in Figure 3.1. For example, Johnson et al. (2007) found a direct path from motives to performance for citizenship performance dimensions, but motives influenced performance indirectly through expectancies for task and adaptive performance dimensions. Research is necessary on specific performance dimensions to determine what elements of the model operate for different types of performance. Certain elements may be consistent across all types of performance, but we expect that most will depend on the performance dimension. Task performance dimensions seem most likely to be influenced by all elements of the model, while citizenship performance and CWB are likely to be determined by a simpler model (Johnson et al. 2007). It is necessary to determine to what extent a single model describes the performance prediction process for performance dimensions within the same broad category (e.g., citizenship performance).

The model is very complex and it is likely not possible to test the whole model in a single study. Therefore, research should be directed at testing portions of the model to determine if and when they hold up. For example, further research like that of Barrick, Stewart, and Piotrowski (2002) should be done to examine the mediating effect of social motives between task-related motives and performance. A measure of goal setting or intentions could be added to examine that as a mediator. Research directions suggested by Tett and Burnett (2003) for evaluating trait activation theory could be combined with aspects of our theory to evaluate the viability of that portion of the model.

This model can be used to guide research on the relationships between specific personality variables and specific performance dimensions by helping to identify theoretically relevant predictors for different criteria. This will be facilitated by the development of a nomological net linking personality variables to the elements of the model. Meta-analyses have been conducted on personality predictors of work attitudes, proactive cognition aspects of motivation, and performance dimensions, but research on personality predictors of the other elements of the model is necessary to help identify likely personality predictors of specific performance dimensions.

In addition, current research on personality predictors of motivation is not at a level that helps us completely understand how specific personality traits are related to specific performance dimensions. Research is necessary to determine how the aspect of performance being studied influences the predictors of motivation. For example, certain personality traits may be highly related to motives, expectancies, self-efficacy, goal content, and goal commitment when the criterion is a dimension of citizenship performance; but have no relationship to these constructs when the criterion is a dimension of task performance. For example, Johnson et al. (2007) found that Agreeableness was related to the components of motivation when predicting citizenship performance, but was not related to motivation when predicting task performance. The opposite relationship would be expected for achievement, although achievement is commonly used as a proxy for motivation for any kind of performance. Research should be directed at creating a taxonomy of personality predictors of motivation for different performance constructs that can be used to facilitate our understanding of how personality influences performance.

Ideally, research guided by this model would be longitudinal. Consistent with previous theories linking job satisfaction to job performance (Judge, Thoreson, et al. 2001), we posit that work attitudes influence job performance. It is probable, however, that over time job performance and organizations' reactions to it (e.g., recognition, promotions, raises) will shape subsequent work attitudes (Judge, Thoreson, et al. 2001). Longitudinal research would enable examination of such reciprocal relationships.

REFERENCES

AJZEN, I. 1985. From intentions to actions: a theory of planned behavior. Pp. 11–39 in *Action Control: From Cognitions to Behavior*, ed. J. Kuhl and J. Beckmänn. New York: Springer-Verlag.

ALLEN, D. G., WEEKS, K. P., and MOFFITT, K. R. 2005. Turnover intentions and voluntary turnover: the moderating roles of self-monitoring, locus of control, proactive personality, and risk aversion. *Journal of Applied Psychology*, 90: 980–90.

ASHTON, M. C., and LEE, K. 2005. Honesty-Humility, the Big Five, and the Five-Factor Model. *Journal of Personality*, 73: 1321–53.

BARRICK, M. R., and MOUNT, M. K. 1991. The Big Five personality dimensions and job performance: a meta-analysis. *Personnel Psychology*, 44: 1–26.

—— 1993. Autonomy as a moderator of the relationships between the Big Five personality dimensions and job performance. *Journal of Applied Psychology*, 78: 111–18.

—— MITCHELL, T. R., and STEWART, G. L. 2003. Situational and motivational influences on trait-behavior relationships. Pp. 60–82 in *Personality and Work: Reconsidering the Role of Personality in Organizations*, ed. M. R. Barrick and A. M. Ryan. San Francisco: Jossey-Bass.

—— MOUNT, M. K., and JUDGE, T. A. 2001. Personality and performance at the beginning of the new millennium: what do we know and where do we go next? *International Journal of Selection and Assessment*, 9: 9–30.

—— STEWART, G. L., and PIOTROWSKI, M. 2002. Personality and job performance: Test of the mediating effects of motivation among sales representatives. *Journal of Applied Psychology*, 87: 43–51.

BARTRAM, D. 2005. The Great Eight competencies: a criterion-centric approach to validation. *Journal of Applied Psychology*, 90: 1185–203.

BATEMAN, T. S., and CRANT, J. M. 1993. The proactive component of organizational behavior: a measure and its correlates. *Journal of Organizational Behavior*, 14: 103–18.

BEATY, J. C., CLEVELAND, J. N., and MURPHY, K. R. 2001. The relation between personality and contextual performance in "strong" versus "weak" situations. *Human Performance*, 14: 125–48.

BING, M. N., LeBRETON, J. M., DAVISON, H. K., MIGETZ, D. Z., and JAMES, L. R. 2007. Integrating implicit and explicit social cognitions for enhanced personality assessment: a general framework for choosing measurement and statistical methods. *Organizational Research Methods*, 10: 346–89.

BONO, J. E., and JUDGE, T. A. 2003. Core self-evaluations: a review of the trait and its role in job performance and job satisfaction. *European Journal of Personality*, 17: S5–S18.

BORMAN, W. C., and PENNER, L. A. 2001. Citizenship performance: its nature, antecedents, and motives. Pp. 45–61 in *The Intersection of Personality and Industrial/Organizational Psychology*, ed., B. W. Roberts and R. T. Hogan. Washington, DC: American Psychological Association.

—— WHITE, L. A., and DORSEY, D. W. 1995. Effects of ratee task performance and interpersonal factors on supervisor and peer performance ratings. *Journal of Applied Psychology*, 80: 168–77.

—— BUCK, D. E., HANSON, M. A., MOTOWIDLO, S. J., STARK, S., and DRASGOW, F. 2001. An examination of the comparative reliability, validity, and accuracy of performance ratings made using computerized adaptive rating scales. *Journal of Applied Psychology*, 86: 965–73.

CAMPBELL, J. P. 1990. Modeling the performance prediction problem in industrial and organizational psychology. Pp. 687–732 in *Handbook of Industrial and Organizational Psychology*, 2nd edn., vol. i, ed. M. D. Dunnette and L. M. Hough. Palo Alto, CA: Consulting Psychologists Press.

COLQUITT, J. A., LePINE, J. A., and NOE, R. A. 2000. Toward an integrative theory of training motivation: a meta-analytic path analysis of 20 years of research. *Journal of Applied Psychology*, 85: 678–707.

CONNOLLY, J. J., and VISWESVARAN, C. 2000. The role of affectivity in job satisfaction: a meta-analysis. *Personality and Individual Differences*, 29: 265–81.

COOPER-HAKIM, A., and VISWESVARAN, C. 2005. The construct of work commitment: testing an integrative framework. *Psychological Bulletin*, 131: 241–59.

COSTA, P. T., and McCRAE, R. R. 1992. *Revised NEO Personality Inventory (NEO-PI-R) and NEO Five-Factor Inventory (NEO-FFI) professional manual*. Odessa, FL: Psychological Assessment Resources.

CULLEN, M. J., and SACKETT, P. R. 2003. Personality and counterproductive workplace behavior. Pp. 150–82 in *Personality and Work: Reconsidering the Role of Personality in Organizations*, ed. M. R. Barrick and A. M. Ryan. San Francisco: Jossey-Bass.

DAY, D. V., BEDEIAN, A. G., and CONTE, J. M. 1998. Personality as predictor of work-related outcomes: test of a mediated latent structure model. *Journal of Applied Social Psychology*, 28: 2068–88.

DORMANN, C., FAY, D., ZAPF, D., and FRESE, M. 2006. A state-trait analysis of job satisfaction: on the effect of core self-evaluations. *Applied Psychology: An International Review*, 55: 27–51.

DUDLEY, N. M., ORVIS, K. A., LEBIECKI, J. E., and CORTINA, J. M. 2006. A meta-analytic investigation of conscientiousness in the prediction of job performance: examining the intercorrelations and the incremental validity of narrow traits. *Journal of Applied Psychology*, 91: 40–57.

ERDHEIM, J., WANG, M., and ZICKAR, M. 2006. Linking the Big Five personality constructs to organizational commitment. *Personality and Individual Differences*, 41: 959–70.

FISHBEIN, M., and AJZEN, I. 1975. *Belief, Attitude, Intention, and Behavior: An Introduction to Theory and Research.* Reading, MA: Addison-Wesley.

FUNDER, D. C. 2001. *The Personality Puzzle*, 2nd edn. New York: Norton.

GELLATLY, I. R., and IRVING, P. G. 2001. Personality, autonomy, and contextual performance of managers. *Human Performance*, 14: 231–45.

GOLDBERG, L. R. 1992. The development of markers for the Big-Five factor structure. *Psychological Assessment*, 4: 26–42.

GRUYS, M. L. 2000. The dimensionality of deviant employee behavior in the workplace. Unpublished doctoral dissertation, University of Minnesota.

GUION, R. M., and GOTTIER, R. F. 1965. Validity of personality measures in personnel selection. *Personnel Psychology*, 18: 135–64.

HECKHAUSEN, H., and KUHL, J. 1985. From wishes to action: the dead ends and short cuts on the long way to action. Pp. 134–60 in *Goal Directed Behavior: The Concept of Action in Psychology*, ed. M. Frese are J. Sabini. Hillsdale, NJ: Erlbaum.

HELMREICH, R. L., SAWIN, L. L., and CARSRUD, A. L. 1986. The honeymoon effect in job performance: temporal increases in the predictive power of achievement motivation. *Journal of Applied Psychology*, 71: 185–8.

HOGAN, J., and HOLLAND, H. 2003. Using theory to evaluate personality and job-performance relations: a socioanalytic perspective. *Journal of Applied Psychology*, 88: 100–12.

HOUGH, L. M. 1992. The "Big Five" personality variables—construct confusion: description versus prediction. *Human Performance*, 5: 139–55.

—— 2003. Emerging trends and needs in personality research and practice: beyond main effects. Pp. 289–325 in *Personality and Work: Reconsidering the Role of Personality in Organizations*, ed. M. R. Barrick and A. M. Ryan. San Francisco: Jossey-Bass.

—— and ONES, D. S. 2001. The structure, measurement, validity, and use of personality variables in industrial, work, and organizational psychology. Pp. 233–77 in *Handbook of Work psychology*, vol. i: *Personnel Psychology*, ed. N. R. Anderson, D. S. Ones, H. K. Sinangil, and C. Viswesvaran. Thousand Oaks, CA: Sage.

—— and OSWALD, F. L. 2005. They're right, well . . . mostly right: research evidence and an agenda to rescue personality testing from 1960s insights. *Human Performance*, 18: 373–87.

—— and SCHNEIDER, R. S. 1996. Personality traits, taxonomies, and applications in organizations. Pp. 31–88 in *Individual Differences and Behavior in organizations*, ed. K. R. Murphy. San Francisco: Jossey-Bass.

—— EATON, N. K., DUNNETTE, M. D., KAMP, J. D., and McCLOY, R. A. 1990. Criterion-related validities of personality constructs and the effect of response distortion on those validities [Monograph]. *Journal of Applied Psychology*, 75: 581–95.

HURTZ, G. M., and DONOVAN, J. J. 2000. Personality and job performance: the Big Five revisited. *Journal of Applied Psychology*, 85: 869–79.

ILIES, R., and JUDGE, T. A. 2002. Understanding the dynamic relationship among personality, mood, and job satisfaction: a field experience sampling study. *Organizational Behavior and Human Decision Processes*, 89: 1119–39.

JAMES, L. R. 1998. Measurement of personality via conditional reasoning. *Organizational Research Methods*, 1: 131–63.

JOHNSON, J. W. 2003. Toward a better understanding of the relationship between personality and individual job performance. Pp. 83–120 in *Personality and Work: Reconsidering the Role of Personality in Organizations*, ed. M. R. Barrick and A. M. Ryan. San Francisco: Jossey-Bass.

JOHNSON, J. W., DUEHR, E. E., HEZLETT, S. A., MUROS, J. P., and FERSTL, K. L. 2007. *Testing a Theory of the Determinants of Individual Job Performance for United States Army Junior Commissioned Officers* (ARI Technical Report). Alexandria, VA: US Army Research Institute for the Behavioral and Social Sciences.

JUDGE, T. A. and BONO, J. E. 2001. Relationship of core self-evaluation traits—self-esteem, generalized self-efficacy, locus of control and emotional stability—with job satisfaction and job performance: a meta-analysis. *Journal of Applied Psychology*, 86: 80–92.

—— and ILIES, R. 2002. Relationship of personality to performance motivation: a meta-analytic review. *Journal of Applied Psychology*, 87: 797–807.

—— BONO, J. E., and LOCKE, E. A. 2000. Personality and job satisfaction: the mediating role of job characteristics. *Journal of Applied Psychology*, 85: 237–49.

—— HELLER, D., and MOUNT, M. K. 2002. Five-factor model of personality and job satisfaction: a meta-analysis. *Journal of Applied Psychology*, 87: 530–41.

—— EREZ, A., BONO, J. E., and THORESON, C. J. 2002. Are measures of self-esteem, neuroticism, locus of control and generalized self-efficacy indicators of a common core construct? *Journal of Personality and Social Psychology*, 83: 693–710.

—— LOCKE, E. A., DURHAM, C. C., and KLUGER, A. N. 1998. Dispositional effects on job and life satisfaction: the role of core evaluations. *Journal of Applied Psychology*, 83: 17–34.

—— THORESON, C. J., BONO, J. E., and PATTON, G. K. 2001. The job satisfaction–job performance relationship: a qualitative and quantitative review. *Psychological Bulletin*, 127: 376–407.

—— PARKER, S., COLBERT, A. E., HELLER, D., and ILIES, R. 2001. Job satisfaction: a cross-cultural review. Pp. 25–52 in *Handbook of Work Psychology (Vol. 2): Organizational Psychology*, ed. N. R. Anderson, D. S. Ones, H. K. Sinangil, and C. Viswesvaran. Thousand Oaks, CA: Sage.

KANFER, R. 1990. Motivation theory and industrial and organizational psychology. Pp. 75–170 in *Handbook of Industrial and Organizational Psychology*, 2nd edn., vol. i, ed. M. D. Dunnette and L. M. Hough. Palo Alto, CA: Consulting Psychologists Press.

—— 1992. Work motivation: new directions in theory and research. Pp. 1–53 in *International Review of Industrial and Organizational Psychology*, vol. vii, ed. C. L. Cooper and I. T. Robertson. Chichester: Wiley.

—— and ACKERMAN, P. L. 1989. Motivation and cognitive abilities: an integrative/aptitude-treatment interaction approach to skill acquisition [Monograph]. *Journal of Applied Psychology*, 74: 657–90.

—— and HEGGESTAD, E. D. 1997. Motivational traits and skills: a person-centered approach to work motivation. Pp. 1–56 in *Research in Organizational Behavior*, vol. xix, ed. L. L. Cummings and B. M. Staw. Greenwich, CT: JAI Press.

KUHL, J. 1985. Volitional mediators of cognition-behavior consistency: self-regulatory processes and action vs. state orientation. Pp. 101–28 in *Action Control: From Cognition to Behavior*, ed. J. Kuhl and J. Beckmänn. New York: Springer-Verlag.

KUNCEL, N. R., and BORNEMAN, M. J. 2007. Toward a new method of detecting deliberately faked personality tests: the use of idiosyncratic item responses. *International Journal of Selection and Assessment*, 15: 220–31.

LANCE, C. E., and BENNETT, W. 2000. Replication and extension of models of supervisory job performance ratings. *Human Performance*, 13: 139–58.

MARCUS, B., LEE, K., and ASHTON, M. C. 2007. Personality dimensions explaining relationships between integrity tests and counterproductive behavior: Big Five, or one in
addition? *Personality Psychology*, 60: 1–34.

—— GOFFIN, R. D., JOHNSTON, N. G., and ROTHSTEIN, M. G. 2007. Personality and
cognitive ability as predictors of typical and maximum managerial performance.
Human Performance, 20: 275–85.

MEYER, J. P., and ALLEN, N. J. 1997. *Commitment in the Workplace: Theory, Research, and
Application.* Thousand Oaks, CA: Sage.

—— STANLEY, D. J., HERSCOVITCH, L., and TOPOLNYTSKY, L. 2002. Affective, continuance,
and normative commitment to the organization: a meta-analysis of antecedents, correlates, and consequences. *Journal of Vocational Behavior*, 61: 20–52.

MITCHELL, T. R., and DANIELS, D. 2003. Motivation. Pp. 225–54 in *Handbook of Psychology*,
vol. xii: *Industrial and Organizational Psychology*, ed. W. Borman, D. Ilgen, and R.
Klimoski. Hoboken, NJ: Wiley.

MORGESON, F. P., CAMPION, M. A., DIPBOYE, R. L., HOLLENBECK, J. R., MURPHY, K., and
SCHMITT, N. 2007. Reconsidering the use of personality tests in personnel selection
contexts. *Personnel Psychology*, 60: 683–729.

MOTOWIDLO, S. J., BORMAN, W. C., and SCHMIT, M. J. 1997. A theory of individual
differences in task and contextual performance. *Human Performance*, 10: 71–83.

MOUNT, M. K., BARRICK, M. R., and RYAN, A. M. 2003. Research themes for the future.
Pp. 326–44 in *Personality and Work: Reconsidering the Role of Personality in Organizations*,
ed. M. R. Barrick and A. M. Ryan. San Francisco: Jossey-Bass.

—— —— and STRAUSS, J. P. 1999. The joint relationship of conscientiousness and ability
with performance: test of the interaction hypothesis. *Journal of Management*, 25: 707–21.

—— ILIES, R., and JOHNSON, E. 2006. Relationship of personality traits and counter-
productive work behaviors: the mediating effects of job satisfaction. *Personnel Psychology*,
59: 591–622.

MURPHY, K. R., and DZIEWECZYNSKI, J. L. 2005. Why don't measures of broad dimensions
of personality perform better as predictors of job performance? *Human Performance*, 18:
343–57.

ONES, D. S., VISWESVARAN, C., and DILCHERT, S. 2005. Personality at work: raising
awareness and correcting misconceptions. *Human Performance*, 18: 389–404.

—— DILCHERT, S., VISWESVARAN, C., and JUDGE, T. A. 2007. In support of personality
assessment in organizational settings. *Personnel Psychology*, 60: 955–1027.

PENNER, L. A., MIDILI, A. R., and KEGELMEYER, J. 1997. Beyond job attitudes: a personality
and social psychology perspective on the causes of organizational citizenship behavior.
Human Performance, 10: 111–31.

PULAKOS, E. D., ARAD, S., DONOVAN, M. A., and PLAMONDON, K. E. 2000. Adaptability in
the workplace: development of a taxonomy of adaptive performance. *Journal of Applied
Psychology*, 85: 612–24.

ROTHSTEIN, M. G., and GOFFIN, R. D. 2006. The use of personality measures in personnel
selection: what does current research support? *Human Resource Management Review*, 16:
155–80.

SACKETT, P. R., and DEVORE, C. J. 2001. Counterproductive behaviors at work. Pp. 145–64
in *International Handbook of Work Psychology*, ed. N. Anderson, D. Ones, H. Sinangil,
and C. Viswesvaran. Thousand Oaks, CA: Sage.

SACKETT, P. R., GRUYS, M. L., and ELLINGSON, J. E. 1998. Ability-personality interactions when predicting job performance. *Journal of Applied Psychology*, 83: 545–56.

SAUCIER, G., and GOLDBERG, L. R. 2003. The structure of personality attributes. Pp. 1–29 in *Personality and Work: Reconsidering the Role of Personality in Organizations*, ed. M. R. Barrick and A. M. Ryan. San Francisco: Jossey-Bass.

SCHMIDT, F. L., HUNTER, J. E., and OUTERBRIDGE, A. N. 1986. Impact of job experience and ability on job knowledge, work sample performance, and supervisory ratings of job performance. *Journal of Applied Psychology*, 71: 432–9.

SCHNEIDER, R. J., HOUGH, L. M., and DUNNETTE, M. D. 1996. Broadsided by broad traits: how to sink science in five dimensions or less. *Journal of Organizational Behavior*, 17: 639–55.

SEIBERT, S. E., CRANT, J. M., and KRAIMER, M. L. 1999. Proactive personality and career success. *Journal of Applied Psychology*, 84: 483–502.

SINCLAIR, R. R., and TUCKER, J. S. 2006. Stress-CARE: an integrated model of individual differences in soldier performance under stress. Pp. 202–31 in *Military Life: The Psychology of Serving in Peace and Combat*, vol. i: *Military Performance*, ed. T. W. Britt, C. A. Castro, and A. B. Adler. Westport, CT: Praeger Security International.

TETT, R. P., and BURNETT, D. B. 2003. A personality trait-based interactionist model of job performance. *Journal of Applied Psychology*, 88: 500–17.

—— and CHRISTIANSEN, N. D. 2007. Personality tests at the crossroads: a response to Morgeson, Campion, Dipboye, Hollenbeck, Murphy, and Schmitt (2007). *Personnel Psychology*, 60: 967–93.

—— JACKSON, D. N., ROTHSTEIN, M., and REDDON, J. R. 1994. Meta-analysis of personality-job performance relations: a reply to Ones, Mount, Barrick, and Hunter (1994). *Personnel Psychology*, 47: 157–72.

—— —— —— —— (1999). Meta-analysis of bi-directional relations in personality-job performance research. *Human Performance*, 12: 1–29.

VAN DEN BERG, P. T., and FEIJ, J. A. 2003. Complex relationships among personality traits, job characteristics, and work behaviors. *International Journal of Selection and Assessment*, 11: 326–39.

WALSH, W. B., and EGGERTH, D. E. 2005. Vocational psychology and personality: the relationship of the five-factor model to job performance and job satisfaction. Pp. 267–95 in *Handbook of Vocational Psychology: Theory, Research, and Practice*, 3rd edn., ed. W. B. Walsh and M. L. Savicks. Mahwah, NJ: Lawrence Erlbaum Associates.

WEISS, H. M. 2002. Deconstructing job satisfaction: separating evaluations, beliefs and affective experiences. *Human Resource Management Review*, 12, 173–94.

WITT, L. A., BURKE, L. A., BARRICK, M. R., and MOUNT, M. K. 2002. The interactive effects of conscientiousness and agreeableness on job performance. *Journal of Applied Psychology*, 87: 164–9.

WOFFORD, J. C., GOODWIN, V. L., and PREMACK, S. 1992. Meta-analysis of the antecedents of personal goal level and of the antecedents and consequences of goal commitment. *Journal of Management*, 18: 595–615.

WRIGHT, P. M., KACMAR, K. M., McMAHAN, G. C., and DELEEUW, K. 1995. P = f(M × A): cognitive ability as a moderator of the relationship between personality and job performance. *Journal of Management*, 21: 1129–39.

4

LEADERSHIP: CURRENT ASSESSMENT AND FUTURE NEEDS

IAIN L. DENSTEN

1. INTRODUCTION

LEADERSHIP continues to dominate the focus of individuals seeking to understand and advance organizations, and thus the literature on leadership has attempted to provide a solution for seemingly endless problems that confront organizations. This review aims to further advance understanding of the interrelationships between leaders, their followers, and the contemporary challenges that face them by identifying (a) the current state of play; (b) the indisputable but not undebatable leadership ideas; (c) how the leadership phenomenon has been sliced up; (d) where contemporary leadership knowledge is going; and (e) the future needs for research.

2. CURRENT STATE OF PLAY

Leadership is ultimately an abstract concept invented by people trying to understand their experiences and identity. While leaders, followers, and situations are indeed observable, leadership itself has no physical form and is constructed in the minds of observers. Individuals who accept the subjective nature of leadership are less susceptible to "naïve realism" which leads them to assume that their perceptions are reality rather than a construction of goal-focused ideas. Further, despite the popularity of leadership, the term is not a scientific term and has no formal or standardized definition (Vroom and Jago 2007) and we must appreciate that the "subject is vast, amorphous, slippery, and, above all, desperately important" (Bennis 2007, 2). However, such views plainly frustrate practitioners who are under pressure from three dialectic divergent challenges, which according to Chemers (2003) are (a) responding to both internal and external environments; (b) accommodating both individual and collective goals and interests; and (c) negotiating a balance between subjective and objective realities. Countless reviews of the leadership research and literature continue to highlight the numerous definitions and theoretical frameworks of leadership which can range from leadership as an influencing process to an exchange relationship. Such diversity creates a fundamental problem as the majority of leadership scholars do not accept a single or definitive definition or framework of leadership. This inability to define leadership inhibits our understanding of this critical organizational phenomenon. However, most definitions of leadership explicitly recognize the role of influence and there is growing acceptance of what leadership is required to influence, namely emotions, cognitions, and behaviors of others.

Few researchers recognize that such a fundamental plank within this field of study is missing and simply portray the leadership research and literature as being inconsistent and unfocused. A key inhibiting influence on achieving a robust definition of leadership, and the subsequent controversy about leadership research, is an insidious need for parsimony. This can be recognized as "Ockham's razor" which was the principle proposed by William of Ockham in the fourteenth century, as "Pluralitas non est ponenda sine necessitate," which translates as "entities should not be multiplied unnecessarily." In practice, researchers have overcome the impossibility of fully considering every strand of complex phenomena and interrelated processes by unsheathing "Ockham's razor" in order to simplify the natural world by putting a fine blade to conceptual knots that confront them and keep things simple.

While this need for simplicity confronts most fields of study, interest in understanding the leadership phenomenon is also driven by the unquenchable thirst of practitioners for usable advice about how to simply understand and lead followers. A prevailing leadership research characteristic is the tendency for evolving theories to reinterpret and reanalyze, rather than eliminate established theories thereby reinforcing a pragmatic and subversive drive that compels researchers to provide simple answers to a complex phenomenon. Leadership theories are judged in terms of face validity and intuitive preconceptions which assume a rational approach to analyzing decisions as well as generating recommendations. This reinforces the basic idea that one can simply modify leadership style to the situation (Vroom and Jago 2007).

Bligh and Meindl's (2005) investigation of popular leadership books found that they were primarily written outside the scientific or research-based approach to the field of leadership. The most common focus was the leader–follower interactions and most projected romantic views of leadership and its potential. They concluded that readers' appetite for leadership books is satisfied in distinctive ways and these were to (a) fascinate the readers with the seemingly inexhaustible power and influence for leaders to enact change; (b) provide easy answers to the ever-quickening pace of change; (c) satisfy the need for wisdom; (d) provide tools from individuals who claim expertise and vast experience; and (e) satisfy a capitalistic, consumer-driven society's desire for self-improvement. According to Krohe (2000, 19), "interest [in leadership books] is ignited by the promise of a miracle cure" where the reader assumes they are already a leader and optimistically can achieve what these books market. The most commercially popular books satisfy the need for simple, understandable, and actionable answers to vexing problems (Schriesheim 2003) and are filled to the brim with maxims (e.g., trust your people). However, these maxims come without sufficient information about how the situational variables determine success or failure (Vroom and Jago 2007) and therefore these books may not transform well-established and tested ideas into more effective organizational practices. Rousseau and McCarthy (2007) argue that managers should be educated from an evidence-based perspective that involves mastering valid behavioral principles and developed procedural knowledge from practice, feedback, and reflection.

3. THE INDISPUTABLE BUT NOT UNDEBATABLE IDEAS

While there is an endless supply of ideas about leadership there is a general lack of commonality, and comprehensiveness that confronts users. However, several themes have emerged from the literature which are well established and are widely recognized as being important to understanding and implementing leadership (i.e., indisputable) but questions still remain about their precise nature and impact (i.e., not undebatable). These themes are that leadership is: romanticized, about "influencing", managing the scene, ruling the game, causing ripple effects, having expertise, using the black box, and giving challenging expectations.

4. LEADERSHIP IS ROMANTICIZED

Heroic leaders have always commanded a disproportionate amount of attention (Bennis 2007). This has led to followers and situations being largely ignored and has produced a predominately romantic view of leaders generally. The tendency to create overly heroic and exaggerated views of leaders and their achievements, termed "romance of leadership", is enhanced by situations where causality is indeterminate and unpredictable events occur (see Meindl, Ehrlich, and Dukerich 1985). Such adverse situations, when combined with susceptible and needy followers, can enable destructive leaders to emerge (Padilla, Hogan, and Kaiser 2007). While the need for leaders to display confidence in their conviction and to use a leadership style that conveys efficacy and control is widely recognized (Meindl, Ehrlich, and Dukerich 1985), Boerner, Eisenbeiss, and Griesser (2007) argue for greater focus on the desired outcomes rather than leadership style. In fact, Vroom and Jago (2007) support disentangling the definition of leadership from organizational effectiveness because many factors, apart from the quality of leadership, have a significant impact.

"Many studies have simply assumed that leaders are powerful and in control while followers are largely powerless, passive, and predictable. Little research attends to followers and their interaction with leaders" (Collinson 2005, 1423). Followers are romantically and unrealistically viewed as "simple" and impatient for the right type of influence given by their leader. In fact, followers may actively attack and isolate leaders in order to reduce their ability to influence (Ruth 2006). While studies that treat followers in a more realistic and proactive light are evident (e.g., Boerner, Eisenbeiss, and Griesser 2007; Densten and Gray 2001), leaders remain the focal point of leadership research and the most prominent element of the socially constructed realities about organizations (Meindl, Ehrlich, and Dukerich 1990) which has led to an overestimation of the influence leaders have on organizational performance (Murphy 2002). Further, the idea that leaders and followers can easily rise above and overcome an inhibiting working environment (e.g., lack of resources) perpetuates romantic notions of leadership; along with the notion that leadership is always associated with positive outcomes.

5. LEADERSHIP IS ABOUT INFLUENCING

Influence is the dominant idea that runs throughout leadership research and involves understanding how leaders and followers alter each others' cognitive, emotional, and motivational processes, in order to exert influence. While leadership can be a substitute for formal controls and mechanisms (i.e., planning, control, organizing), leadership's real value per se is to influence outcomes to be more creative, faster, and effective. Leadership research is primarily focused on how these processes occur in the formal and informal aspect of organizational life and influence the resulting discretionary and non-discretionary behaviors. In other words, how perceptions of working relationships influence the thoughts, commitment, and effort exerted by leaders and followers. These processes are embedded in the organizational context that leaders and followers experience and the perceptions they construct (i.e., "formed impressions" and "make inferences"). Nonverbal, verbal, and interpersonal cues produce these perceptions. However, what cues get noticed by leaders or followers depends on what either is trying to achieve (i.e., their goals) and their own involvement (Klimoski and Donahue 2001). Further, these cues and leadership in general occur within environments where the situational factors, such as culture, task, climate, and organizational level have underlying and unique influences which moderate the influence of leaders (Jaques and Clement 2003; Schein 2004). Studying or applying leadership influence without considering such situational factors is problematic and potentially dangerous.

6. Managing the Scene

Workplace survival requires leaders and followers to actively attempt to display behaviors to present an image which establishes their credibility by appearing competent and trustworthy. Each leader or follower displays attitudes and behaviors that deny common faults and exaggerate personal strengths to project a positive image. These distortions can reflect romantic notions held by the perceivers about what are ideal leaders and followers. Image creation is based on the premise that leaders (and followers) have specific ideas about their own behaviors and what they ideally expect from others (Lord and Hall 2005). A leader's image can be internally distorted by self-deceptive beliefs and externally distorted by image management (Gray and Densten 2007). The matching of these expectations within displayed attitudes and behaviors by leaders and followers is highly influential and can motivate individuals to follow (Hogg 2001; Schyns and Meindl 2005). Image management is also about establishing status within a group which can be accrued through exchanges that gain "idiosyncratic credits" (Chemers 2003). For example, leaders or followers who demonstrate motivation to achieve group goals and display loyalty to group values rather than their own, earn credits which purchase future influence. Image management is also used to establish status which involves encouraging others to accept the capacity or potential to influence others and events through the use of discretion. Leaders and followers gain discretion from organizational policies and procedures that enable them to (a) order, reward, punish, inform, negotiate, persuade, flatter, and provide resources to others; and (b) the need of others for affection, admiration, acceptance, loyalty, and specialized knowledge (French and Raven 1959). While generally leaders tend to use soft tactics (e.g., persuasion) more than hard tactics (e.g., commanding), coercion tactics are more frequent from competent power-holders than from the less competent, and when the power holders are the prime beneficiary from the task performance (Van Knippenberg, Van Knippenberg, and De Cremer 2007).

7. LEADERSHIP IS RULING THE GAME

Relationships between leaders and followers provide critical tacit knowledge about how each should act and how behaviors will be interpreted (i.e., "the rules of the game"). A healthy working relationship enables leaders to influence followers beyond simple command and control and enables them greater access to the motivation, imagination, and expertise of followers which can be critical to complex task completion. The leader and follower relationship provides the rational context and social order within groups and organizations which influence is based upon (Uhl-Bien 2006). Leaders emerge from groups and organizations when they create interdependent relationships that they can directly or indirectly influence. Leaders exchange extrinsic (e.g., job allocation, salary raise) and intrinsic (e.g., praises, sense of empowerment) rewards to gain a position of influence, and use a range of behaviors, such as vision, direction, protection, security, inclusion, and belonging to capitalize on that position. Leaders then use coaching and guiding behaviors to develop and improve their relationships with followers. This gives them greater capacity to influence the development of followers (i.e., skills, abilities, motivation) and confidence about completing tasks successfully (Chemers 2003). Relationships enable the range of exchanges between leaders and followers to be significantly expanded and to provide leaders with more scope to negotiate the followers' commitment to reward for effort. A fundamental challenge for leaders is to discover the uniqueness of each relationship with followers to gain a continual position of influence.

8. Leadership is about Causing Ripple Effects

Successful leadership involves achieving outcomes that are beyond the capacity of what a single individual can accomplish alone and involves leaders using a multiplying effect where their action (e.g., vision) causes ripple effects (or motion) that results in others focusing their outcomes towards a common goal. Leaders are universally time poor and must determine what level of decision-making participation by followers will maximize these ripple effects and how they can exploit the motivation, knowledge, and skills of followers, as individuals and as team members, to ensure these ripple effects achieve the desired outcomes (Chemers 2003). According to Schein (2004), exploitation can occur on at least three levels: (a) visible behaviors; (b) conscious thought, and values; and (c) assumptions, beliefs, and expectations. Clawson (2006) highlights the critical role of leaders in energizing others and themselves. Kark and Van Dijk (2007) suggest that for leaders to energize others and themselves they need to recognize and employ two conflicting motivational syndromes, i.e., the motivation for stability (prevention) versus the motivation for change (promotion) to deploy physical and cognitive resources of their followers. Such deployment enables leaders to overcome their inability to process all the explicit and tacit information critical to effective problem solving. Further, the words and actions of leaders send critical and contextual information to followers about what are acceptable modes of behaviors, and have a major influence on the climate of their group and organization. Sarros and Cooper (2006) highlight that the character of leaders should not be underestimated as an essential building block for socially responsible organizations and ethically sound management practices.

9. Leadership is Having Expertise

Even with this follower assistance, leaders must still be motivated to develop expertise which results from integration of metacognitive skills, learning skills, thinking skills, knowledge, and drive (Sternberg 2007). Further, self-confidence influences the motivation, perceptions, and thought patterns of leaders (Hollenbeck and Hall 2004) which underpin the development of expertise and play an essential role in the ability of leaders to cause this ripple effect. Leaders must use themselves as a source of motivation and control their own thoughts and actions (Yun, Cox, and Sims 2006) to assist them to overcome interference between organizational knowledge and dynamic capabilities caused by power and politics (Prieto and Easterby-Smith 2006), and situational demands that affect the ability of leaders and followers to perceive, understand, and manage their emotions (Cherniss 2006) and cognitions. Failure to overcome these inhibitors would cause the misalignment of leadership with organizational outcomes and be counterproductive, particularly with climate safety (Cox, Jones, and Collinson 2006). Further, from a systems-model view, leadership is a matter of leaders (and followers) formulating, making, and acting on decisions, which to be effective requires a synthesis of intelligence, wisdom, and creativity (Sternberg 2007). Leaders also require expertise in handling conflicting demands and have the breadth of skills, knowledge, and motivation to focus attention on the critical issues and not just the most prevalent problems. After all, leaders are dealing with the complexity of perceptions about reality held within an untouchable black box and not black or white evidence.

10. LEADERSHIP IS USING THE BLACK BOX

Perceptions of leadership behaviors are shaped by the pre-existing knowledge structures (i.e., schemas) that exist within the so-called "black box" or minds of individuals. These schemas are self-motivating cognitive knowledge structures that individuals use to encode and represent new information about leadership (Lord and Maher 1991). Understanding these schemas can give significant insight into how individuals make sense of the world and thus help explain how leaders can exert influence over followers, or vice versa. The potential range of these schemas is large, however those relating to leadership can be narrowed down to include sensitivity, dedication, charisma, attractiveness, intelligence, strength, tyranny, and masculinity (Offermann, Kennedy, and Wirtz 1994) and are unlikely to be affected by experience of leaders or other organizational factors (Golembiewski, Billingsley, and Yeager 1976). Interestingly, the closeness of followers' schemas to the actual or displayed behavior of their leaders influences the quality of exchanges between followers and leaders (Epitropaki and Martin 2005). Chemers (2003) suggests that the ability of potential leaders to match the expectations of their followers requires (a) an understanding of prototypical characteristics and situational schemas of their followers; and (b) the capacity to image manage the expected behaviors and attitudes. Understanding pre-existing knowledge structure should enable leaders to better appreciate how they can easily misinterpret the behaviors and situations they experience and how followers misinterpret their behaviors because of previous expectations.

11. LEADERSHIP IS GIVING CHALLENGING EXPECTATIONS

Challenging performance expectations from leaders and followers can create pressure that motivates them to perform at a higher level. This unique relationship goes beyond leaders and followers simply understanding the expectations of others better which then results in enhanced performance. Rather it acts like a self-fulfilling prophecy where expectation has a profound influence on the leader and follower. This effect is called the Pygmalion effect and operates subconsciously (see White and Locke 2000). According to McNatt (2000, 314), "the Pygmalion effect is a special case of [self-fulfilling prophecies] whereby a person's (perceiver's) expectations of another (target) are transferred to, or otherwise have an influence on, the target such that the target ultimately modifies his or her behaviors or achievement level in conformity with the expectation." In other words, the raising of expectations of the leader or follower (i.e., the Galatea effect) changes the belief that they can achieve, and thus their changed behaviors may result in higher performance. Leadership research appears to imply that successful leadership depends on followers' recognition and compliance with the expectations of others, particularly their leader (Carmeli and Schaubroeck 2007). A dark side of the Pygmalion effect also exists (i.e., the Golem effect) and represents the influence of negative expectations from a leader which subsequently reduces their follower performance. This simplicity of the relationship between expectations and performance has been challenged (see NcNatt 2000; White and Locke 2000). However, the basic idea that interpersonal expectations are a key influence in the self-beliefs which impact on performance is reasonably robust. Further, this effect is most likely continuous and two-way, as both leaders and followers attempt to influence the other's self-belief of what is realistically achievable.

12. THE SLICED-UP LEADERSHIP PHENOMENON

This section goes beyond the indisputable themes and examines how the leadership phenomenon has been sliced to provide key insights.

12.1 The Leader Slice of the Phenomenon

Research into the leader aspects of leadership is dominated by the trait approach, which was the earliest scientific leadership investigation. Researchers reduced the

complexity of the leadership phenomenon down to observable leader characteristics. This approach suggests that "what you see is what you get" and is the most
easily accessible of all leadership theoretical approaches. Trait leadership theories
investigate consistent behavioral patterns and personality persona displayed by
leaders from which traits are then inferred (Hughes, Curphy, and Ginnett 2006).
Trait leadership theories firmly established the process whereby leadership researchers classify sets of characteristics (or behaviors) with abstract labels that
represent an underlying concept, and this approach is characteristic of all subsequent leadership theories. This level of abstraction enables traits to be more
cognitively economical than using individual behaviors when making predictions
about the future behaviors of others, and in determining an appropriate interaction approach (Fiske 1993). The emphasis in trait research has changed. First, it
focused on identifying the qualities of great persons; next, it shifted to include the
impact of situations on leadership; and recently, it has shifted back to re-emphasize
the critical role of traits in effective leadership (Northouse 2007). Further, a review
by Zacarro, Kemp, and Bader (2004) enhanced earlier studies by identifying six
categories of leader traits (or attributes). These were the cognitive abilities (i.e.,
general intelligence and creative thinking capacities), personality (i.e., extroversion, conscientiousness, emotional stability, openness, and agreeableness), motivation (i.e., need for power and achievement, and motivation to lead), social
capacity (i.e., self-monitoring, social intelligence, and emotional intelligence),
problem-solving skills (i.e., problem construction, solution generation, and metacognition), and tacit knowledge. The impact of these traits could vary according to
the context, culture, and hierarchy.

A distinction between "traits that are more distal to behavioral performance and
those that are more proximal to outcomes" is emerging in the form of a multi-stage
model where distal traits predict the proximal traits which in turn predict the
outcomes (Zacarro, Kemp, and Bader 2004, 121). Distal traits (or attributes) are
general cognitive abilities, personality, motives, and values, while proximal traits
(or attributes) are social appraisal skills, problem-solving skills, and expertise/tacit
knowledge. Northhouse (2007) suggests that trait theories offer key insights from a
large body of literature which is primarily focused on the leader component in the
leadership process, and provides benchmarks for individuals wanting to evaluate
their own personal leadership attributes. The trait approach remains instinctively
appealing and builds on a fundamental belief that leaders are unique people who
have special characteristics. Interestingly, an individual belief about the fixedness or
malleability of human attributes (i.e., traits) guides their information processing
and especially their perceptual judgments of others (Dweck 1996). Leaders and
followers who believe traits are fixed and static are more likely to draw global trait
inferences from consistent behavioral patterns and personality, even when plausible situational explanations are evident (Werth, Markel, and Förster 2006). Further, Zacarro (2007) argues that for traits to be a significant precursor of leadership

effectiveness, traits need to be conceptualized into a meaningful framework rather than just used as multiple independent traits and, also, the different impacts that trait types have on leadership outcomes need to be recognized. While the traits approach continues to have a major influence on how leaders and followers manage their image, the lack of success in producing the ultimate set of universal traits encouraged researchers to investigate the behaviors of leaders.

12.2 The Content and Process Slice of the Phenomenon

Research into the content and process aspects of leadership involved reducing the complexity of the leadership phenomenon by focusing on the observable actions of leaders and resulting follower outcomes. This behavioral approach had significant advantages over the trait approach in terms of leader development because behaviors (e.g., inspiring) are more easily observable than traits (e.g., intelligence) and gave individuals the opportunity to recognize ineffective behaviors and empowered them to adopt new behaviors (Hughes, Curphy, and Ginnett 2006). Early behavioral research identified two underlying concepts, namely "consideration" and "initiating structure" which have proven to be among the most robust of leadership ideas (Fleishman 1995). Briefly, "consideration" related to relationship-oriented behaviors that helped followers feel comfortable with themselves, each other, and the situation; and "initiating structure" related to task-oriented behaviors which facilitate followers' goal accomplishment. These concepts enabled the introduction of dialectic reasoning into the selection of leadership behaviors and allowed the logic behind such selection to be intensively scrutinized. Kaplan (2006) has highlighted the detrimental impact of "lopsidedness" in the capacity of leaders to use either dimension. These dimensions also introduced the use of diagrammatic representations of leadership behaviors that significantly improved the understanding and practical use of behaviors. Diagrams are now commonplace amongst most contemporary leadership theories and overcome what Schriesheim (2003) identified as rational boundaries which inhibit a leader's understanding of new knowledge.

Since the discovery of "consideration" and "initiating structure" more than a half-century ago, the validity and measurement of these concepts have been continually questioned, which has resulted in them losing favor in leadership research (Judge, Piccolo, and Ilies 2004). Many prominent leadership researchers have simply dismissed the impact that "consideration" and "initiating structure" has on leadership effectiveness (Northouse 2007). However, such negativity may be unfounded. A recent meta-study by Judge, Piccolo, and Ilies (2004, 44) "revealed that both consideration and initiating structure have important effects on numerous criteria that most would argue are fundamental indicators of effective leadership." Further, a study by Amabile et al. (2004) found that specific types of consideration (i.e., relationship) and initiating structure (i.e., task) and behaviors were intertwined in complex ways. According to Yukl (2006, 63), these two concepts are metacategories within leadership behavior taxonomies and reduce the problem of understanding an almost seemingly unlimited list of behaviors which are "abstract rather than tangible attributes of the real world." These two metacategories are viewed as inadequate and require a third change-oriented metacategory (McCauley 2004; Uhl-Bien, Marion, and McKelvey 2007; Yukl 2006). However, the most comprehensive taxonomy of leadership behaviors is the Competing Values Framework (CVF). This taxonomy builds on substantial organizational behavioral theory and provides eight paradoxical metacategories (or roles) that enact leadership strategies aimed at achieving specific organizational effectiveness outcomes (Quinn et al. 2003). The CVF is able to graphically represent complexity of leadership and the range and depth of expertise required to function as leader.

The difficulty in developing leadership taxonomies is the problem of (a) attempting to "identify observed behavior in order to organize perceptions of the world and make them meaningful [...when they] do not exist in any objective sense" (Yukl 2006, 63); (b) determining the appropriate level of abstraction or generality; (c) the choice of leadership outcomes; and (d) the method (e.g., factor analysis) used to develop each metacategory (Fleishman et al., 1991). However, ideas about dynamic situations and unforeseen surprises are not a central feature of these leadership approaches which assume an equilibrium end state (Plowman et al. 2007). Further, Yukl (2006) continues to remind us that a half-century of research on leadership behavior has taught us the dangers of relying exclusively on behavior constructs that are very broad and abstract. Finally, the success of trait and behavioral approaches is based on the assumption that leaders through planning, directing, organizing, and controlling can purposely create a context capable of attaining a well-articulated future state (Marion and Uhl-Bien 2001).

12.3 The Contingency Slice of the Phenomenon

Research into the contingency and situational aspects of leadership focuses on the selection of leadership traits and behaviors to specific contextual demands that directly relate to performance. The traits and behaviors of leaders are viewed as mediating variables between structural antecedents and organizational outcomes. The irrelevancy of the traits and behaviors of leaders to organizational effectiveness is recognized and challenged based on the observations that (a) leaders have much less power that is attributed to them; (b) the selection process for leaders drastically curtails their differences; and (c) leaders can be overwhelmed by the situational demands of the leadership role (Vroom and Jago 2007). Contingent influences are usually treated as moderator variables which assume independent variables (i.e., the leader's characteristics) and dependent variables (i.e., the outcomes) are not related but whose presence changes the nature of the relationship (Ayman 2004). Interestingly, conducive environments to destructive leadership are characterized by instability, perceived threat, cultural values, absence of checks and balances, and institutionalization (Padilla, Hogan, and Kaiser 2007). Also, the organizational level at which leaders operate requires different cognitive ability (Jaques and Clement 2003) and an appreciation of the importance of space and time when modeling leadership (Grint 2005).

   Yun, Cox, and Sims (2006) identified the significant role follower attributes play in a contingency leadership approach. They identified how empowering leadership and the followers' need for autonomy interacted to influence the subsequent follower self-leadership, and demonstrated why followers should not be forgotten as an important contingency factor. Another contingency, follower vulnerability, clarified the link between leadership behaviors and the likelihood of the erosion of trust (Lapidot, Kark, and Shamir 2007). Followers susceptible to destructive leadership are characterized as having unmet basic needs such as negative core self-evaluations, low maturity, ambition, congruent values and beliefs, and unsocialized values (Padilla, Hogan, and Kaiser 2007). Finally, Jörg and Petersen (2007) identified the adverse impact that the romance of leadership had on managerial and political practices when situational information was lacking.

   Contingent and situational variables remain important moderators of leader behaviors because leaders and followers constantly assess their situation and attempt to respond accordingly in order to maximize performance and reward. Organizational culture and leadership remain fundamental explanatory constructs for understanding organizational performance, innovation, and change (Epitropaki and Martin 2005; Schein 2004) which are strongly influenced by the leadership from top management (Elenkov and Manev 2005). Further, the focus on explicating the contingency or contextual factors and how they moderate the relationship between various leadership behaviors to performance represent surface structure-level leadership theory (Lord and Hall 2005). Finally, "viewing leadership in purely dispositional or purely situational terms is to miss a major portion of the phenomenon" (Vroom and Jago 2007, 23). After all, the majority of traits and behaviors possessed by traditional brick and mortar leaders will remain equally relevant in the digital organizations. However, the propensity for risk taking, entrepreneurialism, networking ability, and requisite technical skills will give leaders advantage (Horner-Long and Schoenberg 2002).

12.4   The Information-Processing Slice of the Phenomenon

Leadership research that aims to isolate precise traits and behaviors of leaders fails to recognize that leadership results from social-cognitive or information processes

(Brown and Lord 2001; Lord and Maher 1991). According to Calder (1977), such research is likely to produce what may be termed as "common sense" assessments of leadership (i.e., easily observable behaviors or first-order constructs) rather than more scientifically supported investigations (i.e., perceptually based understanding of events, or second-order constructs). While first-order constructs ultimately represent key observable components of leadership (Calder 1977; Hollander 1992) aspects of followers that moderate their responses (i.e., second-order constructs) to leadership are neglected which produce a leader-centric perspective (Lord and Brown 2004). Brown and Lord (2001, 182) have consistently argued that the study of leadership must be sensitive to the information processing of perceivers, rather than just the characteristics and actions of leaders. After all, the collection of perceived leadership actions, most typically from followers, often capture surface aspects of leadership (Lord and Hall 2005). Further, Vroom and Jago (2007, 23) suggest a "leadership paradox" which "leads one to see stability and consistency in leader behaviors and its outcomes, despite compelling evidence for the role of situation and context."

Lord and Brown (2004) have suggested that the effect of leadership on outcomes remains disappointingly understood because research has not advanced our understanding of followers and the mechanisms that connect leaders and followers. Understanding the content, creation, and deployment of knowledge is central to the information-processing approach (Brown, Scott, and Lewis 2004). For example, when individuals believe that human attributes are dynamic qualities that change and develop, situational moderators have an impact on their information processing and especially their perceptual judgments of others (Werth, Markel, and Förster 2006). Interestingly, several studies have concluded that the gender of individuals in leadership roles does not provide them with any unique advantage (e.g, Hyde 2006), but rather the incongruity in the expectations of observers may present obstacles to leader effectiveness (Vecchio and Brazil 2007). For example, the traits of the male stereotype may more closely match those of the leader stereotype (i.e., schema) which includes the information that leaders in general are strong, intelligent, and masculine (Epitropaki and Martin 2004; Offermann, Kennedy, and Wirtz 1994). Scott and Brown (2006) suggest it may be easier for perceivers to activate leadership categories when observing men rather than when observing women. Further, they argue that "easily observed relationships do not necessarily reflect the underlying causal structure of events." Several researchers are arguing that leadership theory must elaborate on how leaders and followers create meaning from leadership traits and behaviors, and how this inference impacts on their evaluations and self-regulation in specific contexts (Lord and Brown 2004; Werth, Markel, and Förster 2006).

12.5 The Leader and Follower Exchanges Slice of the Phenomenon

The exchanges between leaders and followers aspect of leadership focuses on the quality interactions between leaders and followers over time, and recognizes that leaders can personalize their relationships with each follower, and is encapsulated within the Leader Member Exchange (LMX) Theory. Liden et al. (2006) examined whether leader differentiations among followers hurt or enhanced performance, and they found that leaders' "differentiation" influenced (a) the performance of members with low LMX (i.e., self-interest, low trust, and close score keeping), rather than members with high LMX (mutual interest, trust, and equivalence); and (b) the group performance when task interdependence was high. Hogg, Martin, and Weeden (2003) highlight two key criticisms—(a) LMX is located within a dyadic relationship and ignores the entire network of member–member relationships, and (b) the process by which followers evaluate their LMX relationships is oversimplified. Further, they suggest that the nature of leader–follower exchanges should be understood within a deeper, more textual analysis of group process, inter-group behavior, and group membership; and consequently argue that LMX must be understood in terms of how the followers' membership of a group influences their self-identity.

12.6 The Charismatic and Transformational Slice of the Phenomenon

Research into the charismatic and transformational aspects of leadership reduced the complexity of leadership down to three dimensions—leaders' characteristics (traits), leader behavior, and the situational context of leadership (Sashkin 2004). These approaches emphasize how the personal power of leaders motivates individuals to follow them (Hughes et al. 2006). Charismatic leadership theories focus on leaders being "extraordinary" and are strongly influenced by Max Weber, the early sociologist who identified this non-formal authoritarian influence. Modern versions of charismatic leadership have emphasized the motives and behaviors of "extraordinary" leaders and their influence on the psychological processes of followers. These theoretical frameworks highlight the positive impacts resulting from followers (a) attributing qualities of charisma to leaders based on their behaviors, expertise, and certain situational aspects; (b) having their enthusiasm and commitment raised from compelling vision and increased follower confidence; (c) internalizing new values and beliefs; and (d) having a strong personal identification with their leader.

Charismatic research has identified how the attributing of charisma to leaders by followers occurs from (a) a feeling of inadequacy (i.e., fear, guilt, or alienation); (b) the spontaneous spreading of emotions and behavioral reactions (i.e., social contagion); (c) the frequency and nature of interactions among followers; and (d) rites and ceremonies during the changing of leaders (see Yukl 2006). Recently, Mumford (2007) expanded the debate on outstanding leaders by suggesting two alternative metacategories besides charismatic, which are ideologues and pragmatic leaders. Each type has cognitive, behavioral, and development differences which have different methods of influence. For example, the charismatic emotionally evoke a future-oriented vision that provides a sense of shared experiences and shared future; ideologues emotionally evoke a tradition-oriented vision where the emphasis is on a shared collective past, and the values and standards necessary for a just society; and the pragmatic focus primarily on the problem and need for solution. Interestingly, a study by Bedell et al. (2006) indicates that various levels of Machiavellian tendencies cross all of these metacategories. The literature supports an empirical link between charisma and destructive leadership and highlights that "even when charismatic leaderships are not destructive they are still dangerous" (Padilla, Hogan, and Kaiser 2007, 108). A common trait among charismatic leaders appears to be their willingness to deliberately fracture organizations as a means to effect change (Storey 2004, 32).

Transformational leadership theories are strongly influenced by James McGregor Burns who conceptualized two contrasting leadership types, transforming (i.e., the leader appeals to the moral values of followers) and transactional leadership (i.e., the leader appeals to self-interest and benefit exchange) to influence followers. These theories focus on the idea that leadership behaviors can transform and motivate followers by raising their consciousness (i.e., big picture awareness) and encouraging them to rise above their own self-interest and are more concerned with pragmatic task objectives achievement than follower moral elevation or social reform (Yukl 2006). These theories expanded and integrated the "relationship," "change-oriented," and "initiating structure" behaviors into more dynamic frameworks which emphasized achievement of above average results. Each framework is primarily an extension of motivation theories and linked to a range of organizational outcomes (Sarros, Gray, and Densten 2003). For some time, concerns about the conceptual rigor, theoretical dimensions, measurement of concepts, and lack of details about how the underlying influencing processes are operationalized have been raised (Densten 2005; Yukl and Lepsinger 2004). However, the idea that leaders can transform their followers into amazing, creative, and committed achievers continues to drive research, and a ready market for this romantic idea is evident.

The predominant transformational leadership framework currently used by researchers was developed by Bass (1985), which reconceptualized leadership behaviors into three metacategories of transformational, transactional, and laissez-faire leadership. Structural validity and reliability findings about the measurements of these metacategories remain controversial. Sosik (2006) concluded that further research was still required to draw firm conclusions about the factor structure of these metacategories. The most recent version of Bass's (1985) transformational leadership framework is called Full Range Leadership. However, an extensive review of the leadership literature and existing transformational leadership frameworks by Podsakoff et al. (1990) developed a more comprehensive framework and instrument (i.e., the Transformational Leadership Inventory) which measures six reflective latent constructs. Transformational leadership has significant romantic appeal and popularity which has resulted in transactional leadership research being largely ignored, despite its common use in most working environments. Transactional leadership focuses on contingent and non-contingent exchanges between leaders and followers which can be rewards or punishments. Fundamentally, the contingent exchanges enable the leaders to focus and maintain the effort of followers toward a goal (House 1996) and has significant similarities to the negotiating processes to framing, clarifying, and rewarding (Densten 2006).

12.7 The New Leadership Slice of the Phenomenon

New evolving research has aimed at identifying outstanding leadership beyond the primary typologies of transformational and charismatic leadership (Bedell, Angie, and Vert 2006). Several new leadership approaches have now emerged which are distributed (Gronn 2002), distributive (Brown and Gioia 2002), shared (Pearce and Conger 2003), post-heroic (Fletcher 2004), authentic leadership (Luthans, Norman, and Larry 2006), relationship (Uhl-Bien 2006), and complexity leadership (Uhl-Bien, Marion, and McKelvey 2007). These new forms are based on relationships rather than authority, superiority, or dominance (Drath 2001). Uhl-Bien, Marion, and McKelvey (2007) proposed the Complexity Leadership Theory (CLT), which recognizes the nature of interactions and interdependencies among agents (people, ideas, etc.), hierarchical divisions, organizations, and environments which form the basis of the socially constructed context, and focuses on identifying and exploring the strategies and behaviors that enable organizational and sub-unit creativity, learning, and adaptability. Their leadership framework attempts to provide an understanding of leadership within the fast-paced, volatile context of the Knowledge Era (see Marion and Uhl-Bien 2001; Schneider and Somers 2006) and as a function of interactions.

13. WHERE IS CONTEMPORARY LEADERSHIP KNOWLEDGE GOING?

The vast majority of researchers have studied leadership in formal, most often managerial roles (Bedeian and Hunt 2006) and have a strong North American flavor which flows through most leadership theories, models, and measures within the mainstream social science literature. The most commonly used method for investigating leadership is surveys, and the most frequently recognized limitation of leadership research is the lack of longitudinal and qualitative studies. Many measure issues confront leadership researchers. In terms of Type I and Type II errors there are (a) "measurement bias" that distorts relationships between multiple indicators and the unobserved or latent variables they are reputed to represent which has the potential for accepting incorrect alternative models (Spector 2006); and (b) the misspecification of reflective and formative constructs which can result in the acceptance of incorrect models when using structural equation modeling (MacKenzie, Podsakoff, and Jarvis 2005). Both issues are critical to defining, identifying, and measuring the theoretical concepts of leadership. Such concepts are susceptible to the "fallacy of the wrong level" when they attribute something (an effect, a variable, a relationship) to one level of analysis (e.g., an individual) when it is actually attributable to another level (i.e., a group) (Dansereau, Cho, and Yammarino 2006, 537). Additional issues are the overuse of convenient short-term measures (Osborn and Hunt 2007), the impact of quality and quantity observations on the perceptions of leadership (Jones and Kelly 2007), the avoidance of multi-or meso-level relationships (Yun et al. 2006), and finally, the correct classification of moderator and mediator variables (Ayman 2004). Three key issues that are driving research into leadership are inhibitors, processes, and the development of leaders.

14. What is Inhibiting Leaders from Being Effective?

Interest in leadership and emotional intelligence is being stimulated by claims that it is more important for effective leadership than cognitive abilities (Cherniss 2006). Support for this claim comes from several studies that demonstrate the impact of emotional self-awareness on leaders' capacity to (a) become more savvy users of their gut feelings (Morse 2006); and (b) reduce the likelihood of them ignoring critical information (Bazerman and Chugh 2006). However, research into the cognitive aspect of how leaders think about themselves has been relatively ignored by leadership research (Murphy 2002) and such self-insight is a recognized prerequisite for understanding others and the environment (London 2002). In fact, the way leaders and followers see themselves is so fundamental to how they behave and is yet so "invisible" because this process is internal and often privately held in their minds (Hall 2004), and may explain why leaders can lack true insight into the real impact of their behaviors (Kets De Vries 2006; Van Dierendonck et al. 2007). For example, limited insights can handicap leaders in understanding the importance of relationship-based leadership behaviors which, according to Lapidot, Kark, and Shamir (2007) enable leaders to demonstrate (a) an ability and integrity that reduce the impact of trust-erosion incidents; and (b) benevolence that enhances the impact of trust-building incidents. Further, leaders need to appreciate how their prevention or promotion motivation is influencing their choice of behaviors (Kark and Van Dijk 2007). Finally, despite the widely recognized phenomenon of followers punishing their leaders by attacking and isolating them, few systematic investigations have been conducted (Ruth 2006). In fact, the relationship between leadership and misbehaviors in organizations appears to be inadequate.

15. UNDERLYING INFLUENCE PROCESSES

Few studies have investigated the underlying influence processes that account for the positive relationship found between leader behavior and follower performance (Kark and Van Dijk 2007; Yukl 2006). The Social Identity Theory of Leadership (Hogg 2001) addresses this limitation and suggests that the leaders' ability to influence their followers is contingent on the (a) extent to which group identity is an important aspect of the self-identity for each follower; and (b) capacity of leaders to match the defining features of the group or individual. Leadership and identity are mutually interdependent features of group life (Haslam and Platow 2001) and is implicated in all forms of leadership (Van Knippenberg and Hogg 2003). Followers will strongly identify with leaders and thus endorse them, when they are perceived as quintessentially embodying the values of the groups (Hogg, Martin, and Weeden 2003). Further, Lord and Brown (2004) and colleagues have consistently argued that research needs to examine how followers determine what they are going to do (i.e., self-regulate). This involves understanding how internal self-altering cognitive, emotional, and motivational processes are influenced by the pre-existing knowledge structures housed within the self-concept of followers.

Self-concept is a multifaceted schema and has three levels of identities, i.e., individual-level identities define one's uniqueness and differentiation of the self from others; relational identities define the self in terms of specific roles or relations and often include others in the definition of one's own self-identity; and the collective identities define the self in terms of specific collectives such as groups or organizations, and creating a desire to develop in oneself the qualities that are prototypical of these collectives. Each level has its own self-regulating and interpersonal processes but self-regulation depends on the currently activated identity level. However, Hall (2004) asserts that key questions about identity remain unanswered, such as, how does identity (a) influence motivation; (b) change over time; (c) alter when role and environment changes occur; and (d) become enhanced. Further, the identity processes are fundamentally ambiguous and always in a state of flux and reconstruction, and can be characterized by paradox and contradiction (Collinson 2006) which will require significant cognitive ability from leaders to "lead" the identity of followers, in order to influence their behaviors.

16. Developing Leaders

The ultimate achievement for any leadership researcher is to develop ideas that change the behaviors of "leader practitioners" which then results in significant improvements for individuals, groups, organizations, and ultimately society. Heifetz and his colleagues (cited Parks 2005) suggest that most leaders are resistant to new leadership ideas and remain heavily reliant on long-held habits of thoughts and actions. Such defensive reasoning can be counter-productive for leaders who instinctively avoid complexity and attempt to ensure tangible detached control in order to limit the damage and insecurity of uncertainty (Mitchell and Rossmoore 2001). Argyris (2005) has consistently argued that individuals (i.e., leaders) only benefit from new knowledge when they adopt productive reasoning (i.e., validating knowledge, creating informed choices, and emphasizing personal responsibility for the effectiveness of actions) rather than defensive reasoning (i.e., avoiding transparency, valid testing of ideas, and personal responsibility for one's action). Such maturity requires personal growth (Lyons 2002), which according to Mintzberg (2004) builds on the rationale that the cornerstone of all insight is self-knowledge. This development is extremely difficult for leaders experiencing the hectic pace of managerial work where responsibility is overriding and control is imperfect. Further, leadership researchers have to overcome leaders who are only interested in (a) learning techniques (e.g., skills, tactics, or a tool kit); (b) sorting out career challenges and prospects (i.e., have they got what it takes to get promoted); and (c) validating their own competencies (Parks 2005). Kempster (2006) suggests that leaders need to learn through lived experiences which involves apprenticeship that develops their identity as a leader.

17. FUTURE NEEDS

While previous reviews have assessed the leadership knowledge as being very complex, not complete, and difficult to apply, the current review presents several themes that are indisputable but not undebatable, in order to establish the knowledge boundaries of leadership and enable future needs to be identified. These themes encompass that leadership is: romanticized, about "influencing," managing the scene, ruling the game, causing ripple effects, having expertise, using the black box, and giving challenging expectations which provide a very strong theoretical foundation to further develop leadership understanding. Unfortunately, "popular" leadership books distort leadership by presenting it as an easily definable concept and create expectations that simple answers can easily be identified and implemented in a rational step-by-step manner. This situation has not been helped by the slicing up of the leadership phenomenon into focused aspects (e.g., traits) thus creating lack of idea integrations, even though ideas tend to be reconceptualized rather than eliminated. Nevertheless, leadership research continues to provide thought-provoking insights into the phenomenon, in terms of providing more sophisticated views of how combinations of traits affect the potential of leaders, what types of behaviors are available to leaders, where the situational and contingency factors influence decisions of leaders and effectiveness of outcomes, and why influence between leaders and followers gets distorted and changed.

Further, research continues to refine what Quinn and Spreitzer (2006) call the "fundamental state of leadership" which enables a psychologically elevated state to exist where leaders and followers experience an increase in intention, integrity, subordination, and adaptation. Insights into when to create such transformational and inspiring states are readily available and are being enriched by new leadership theories. However, the essential challenge for leadership researchers is to provide compelling reasons and strong evidence for leaders to move from a heuristic processing of leadership situations (i.e., the reliance on prior knowledge such as schemas, stereotypes, and expectancies that can be imposed on information into existing knowledge structures) to a systematic processing which involves meticulous appraisal of the qualities and behaviors of others, as well as re-examination of personal thoughts and prior beliefs about the stimuli (see Moskowitz 2005). Further, any new leadership framework must have a level of complexity that enables realistic interpretations and understanding of leadership challenges which leaders have the cognitive and emotional capacity to operate. After all, the prevalence of two and three metacategory dimensions in leadership theories may result from the inability of leaders to process any additional dimensions. Further, inadequate "common sense" theories may be clogging up the minds of leaders and stop potentially beneficial leadership ideas being accepted and implemented.

Currently, the vast majority of theories provide little appreciation of leaders' limitations, which perpetuates the romantic views of leadership (e.g., leaders can achieve everything). Most theories present multidimensional models that impact on numerous outcomes and, therefore, how dimensions (i.e., metacategories or concepts) are defined, measured, and examined is of critical importance and, perhaps, contemporary theory-developing approaches maybe inadequate. For example, the current practice of identifying underlying or latent concepts (e.g., visioning behaviors) may be inadequate because they are based purely on reflective indicators that are highly correlated, exhibit high levels of internal consistency reliability, and are interchangeable. Researchers need to consider incorporating formative indicators (e.g., the organizational level of leaders), after all, a large body of leadership research highlights the importance of recognizing the "causal" impact of contingency and contextual issues. Further, the benchmark for new leadership theories is the requirement to establish the logic and provide the evidence of how leadership concepts create influence. Furthermore, significant conceptual development and supporting research will be required to explain how these leadership concepts influence (a) processes that connect or bond individuals with others (Uhl-Bien 2006); and (b) the power dynamics (Van Knippenberg, Van Knippenberg, and De Cremer 2007).

The very nature of leadership research means that explicit rather than tacit knowledge will always be developed. However, leaders require tacit knowledge to implement explicit leadership ideas and thus researchers need to provide the mechanisms (or theory) to enable leaders to create their own tacit knowledge that supports and enhances the theoretical model they propose leaders adopt. Such models need to slice the leadership phenomenon into aspects that can be implemented (e.g., what "front-level" leaders need to know about leadership) rather than the traits that leaders of all levels require. The leadership phenomenon will always be extremely complex and the real challenge for researchers is to reduce the unnecessary clutter and redundant concepts to produce actionable ideas that are far superior to "intuitive or established practice" approaches to leadership.

References

AMABILE, T. M., SCHATZEL, E. A., MONETA, G. B., and KRAMER, S. J. 2004. Leader behaviors and the work environment for creativity: perceived leader support. *Leadership Quarterly*, 15 (1): 5–32.

ARGYRIS, C. 2005. A next challenge in organizational leadership. Pp. 163–84 in *Leadership and Management in the 21st Century: Business Challenges of the Future*, ed. C. L. Cooper. Oxford: Oxford University Press.

AYMAN, R. 2004. Situational and contingency approaches to leadership. Pp. 148–70 in *The Nature of Leadership*, J. Antonakis, A. T. Cianciolo and R. J. Sternberg. London: Sage.

BASS, B. M. 1985. *Leadership and Performance beyond Expectations*. New York: Free Press.

BAZERMAN, M. H., and CHUGH, D. 2006. Decisions without blinders. *Harvard Business Review*, 84 (1): 88–97.

BEDEIAN, A. G., and HUNT, J. G. 2006. Academic amnesia and vestigial assumptions of our forefathers. *Leadership Quarterly*, 17 (2): 190–205.

BEDELL, K., HUNTER, S., ANGIE, A., and VERT, A. 2006. A historiometric examination of Machiavellianism and a new taxonomy of leadership. *Journal of Leadership and Organizational Studies*, 12 (4): 50–72.

BENNIS, W. G. 2007. The challenges of leadership in the modern world: Introduction to the Special Issue. *American Psychologist*, 62 (1): 2–5.

BLIGH, M. C., and MEINDL, J. R. 2005. The cultural ecology of leadership: an analysis of popular leadership books. Pp. 11–52 in *The Psychology of Leadership: New Perspectives and Research*, D. M. Messick and R. M. Krammer. Mahwah, NJ: Lawrence Erlbaum Associates.

BOERNER, S., EISENBEISS, S. A., and GRIESSER, D. 2007. Follower behavior and organizational performance: the impact of transformational leaders. *Journal of Leadership and Organizational Studies*, 13 (3): 15–26.

BROWN, D. J., and LORD, R. G. 2001. Leadership and perceiver cognition: moving beyond first order constructs. Pp. 181–202 in *How People Evaluate Others in Organization*, ed. M. London. Mahwah, NJ: Lawrence Erlbaum Associate.

—— SCOTT, K. A., and LEWIS, H. 2004. Information processing and leadership. Pp. 125–47 in *The Nature of Leadership*, ed. J. Antonakis, A. T. Cianciolo and R. J. Sternberg. London: Sage.

BROWN, M. E., and GIOIA, D. A. 2002. Making things "click": distributive leadership in an online division of an off line organization. *Leadership Quarterly*, 13 (4): 397–419.

CALDER, B. J. 1977. An attribution theory of leadership. In *New Directions in Organizational Behavior*, ed. B. M. Staw and G. R. Salancik. Chicago: St Clair Press.

CARMELI, A., and SCHAUBROECK, J. 2007. The influence of leaders' and other referents' normative expectations on individual involvement in creative work. *Leadership Quarterly*, 18: 35–48.

CHEMERS, M. M. 2003. Leadership effectiveness: functional, constructivist and empirical perspectives. Pp. 5–17 in *Leadership and Power: Identity Processes in Groups and Organization*, ed. D. van Knippenberg and M. A. Hogg. London: Sage.

CHERNISS, C. 2006. Leadership and emotional intelligence. Pp. 132–48 in *Inspiring Leaders*, ed. R. J. Burke and C. L. Cooper. London: Routledge.

CLAWSON, J. G. 2006. The inspirational nature of level three leadership. In *Inspiring Leaders*, ed. R. J. Burke and C. L. Cooper. London: Routledge.

COLLINSON, D. 2005. Dialectics of leadership. *Human Relations*, 58 (11): 1419–42.

—— 2006. Rethinking followership: a post-structuralist analysis of follower identities. *Leadership Quarterly*, 17 (2): 179–89.

COX, S., JONES, B., and COLLINSON, D. 2006. Trust relations in high-reliability organizations. *Risk Analysis*, 26 (5): 1123–38.

DANSEREAU, F., CHO, J., and YAMMARINO, F. J. 2006. Avoiding the "fallacy of the wrong level": a within and between analysis (WABA) approach. *Group and Organization Studies*, 31 (5): 536–77.

DENSTEN, I. L. 2005. The relationship between visioning behaviours of leaders and follower burnout. *British Journal of Management*, 16 (2): 105–18.

DENSTEN, I. L. 2006. Negotiating extra effort through contingent rewards. *Leadership and Organizational Development Journal*, 27 (1): 38–49.

—— and GRAY, J. H. 2001. The links between followership and the experiential learning model: followership coming of age. *Journal of Leadership Studies*, 8 (1): 69–76.

DRATH, W. H. 2001. *The Deep Blue Sea: Rethinking the Source of Leadership.* San Francisco, CA: Jossey-Bass.

DWECK, C. S. 1996. Implicit theories as organizers of goals and behavior. Pp. 69–90 in *The Psychology of Action: Linking Cognition and Motivation to Behavior*, ed. P. M. Gollwitzer and J. A. Bargh. New York: Guilford Press.

ELENKOV, D. S., and MANEV, I. M. 2005. Top management leadership and influence on innovation: the role of sociocultural context. *Journal of Management*, 31 (3): 381–402.

EPITROPAKI, O., and MARTIN, R. 2004. Implicit leadership theories in applied settings: factor structure, generalizability, and stability over time. *Journal of Applied Psychology*, 89 (2): 293–310.

—— —— 2005. From ideal to real: a longitudinal study of the role of implicit leadership theories on leader-member exchanges and employee outcomes. *Journal of Applied Psychology*, 90 (4): 659–76.

FISKE, S. T. 1993. Social cognition and social perception. *Annual Review of Psychology*, 44: 155–94.

FLEISHMAN, E. A. 1995. Consideration and structure: another look at their role in leadership research. In *Leadership: The Multiple-Level Approaches*, ed. F. Dansereau and F. J. Yammarino. Stamford, CT: JAI Press.

—— MUMFORD, M. D., ZACARRO, S. J., LEVIN, J., KOROTKIN, A. L., and HEIN, M. B. 1991. Taxonomic efforts in the description of leader behavior: a synthesis and functional interpretation. *Leadership Quarterly*, 2: 245–87.

FLETCHER, J. K. 2004. The paradox of postheroic leadership: an essay on gender, power, and transformational change. *Leadership Quarterly*, 15 (5): 647–61.

FRENCH, J., and RAVEN, B. H. 1959. The bases of social power. In *Studies of Social Power*, ed. D. Cartwright. Ann Arbor: Institute for Social Research.

GOLEMBIEWSKI, R. T., BILLINGSLEY, K., and YEAGER, S. 1976. Measuring change persistency in human affairs: types of changes generated by OD designs. *Journal of Applied Behavioral Sciences*, 12: 133–57.

GRAY, J. H., and DENSTEN, I. L. 2007. How leaders woo followers in the romance of leadership. *Applied Psychological: An International Review*, 4.

GRINT, K. 2005. Twenty-first-century leadership: the god of small things; or putting the "Ship" back into leadership. In *Leadership and Management in the 21st Century: Business Challenges of the Future*, ed. C. L. Cooper. Oxford: Oxford University Press.

GRONN, P. 2002. Distributed leadership as a unit of analysis. *Leadership Quarterly*, 13 (4): 423–51.

HALL, D. T. 2004. Self-awareness, identity and leader development. Pp. 153–76 in *Leader Development for Transforming Organizations: Growing Leaders for Tomorrow*, ed. D. V. Day, S. J. Zacarro, and S. M. Halpin. London: Lawrence Erlbaum Associates.

HASLAM, S. A., and PLATOW, M. J. 2001. The link between leadership and followership: how affirming social identity translates vision into action. *Personality and Social Psychology Bulletin*, 27: 1469–79.

HOGG, M. A. 2001. A social identity theory of leadership. *Personality and Social Psychology Review*, 5: 184–200.

—— MARTIN, R., and WEEDEN, K. 2003. Leader-member relations and social identity. Pp. 18–33 in *Leadership and Power: Identity Processes in Groups and Organizations*, ed. D. van Knippenberg and M. A. Hogg. London: Sage.

HOLLANDER, E. P. 1992. Leadership, followership, self, and others. *Leadership Quarterly*, 3 (2): 5–11.

HOLLENBECK, G. P., and HALL, D. T. 2004. Self-confidence and Leader Performance. *Organizational Dynamics*, 33 (3): 254–69.

HORNER-LONG, P., and SCHOENBERG, R. 2002. Does e-business require different leadership characteristics? An empirical investigation. *European Management Journal*, 20 (6): 611–19.

HOUSE, R. J. 1996. Path-goal theory of leadership: lessons, legacy, and a reformulated theory. *Leadership Quarterly*, 7 (3): 323–52.

HUGHES, R. L., CURPHY, G. J., and GINNETT, R. C. 2006. *Leadership: Enhancing the Lessons of Experience*, 5th edn. Homewood, IL: Irwin.

HYDE, J. S. 2006. The gender similarities hypothesis. *American Psychologist*, 60: 581–92.

JAQUES, E., and CLEMENT, S. D. 2003. *Executive Leadership: A Practical Guide to Managing Complexity*. Oxford: Cason Hall and Co. Publishers.

JONES, E. E., and KELLY, J. R. 2007. Contributions to a group discussion and perceptions of leadership: does quantity always count. *Group Dynamics: Theory Research and Practice*, 11 (1): 15–30.

JÖRG, F., and PETERSEN, L.-E. 2007. Romance of leadership and management decision making. *European Journal of Work and Organizational Psychology*, 16 (1): 1–24.

JUDGE, T. A., PICCOLO, R. F., and ILIES, R. 2004. The forgotten ones? The validity of consideration and initiating structure in leadership research. *Journal of Applied Psychology*, 89 (1): 36–51.

KAPLAN, R. E. 2006. Lopsidedness in leaders. In *Inspiring Leaders*, ed. R. J. Burke and C. L. Cooper. London: Routledge.

KARK, R., and VAN DIJK, D. 2007. Motivation to lead, motivation to follow: the role of self-regulatory focus in leadership processes. *Academy of Management Review*, 32 (2): 500–28.

KEMPSTER, S. 2006. Leadership learning through lived experience: a process of apprenticeship? *Journal of Management and Organization*, 12 (1): 4–22.

KETS DE VRIES, M. 2006. *The Leader on the Couch: A Clinical Approach to Changing People and Organizations*. Chichester: Jossey-Bass.

KLIMOSKI, R. J., and DONAHUE, L. M. 2001. Person perception in organizations: an overview of the field. Pp. 5–44 in *How People Evaluate Others in Organizations*, ed. M. London. Mahwah, NJ: Lawrence Erlbaum Associates.

KROHE, J. 2000. Leadership books: why we buy them. *Across the Board*, 37 (1): 28–34.

LAPIDOT, Y., KARK, R., and SHAMIR, B. 2007. The impact of situational vulnerability on the development and erosion of followers' trust in their leader. *Leadership Quarterly*, 18 (1): 16–34.

LIDEN, R. C., ERDOGAN, B., WAYNE, S. J., and SPARROWE, R. T. 2006. Leader-member exchange, differentiation, and task interdependence: implications for individual and group performance. *Journal of Organizational Behavior*, 27: 723–46.

LONDON, M. 2002. *Leadership Development: Paths to Self-insight and Professional Growth*. London: Lawrence Erlbaum Associates.

LORD, R. G., and BROWN, D. J. 2004. *Leadership Processes and Follower Self-Identity*. London: Lawrence Erlbaum Associates.

—— and HALL, R. J. 2005. Identity, deep structure and the development of leadership skill. *Leadership Quarterly*, 16 (4): 591–615.

—— and MAHER, K. J. 1991. *Leadership and Information Processing: Linking Perceptions and Performance*. Cambridge: Unwin Hyman Ltd.

LUTHANS, F., NORMAN, S., and LARRY, H. 2006. Authentic leadership: a new approach for a new time. Pp. 84–104 in *Inspiring Leaders*, ed. R. J. Burke and C. L. Cooper. London: Routledge.

LYONS, D. 2002. Freer to be me: the development of executives at mid-life. *Consulting Psychology Journal: Practice and Research*, 54: 15–27.

McCAULEY, C. D. 2004. Successful and unsuccessful leadership. Pp. 199–221 in *The Nature of Leadership*, ed. J. Antonakis, A. T. Cianciolo, and R. J. Sternberg. Thousand Oaks, CA: Sage.

MacKENZIE, S. B., PODSAKOFF, P. M., and JARVIS, C. B. 2005. The problem of measurement of model: misspecification in behavioral and organizational research and some recommended solutions. *Journal of Applied Psychology*, 90 (4): 710–30.

McNATT, D. B. 2000. Ancient pygmalion joins contemporary management: a meta-analysis of the results. *Journal of Applied Psychology*, 85 (2): 314–22.

MARION, R., and UHL-BIEN, M. 2001. Leadership in complex organizations. *Leadership Quarterly*, 12 (4): 389–418.

MEINDL, J. R., EHRLICH, S. B., and DUKERICH, J. M. 1985. The romance of leadership. *Administrative Science Quarterly*, 30: 78–102.

—— —— —— 1990. On leadership: an alternative to conventional wisdom. Pp. 159–203 in, *Research in Organizational Behavior*, vol. xii, ed. B. M. Staw and T. G. Cummings. Greenwich, CT: JAI Press.

MINTZBERG, H. 2004. *Managers not MBAs*. San Francisco, CA: Berrett-Koehler.

MITCHELL, R. C., and ROSSMOORE, D. 2001. Why good leaders can't use good advice. *Journal of Leadership Studies*, 8 (2): 79–104.

MORSE, G. 2006. Decision and desire. *Harvard Business Review*, 84 (1): 42–51.

MOSKOWITZ, G. B. 2005. *Social Cognition: Understanding Self and Others*. New York: Guilford Press.

MUMFORD, M. D. 2007. *Pathways to Outstanding Leaders: A Comparative Analysis of Charismatic, Ideological, and Pragmatic Leadership*. Mahwah, NJ: Erlbaum Press.

MURPHY, S. E. 2002. Leader self-regulation: the role of self-efficacy and multiple intelligences. Pp. 163–86 in *Multiple Intelligences and Leadership*, ed. R. E. Riggio, S. E. Murphy, and F. J. Pirozzolo. London: Lawrence Erlbaum Associates.

NORTHOUSE, P. G. 2007. *Leadership: Theory and Practice*, (4th edn.) Thousand Oaks, CA: Sage.

OFFERMANN, L. R., KENNEDY, J. K., and WIRTZ, P. W. 1994. Implicit leadership theories: content, structure, and generalizability. *Leadership Quarterly*, 5: 43–58.

OSBORN, R. N., and HUNT, J. G. 2007. Leadership and the choice of order: complexity and hierarchical perspectives near the edge of chaos. *Leadership Quarterly*, 18 (4): 319–40.

PADILLA, A., HOGAN, R., and KAISER, R. B. 2007. The toxic triangle: destructive leaders, susceptible followers, and conducive environments. *Leadership Quarterly*, 18 (3): 176–94.

PARKS, S. D. 2005. *Leadership Can Be Taught*. Boston: Harvard Business Review.

PEARCE, C. L., and CONGER, J. A. 2003. *Shared Leadership: Reframing the How and Whys of Leadership*. Thousand Oaks, CA: Sage.

PLOWMAN, D. A., SOLANSKY, S., BECK, T. E., BAKER, L., KULKARNI, M., and TRAVIS, D. V. 2007. The role of leadership in emergent, self-organization. *Leadership Quarterly*, 18 (4): 341–56.

PODSAKOFF, P. M., MACKENZIE, S. B., MOORMAN, R. H., and FETTER, R. 1990. Transformational leader behavior and their effects on followers' trust in leader, satisfaction, and organizational citizenship behavior. *Leadership Quarterly*, 1 (2): 107–42.

PRIETO, I. M., and EASTERBY-SMITH, M. 2006. Dynamic capabilities and the role of organizational knowledge: an exploration. *European Journal of Information Systems*, 15: 500–10.

QUINN, R. E., and SPREITZER, G. M. 2006. Entering the fundamental state of leadership: a framework for the positive transformation of self and others. Pp. 67–83 in *Inspiring Leaders*, ed. R. J. Burke and C. L. Cooper. London: Routledge.

——— FAERMAN, S. R., THOMPSON, M. P., and MCGRATH, M. R. 2003. *Becoming a Master Manager: A Competency Framework*, 3rd edn. New York: John Wiley and Sons.

ROUSSEAU, D. M., and MCCARTHY, S. 2007. Educating managers from an evidence-base perspective. *Academy of Management Learning and Education*, 6 (1): 84–101.

RUTH, S. 2006. *Leadership and Liberation: A Psychological Approach*. London: Routledge.

SARROS, J. C., and COOPER, B. 2006. Building character: a leadership essential. *Journal of Business and Psychology*, 21 (1): 1–22.

——— GRAY, J. H., and DENSTEN, I. L. 2003. Leadership and its impact on organizational culture. *International Journal of Business Studies*, 10 (2): 1–26.

SASHKIN, M. 2004. Transformational leadership approaches. Pp. 171–96 in *The Nature of Leadership*, ed. J. Antonakis, A. T. Cianciolo, and R. J. Sternberg. London: Sage.

SCHEIN, E. H. 2004. *Organizational Culture and Leadership*, 3rd edn. San Francisco: Jossey-Bass.

SCHNEIDER, M., and SOMERS, M. 2006. Organizations as complex adaptive systems: implications of Complexity Theory for leadership research. *Leadership Quarterly*, 17 (4): 351–65.

SCHRIESHEIM, C. A. 2003. Why leadership research is generally irrelevant for leadership development. Pp. 181–97 in *The Future of Leadership Development*, ed. S. E. Murphy and R. E. Riggio. Mahwah, NJ: Lawrence Erlbaum Associates.

SCHYNS, B., and MEINDL, J. R. 2005. An overview of implicit leadership theories and their application in organization practice. Pp. 15–36 in *Implicit Leadership Theories: Essays and Explorations*, ed. B. Schyns and J. R. Meindl. Greenwich, CT: Information Age Publishing.

SCOTT, K. A., and BROWN, D. J. 2006. Female first, leader second? Gender bias in the encoding of leadership behavior. *Organizational Behavior and Human Decision Processes*, 101 (2): 230–42.

SOSIK, J. J. 2006. Full range of leadership: model, research, extensions, and training. Pp. 33–66 in *Inspiring Leaders*, ed. R. J. Burke and C. L. Cooper. New York: Routledge.

SPECTOR, P. E. 2006. Method variance in organizational research. *Organizational Research Methods*, 9 (2): 221–32.

STERNBERG, R. J. 2007. A systems model of leadership: WICS. *American Psychologist*, 62 (1): 34–42.

STOREY, J. 2004. Changing theories of leadership and leadership development. Pp. 11–38 in *Leadership in Organizations: Current Issues and Key Trends*, ed. J. Storey. London: Routledge.

UHL-BIEN, M. 2006. Relational Leadership Theory: exploring the social processes of leadership and organizing. *Leadership Quarterly*, 17 (6): 654–76.

—— MARION, R., and MCKELVEY, B. 2007. Complexity Leadership Theory: shifting leadership from the industrial age to the knowledge era. *Leadership Quarterly*, 18 (4): 298–318.

VAN DIERENDONCK, D., HAYNES, C., BORRIL, C., and STRIDE, C. 2007. Effects of upward feedback on leadership behavior toward subordinates. *Journal of Management Development*, 26 (3): 228–38.

VAN KNIPPENBERG, B., VAN KNIPPENBERG, D., and DE CREMER, D. 2007. Why people resort to coercion: the role of utility and legitimacy. *European Journal of Social Psychology*, 37: 276–87.

VAN KNIPPENBERG, D., and HOGG, M. A. 2003. *Leadership and Power: Identity Processes in Groups and Organizations*. London: Sage.

VECCHIO, R. P., and BRAZIL, D. M. 2007. Leadership and sex-similarity: a comparison in a military setting. *Personnel Psychology*, 60 (2): 303–35.

VROOM, V. H., and JAGO, A. G. 2007. The role of the situation in leadership. *American Psychologist*, 62 (1): 17–24.

WERTH, L., MARKEL, P., and FÖRSTER, J. 2006. The role of subjective theories of leadership evaluation. *European Journal of Work and Organizational Psychology*, 15 (1): 102–27.

WHITE, S. S., and LOCKE, E. A. 2000. Problems with the Pygmalion effect and some proposed solutions. *Leadership Quarterly*, 11 (3): 389–415.

YUKL, G. A. 2006. *Leadership in Organizations*, 6th edn. Upper Saddle River, NJ: Pearson Prentice Hall.

—— and LEPSINGER, R. 2004. *Flexible Leadership: Creating Value by Balancing Multiple Challenges and Choices*. San Francisco, CA: Jossey-Bass.

YUN, S., COX, J., and SIMS, H. P. J. 2006. The forgotten follower: a contingency model of leadership and follower self-leadership. *Journal of Managerial Psychology*, 21 (4): 374–88.

ZACARRO, S. J. 2007. Trait-based perspectives of leadership. *American Psychologist*, 62 (1): 6–16.

ZACARRO, S. J., KEMP, C., and BADER, P. 2004. Leader traits and attributes. Pp. 101–24 in *The Nature of Leadership*, ed. J. Antonakis, A. T. Cianciolo, and R. J. Sternberg. Thousand Oaks, CA: Sage.

5

A PERSONALITY APPROACH TO ENTREPRENEURSHIP

ANDREAS RAUCH

MICHAEL FRESE

1. INTRODUCTION

THERE are numerous books and articles with anecdotal stories about successful entrepreneurs, and most of them attribute successful business creation and venture performance to the efforts of extraordinary entrepreneurs. W. Smith, for example, who was able to raise the huge start-up capital he needed to set up FedEx, was described as a visionary person who loved working hard and who displayed enormous conviction and commitment to his idea (Academy of Achievement 1998). These are the kinds of characteristics that are examined in a personality approach to entrepreneurship, which focuses on individual-level differences to explain entrepreneurial behavior, such as business creation, business success, and survival. The personality approach tries to explain which traits make people decide to become entrepreneurs, and play a crucial role in determining subsequent business success.

The personality approach to entrepreneurship has been given much attention in early entrepreneurship literature. Its most fundamental criticism comes from the ecological approach, which assumes that individual entrepreneurs can be ignored when we look at business start-ups and their success and failure at a population level (Aldrich and Wiedenmayer 1993). However, while the ecological approach is useful in explaining "when" variations in business populations occur, it cannot explain "why" individual people decide to become entrepreneurs at a specific point of time. The personality approach to entrepreneurship has also been criticized because of inconsistencies in findings, small sample sizes, heterogeneity of concepts used to describe entrepreneurs (Brockhaus and Horwitz 1985), and the descriptive design that tends to dominate research into the traits of entrepreneurs (Low and MacMillan 1988). Gartner (1989) criticized that traits like innovativeness amount to little more than a simple relabeling of the term entrepreneur, without adding any useful insight to the phenomenon of entrepreneurship. Moreover, he argued that entrepreneurs are a highly heterogeneous population, making it impossible to draw any general definition that includes their individual traits (Gartner 1989). Based on these arguments, very few studies that were conducted in the late 1980s paid much attention at all to the character traits of entrepreneurs.

We argue that, although the personality approach to entrepreneurship may help us explain entrepreneurial behavior, it should be supplemented by sound and theoretically justified developments of modern personality psychology. Firstly, personality traits have to be related theoretically to entrepreneurship to make predictions more accurate, as was done in early economic theories. Schumpeter (1935), for example, used traits to describe why entrepreneurs destroy market equilibrium by introducing innovations, while Knight (1921) explained how entrepreneurs have to make decisions in the face of uncertainty and risk. Later, McClelland (1961) explained economic growth by achievement motivation theory. Some of the later studies, by contrast, were predominantly descriptive (Low and MacMillan 1988), which increased the probability of finding non-significant results (Tett, Steele, and Beauregard 2003). It is, therefore, essential to establish a theoretical relationship between a person's character traits and the domain of entrepreneurship. This leads to the following proposition: Traits that are related to the domain of entrepreneurship need to be more specific. Specific concepts related to entrepreneurship may include facets of Big Five factors and motivational traits. These characteristics are more directly related to entrepreneurial behavior, and as such allow for a better prediction than broad Big Five traits.

Second, we argue that it is essential to include a process view: Prime candidates for mediating processes are characteristics that are more proximal to the actions and the behavior of entrepreneurs (Kanfer 1992). Such mediators include task-specific traits, motivation, and action processes.

Third, the prediction of entrepreneurial behavior depends on the interaction between personality traits and situational conditions (Mischel 1968).

Fourth, specific traits and motivation are less stable than Big Five traits, which means that the effect they have on entrepreneurial behavior may be increased by situational conditions. Thus, because an individual's personality consists of stable trait components as well as of less stable state components, a personality approach also needs to consider the process dynamics of personality constructs (Mischel and Shoda 1998; Baron 2007). Figure 5.1 integrates the propositions described above.

The aim of this chapter is to review the personality approach on the basis of our theoretical framework (Figure 5.1), which assumes that the effects of a person's traits on his or her entrepreneurial behavior are mediated by specific traits and motivations, and moderated by environmental conditions. Thereby, we try to integrate the empirical evidence in the context of entrepreneurship. In our discussion we rely to a considerable extent on meta-analytical evidence.

2. THE PERSONALITY APPROACH TO ENTREPRENEURSHIP

Personality traits can be defined as relative stable tendencies of behavior across situations and across time (Paunonen and Aston 2001). It is important to consider three issues related to this definition. First of all, traits are dispositions rather than determinations of behavior. Therefore, traits are factors that explain entrepreneurial behavior in a certain context and should not be used to define entrepreneurs. Second, traits cannot predict specific behavior. Rather, since traits are aggregated across situations and time points, they are predictive for broad classes of behavior (Epstein and O'Brien 1985). Third, if we are to understand how traits affect behavior, we need to include additional individual difference concepts that are less stable and more proximal to the way people actually behave (Kanfer 1992) into our prediction of entrepreneurial behavior. Consequently, we include in our theory several conceptualizations of personality characteristics (broad Big Five traits, task-specific traits, and specific motivation), and we discuss process issues that should be considered when discussing the characteristics of successful entrepreneurs.

2.1 The Big Five Trait Taxonomy and Entrepreneurial Behavior

The Big Five model has conveniently categorized traits into the dimensions conscientiousness, extraversion, emotional stability, assertiveness, and openness to experience (Costa and McCrae 1988). In organizational behavior it is well established that conscientiousness is the factor most strongly and positively related to

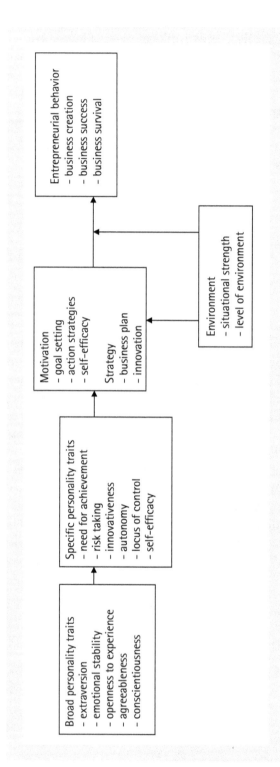

Fig. 5.1 A model of entrepreneurs' personality characteristics and entrepreneurial behavior

Source: Adapted from Rauch and Frese 2000.

job performance; meta-analytical evidence suggests that the weighted effect size is $r = .22$ across occupations (Barrick and Mount 1991).

Several studies have tested the validity of such broad trait taxonomies in entrepreneurship (Brandstätter 1988; Ciaverella et al. 2004; Wooton and Timmerman 1999). In the meta-analysis they conducted, Zhao and Seibert (2006) analyzed twenty-three studies by categorizing traits according to the five-factor taxonomy. The results indicated that, with the exception of extraversion, the five factors discriminated well between entrepreneurs and managers. As in the meta-analysis carried out by Barrick and Mount (1991), conscientiousness produced the highest effect sizes in entrepreneurship as well ($r = .22$, Zhao and Seibert 2006). Several issues still need to be addressed if we are to generalize the effects of Big Five traits among entrepreneurs. First, while the Big Five taxonomy is useful in differentiating between entrepreneurs and non-entrepreneurs, it has not been established whether or not Big Five traits are related to business success (with the exception of one study, in which it was indicated that Big Five traits are related to survival (Ciaverella et al. 2004). A positive relationship between Big Five traits and business performance is likely when one assumes that entrepreneurial behavior is similar to organizational behavior (e.g., hard work is important to both entrepreneurs and employees) and given the empirical evidence found in organizational behavior. However, if we assume there is a difference between entrepreneurial behavior and organizational behavior, such a relationship cannot be taken for granted. For example, specific traits may produce higher relationships with entrepreneurial behavior than Big Five traits, because they maximize criterion-related variance. Moreover, broad trait taxonomies are relatively weak in explaining how the effects of traits are transmitted into entrepreneurial behavior.

2.2 Traits Specifically Related to Entrepreneurial Behavior

A majority of the studies that adopt the personality approach to entrepreneurship did not analyze Big Five factors, looking instead at more specific facets of the Big Five taxonomy. One advantage of specific traits is that they are closer to behavior and, therefore, more directly related to entrepreneurial behavior (Rauch and Frese 2006). Moreover, specific traits rely on the explicit description that may be situated in time, place, or roles (Barrick and Mount 2005, 367). Finally, specific traits maximize criterion-related variance: Therefore, predictors of entrepreneurial behavior may very well belong to different Big Five factors (Paunonen and Aston 2001). All these arguments support the assumption that specific traits are valid predictors of entrepreneurial behavior.

It is noteworthy that the number of different traits being studied in the domain of entrepreneurship exceeded forty as early as 1971 (Hornaday and Aboud 1971), and this number has certainly grown considerably by now. The very fact that so many different traits have been associated with entrepreneurial behavior has raised doubts as to the validity of the results. This means that it is useful to examine traits that are theoretically justified. For example, tenacity, proactive attitude, and passion are important to entrepreneurs, because entrepreneurs need to love their work, be enthusiastic, and be able to overcome obstacles when they pursue their goals (Baum and Locke 2004).

The two traits that have probably been studied most frequently in entrepreneurship research are "need for achievement" and "risk-taking propensity" (Rauch and Frese 2006), which both appear to be particularly important to entrepreneurship (Schumpeter 1935; McClelland 1961). Need for achievement is related to entrepreneurship because entrepreneurs need to perform well at challenging tasks of moderate difficulty, seek feedback on performance, take responsibility, and look for new ways to accomplish tasks. Several meta-analyses showed that entrepreneurs have consistently higher levels of achievement motivation than non-entrepreneurs (Collins, Hanges, and Locke 2004; Rauch and Frese 2007; Stewart and Roth 2004b). Moreover, need for achievement is positively related to venture performance (Rauch and Frese 2007). Effect sizes reported in these studies ranged between $r = .227$ and $r = .314$. These are moderate effects (Cohen 1977) that indicate support for a personality approach to entrepreneurship.

Risk taking can be defined as an individual disposition toward risk, such as a preference to pursue a business opportunity when the probability of success is low (Chell, Haworth, and Brearley 1991). Entrepreneurs have to make decisions under uncertainty and risk (Knight 1921). There is some controversy in the theoretical literature about whether risk taking is related to entrepreneurship behavior in a linear or curve-linear way (Stewart and Roth 2001). A majority of empirical studies tested linear relationships between risk taking and performance. Meta-analytical results confirmed the proposition that entrepreneurs have a higher risk-taking propensity than managers and non-entrepreneurs ($r = .11$ and $r = .118$, Stewart and Roth 2004a; Rauch and Frese 2007, respectively). Moreover, risk taking showed positive overall relationships with venture success ($r = .092$, Rauch and Frese 2007). While these effect sizes are positive and significant, they seem to be smaller than the effect sizes of achievement motivation. We suggest that future research should test curve-linear relationships between risk taking and venture performance on a more frequent basis.

Other personality traits validated in a meta-analysis are generalized self-efficacy, innovativeness, stress tolerance, need for autonomy, dominance, and proactivity (Rauch and Frese 2007). There are other potentially important specific traits, such as tenacity or passion (Baum, Locke, and Smith 2001), that have not been studied frequently enough to include them in a meta-analysis. At this point we can conclude that specific traits that are theoretically related to the domain of entrepreneurship are valid predictors of both business creation and business performance.

2.3 Motivation Related to Entrepreneurial Behavior

While traits are general dispositions, motivation pushes or pulls the direction, the effort, and the persistence of a person's behavior (Locke and Baum 2007). Therefore, motivation is more proximal to behavior than traits (Kanfer 1992). Entrepreneurship theory with regard to motivation has focused predominantly on cognitive approaches to motivation, such as specific self-efficacy (Bandura 1997), goal-setting theory (Locke and Baum 2007), and action strategies (Frese 2007). All these approaches directed the attention to situational-specific motivation, reflecting the effect of motivation on specific tasks in specific situations. Consequently, these concepts can be applied directly to the tasks of entrepreneurs.

Specific self-efficacy can be defined as a belief that one is able to perform a specific task effectively, and it includes judgments about one's capabilities to meet given situational demands (Bandura 1997). Thus, in contrast to generalized self-efficacy, which generalizes across situations, specific self-efficacy refers to specific situations (Eden and Aviram 1993). In entrepreneurship research, most studies addressed either generalized self-efficacy (see above), or used a conceptualization of moderate specificity (Chen, Greene, and Crick 1998; Zhao, Seibert, and Hills 2005). Specific self-efficacy is usually measured by asking people about their confidence level with regard to performing a certain task or achieving a goal (Locke and Baum 2007). Baum, Locke, and Smith (2001) showed that specific self-efficacy is related to performance and, most importantly, that this is a causal effect: the self-efficacy of CEOs affects their subsequent performance (Baum and Locke 2004).

Goal-setting theory suggests that having difficult and specific goals motivates people to work harder, making them perform better than they would if the goals were easy and general in nature (Locke and Latham 1990). The positive effects of goal setting are well known in organizational behavior (Tubbs 1986), and they have been tested in entrepreneurship as well. Two studies indicated that goal setting has a direct and positive effect on venture performance (Baum and Locke 2004; Tracy, Locke, and Renard 1999).

Action theory assumes that actions are goal-oriented behavior, and it is concerned with how people regulate their actions in a given situation (Frese and Zapf 1994). While goal-setting theory assumes that the goal itself forces people to work harder and be successful, action theory focuses more heavily on the means and processes by which goals are attained. In entrepreneurship research, there are two concepts related to action theory that have received a degree of attention (Frese 2007). First, entrepreneurs have to be active and persistent in managing their environment, which requires a high amount of personal initiative. Second, they need to determine the actions needed to achieve their goals and, therefore, develop action plans.

Personal initiative involves self-starting behavior, overcoming barriers and preparing for future opportunities and threats (Frese et al. 1997). Entrepreneurs typically need to be more active than non-entrepreneurs (Crant 1996), e.g., they have to search actively for opportunities (Fiet, Piskounov, and Patel 2005), scan and change their environment, anticipate changing demands, and learn to align tasks to their knowledge and abilities. Empirical evidence suggests that entrepreneurs show higher degrees of initiative than non-entrepreneurs (Crant 1996) Moreover, initiative is related to venture performance (Frese et al. 1997).

Action plans have to do with a person's everyday planning rather than the development of formal business plans. Four different types of planning can be distinguished along lines of goal orientation, long-term planning, knowledge base, situational responsiveness, and proactiveness (Frese, van Gelderen, and Ombach 2000). Comprehensive planning means a high goal orientation, a highly proactive attitude, and long-term planning. Critical point strategy concentrates on the most difficult and most important point first. Opportunistic strategy involves some rudimentary planning, although a deviation from these plans is likely when opportunities arise. Finally, a reactive strategy involves little planning and a propensity to react to a situation. Empirical results indicate that reactive planning is negatively related to venture performance (Frese 2000; Frese, van Gelderen, and Ombach 2000). Moreover, proactive planning (complete planning and critical point strategy) is positively related to success (Frese et al. in press).

Thus, situation-specific motivations are useful predictors of entrepreneurial behavior. It is somewhat surprising that most studies addressed the effect of specific motivation on performance rather than on business creation. Moreover, given the aim of this chapter to review stable dispositions, one may question our decision to include situation-specific motivation into our review, because specific motivation is not stable across situations and time. The reason for this is that specific motivation mediates the effects of stable traits (Baum and Locke 2004; Baum, Locke, and Smith 2001), which we discuss in the next section.

2.4 Processes that Mediate the Role of Personality Traits

To complete a personality approach, one also needs to look at the mediating processes by which personality affects entrepreneurial behavior (Rauch and Frese 2000). Prime candidates for such mediating processes are concepts that are closer to actual behavior, such as specific traits and specific motivation (Kanfer 1992; Johnson 2003). For example, conscientiousness may help people develop difficult and specific goals, and as such is related to success.

Empirical literature indicates support for two different mediating processes: proximal/motivational concepts and venture strategy. The former concepts assume that traits affect an entrepreneur's motivation and action strategies that help him or her to run a business successfully. For example, Frese (2007) showed that proactive and elaborated action planning mediated the relationship between motivation and success in micro-business enterprises. Baum and Locke (2004) showed that both specific motivation (goal setting, self-efficacy) and competitive strategies mediate the relationship between personality traits and success. Moreover, elaborated formal planning and innovative strategies have been identified as mediators in previous studies (Rauch, Frese, and Sonnentag 2000; Utsch and Rauch 2000, respectively).

Thus, mediating processes should be included in the prediction of entrepreneurial behavior. Identifying mediators in the personality–success relationship is important in theoretical and practical interventions. Theoretically, knowing mediators leads to a better understanding of the processes that connect broad personality traits to specific entrepreneurial behavior. Moreover, while it is difficult to modify Big Five traits, specific motivation can be modified by intervention.

2.5 Processes that Affect the Role of Personality Traits

Understanding the effects of personality traits on entrepreneurial behavior involves considering the situational demands that influence these effects. Holland (1985) suggests that the person–situation interaction explains someone's occupational choice, for example their decision in favor of entrepreneurship.

Mischel (1968) argued that traits may affect outcomes only in environments in which they can be expressed. Therefore, one situational moderator is the strength of the situation: Weak situations allow the expression of dispositions that affect behavior, strong ones do not (Mischel and Shoda 1998). For example, it may be difficult to develop high and specific goals when easy goals are provided and required in a particular job. Thus, personality traits need to be applied in situations. Unfortunately, it is difficult to apply such a contingency theory to entrepreneurship, because there are a number of different levels of relevant situations, such as the resource environment, the organizational environment, the task environment, and the macroenvironment (Castrogiovanni 1991). One may argue that entrepreneurship is generally speaking a weak situation, because entrepreneurs are in a position to make their own decisions and determine their own actions in a way that is often not possible in other jobs. One study of 201 business founders analyzed the effect of the task environment on success (Hmielski and Baron 2006). The results indicated that optimism has a negative impact on venture performance. In stable environments, however, the relationship between optimism and performance was positive. Thus, favorable environments rather than unfavorable environments may allow for the positive effects of traits.

We need more studies that address the moderating effects of different situational strengths. A number of method moderators has been identified in previous meta-analyses, such as type of instrument, type of criterion, and type of sample used (Collins, Hanges, and Lake 2004; Rauch and Frese 2007; Stewart and Roth 2004a). Thus, entrepreneurship research needs to look at interactions between personality and situational conditions. This is all the more important in light of the above-mentioned need for more specific traits and motivation to be used. Specific traits and motivation link personality to situations, because more specific concepts of individual differences rely more heavily on those situations. For example, motivation is already aimed in a certain direction and goal setting implies the presence of an object or aim of the action. Thus, a personality approach needs to consider situational dynamics as well.

2.6 A Process View of the Personality Approach to Entrepreneurship

Given the situational dynamics, recent entrepreneurship theory has focused on a process view of entrepreneurship, and criticized the static view of the personality approach to entrepreneurship. However, there have been attempts to conceptualize the role of traits within the process of entrepreneurship. A process perspective assumes that entrepreneurs perform different and changing tasks during the entrepreneurial process. As a result, the relative importance of specific predictors and criteria of entrepreneurial behavior changes in the course of that process (Baron 2007). For example, while leadership skills may be relatively unimportant when it comes to recognizing an opportunity, such skills may become more important when the enterprise is established and experiences a certain growth.

Shane and Vankatamaran (2000) described entrepreneurship as a process involving the recognition and exploitation of existing opportunities and, thus, as a process that evolves over time. Within each phase of this process, situational variables as well as individual difference variables play a role. Individual differences that are important to the recognition and discovery of opportunities are mainly cognitive variables. Personality characteristics influence above all the exploitation of opportunities.

Baron and Markman (2004) distinguished three major phases in the entrepreneurial process: pre-launch phase, launch phase, and post-launch phase. They examined 131 individuals who received a patent for internet-related inventions. The results of their study indicate that extraversion was related to intentions in the pre-launch phase, to the amount of capital raised in the launch phase, and to personal income in the post-launch phase. Other authors argued that personality traits affect people's decision to start an enterprise more strongly than subsequent business success, because the impact of the individual business owner is reduced as the enterprise grows (Begley and Boyd 1987; Frese, van Gelderen, and Ombach

2000). However, meta-analytical evidence has challenged this proposition (Collins, Hanges, and Locke 2004; Rauch and Frese 2007).

While a process approach to entrepreneurial personality traits is in line with mainstream theorizing in the field of entrepreneurship (e.g., Shane and Venkataraman 2000), existing empirical evidence is preliminary and inconsistent in nature. Nevertheless, a process approach provides a useful framework for integrating past and future research, and it provides a basis for strong theoretical and practical recommendations (Baron 2007).

2.7 A Multi-Level Model of Entrepreneurial Behavior

While the personality approach to entrepreneurship by its very definition is an individual-level approach, a theory of entrepreneurship needs to look at other levels as well. McMullen and Shepherd (2006), for example, have combined individual-level approaches (knowledge and motivation) with system-level approaches (theories of economic growth), by referring to the concept of uncertainty. Moreover, entrepreneurs make choices and decisions that affect firm-level variables and performance in the long term. Even an ecological approach, which usually neglects individual-level differences, may be able to include individual-level variables in its predictions. The ecological approach assumes that selection processes determine start-up rates, survival, and changes of business populations (Aldrich and Wiedenmayer 1993). However, individuals can affect such selective forces, e.g., by choosing the right time point for entry (e.g., growing industry), adapting their strategies to their environment (e.g., by specializing in concentrated markets), selecting the right environment (e.g., a dynamic environment), and choosing a bigger start-up size when creating the company. Therefore, theories of entrepreneurships need to include different levels of constructs into entrepreneurship theorizing. Otherwise models are specified incorrectly and do not allow for a consistent prediction of entrepreneurial behavior.

3. CONCLUSION

The personality approach has been one of the early approaches to entrepreneurship and has received a considerable amount of empirical attention. However, it also has been the subject of serious criticism. We have presented a framework that may help mitigate some of the concerns involved. The framework describes how the effects of traits on entrepreneurial behavior are transmitted via specific traits and motivation, and moderated by environmental influences. By bringing the situation into the model and different types of behavior, the model can address process dynamics of entrepreneurship as well as different levels of constructs. Some of the propositions included in the framework are supported by the empirical evidence.

First, we are able to reject the criticism to the personality approach to entrepreneurship, because meta-analyses have proved quite consistently that broad traits (e.g., conscientiousness) as well as more specific traits (e.g., need for achievement) are related to entrepreneurial behavior, such as business creations and success. Moreover, situation-specific motivation (e.g., goal setting) is also related to entrepreneurial behavior. Additionally, we have found that such individual difference variables affect different types of entrepreneurial behavior, such as business creation and business performance. Second, we can assume that broad traits have an effect on specific traits and motivation, and thereby on business success. Therefore, more specific individual-level constructs need to be included into the prediction of entrepreneurial behavior. Moreover, while Big Five traits may be effective in predicting broad classes of behavior, predicting specific behavior requires the consideration of more specific individual-level constructs that go beyond the Big Five traits.

Although our review provided some evidence with regard to moderating and mediating processes, it is our conclusion that more empirical research is needed to analyze the process dynamics of personality traits. If we are to predict entrepreneurial behavior with accuracy, we also need to look at the specific contexts in which (would-be) entrepreneurs operate. Thus, our review challenges the assumption that the effect of personality characteristics on entrepreneurial behavior is static by bringing specific mediating processes and situational dynamics into the equation. In reality, the environment as well as the firms that operate in that environment are constantly changing. Our framework includes the environment in which people and firms operate, thereby linking contextual and processing dynamics to stable dispositions (Mischel and Shoda 1998). We conclude that a personality approach can be included in a process view of entrepreneurship. However, such process dynamics need to be addressed in entrepreneurship research more frequently if we are to draw more definite conclusions at this point.

It is interesting to discuss the issue of processes with regard to interventions as well, because more specific personality traits can be modified more easily than broad Big Five traits. For example, self-efficacy can be improved by mastery experience (Eden and Aviram 1993) and need for achievement can be increased by training as well (Spencer and Spencer 1993). Therefore, a process view also needs to address the causal links between entrepreneurial characteristics and outcomes.

In our review we have not addressed cognitive approaches that focus on individual differences and that have entered entrepreneurship theory more recently than personality approaches. Compared to personality traits, cognitive processes involve different underlying processes. While traits focus on dispositions that are in part genetically determined, cognitions have to do with mental processes involving people's memory and their information-processing capacity. Moreover, cognitions and traits focus on different aspects of the entrepreneurial process. While the trait approach focuses predominantly on a person's decision to start an enterprise and business success, cognitions are mainly related to the recognition of opportunities and the decision to start an enterprise (Baron 1998; Busenitz 1996; Mitchell et al. 2002).

To conclude, we have tried to make a contribution to the understanding of the personality approach to entrepreneurship and, thereby, we hope to provide some answers to criticism of the personality approach. We have emphasized that a sophisticated personality approach that includes context and process dynamics can offer a meaningful contribution to explaining the phenomenon of entrepreneurship.

REFERENCES

ACADEMY OF ACHIEVEMENT. 1998. Interview: Frederick W. Smith. Founder, Federal Express. May 23, 1998 Jackson Hole, Wyoming

ALDRICH, H. E., and WIEDENMAYER, G. 1993. From traits to rates: an ecological perspective on organizational foundings. Pp. 145–95 in *Advances in Entrepreneurship, Firm Emergence, and Growth*, vol. i, ed. J. A. Katz and R. H. Brockhaus. Greenwich, CT: JAI Press.

BANDURA, A. 1997. *Self-efficacy: The Exercise of Control*. New York: Freeman and Co.

BARON, R. A. 1998. Cognitive mechanisms in entrepreneurship: why and when entrepreneurs think differently than other people. *Journal of Business Venturing*, 13: 275–94.

—— 2007. Entrepreneurship: a process perspective. In *The Psychology of Entrepreneurship*, ed J. R. Baum, M. Frese and R. A. Baron. London: Lawrence Erlbaum Associates.

—— and MARKMAN, G. D. 2004. Toward a process view of entrepreneurship: the changing impact of individual-level variables across phases of new firm development. In *Current Topics in Management*, vol. ix, ed. M. A. Rahim, R. T. Golembiewski and K. D. McMackenzie. New Brunswick, NY: Transaction Publishers.

BARRICK, M. R., and MOUNT, M. K. 1991. The big five personality dimensions and job performance: a meta-analysis. *Personnel Psychology*, 44 (1): 1–26.

—— —— 2005. Yes, personality matters: moving on to more important matters. *Human Performance*, 18: 359–72.

BAUM, J. R., and LOCKE, E. A. 2004. The relation of entrepreneurial traits, skill, and motivation to subsequent venture growth. *Journal of Applied Psychology*, 89 (4): 587–98.

—— —— SMITH, K. G. 2001. A multidimensional model of venture performance. *Academy of Management Journal*, 44 (2): 292–303.

BEGLEY, T. M., and BOYD, D. P. 1987. Psychological characteristics associated with performance in entrepreneurial firms and smaller businesses. *Journal of Business Venturing*, 2: 79–93.

BRANDSTÄTTER, H. 1988. Becoming an entrepreneur:—a question of personality structure? Paper presented at the 13th Annual Colloquium of IAREP, Leuven.

BROCKHAUS, R. H., and HORWITZ, P. S. 1985. The psychology of the entrepreneur. In *The Art and Science of Entrepreneurship*, ed. D. L. Sexton and R. W. Smilor. Cambridge, MA: Ballinger.

BUSENITZ, L. W. 1996. Research on entrepreneurial alertness. *Journal of Small Business Management*, 34 (4): 35–44.

CASTROGIOVANNI, G. J. 1991. Environmental munificence: a theoretical assessment. *Academy of Management Review*, 16 (1): 542–65.

CHELL, E., HAWORTH, J. M., and BREARLEY, S. 1991. *The Entrepreneurial Personality*. London: Routledge.

CHEN, C. C., GREENE, P. G., and CRICK, A. 1998. Does entrepreneurial self-efficacy distinguish entrepreneurs from managers? *Journal of Business Venturing*, 13 (4): 295–316.

CIAVERELLA, M. A., BUCHHOLTZ, A. K., RIORDAN, C. M., GATEWOOD, R. D., and STOKES, G. S. 2004. The big five and venture survival: is there a linkage? *Journal of Business Venturing*, 19: 465–83.

COHEN, J. 1977. *Statistical Power Analysis for the Behavioral Science*. New York: Academic Press.

COLLINS, C. J., HANGES, P. J., and LOCKE, E. E. 2004. The relationship of achievement motivation to entrepreneurial behavior: a meta-analysis. *Human Performance*, 17 (1): 95–117.

COSTA, P. T., and McCRAE, R. R. 1988. From catalog to classification: Murray's needs and the five-factor model. *Journal of Personality and Social Psychology*, 55: 258–65.

CRANT, J. M. 1996. The proactive personality scale as a predictor of entrepreneurial intentions. *Journal of Small Business Management*, 34 (3): 42–9.

EDEN, D., and AVIRAM, A. 1993. Self-efficacy training to speed reemployment: helping people to help themselves. *Journal of Applied Psychology*, 78: 352–60.

EPSTEIN, S., and O'BRIEN, E. J. 1985. The person-situation debate in historical and current perspective. *Psychological Bulletin*, 98: 513–37.

FIET, J., PISKOUNOV, A., and PATEL, P. 2005. Still searching (systematically) for entrepreneurial discoveries. *Small Business Economics*, 25: 489–504.

FRESE, M., ed. 2000. *Success and Failure of Microbusiness Owners in Africa: A New Psychological Approach*. Westport, CT: Greenwood.

—— 2007. The psychological actions and entrepreneurial success: an action theory approach. In *The Psychology of Entrepreneurship*, ed. J. R. Baum, M. Frese, and J. Baron. Mahwah, NJ: Lawrence Erlbaum Associates.

—— and ZAPF, D. 1994. Action as the core of work psychology: a German approach. In *Handbook of Industrial and Organizational Psychology*, 2nd edn., vol. iv, ed. H. C. Trinadis, M. D. Dunnette and L. M. Hough. Palo Alto, CA: Consulting Psychologists Press.

—— VAN GELDEREN, M., and OMBACH, M. 2000. How to plan as a small scale business owner: Psychological process characteristics of action strategies and success. *Journal of Small Business Management*, 38 (2): 1–18.

—— FAY, D., HILBURGER, T., LENG, K., and TAG, A. 1997. The concept of personal initiative: operationalization, reliability and validity in two German samples. *Journal of Organizational and Occupational Psychology*, 70: 139–61.

—— KRAUSS, S.I., KEITH, N., ESCHER, S., GRABARKIEWICZ, R., LUNENG, S. T., HEERS, C., UNGER, J. M., and FRIEDRICH, C. In press. Business owners' action planning and its relationship to business success in three African countries. *Journal of Applied Psychology*.

GARTNER, W. B. 1989. "Who is an entrepreneur?" is the wrong question. *Entrepreneurship Theory and Practice*, 12 (2): 47–68.

HMIELSKI, K. M., and BARON, R. A. 2006. Optimism and environmental uncertainty: implications for entrepreneurial performance. In *Frontieres of Entrepreneurship Research*, ed. A. Zacherakis, S. Alvarez, P. Davidsson, J. Fiet, G. George et al. Wellesley, MA: Babson College.

HOLLAND, J. L. 1985. *Making Vocational Choices*. Englewood Cliffs, NJ: Prentice Hall.

HORNADAY, J. A., and ABOUD, J. 1971. Characteristics of successful entrepreneurs. *Personnel Psychology*, 24: 141–53.

JOHNSON, J. W. 2003. Toward a better understanding of the relationship between personality and individual job performance. Pp. 83–120 in *Personality and Work: Reconsidering the Role of Personality in Organizations*, ed. M. R. Barrick and A. M. Ryan. San Francisco, CA: Jossey-Bass.

KANFER, R. 1992. Work motivation: new directions in theory and research. Pp. 1–53 in *International Review of Industrial and Organizational Psychology*, vol. vii, ed. C. L. Cooper and I. T. Robertson. London: John Wiley and Sons.

KNIGHT, F. H. 1921. *Risk, Uncertainty, and Profit*. New York: Kelly and Millman.

LOCKE, E. A., and BAUM, J. R. 2007. Entrepreneurial motivation. In *The Psychology of Entrepreneurship*, ed. J. R. Baum, M. Frese, and J. Baron. London: Lawrence Erlbaum Associates.

—— and LATHAM, G. P. 1990. *A Theory of Goal Setting and Task Performance*. Englewood Cliffs, NJ: Prentice-Hall.

LOW, M. B., and MACMILLAN, B. C. 1988. Entrepreneurship: past research and future challenges. *Journal of Management*, 14 (2): 139–62.

MCCLELLAND, D. C. 1961. *The Achieving Society*. New York: Free Press.

MCMULLEN, J. S., and SHEPHERD, D. A. 2006. Entrepreneurial action and the role of uncertainty in the theory of the entrepreneur. *Academy of Management Review*, 31 (1): 132–52.

MISCHEL, W. 1968. *Personality and Assessment*. New York: Wiley.

—— and SHODA, Y. 1998. Reconciling processing dynamics and personality dispositions. *Annual Review of Psychology*, 49: 229–58.

MITCHELL, R. K., BUSENITZ, L., LANT, T., MCDOUGALL, T. T., MORSE, E. A., and SMITH, J. B. 2002. Toward a theory of entrepreneurial cognition: rethinking the people side of entrepreneurship research. *Entrepreneurship Theory and Practice*, 4: 93–104.

PAUNONEN, S. V., and ASTON, M. C. 2001. Big five factors and the prediction of behavior. *Journal of Personality and Social Psychology*, 81 (3): 524–39.

RAUCH, A., and FRESE, M. 2000. Psychological approaches to entrepreneurial success: a general model and an overview of findings. Pp. 101–41 in *International Review of Industrial and Organizational Psychology*, vol. xv, ed. C. L. Cooper and I. T. Robertson. New York: John Wiley and Sons.

—— —— 2006. Meta-analysis as a tool for developing entrepreneurship research and theory. Pp. 29–52 in *Advances in Entrepreneurship, Firm Emergence, and Growth*, vol. ix, ed. J. Wiklund, D. P. Dimov, J. Katz and D. Shepherd. London: Elsevier.

—— —— 2007. Let's put the person back into entrepreneurship research: a meta-analysis of the relationship between business owners' personality traits, business creation and success. *European Journal of Work and Organizational Psychology*, 16 (4): 353–85.

RAUCH, A., FRESE, M., and SONNENTAG, S. 2000. Cultural differences in planning/success relationships: a comparison of small enterprises in Ireland, West Germany, and East Germany. *Journal of Small Business Management*, 38 (4).

SCHUMPETER, J. 1935. *Theorie der wirtschaftlichen Entwicklung (Theory of Economic Growth)*. Munich: Von Duncker und Humbolt.

SHANE, S., and VENKATARAMAN, S. 2000. The promise of entrepreneurship as a field of research. *Academy of Management Review*, 25 (1): 217–26.

SPENCER, L. M., and SPENCER, S. M. 1993. *Competence at Work: Models for Superior Performance*. New York: Wiley.

STEWART, W. H., and ROTH, P. L. 2001. Risk propensity differences between entrepreneurs and managers: a meta-analytic review. *Journal of Applied Psychology*, 86 (1): 145–53.

—— —— 2004a. Data-quality affects meta-analytic conclusions: a response to Miner and Raju (2004) concerning entrepreneurial risk propensity. *Journal of Applied Psychology*, 89 (1): 14–21.

—— —— 2004b. A meta-analysis of achievement motivation and entrepreneurial status. Paper presented at the Academy of Management Conference, New Orleans, August 6–11.

TETT, R. P., STEELE, J. R., and BEAUREGARD, R. S. 2003. Broad and narrow measures on both sides of the personality-job performance relationship. *Journal of Organizational Behavior*, 24: 335–56.

TRACY, K., LOCKE, E. A., and RENARD, M. 1999. Conscious goal setting versus subconscious and motives: longitudinal and concurrent effects on the performance of entrepreneurial firms. Paper presented at the Academy of Management Conference, Chicago.

TUBBS, M. E. 1986. Goal-setting: a meta-analytic examination of the empirical evidence. *Journal of Applied Psychology*, 71: 474–83.

UTSCH, A., and RAUCH, A. 2000. Innovativeness and initiative as mediators between achievement orientation and venture performance. *European Journal of Work and Organizational Psychology*, 9: 45–62.

WOOTON, K. C., and TIMMERMAN, T. A. 1999. The use of personality and the five factor model to predict business ventures: from outplacement to start-up. *Journal of Vocational Behavior*, 58: 82–101.

ZHAO, H. S., and SEIBERT, S. E. 2006. The big five personality dimensions and entrepreneurial status: a meta-analytical review. *Journal of Applied Psychology*, 91 (2): 259–71.

—— —— and HILLS, G. E. 2005. The mediating role of self-efficacy in the development of entrepreneurial intentions. *Journal of Applied Psychology*, 90 (6): 1265–72.

PART II

PERSONNEL SELECTION

6

JOB ANALYSIS AND COMPETENCY MODELING

OLGA F. VOSKUIJL

ARNE EVERS

IT has been argued that job analysis is not relevant to the changing world of work; some authors find it is outdated or are of the opinion that it even could be declared dead (Schuler 1989). Although there might be a bit of an image problem (Harvey 1999), the arguments against job analysis appear not to be strong enough to abolish one of the oldest human resource management tools. Competency modeling is often seen as the solution to the problem; the term is fashionable and probably more marketable, but of course there is more to it than that. This chapter focuses on the role of "conventional" job or work analysis, now and in the future, and discusses the differences between these approaches of analysis of work and competency modeling. In the first section the characteristics of job analysis and some well-known instruments and methods of job analysis are described. The second section presents a variety of approaches of competency modeling. In the third section job analysis and competency modeling are contrasted and integrated. The fourth section summarizes the consequences of past developments in work for job analysis.

1. Job Analysis

Job analysis has been defined as "the collection and analysis of any type of job related information by any method for any purpose" (Ash 1988, 1) or more specifically, according to Cascio (1991, 188): "The objective of job analysis is to define each job in terms of the behaviors necessary to perform it. Job analysis comprises of two major elements: job descriptions and job specifications." Job descriptions refer to defining the job in terms of its task requirements and include characteristics of the job such as the procedures, methods, and standards of performance. Job specifications refer to "people requirements," that is, what the job calls for in terms of behaviors, knowledge, abilities, skills and other personal characteristics. The latter definition reflects the well-known distinction of job-related behavior of McCormick and his associates (e.g., McCormick, Jeanneret, and Mecham 1972) in generalized worker activities and attribute requirements. In relation to the purpose of job analysis the *type of job data* to collect is one of the choices to be made when applying job analysis. McCormick (1976) mentioned several other aspects that must be considered, for example: *the method of data collection* and *the agent or source of the information.*

Job data. McCormick (1976) distinguished the following types of information: work activities; work performance (e.g., time taken and error analysis); job context (e.g., social context and physical working conditions); machines, tools, equipment, and work aids used; job-related tangibles and intangibles such as materials processed and services rendered; and personnel requirements. Work activities and personnel requirements in particular were subject of research. Work activities are divided in job-oriented and worker-oriented activities; job-oriented activities are usually expressed in job terms and indicate what is accomplished. Worker-oriented activities refer, for example, to behaviors performed in work (e.g., decision making). Personnel requirements include knowledge, skills, attributes, and other personal characteristics, known as KSAOs. It must be noted, however, that Harvey (1991) and Harvey and Wilson (2000) excluded the process of inferring required worker traits or abilities, thereby referring to the American Uniform Guidelines on Employee Selection Procedures (Equal Employment Opportunity Commission 1978). In their opinion job analysis methods should describe observable work behavior, independent of the characteristics of the people who perform the job, and job analysis data should be verifiable and replicable. Required personal traits do not meet these characteristics. Sanchez and Levine (2001), on the other hand, describe the derivation of human attributes, as the psychological part of doing job analysis and Sackett and Laczo (2003) perceive a growing trend toward the incorporation of personality variables in job analysis (e.g., Raymark, Schmit, and Guion 1997). Cucina, Vasilopoulios, and Sehgal (2005) find the justification for using personality-based job analysis in the fact that several personality dimensions proved to be valid predictors of work performance (Salgado and De Fruyt 2005). They suggest that the use of personality-based job analysis increases the likelihood that the most important personality traits required for a job are identified.

Method of data collection. There are various methods for collecting job information; Sackett and Laczo (2003) distinguish qualitative versus quantitative methods and taxonomy-based versus blank slate. Taxonomy-based approaches make use of existing taxonomies of characteristics of jobs; in blank slate approaches lists of job activities or attributes are generated. Quantitative and taxonomy-based methods mostly involve standardized questionnaires. In the qualitative and/or blank slate approaches interviews with (groups of) incumbents, direct observation of job incumbents, and diaries kept by incumbents are more appropriate. The more contemporary methods include recordings of job activities by means of videotapes or electronic records. Combinations of several methods are possible. Multi-method approaches result in more complete pictures of the jobs (Morgeson and Campion 1997).

Agent or source of the information. Traditionally, job incumbents, supervisors, and professional job analysts were the most important sources of job information. As the boundaries of jobs become less clear-cut job analysis demands a broader range of information agents; for example, customers or training experts. Besides people, devices can be used also as a source of job information; we mentioned already the use of videotapes and other electronic information; in those cases cameras, tape recorders, and computers are the sources. Sanchez and Levine (2001) stress the importance of electronic records of performance (i.e., in call centers the number of calls handled) as reliable sources of work information. Each type of resource has its particular strengths and weaknesses; for example, incumbents might have the most information about the content of a job, but professional job analysts might be more familiar with job analysis methods.

Sanchez (2000) states that job analysts prefer incumbent ratings because these ratings have high face validity. He also describes several disadvantages of the use of incumbent job analysis data as well: (a) it takes valuable time of large numbers of incumbents; (b) incumbents are not always motivated to rate their jobs conscientiously; (c) rating instructions and survey format are not always well understood; (d) there is no empirical evidence that incumbents are most qualified to ensure valid job information.

Several studies show variability in incumbent ratings that might be unrelated to job content, such as work attitudes (e.g., job satisfaction, organizational commitment, and job involvement; Conte et al. 2005; Sanchez, Zamora, and Visweswaran 1997), and job tenure (Tross and Maureo, 2000). Differences within incumbents and between incumbents and others might reflect real differences; for example, employees with longer job tenure might have more freedom to develop unique patterns or profiles of activities (Lindell et al. 1998), which are all correct. The meta-analyses of Dierdorff and Wilson (2003) revealed that rater source did affect the reliability coefficients but there were other important moderators as well. This brings us to the psychometric properties of job analysis instruments.

1.1 Validity and Reliability of Job Analysis Data

Job analysis outcomes are often the result of subjective judgments, and human judgment has proven to be fallible, thus leading to inaccuracy. Morgeson and Campion (1997) distinguished two broad categories of inaccuracy: social (e.g., conformity pressures, and social desirability) and cognitive (e.g., information overload and extraneous information). They mention likely effects of those sources on psychometric aspects of job analysis data, for example on interrater reliability and factor structures. These effects refer to different aspects of validity or, in terms of Morgeson and Campion (1997; 2000), accuracy. However, most of the hypothesized effects have not yet been the subject of research.

Interesting in this context are the differing views about accuracy and validity of Sanchez and Levine (2000), on the one hand, and Harvey and Wilson (2000) on the other hand. Sanchez and Levine question the meaning of accuracy in terms of the correspondence between job analysis data and the "true" job characteristics. They argue that it is not possible to assess the true job content and therefore accuracy cannot be expressed in terms of deviation of an objective and absolute standard. Harvey and Wilson state that this view only holds for highly questionable data collection methods (e.g., using inexperienced raters and poorly anchored scales and drawing unverifiable inferences from abstract job dimensions). In their opinion it is possible to assess jobs correctly and accurately if one uses the "right" combination of the work descriptors and rating scales (this is extended upon in the next section). Less controversial is the best-documented aspect of accuracy: interrater or intrarater reliability.

Almost every study on job analysis presents some measure of interrater reliability or intrarater reliability. Interrater reliability refers to consistency across raters, often expressed in intraclass correlations and means of pair-wise correlations. Intrarater reliability refers, for example, to a type of test-retest measurement. The meta-analysis of Dierdorff and Wilson (2003) shows that tasks generally have a higher interrater reliability than generalized worker activities. However, task data showed lower estimates of intrarater reliability. Professional analysts display higher interrater reliabilities than other sources (e.g., incumbents, supervisors, trained students).

1.2 Some Methods and Questionnaires to Collect Work-Related Information

Harvey (1991) developed a taxonomy of job analysis methods, based on two dimensions: (a) specificity of job analysis information; and (b) type of rating scale used. Specificity of information refers to the degree of behavioral and technological detail provided by the job descriptor items, ranging from specific, observable, and verifiable to holistic, abstract, and multidimensional. The earlier described job- and worker-oriented activities are respectively highly and moderately specific. The degree of specificity has an effect on the possibility of cross-job comparisons. The possibility of cross-job comparisons refers to the other dimension in the taxonomy of Harvey, the type of judgment that is required of the rater analysing the job. This judgment depends, for example, on the type of rating scale used. This dimension ranges from verifiable scale anchors, with a constant meaning across jobs (thus facilitating cross-job comparisons), to non-verifiable anchors in term of within-job relativity (the items are rated relative to the other items) that make comparisons between different jobs impossible. For example, in relative-time-spent scales or in relative importance scales, the other items are the standard. Harvey advises against the use of instruments that do not allow cross-job comparisons because the usefulness of those instruments is limited in job classification, career planning placement, and other personnel activities. Furthermore, he objects to methods that directly rate abstract and holistic aspects of work. In fact, only the methods that are verifiable in terms of both dimensions meet the conditions set forth by Harvey in 1991. However, Harvey and Wilson (2000) do not raise objections to all abstract job analysis data (job dimensions), provided that such data are based on a combination of a number of moderate-specificity ratings. They consider the Position Analysis Questionnaire (PAQ; McCormick, Jeanneret, and Mecham 1972) and the Common-Metric Questionnaire (CMQ; Harvey, 1991) examples of this type of acceptable instruments.

Most of the standardized questionnaires belong to the category that combines the moderate level of both dimensions: moderate behavioral specificity and within-job-relative scales. Some instruments incorporate several sections and cover more than one category of the taxonomy, for example the Functional Job Analysis (FJA; Fine 1988). In the next section, some well-known instruments and methods will be described. An exhaustive overview is presented in the handbook by Gael (1988).

1.2.1 *Position Analysis Questionnaire (PAQ)*

The PAQ, developed by McCormick and co-workers (1972; 1976) is based on the worker-oriented approach. This means that generalized worker behaviors (behaviors that are involved in work activities, e.g., advising) are rated and that the instrument has a moderate level of behavioral specificity. The term generalized refers to the fact that the elements are not job specific, in order to make it possible to compare different jobs.

1.2.2 *Functional Job Analysis (FJA) and the Occupational Information Network (O*Net)*

Functional Job Analysis resulted from the development of the Dictionary of Occupational Titles (DOT; US Department of Labor), which describes the characteristics, methods, work requirements, and activities required to perform almost all jobs in the United States. Functional Job Analysis aims at generating task statements and identifies for each task what the worker does (behavior), why and how he does it, and what is accomplished by his work (Fine 1988). The job analyst describes for each task the orientation and level of involvement of the worker with data, people, and things, the well-known Worker Functions. The method is a combination of the worker-oriented approach (e.g., the Worker Functions), the work-oriented approach (a task inventory), and the qualitative approach (the description of job-specific tasks). The worker-oriented scales do allow cross-job comparisons but the job-specific task descriptions do not.

In the 1980s the task-based DOT was evaluated as no longer apt to reflect changes in the nature and conditions of work. The Occupational Information Network (O*Net; Peterson et al. 1999) is an automated job classification system that replaces the DOT; it focuses in particular on cross-job descriptors. O*NET is based on a content model that consists of five categories of job descriptors: (a) worker requirements (e.g., basic skills, cross-functional skills); (b) worker characteristics (e.g., abilities, values); (c) experience requirements (e.g., training); (d) occupational requirements (e.g., generalized work activities, work context); (e) occupation-specific requirements (e.g., tasks, duties).

1.2.3 *Critical Incidents Technique (CIT)*

As the name indicates the CIT is not a questionnaire but a technique (Flanagan 1954). This approach generates critical behaviors observed by incumbents or others who have experience with the job being studied. These job experts describe anecdotes or incidents that illustrate effective, and ineffective (and sometimes also average) job performance. Each incident must describe: (a) what led up to the incident; (b) what the individual did; (c) what the consequences of the behavior of the employee were; and (d) whether the consequences were within the employee's control. The incidents are categorized in performance dimensions. The technique is especially suited for the development of Behaviorally Anchored Rating Scales (the incidents form the scale anchors) and the development of situational interviews. In the last decade, this technique has been recommended to identify competencies (e.g., Robinson et al. 2007). However, the development of instruments by means of the CIT is time consuming and the applicability is limited according to the taxonomy of Harvey. This approach can be considered as high on behavioral specificity with very limited possibilities to compare jobs.

1.2.4 *Ability Requirements Scales (ARS)*

The Ability Requirement Scales are developed by Fleishman and several co-workers (e.g., Fleishman and Mumford 1988; 1991). Through the abilities requirements approach information about the characteristics of job incumbents are identified.

Abilities are defined as "relatively enduring attributes of the individual that influence a broad range of task performance" (Fleishman and Mumford 1988, 918). Examples of abilities are: verbal comprehension, inductive reasoning, mathematical reasoning, and knowledge. The results of this type of job analysis provide directly the information to guide selection or development of selection procedures. The scales are based on the development of a taxonomy of abilities that might describe work activities, based on factor analytic studies. Because the information is not directly tied to fluctuating tasks but to relatively stable characteristics of individuals this approach pretends to offer a taxonomic system that is likely to be stable in a changing environment. It is said to be generalizable to different jobs and different circumstances, so cross-job comparisons are possible. Although the scale anchors are defined in terms of behavior, the behavioral specificity is low.

1.2.5 Job Element Method (JEM)

Primoff and Dittrich Eyde (1988, 807) described the purpose of the Job Element Method of job analysis as "to identify the behaviors and their evidences, as revealed in achievements, that are significant to job success." So, elements refer to behaviors and their evidences, or to the well-known Knowledge, Skills, Abilities, and Other personal characteristics (KSAOs) and their evidences. Elements that are relevant for a job are identified and evaluated by subject-matter experts. Most elements are expressed in terms of job-specific KSAOs; because of the job specificity some of them can be considered as work oriented (e.g., an element for the job police officer is "ability to enforce laws"). The elements show a moderate or low level of behavioral specificity. The elements for each job are gathered in a rather unstructured way in sessions of subject-matter experts (SME) panels, therefore cross-job comparisons are very limited.

1.2.6 Task inventory analysis

Task inventories are probably the oldest and most traditional approaches of job analysis. When job analysis is accused of being archaic and not relevant to the changing world of work (e.g., Sanchez and Levine 2001; Schuler 1989) it is mostly this type of job analysis that is being referred to.

   Task inventory approaches start with the identification of tasks in order to develop a questionnaire or checklist for a specific job. Tasks can be described as activities or sequences of related activities directed at specified job objectives (Levine 1983). Task inventories consist of lists of activities or task statements. In general a statement is in its most basic form a description of what the worker does in terms of an action verb, the purpose of that action, and the methods and equipment used. In short: what does the worker do, how does he or she do it, and why? Each task is rated on one or more scales: relative-time-spent (relative to the other tasks), importance, difficulty, and criticality. When using more than one scale per task it is possible to calculate a task importance value, for example by adding and/or multiplying the different scale values. Task inventories are behavioral specific and comparisons between jobs are not possible.

1.2.7 *Personality-Related Position Requirements Form (PPRF)*

Raymark, Schmit, and Guion (1997) view the existing methods as lacking the possibility to identify some aspects of personality-related position requirements to formulate selection hypotheses. They stated that if personality traits are relevant to job performance, and if they are not identified and measured because job analysis instruments do not cover these variables, they will be overlooked for selection. The authors developed an instrument that is meant to generate hypotheses about relevant personality variables: the Personality-Related Position Requirements Form (PPRF). The PPRF is meant as an addition to other job analysis instruments that cover other job-related information. Raymark et al. departed from the "Big Five", but found that the five factors were too broad to describe work-related employee characteristics, so they defined twelve subdimensions (for example, Conscientiousness was covered by the subscales: General Trustworthiness, Adherence to a Work Ethic, and Thoroughness and Attentiveness). Respondents are asked to indicate the extent to which the requirements are necessary for effective performance. The instrument is low on behavior specificity and high on cross-job comparability.

1.3 Purpose of Methods

Which method (or combination of methods) is appropriate in a specific context depends on the purpose of the analysis. Levine et al. (1983) compared some of the instruments described above and the Threshold Trait Analysis (TTA; Lopez 1988), an instrument to identify the personal characteristics that are important to perform a job acceptably; the task inventory in their study was paired with the Comprehensive Occupational Data Analysis Program (CODAP). They asked experienced job analysts to rate the effectiveness (quality and comprehensiveness) of seven instruments in relation to eleven purposes on a five-point scale (a score of 1 indicates that a method is not at all comprehensive and is low in quality; 3 means that the method is moderately high in quality for the stated purpose and provides information that covers about half of the job's features). Table 6.1 gives examples of possible combinations of job analysis methods and the purposes they might serve. The instruments marked with an asterisk had a mean higher than 3.5 in the study of Levine et al.

Besides purpose, time and cost may guide the choice for the use of specific job analysis methods. The application of some methods is very time consuming and thus expensive, for example: the CIT, task inventories, and FJA.

Table 6.1 Combinations of job analysis methods and purposes

Purpose	Method
Selection/placement	TTA*, ARS*, PPRF, PAQ, FJA*
Development of AC exercises	PAQ, CIT, Task inventories, FJA
Job design and restructuring	TI/CODAP*, FJA*
Job evaluation	PAQ*, FJA*
Performance appraisal	CIT*, FJA*
Training	TI/CODAP*, CIT*
Validity generalization	TTA, PAQ*, TI/CODAP*, FJA*

* Mean>3.5 in the study of Levine et al. (1983)
Source: Voskuijl (2005), based upon Levine et al. (1983).

In the study of Levine et al., 86 percent of the 93 respondents preferred the use of a combination of job analysis methods. To cover the content of jobs in full extension, especially work that goes beyond the borders of "traditional" jobs, a combination of different methods might be even more appropriate nowadays.

The methods and instruments presented above show that job analysis can be more than the identification of lists of tasks, as some opponents suggest. Of course it is wise to look further than the often artificial boundaries of jobs; therefore Sanchez and Levine (2001) propagated the use of the term work analysis to indicate that the analysis is not limited to a fixed set of tasks that defines one job within clear boundaries. It is easy to apply most of the described job analysis instruments to a broader interpretation of the concept job. Furthermore, it is often difficult to avoid describing or thinking in terms of more or less delimited "portions" of work; even an ever-changing amoeba has boundaries and, in the case of work, job or work analysis can help to identify those boundaries and what they enclose.

1.4 Recent Developments

In answer to the increased instability of jobs and the supposed inadequacy of job analysis to cover changes in jobs, in the last decennia several "new" techniques have been developed; techniques that pretend to grasp the content of existing but changing work and work yet to be created: strategic job analysis, strategic job modeling, future-oriented job modeling, competency modeling. Whether these techniques are really new or whether they are a rearrangement or adaptation of existing techniques is not always clear. Schneider and Konz (1989) introduced the term strategic job modeling referring to "a process through which the skills required by jobs in the future can be identified" (p. 53). Their approach is based on a combination of traditional job analysis procedures ("Multimethod Job Analysis"). Information about jobs in the future and required KSAs is gathered by "simply" asking subject-matter experts (e.g., job incumbents and supervisors) and job analysts about their expectations of the future. The method resembles the Combined Job Analysis Method (C-JAM), described by Levine (1983). Whilst in the C-JAM the task statements, their importance ratings, and the identification of KSAOs are related to existing jobs, in strategic job analysis they refer to the expected content of future jobs. A comparable but extended approach was applied by Landis, Fogli, and Goldberg (1998). They used a future-oriented job analysis (FOJA) procedure to gain an understanding of three newly formed entry-level positions. This procedure includes seven developmental steps that were based on a combination of traditional job analysis methods (task inventories, task-KSA linkage questionnaires) and new instruments. New in this procedure was the development and use of the Task Sort Questionnaire (TSQ). The TSQ consisted of a list of 459 task statements for the three jobs, which were gathered in the preceding steps. SMEs were asked to indicate in which of the three future positions each task was likely to be performed. The percentages of correct sorts (that is, tasks attributed to the job it was written for) were considered as indicators of accuracy and were input for discussions about misunderstandings and differences of opinions about the content of the jobs. Because Landis et al. collected only future-oriented information this procedure could be completed within six weeks. However, if practitioners follow the recommendations of Schneider and Konz to also analyze the jobs as they currently exist, the procedure would be very time consuming.

2. COMPETENCY MODELING

Schippmann (1999, p. x) uses the term strategic job modeling to describe an approach of job analysis that focuses at "the strategic and future-oriented needs of today's organisations." He considers competencies as one of the building blocks of strategic job modeling.

Competency modeling seems to be the most extreme "replacement" for job analysis, although some authors view job analysis as an important technique to identify competencies (e.g., Woodruffe 1993). However, it is still a problem that definitions of the term competency are not univocal and sometimes even contradictory. McClelland (1973) introduced the term as a predictor of job performance because he doubted the predictive validity of cognitive ability tests. He proposed to replace intelligence testing with competency testing. Though he did not define the term competency, he made it explicitly clear that the term did not include intelligence. Today, we know that general mental ability is the most valid predictor of job performance (e.g., Schmidt and Hunter 1998), but in spite of the paucity of empirical evidence that competencies add something to the traditional concepts in the prediction or explanation of job success (KSAOs), competencies, competency modeling, and competency frameworks[1] are very popular (e.g., Schippmann et al. 2000). It is beyond doubt that there is more than intelligence, but the question is how to define and measure the characteristics that one needs in addition to intelligence. Is the answer the Big Five or do we need other concepts, such as competencies? In defining personality traits we rely on a history of theory building and empirical research (e.g., Salgado and De Fruyt 2005), but the theoretical base of competencies is very weak (Harvey 1999; Lievens, Sanchez, and De Korte 2004). In part, the lack of consensus in the different approaches of competencies originates in the diversity of disciplines in which the concept is developed and applied: law, clinical psychology, vocational counseling, education, training, management, and even politics (e.g., Schippmann et al. 2000). In the next section examples will be given of the diversity in definitions and some typologies of competency approaches will be described.

2.1 Definitions

Because it is impossible to discuss without misunderstanding any concept without a clear definition of the term, most of the publications with a focus on competencies start with an anthology of definitions; we follow this "tradition" by presenting various meanings of the term formulated by different authors. Probably the most cited definition is that of Boyatzis (1982, 21): "an underlying characteristic of a person, which results in an effective and/or superior performance of a job." This definition is based on the data of McClelland (1973) and refers to KSAs, motives, traits, and aspects of one's self-image or social roles of individuals, related to job performance. Somewhat smaller in scope are the definitions that refer just to combinations of KSAOs that are needed to perform a group of related tasks or to bundles of *demonstrated* KSAOs (Garavan and McGuire 2001). The term *demonstrated* in the latter definition appears to refer to behavior. Other authors refer more explicitly to behaviors. For example, Tett et al. (2000, 215) describe a competency as: "an identifiable aspect of prospective work behavior attributable to the individual that is expected to contribute positively and/or negatively to organisational effectiveness." They conclude: "In short, a competency is future-evaluated work behavior" (p. 215). The focus on behavior is less univocal in the definition of Woodruffe (1993, 29): "A competency is the set of behavior patterns that the incumbent needs to bring to a position in order to perform its tasks and functions with competence" and "a dimension of overt manifest behavior that allows a person to perform competently." However, other authors (e.g., Kurz and Bartram 2002; Roe 2002)

---

[1] The term competency framework is developed in the UK; the term competency modeling is most common in the US.

are of the firm opinion that a competency is *not* behavior. Kurz and Bartram (2002, 230), for example, stated: "A competency is not the behavior or perform-ance itself, but the repertoire of capabilities, activities, processes and responses available that enable a range of work demands to be met more effectively by some people than by others" and "Competence is what enables the performance to occur." However, elsewhere Bartram, Kurz, and Baron (2003) define compe-tencies as "sets of desirable behaviours" (p. 23). In their definitions the diffe-rence between behaviors and sets of behaviors appears very subtle and may be confusing.

The above-mentioned examples focus on characteristics of the individual job holder (person based); however, some definitions focus on the job or tasks. The latter are part of the UK model, which will be described in the next section.

In conclusion, it can be said that competencies appear to be close to anything one wants them to be. The definitions vary from abstract psychological constructs to direct observable behavior, from "old wine in new barrels" (e.g., traditional KSAOs) to something innovative and refreshing, and from "a ghastly piece of jargon" (Woodruffe 1991, 31) to something highly desirable.

2.2 Typologies

Competencies are categorized in different ways, for example, by scope (e.g., person, job, occupation, organization) or by origin (UK or US). On the whole, the predominant typologies can be combined and summarized into two broad cat-egories: (1) the person-based approach; and (2) the job/work-based approach.

2.2.1 *Person-based versus job-based*

The person-based approach finds its origin in the US. Within this approach competencies are conceived as individual characteristics that are related to excel-lent or *superior* performance. This perspective is worker-oriented and is concerned with the input of individuals in terms of behavior, skills, or underlying personal characteristics required by job holders (Garavan and McGuire 2001; Stuart and Lindsay 1997).

The job-based approach is based on the UK's national Occupational Standards for Management, developed by the Management Charter Initiative (Frank, 1991). The approach is task centered and focuses on the purpose of the job or occupation, rather than the job holder. In the "occupational standards model" or "job com-petence model" (Cheetham and Chivers 1996, 21) competencies (mostly called competences) are described in terms of minimum standards of performance (*threshold performance*). This approach is directed at job output; in this perspective the characteristics required by job holders are assumed to exist when the standards are met (Garavan and McGuire 2001; Stuart and Lindsay 1997).

Although the terms *competence* and *competency* are often used interchangeably, the British approach makes an explicit distinction between them (Stuart and Lindsay 1997; Woodruffe 1991). The differences between the terms parallel the differences between the job-based versus the person-based perspectives. In the UK, in particular, the term competence is generally associated with the job-based approach, especially in the public and educational sector (Hoffmann 1999). Person-based competency frameworks appear to be more relevant in the area of management, especially in selection and assessment.

In the UK there is a trend to integrate both approaches. For example, Stuart and Lindsay (1997) distinguish in their model "competence domains," competencies and components of competencies. Competence domains are "areas of activity regarded as an important focus for performance excellence" (p. 28). In defining competencies they follow the definition of Woodruffe (1991, 28): "Competencies are described as integrated sets of behaviors which can be directed towards successful goal achievement within competence domains." The components of competencies (the "constituents of competencies") refer to KSAOs "which make up, contribute and add 'style' to the competencies." The authors state that their competence domains overlap with the competences associated with the UK approach of managerial competence; their components of competencies overlap with the competencies generally associated with the US approach.

Garavan and McGuire (2001) consider the UK approach as representative for other European countries, but the situation in Europe seems less clear cut. In the Netherlands and Belgium (e.g., Lievens, Sanchez, and De Corte 2004), for example, person-based approaches as well as job-based and more organization-oriented approaches are found (Roe 2002; Van der Maessen de Sombreff and Schakel 1999). The latter approach refers to "core competencies."

2.2.2 Core competencies

In addition to the two broad categories presented above, some authors distinguish a third category, the organization-based approach. In this perspective Prahalad and Hamel (1990) introduced the term *core* competence (plural: core competencies, according to Prahalad and Hamel). They refer to core competencies as "the collective learning in the organisation, especially how to coordinate diverse production skills and integrate multiple streams of technologies" (p. 82). Again, this concept lacks a clear definition. Prahalad and Hamel give many examples of well-known organizations (especially in the business of high technology) and they attribute the success of those organizations to their core competencies. However, Prahalad and Hamel did not exactly define the concept, but presented three functions of core competences instead: (1) core competencies provide access to a variety of markets (e.g., competence in display systems); (2) core competencies should make an important contribution to the perceived customer benefits of the end product; and (3) core competencies should be firm specific, in order to be difficult for competitors to imitate. It can be concluded that core competencies have something to do with business strategy.

Sparrow (1997) defines an organizational competence as a characteristic of the organization that is developed by individuals in the organization. He perceives these competences as internal resources and capabilities of the organization linked with business performance in order to make the organization more successful than others. Stuart and Lindsay (1997) view organizational competence as a lens focusing on the world of managerial competence. In this view, the lens connects the environment and the culture of the organization to the required individual competencies and "competence domains," described above.

Another interpretation of the term core competencies is "general," "generic," or "universal" management competencies, that is, competencies that hold for all or most managers. Although most of the typologies do not include competences at the organizational level, their link with business strategy appears to be seen as a typical characteristic of competencies in general, as the study of Schippmann et al. (2000, see next section) shows.

2.3 Benefits and Drawbacks

2.3.1 *Drawbacks*

Some of the drawbacks of the development and use of competencies have already been mentioned (e.g., the lack of a coherent definition and a theoretical framework). Jubb and Robotham (1997) summarize the problems as follows: "The whole competence movement appears to have grown up around a series of assumptions which, on closer examination, either lack theoretical support, or simply do not stand up" (p. 174). The validity and methodology of the competency approach is questioned (Barrett and Depinet 1991; Garavan and McGuire 2001). In this context one might also wonder whether competencies are the *predictors* of workplace behavior (the criteria), or the criteria themselves (the workplace behaviors to be predicted). Bartram, Kurz, and Baron (2003) perceive competencies as criteria and they developed a competency model with eight factors as the result of factor analysis of ratings of workplace behaviors (by supervisors). Their study showed that personality and ability tests (measures of "competency potential", p. 6) predict competency performance ratings in a meaningful fashion. Others consider competencies as predictors of workplace performance (e.g., Barrett and Depinet 1991; Garavan and McGuire 2001).

The study of Lievens et al. (2004) is among the first to empirically examine the quality of the inferences made in competency modeling. They characterize competency modeling as tying job specifications to the organization's strategy, and the generation of a set of human attributes or competencies, derived from the strategic requirements in combination with non-strategic job requirements. Based on three studies, they concluded that the quality of inferences in competency modeling should not be taken for granted. Their results indicated that presentation of task information and the use of a variety of job experts could enhance the quality of the inference process. They found that combining a task analysis approach with a competency-based approach might enhance the quality of the inferences job experts draw about competency requirements in terms of interrater reliability among the experts, and their ability to discriminate between jobs.

Most of the criticism against the use of competencies refers to matters of validity and theoretical background of the concept, but there are practical disadvantages too. Mansfield (1996) stated that the oldest competency models were developed for single jobs. These models included extensive data gathering (e.g., interviews, focus groups, surveys, observation) with subject-matter experts (e.g., managers, job holders, customers). From the colleted data lists of ten to twenty skills or traits (the competencies) were distilled. The obvious disadvantages of this procedure are time, costs, and effort. Besides, when jobs are changing the competency models have to be changed too. Another drawback of single-job models is the fact that jobs are difficult to compare, for example, for selection or promotion purposes. In short, these models are too expensive to be practical.

The other model Mansfield describes, the "one-size-fits-all" model, defines one set of competencies for a broad category of (related) jobs, for example, all managerial jobs. The most important drawback of this model is the impossibility of describing the typical requirements of specific jobs; therefore it is of limited use in several HRM practices, such as selection and promotion procedures. Mansfield suggests a kind of in-between model, the "multiple job model" that assumes, for example, experience in building competency models, the existence of many single-job models, and consultants specialized in competency work. If such conditions are met, it might be possible to develop a competency model for a specific job in a quick, low-cost way.

Jubb and Robotham (1997) warn against oversimplifying the concept of competency and its context; they are afraid that attempting to derive an operational definition of managerial competence may unacceptably simplify the complex realities of management behaviors. They stated that the measurability of competencies has not yet been proven.

Because of the mentioned shortcomings, academics have been reserved in adopting the concept of competence, but as Garavan and McGuire (2001, 159) put it: "On the surface, notions of competency appear so obviously useful that they cannot be ignored." And, indeed there are (claimed) advantages too.

2.3.2 *Benefits*

Sparrow (1997) argues that the strength of the behavioral competency approach is the use of criterion samples. He claims that the approach focuses on those behaviors that have "proven" to result in successful performance in a sample of job holders who have had success in their jobs. He presents a list with no less than twenty-eight claimed benefits from the use of behavioral competencies in the areas of recruitment and selection, career development, performance management, and HRM processes. This seems impressive, but Sparrow also notices that many of the benefits claimed by practitioners are as yet untested. However, according to Sparrow, many claims "do not need supporting through independent study since they are based on accepted practice or tenets of occupational psychology" (p. 350). This holds especially for process benefits related to the consulting process such as higher ownership of the competency profile as a result of the contribution, of job holders as well as managers, to the competency development process. He concludes that it is difficult to assess the unique benefits, because competency modeling often occurs simultaneously with other changes in the organization. Although Jubb and Robotham (1997) stress several weaknesses of the use of competences in the context of management development, they appreciate the fact that the competence approach concentrates on what managers actually do, rather than on beliefs about what managers do.

Referring to the single-job competency model, Mansfield (1996) mentions the following benefits: the description of specific behaviors tell job holders what they must do to perform successfully; competencies provide a framework for describing job requirements; a competency model might be better than what existed before. The latter is in line with the opinion of Woodruffe (1991) who stated that the word competency could have offered a fresh start to replace the often misunderstood terms of traits and motives. Harvey (1999) suggested that the term competency analysis, *as a new name for job analysis* (in terms of the capacity to perform essential job functions) might solve the image problem of job analysis.

2.4 The Practice of Competency Modeling

In general, competency frameworks or competency models describe the competencies required for effective (or excellent) performance on the job; they mostly consist of lists of competencies (typically 10–20), each with a definition and examples of specific behaviors. Competency models are often based on content analysis of existing job performance models and managerial performance taxonomies (e.g., Bartram, Kurz, and Baron 2003; Tett et al. 2000). In addition, organization- (industry-, job-) specific competencies are identified. As in job analysis, there are several methods for identifying competencies: direct observation, critical incident technique, panels or teams of subject-matter experts or focus groups, questionnaires, repertory grid technique (RGT), or conventional job analysis (Garavan and McGuire 2001; Robinson et al. 2007; Woodruffe 1993). The method Boyatzis (1982) originally suggested was the *Behavioral Event Interview* (BEI): individuals were asked to tell what made them successful in their job, by describing three incidents in which they felt effective and three incidents in which they felt ineffective. This approach has been heavily criticized (e.g., Barrett and Depinet 1991), because of unsatisfactorily empirical evidence of validity. Today, combinations of qualitative methods (like the CIT and the RGT), and quantitative measures (questionnaires) are advocated (e.g., Robinson et al. 2007). The choice of techniques depends on the kind of competency or competence one is focusing on. For example, grouping specific types of behavior into competencies, for instance, by means of the critical incident technique, can derive person-related competencies. Job-related competencies (competences or areas of competence) could be analyzed with questionnaires, in this context often labeled as functional analysis. Functional analysis resembles task analysis and identifies key roles and elements of the job and focuses on what job holders do, what they must be competent at (Woodruffe 1991).

As in job analysis, the sources of information for the identification of competencies are job holders, their supervisors, their subordinates, and their clients. It appears that there are several similarities between competency modeling and job analysis (e.g., in methods of data collection). A remarkable example is the Job Element Method (Primoff and Dittrich Eyde 1988), a job analysis method that focuses on behaviors that are relevant to successful job performance. This comes close to the person-based approach of competency modeling. The question is whether competency modeling could or should replace job analysis to facilitate the adaptation and orientation to the changes in the world of work.

3. JOB ANALYSIS VERSUS COMPETENCY MODELING

The members of the Job Analysis and Competency Modeling Task Force (JACMTF; Schippmann et al. 2000) compared and contrasted competency modeling and job analysis. They conducted a literature search and interviewed thirty-seven subject-matter experts, such as human resources consultants, former presidents of the Society for Industrial and Organizational Psychology, leaders in the area of competency modeling and industrial and organizational psychologists who represent a traditional job analysis perspective. The sample of experts represented advocates as

Table 6.2 Differences between job analysis and competency modeling

Job analysis	Competency modeling
Focus on	Focus on
a. work and tasks	a. worker
b. technical skills	b. personal values, personality
c. differences between jobs	c. core competencies, common for several jobs
d. short-term job match	d. long-term organizational fit
Advantage:	Advantage:
Psychometrically sound	Link to business goals and strategies

Source: Voskuijl (2005), based upon Schippmann et al. (2000).

well as opponents of either job analysis or competency modeling. The task force asked the experts to define a competency and to describe the differences between job analysis and competency modeling. Their search revealed, again, a variety of definitions of a competency. The comparison of job analysis and competency modeling resulted in a superior overall evaluation of job analysis: job analysis is considered as more psychometrically sound. Based on the interviews with the experts the task force members rated both approaches on ten evaluative criteria (e.g., method of investigation, procedures for developing descriptor content, detail of descriptor content) according to the level of rigor with which they were practiced. The differences are summarized in Table 6.2.

Except for the evaluation variable "link to business goals and strategies," job analysis demonstrated medium/high and high rigor with reference to the criteria. In contrast, competency profiling has a strong link to business goals and strategies but demonstrates low/medium to medium rigor with respect to the other criteria. The link to business goals and strategies is also reflected in the opinions of the experts about other characteristics of both approaches: competency modeling is more focused on core competencies that are common to several jobs (or even to the whole organization), and on aspects that are related to long-term organizational fit; the focus of job analysis is supposed to be on differences between jobs and on short-term job match. Furthermore, job analysis focuses more on technical skills and competency modeling tends to emphasize personal values and personality orientations more. The findings of Schippmann et al. are no reason to replace job analysis with competency modeling. Job analysis is even necessary to identify competencies, according to several authors (e.g., Woodruffe 1993). Sanchez and Levine (2001) state that the difference between both approaches is blurry. However, they stress, like Schippmann et al., that (non-strategic) job analysis fails to reflect the strategy, goals, and future needs of the organization. Apparently, their view and the results of the study of Schippmann et al. refer especially to organizational competencies. Based on the results of

Schippmann et al., Sacket and Laczo (2003) concluded that competency modeling is a form of worker-oriented job analysis that focuses on broader characteristics of individuals.

In contrasting job analysis and competency modeling the conclusion is that
integration of the strengths of both approaches could enhance the quality of the
results (Lievens, Sanchez, and De Corte 2004; Sackett and Laczo, 2003; Sanchez
and Levine 2001; Schippmann et al. 2000). A study by Siddique (2004) indicated
that a company-wide policy of job analysis is an important source of competitive
advantage. He found a relationship between frequency/regularity of conducting
job analysis and organizational performance (e.g., administrative efficiency,
quality of organizational climate, financial performance, overall sales growth).
The relationship was stronger when the job analysis approach was competency
focused. By that Siddique meant approaches that placed greater emphasis on
"characteristics of employees considered essential for successful job performance" (pp. 225–6; for example, motivation, adaptability, teamwork orientation,
interpersonal skills, innovative thinking, self-motivation). It seems that Siddique
refers to the definition of Boyatzis (1982). The author developed a measure of the
degree of competency focus by reviewing several documents used by the companies under investigation (job analysis forms, job application forms, performance evaluation forms). Despite several limitations of the study, one of them
being the lack of a clear definition of a competency, this type of studies might
shed light on the impact of job analysis and the possible role of competencies in
approaches of work analysis.

4. CONCLUDING REMARKS
AND SUGGESTIONS

Detailed job analysis in terms of fixed tasks within strict job boundaries is more
and more inappropriate considering the changing world of work. Job boundaries
have become blurry, new jobs emerge, work is described in flexible and changeable
work roles, and employees take on broader responsibilities. However, in several
work settings a tight and detailed description of tasks and duties within jobs is
inevitable. For example, in areas with high safety risks, such as an oil refinery, safety
rules prescribe in detail the actions of the workers. Creativity and flexibility might
result in disasters in this kind of industry. Similar examples can be found in the
medical world; imagine the surgical nurse who is exploring the boundaries of her
job during surgery. Less disastrous but yet embarrassing consequences are to be
expected if tasks and responsibilities are not prescribed in detail in hierarchical

settings and settings wherein people work under time pressure (e.g., the chef-cook and the apprentice in the kitchen of a restaurant). Weick (1996) noted that those "strong" situations, that is, situations where there are clear guidelines and rules about how one should behave, are quite common also in cultures high in power distance and collectivism. However, many future work situations are more ambiguous and ask for adaptations in the focus of work analysis. Although Fleishmann and Mumford (1988) stated that the successful performance of a large number of tasks in different jobs may require a limited amount of abilities, changing jobs or newly created jobs may ask for the identification of "new" KSAOs that contribute to the process of business planning (such as openness to innovation, Sanchez 1994) and teamwork (such as interpersonal skills relevant for cooperation). The creation of (cross-functional and temporary) teams is seen as an answer to the increased (international) competition in terms of innovation and speed. Employees have become highly interdependent in teamwork. Sanchez (1994) states that the greater the emphasis on analyzing task interdependencies and workflows, the better the teamwork. A related trend is a focus on descriptions of broad roles (Altink, Visser, and Castelijns 1997). Role descriptions should reflect the strategies and goals of the organization and go beyond the tasks within traditional jobs. As said before, in conventional job analysis no link to business goals and strategies was made. However, in the study of Schippmann et al. (2000), this aspect appeared to be the strongest characteristic of competency modeling. Without embracing competency modeling wholeheartedly, it might be wise to learn from the broader focus of this approach.

Finally, to be able to adapt continuously to changing information about work and workers it is advised to develop or optimize automated work-analytic systems and databases (e.g., Sanchez 2000). Relations between different categories of information within a system, for example, between work characteristics and worker characteristics, can be explored (Hanson et al. 1999).

In conclusion, it can be said that job analysis is still alive. It continues to be an essential instrument in human resource applications. It forms the basis for personnel decisions in focusing on answers to questions such as: Selection for what? Compensation for what? Appraisal of what? An integration of the strengths of both job analysis (e.g., psychometric soundness) and competency modeling (links with business strategy) could benefit the quality of both or of the combination of both approaches. Developments in the structure of work stress the urgency to concentrate as well on the traditional aspects of work (e.g., job-oriented and worker-oriented activities) as on the strategic and future-oriented needs and goals of the organization as a whole and the related "new" KSAOs (e.g., creativity), roles and processes. Furthermore, job descriptors should also include contextual and environmental dimensions, in order to cover jobs in their broadest meaning with possibilities to capture continuous changes.

Research in the field of job analysis and competency modeling would profit from the suggested "Pragmatic Science" quadrant of the fourfold typology of research in industrial, work, and organizational psychology from Anderson, Herriot, and Hodgkinson (2001). This quadrant refers, for example, to studies that add to knowledge with practical implications *and* appropriate design rigor, to studies that are grounded upon current issues in HRM practice *and* upon relevant theory and past findings; furthermore, practitioners as well as researchers should find the study valuable. In this way the benefits from job modeling and competencies can be combined.

References

ALTINK, W. M. M., VISSER, C. F., and CASTELIJNS, M. 1997. Criterion development: the unknown power of criteria as communication tools. Pp. 287–302 in *International Handbook of Selection and Assessment*, ed. N. Anderson and P. Herriot. New York: Wiley.

ANDERSON, N., HERRIOT, P., and HODGKINSON, G. P. 2001.The practitioner–researcher divide in industrial, work and organizational (IWO) psychology: where are we now, and where do we go from here? *Journal of Occupational and Organizational Psychology*, 74: 391–411.

ASH, R. A. 1988. Job analysis in the world of work. Pp. 3–13 in *The Job Analysis Handbook for Business, Industry and Government*, vol. i, ed. S. Gael. New York: Wiley.

BARRETT, G., and DEPINET, R. 1991. Reconsideration of testing for competence rather than intelligence. *American Psychologist*, 46: 1012–23.

BARTRAM, D., KURZ, R., and BARON, H. 2003. The great eight competencies: meta-analysis using a criterion-centric approach to validation. Paper presented at SIOP, Orlando, April.

BOYATZIS, R. E. 1982. *The Competent Manager*. New York: Wiley.

CASCIO, W. F. 1991. *Applied Psychology in Personnel Management*. London: Prentice-Hall.

CHEETHAM, G., and CHIVERS, G. 1996. Towards a holistic model of professional competence. *Journal of European Industrial Training*, 20: 20–30.

CONTE, J. M., DEAN, M. A., RINGENBACH, K. L., MORAN, S. K., and LANDY, F. J. 2005. The relationship between work attitutudes and job analysis ratings: do rating scale type and task discretion matter? *Human Performance*, 18: 1–21.

CUCINA, J. F., VASILOPOULOS, N. L., and SEHGAL, K. G. 2005. Personality-based job analysis and the self-serving bias. *Journal of Business and Psychology*, 20: 275–90.

CUNNINGHAM, J. W. 1996. Generic job descriptors: a likely direction in occupational analysis. *Military Psychology*, 8: 247–62.

DIERDORFF, E. C., and WILSON, M. A. 2003. A meta-analysis of job analysis reliability. *Journal of Applied Psychology*, 88: 635–46.

EQUAL EMPLOYMENT OPPORTUNITY COMMISSION. 1978. Uniform guidelines on employee selection procedures. Federal Register, 43: 38290–38315.

FINE, S. A. 1988. Functional job analysis. Pp. 1019–35 in *The Job Analysis Handbook for Business, Industry and Government*, vol. ii, ed. S. Gael. New York: Wiley.

FLANAGAN, J. C. 1954. The critical incidents technique. *Psychological Bulletin*, 51: 327–58.

FLEISHMAN, E. A., and MUMFORD, M. D. 1988. Ability Requirement Scales. Pp. 917–35 in *The Job Analysis Handbook for Business, Industry and Government*, vol. ii, ed. S. Gael. New York: Wiley.

FRANK, E. 1991. The UK's management Charter Initiative: the first three years. *Journal of European Industrial Training*, 15: 3–12.

GAEL, S., ed. 1988. *The Job Analysis Handbook for Business, Industry and Government*. New York: Wiley.

GARAVAN, T. N., and McGUIRE, D. 2001. Competencies and workplace learning: some reflections on the rhetoric and the reality. *Journal of Workplace Learning*, 13: 144–163.

HANSON, M. A., BORMAN, W. C., KUBISIAK, U. C., and SAGER, C. E. 1999. Cross-domain analyses. Pp. 247–58 in *An Occupational Information System for the 21st Century: The Development of O*NET*, ed. N. G. Peterson, M. D. Mumford, W. C Borman, P. R. Jeanneret, and E. A. Fleishman. Washington, DC: APA.

HARVEY, R. J. 1991. Job analysis. Pp. 71–162 in *Handbook of Industrial and Organizational Psychology*, vol. ii, ed. M. D. Dunnette and L. M. Hough. Palo Alto, CA: Consulting Psychologists Press.

—— (1999). Dr. CompetencyLove: how I learned to stop worrying and love "competencied." Invited presentation in the use of structured job analysis methods to address issues involved in competency modeling for the North Carolina/Organizational Psychologists Association (March) given at the Center for Creative Leadership, Greenslero.

—— and WILSON, M. A. 2000. Yes Virginia, there *is* an objective reality in job analysis. *Journal of Organizational Behaviour*, 21: 829–54.

HOFFMANN, T. 1999. The meanings of competency. *Journal of European Industrial Training*, 23: 275–85.

JUBB, R., and ROBOTHAM, D. 1997. Competences in management development: challenging the myths. *Journal of European Industrial Training*, 21: 171–5.

KURZ, R., and BARTRAM, D. 2002. Competency and individual performance: modeling the world of work. Pp. 227–55 in *Organizational Effectiveness: The Role of Psychology*, ed. I. T. Robertson, M. Callinan and D. Bartram. Chichester: Wiley.

LANDIS, R. S., FOGLI, L., and GOLDBERG, E. 1998. Future-oriented job analysis: a description of the process and its organizational implications. *International Journal of Selection and Assessment*, 6: 192–7.

LEVINE, E. L. 1983. *Everything You Always Wanted to Know about Job Analysis*. Tampa, FL: Mariner Publishing.

—— ASH, R. A., HALL, H., and SISTRUNK, F. 1983. Evaluation of job analysis methods by experiences job analysts. *Academy of Management Journal*, 26: 339–48.

LIEVENS, F., SANCHEZ, J. I., and DE CORTE, W. 2004. Easing the inferential leap in competency modeling: the effects of task-related information and subject-matter expertise. *Personnel Psychology*, 57: 881–904.

LINDELL, M. K., CLAUSE, C. S., BRANDT, C. J., and, LANDIS, R. S. 1998. Relationship between organizational context and job analysis task ratings. *Journal of Applied Psychology*, 83: 769–76.

LOPEZ, F. M. 1988. Threshold Traits Analysis System. Pp. 880–901 in *The Job Analysis Handbook for Business, Industry and Government*, vol. ii, ed. S. Gael. New York: Wiley.

McCLELLAND, D. C. 1973. Testing for competence rather than for "intelligence." *American Psychologist*, 28: 1–14.

McCormick, E. J. 1976. Job and task analysis. Pp. 651–97 in *Handbook of Industrial and Organizational Psychology*, ed. M. D. Dunnette. Chicago: Rand McNally.

—— Jeanneret, P. R., and Mecham, R. C. 1972. A study of job characteristics and job dimensions as based on the Position Analysis Questionnaire (PAQ). *Journal of Applied Psychology*, 56: 347–68.

Mansfield, R. S. 1996. Building competency models: approaches for HR professionals. *Human Resource Management*, 35: 7–18.

Morgeson, F. P., and Campion, M. A. 1997. Social and cognitive sources of potential inaccuracy in job analysis. *Journal of Applied Psychology*, 82: 627–55.

—— —— 2000. Accuracy in job analysis: toward an inference-based model. *Journal of Organizational Behaviour*, 21: 819–27.

Peterson, N. G., Mumford, M. D., Borman, W. C., Jeanneret, P. R., and Fleishman, E. A. 1999. *An Occupational Information System for the 21st Century: The Development of O*NET*. Washington, DC: APA.

Prahalad, C. K., and Hamel, G. 1990. The core competence of the corporation. *Harvard Business Review* (May-June): 79–91.

Primoff, E. S., and Dittrich Eyde, L. 1988. Job element analysis. Pp. 807–24 in *The Job Analysis Handbook for Business, Industry and Government*, vol. ii, ed. S. Gael. New York: Wiley.

Raymark, P. H., Schmit, M. J., and Guion, R. M. 1997. Identifying potentially useful personality constructs for employee selection. *Personnel Psychology*, 50: 723–36.

Robinson, M. A., Sparrow, P. R., Clegg, C., and Birdi, K. 2007. Forecasting future competency requirements: a three-phase methodology. *Personnel Review*, 36: 65–90.

Roe, R. A. 2002. Competenties—Een sleutel tot integratie in theorie en praktijk van de A & O-psychologie [Competences—A key towards the integration of theory and practice in work and organizational psychology]. *Gedrag and Organisatie*, 15: 203–24.

Sackett, P. R., and Laczo, R. M. 2003. Job and work analysis. Pp. 21–37 in *Handbook of Psychology*, xii: *Industrial and Organizational Psychology*, ed. W. C. Borman, D. R. Ilgen, and R. J. Klimoski. Hoboken, NJ: Wiley.

Salgado, J. F., and De Fruyt, F. 2005. Personality in Personnel Selection. Pp. 174–98 in *The Blackwell Handbook of Personnel Selection*, ed. A. Evers, N. Anderson, and O. F. Voskuijl. Oxford: Blackwell.

Sanchez, J. I. 1994. From documentation to innovation: reshaping job analysis to meet emerging business needs. *Human Resource Management Review*, 4: 51–74.

—— 2000. Adapting work analysis to a fast-paced electronic business world. *International Journal of Selection and Assessment*, 8: 207–15.

—— and Levine, E. L. 2000. Accuracy or consequential validity: which is the better standard for job analysis data? *Journal of Organizational Behaviour*, 21: 809–18.

—— —— 2001. The analysis of work in the 20th and 21st centuries. Pp. 71–89 in *Handbook of Industrial, Work, and Organizational Psychology*, vol. i, ed. N. Anderson, D. S. Ones, H. Kepir Sinangil, and C. Viswesvaran. London: Sage Publications.

—— Zamora, A., and Visweswaran, C. 1997. Moderators of agreement between incumbent and non-incumbent ratings of job characteristics. *Journal of Occupational and Organizational Psychology*, 70: 209–18.

Schippmann, J. S. 1999. *Strategic Job Modeling: Working at the Core of Integrated Human Resources*. London: Lawrence Erlbaum.

SCHIPPMANN, J. S., ASH, R. A., BATTISTA, M., CARR, L., EYDE, L. D., HESKETH, B., et al. 2000. The practice of competency modeling. *Personnel Psychology,* 53: 703–39.

SCHMIDT, F. L., and HUNTER, J. E. 1998. The validity and utility of selection methods in personnel psychology: practical and theoretical implications of 85 years of research findings. *Psychological Bulletin,* 124: 262–74.

SCHNEIDER, B. S., and KONZ, A. M. 1989 Strategic job analysis. *Human Resource Management,* 28: 51–63.

SCHULER, H. 1989. Some advantages and problems of job analysis. Pp. 31–42 in *Advances in Selection and Assessment,* ed. M. Smith and I. Robertson. London: Wiley.

SIDDIQUE, C. M. 2004. Job analysis: a strategic human resource management practice. *International Journal of Human Resource Management,* 15: 219–44.

SPARROW, P. R. 1997. Organizational competencies: creating a strategic behavioural framework for selection and assessment. Pp. 343–68 in *International Handbook of Selection and Assessment,* ed. N. Anderson. and P. Herriot. Chichester: Wiley.

STUART, R., and LINDSAY, P. 1997. Beyond the frame of management competenc(i)es: towards a contextually embedded framework of managerial competence in organizations. *Journal of European Industrial Training,* 21: 26–33.

TETT, R. P., GUTERMAN, H. A., BLEIER, A., and MURPHY, P. J. 2000. Development and content validation of a "hyperdimensional" taxonomy of managerial competence. *Human Performance,* 13: 205–51.

TROSS, S. A., and MAURER, T. J. 2000. The relationship between SME job experience and job analysis ratings: findings with and without statistical control. *Journal of Business and Psychology,* 15: 97–110.

VAN DER MAESSEN DE SOMBREFF, P., and SCHAKEL, L. 1999. Wat zijn competenties niet? [What are competencies not?]. *Opleiding en Ontwikkeling,* 12: 11–17.

VOSKUIJL, O. F. 2005. Job analysis: current and future perspectives. Pp. 98–117 in *The Blackwell Handbook of Personnel Selection,* ed. A. Evers, N. Anderson, and O. F. Voskuijl. Oxford: Blackwell.

WEICK, K. E. 1996. Enactment and the boundaryless career: organizing as we work. Pp. 40–55 in *The Boundaryless Career: A New Employment Principle for a New Organizational Era,* ed. M. B. Arthur and D. Rousseau. Oxford: Oxford University Press.

WOODRUFFE, C. 1991. Competent by another name. *Personnel Management* (Sept.): 30–3.

—— 1993. What is meant by a competency? *Leadership and Organization Development Journal,* 14: 29–36.

7

VALIDITY OF SELECTION PROCEDURES

NEAL SCHMITT

JESSICA FANDRE

1. INTRODUCTION

IN this chapter we address two major issues: (a) how psychologists conceptualize the validity of the procedures they develop and use to select employees; and (b) what are reasonable estimates of the validity of those procedures. In both areas, we have seen considerable new development in the past two decades in a field that is at least a century old in its modern manifestation (Vinchur 2007). Changes in the way we conceptualize validity are obvious in the APA Guidelines (American Educational Research Association, American Psychological Association, and National Council on Measurement in Education 1999), the SIOP Principles (Society for Industrial and Organizational Psychology 2003) as well as recent textbook treatments of validity (Guion and Highhouse 2006; Ployhart, Schneider, and Schmitt 2006). At the same time that these changes in our ideas about measure validity have occurred, the use of meta-analysis has radically changed the discipline's thinking regarding the magnitude of the validity and utility of selection procedures as well as their generalizability. Procedures developed to assess the extent of validity generalization (e.g., Schmidt and Hunter 1977; Schmidt and Hunter 1998) have prompted a focus on true validity (as opposed to empirical estimates).

2. The Conceptualization of Validity

Early versions of the APA Standards and Principles generally described three types of validity (i.e., construct, content, and criterion-related validity). Construct validity was usually defined as the degree to which scores on a test were consistent with our theoretical ideas about what a predictor measure assessed. Content validity was seen as the degree to which the responses required of job candidates represented the behaviors required to successfully perform some job and about which we wanted to make inferences. Criterion-related validity referred to the extent to which test scores used to make selection decisions were correlated with measures of job performance. For a variety of reasons, criterion-related validation studies were preferred by industrial/organizational psychologists. Thousands of such studies have been conducted over the course of the previous century and these data are the basis for the meta-analyses summarized in a substantial portion of this chapter.

The most recent statements in the Standards (1999) and Principles (2003) have represented a recognition that psychologists are always interested in the predictor construct they are measuring and in making inferences about the degree to which that construct allows them to predict a theoretical job performance construct (Binning and Barrett 1989). The Standards describe eight sources of validity evidence. Direct examination of the content of a test (and its similarity to the content of a job) and documentation of test-criterion relationships are evidence that used to be labeled content and criterion-related validity. In addition, evidence based on response processes, the internal structure of a test, relationships to variables external to the test, validity generalization, and convergent and discriminant validity are sources of evidence that used to be called construct validity. Evidence related to the unintended consequences of testing (e.g., unequal proportions of members of various demographic groups being selected), termed consequential validity by Messick (1998), is also discussed in Standards. The discussion of various sources of validity evidence in Principles generally parallels that of the Standards with the exception of consequential validity.

As stated above, criterion-related validity evidence usually consists of a study in which the researcher estimates the correlation between a test score and some criterion(a) of job performance including performance ratings, sales performance, productivity measures, and turnover among others. There are problems with this approach, however. Perhaps, the single largest issue involves the availability of a sufficiently large sample from which to derive a stable estimate of criterion-related validity. Reliance on small sample criterion-related studies means that estimates of validity vary a great deal from one study to another simply as a result of sampling error making generalizations to some larger population difficult. Second, the major objective of criterion-related research is to provide data that serve as the bases on which to predict the job performance of applicants, but to do that, we must wait months or years before we have a credible measure of job performance. This has led to the simultaneous collection of test and performance data from job incumbents and correlating these two variables as an estimate of predictive criterion-related validity. However, job incumbents whose test scores and job performance represent the full range of scores in an applicant group are not usually available producing what the literature calls a restriction of range. Third, it is often the case that the criterion measure against which a predictor is validated is unreliable or deficient. The effects of criterion unreliability and restriction of range on mean validity estimates can be corrected for statistically and often are in meta-analytic research yielding what that body of literature commonly labels true validity. Some meta-analytic researchers, especially those summarizing the personality research, also correct for unreliability in the predictor. In all cases, we reported the authors' estimates of ρ in our tables. The variability in observed estimates of validity (VE) is a function of sampling error as well as variability in restriction of range and criterion unreliability across studies. Corrections for these sources of variance can be made, and are made, in meta-analytic efforts to summarize criterion-related validity research.

Some variations on traditional criterion-related research designs have also been used by researchers. Synthetic validation is an approach whereby validity of tests for a given job is estimated by examining the validity of these tests in predicting different aspects of the job present in other occupations or organizations. These estimates are combined to calculate the validity of a new battery of instruments for the target job. Validity streaming is a design in which a performance data bank is constructed from data collected from all employees in an organization over a period of time. Proposed selection instruments can then be administered to a group of incumbents at any time and subsequently related to measures existing in the performance data bank. Use of this design overcomes the small sample size problem existing even in large organizations whose hiring decisions are not made en masse, but rather in small ad hoc groups as the need arises. This design does not overcome the fact that the motivation of the incumbents who complete the new instruments may differ from the motivation of those who are applying for positions.

The content of a measure should be of concern whether or not other types of validity evidence are collected, but if a researcher is to rely only on careful specification of the content of a selection instrument then several issues are paramount:

1. The job performance domain must be carefully specified;

2. The objectives of the test user must be clearly formulated; and

3. The method of sampling item content from the performance domain must be adequate.

In these cases, a careful and reliable job analysis is critical. The knowledge, skills, abilities, and other characteristics (KASO) and/or the tasks required for successful job performance and their relative necessity for successful performance must be identified. The results of this job analysis must be used to determine the content areas around which the selection measures are built. It is also important that the format of written test items or the nature of test exercises correspond as closely as possible to actual performance required on the job. A personality test measuring extroversion, for example, would ordinarily not be defensible as a sample of the work behavior required of salesmen. Content of tests, based on careful job analyses, is also usually evaluated by subject-matter experts who are asked to evaluate each item on the degree to which it reflects some important job-related KASO or task.

As stated above, more attention has recently been directed to the theoretical meaningfulness of tests as valid measures of constructs. Constructs are psychological explanations of variance in behavior on a test or job. We may believe that extroversion is an important element of salesmanship, but we do not directly see extroversion. We observe that some job applicants introduce themselves to others and initiate conversations. We find later that these same persons initiate contacts with clients or customers and engage in behavior designed to please these customers. We also find that the person states she/he likes people, has joined and led various clubs and social organizations, and seeks out people with whom to enjoy various activities. All of these behaviors or statements would be explained by saying that the person is extroverted.

Information about the degree to which tests are adequate indices of some construct can take many forms. The different measures or observations themselves should correlate highly if they are measures of a single construct. The possible indices of extroversion mentioned above should correlate with each other and ratings of extroversion collected from peers or colleagues, the amount of time individuals spend alone or with others, and scores on self-reported personality measures of extroversion. Positive correlations between these different indices constitute what is sometimes called convergent validity. These various indices or behaviors would not necessarily be related to the time individuals spend on outdoor activities or their scores on physics exams. The latter data constitute discriminant or divergent validity.

Correlational data of this type can be used to analyze the internal structure of a test as well. If items on a test are all supposed to measure extroversion, but an examination of item intercorrelations suggests that some subset of items are more highly correlated with each other than with another item subset, we have evidence that more than one construct is being measured. Both exploratory and confirmatory factor analyses can be used to examine the internal structure of a test as well as its relationship to other measures.

In some studies of constructs, we also try to assess the underlying processes that determine test behavior or responses. We might try to measure the ability of a mechanic to operate various pieces of equipment and provide instructions to do so in written format. If we find that these instructions correlate highly with a test of vocabulary, we might conclude that the applicants' ability to operate the equipment was a function of their vocabulary, not necessarily their mechanical ability. The relevant question then becomes the degree to which operating similar pieces of equipment on the job require that similar vocabulary be available to read and understand instructions. Selection researchers have spent a great deal of time trying to understand the processes underlying test item responses that might be related to race, gender, or cultural background of examinees (Raju and Ellis 2002) or to artificially inflated responses to non-cognitive measures (Ones and Viswesvaran 1998; Paulhus 1991).

Validity generalization research using meta-analysis has also contributed to our understanding of the constructs underlying tests and job performance. A good portion of this chapter will summarize the existing meta-analytic database which now constitutes our best knowledge of the validity of selection procedures. Early criterion-related studies indicated that test validity was highly variable across studies. That variability was often attributed to aspects of the organizational situation that were not understood. Schmidt and Hunter (1977) demonstrated that much of this variability was a function of small sample sizes and study differences in range restriction and criterion unreliability. Their re-examination of the validity of cognitive ability employing corrections for these problems demonstrated that the validity of cognitive ability was non-zero in most instances. Subsequent research indicated that the magnitude of the validity of cognitive ability measures was a function of job complexity (Hunter and Hunter 1984). Their research and that of others summarized below has resulted in increased confidence among researchers of the meaningfulness and interpretation of the constructs underlying tests and job performance. However, it will become obvious when we review these meta-analyses that important gaps in our understanding of ability–performance relationships remain.

In the most recent version of the Standards (1999), discussion of evidence for test validity is extended to include consequential validity, a consideration of the intended and unintended consequences of tests (Messick 1998). This represents a concern that disproportionate numbers of race and gender subgroups are selected or rejected using tests in academic and employment situations. Staffing researchers have usually maintained that disproportionate impact is not a validity issue; that validity involves only a demonstration that the constructs measured by our tests are relevant to the job performance outcomes we hope to maximize. This is the position that is at least implied by the discussion of test score differences and their impact on various groups in the Principles (2003). Whether considered an integral part of validity or not, staffing researchers cannot ignore the impact of selection procedures on minority and women applicants. Doing so invites social, economic, and legal consequences in most Western countries and involves the potential loss of important human talent.

Thus, the meaning of validity as understood by personnel selection researchers has changed significantly in the last couple of decades. We now understand that all validity research and evidence does inform us about the constructs that underlie our measures. Today multiple lines of evidence are used to support the conclusion that an inference about future job performance based on a test score is appropriate. Beginning with test construction, there should be evidence that test items represent some hypothetical construct or job relevant domain of interest.

We also want to find that test scores relate to measures of job performance. We hope our measures correlate with theoretically related measures and not with measures or variables that might be considered irrelevant or representative of some sort of bias. We can also assess construct validity by cumulating evidence over the many previous studies of test-criterion relationships that have been conducted across varying situations and organizations. This body of evidence is by far the largest and best documented available to staffing researchers; in the remainder of this chapter, we try to summarize this work and draw justifiable conclusions about the validity of various selection procedures. We have limited our review in several ways. First, we included only meta-analyses published in peer-reviewed outlets. Second, we did not include studies that summarized research on particular occupations; our rationale is that these data were also part of other meta-analyses that were focused on the validity of measures of specific constructs or methods. For the most part, we have also limited the personality meta-analyses to those focusing on the Big Five though studies such as that by Hough (1992) provide a great deal of data on constructs that don't fit the Big Five taxonomy very well. We have tried to avoid excessive overlap when studies included data that were part of more than one meta-analysis, but we have undoubtedly failed to some degree in this effort.

3. COGNITIVE ABILITY

Meta-analytic evidence of the validity of cognitive ability and measures of specific cognitive abilities was first examined, perhaps because evidence about this construct was most frequently reported. We have provided a summary of the major studies in Table 7.1. These data are from three major sources. Hunter (1983) reported the validity of the General Aptitude Test Battery used by the US Department of Labor and he and his colleagues have cited this evidence in other papers published later (e.g., Hunter and Hunter 1984; Schmidt and Hunter 1998). The second source of data on the validity of cognitive ability is provided by Schmitt et al. (1984) who provided a meta-analysis of all studies on cognitive ability published in *Personnel Psychology* and *Journal of Applied Psychology* between 1964 and 1982. Finally, Salgado and his colleagues have provided several analyses and papers based on European studies of the validity of cognitive ability (Salgado 1997; Salgado et al. 2003a; Salgado et al. 2003b).

As can be seen in Table 7.1, these databases included an impressive number of participants and equally impressive estimates of the validity of general cognitive ability as well as specific cognitive abilities. The observed values of the validity coefficients for training success and job performance are nearly equal and mostly in the .20s. Estimates of true validity (ρ) which involve corrections for range restriction and unreliability in the criterion are all much higher, mostly in the .40 to .60 range. The 90 percent credibility interval above which an investigator can expect estimates of ρ from future similar studies to fall are all above .00 (mostly in the .30s). The fact that all credibility values are above zero has been taken as evidence that cognitive ability measures are valid across all jobs in the US economy (Schmidt 1992; Schmidt and Hunter 1981). Interestingly, the estimates of the validity of specific cognitive abilities are almost exactly the same as those reported for general cognitive ability suggesting that these specific abilities are interchangeable and that all are equally representative of a general factor, g. This argument, in fact, has been espoused by some researchers (e.g., Ree and Earles 1991; 1992).

With the exception of the Hunter (1983) work, moderators of the validity of cognitive ability have not been widely examined. Hunter found that job complexity moderated the validity of cognitive measures such that validities were higher for jobs high in complexity than for less complex jobs. Because large portions of the variance in coefficients in many of these meta-analyses (VE in our tables) were explained by the artifacts examined (i.e., sample size, restriction of range, and criterion unreliability), it is not likely that moderators would have included subsets of situations that would yield 90 percent credibility values below zero.

Another aspect of these data that is worth noting is that the US samples were collected at least twenty-five years ago and for many of the studies perhaps as long as fifty or more years ago. With perhaps one significant exception, not many primary studies of the validity of cognitive ability (and no new meta-analyses) have been reported in the last twenty years in peer-reviewed journals. Because of the very large sample size ($N = 4,039$) and the widely different set of military jobs for which criterion-related validity was examined, a study by McHenry et al. (1990) rivals some of the earlier meta-analytic examinations of the validity of cognitive

Table 7.1 Meta-analyses of the validity of cognitive ability measures

	ρ	r̄	Sample	(N)	Criterion	90%CV	%VE	Moderators
General Cognitive Ability								
GMA								
Bertua, Anderson, and Salgado (2005)	.48	.22	UK	2,469	Job performance	.17	45	Occupation[a]
	.50	.29		17,982	Training success	.33	64	
Hunter (1983)	.45	.25[b]	US	32,124	Job proficiency	.35	NA	Job complexity[c]
	.54	.25[b]		6,496	Training success	.34	NA	
Salgado et al (2003a)	.62	.29	European community[d]	9,554	Job performance	.37	75	Job complexity[e]
	.54	.28		16,065	Training success	.29	47	
Schmitt et al. (1984)	NA	.25	US	40,235	Job performance	NA	30	Criterion
Miller Analogies Test[f]								
Kuncel, Hezlett, and Ones (2004)	.41	.26	US	598	Job performance	.21	NA	
Specific Cognitive Abilities								
Memory								
Salgado et al. (2003a)	.56	.26	European community	946	Job performance	.56	100	
	.34	.17		3,323	Training success	.08	35	
Numerical ability								
Bertua, Anderson, and Salgado (2005)	.42	.19	UK	3,410	Job performance	.26	75	
	.54	.32		15,925	Training success	.43	81	
Salgado et al. (2003a)	.52	.24	European community	5,241	Job performance	.52	100	
	.48	.25		10,860	Training success	.24	46	
Perceptual Ability								
Bertua, Anderson, and Salgado (2005)	.50	.23	UK	1,968	Job performance	.50	242	
	.50	.30		13,134	Training success	.35	66	
Hunter (1983)	.37	.25[b]	US	32,124	Job performance	.24	NA	Job complexity[g]
	.41	.25		6,496	Training success	.33	NA	

Study			Region	Criterion	N		Job complexity[h]
Salgado et al. (2003a)	.52	.24	European community	Job performance	3,798	.28	73
	.25	.13		Training success	3,935	.00	34
Psychomotor Ability							
Hunter (1983)	.37	.25[b]	US	Job performance	32,124	.20	NA
	.26	.25		Training success	6,496	.14	NA
Spatial Ability							
Bertua, Anderson, and Salgado (2005)	.35	.15	UK	Job performance	1,951	.35	348
	.42	.24		Training success	15,591	.42	149
Spatial-Mechanical Ability							
Salgado et al. (2003a)	.51	.23	European community	Job performance	3,750	.13	52
	.40	.20		Training success	15,834	.16	43
Verbal Ability							
Bertua, Anderson, and Salgado (2005)	.39	.17	UK	Job performance	3,464	.20	61
	.49	.29		Training success	12,679	.36	64
Salgado et al. (2003a)	.35	.29	European community	Job performance	4,781	.04	53
	.44	.23		Training success	11,123	.20	45

Notes: Hunter (1983) constitutes a study conducted for the US Department of Labor that was the source of data for the GMA validities cited in Hunter and Hunter (1984) and Schmidt and Hunter (1998). Values here differ from those reported in Schmidt and Hunter (1998). Values here differ from those reported in Schmidt and Hunter because they span across complexity levels. There is substantial overlap between the primary studies used in Bertua et al. (2005) and Salgado et al. (2003a). NA = not available.
[a] Validity was higher for more complex occupations (e.g., ρ = .14 for clerical jobs and ρ = .33 for engineers).
[b] The number for observed validities represents a collapse across criteria (job performance and training success) as this was the only figure available in Hunter (1983). This is the case for both general cognitive ability, perceptual ability, and psychomotor ability.
[c] Validity increases along with job complexity (ρ = .23 for the lowest level and ρ = .56 for the highest out of five levels of complexity).
[d] The countries represented in the analysis are Belgium, France, Germany, Ireland, the Netherlands, Portugal, the Scandinavian countries, Spain, and the United Kingdom.
[e] In a separate report (Salgado et al., 2003b), validity was shown to increase along with job complexity (ρ = .51, ρ = .53, and ρ = .64 for low-, medium-, and high–complexity jobs, respectively).
[f] The Miller Analogies Test displays a true correlation of .75 with general ability measures.
[g] Validity increases along with job complexity (ρ = .24 for the lowest and ρ = .52 for the highest level).
[h] Validity decreases as a function of job complexity (ρ = .48 for the highest and ρ = .30 for the lowest level).

ability. In their military study, commonly called Project A, the true validity of cognitive ability measures was .63 and .65 against supervisory ratings of core technical proficiency and general task proficiency, respectively. These validities certainly reaffirm earlier meta-analytic efforts given that this military project was exceptionally well designed.

We believe that new studies of the validity of cognitive ability measures should be conducted and reported. We do not believe that these studies will change the conclusion that cognitive validity measures do have validity across all, or nearly all, jobs. However, there have been improvements (or at least changes) in the manner in which cognitive ability and other constructs are measured (e.g., Embretson 1998; Kyllonen 1994). Performance is now viewed as a multidimensional construct and it is important that we continue to develop a database that expands on that provided in the Project A study described above which showed much lower validities for other performance outcomes than those described above. It is also the case that we now understand better the impact of study design issues (e.g., use of job incumbents) that may produce inadequate validity estimates and how to improve upon the quality of performance ratings which are usually used as the criteria in these studies. A large multi-organization study of the validity streaming type described earlier should yield valuable information about the validity of cognitive ability tests as well as the manner in which such estimates may be underestimating their worth because of study inadequacies and ways in which measurement of the predictor and criterion constructs may be better understood. They may also contribute to the broader literature in organizational behavior and personnel selection that has begun to address multi-level hypotheses (Klein and Kozlowski 2000; Ployhart and Schneider 2005).

4. PERSONALITY MEASURES

In Table 7.2, we present a summary of the meta-analyses of personality measures, all of which were conducted since the Barrick and Mount (1991) analysis. Estimates of both observed and true validity are markedly lower than those reported for cognitive ability. Most of these meta-analyses consider the Big Five constructs; only Conscientiousness shows true validity against job performance measures exceeding .20. Ninety percent credibility values are consistently above .00 for Conscientiousness and in several instances for Emotional Stability.

When criteria other than job performance are considered, the validities are somewhat higher though the meta-analyses are typically conducted on smaller numbers of people than are those analyses considering job performance. When

Table 7.2 Meta-analyses of the validity of personality measures

	ρ	r̄	Sample	(N)	Criterion	90%CV	%VE	Moderators
FFM								
Barrick and Mount (1991)								
Extroversion	.13	.08	US	19,721	Job proficiency, Training proficiency, Personnel data	−.01	47	Criterion, Occupation[a]
Emotional stability	.08	.05		18,719		−.05	60	
Agreeableness	.07	.04		17,520		−.05	68	
Conscientiousness	.22	.13		19,511		.08	57	Criterion[b]
Openness to experience	.04	.03		14,326		−.02	51	Criterion[c]
Barrick, Mount and Judge (2001)[a]								
Extroversion	.15	.06	US	39,432	Supervisor ratings, Objective performance, Training performance, Teamwork	−.07	43	Criterion, Occupation[d]
Emotional stability	.13	.06		38,817		.01	66	Criterion, Occupation[e]
Agreeableness	.13	.06		36,210		−.01	47	Criterion[f]
Conscientiousness	.27	.12		48,100		.10	30	
Openness to experience	.07	.03		23,255		−.09	53	Criterion[g]
Hurtz and Donovan (2000)								
Extroversion	.10	.06	US	6,453	Job performance and Training performance	−.04	57	
Emotional stability	.14	.09		5,671		.06	85	
Agreeableness	.13	.07		6,447		−.01	62	
Conscientiousness	.22	.14		8,083		.03	44	
Openness to experience	.07	.04		5,525		−.04	70	

(continued)

Table 7.2 (continued)

	ρ	r̄	Sample	(N)	Criterion	90%CV	%VE	Moderators
Salgado (1997)[h]								
Extroversion	.12	.05	European Community	3,806	Job performance, Training success, and Personnel data	−.08	42	Occupation[i]
Emotional stability	.19	.09		3,877		.10	78	
Agreeableness	.02	.01		3,466		−.07	79	Criterion, Occupation[j]
Conscientiousness	.25	.10		3,295		.13	66	
Openness to experience	.09	.04		2,722		.01	81	Criterion[k]
Tett, Jackson, and Rothstein (1991)[l]								
Extroversion	.16	.10	US	2,302	Overall job performance		7	Study type, Validation sample[m]
Emotional stability	.22	.15		900			24	
Agreeableness	.33	.22		280			9	
Conscientiousness	.18	.12		450			16	
Openness to experience	.27	.18		1,304			4	
Other criteria								
Borman et al. (2001)								
Conscientiousness	NA	.24	US	2,378	Citizenship performance	NA	NA	
Agreeableness	—	.13		1,554		NA	NA	
Positive affectivity	—	.18		985		NA	NA	
Extroversion	—	.08		1,832		NA	NA	
Negative affectivity	—	−.14		1,151		NA	NA	
Mount, Barrick, and Stewart (1998)[n]								
Extroversion	.14	.09	US	1,412	Interaction with others	NA	100	

				N	Outcome		%	
Emotional stability	.19	.12		1,491		NA	100	Occupation°
Agreeableness	.27	.17		1,491		NA	100	Occupation°
Conscientiousness	.20	.13		1,491		NA	100	
Openness to experience	.10	.06		1,412		NA	100	
Organ and Ryan (1995) Conscientiousness	.23	.17	US	1,231	OCB (Generalized compliance)	.15	69	Ratings source[p]
Agreeableness	.11	.08		916		.11	100	
Positive affectivity	.07	.06		934		−.06	52	
Negative affectivity	−.12	−.09		847		−.03	65	
Conscientiousness	.04	.04		1,231	OCB (Altruism)	−.03	76	Ratings source[p]
Agreeableness	.13	.10		916		.06	80	
Positive affectivity	.08	.08		869		−.03	55	Ratings source[p]
Negative affectivity	−.06	−.05		1,201		−.00	76	
Other personality traits								
Frei and McDaniel (1998) Customer service orientation	.50	.24	US	6,945	Job performance	0.5	100	
Judge and Bono (2001) Core self-evaluation: Self-esteem	.26	.18	US	5,145	Job performance	−0.1	20	
Generalized self-efficacy	.23	.19		1,122		0.1	66	
Internal locus of control	.22	.14		4,310		0.08	62	
Emotional stability	.19	.16		4,106		0.11	.269	

(continued)

Table 7.2 (continued)

	ρ	r̄	Sample	(N)	Criterion	90%CV	%VE	Moderators
Ones, Viswesvaran and Schmidt (1993)								
Integrity tests	.34	.21		68,772	Job performance	.20	53	Validation sample[q]
	.47	.33		507,688	CWB	.05	9	Validation sample and strategy; Criterion measure[r]

Note: FFM = Five Factor Model. CWB = Counter-productive Work Behaviors. NA = not available.

[a] Validity was highest for training proficiency (ρ = .26) and for managers and salespeople (ρ = .18 and ρ = .15, respectively).
[b] Validity was higher for subjective (ρ = .26) than objective criteria (ρ = .14).
[c] Validity was higher for training proficiency (ρ = .14).
[d] Validity was higher for training performance (ρ = .28) and for managers (ρ = .21).
[e] Validity was higher for teamwork (ρ = .22) and for police (ρ = .12).
[f] Validity was higher for teamwork (ρ = .34).
[g] Validity was higher for training performance (ρ = .33).
[h] The reported correlations were also corrected for construct validity.
[i] Validity was higher for police (ρ = .20).
[j] Validity was higher for training proficiency (ρ = .31) and professionals (ρ = .14).
[k] Validity was higher for training proficiency (ρ = .17).
[l] A reanalysis employing improved corrections for using absolute value correlations (Tett et al. 1994) indicates that the values reported here may be slightly inflated.
[m] For the Big Five, in general, validity was higher for confirmatory (vs. exploratory) studies, recruits (vs. incumbents), military (vs. civilian) samples, and articles (vs. dissertations).
[n] The criterion used was supervisory ratings of interaction with others in jobs within service or team settings. Validities reported are true validities (they are corrected for range restriction and unreliability in predictor and criterion). The variance explained by artifacts was truncated at 100% for all predictors and no credibility intervals included zero.
[o] Validity was higher for jobs involving teamwork (ρ = .25 and ρ = .35 for emotional stability and agreeableness, respectively) than for dyadic service jobs (ρ = .14 and ρ = .22 for emotional stability and agreeableness, respectively).
[p] The reported validities are for those studies excluding self-reports of OCB. The validities were higher for self-reported OCB: conscientiousness-generalized compliance (ρ = .30), conscientiousness-altruism (ρ = .22), and positive affectivity-altruism (ρ = .15).
[q] Validity was higher for applicant samples (ρ = .40) than for incumbent samples (ρ = .18).
[r] Validity was higher for incumbent samples (ρ = .54) than for applicant samples (ρ = .44). Validity was higher for concurrent studies (ρ = .56) than predictive studies (ρ = .36). Validity was higher for predicting admissions criteria (ρ = .58) than for external criteria (ρ = .32).

considering measures of Interaction with Others as the criterion, Agreeableness was the most valid predictor. Because of the smaller sample sizes available for the analyses that included these alternate criteria, the 90 percent credibility values are still mostly near zero or negative. When other than the Big Five constructs are considered (e.g., customer service orientation; Frei and McDaniel 1998), the observed and true validities are higher, though again the total sample sizes are relatively small. Integrity tests whose construct validity is often questioned appear to have validity in the prediction of job performance ($\rho = .34$) as well as counter-productive work behavior ($\rho = .47$). The importance of the criteria against which personality measures are validated is underscored by a meta-analysis not reported in Table 7.2. Hogan and Holland (2003) showed that when theoretically appropriate criteria (those aligned with the personality constructs) were considered in validating subscales of the Hogan Personality Inventory, the average validities were higher and that, with the exception of school success, the lower bound 90 percent credibility values were all greater than or equal to .20.

As the footnote to Table 7.2 indicates, the personality meta-analyses found evidence for a large number of moderators relative to those reported for cognitive ability. This would be the case if what is combined under the umbrella of personality, or even the Big Five constructs, is really multidimensional. In this context, it is important to note that most of the major personality measures used in the employment context—e.g., NEO-PI (Costa and McCrae 1992), Hogan Personality Inventory (Hogan and Hogan 1992), the IPIP (Goldberg 1999)—include scores for various facets of each of the Big Five constructs along with evidence that these facet measures are somewhat independent of each other. If this is the case, then combining information from studies that represented different facets of one of the Big Five dimensions would have the potential to produce variability in validity coefficients. In recognition of this issue and with a different purpose in mind, Mount and Barrick (1995) and Salgado (1997) "corrected for construct validity" in recognition of the fact that some studies involved only a narrow facet of some Big Five dimension.

McHenry et al. (1990) provide primary validity data from Project A military work on more cases ($N = 4,039$) than several of the meta-analyses included in Table 7.2. Corrected validities for personality measures in that study were .26 and .25 for Core Technical Proficiency and General Soldiering Proficiency and in the low to mid .30s for "will do" criterion measures. Unless there is something unique about the military context in which the data were collected, this study suggests that some of the meta-analytic database used in the studies summarized in Table 7.2 underestimates the validity of personality tests, especially for motivational criteria.

These meta-analytic data appear to point to the need for additional primary studies in which personality measures are linked to outcomes that are more theoretically appropriate. For example, personality measures are related to overall job proficiency, but it might be more appropriate to link personality to the motivational components of performance (see Judge and Ilies 2003) for a relevant meta-analysis of personality-motivation relationships). It also may be worthwhile to consider more specific aspects of personality than the Big Five as some have argued and demonstrated with meta-analytic results not present in Table 7.2 (Conway, Lombardo, and Sanders 2001; Dudley et al. 2006; Hough 1992; 1998). The Conway et al. study also found higher correlations between peer ratings and personality variables than the correlations between subordinate ratings and personality. Finally, Ones, Viswesvaran, and Dilchert (2005) have argued that we should consider the validity of composites of the Big Five and maybe other composites as well. Their thesis is that each of the Big Five (or aspects of the Big Five) captures different portions of relevant criterion variance and that the validity of any one component underestimates the potential contribution of personality in the prediction of job performance criteria. Their position is supported by the findings in Table 7.2 for customer orientation and core self-evaluation as well as similar data for measures of violence, stress tolerance, and managerial potential (Ones, Hough, and Viswesvaran 1998; Ones and Viswesvaran 2000). These measures usually include items tapping different aspects of personality and the observed and corrected validities tend to be higher than those observed for individual aspects (i.e., one of the Big Five dimensions) of personality.

5. OTHER CONSTRUCTS

Beyond personality and cognitive ability, meta-analytic data on the validity of a variety of other constructs are available. Two meta-analyses of fit have been conducted and some of the available data from these two studies are presented in Table 7.3 broken down by the type of fit being measured. It appears that fit may be a valid predictor of job performance with validities between .15 and .20, but in all but one case the lower value of the confidence interval included zero and large portions of the variance in validities remained unexplained suggesting the importance of the moderator analyses performed by Kristof-Brown, Zimmerman, and Johnson (2005). It is also the case that measures of fit are more likely to predict other criteria than job performance such as commitment, satisfaction, and turnover as suggested by the meta-analyses provided by Kristof-Brown et al.

Hunter and Hunter (1984) examined experience and reported a corrected validity of .18 which was lower than that (.32) reported in a subsequent meta-analytic effort by McDaniel, Schmidt, and Hunter (1988). Quiñones, Ford, and Teachout (1995) have pointed out, though, the importance of the manner in which

Table 7.3 Meta-analyses of other constructs

	ρ	r̄	N	Criterion	90%CV	%VE	Moderators
Age							
Hunter and Hunter (1984)	−.01	NA	NA	Job performance	NA	NA	
McEvoy and Cascio (1989)	−.01	NA	NA	Training success	NA	NA	
	NA	.06	38,983	Job performance	−.09	15	Age range in sample[a]
Waldman and Avolio (1986)	NA	.06	3,660	Job performance	NA	18	Performance Criterion, Occupation[b]
Experience							
Hunter and Hunter (1984)	.18	NA	NA	Job performance	NA	NA	
	.01	NA	NA	Training success	NA	NA	
McDaniel, Schmidt, and Hunter (1988)	.32	.21	16,058	Job performance	.08	NA	Experience of sample, Job complexity[c]
Quiñones, Ford, and Teachour (1995)	.27	.22	25,911	Job performance	.12	13	Performance criterion, Type and specificity of experience measure[d]
Fit							
Arthur et al. (2006)	.15	.12	5,377	Job performance	−.05	32	Performance criterion[e]
Kristof-Brown, Zimmerman, and Johnson (2005)[f]	.20	.16	1,938	Overall job performance	−.04	30	Fit measurement method[g], Conceptualization of fit[h]
	.07	.05	5,827	Person–organization fit	−.14	18	Fit measurement method, Performance criterion[i]

Person–organization fit (Arthur et al. 2006 row), Person–job fit (Kristof-Brown row), Person–organization fit (last row)

(*continued*)

Table 7.3 (continued)

		ρ	r̄	N	Criterion	90%CV	%VE	Moderators
	Person-group fit	.15	.19	1,946		.03	100	Performance criterion[j]
	Person-supervisor fit	.15	.18	3,461		-.12	20	Fit measurement method
Grades								
Hunter and Hunter (1984)		.11	NA	1,089	Job performance	NA	NA	
		.30	NA		Training success	NA	NA	
Roth et al. (1996)	Grades	.35	.16	13,984	Job performance	.17	NA	Study publication year, Time since graduation[k]
Physical Ability								
Blakely et al. (1994)	Isometric Strength	.32	.28	1,364	Physical ability ratings	.32	100	
		.55	.55	1,364	Work simulation composite	.36	10	
Lewis (1989)[l]	Anthropometric	.26	NA	1,426	Supervisor ratings	NA	NA	Criterion[m]
	Muscular endurance	.23	NA	2,022		NA	NA	
	Muscular power	.26	NA	1,699		NA	NA	Criterion[n]
Schmitt et al. (1984)	Physical ability	NA	.32	3,103	Job performance	NA	12	
Other								
Hunter and Hunter (1984)	Education	.20	NA	NA	Job performance	NA	NA	
		.10	NA	NA	Training success	NA	NA	
	Interests	.10	NA	NA	Job performance	NA	NA	

| Job knowledge | .18 | NA | NA | Training success | NA | NA |
| | .48 | NA | NA | 3,078 | Job performance | .38 | NA |

Note: NA = not available.

[a] Validity was substantially higher for very young workers (17–22 years old) than all other workers; they highlight the potential for inflation depending on the age range of the validation sample.

[b] Validity varied by performance criterion: supervisory ratings ($r=-.14$), peer ratings ($r=.10$), and productivity ($r=.27$). Supervisory ratings were less negative for professional than non-professional occupations ($r=-.05$) and, likewise, peer ratings were more positive for professional than non-professional occupations ($r=.30$).

[c] Validity was higher for samples with lower mean levels of experience. Validity was generally higher for less complex jobs.

[d] Validity was higher for hard ($\rho=.39$) than for soft ($\rho=.24$) performance criteria. Validity was higher when experience was operationalized as amount of relevant task performance ($\rho=.43$) than when a measure of length of time or type of prior experience was used ($\rho=.27$ and $\rho=.21$, respectively). Validity was higher for task experience ($\rho=.41$) than for job experience ($\rho=.27$) and organization experience ($\rho=.16$).

[e] Validity was higher for contextual performance ($\rho=.22$) than for task performance ($\rho=.10$).

[f] Study included meta-analyses of a large number of other criteria; for the sake of space, we have presented results only for the outcome of overall performance. Authors presented the lower bound of the 95% confidence interval and that is what we report here as well. It is important to note that substantial variance remained unexplained after accounting for significant moderators.

[g] Direct measurement of fit (i.e., perceived fit) demonstrated higher validity than both indirect methods (subjective and objective fit based on person and environment variables). This same pattern was observed for fit with job, organization, and supervisor.

[h] Validity was higher for needs-supplies ($\rho=.20$) than for demands-abilities ($\rho=.12$) fit.

[i] Validity was higher for task performance ($\rho=.13$) and for contextual performance ($\rho=.27$).

[j] Validity was slightly higher for contextual performance ($\rho=.23$).

[k] Validity of grades was higher for studies published before 1961. Validity decreased as time elapsed since graduation increased.

[l] The findings from Lewis (1989) can be found in Hogan (1991). Muscular strength did not have a corresponding validity for supervisory ratings ($\rho=.82$ and $\rho=.23$ for work sample and training criteria, respectively).

[m] Validity was similar for training criteria but substantially higher for work samples ($\rho=.49$).

[n] Validity was higher for training criteria and work samples ($\rho=.30$ and $\rho=.37$, respectively).

experience is operationalized in considering its relationship to performance. Job knowledge also appears to be a reliable and substantial predictor of job performance ($\rho = .48$). Education and grades are also strong predictors of performance with Roth et al. (1996) reporting a relatively high ($\rho = .35$) validity; earlier estimates by Hunter and Hunter (1984) were not that encouraging. Physical ability displays substantial validity for predicting performance in jobs that require significant manual labor. Interests and age do not appear to be highly related to job performance though interests do appear to be related to training performance.

6. META-ANALYSIS OF METHODS OF MEASUREMENT

Personnel selection researchers have often failed to discriminate between the constructs they hope to measure and the methods whereby these constructs are measured (Schmitt, Clause, and Pulakos 1996). We often speak of the validity of interviews, work samples, or biodata; hence it is not surprising that we have meta-analyses of the validity of different types of methods. These meta-analyses are summarized in Table 7.4. Since these methods can be and are adapted to measure a variety of constructs including personality and cognitive ability, we should see that there are moderators of the validity of these methods. This is the case particularly for those meta-analytic results based on substantial numbers of studies and associated with relatively low levels of second-order sampling error (Arthur et al. 2003), interviews (Huffcutt and Arthur 1994; McDaniel et al. 1994; Wiesner and Cronshaw 1988), situational judgment tests (McDaniel et al. 2001), and work samples (Roth, Bobko, and McFarland 2005). In all of these cases, the percent of variance in validities after correction for statistical artifacts is quite high, indicating the possible presence of moderators. As the footnote to that table indicates, in some of these meta-analyses, moderators were identified.

Assessment centers have been used widely as a means of selecting and promoting managerial personnel. All meta-analyses of this method produce relatively high validity coefficients; the last and most comprehensive by Arthur et al. (2003) indicates an average corrected validity of .36 with a 90 percent credibility value of .23. The dimension (or construct) being evaluated was identified as a moderator.

The most comprehensive meta-analysis of biodata was reported by Rothstein et al. (1990). The average corrected validity was .32 with a 90 percent credibility value of .29. A surprisingly high percent of the variance (82 percent) was accounted for by the usual artifacts. This suggests that this method of measurement may be more consistently operationalized in terms of the construct(s) measured than are

Table 7.4 Meta-analyses of the validity of selection methods

	Predictor or Scale	ρ	r̄	N	Criterion	90%CV	%VE	Moderators
Assessment Centers								
Arthur et al. (2003)	OAR	.36	.28	83,761	Job performance	.23	34	Dimension[a]
Gaugler, et al. (1987)	OAR	.36	.25	4,180	Job performance	.18	57	Criterion, Purpose of center, Gender composition of group, Days of observation[b]
Hunter and Hunter (1984)[c]		.43	NA	NA	Job performance	NA	NA	
Schmitt et al. (1984)		NA	.41	3,103	Job performance	NA	100	
Biodata								
Rothstein et al. (1990)	SPR	.32	.26	11,332	Job performance	.29	82	
Hunter and Hunter (1984)		.37	NA	4,429	Job performance	.24	NA	
		.30	NA	9,024	Training success	.13	NA	
Schmitt et al. (1984)		NA	.32	3,998	Job performance	NA	16	
Interviews								
Huffcutt and Arthur (1994)		.37	.22	18,652	Job performance	.06	NA	Structure[d]
Hunter and Hunter (1984)		.14	.11	2,694	Job performance	NA	NA	
		.10	NA	3,544	Training success	.01	NA	
McDaniel et al. (1994)		.37	.15	25,244	Job performance	.08	NA	Content, Structure, Purpose of interview[e]

(continued)

Table 7.4 (continued)

Predictor or Scale	ρ	r̄	N	Criterion	90%CV	%VE	Moderators
Schmidt and Rader (1999)							
telephone interview	.36	.09	59,844	Training success	.24	NA	NA
	.40	.19	2,539	Job performance	.16	NA	Criterion[f]
Taylor and Small (2002)[g]							
situational questions (structured interviews)	.47	.26	2,142	Job performance	.19	NA	
past behavior questions (structured interviews)	.63	.35	1,119		.54	NA	
Wiesner and Cronshaw (1988)							
	.47	.26	51,549	Job performance	NA	14	Structure, Job analysis[h]
Wright, Lichtenfels, and Pursell (1989)							
structured interview	.39	.29	833	Job performance	.30	NA	
Peer Ratings							
Hunter and Hunter (1984)	.49	NA	8,202	Job performance	.30	NA	
Hunter and Hunter (1984)	.36	NA	1,406	Training success	.10	NA	
Reference Checks							
Hunter and Hunter (1984)	.26	NA	5,389	Job performance	.14	NA	
Hunter and Hunter (1984)	.23	NA	1,553	Training success	NA	NA	
Situational Judgment Tests							
McDaniel et al (2001)	.34	.26	10,640	Job performance	.16	45	Test development[i]
Training and Experience Methods							
McDaniel, Schmidt, and Hunter (1988)							
Point method	.11	.06	6,741	Job performance	−.20	44	Job experience[j]

Method / Study			N	Criterion			Job experience[j] / Year of study[k]
Illinois job element method	.20	.11	3,168	Job performance	.20	119	
Task method	.15	.08	991	Job performance	−.19	31	
Behavioral consistency method	.45	.25	1,148	Job performance	.33	82	
Work Sample							
Roth, Bobko, and McFarland (2005)	.33	.26	10,469	Job performance	.24	55	
Hunter and Hunter (1984)[i]	.54	NA	NA	Job performance	NA	NA	
	.50	NA	NA	Training success	NA	NA	
Schmitt et al. (1984)	NA	.32	3,998	Job performance	NA	100	

Notes: OAR = Overall Assessment Rating. SPR = Supervisory Profile Record (Richardson, Bellows, Henry and Co., Inc. 1981). NA = not available.

[a] Validity was highest for the dimensions of problem solving (ρ = .39), organization/planning (ρ = .37), and influencing others (ρ = .38).

[b] Validity was higher for the criterion of potential ratings (ρ = .53) than for job performance. The lowest validity observed was for those assessment centers with the purpose of promoting employees (ρ = .30). When job performance was the criterion, a larger proportion of female assessees was associated with higher validity as was a shorter period of AC observation.

[c] It is not clear whether the authors performed the meta-analysis resulting in the estimate for assessment center validity, because they included no discussion of its derivation or sources of data.

[d] Validity increased along with level of structure but reached a plateau (level 1, ρ = .20; level 2, ρ = .35; level 3, ρ = .56; level 4, ρ = .57).

[e] Validity varied by interview content such that it was higher for situational (ρ = .50) than for job-related (ρ = .39) or psychological (ρ = .29) interviews. Validity was higher for structured (ρ = .44) than for unstructured (ρ = .33) interviews. There was a downward bias in interview validity when the purpose was administrative (ρ = .36) versus research-based (ρ = .47).

[f] The reported validity was for supervisory ratings. Validity was equally high for production records (ρ = .40) and job tenure (ρ = .39) but lower for sales performance (ρ = .24) and absenteeism (ρ = .19).

[g] Rating scale type was identified as a confound. Results refer to those studies employing descriptively anchored rating scales.

[h] Validity of structured interviews (ρ = .62) was double that of unstructured interviews (ρ = .31). Validity was higher when questions were based on formal job analyses (ρ = .87) than "armchair" (ρ = .59) or unknown (ρ = .56) job analytic methods.

[i] Validity was higher for tests developed on the basis of a job analysis (ρ = .38 as opposed to ρ = .29).

[j] Based on a moderator analysis on one set of data (Molyneaux 1953), McDaniel, Schmidt, and Hunter (1988) provide evidence that the validity of point and task methods of training and experience ratings decreases with higher mean levels of applicant pool experience. Supposedly, the point and task methods assess variables that are less relevant at higher levels of experience.

[k] Validity was slightly higher for those studies published pre-1982 (ρ = .40) compared to later studies (ρ = .31).

[l] As noted by Roth, Bobko, and McFarland (2005), none of the studies contributing toward the estimate for work sample validity reported by Hunter and Hunter (1984) were named. Hence, it is not clear whether Hunter and Hunter performed the meta-analysis resulting in this figure.

the other methods summarized in Table 7.4. The Schmitt et al. (1984) meta-analysis containing studies representing far fewer people accounted for only 16 percent of the variance though they considered only sampling error as an explanation for the variance in validity coefficients.

Recent meta-analyses of interviews report corrected validities in the .30s and .40s. In all cases, interview structure moderated the validity such that more structured interviews were more valid than those that were unstructured. Beyond the effects of structure, as it is defined by Huffcutt and Arthur (1994), there is evidence that question type (Taylor and Small 2002) and interviewer training (Huffcutt and Woehr 1999) provide incremental validity. In all of the recent and relatively large-scale meta-analyses, a very large proportion of the variance in validity remains unexplained. Of the moderators examined, structure and content appear to be most often related to the magnitude of the validity.

A meta-analysis of situational judgment tests yielded a high average corrected validity (.34), but over half the variance in validity coefficients was not explained on the basis of artifacts. A similar finding for work samples was reported by Roth, Bobko, and McFarland (2005); they also reported that studies conducted before 1982 yielded higher validities than did those conducted after that date. This is consistent with the Hunter and Hunter (1984) analysis conducted twenty years before which yielded higher validity. Peer ratings, which are most frequently used in military contexts, yielded high average validities (corrected .49 against job performance) though the last meta-analysis conducted was that of Hunter and Hunter. The validity of reference checks was last examined meta-analytically by Hunter and Hunter also; they reported an average corrected validity of .26. Different types of documenting and scoring training and experience have been meta-analyzed (McDaniel, Schmidt, and Hunter 1988) with mostly disappointing results though there seems to be some evidence based on a relatively small sample that behavioral consistency methods may be promising.

Minimal and largely disappointing data on self-assessments, expert judgments, and projective tests (untabled) were reported by Reilly and Chao (1982). In an unpublished report that predates contemporary meta-analyses, Dunnette (1972) reported that the average corrected validity of ratings of performance during a job tryout period of workers in the petroleum industry was .44.

The credibility interval of most of these methods of measurement does not include zero, which means they can be useful in the assessment of worker potential along various dimensions, at least those assessed in the primary research that is summarized in Table 7.4. Most often it is likely that the dimensions measured are non-cognitive or motivational (e.g., interviews, biodata, assessment centers) though, even in the case of these methods, there is evidence that cognitive ability also plays a role (see Campion, Pursell, and Brown 1988 for a description of an interview that is highly cognitively loaded). Most assessment centers include an actual test of cognitive ability as well as ratings of performance in various exercises designed to produce information about interpersonal or motivational constructs. As mentioned above, describing the validity of methods of measurement is not too helpful if we want to understand the construct or knowledge, skill, or ability that is responsible for successful prediction. We do know that whatever construct(s) are being measured are in some way represented in the job performance domain. Practically, however, the data in Table 7.4 suggest that there are a variety of methods from which practitioners can choose to produce useful levels of predictions of worker performance.

6.1 Summative Statements

This review emphasized to us the very large body of data both in terms of primary studies and meta-analytic efforts to summarize the research that is available. It is also the case that we have chosen not to include some efforts that might be relevant to some researchers and we may have inadvertently missed other efforts that are pertinent. However, we believe that the research reviewed in this chapter supports some obvious conclusions. First, most obvious and most frequently stated by others, is the fact that many of the measures used in personnel selection can be used with great confidence that the validity of these measures in the prediction of job performance and training success will be non-zero and practically significant.

Second, for many of the constructs and methods used to assess human potential, the database we have is relatively old. As discussed above, this seems particularly true for cognitive ability where advancements in research design, measurement, and conceptualization of the job performance domain all suggest that large-scale multi-organization and multi-level studies (e.g., Ployhart and Schneider 2005) be conducted to update our database. We suspect that such studies could much more clearly articulate the role that cognitive ability plays in determining individual and organizational success. The Project A study that we have referenced several times in this chapter is a good example of a single study that provides more definitive data than do the many small studies that represent the existing database relevant to many important questions in personnel selection.

Third, we believe that large-scale carefully conducted studies of personality and other motivational constructs would have value. These studies should estimate the relationship of these measures with criteria other than simply task performance. More theoretically grounded relationships should be investigated that often will involve measures that are more specific than are the Big Five measures. At the same time, if broader overall performance is the criterion of interest, then we should assess the validity of the combination of measures used.

Fourth, it is certainly the case that one can combine measures of different constructs to achieve better predictability than is the case for the bivariate validity coefficients that are summarized in most of the meta-analyses described in this chapter. This has been demonstrated in many primary validity studies (e.g., Wise, McHenry, and Campbell 1990) as well as in meta-analytic efforts (e.g., Bobko, Roth, and Potosky 1999). Measures of motivational constructs are often not highly correlated with measures of cognitive ability; if both are related to performance, the combination of these two types of predictors will produce a composite that has superior validity.

Fifth, scientific ideas about validation have changed significantly in the last two decades. The relatively simple criterion-related study that is the basis of the meta-analyses summarized in our tables represents a very narrow, inadequate, and at times, overly restrictive operationalization of the validity of psychological measures. Employing the alternate methods of validation discussed at the beginning of this chapter may not provide the validity coefficients with which selection specialists are most familiar, but they should provide much better answers to scientific questions. These answers should also provide long-term practical improvements in personnel selection.

Finally, we hope our discussion and the data presented in Tables 7.1–7.4 represent practical and theoretical guidance to future researchers and practitioners in personnel selection.

References

AMERICAN EDUCATIONAL RESEARCH ASSOCIATION, AMERICAN PSYCHOLOGICAL ASSOCIATION, and NATIONAL COUNCIL ON MEASUREMENT IN EDUCATION. 1999. *Standards for Educational and Psychological Testing.* Washington, DC: American Educational Research Association.

ARTHUR, W. A., DAY, E. A., McNELLY, T. L., and EDENS, P. S. 2003. A meta-analysis of the criterion-related validity of assessment center dimensions. *Personnel Psychology,* 56: 125–54.

—— BELL, S. T., VILLADO, A. J., and DOVERSPIKE, D. 2006. The use of person-organization fit in employment decision making: an assessment of its criterion-related validity. *Journal of Applied Psychology,* 91: 786–801.

BARRICK, M. R., and MOUNT, M. K. 1991. The Big Five personality dimensions and job performance: a meta-analysis. *Personnel Psychology,* 44: 1–26.

—— —— and JUDGE, T. A. 2001. Personality and performance at the beginning of the new millennium: what do we know and where do we go next? *International Journal of Selection and Assessment,* 9: 9–30.

BERTUA, C., ANDERSON, N., and SALGADO, J. F. 2005. The predictive validity of cognitive ability tests: a UK meta-analysis. *Journal of Occupational and Organizational Psychology,* 78: 387–409.

BINNING, J., and BARRETT, G. V. 1989. Validity of personnel decisions: a conceptual analysis of the inferential and evidential bases. *Journal of Applied Psychology,* 74: 478–94.

BLAKELY, B. R., QUIÑONES, M. A., CRAWFORD, M. S., and JAGO, I. A. 1994. The validity of isometric strength tests. *Personnel Psychology*, 47: 247–474.

BOBKO, P., ROTH, P. L., and POTOSKY, D. 1999. Derivation and implications of a meta-analytic matrix incorporating cognitive ability, alternative predictors, and job performance. *Personnel Psychology*, 52: 561–90.

BORMAN, W. C., PENNER, L. A., ALLEN, T. D., and MOTOWIDLO, S. J. 2001. Personality predictors of citizenship performance. *International Journal of Selection and Assessment*, 91: 52–69.

CAMPION, M. A., PURSELL, E. D., and BROWN, B. K. 1988. Structured interviewing: raising the psychometric properties of the employment interview. *Personnel Psychology*, 41: 25–42.

CONWAY, J. M., LOMBARDO, K., and SANDERS, K. C. 2001. A meta-analysis of incremental validity and nomological networks for subordinate and peer ratings. *Human Performance*, 14: 267–304.

COSTA, P. T., Jr., and McCRAE, R. R. 1992. *Revised NEO Personality Inventory (NEO PI-R) and NEO Five Factor Inventory (FFI) Professional Manual*. Odessa, FL: Psychological Assessment Resources.

DUDLEY, N. M., ORVIS, K. A., LEBIECKI, J. E., and CORTINA, J. M. 2006. A meta-analytic investigation of conscientiousness in the prediction of job performance: examining the intercorrelations and the incremental validity of narrow traits. *Journal of Applied Psychology*, 91: 40–57.

DUNNETTE, M. D. 1972. *Validity Study Results for Jobs Relevant to the Petroleum Refining Industry*. Washington, DC: American Petroleum Institute.

EMBRETSON, S. E. 1998. A cognitive design system approach to generating valid tests: application to abstract reasoning. *Psychological Methods*, 3: 380–96.

FREI, R. L., and McDANIEL, M. A. 1998. Validity of customer service measures in personnel selection: a review of criterion and construct evidence. *Human Performance*, 11: 1–27.

GAUGLER, B. B., ROSENTHAL, D. B., THORNTON, G. C., and BENTSON, C. 1987. Meta-analysis of assessment center validity. *Journal of Applied Psychology*, 72: 493–511.

GOLDBERG, L. R. 1999. A broad-bandwidth public-domain personality inventory measuring the lower-level facets of several five-factor models. Pp. 7–28 in *Personality Psychology in Europe*, vol. vii, ed. I. Mervielde, I. Deary, F. De Fruyt, and F. Ostendorf. Tilburg: Tilburg University Press.

GUION, R. M., and HIGHHOUSE, S. 2006. *Essentials of Personnel Assessment and Selection*. Mahwah, NJ: Lawrence Erlbaum and Associates.

HOGAN, J. 1991. Physical abilities. Pp. 753–831 in *Handbook of Industrial and Organizational Psychology*, 2nd edn., vol. ii, ed. M. D. Dunnette, and L. M. Hough. Palo Alto, CA: Consulting Psychologists Press.

—— and HOLLAND, B. 2003. Using theory to evaluate personality and job-performance relations: a socioanalytic perspective. *Journal of Applied Psychology*, 88: 100–12.

HOGAN, R., and HOGAN, J. 1992. *Manual for the Hogan Personality Inventory*. Tulsa, OK: Hogan Assessment Systems.

HOUGH, L. M. 1992. The "Big Five" personality variables—construct confusion: description versus prediction. *Human Performance*, 5: 139–55.

—— 1998. Personality at work: issues and evidence. In *Beyond Multiple Choice: Evaluating Alternatives to Traditional Testing for Selection*, ed. M. D. Hakel. Mahwah, NJ: Lawrence Erlbaum and Associates.

HUFFCUTT, A. I., and ARTHUR, W. 1994. Hunter and Hunter (1984) revisited: interview validity for entry-level jobs. *Journal of Applied Psychology*, 79: 184–90.

—— and WOEHR 1999. Further analysis of employment interview validity: a quantitative evaluation of interviewer-related structuring methods. *Journal of Organizational Behavior*, 20: 549–60.

HUNTER, J. E. 1983. *Test Validation for 12,000 Jobs: An Application of Job Classification and Validity Generalization Analysis to the General Aptitude Test Battery*. Washington, DC: US Department of Labor, Employment Services.

—— and HUNTER, R. F. 1984. Validity and utility of alternative predictors of job performance. *Psychological Bulletin*, 96: 72–95.

HURTZ, G. M., and DONOVAN, J. J. 2000. Personality and job performance: the Big Five revisited. *Journal of Applied Psychology*, 85: 869–79.

JUDGE, T. A., and BONO, J. E. 2001. Relationship of core self-evaluation traits—self-esteem, generalized self-efficacy, locus of control, and emotional stability—with job satisfaction and job performance: a meta-analysis. *Journal of Applied Psychology*, 86: 80–92.

—— and ILIES, R. 2003. Relationship of personality to performance motivation: a meta-analytic review. *Journal of Applied Psychology*, 87: 797–807.

KLEIN, K. J., and KOZLOWSKI, S. W. J. 2000. *Multilevel Theory, Research, and Methods in Organizations*. San Francisco: Jossey-Bass.

KRISTOF-BROWN, A. L., ZIMMERMAN, R. D., and JOHNSON, E. C. 2005. Consequences of individuals' fit at work: a meta-analysis of person-job, person-organization, person-group, and person-supervisor fit. *Personnel Psychology*, 58: 281–342.

KUNCEL, N. R., HEZLETT, S. A., and ONES, D. S. 2004. Academic performance, career potential, creativity, and job performance: can one construct predict them all? *Journal of Personality and Social Psychology*, 86: 148–61.

KYLLONEN, P. C. 1994. Cognitive abilities testing: an agenda for the 1990s. In *Personnel Selection and Classification*, ed. M. G. Rumsey, C. B. Walker, and J. B. Harris. Hillsdale, NJ: Lawrence Erlbaum and Associates.

LEWIS, R. E. 1989. Physical ability tests as predictors of job-related criteria: a meta-analysis. Unpublished manuscript.

McDANIEL, M. A., SCHMIDT, F. L., and HUNTER, J. E. 1988. A meta-analysis of the validity of methods for rating training and experience in personnel selection. *Personnel Psychology*, 41: 283–309.

—— WHETZEL, D. L., SCHMIDT, F. L., and MAURER, S. D. 1994. The validity of employment interviews: a comprehensive review and meta-analysis. *Journal of Applied Psychology*, 79: 599–616.

—— MORGESON, F. P., FINNEGAN, E. B., CAMPION, M. A., and BRAVERMAN, E. P. 2001. Use of situational judgment tests to predict job performance: a clarification of the literature. *Journal of Applied Psychology*, 86: 730–40.

McEVOY, G. M., and CASCIO, W. F. 1989. Cumulative evidence of the relationship between employee age and job performance. *Journal of Applied Psychology*, 74: 11–17.

McHENRY, J. J., HOUGH, L. M., TOQUAM, J. L., HANSON, M. A., and ASHWORTH, S. 1990. Project A validity results: the relationship between predictor and criterion domains. *Personnel Psychology*, 43: 335–54.

MESSICK, S. 1998. Test validity: a matter of consequence. *Social Indicators Research*, 45: 35–44.

MOLYNEAUX, J. W. 1953. An evaluation of unassembled examinations. Unpublished master's thesis, The George Washington University, Washington, DC.

MOUNT, M. K., and BARRICK, M. R. 1995. The Big Five personality dimensions: implications for research and practice in human resources management. Pp. 153–200 in *Research in Personnel and Human Resources Management*, vol. xiii, ed. K. M. Rowland and G. Ferris. Greenwich, CT: JAI Press.

—— —— and STEWART, G. L. 1998. Five Factor Model of personality and performance in jobs involving interpersonal interactions. *Human Performance*, 11: 145–65.

ONES, D. S., and VISWESVARAN, C. 1998. The effects of social desirability and faking on personality and integrity assessment for personnel selection. *Human Performance*, 11: 245–70.

—— —— 2000. Personality-based stress tolerance scales used in personnel selection. Paper presented at the 108th Annual Convention of the American Psychological Association, Washington, DC, August.

—— HOUGH, L. M., and VISWESVARAN, C. 1998. Validity and adverse impact of personality-based managerial potential scales. Paper presented at the thirteenth annual meeting of the Society for Industrial-Organizational Psychology, Inc., Dallas, TX.

—— VISWESVARAN, C., and DILCHERT, S. 2005. Personality at work: raising awareness and correcting misconceptions. *Human Performance*, 18: 389–404.

—— —— and SCHMIDT, F. L. 1993. Comprehensive meta-analysis of integrity test validities: findings and implications for personnel selection and theories of job performance. *Journal of Applied Psychology*, 78: 679–703.

ORGAN, D. W., and RYAN, K. 1995. A meta-analytic review of attitudinal and dispositional predictors of organizational citizenship behavior. *Personnel Psychology*, 48: 775–802.

PAULHUS, D. L. 1991. Measurement and control of response bias. Pp. 17–59 in *Measures of Personality and Social Psychology Attitudes*, ed. J. P. Robinson, P. R. Shaver, and L. S. Wrightsman. San Diego: Academic Press.

PLOYHART, R. E., and SCHNEIDER, B. 2005. Multilevel selection and prediction: theories, methods, and models. Pp. 495–516 in *Handbook of Personnel Selection*, ed. A. Evers, O. Smit-Voskuyl, and N. R. Anderson. Chichester/London: Wiley.

—— —— and SCHMITT, N. 2006. *Staffing Organizations: Contemporary Practice and Theory*. Mahwah, NJ: Lawrence Erlbaum and Associates.

QUIÑONES, M. A., FORD, J. K., and TEACHOUT, M. S. 1995. The relationship between work experience and job performance: a conceptual and meta-analytic review. *Personnel Psychology*, 48: 887–910.

RAJU, N. S., and ELLIS, B. B. 2002. Differential item and test functioning. Pp. 156–88 in *Measuring and Analyzing Behavior in Organizations*, ed. F. Drasgow and N. Schmitt. San Francisco: Jossey-Bass.

REE, M. J., and EARLES, J. A. 1991. Predicting training success: not much more than g. *Personnel Psychology*, 44: 321–32.

—— —— 1992. Intelligence is the best predictor of job performance. *Current Directions in Psychological Science*, 1: 86–9.

REILLY, R. R., and CHAO, G. T. 1982. Validity and fairness of some alternative employee selection procedures. *Personnel Psychology*, 35: 1–62.

RICHARDSON, BELLOWS, HENRY AND CO., INC. 1981. Supervisory Profile Record (Tech. Reps., vols. i, ii, and iii). Washington, DC: Author.

ROTH, P. L., BOBKO, P., and McFARLAND, L. A. 2005. A meta-analysis of work sample test validity: updating and integrating some classic literature. *Personnel Psychology*, 58: 1009–37.

—— BeVIER, C. A., SWITZER, F. S., and SCHIPPMANN, J. S. 1996. Meta-analyzing the relationship between grades and job performance. *Journal of Applied Psychology*, 81: 548–56.

ROTHSTEIN, H. R., SCHMIDT, F. L., ERWIN, F. W., OWENS, W. A., and SPARKS, C. P. 1990. Biographical data in employment selection: can validities be made generalizable? *Journal of Applied Psychology*, 75: 175–84.

SALGADO, J. F. 1997. The Five Factor Model of personality and job performance in the European Community. *Journal of Applied Psychology*, 82: 30–45.

—— ANDERSON, N., MOSCOSO, S., BERTUA, C., and DE FRUYT, F. 2003a. International validity generalization of GMA and cognitive abilities: a European Community meta-analysis. *Personnel Psychology*, 56: 537–605.

—— —— —— —— —— and ROLLAND, J. P. (2003b). A meta-analytic study of general mental ability validity for different occupations in the European Community. *Journal of Applied Psychology*, 88: 1068–81.

SCHMIDT, F. L. 1992. What do data really mean? Research findings, meta-analysis, and cumulative knowledge in psychology. *American Psychologist*, 47: 1173–81.

—— and HUNTER, J. E. 1977. Development of a general solution to the problem of validity generalization. *Journal of Applied Psychology*, 62: 529–40.

—— —— 1981. Employment testing: old theories and new research findings. *American Psychologist*, 36: 1128–37.

—— —— 1998. The validity and utility of selection methods in personnel psychology: practical and theoretical implications of 85 years of research findings. *Psychological Bulletin*, 124: 262–74.

—— and RADER, M. 1999. Exploring the boundary conditions for interview validity: meta-analytic validity findings for a new interview type. *Personnel Psychology*, 52: 445–64.

—— CLAUSE, C., and PULAKOS, E. D. 1996. Subgroup differences associated with different measures of some common job-related constructs. Pp. 115–40 in *International Review of Industrial and Organizational Psychology*, vol. xi, ed. C. R. Cooper and I. T. Robertson. New York: Wiley.

—— GOODING, R. Z., NOE, R. A., and KIRSCH, M. 1984. Meta-analyses of validity studies published between 1964 and 1982 and the investigation of study characteristics. *Personnel Psychology*, 37: 407–22.

SOCIETY FOR INDUSTRIAL AND ORGANIZATIONAL PSYCHOLOGY. 2003. *Principles for the Validation and Use of Personnel Selection Procedures*. Bowling Green, OH: Author.

TAYLOR, P. J., and SMALL, B. 2002. Asking applicants what they would do versus what they did do: a meta-analytic comparison of situational and past behaviour employment interview questions. *Journal of Occupational and Organizational Psychology*, 75: 277–94.

TETT, R. P., JACKSON, D. N., and ROTHSTEIN, M. 1991. Personality measures as predictors of job performance: a meta-analytic review. *Personnel Psychology*, 44: 703–42.

—— —— —— and REDDON, J. R. 1994. Meta-analysis of personality-job performance relations: a reply to Ones, Mount, Barrick, and Hunter (1994). *Personnel Psychology*, 47: 157–72.

VINCHUR, A. J. 2007. A history of psychology applied to employee selection. In *Historical Perspectives in Industrial and Organizational Psychology*, ed. L. L. Koppes. Mahwah, NJ: Lawrence Erlbaum and Associates.

WALDMAN, D. A., and AVOLIO, B. J. 1986. A meta-analysis of age differences in job performance. *Journal of Applied Psychology*, 71: 33–8.

WIESNER, W. H., and CRONSHAW, S. F. 1988. A meta-analytic investigation of the impact of interview format and degree of structure on the validity of the employment interview. *Journal of Occupational Psychology*, 61: 275–90.

WISE, L. L., MCHENRY, J., and CAMPBELL, J. P. 1990. Identifying optimal predictor composites and testing for generalizability across jobs and performance factors. *Human Performance*, 43: 355–66.

WRIGHT, P. M., LICHTENFELS, P. A., and PURSELL, E. D. 1989. The structured interview: additional studies and a meta-analysis. *Journal of Occupational Psychology*, 62: 191–9.

8

THE EFFECTIVE INTERVIEW

MELINDA BLACKMAN

1. INTRODUCTION

THE face of the employment interview has been gradually transforming over the past fifty years with the culmination of new research, theory, and practices. Now more than ever, researchers and human resource professionals are demanding interview formats that accurately and reliably predict a plethora of criteria (e.g. organizational citizenship, integrity, personality traits, person–organization fit, the candidate's motivation and true behavior) in addition to the job candidate's skill set. No longer is the implementation of the traditional structured interview format sufficient for screening applicants. Campbell and Fiske's (1959) convergent multiple trait multiple method approach is becoming the standard in many organizations as several interview venues (e.g., panel interviews, multiple applicant interviews, face-to-face media) and interviewers are being implemented to increase the interview's predictive validity and subsequently decrease employee turnover. The effective interview is on its way to being transformed into a multifaceted instrument that aims to surpass the predictive precision of standardized selection tests.

2. THE EFFECTIVE INTERVIEW: A CULMINATION OF RESEARCH, THEORY, AND PRACTICE

Good morning Ms Anderson, I'm Mr Randall and I will be conducting your interview. Please, have a seat. So, tell me about yourself and why you applied for this position at our company?

Up until the 1990s, this basic scenario is what an applicant could expect to encounter during an employment interview. Since this time, the face of the employment interview has rapidly evolved. To illustrate the employment interview's tremendous metamorphosis over the past five decades, take a glimpse at what current and future job applicants should now anticipate their interview process to entail:

Good morning Ms Anderson, I'm Mr Randall and I will be conducting your first interview this morning. Here is your agenda of interview activities that you will be participating in. As you see, after our interview concludes, you will participate in a panel interview with Ms Zavala, Mr Mears, and Ms Kahne. Next, you will proceed to that computer terminal for an online knowledge and personality test. After that, you will enter that cubicle and complete all of the tasks that are located in your "In-Basket." Also, the CEO of our organization would like to meet you, though he is out of the country at this time, so you will have a brief videoconference with him. Last, Mr Harrigan will give you an informal tour of the organization over coffee. The entire process usually lasts no longer than six hours.

The transformation of the employment interview from a staid two-person inter-action with a predictable script of questions to a dynamic, multifaceted, multi-person encounter did not occur over night. Not only did the format of the employment interview receive a face-lift over the past five decades, but the criterion that the interview was originally meant to predict (job performance) has increased twofold to encompass aspects such as person–job fit, person–organization fit, organizational citizenship, and personality characteristics such as honesty and integrity. This chapter will lead you through the metamorphosis of the employment interview over the last five decades, it will outline the impetus of research, theory, and practice that spurred on the interview's transformation and the long-term payoff that employers are receiving from the changes. You will also receive a glimpse of where the employment interview is headed in the upcoming decade and the factors that make today's employment interview so effective.

3. A Retrospective Examination of the Employment Interview: Research, Theory, and Practice through the 1980s

Professional and scholarly interest in the functionality of the employment interview has steadily increased over the past fifty years (Posthuma, Morgeson, and Campion 2002). To illustrate this point, I conducted a keyword search for the words "employment interview" on Psych Info, an electronic database, during each of the past five decades. From 1960 to 1969, a mere 6 articles/dissertations were published on the topic of employment interviews, with the 1970s showing a slight increase with 17 articles produced. The 1980s and 1990s produced a steady increase in articles, 41 and 49 articles respectively. My search from the year 2000 to the present, 2007, revealed that 86 articles were published on the topic of employment interviews, a definite marked increase from the 1960s. Keep in mind that this search does not include unpublished works or papers presented at conferences.

This abridged retrospective look at employment interview theory, research, and practice over each of the five decades will unfold some of the events for you that have led to the transformation of the "employment interview" as we now know it in the twenty-first century. Through the 1960s, 1970s, and 1980s, theory about the factors that affect an employment interview's validity and reliability was extremely limited and fragmented (Campion, Palmer, and Campion 1998; McDaniel, Whetzel, and Schmidt 1994). Research on the topic of employment interviews during this time period was just entering its infancy. At this time many researchers tended to put the carriage before the horse and incorrectly assume that the employment interview, for the most part, was a reliable and valid measure or they simply ignored the issue of its validity altogether. Instead, these researchers focused on ancillary aspects of the employment interview that were timely and on the front burner of society's concerns, such as discrimination in the interview process (Anderson 1960; Arvey 1979; Fugita, Wexley, and Hillery 1974; Rand and Wexley 1975; Wexley, Yuke, and Kovacs 1972). The practical impetus for much of the employment interview research during the 1960s and 1970s was the legal ramifications that employers could face if their interview process was biased in nature and discriminated against under-represented groups such as blacks, females, the elderly, and disabled persons. Many researchers believed that the interviewer's perception of the applicant's non-verbal behavior and their expectancies were the keys to eliminating non-discriminatory interviews (Arvey 1979; Fugita, Wexley, and Hillery 1974; Rand and Wexley 1975; Washburn and Hakel 1973; Young and Beier 1977). Specific aspects such as the applicant's visual cues and verbal content, and contrast effects between the applicants, were studied to determine their possible contributory effects in biasing the interviewer's perception of the minority applicant (Wexley, Yukl, and Kovacs 1972).

With two decades of research under their belts, researchers felt that they had a handle on eliminating discriminatory interview practices. The answer after twenty years of research pointed to the retraining of interviewers' person perception skills and their expectancies (Cogger 1982; Graves and Powell 1988; Posthuma, Morgeson, and Campion 2002). As researchers in the 1980s dug into improving the interviewer's processing skills, another related issue reared its head, that of generalizability (Posthuma, Morgeson, and Campion 2002). Up until this time, much of the research on the employment interview was conducted with fictitious applicants or "paper applicants" (Gorman, Clover, and Doherty 1978; Graves and Powell 1988). The push and necessity to use real applicants became apparent during this time period as the validity of two decades of "interview" research was starting to be questioned (Cogger 1982; Gorman, Clover, and Doherty 1978;).

Mainstream interview practices up through the 1980s were in some sense a "fly by the seat of your pants" process. Employers who conducted what they thought were structured interviews, sometimes would have a list of questions that they would ask each applicant or modify and create questions along the way. However, their method of administering the questions was far from standardized, leaving itself short of the true definition of a structured interview, in which standardization of the questions and procedures with each applicant is required (Baker and Spier 1990; Campion, Palmer, and Campion 1998; McDaniel, Whetzel, and Schmidt 1994). Also, the interviewers had no real way of knowing the predictive validity of the questions that they chose to ask and instead relied on the "we have always done it this way" approach to the interview process. Interestingly enough, interviewers who thought they were conducting structured interviews were probably implementing unstructured interview formats unbeknownst to them (Campion, Palmer, and Campion 1998).

4. RESEARCH, THEORY, AND PRACTICE IN THE 1990S

During the 1990s, the need for "interview" theory became apparent as it was very fragmented up until this point. The delineation between a structured and unstructured interview format at this time was simplistic and vague at most (Campion, Palmer, and Campion 1998). Suddenly the issue of discriminatory interview practices was now being overtaken by validity and reliability concerns, and for the first time, the carriage was being put behind the horse with regard to interview research and theory (Biesanz, Newberg, and Judice 1999; Campion, Palmer, and Campion 1998; Kacmar and Hochwarter 1996; McDaniel, Whetzel, and Schmidt 1994).

Campion, Palmer, and Campion (1998) attacked the lack of theory head on in reiterating formal definitions and delineations between the structured and the unstructured interview formats. Campion et al. detailed specifically how to improve the reliability and validity of one's interview process by creating a structured interview that adheres strictly to its definition (e.g., questions derived from a job analysis, standardization of questions, etc.). Campion and colleagues were also strong advocates of critically examining the effect sizes of interview studies before giving credence to their findings. Obtaining accurate and predictive interview results was now at the forefront of researchers' minds, replacing their short-sighted concerns of discriminatory perceptual biases in the interview process.

With the advent of the internet and burgeoning technology in the 1990s, many new interview formats were becoming available to interviewers to implement. Applicants and interviewers who, for whatever reason, could not be available in the same location for the interview to occur, could turn to telephone conference calls or videoconferencing. Panel interviews, in which multiple persons simultaneously interview the applicant, were being used more frequently to increase the reliability and predictive validity of the interview process (Dipboye, Gaugler, and Hayes 1997; Kacmar and Hochwarter 1996). And organizations that were either constrained by time or finances were turning to the group interview or multiple applicant interview, in which several applicants are interviewed simultaneously by one interviewer, as their panacea (Tran and Blackman 2006). However, with these new and varied interview practices came the unknown with regard to their validity and reliability, an issue researchers later tackled (Blackman 2002a; 2002b; Chapman and Rowe 2002; Straus, Miles, and Levesque 2001; Tran and Blackman 2006).

During this time period, organizations such as the Society for Human Resource Management, the Academy of Management, and the American Society of Personnel Administration were more prominently serving as liaisons between researchers and the human resource practitioner out in the field. These organizations and their publications were instrumental in disseminating knowledge about ensuring the validity and reliability of interview practices and formulating predictive interview questions based upon job analyses. Up until this time, most practitioners developed their own interview questions from scratch, oblivious to validity issues. Savvy researchers, however, were beginning to see the need for interview questions that actually predicted the criteria of individual and varied job descriptions. With this clear need identified, some researchers took it upon themselves to give this service to the practitioner by creating predictive tailor-made interview questions. Suddenly, companies, consulting services, and software programs that offered the service of providing predictive interview questions, tailor made for each practitioner's job description, moved into the limelight (Reid London House 2007). These types of companies helped to increase the validity and reliability of interviews for organizations who could afford their services or software, yet many organizations remained in the dark as to the validity and reliability concerns that potentially plagued their interview practices.

The lucrative liaison between researchers and practitioners also produced an unexpected turnaround in the academic community. These forged relationships facilitated researchers' access to applied, real-world samples of interview behavior. No longer were academicians limited to basing their studies on fictitious paper-and-pencil applicants or utilizing the college student as their pseudo job applicant (Arvey and Campion 1982; Gorman, Clover, and Doherty 1978; Posthuma, Morgeson, and Campion 2002). Researchers now had more opportunities to link their research to actual outcome measures such as job offers and acceptance rates.

5. Research, Theory, and Practice in the Twenty-First Century

Research and theory development in the 1990s gave researchers and practitioners alike confidence in the utility of the structured interview (if conducted properly) as a valid and reliable method for predicting a candidate's future job performance. But being able to predict a job applicant's skill set was not enough for practitioners in the 1990s, as it did not fix the ever present problem that many employers are plagued with, that of turnover. Yes, the incumbent may be able to effectively execute his or her job on a daily basis, but in many cases the long-term costs of hiring that person would sooner or later take their toll on the organization. Practitioners were finding that even "qualified" new hires were still either leaving the organization or being terminated from their positions for reasons unrelated to their skills set. Researchers and practitioners alike were coming to the realization that assessing a job candidate's skill set is simply not an adequate criterion to ensure that the individual will have a long tenure with the organization. "What constructs are we really assessing in the interview process and what constructs should we be assessing?" became prominent research queries that researchers are now vigorously pursuing in the twenty-first century (Posthuma, Morgeson, and Campion 2002; Raymark, Schmit, and Guion 1997; Werbel and Gilliland 1999).

6. Constructs Relevant to the Employment Interview

By examining contributory sources of turnover, researchers were able to pinpoint crucial constructs that were overlooked and simply not assessed during employment interviews, but would undoubtedly lead to turnover if not assessed (Chuang 2001; Cook and Vance 2000). The most prominent overlooked broad construct during the employment interview was "personality" (Cook and Vance 2000; Christiansen, Wolcott-Burnam, and Janovics 2005; Roth et al. 2005; Townsend, Bacigalupi, and Blackman 2007; Van Dam 2003). Sure most practitioners come away from an interview with a gut feeling as to whether the candidate was a nice person or not, but without using any specific criterion-related questions. What are the implications for an organization which does not accurately assess an individual candidate's personality? The implications are far and wide, especially if this candidate is hired (Cook and Vance 2000; Townsend, Bacigalupi, and Blackman 2007). An accurate assessment of a job candidate's personality can predict an entire host of behaviors that could ultimately lead to turnover, either initiated by the candidate or the organization in the form of termination (Barrick, Patton, and Haugland 2000). First, consider the concept of person–job fit. Does the applicant have personality traits that are a conducive fit with the job description or better yet with the climate of the entire organization? For example, suppose an introverted applicant interviews for an accounting position with an advertising firm and if hired will be dealing with many extroverted, high-energy salespersons. The climate of the organization will probably be too overpowering for this applicant, resulting in a lack of person–job fit or more specifically person–organization fit, ultimately perhaps ending in the candidate leaving the organization (Werbel and Gilliland 1999).

An applicant's potential to engage in counter-productive behavior is another personality-related factor that can contribute to turnover (Ones and Viswesvaran 1998; Townsend, Bacigalupi, and Blackman 2007). Ideally, during the interview process, savvy interviewers should ask themselves these questions about the candidate's integrity: "Will he, if denied a raise or a fringe benefit, steal from the organization, sabotage co-workers' projects or the reputation of the organization? Can I trust him to keep track of his work hours correctly without having him punch in on a time clock? If the amount of cash in the till at the end of the day is short, will he fudge the numbers to try to rectify the problem?" These are the type of integrity-related issues that need to be considered when interviewing applicants.

Some personality characteristics that are linked to a candidate's potential to engage in counter-productive behavior are dependability and conscientiousness (Organ 1988; Townsend, Bacigalupi, and Blackman 2007; Van Dam 2003). The lack of these prominent tendencies could lead to an entire gamut of counter-productive actions such as tardiness, absenteeism, volatile behavior, or even lack of attention to detail in tasks in which human life is at risk (e.g., air traffic controling, 911 dispatching, medical laboratory technicians, etc.) (Taylor and Small 2002). No doubt the long-term repercussions of failing to assess these crucial traits would be financial loss, human life lost, and of course turnover.

The construct of organizational citizenship is related as well to the personality characteristics of dependability and conscientiousness. Originally Organ (1988) proposed that organizational citizenship behavior consists of five categories of behavior that, over time and across people, influence an organization's effectiveness. These five personality-relevant categories are:

1. Conscientiousness—will the employee exert effort beyond their formal requirement?
2. Altruism—will the employee help new colleagues and give freely of their time?
3. Sportsmanship—will the employee engage in complaining, whining, and carping when things do not go their way?
4. Courtesy—will the employee give advance notice if he or she is to take the day off?
5. Civic virtue—will the employee voluntarily participate on committees and other relevant activities?

More recently there are several models proposed as to the exact personality constructs that make up organizational citizenship (DiPaola and Tschannen-Moran 2001; Skarlicki and Latham 1995). Nonetheless, a job candidate's potential to engage in prosocial behavior should be assessed and regarded highly.

Recent national events and the mass media have brought the concept of workplace counter-productive behavior into the public's view. And this in turn has initiated a surge of interest by researchers, in proactive methods to reduce employee counter-productive behavior. One proactive method that has received a lot of attention is personality assessment. More specifically, researchers believe that by being able to accurately assess a job candidate's personality traits during an employment interview, future workplace counter-productive behavior will be reduced (Blackman 2002a; 2002b; Cook and Vance 2000; Townsend, Bacigalupi, and Blackman 2007; Tran and Blackman 2006; Van Dam 2003). The first priority of interest for many of these researchers is determining "How accurate is the average practitioner or lay interviewer at detecting job-relevant personality traits during the employment interview?" Of course, this question is not nearly as relevant for organizations that rely solely on the use of personality inventories to assess their criteria. However, the answer for the previous question is crucial for the thousands upon thousands of organizations that do not have the time or the finances to take this route, and rely on their gut impression of the candidate's personality characteristics during the employment interview. So, how accurate an impression of the candidate's personality do these lay interviewers come away from the interview with? According to Blackman (2002a; 2000b) it depends upon the type of interview format that is used and not necessarily the type of personality-relevant questions that are asked. Blackman (2002a) compared the accuracy of personality judgments made by lay judges who either administered a structured interview format or an unstructured interview format. Blackman found that lay interviewers produced significantly more accurate personality judgments of the job applicants when an unstructured interview format was used, and self–interviewer and peer–interviewer agreement were used as the criteria for accuracy. Even more interesting was the finding that the structured interview format contained significantly more personality-relevant interview questions than did the unstructured format. Interviewers in the structured format were told to stick to asking the eleven personality-relevant questions developed from a job analysis and to not deviate from their scripts. Interviewers in the unstructured condition were told to ask any questions that came to mind and that they thought were relevant to the job description. A neutral third party recorded each of the questions asked during both interview formats and timed both formats, while coding the verbal and non-verbal behavior of both the interviewer and applicant. Ultimately, it was found that the applicants in the unstructured format appeared more at ease and talked significantly longer than those applicants in the structured format, offering more information about themselves. Also, interviewers in the unstructured format asked significantly more follow-up questions than those interviewers in the structured format.

Blackman (2002a) believes that the casual nature of the unstructured format and the unpredictability of the interview questions acts as a catalyst, so that applicants will volunteer more information about themselves. This increased supply of information allows the interviewer of personality more information to base their judgment on in comparison to the interviewers in the structured format. Based upon past research (Campion, Palmer, and Campion 1998; Conway, Jako, and Goodman 1995), Blackman advises that an unstructured interview should be used as a follow-up to the structured interview, which is still superior to the unstructured interview in predicting a candidate's future performance skills. In other words, the structured interview should serve as a screening device for performance-based skills. Then, the promising candidates culled from this interview format should be screened for relevant personality traits during the unstructured interview.

7. Personality Assessment and a Myriad of Interview Formats

In addition to the structured and unstructured interview format, researchers have turned their attention to examining other increasingly popular interview formats in hopes of determining their validity to assess a job candidate's personality (Blackman 2002b; Chapman and Rowe 2002; Dipboye, Gaugler, and Hayes 1997; Tran and Blackman 2006; Straus, Miles, and Levesque 2001; Townsend, Bacigalupi, and Blackman 2007). Blackman (2002b), for instance, looked at the structured face-to-face interview format vs. the structured telephone conference call. Many organizations routinely use the telephone conference call as a first point of contact with their job applicants. Even though the telephone conference call is an efficient preliminary screening tool, does efficiency have its price, Blackman wondered (2002b)? Through the course of her research, Blackman found that significantly more accurate personality judgments about the candidates were made by the lay interviewers when the face-to-face interview format was utilized instead of the telephone conference call. Why would this be, when both formats contained the same interview questions? Again the verbal and non-verbal behavior of both the candidate and interviewer was coded in Blackman's study. It was found that the candidates in the face-to-face interview gave longer responses to each of the interview questions in comparison to the telephone candidates. Also, interviewers in the face-to-face condition (even though they were forbidden to do so) asked significantly more follow-up questions than those interviewers in the telephone format. It is believed that the interviewers in the face-to-face format were detecting the applicants' non-verbal behavior and, if their non-verbal cues were not clear or were inconsistent, they would seek clarification with a follow-up question. However, the telephone interviewers did not have the opportunity to detect the candidate's non-verbal behavior, thus they were not prompted to ask follow-up questions in response to vague non-verbal behavior and subsequently gain more information about the candidate. The take-home message from Blackman's (2002b) study was that the interviewer's detection of the candidate's non-verbal behavior plays an important role in accurate personality assessment, and interview formats that reduce or eliminate the opportunity for the interviewer to detect this behavior are sacrificing accuracy for cost efficiency.

Tran and Blackman (2006) followed up further on another cost-efficient interview method, the group interview, and its ability to accurately predict the job candidate's personality traits. The group interview, or the multiple applicant interview format, consists of two or more job applicants being interviewed simultaneously by one interviewer. This interview format has grown in popularity over the years by organizations that hire seasonal help and need to interview a large number of applicants in a short period of time. The researchers compared the accuracy of the personality judgments made by the interviewers who implemented the group interview, with the personality judgments made by the interviewers who implemented the traditional structured one-on-one interview format. As you could have probably surmised, the interviewers in the one-on-one format were significantly more accurate in their personality assessments of the candidates than those interviewers in the group interview format. The data from the study suggest that it is the inherent cognitive multitasking that the group interviewer relies on that compromises the interviewer's overall judgment process, helping to explain this previous finding. Tran and Blackman caution organizations that use the group interview to only use it as a preliminary skills screening measure and then to follow up with those qualified applicants by using an unstructured or at least a one-on-one format. Blackman and her colleagues have found that cost-efficient interview formats all seem to have one aspect in common, they sacrifice accuracy for efficiency and this sacrifice can be detrimental to the health of any organization in the long run.

8. Implementing the MTMM within the Context of the Employment Interview

With the concept of personality assessment now on the minds of interview researchers, suddenly determining what true constructs the employment interview was measuring (the applicant's motivation level or the applicant's true behavior) became another priority with the twenty-first-century researchers. Questions like, "Is this applicant merely acting the role of the model job candidate or is this her true inner self that is being revealed?" began to be fielded by researchers (Ellis et al. 2002; Levashina and Campion 2006; Ones and Viswesvaran 1998; Snell, Sydell, and Lueke, 1999). To examine this query, researchers and practitioners began relying more on multiple criteria or persons' judgments to get to the bottom of this quandary. One could say that Campbell and Fiske's (1959) multi-trait, multi-method (MTMM) approach to research had come in vogue again, as researchers were simply not finding the whole truth from single criterion studies—a point that we will revisit in the latter part of this chapter. In laboratory studies, peer judgments of interview participants were becoming more commonly solicited to serve as another criterion in addition to the interviewer's judgment of the target's personality (Blackman 2002a; 2002b; Funder and Colvin 1997; Tran and Blackman 2006; Townsend, Bacigalupi, and Blackman 2007). Specifically, self–interviewer and peer–interviewer agreement became the criteria for accurate personality judgment for these previously mentioned studies. Funder and colleagues even went so far as to solicit personality judgments from the parents and peers of the target participant, in order to provide judgments from varying viewpoints and contexts. These multiple judgments and criteria provided reassuring evidence that, for the most part, people's behavior is cross-situationally consistent, whether it be at home, at school, or at an employment interview. In other words, the personality characteristics that the job candidate reveals during the interview are generally his or her true nature (Blackman 2002a; 2002b; Blackman and Funder 2002; Funder 1995; Funder and Colvin 1997; Townsend, Bacigalupi, and Blackman 2007; Tran and Blackman 2006). These studies however, do not dismiss the idea that job candidates could be engaging in impression management tactics during their employment interviews either to purposely put forth a false image or to enhance their existing image (Ellis et al. 2002; Levashina and Campion 2006; Snell, Sydell, and Lueke 1999). But again, despite the concern of candidates engaging in impression management tactics during employment interviews, research by Blackman (2002a; 2002b), Funder and Colvin (1997), and Townsend, Bacigalupi, and Blackman (2007) assures us that it does not significantly impair even a lay judge's personality judgment of that individual.

Another comforting outcome from this previously mentioned group of studies was that they revealed that lay employment interviewers are fairly accurate judges of personality when self–interviewer and peer–interviewer agreement are used as the criteria for accuracy. But this confirmation was not enough for researchers as they began to wonder, "How accurate and predictive are lay interviewers' personality judgments when compared to the results of an integrity inventory, for instance?" Simply put, "should we be investing in the future of the *online integrity test* or in the future of the *well-trained interviewer*?"

9. Interviewer Assessment vs. Standardized Test Assessment

Let's take a look for a moment at the most commonly administered integrity test in the United States, the Reid Report (Reid London House 2007). The Reid Report helps identify job applicants with high levels of integrity, who are likely to become productive employees. The Reid Report is administered to job applicants by high-profile organizations such as Disney, Home Depot, and Linens and Things. This assessment can be given in several ways, such as a paper-and-pencil assessment or an on-line assessment. For some organizations, the Reid Report is a pre-screening device, and if the applicant meets the test's criteria, then he or she is scheduled for a human-conducted interview. The following are the four main dimensions that the Reid Report assesses:

• *Integrity*—An applicant's attitudes and behaviors that are likely to influence honesty, performance, and trustworthiness.

- *Social Behavior*—An applicant's behaviors regarding theft and criminal activities.
- *Substance Use*—An applicant's behaviors regarding the use of illegal drugs at or before work.
- *Work Background*—A brief summary of an applicant's employment history.

After the applicant has completed the test, it is either faxed or sent electronically to the test maker's organization for scoring and then feedback about the applicant's potential to engage in counter-productive behavior while on the job. The purchase and scoring of one job applicant's inventory costs about $16–$18. Of course, the Reid Report scoring routine is not made available to the public. For many small organizations, the costs of integrating this screening tool into their employee selection process may be too much, even though the average return of investment is 13 to 1. Some of the benefits that the Reid Report customers can expect (according to the organization) are the following:

- Inventory shrinkage reductions by 10–30 percent
- Employee retention increases averaging 25 percent
- Net profit gains 66 percent greater for one of our clients, as compared to a top competitor using a different selection program
- A 39 percent drop in on-the-job accident rates over a six-month period, resulting in savings of over $1.4 million in associated costs (Reid London House 2007).

Townsend, Bacigalupi, and Blackman (2007) set out to determine how much of an edge an employer who utilized the Reid Report would have over an employer who relied solely on his gut impression from the face-to-face interview of the job candidate's integrity level. In other words, can employers who forgo implementing integrity tests be guaranteed any predictive validity about the candidate's counter-productive behavior by just using the information gleaned about the candidate from the interview itself? In Townsend and his colleagues' study, they administered an integrity test very similar in content and format to the Reid Report to their job applicants. Next, peers who knew the applicants well provided assessments of the job candidates using the integrity inventory, providing an additional perspective of the candidate. Each job applicant also participated in a structured 10–12-minute face-to-face interview. After each interview was complete, the interviewer completed the integrity inventory on the candidate. Self–interviewer, peer–interviewer agreement on the inventory were then used as the criteria for accuracy. What Townsend et al. found was very surprising as well as encouraging. The degree of self–interviewer agreement on the integrity survey was quite impressive, however it was not significantly different from the equally impressive levels of peer–interviewer agreement obtained. In summary, employers can feel quite confident that their integrity assessment of a job applicant, gathered from an interview, is just as predictive as an integrity assessment made by a well-acquainted peer or the applicant himself.

Townsend, Bacigalupi, and Blackman (2007) conducted a further investigation with these promising findings. The question that Townsend and his colleagues now asked was, "Could we obtain even higher levels of self–interviewer and peer–interviewer agreement about the job applicant's integrity level if the interview format was unstructured instead of structured?" The researchers created a between-subjects design in which the job applicants participated either in a structured, unstructured, or informal interview format. The informal interview condition involved an unstructured interview in which the interviewer walked with the applicant over to a nearby alfresco coffee stand and asked whatever questions came to mind while walking and over coffee. All three interview formats were controlled to ensure that they did not differ with regard to the length of interview time.

Townsend and his colleagues (2007) found that the informal interview format produced significantly higher self–interviewer and peer–interviewer integrity assessment agreement scores than either the structured or unstructured formats. The researchers found that the candidates spent a significantly longer amount of time talking about themselves than did the candidates in the two other conditions. Also, the interviewers in the informal interview format asked significantly more follow-up questions to the candidates than did the interviewers in the other two conditions.

Townsend, Bacigalupi, and Blackman (2007) relied on Funder's Realistic Accuracy Model (RAM) of personality judgment (1995) to explain their findings. According to RAM there are four moderators of personality judgment. The first moderator is the "good judge." Simply put, some people are better judges of personality than others. The second moderator is the "good trait," implying that there are some traits that are easier to judge than others. For instance, some traits are simply more visible to the human eye than others (e.g., "is talkative" vs. "likes to daydream"). More specifically, those traits that have more visible cues are more likely to be judged accurately. The third moderator of RAM is the "good target," as some people or targets are easier to judge than others as their behavior is more consistent. With these "good targets," the lay judge is more likely to be accurate when judging their personality traits. And the last moderator of personality judgment and the most relevant to Townsend et al.'s study, is "good information." RAM posits that as the judge of personality is exposed to a greater quantity of information about the target subject, he or she will have a greater likelihood of making an accurate personality judgment. Likewise, as the judge of personality sees the target subject in a variety of diverse and meaningful interactions, he or she is exposed to a better quality of information about the target subject and has a better chance of making an accurate personality judgment about him or her. Townsend et al. believe that the informal interview format is unique in that it gives the interviewer "good information" about the target subject that they would not receive during a structured interview format. RAM would categorize the structured interview format as a "strong" situation in which there are strong cues or scripts for the target subject's behavior and little room for deviation. The informal interview format would be coined by RAM as a "weak" situation in which the cues for appropriate behavior or scripted behavior are muddied and less apparent. Candidates interviewed with this format in the Townsend et al. study were probably caught off guard with the informal nature of the conversation and casual atmosphere of the alfresco coffee stand. Needless to say, many of these candidates felt so comfortable that they probably let down their guard and inadvertently revealed many telling aspects about their personality which they would have never done in a "strong" or structured situation. It also may have been that the candidates in this casual atmosphere began to see the interviewer more as a friend than authority figure and revealed more information verbally and non-verbally about themselves. With the candidates guarding their behavior less in the informal format, the interviewers were undoubtedly exposed to a better quality of information and an increased quantity of information with regard to the candidate's personality on which to formulate their personality judgments. Ultimately, the increased quality and quantity of information that the interviewer has at his or her disposal facilitates making a more accurate personality judgment.

10. Using What We Have Learned through the Years to Create the Effective Interview for the Twenty-First Century

There have been enormous changes to the employment interview over the past fifty years. The context of the interview is one of the most prominent changes we have seen. Employers have gone from conducting interviews while seated behind their desks, to conducting interviews over coffee at Starbucks, or via a satellite connection. The job applicant over the years has also seen changes in the types of questions that they are being asked and the number of interviewers that they can expect to encounter while interviewing for one position. No longer can the job applicant expect the hackneyed questions such as, "Why do you want to work for our organization?" or "What skills could you bring to our organization?" Today's job applicants must be ready to answer an array of situationally/behaviorally based interview questions, such as "Give us an instance when you effectively resolved a dispute between two of your co-workers. First tell me what the dispute was about and then what action you took to resolve it" (Ellis et al. 2002). And now, just when the applicant begins to breathe a sigh of relief, thinking that their interview is over, he or she is moved along to another room only to be interviewed by a panel of incumbents. And last, but not least, the job applicant is finally escorted to a computer to take an on-line test known as the Reid Report. And to his or her surprise, the original interviewer approaches him or her with a pair of scissors and asks to cut a lock of hair for drug testing. Yes, the employment interview has changed over the past five decades.

What constitutes an "effective interview" in the twenty-first century? The biggest lesson that we have learned over time is the "employment interview" should not be conceptualized as a single event, but instead as a series of multifaceted interviews and assessments. Developing a successful interview format should revolve around embracing Campbell and Fiske's (1959) multi-trait, multi-method philosophy with the ultimate aim of obtaining convergent validity about the candidate's skills, personality traits and background. I have listed some sources and assessment measures that could serve to increase the convergent validity of the interview process.

Varying Interview Formats (choose more than one):

a. structured
b. unstructured
c. panel
d. multiple applicant or group interview
e. conference call
f. satellite interview

Sources of judgments with regard to the candidate's skills or personality traits (choose more than one):

a. main interviewer
b. incumbents
c. potential subordinates in the organization (e.g., staff members)
d. potential peers in the organization
e. long-standing clients or customers who the organization works with
f. past employer (though this situation as you know can get a bit sticky)
g. past co-workers
h. hometown friends or peers
i. friends or family members
j. a private investigator (e.g., background check)
k. the candidate himself

Assessment (skills and personality) techniques (choose more than one):

a. integrity testing
b. drug testing
c. in-basket task

d. achievement test

e. aptitude test

f. personality testing

g. tests of skill (e.g., physical agility, lifting of heavy boxes, word-processing).

Here are some very general tips that interviewers can use as a springboard in developing their multifaceted interview process:

Pre-Interview Preparation:

1. *The Job Description.* First, access the job description for the impending open position.

2. *Predictive Interview Questions.* Second, develop skill-related questions by either using a job analysis or hiring the project out to a reputable organization. Make sure that situational/behavioral interview questions are included.

3. *Find "Good Judges."* Identify key colleagues who are "good judges of personality," and ideally extroverts, who would be willing to interview the candidates at various stages during the interview process. Research indicates that extroverted individuals have more opportunities for social interactions and thus have more practice and are more accurate at decoding others' non-verbal and verbal behavior (Funder 1995).

4. *Choose Your Methods.* Decide upon which methods (plural) you will utilize to obtain a degree of convergent validity about the candidate's relevant job experience and skills (e.g. structured interview, in-basket task, achievement test).

5. *Find Situations that Will Yield "Good Information" about the Candidate.* Decide upon which situations you will utilize to obtain a degree of convergent validity about the candidate's personality (e.g., potential for counter-productive behavior, organizational citizenship behavior, person–job fit). Keep in mind the more unstructured the interview (e.g., over dinner, during a tour of the organization, during casual conversation in the hallways with passing colleagues) and the more colleagues who are able to interact with the candidate, the higher your convergent validity will be. Candidates who have something to hide will eventually leak these clues to us when they let down their guard in an unstructured situation. By having multiple interviewers present during various portions of the interview process, one or two of them will undoubtedly see any "red flags" that the candidate's behavior may raise.

The Actual Interview Process:

1. *The Element of Surprise.* Ideally, candidates should not be tipped off in too much detail as to what the actual interview entails (such as a structured and unstructured format or an "integrity test." The element of surprise will hopefully catch even the most polished actor off guard and at the same time will highlight true talent.

2. *Résumé Fraud.* During the structured interview keep a copy of the candidate's résumé in hand (or even better have a third party present) to check for any

glaring discrepancies between what the candidate says during the process and what is written on his or her résumé.

3. *Standardized Rating Forms.* For the structured and unstructured interviews make sure that you have a standardized rating form that you can compare scores with, for each of the candidates.

4. *Tune into Both Channels.* Interviewers should be prepared to multitask while interviewing a job applicant. Not only must they direct the interview by asking the questions, but they must be tuned to the applicant's verbal as well as non-verbal responses. Be aware of the candidate's handshake (weak vs. strong), level of eye contact, posture, indications of state (e.g., nervous twitching, shakes, or confident mannerisms).

Post Interview:

1. *Feedback to the Candidate.* Let the candidate know after the conclusion of the interview process as quickly as possible (e.g., a week after the interview) where they stand. Remember that even negative feedback is better than no feedback at all. How the candidate views your organization, regardless of whether he or she is hired, can come back to the organization through various channels.

2. *Gather your Sources' Judgments.* Look for a pattern in the multiple assessments and judgments made about your candidate. Also, look for any anomalies or red flags (e.g., these can be written in subtle language in letters of recommendation about the candidate from past employers, so keep your eyes open).

3. *Leave No Rock Unturned.* If you feel that you have tapped all of your interview resources, and their judgments and assessments seem to converge prominently in one direction, then you have conducted a twenty-first-century interview. Congratulations!

As you can see "it takes a village" to conduct an interview in the twenty-first century. If you want to be assured of a return on your investment of a new hire, then conducting a twenty-first-century interview is your best bet. It is the increasingly strong alliance between researchers and practitioners that has and is continually carving out the path for the effective interview. Though the path may be ever-changing it is becoming very well lit!

REFERENCES

ANDERSON, C. W. 1960. The relation between speaking times and decision in the employment interview. *Journal of Applied Psychology*, 44 (4): 267–8.

ARVEY, R. D. 1979. Unfair discrimination in the employment interview: legal and psychological aspects. *Psychological Bulletin*, 86: 736–65.

—— and CAMPION, J. E. 1982. The employment interview: a summary review of the present research. *Personnel Psychology*, 35: 281–322.

BAKER, H. G., and SPIER, M. S. 1990. The employment interview: guaranteed improvement in reliability. *Public Personnel Management*, 19: 85–90.

BARRICK, M. R., PATTON, G. K., and HAUGLAND, S. N. 2000. Accuracy of individual judgments of job applicant personality traits. *Personnel Psychology*, 53: 925–51.

BIESANZ, J. C., NEUBERG, S. L., and JUDICE, N. T. 1999. When interviewers desire accurate impressions: the effects of note taking on the influence of expectations. *Journal of Applied Social Psychology*, 29: 2529–49.

BLACKMAN, M. C. 2002a. Personality judgment and the utility of the unstructured employment interview. *Basic and Applied Social Psychology*, 24 (3): 240–9.

—— 2002b. The employment interview via the telephone: are we sacrificing accurate personality judgments for cost efficiency? *Journal of Research in Personality*, 36 (3): 208–23.

—— and FUNDER, D. C. 2002. Effective interview practices for accurately assessing counterproductive traits. *International Journal of Selection and Assessment*, 10 (1/2): 109–16.

CAMPBELL, D. T., and FISKE, D. W. 1959. Convergent and discriminant validation by the multitrait-multimethod matrix. *Psychological Bulletin*, 56: 81–105.

CAMPION, M. A., PALMER, D. K., and CAMPION, J. E. 1998. Structuring employment interviews to improve reliability, validity and users' reactions. *Current Directions in Psychological Science*, 7: 77–82.

CHAPMAN, D. S., and ROWE, P. M. 2002. The influence of videoconferencing technology and interview structure on the recruiting function of the employment interview: a field experiment. *International Journal of Selection and Assessment*, 10: 185–97.

CHRISTIANSEN, N. D., WOLCOTT-BURNAM, S., and JANOVICS, J. E. 2005. The good judge revisited: individual differences in the accuracy of personality judgments. *Human Performance*, 18: 123–49.

CHUANG, A. 2001. *The Perceived Importance of Person-Job Fit and Person Organization Fit between and within Interview Stages*. Dissertation Abstracts. Section B. The Sciences and Engineering, Vol. 62 (3-B).

COGGER, J. W. 1982. Are you a skilled interviewer? *Personnel Journal*, 61: 840–3.

CONWAY, J. M., JAKO, R. A., and GOODMAN, D. R. 1995. A meta-analysis of interrater and internal consistency reliability of selection interviews. *Journal of Applied Psychology*, 87: 1200–8.

COOK, K. W., and VANCE, C. A. 2000. The relation of candidate personality with selected interview outcomes. *Journal of Applied Social Psychology*, 30: 867–85.

DIPAOLA, M. F., and TSCHANNEN-MORAN, M. 2001. Organizational citizenship behavior in school and its relation to school climate. *Journal of School Leadership*, 11: 424–47.

DIPBOYE, R. L., GAUGLER, B. B., and HAYES, T. L. 1997. The validity of unstructured panel interviews: more than meets the eye? *Journal of Business and Psychology*, 16: 35–49.

ELLIS, A. P. J., WEST, B. J., RYAN, A. M., and DESHON, R. P. 2002. The use of impression management tactics in subject interviews: a function of question type? *Journal of Applied Psychology*, 87: 1200–8.

FUGITA, S. S., WEXLEY, K. N., and HILLERY, J. M. 1974. Black–white differences in nonverbal behavior in an interview setting. *Journal of Applied Social Psychology*, 4: 343–50.

FUNDER, D. C. 1995. On the accuracy of personality judgment: a realistic approach. *Psychological Review*, 102: 652–70.

—— and COLVIN, C. R. 1997. Congruence of self and others' judgments of personality. Pp. 617–47 in *Handbook of Personality Psychology*, ed. R. Hogan, J. Johnson, and S. Briggs. Orlando, FL: Academic Press.

GORMAN, C. D., CLOVER, W. H., and DOHERTY, M. E. 1978. Can we learn anything about interviewing real people from "interviews" of paper people? Two studies of the external validity of a paradigm. *Organizational Behavior and Human Performance*, 22: 165–92.

GRAVES, L. M., and POWELL, G. N. 1988. An investigation of sex discrimination in recruiters' evaluations of actual applicants. *Journal of Applied Psychology*, 73: 20–9.

KACMAR, M. K., and HOCHWARTER, W. A. 1996. Rater agreement across multiple data collection media. *Journal of Social Psychology*, 136: 469–75.

LEVASHINA, J., and CAMPION, M. 2006. A model of faking likelihood in the employment interview. *International Journal of Selection and Assessment*, 14: 299–316.

MCDANIEL, M. A., WHETZEL, D. L., and SCHMIDT, F. L. 1994. The validity of the employment interview: a comprehensive review and meta-analysis. *Journal of Applied Psychology*, 79: 599–616.

ONES, D. S., and VISWESVARAN, C. 1998. The effects of social desirability and faking on personality and interview assessment for personnel selection. *Human Performance*, 11: 245–69.

ORGAN, D. W. 1988. *Organizational Citizenship Behavior*. Lexington, MA: D. C. Heath and Co.

POSTHUMA, R. A., MORGESON, F. P., and CAMPION, M. A. 2002. Beyond employment interview validity: a comprehensive narrative review of recent research trends over time. *Personnel Psychology*, 55: 1–81.

RAND, T. M., and WEXLEY, K. N. 1975. Demonstration of the effect "similar to me" in simulated employment interviews. *Psychological Reports*, 36: 535–44.

RAYMARK, P. H., SCHMIT, M. J., and GUION, R. M. 1997. Identifying potentially useful personality constructs for personnel-selection. *Personnel Psychology*, 50: 723–36.

Reid London House. 2007. *Abbreviated Reid Report*. Minneapolis: NCS Pearson.

ROTH, P. L., VAN IDDEKINGE, C. H., HUFFCUTT, A. I., EIDSON C. E., Jr., and SCHMIT, M. J. 2005. Personality saturation in structured interviews. *International Journal of Selection and Assessment*, 13: 261–3.

SKARLICKI, D., and LATHAM, G. 1995. Organizational citizenship behavior in a university setting. *Canadian Journal of Administrative Sciences*, 12: 175–81.

SNELL, A. F., SYDELL, E. J., and LUEKE, S. B. 1999. Towards a theory of applicant faking: integrating studies of deception. *Human Resource Management Review*, 9: 219–41.

STRAUS, S. G., MILES, J. A., and LEVESQUE, L. L. 2001. The effects of videoconference, telephone, and face to face media on interviewer and applicant judgments in employment interviews. *Journal of Management*, 27: 363–81.

TAYLOR, P. J., and SMALL, B. 2002. Asking applicants what whey would do versus what they did do: a meta-analytic comparison of situational and past behavior employment interview questions. *Journal of Occupational and Organizational Psychology*, 75: 277–94.

TOWNSEND, R. J., BACIGALUPI, S. C., and BLACKMAN, M. C. 2007. The accuracy of lay integrity assessments in simulated employment interviews. *Journal of Research in Personality*, 41: 540–57.

TRAN, T., and BLACKMAN, M. C. 2006. The dynamics and validity of the group selection interview. *Journal of Social Psychology*, 146 (2): 183–201.

VAN DAM, K. 2003. Trait perception in the employment interview: a five factor model perspective. *International Journal of Selection and Assessment*, 11: 43, 55.

WASHBURN, P. V., and HAKEL, M. D. 1973. Visual cues and verbal content as influences on impressions formed after simulated employment interviews. *Journal of Applied Psychology*, 58: 137–41.

WERBEL, J. D., and GILLILAND, S. W. 1999. Person–environment fit in the selection process. *Research in Personnel and Human Resources Management*, 17: 209–45.

WEXLEY, K. N., YUKL, G. A., and KOVACS, S. Z. 1972. Importance of contrast effects in employment interviews. *Journal of Applied Psychology*, 56: 45–8.

YOUNG, D. M., and BEIER, E. G. 1977. The role of applicant nonverbal communication in the employment interview. *Journal of Employment Counseling*, 14: 154–65.

9

CURRENT THEORY AND PRACTICE OF ASSESSMENT CENTERS: THE IMPORTANCE OF TRAIT ACTIVATION

FILIP LIEVENS

LIESBET DE KOSTER

EVELINE SCHOLLAERT

1. INTRODUCTION

ASSESSMENT centers have always had a strong link with practice. This link is so strong that the theoretical basis of the workings of an assessment center is sometimes questioned. In this chapter, we posit that trait activation theory (Tett and Burnett 2003) might be fruitfully used to explain how job-relevant candidate behavior is elicited and rated in assessment centers. Trait activation theory is a recent theory that focuses on the person–situation interaction to explain behavior based on responses to trait-relevant cues found in situations. These observable responses serve as the basis for behavioral ratings on dimensions used in a variety of assessments such as performance appraisal, interviews, but also assessment centers.

The outline of this chapter is as follows. We start by explaining the basic tenets behind the assessment center method and trait activation theory. We thereby clarify the relevance of trait activation to the assessment center paradigm. Second, we delineate the implications of trait activation theory for assessment center practice. Finally, we show how trait activation theory might have key implications for current and future assessment center research. We also provide various directions for future assessment center studies.

2. ASSESSMENT CENTERS

The International Task Force on Assessment Center Guidelines (2000) defines an assessment center as "a standardized evaluation of behavior based on multiple inputs. Several trained observers and techniques are used. Judgments about behavior are made, in major part, from specifically developed assessment simulations. These judgments are pooled in a meeting among the assessors or by a statistical integration process." In other words, in an assessment center procedure, the candidate or assessee is observed by multiple assessors on job-related dimensions (competencies) across several exercises. These exercises are job-related simulations, for example in-basket exercises, group exercises, interview simulations, oral presentations, and fact-finding exercises.

Assessment centers can be part of selection, diagnostic and training programs (Thornton 1992). The specific design of the assessment center is contingent upon these different purposes. Given that assessment centers for selection are aimed at selecting the best candidate for a specific job, assessors often act primarily as observers and evaluators. Conversely, in diagnostic programs, assessment centers (also known as "development centers") are primarily developed to shed light on the strengths and weaknesses of assessees. Assessors are no longer observers as they also provide assessees with feedback for improvement and development upon completion of the development center. Finally, participants of so-called "training centers" are trained in job-related skills which are required for their current job or promotion. In this application, assessors typically serve as individual coaches and trainers, who provide instant feedback to participants during the exercises. In the design of an assessment center, one has to carefully ensure that all assessment center attributes and characteristics match the purpose of the assessment center.

Worldwide, assessment centers are quite popular. This is probably due to their psychometric advantages. On average, assessment centers have good criterion-related validity, ranging from .25 to .39, depending on the dimension measured (Arthur et al. 2003). Overall, the interrater reliability is found to be moderate to high (.60-.90), depending on the level of experience and the training of assessors (Lievens 2002). Assessment centers further demonstrate good utility (Hoffman and Thornton 1997) and little adverse impact (Terpstra, Mohamed, and Kethley 1999). Finally, assessees react positively to the procedure (Hausknecht, Day, and Thomas 2004). This is not to say that assessment centers enjoy a perfect psychometric record. In particular, over the last years questions have been raised with respect to the quality of construct measurement in assessment centers (Lievens and Conway 2001; Lance et al. 2004; Sackett and Tuzinski 2001) because ratings of the same dimension do not seem to converge well across exercises (i.e., poor convergent validity). In addition, there appears to be little distinction between dimensions within a specific exercise as within-exercise dimension ratings are highly correlated (i.e., poor discriminant validity).

3. TRAIT ACTIVATION THEORY

In assessment centers, candidates participate in various exercises, which is essentially similar to individuals acting in different situations. To make well-grounded evaluations about a candidate's performance in assessment centers, it is of major importance to understand how behavior is expressed and evaluated in different situations. The answer to this issue has its foundations in the long debate in personality and social psychology over the relative importance of traits and situations as sources of behavioral variance. Along these lines, interactional psychology recognizes that people can behave consistently across distinct situations as well as that situations can cause several individuals to behave similarly (Tett and Guterman 2000).

Trait activation theory is a recent theory that focuses on this person–situation interaction to understand how individual traits express as work-related behavior and how this behavior is related to job performance (Tett and Burnett 2003). Figure 9.1 gives a schematic overview of the main ideas behind trait activation theory. As shown in Figure 9.1, trait activation theory starts with the common notion that a person's trait level is expressed as trait-relevant behavior at work. Apart from the main effect of situations on work behavior (and vice versa), a first key axiom underlying trait activation theory is that traits will manifest as trait-expressive work behaviors only when trait-relevant cues are present (Tett and

Burnett 2003). According to trait activation theory, these trait-relevant cues can be categorized into three broad interrelated groups: task, social, and organizational. That is, specific task features (e.g., a messy desk), social features (e.g., problem colleagues), and organizational features (e.g., team-based organizational culture) are posited to moderate whether and how traits are expressed in trait-relevant behavior. For example, a trait such as Autonomy is likely not to be expressed in routine monotonous jobs (task level), in the presence of a controlling supervisor (social level), or in a rigid autocratic culture (organizational level), whereas it is likely to be activated in the reverse conditions. In trait activation theory, situations are then described on the basis of their *situation trait relevance,* which can be referred to as a qualitative feature of situations that is essentially trait specific. It is informative with regard to which cues are present to elicit behavior for a given latent trait. For example, when an employee opens a messy drawer full of odds and ends, this situation is relevant for the trait order (Conscientiousness). Similarly, when someone is confronted with an angry customer, this situation provides cues for traits such as Calmness (Emotional Stability).

A second axiom underlying trait activation theory is that trait expression is not only dependent upon the relevance of the situation. The strength of the situation also plays a role (Tett and Burnett 2003). This notion of *situation strength* builds on the research about strong and weak situations. In contrast to situation trait relevance, situation strength is a continuum that refers to how much clarity there is with regard to how the situation is perceived. Strong situations contain unambiguous behavioral demands where the outcomes of behavior are clearly understood and widely shared (Mischel 1973). Strong situations and their relatively uniform expectations are therefore likely to result in few differences in how individuals respond to the situation, obscuring individual differences on underlying personality traits even where relevant. Conversely, weak situations are characterized by more ambiguous expectations, enabling much more variability in behavioral responses to be observed. In Figure 9.1, this notion of situation strength is captured by the box "intrinsic and extrinsic rewards" (Tett and Burnett 2003). The rationale is that trait-relevant work behavior that is favourably regarded in light of task, social, and/or organizational demands is likely to receive positive responses (e.g., bonuses, approval). Conversely, behavior at work that is unfavorably regarded is likely to get negative responses. Building on the research on weak situations, trait activation theory posits that a requirement for trait expression is that the associated rewards are modest or ambiguous. Staying with the same example as above, when a supervisor instructs the employee to clean the messy drawer, it will be much more difficult to observe individual differences related to the trait Order, whereas the opposite might be true in the absence of such clear-cut supervisory instructions.

Thus, the above shows that the greatest variability in trait-expressive behavior might be expected when individuals act in situations (1) that offer trait-relevant

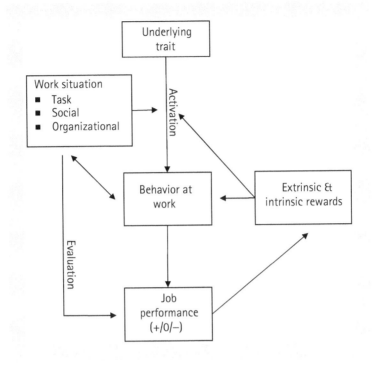

Fig. 9.1 Schematic overview of trait activation theory

Source: Adapted from Tett and Burnett 2003.

cues (the notion of "situation trait relevance"); and (2) where extrinsic rewards are modest or ambiguous (the notion of "situation strength"). Both of these distinct characteristics[1] of situations determine a situation's trait activation potential (Haaland and Christiansen 2002; Tett and Burnett 2003). So, a situation's trait activation potential is defined as the ability to observe differences in trait-related behaviors within a certain situation. The more probable it is to observe these differences, the higher that situation's trait-activation potential is considered.

As trait activation theory describes situations on the basis of the traits activated by the situations, trait activation theory offers a substantial advancement as compared to earlier theories of interactional psychology by providing a trait-based frame to define situations. Specifically, the Big Five personality traits are typically used for describing the situations because these traits consist of clearly understood behavioral domains and represent the natural categories that individuals use to describe and evaluate social behavior (e.g., Costa and McCrae 1992;

---

[1] The analogy used by Tett and Burnett (2003) to distinguish between the two concepts is that trait relevance is akin to which channel a radio is tuned to, whereas situation strength is more similar to volume; relevance determines what is playing and strength whether it will be heard.

Goldberg 1992; Haaland and Christiansen 2002; Lievens, De Fruyt, and Van Dam 2001). Hence, they facilitate classification of situations with similar situational demands.

Third, trait activation theory distinguishes trait-expressive work behavior from job performance, the latter defined as valued work behavior (Tett and Burnett 2003). As indicated by Figure 9.1, trait-related work behavior is rated positively ($+$), negatively ($-$), or mediocre (o) depending on whether the behaviors expressed meet task (e.g., does the work meet the performance objectives), social (e.g., does the person fit in the group), and organizational (e.g., do the behaviors shown match the organizational values) demands. This shows that the situational features serve as reference points for evaluating work behaviors. We refer interested readers to Tett and Burnett (2003) for a detailed and excellent primer on trait activation theory.

3.1 Assessment Center Workings Framed in Trait Activation Theory

Figure 9.2 shows how assessment centers can be framed in trait activation theory. In assessment centers, a person's trait level is measured as a score on a trait-related competency (e.g., Stress Tolerance as being related to Emotional Stability) that is based on behavior in various assessment center exercises. Assessment center exercises represent situations that differ in terms of their trait activation potential. The more likely behavior can be observed within an exercise that is relevant to a particular Big Five trait, the higher the exercise's activation potential would be for that trait. As posited by trait activation theory, the trait activation potential of assessment center exercises will be determined by two factors: the availability of trait-relevant exercise cues and the rewards provided (also known as the strength of the exercise). With respect to the former, assessment center exercise descriptions typically contain information about the three levels: job demands, social demands, and organizational demands. That is, a given assessment center exercise tries to simulate these demands, hereby eliciting trait-relevant behavior. Apart from the fact that exercise descriptions contain information about the work itself (task demands), unique advantages of assessment center exercises over other predictors are that they also simulate working with others such as clients, colleagues, supervisors (played by role players or other candidates) and that they are embedded in a specific organizational culture.

In assessment center exercises, the rewards are represented by the specific exercise instructions that provide information and expectations to candidates about what to do or not to do. For example, exercise instructions might mention that the general aim of the exercise is "to reach consensus," "to motivate the

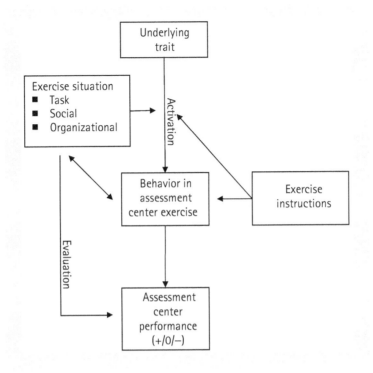

Fig. 9.2 Schematic overview of trait activation theory applied to assessment center exercises

problem subordinate," "to make a good impression," or "to give an oral presentation on strategic issues." Instructions and cues about effective behavior do not come only from the exercise instructions. Candidates might also get a sense of what is effective through prior experience in assessment center exercises, information from other candidates, prior coaching, etc.

4. IMPLICATIONS OF TRAIT ACTIVATION THEORY FOR ASSESSMENT CENTER PRACTICE

Trait activation theory does not need to be reserved as a theoretical framework. If desired, one can go even further by using trait activation theory as a useful prescriptive framework in assessment centers. Prior to presenting some implications, we want to emphasize that trait activation theory does *not* mean that assessors should directly rate traits and that dimensions should be removed from assessment centers. Organizations choose dimensions for a variety of reasons, only one of which is their representation of traits. An important advantage of dimensions is that they are often formulated in the language of work behavior, increasing their apparent relevance to management. In fact, dimensions capture acquired work skills (e.g., negotiation and organization skills) and are closely linked to job activities and organizations' competency models (Lievens, Sanchez, and De Corte 2004).

We believe that the theory-based implications of trait activation for assessment center practice are diverse. First, one way to use the logic of trait activation in practice concerns the development of *exercises*. In current assessment center practices, exercises are primarily developed to increase fidelity and criterion-related validity. We are not proposing that these practices should be abandoned. However, trait activation theory should *also* play a role. Specifically, trait activation emphasizes the importance of characteristics of the situations for observing differences in trait-relevant behavior in assessment center exercises. As noted above, the opportunity to observe these differences in trait-relevant behavior depends primarily upon the relevance and strength of the situation. This leads to two implications. On the one hand, substantial efforts should be undertaken to increase the situation trait relevance of exercises. For example, if organizations want to assess candidates on a dimension such as resistance to stress that is related to the trait of Emotional Stability, they must use exercises that put people in a situation that might activate behavior relevant to the trait of interest. An oral presentation with challenging questions might be a good example as this kind of situation is likely to evoke dimension-relevant behavior. Other examples might be the inclusion of stringent time limits, sudden obstacles, or information overload in exercises. In addition, assessment center developers might ensure that cues at the three different levels (task, social, and organizational) are embedded in the exercises. On the other hand, trait activation theory highlights that exercises should not represent strong situations. If organizations design exercises with clearly defined tasks and role players with strict rules about what to say or do, there might be few options left open for the assessees. Examples in a role play might be exercise instructions that prescribe candidates to fire the employee (instead of leaving this option open). Such exercise instructions with clear-cut expectations invoke too strong situations, reducing the variability in the expression of relevant dimensions. Therefore, organizations typically design exercises with a certain amount of vagueness and ambiguity so that differences in how assessees tackle the situation are more easily elicited and observed.

Second, there are various implications for assessment center *dimensions*. Assessment center dimensions are typically based on job analysis. However, once job analysis has identified the dimensions to be measured, trait activation theory might be used to eliminate or combine dimensions within an exercise that seem to capture the same underlying trait (e.g., "Innovation" and "Adaptability" are based on behaviors that might be expressions of Openness). In addition, trait activation theory advocates using specific dimensions instead of general concepts (Tett and Schleicher 2001). At a practical level, use of specific dimensions allows precise diagnosis for developmental purposes (Thornton 1992) and more points of comparison in matching individuals to work environments (Tett and Guterman 2000).

Third, there are implications for the development of *scoring* methods (Tett 1999). That is, trait activation prescribes that the observation of behavior has to be well separated from the evaluation. Evaluation based immediately on observations obscures the relation between behaviors which on the surface may seem opposite or even are related to different dimensions, but in fact share the same underlying trait. In addition, trait activation theory suggests developing scoring checklists that include behavioral clusters, i.e. behaviors sharing a common underlying dimension and trait (see also Lievens 1998).

Fourth, trait activation theory provides a theoretical underpinning for the provision of *training* to assessors. Specifically, the clear distinction in trait activation theory between observation and evaluation suggests that assessor training should not only provide assessors with information about the behaviors to be observed but also about the evaluation of these behaviors. This is exactly what frame-of-reference training aims to accomplish (Lievens 2001; Schleicher et al. 2002). In frame-of-reference training, a performance theory is imposed on assessors to ensure that they rate candidates in accordance with the norms and values of a specific organization. This performance theory consists of competency-relevant behaviors and their effectiveness levels. Accordingly, trait activation theory provides a theory-based underpinning for the importance of providing a frame-of-reference training to assessors.

Fifth, assessment center users might fruitfully build on trait activation theory when constructing *role-player* instructions. In current assessment center practice, role players are typically given a specific list of things to do and to avoid. Role players are also trained to perform realistically albeit consistently across candidates. Although these best practices have proven their usefulness over the years, a key function of trained role players consists of evoking dimension-related behavior from candidates (Thornton and Mueller-Hanson 2004). Trait activation might help identify which specific traits can be evoked by specific role player stimuli (i.e., specific statements or actions). These role-player cues should *subtly* elicit assessee behavior because otherwise the situations might become too strong.

Finally, trait activation theory has also implications for *assessment center feedback*. There has been some debate about whether assessment center feedback reports should be built around dimensions versus exercises (Thornton et al. 1999). When feedback is built around dimensions (e.g., "You score weak on resilience"), the advantage is that such dimension-specific feedback is relevant across a wide variety of situations. Yet, this feedback assumes that these dimensions are indeed measured across many situations (exercises). Research shows this is often not the case. Conversely, feedback might also be built around exercises (e.g., "You score weak in the oral presentation"). This is in line with most of the research evidence showing that exercises capture much of the variance in assessment center ratings. Yet, this feedback lacks depth as it generalizes to only one specific situation (one exercise). The interesting point is that trait activation theory takes a middle of the road position between these two extremes. Specifically, trait activation theory suggests building feedback reports around the situations that activate the traits (e.g., "You score weak in situations where you are put under pressure").

5. Implications of Trait Activation Theory for Assessment Center Research

5.1 Convergent Validity of Assessment Center Ratings

One of the strongest implications of trait activation for current assessment center research is related to the research stream on the convergent validity of assessment center ratings. As described above, assessment centers are found to lack convergent validity, since common MTMM findings indicate that ratings of the same dimension do not converge well across assessment center exercises (see Sackett and Tuzinski 2001). From a theoretical point of view, these findings undermine the position of dimensions as cornerstones of assessment centers. In addition, the common use of final dimension ratings for giving feedback can be questioned. After all, for this feedback to be meaningful, it is essential that there is indeed evidence that these final dimension ratings measure the dimensions consistently across various situations (exercises).

Trait activation theory provides an alternative theory-based approach for looking at the convergent validity findings. As exercises differ in their trait activation potential, it will be difficult to observe consistent behavior across exercises. Therefore, convergence will be poor for ratings of a dimension related to a given personality trait, when exercises differ in their activation potential for that trait. Trait activation theory predicts that stronger convergence should be expected when ratings are based on exercises in which there is significant opportunity to observe trait-relevant behavior in each exercise. For example, consider ratings on the dimension of Interpersonal Influence, which are based on behaviors that are expressions of the Big Five trait of Extroversion. As a leaderless group discussion and a role-play exercise can be both expected to provide cues relevant to this trait, convergence between ratings should be expected. However, as a planning exercise probably does not provide as many cues for expression of trait-relevant behavior, ratings on the Interpersonal Influence dimension from this exercise should not be expected to correlate very strongly with those from other exercises.

There is growing evidence to support this argument. Highhouse and Harris (1993) found higher convergence across exercises in which the same behavior can be observed. However, it is noteworthy that the trait activation approach extends beyond pure behavior, because the exact same behavior need not be observed in two exercises to be considered similar; behaviors can appear different on the surface, but in fact are related to the same personality trait (Haaland and Christiansen 2002). The example used by the researchers to illustrate this involved consideration of one exercise that requires risk-taking behavior to successfully resolve the situation and one that involves persuading a group of people to adopt the candidates' position. Given that these behaviors can be seen as falling within the construct domain of Extroversion, convergence on ratings from a dimension linked to this Big Five trait could be expected across these exercises.

Direct empirical support for this implication of trait activation theory can be found in a recent study by Haaland and Christiansen (2002). They examined whether poor convergence of assessment centers across exercises was due to correlating ratings from exercises that differed in trait activation potential. Subject-matter experts were asked to judge whether it could be possible to observe behavior relevant to the Big Five traits in a given exercise. The subject-matter experts were then instructed to link the dimensions of the assessment center with the Big Five traits, because greater convergence should only be expected on dimensions that were conceptually relevant to a given trait. The correlations between ratings from exercises high in trait activation potential were compared to the correlations between ratings from exercises low in trait activation potential, providing support for the implication that the trait activation potential of the exercises plays an important role in the convergent validity of ratings. Lievens et al. (2006) found support for trait activation as a theoretical framework for understanding convergent validity across a large number of assessment centers. That is, they found support for the proposition that convergence is better between exercises that provide an opportunity to observe behavior related to the same trait. Effects were small, though.

In sum, trait activation provides a deeper and more sophisticated approach for looking at the convergence of ratings of the same dimensions across assessment center exercises. An advantage of using trait activation theory is that convergence should not be expected among all dimension ratings. In fact, trait activation posits that convergence should be expected only between exercises that provide an opportunity to observe behavior related to the same trait. Furthermore, the greater psychological depth of trait activation is illustrated by the fact that convergence is also expected across exercises that look different on the surface, but activate the same traits on a deeper trait level.

5.2 Discriminant Validity of Assessment Center Ratings

Trait activation theory also provides a novel look at discriminant validity research in assessment centers. As mentioned above, assessment centers have weak discriminant validity, because MTMM research has found high correlations between dimensions within exercises (see Sackett and Tuzinski 2001). These findings are not consonant with theoretical inferences, since assessment center theory emphasizes distinct dimensions as cornerstones of assessment centers. Instead, these findings suggest that ratings cluster within exercises, which again has implications for assessment center practice. For example, one might wonder whether it is still justified to organize evaluations and feedback around dimensions instead of exercises.

To our knowledge, all prior assessment center studies correlated all dimensions within a particular exercise to obtain an index of discriminant validity. Such a broad approach focuses only on the surface dimensions and ignores that these dimensions are conceptually related to underlying traits. Specifically, exercises may have cues for behaviors that are related to different dimensions, but are in fact expressions of the same trait. These dimensions will therefore correlate more strongly, because they share a common cause. Trait activation theory suggests that discriminant validity will be worse in part, because prior research assumes that assessment center dimensions are totally discrete whereas they may not be.

By specifying links to underlying traits as a causal explanation for strong dimension correlations within exercises, trait activation theory again goes beyond the simple conceptualization that dimensions may overlap because they require the same behaviors. For example, ratings on dimensions of Oral Communication and impact may be based on very different behaviors but may both be expressions of the Big Five trait of Extroversion. Conversely, better discrimination might be observed when correlating ratings of Problem Solving and Interpersonal Skills because these dimensions are not expressions of the same underlying trait(s).

Support for this idea can be found in Kleinmann et al. (1995). In this study, use of conceptually distinct dimensions had positive effects on discriminant validity. With interchangeable dimensions, assessors gave interdependent ratings which did not differ meaningfully from each other. Lievens et al. (2006) provide even more direct support. In this large-scale study, subject-matter experts were asked to link the dimensions of the assessment center to the Big Five traits. When examining discriminant validity, Lievens et al. (2006) took the relation between the dimensions and the underlying traits into account. Results revealed that discrimination among ratings within exercises was better for dimensions that were not expressions of the same underlying traits than for dimensions that were. Again, effects were small.

In sum, trait activation theory has key implications for the discriminant validity of assessment center ratings. Traditional approaches for examining the discriminant validity of assessment center ratings have typically involved analyzing all correlations among all dimension ratings, without regard for underlying traits. Conversely, trait activation theory suggests that part of the reason dimension ratings correlate so highly, is that they may be based on behavioral cues related to a common underlying trait. From this point of view, weak discriminant validity between some assessment center dimensions can be expected.

5.3 Correlations with Other Assessment Methods

External validation research on assessment centers might also benefit from taking trait activation theory into account. In external validation, assessment center scores are linked in a nomological network to other instruments such as personality inventories, 360 degree feedback ratings, and cognitive ability tests. As argued by Tett and Burnett (2003), trait activation is a framework that applies to many assessment methods, such as assessment centers as well as other predictor assessment methods (personality inventories, 360 degree feedback inventories, structured interviews, etc.). Essentially, as long as these predictor methods create the opportunity to observe similar trait-relevant behavior as assessment center exercises, one can expect these methods to obtain convergent results. Conversely, when various assessment methods do not lend themselves to observe similar trait-relevant behavior, divergent results might be expected. Therefore, trait activation theory might also provide a novel look at research that correlates assessment center ratings with other assessment instruments. In particular, an intriguing avenue for future studies consists of incorporating trait activation ideas when externally validating assessment center ratings with those from non-assessment center methods with similar activation potential.

The value of this idea can be indirectly tested by reinterpreting the results of prior external validation research in the assessment center field. Although these prior studies did not rely on trait activation theory, it was striking that specific personality traits were correlated with specific assessment center exercises. For instance, Spector et al. (2000) discovered that "interpersonal" exercises correlated with personality constructs such as Emotional Stability, Extroversion, and Openness, whereas "problem-solving" exercises correlated with Cognitive Ability and Conscientiousness. In another study, Craik et al. (2002) reported that in-basket performance was related to Conscientiousness, Openness, and strategic dimensions such as Decision Making. Conversely, group discussion performance was best described by Interpersonal dimensions and personality constructs such as Agreeableness, Extroversion, and

Openness. Similar a priori formulated hypotheses were tested about relations between assessment center exercises and cognitive ability. Goldstein et al. (1998) reported that the relationship between assessment centers and cognitive ability tests varied as a function of the cognitive "loading" of assessment center exercises. When exercises (e.g., in-basket exercise) tapped cognitively oriented dimensions (e.g., Problem Analysis), there were stronger relationships between the exercise and the cognitive ability test. Similarly, Thornton et al. (1997) found that the correlations of assessment center ratings with dimensions measured by comparable cognitive ability tests were higher than the correlations with dimensions measured by non-comparable cognitive ability tests. For example, assessment center ratings on routine problem solving correlated on average higher with tests of general intelligence, creativity, logic, and mechanical ability than with tests of spatial perception, accuracy of perception, writing ability, oral ability, and graphical ability.

More direct support for the idea to include trait activation potential in external validating research can be found in Lievens, De Fruyt, and van Dam (2001). They studied trait descriptors in assessor notes and found differences between assessment center exercises in terms of the personality adjectives noted, with particular personality traits linked to specific exercises. For example, in group discussions, assessors reported mainly Extroversion adjectives, while Conscientiousness markers were more frequently noted in the in-basket exercise. Haaland and Christiansen (2002) actually tested inferences of trait activation theory. They asked subject-matter experts to evaluate assessment center exercises on their trait activation potential. These evaluations were taken into account when correlating the exercises with 16PF scores, resulting in higher correlations between the personality scores and exercises judged to be high in trait activation potential for that personality trait than correlations with exercises low in trait activation potential.

Besides looking at the personality trait inventories, another research suggestion consists of studying the relations between assessment center ratings and 360 degree feedback ratings. Prior studies (Atkins and Wood 2002; Hagan et al. 2006) that validated a 360-degree feedback program against an assessment center found high correlations between the overall assessment rating and the aggregated 360 degree ratings. Unfortunately, no analyses at the level of the dimension ratings were conducted. Future studies might employ trait activation theory to make more fine-grained predictions and to examine under which conditions both procedures yield convergent results. For example, trait activation theory suggests that ratings of Interpersonal Sensitivity in assessment center exercises that are high in trait activation potential for Agreeableness might correlate higher with peer ratings on Interpersonal Sensitivity in 360 degree feedback than with supervisor ratings of Interpersonal Sensitivity. The rationale is that peers might provide good insight in these interpersonal aspects because they have the opportunity to observe behavior related to the trait of Agreeableness, whereas supervisors have less opportunity to observe such behavior. Similar hypotheses might be posited for the convergence of assessment center exercises with dimensions rated by other rating sources in 360-degree feedback programs.

In sum, prior research has externally validated assessment center ratings without paying attention to trait activation theory. Trait activation theory presents a more sophisticated and theory-driven strategy as it consists of mapping the trait activation potential of the assessment center exercises and the trait activation potential of the external criteria (personality inventories, 360-degree feedback, etc.). A similar theory-driven strategy can be followed when correlating assessment center exercises with construct-oriented situational judgment tests or structured interview ratings. So far, trait activation theory has been used only as an internal validation approach within assessment centers. However, the above shows that we can also easily apply the trait activation principles in an external nomological network.

5.4 Criterion-Related Validity of Assessment Center Ratings

Prior criterion-related validity research has shown that assessment centers are good predictors of job performance and potential, at the level of both the overall assessment rating and the final dimension rating (Arthur et al. 2003; Gaugler et al. 1987; Hermelin, Lievens, and Robertson 2007). Given the variability in assessment center design, it is feasible to search for factors that moderate the criterion-related validity of assessment centers. In Gaugler et al. (1987), assessment centers were more valid when a greater number of different types of exercises were used, a form of peer evaluation was applied, assessors were both psychologists and managers, the research methodology was solid, and the percentage of female candidates was high.

On the basis of trait activation theory other moderators might be suggested. In fact, the *behavior consistency model* of predictor validity (Wernimont and Campbell 1968) posits that the precision in predicting future performance improves if the correspondence between predictor and criterion measures is increased. These ideas can be linked to trait activation theory (see Tett and Schleicher 2001) which might present a theoretical basis for this behavior consistency model and for increasing assessment center validity. According to trait activation theory, the implementation of trait-relevant cues in situations is very important—as already emphasized earlier in the chapter. As an evident consequence, assessment centers that include work settings that activate the traits required for successful performance in the job might be more valid. To this end, cues related to the different levels (task, social, and organizational) might be built into the exercise descriptions. Another straightforward consequence is that assessment centers wherein assessors use the same standards for evaluating candidates as supervisors on the job will show higher predictive validity. Low predictive validity could then be due to the fact that situations in the assessment center exercises evoked different traits than those needed for the job or that the evaluative standards in the assessment center do not converge with the ones on the job (Tett and Schleicher 2001). Finally, trait activation theory suggests that the conceptual accordance between assessment center scores and criteria might be enhanced by using the same dimensions in both the predictor and the criterion. For instance, assessment center dimensions (e.g., "Detail Oriented" or "Being Prepared" as expressions of the underlying trait of Conscientiousness) are then correlated with similar dimensional criteria.

In sum, assessment centers should be designed to ensure their predictive validity. Along these lines, trait activation proposes several interesting insights (use of similar dimensions, use of exercises that elicit the relevant traits, etc.) that are related to increasing the overlap between assessment center ratings and criterion ratings.

6. Conclusion

It is generally acknowledged that the behavior of candidates in assessment centers is neither determined solely by dispositional factors (i.e., stable personality traits) nor solely by situational factors (i.e., assessment center exercises) but by the interaction of the person and the situation. Therefore, it is appropriate to conceptualize the occurrence of behavior in assessment center exercises and its evaluation in terms of a recent interactionist theory such as trait activation theory. A central concept within this theory is *trait activation potential*, which refers to the ability to observe differences in trait-related behavior within a given situation. The trait activation potential of a situation is determined by its strength and relevance.

The implications of trait activation theory for assessment center practice are far reaching as trait activation theory can be used as a prescriptive framework for assessment center design. First, one should keep the logic behind trait activation potential in mind during exercise development. Second, trait activation theory might be used to eliminate or combine dimensions that seem to capture the same underlying trait. In addition, trait activation theory advocates the use of specific dimensions instead of general concepts. Third, the underlying relations between dimensions and traits should be taken into account while developing scoring methods. Fourth, frame-of-reference training might be fruitfully used to impose both behaviors and effectiveness levels to assessors, two main components of trait activation theory. Fifth, assessment centers might benefit from trait activation theory when constructing role-player instructions. Sixth, trait activation theory suggests building feedback reports around situations that activate a specific dimension or trait.

Finally, this chapter shows that trait activation theory has also important implications for assessment center research. First, trait activation theory provides a deeper and more sophisticated explanation for the construct validity findings in assessment centers. Traditionally, multi-trait multi-method (MTMM) research posits that ratings on a specific dimension should correlate highly across all exercises, evidencing convergent validity. Conversely, according to trait activation theory, one should expect only high correlations across exercises which are high in trait activation potential for that dimension. In addition, trait activation theory also provides insights into the lack of discriminant validity evidence. Again, according to the MTMM approach, to establish discriminant validity, dimensions within an exercise should not correlate highly. To this end, all dimensions within a particular exercise are correlated. Instead, trait activation theory argues that this approach is too broad. That is, underlying relations between dimensions and traits are being ignored, because the MTMM approach assumes that assessment center dimensions are totally discrete whereas they may not be. From this point of view, particular dimensions which are related to the same underlying trait may correlate rather highly, establishing weak discriminant validity evidence. Besides offering valuable perspectives on these internal validation research efforts, external validation research may also benefit from trait activation theory. In particular, as long as assessment methods yield equal activation potential for a given dimension or trait, convergent results should be expected, whereas trait activation theory predicts divergent results between methods which are dissimilar in trait activation potential. So, trait activation theory offers a theory-driven strategy to develop a nomological network and externally validate assessment centers. Finally, trait activation theory has implications for predictive validity research. Although previous studies have already provided evidence for good predictive validity of assessment centers, it may even be increased by improving the similarity in trait activation potential between predictor and criterion.

In closing, this chapter outlined the value of trait activation theory and its opportunities for assessment center practice and research. Our contribution should encourage both practitioners and researchers to conceptualize assessment centers that are in line with the tenets underlying trait activation theory.

REFERENCES

ARTHUR, W., DAY, E. A., McNELLY, T. L., and EDENS, P. S. 2003. A meta-analysis of the criterion-related validity of assessment center dimensions. *Personnel Psychology*, 56: 125–54.

ATKINS, P. W. B., and WOOD, R. E. 2002. Self- versus others' ratings as predictors of assessment center ratings: validation evidence for 360-degree feedback programs. *Personnel Psychology*, 55: 871–904.

COSTA, P. T., and McCRAE, R. R. 1992. *Revised NEO Personality Inventory (NEO-PI-R) and NEO Five-Factor Inventory (NEO-FFI): Professional Manual.* Odessa, FL: Psychological Assessment Resources.

CRAIK, K. H., WARE, A. P., KAMP, J., O'REILLY, C. III, STAW, B., and ZEDECK, S. 2002. Explorations of construct validity in a combined managerial and personality assessment programme. *Journal of Occupational and Organizational Psychology*, 75: 171–93.

GAUGLER, B. B., ROSENTHAL D. B., THORNTON, G. C., and BENTSON, C. 1987. Meta-analysis of assessment center validity. *Journal of Applied Psychology*, 72: 493–511.

GOLDBERG, L. R. 1992. The development of markers for the big five-factor structure. *Psychological Assessment*, 4: 26–42.

GOLDSTEIN, H. W., YUSKO, K. P., BRAVERMAN, E. P., SMITH, D. B., and CHUNG, B. 1998. The role of cognitive ability in the subgroup differences and incremental validity of assessment center exercises. *Personnel Psychology*, 51: 357–74.

HAALAND, S., and CHRISTIANSEN, N. D. 2002. Implications of trait-activation theory for evaluating the construct validity of assessment center ratings. *Personnel Psychology*, 55: 137–63.

HAGAN, C. M., KONOPASKE, R., BERNARDIN, H. J., and TYLER, C. L. 2006. Predicting assessment center performance with 360-degree, top-down, and customer-based competency assessments. *Human Resource Management*, 45: 357–90.

HAUSKNECHT, J. P., DAY, D. V., and THOMAS, S. C. 2004. Applicant reactions to selection procedures: an updated model and meta-analysis. *Personnel Psychology*, 57: 639–83.

HERMELIN, E., LIEVENS, F., and ROBERTSON, I. T. 2007. The validity of assessment centers for the prediction of supervisory performance ratings: a meta-analysis. *International Journal of Selection and Assessment*, 15: 405–11.

HIGHHOUSE, S., and HARRIS, M. M. 1993. The measurement of assessment-center situations: Bem Template Matching technique for examining exercise similarity. *Journal of Applied Social Psychology*, 23: 140–55.

HOFFMAN, C. C., and THORNTON, G. C. I. 1997. Examining selection utility where competing predictors differ in adverse impact. *Personnel Psychology*, 50: 455–70.

INTERNATIONAL TASKFORCE ON ASSESSMENT CENTERS GUIDELINES. 2000. Guidelines and ethical considerations for assessment center operations. *Public Personnel Management*, 29: 315–31.

KLEINMANN, M., EXLER, C., KUPTSCH, C., and KÖLLER, O. 1995. Independence and Observability of Dimensions as Moderators of Construct-Validity in the Assessment-Center. *Zeitschrift für Arbeits und Organisationspsychologie*, 39: 22–8.

LANCE, C. E., LAMBERT, T. A., GEWIN, A. G., LIEVENS, F., and CONWAY, J. M. 2004. Revised estimates of dimension and exercise variance components in assessment center post-exercise dimension ratings. *Journal of Applied Psychology*, 89: 377–85.

LIEVENS, F. 1998. Factors which improve the construct validity of assessment centers: a review. *International Journal of Selection and Assessment*, 6: 141–52.

—— 2001. Assessor training strategies and their effects on accuracy, inter-rater reliability, and discriminant validity. *Journal of Applied Psychology*, 86: 255–64.

—— 2002. An examination of the accuracy of slogans related to assessment centers. *Personnel Review*, 31: 86–102.

—— and CONWAY, J. 2001. Dimension and exercise variance in assessment center scores: a large-scale evaluation of multitrait-multimethod studies. *Journal of Applied Psychology*, 86: 1202–22.

—— DE FRUYT, F., and VAN DAM, K. 2001. Assessors' use of personality traits in descriptions of assessment center candidates: a five-factor model perspective. *Journal of Occupational and Organizational Psychology*, 74: 623–36.

—— SANCHEZ, J. I., and DE CORTE, W. 2004. Easing the inferential leap in competency modeling: the effects of task-related information and subject-matter expertise. *Personnel Psychology*, 57: 881–904.

—— CHASTEEN, C. S., DAY, E. A., and CHRISTIANSEN, N. D. 2006. Large-scale investigation of the role of trait activation theory for understanding assessment center convergent and discriminant validity. *Journal of Applied Psychology*, 91: 247–58.

MISCHEL, W. 1973. Toward a cognitive social learning reconceptualization of personality. *Psychological Review*, 80: 252–83.

SACKETT, P. R., and TUZINSKI, K. 2001. The role of dimensions and exercises in assessment center judgements. Pp. 111–29 in *How People Evaluate Others in Organizations*, ed. M. London. Mahwah, NJ: Erlbaum.

SCHLEICHER, D. J., DAY, D. V., MAYES, B. T., and RIGGIO, R. E. 2002. A new frame for frame of reference training: enhancing the construct validity of assessment centers. *Journal of Applied Psychology*, 87: 735–46.

SPECTOR, P. E., SCHNEIDER, J. R., VANCE, C. A., and HEZLETT, S. A. 2000. The relation of cognitive ability and personality traits to assessment center performance. *Journal of Applied Social Psychology*, 30: 1474–91.

TERPSTRA, D. E., MOHAMED, A. A., and KETHLEY, R. B. 1999. An analysis of federal court cases involving nine selection devices. *International Journal of Selection and Assessment*, 7: 26–34.

TETT, R. P. 1999. Assessment center validity: new perspectives on an old problem. Paper presented at the 14th Annual Convention of the Society of Industrial and Organizational Psychology.

—— and BURNETT, D. D. 2003. A personality trait-based interactionist model of job performance. *Journal of Applied Psychology*, 88: 500–17.

—— and GUTERMAN, H. A. 2000. Situation trait relevance, trait expression, and cross-situational consistency: testing a principle of trait activation. *Journal of Research in Personality*, 34: 397–423.

—— and SCHLEICHER, D. J. 2001. Assessment Center Dimensions as "traits": new concepts in AC design. In M. Born (Chair), Assessment Center Dimension Validation: Are We Asking the Wrong Questions? Symposium conducted at the 16th Annual Conference of the Society for Industrial and Organizational Psychology, San Diego, CA, April.

THORNTON, G. C. 1992. *Assessment Centers and Human Resource Management*. Reading, MA: Addison-Wesley.

—— and MUELLER-HANSON, R. A. 2004. *Developing Organizational Simulations: A Guide for Practitioners and Students*. Mahwah, NJ: Lawrence Erlbaum Associates, Inc.

—— LARSH, S. L., LAYER, S., and KAMAN, V. S. (1999). Reactions to attribute- versus exercise-based feedback in developmental assessment centers. Paper presented at the Society for Industrial and Organizational Psychology, Atlanta, GA, April.

—— TZINER, A., DAHAN, M., CLEVENGER, J. P., MEIR, E. 1997. *Journal of Social Behavior and Personality*, 12: 109–28.

WERNIMONT, P. F. and CAMPBELL, J. P. 1968. Signs, samples, and criteria. *Journal of Applied Psychology*, 52: 372–6.

10

THE ADVANTAGES AND DISADVANTAGES OF ON-LINE TESTING

DAVE BARTRAM

1. THE EMERGENCE OF ON-LINE TESTING

PRIOR to the invention of the printing press, the written word was controlled by a small number of skilled experts; literary "guardians" who managed the flow of knowledge and information to others. The ability to mass produce books changed that for ever. Within a few decades of the invention of movable type, marked by the publication of Gutenberg's Bible in 1455, the mass production of books meant that anyone could have access to this information first hand. The impact of this was profound though slow to spread, as it relied on people developing the literacy skills necessary to take advantage of the new-found access to books. Up until the development of the World Wide Web (hereafter referred to as "the Web": Berners-Lee 1999), employment testing had remained in the Gutenberg era of print. Through his invention of the Web, Tim Berners-Lee created as big a revolution in how information flows as Gutenberg had done over half a millennium earlier.

What is different now is the speed with which such technological changes make an impact on us. In the last century it took radio about thirty-eight years to develop a worldwide audience of 50 million people; for television, this time shrank to thirteen years. For the Web, it took a mere four years.

In this chapter we will consider the impact the development of the Web has had on employment testing. The main focus will be on the impact the use of remote forms of assessment has had on practice and on the development of new ways of managing the risks associated with assessment "at a distance," especially in high-stakes situations. The use of the internet for assessment raises many other issues, such as the impact of remote assessment on applicant reactions (Anderson 2003), implications for the design of robust systems, the use of complex test forms, and on-line simulations to name but a few. While some of these issues will be touched on here, for a more extensive treatment the interested reader is referred to Bartram (2006) and to Bartram and Hambleton (2006).

1.1 Growth of the Web

Prior to the development of the Web, the main use of computers in testing had been in the area of report generation. Some of the earliest systems (back in the days before personal computers) were designed to automate the scoring and interpretation of instruments like the Minnesota Multiphasic Personality Inventory (MMPI). With the advent of the personal computer, we saw the development of computer-administered versions of paper-and-pencil tests. These provided some advantages over paper and pencil, in terms of control of administration, and some disadvantages (e.g., the need for sufficient hardware to test groups of people). Despite the potential offered by technology for novel forms of assessment, the literature on computer-based assessment (CBA) within employment settings has been largely confined to a small number of issues. These were dominated by the issue of the equivalence of computer-based and paper-based versions of the same tests. This remains an issue of concern, but we will see that on-line testing has introduced a range of new issues, not least that of unsupervised, remote, or unproctored testing. In this chapter we will review the evidence relating to issues of equivalence of on-line and off-line testing and also consider the impact on-line testing has had on modes of administration, especially the rise of unproctored or unsupervised administration modes.

In reviews going back from the mid-1990s, Bartram (Bartram and Bayliss 1984; Bartram 1994) commented that while there was a great deal of research on computer-based testing (CBT) there was relatively little evidence of it having had an impact on practice in the area of employment testing. The reasons for this were clear: Computer technology was expensive, difficult to use, and unreliable. During the early 1990s there were a number of changes in technology that resulted in a step change in the way CBT was used. On the hardware side, we saw an increase in computing power, memory, and an associated driving down of prices. The adoption of a standard software operating system (the ubiquitous Windows) made interoperability of hardware a reality. Both factors helped to make computers a familiar, standard piece of office equipment. However, it was the emergence of the Web that signaled the real beginning of widespread CBT in the world of workplace assessment.

The Internet has been around since the 1950s, but it was originally a very unfriendly environment within which to operate. Prior to the 1990s it was mainly the province of specialists operating in the military and the university communities. Two factors changed that. One was the availability of low-cost hardware with user-friendly operating systems and applications and the other was the introduction of an easy-to-use hypertext-based system of interacting with the Internet. Tim Berners-Lee proposed the idea of using a standard graphical browser and a communication standard to provide access to data from any source in 1989 and launched the first web browser in 1991. However, we can probably look on 1995 as the real beginning of the widespread use of the Internet, the time at which it started to become part of the fabric of many people's everyday lives. Since 1995, the Web audience has grown to over 1,000 million people (figures from Computer Industry Almanac Inc 2006: <http://www.c-i-a.com>), representing some 15 percent of the world's population. What is more, the level of use in countries in Europe, North America, and parts of Asia is now in the region of 70 percent or more of the population.

In less than a decade, computers and the Internet became a part of many people's everyday life at home and at work. We use it for information, for shopping, for booking holidays, and managing our finances. For testing, the impact has been very significant. Not only has the volume of testing increased with the move to the Web but the way in which tests are used in employment settings is changing as a result of it.

An obvious impact of the internet is that tests and documents can be downloaded directly to users. This means that the Web can be used as a complete commercial solution for test publishers. There is no longer any need for printing and production, warehousing, and postal delivery services. More significant for testing, however, is the shift in locus of control provided by the Web from the "client-side" to the "server-side." For paper and pencil testing, publishers have had to provide users with test items, scoring keys, and interpretation algorithms. As these are "public" so the danger of compromise and security breaches are high. Test users can (and do) pass these materials on to people who are not authorized to use them. All the test data also reside with the user. The process of developing norms, checking the performance of test items, and carrying out validation studies is dependent upon costly procedures for recovering data from users. For the internet that situation is reversed. The data and the intellectual property reside on the publisher's server. The user has access only to those parts of the process that they need. In formal terms, the test user takes on the role of a "data controller," while the publisher has the role of "data processor."

The most rapid expansion in the use of on-line testing has been in the area of recruitment. Here there has been an insatiable demand for fast, reliable, and valid assessment at the front end of the recruitment funnel. For post-hire applications, we have seen the mushrooming of personnel appraisal and personal development planning systems (360-degree feedback) as the logistical advantages of managing distributed assessment over the internet are realized.

1.2 Modes of On-line Delivery

We shall see that on-line testing offers many potential benefits and advantages for publishers, test users, and test takers. However, it also poses some problems and new challenges. In order to clarify these, it is necessary to distinguish between different modes of on-line test administration (Bartram 2001). These modes form the basis for the current International Test Commission's (ITC) Guidelines on Computer-Based Testing and the Testing on the Internet (ITC 2006).

1. Open Mode. These are conditions where there is no means of identifying the test taker and there is no human supervision. Examples of this include tests that can be accessed openly on the internet without any requirement for test taker registration. One of the problems the internet has created is the growth of "testing sites" that offer all sorts of free or cheap tests with little or no information available about their technical properties. While many are offered for use for "amusement" or "fun," others are offered for use in real decision making (such as job selection). Partly because of pressure from the public to make clearer the differences between properly developed psychometric tests and those produced for amusement, the British Psychological Society (BPS) launched a test registration procedure to help the unwary test taker know when they are taking a "real" test and when they are not. Test registration is also taking place in Norway and a number of other countries are considering the need for this.

2. Controlled Mode. This is similar to the Open Mode in that no human supervision of the test session is assumed. However, the test is only made available to known test takers. For the internet this is controlled through the requirement for the test taker to be provided with a logon username and password. This is the most widely used mode for the delivery of the major personality inventories and other self-report measures (for example, the OPQ32, 16PF, HPI, MBTI, and so on). Within the research community, this mode is also identified as "unproctored internet testing" or UIT (Tippins et al., 2006).

3. Supervised Mode. For this mode, a level of human supervision is assumed, whereby the identity of the test taker can be authenticated and test-taking conditions validated. This mode also provides a better level of control over dealing with unexpected problems or issues. For internet testing, this mode is achieved by requiring the test administrator or proctor to log in the candidate and to confirm at the end of the session that the testing was completed correctly.

4. Managed Mode. This is a mode where a high level of human supervision is assumed and there is also control over the test-taking environment. For computer-based testing this is achieved through the use of dedicated testing centres where the location is specified, the physical security levels are definable and known, and the nature and technical specification of the computer equipment is under control. In addition the competences of the staff are known and they may be required to have higher levels of qualification as test administrators than simply acting as proctors or invigilators. As a consequence, test materials can be securely downloaded and item types can be used which make particular demands on the user work station (e.g., audio and streaming video).

2. THE BUSINESS CASE THAT IS DRIVING TESTING ON-LINE

A big disadvantage of on-line testing from the publisher's view point is the cost of developing on-line delivery systems and the cost of keeping these maintained and up to date. It is often assumed by people on the receiving end that the Web is "free." In one sense it is, in that one does not pay for the infrastructure directly (though you do pay indirectly through service provider charges). However, the costs of developing the software and databases necessary to deliver high volumes of tests with high levels of robustness are in the millions of pounds—far higher than the start-up costs for producing new tests in print. As many of the smaller publishers cannot afford this level of investment, we have also seen the rise of the "ASP" or application service provider who provides a platform on which other publishers can "rent" space.

If going on-line is such a major cost for test publishers, why have they done it? Why not stick to traditional paper-and-pencil methods which have relatively low entry costs and which do not require major investments in IT infrastructure and products, or why not just use the internet as a delivery mechanism for e-book publishing? It is true that the on-line testing technologies open up possibilities for new ways of designing tests, but that is not what has driven the change. The pressure for change has been a pull coming from the market rather than a push from the publishers of tests. From the user point of view, on-line testing is more accessible, and within the employment testing sector, it provides the opportunity for increasing the speed, reach, and efficiency of recruitment and selection, with consequent major cost savings.

The move to online selection by organizations has in turn been pushed by the increasing use of the Web by job seekers and the mushrooming of job boards to service that demand (Bartram 2000). In the UK, the Chartered Institute for Personnel and Development report (CIPD 2006) that almost two-thirds of the organizations they surveyed now use e-recruitment methods, with the number and amount of use continuing to increase rapidly in comparison to what it was three years earlier. On-line testing is still only used by a minority of organizations from their survey, but 60 percent of those reported increased use and 33 percent no change over the past three years. What is interesting is that e-recruitment methods are seen as increasing the volume of applicants and also the number of unsuitable applicants. This is where on-line testing presents its biggest potential value: in sifting out unsuitable applicants early on in the selection process. Because of this we are likely to see on-line testing use grow at an even faster rate as these benefits start to become more widely known and understood.

In the area of graduate recruitment, the on-line environment is now the environment of choice for applicants. Graduates are using on-line job boards and organizations' career websites as the normal mode of job searching. No major organization would now dream of recruiting from the graduate community without doing it online. The UK Association of Graduate Recruiters' 2007 survey of 219 organizations (AGR 2007) showed that the number only accepting on-line applications had increased from 65 percent in 2006 to 76.9 percent in 2007. With regard to the use of testing, they found a much higher incidence of use in graduate recruitment than CIPD had found in more general recruitment, with 92 percent of graduate recruiters saying that psychometric testing methods are "useful" or "very useful," and over 90 percent saying they have some influence on the final hiring decisions. The most commonly used psychometric tools were numerical reasoning tests (80.3 percent), verbal reasoning tests (71.8 percent), and personality inventories (29.6 percent). With the recruitment process moving on-line, it is natural to move the selection assessment tools on-line as well in order to provide applicants with an efficient, seamless process and to reduce the workload for hiring managers.

2.1 Cost Savings Associated with Remote Administration in Selection and Recruitment

It is the ability to administer tests at a distance that has been the major driver of the growth in on-line testing. Significant savings in costs can be realized by the use of unsupervised or unproctored Internet testing (UIT) and these can be converted into more efficient hiring procedures so long as there are sufficient controls in place to ensure that the validity of the assessment procedures are not affected by the move from proctored to unproctored modes of administration.

Baron, Miles, and Bartram (2001) reported data from the use of a short on-line numerical reasoning test designed for use as an unproctored sift. This used test generation technology (discussed later) to ensure that every candidate received a different version of the test. Following the initial sift, short-listed candidates were retested under proctored conditions with a full-length numerical reasoning test. Prior to use of this sift, 880 applicants were short-listed for assessment centers each year. Of these only 30 percent passed the numerical reasoning test given at the assessment center and 211 of these met the overall criterion for hiring. Following introduction of the screening test, the number going forward for assessment was reduced to 700, the pass rate on the proctored numerical reasoning test rose to 50 percent, and 280 of those people met the criterion for hiring. The estimated savings in recruitment costs were $1,000 per hire or around $0.25 million per year.

Beaty, Fallon, and Sheperd (2002) reported a study in which a government agency implemented an on-line selection system for recruitment into an information technology training course. Employees who met the necessary requirements were sent an email invitation to take a Web-based test (unproctored). Of the 450 people who did this, 76 were selected for the next stage, in which they took a proctored test similar to the one they had taken unproctored. Those who passed this stage were invited for an interview and finally 60 were selected. If the test had not been given on-line, it would have taken an estimated six weeks to carry out procotored administrations, and the costs would have been considerable. The savings in time alone were around 500 percent.

McCook (2007) reported results of a comparison of administration modes for a battery of scales covering work-related personality characteristics, basic abilities, work ethics or integrity, job willingness or fit, and a positive response (unlikely virtues) measure. These were used for selection with a retail organization that had around 50,000 applicants per year. The organization moved from traditional proctored assessment to unproctored Web-based assessment in 2006. McCook reports on data from $n = 48,292$ applicants who had completed proctored administration during the peak hiring period in 2005 and $n = 98,865$ who completed the unproctored Web system in the 2006 peak hiring period. The change to Web-based testing had the effect of increasing the candidate flow by over 100 percent, relative to 2005. The quality of hires was maintained with similar trends in the key performance index measure for hires from both procotored and unproctored selection procedures. The move to on-line testing provided significant efficiency savings and increased the size of the applicant pool without any downside in terms of lower quality of hires.

Thus, we have a win–win situation where the test users, by doing more testing (which is a "win" for the publisher) actually benefit from a more effective recruitment process (which is a "win" for the test user) either in direct cost savings, or in improvements or quality or both. There is also a "win" for test takers in that they engage in a recruitment process that is faster and more transparent than it was in the pre-on-line days. Good on-line recruitment systems provide feedback to applicants about the process of their application—just as you can track your parcels through UPS or FedEx websites. The time between application and decision can also be greatly reduced—to a matter of hours rather than days or weeks.

2.2 Benefits of On-line Testing for Post-hire Assessments

While most of the literature on on-line testing focuses on the use of tests in selection and recruitment, another area where there has been a quiet revolution has been that of post-hire assessment within organizations. Perhaps the best example of this is in the use of on-line delivery for managing 360-degree feedback. This is one of the most logistically complex assessment procedures. One first has to identify, for each individual focus of the assessment, a set of people (manager, peers, subordinates, others) who will provide ratings of the target person's competencies or other attributes. These people then need to be asked to complete the assessments and the results brought together into a report that a feedback provider can receive and use in the feedback discussion with the target of the assessment. Carrying out an organization-wide 360-degree feedback process used to be an HRM nightmare and consumed enormous amounts of time and resource before on-line tools were available. Indeed, the costs of such procedures were so high that they were little used.

With on-line testing, the whole process of managing the 360-degree assessment and feedback process is dealt with by the on-line software: Depending on the organization's 360-degree policy, this can be handled by the target of the assessment, their line manager, or the feedback provider (if that is not the line manager).

The benefits of using on-line testing tools for assessments within organizations become even more apparent when one considers the impact on multinationals, where people may not only be in different buildings, but also be in different countries. Globalization has been another major driver of testing having to move on-line. Commercial organizations no longer operate within close national boundaries and they no longer want to draw their talent from a single location when they can seek it from the whole of the world.

For both recruitment and post-hire assessment, on-line testing has opened up the whole area of multinational assessment projects. Applicants for management positions in an organization may now come from a wide range of countries and they may need to be able to complete assessments in a variety of different languages. Within organizations, assessment programmes for the identification of people for fast-track senior management development or leadership development need to draw from employees in all the countries the organization operates in. This is a real challenge for the providers of assessment as they increasingly need to support multiple language versions of tests that are sufficiently well adapted to allow their use when making comparisons between people from different countries (Bartram 2007).

3. THE TRANSITION FROM PAPER AND PC TO ON-LINE DELIVERY

The move from paper to Web delivery has passed through two "generations." In the first the main emphasis was on existing paper-and pencil tests being put on-line. In the second we are seeing the development of assessment tools that have been designed with Web delivery in mind from the outset. We shall see that the latter provide solutions to many of the problems raised by the former.

The growth of on-line delivery resulted in publishers having to confront a whole new set of problems, which are in many cases far more complex and difficult to control than they were for paper production. For paper-based testing, the publisher was in full control of the production process and could quality check the final product before it left the warehouse. For Web-based testing, the publisher has to deal with a large variety of browsers and browser versions, each of which can produce different effects on how items might be rendered on-screen. In addition, there are interactions of all these effects with the recipient's operating system.

For self-report inventories, the transition from paper was relatively simple. There was no need for timing controls and Web-based browsers provide sufficient functionality for delivering simple items that involve rating scales and even some more complex item formats, such as forced choice. For cognitive ability tests, the issues are more complex. Typically these are timed and we require a much greater degree of control over design and layout of the item on the screen than standard html browsers can provide. As a result such tests tend to be written as downloadable applets using languages such as Java or Flash. While these developments provide a solution to some of the control and display issues, they also introduce other issues. Especially for testing within organizations, internet firewall settings can pose a real problem for test providers. Many organizations set their firewalls to prevent downloads and many IT departments lock down user PCs so that they do not have permission, for example, to download a Java applet or to install or turn on Java.

Waters and Pommerich (2006) present a review of "context" effects in internet testing. Such effects cover factors like connection speed, screen size and resolution, web browser settings, font size, use of scrolling, and monitor or computer type. Of these, connection speed is probably the main issue as slow downloads can increase test-taker anxiety. While download speed could affect timed tests, best practice dictates that if timing is important, the test should run as a downloadable applet and not be dependent on Internet connection speeds. Screen size, resolution, monitor or computer type (e.g., CRT versus LCD displays; desktops versus laptops), web browser setting, and font size are all related to issues of legibility. Scrolling is a related issue in that for some screen resolutions it may be necessary to allow screen scrolling to ensure legibility. However, scrolling should be avoided wherever possible as test takers report that it interferes with test taking. In particular, scrolling should not be required for some test takers but not others. The bottom line is that test takers find problems with small, illegible, or inaccessible content whatever the reason for it.

It is now necessary for publishers distributing tests on the web to have a well-defined policy that defines which browser and operating system combinations they support and to implement checking procedures in their software if they are to ensure that tests do not get used on systems where the appearance or the operation of the test is incorrect. This is relatively easy to do for Managed Mode administration, but for the other three modes (Open, Controled, and Supervised) there is little the publishers can do to ensure that the hardware and software at the test-taker end are suitable—apart from carrying out software-based checks and denying the service if these indicate an unsuitable system. Clearly, such denials of service have to be managed carefully with support and alternate methods being offered to the test taker.

3.1 The Second Generation: The Rise of True On-line Tests

Many of the problems associated with on-line delivery of tests of ability are ones of test security. The more accessible such tests become both through wider circulation and through more "open" access, the more likely it is that they will be compromised. We will discuss later the whole issue of managing the risks of cheating in assessment on-line. For now it is worth noting that one impact of the move to on-line ability testing has been a related move away from classical test theory to item response theory (IRT) as the basis for test construction. IRT provides the psychometric technology needed to provide regular changes of test content, randomization of items within tests, and a range of other advances which are not possible using classical test theory approaches to test design. It also opens up the possibility of providing real-time adaptive testing on-line.

The main drivers from the market have been the push to move testing earlier on in the recruitment process, when applicants first enter the selection "funnel," and an associated push to make tests shorter and less of a "barrier" to applicants. IRT also provides the solution to both of these pressures in that it enables test designers to be much more efficient in measurement terms and hence get the same level of measurement precision with fewer items, as well as being able to vary test content in an unpredictable way that makes "cheating" very difficult.

We are also beginning to see some interesting new innovations in the area of self-report measures. In the next few years we can expect to see some radical changes in the way self-report measures are designed and delivered on the Web, with IRT models being extended to the area of multidimensional assessments and new item types appearing that make more use of the information-capturing potential of on-line systems.

4. RESEARCH ON ON-LINE TESTING

Despite the dramatic impact that the internet, through the Web, has had on the practice of testing in the occupational field, relatively little has been published in terms of research. What has been done tends to have been either concerned with issues of equivalence of Internet-based and earlier paper versions of tests or with the issue of applicant reactions to on-line testing.

For tests that have been moved from paper to computer delivery, a major issue has been that of equivalence. The question raised is whether the results from a test delivered by computer can be regarded as being comparable to the results from the same test when administered in traditional paper form. Mead and Drasgow (1993) reported a meta-analysis of equivalence studies, King and Miles (1995) reviewed cross-mode equivalence of non-cognitive tests and Bartram (1994) reviewed the literature in relation to both ability tests and inventories, questionnaires, and survey instruments. The general consensus from all these reviews was that there was no problem associated with computerization of non-cognitive tests, so long as due care was taken in the process of designing the computerized delivery. The same was true for tests of ability that were not highly speeded. The only area where equivalence is an issue is where speeded ability tests are concerned. Mead and Drasgow reported mean disattenuated cross-mode correlations of 0.97 for power tests and 0.72 for speeded ones.

The main issue is one of ergonomics. Under time pressure, differences in mode of response may act to significantly change the nature of the task. Thus, speeded tests, like clerical checking tasks, may need to be carefully redesigned and renormed when computerized. For most other ability tests, whether timed or untimed, so long as the timing does not introduce a high degree of speededness, paper and computer versions can be treated as equivalent forms. An important caveat to this, however, is that the implementation of the test in computer form must have been carried out carefully with due regard to readability and legibility of content (Waters and Pommerich 2006). Problems can arise for tests that rely on the test taker having to make use of various resource materials (charts, diagrams, reference materials, etc). Where it is not possible to fit these onto the computer screen, the nature of the task may be adversely affected by computerization.

More recent studies have supported these general conclusions. Gibson and Weiner (1997) report an elegantly designed study in which two forms of each of a number of different ability tests are presented in both computer and paper modes with complete balancing of forms and orders of modes of administration. They found that the average disattenuated correlation between modes was 0.94, and was greater for unspeeded tests than for speeded tests. For the latter they found an average disattenuated correlation of 0.86. For unspeeded tests, the average disattenuated correlation was close to unity (0.98).

There is a growing body of data to suggest that on-line delivery of tests does not impact on their psychometric properties (e.g., Bartram 2006). What evidence there is suggests that, given due care has been exercised in the implementation to ensure that ergonomic factors do not cause differences, there is unlikely to be any major impact of Web delivery on equivalence.

However, on-line testing has introduced another factor that needs to be considered: the difference between proctored and unproctored administration. The evidence of equivalence considered so far is based on changing the medium from paper to computer but keeping the mode of administration the same (i.e. supervised or proctored).

4.1 Equivalence and Unsupervised On-line Testing Mode

The issue that concerns most people about on-line testing is the use of what are variously referred to as controlled (ITC 2006), unsupervised, or unproctored modes of testing (Tippins et al. 2006). However, there is a growing body of research now that suggests the use of this mode does not have any adverse effect on the properties of self-report inventories or, under certain conditions, cognitive ability tests.

Lievens and Harris (2003) noted that "initial evidence seems to indicate that measurement equivalence between web-based and paper-and-pencil tests is generally established. In addition, no large differences are found between supervised and unsupervised testing. . . . these results should be interpreted with caution because of the small number of research studies involved." Oswald, Carr, and Schmidt (2001) examined the effects of presentation medium for both supervised and unsupervised administrations of a Big Five personality measure and found that in the supervised conditions there were some differences between the means and SDs for the two media. In the unsupervised conditions the means and SDs were very similar. Both of these studies were performed in laboratory conditions and only explored effects of the medium of presentation with fixed administration mode.

A key issue is how people behave in real high-stakes situations. Can practitioners use on-line personality measures for recruitment, selection, or development? Can they get valid and reliable personality profiles and can they use the same norms? Are there any issues or concerns for test takers that might affect their perception of a personality measure or create any systematic bias?

Bartram and Brown (2004) report on the comparison between matched samples completing the ipsative version of the SHL Occupational Personality Question-naire (OPQ32i) under real high-stakes conditions either in paper-and-pencil supervised conditions or on-line unsupervised. They found no substantive differ-ence in scales means, SDs, or reliabilities as a function of mode of administration. Furthermore, the relationships between scales were not affected by mode of administration. Comparable results were also reported for the normative version of the OPQ32 and for the SHL Motivation Questionnaire (Brown et al. 2005).

More recently, Do, Shepard, and Drasgow (2007) looked at response equiva-lence in terms of response rates and patterns at the scale and structure level. In one study they compared proctored and unproctored administration of a selec-tion battery for hourly call center employees ($n = 415$) with scales on education and work-related experience, conscientiousness, customer service, sales poten-tial, and working with information. Participants were randomly assigned to either the proctored or unproctored conditions. For scale-level data, the unproc-tored group had lower rather than higher scores on all scales apart from the education and work-related experience (where there was no difference). While the scale correlations and variances were larger for the unproctored group, IRT analyses showed little evidence of either differential item functioning (DIF) or differential test functioning (DTF).

In a second study, they compared a job incumbent sample who had applied for team leader or distribution center supervisor positions in a large retailer. Here the participants chose whether to have the proctored or unproctored conditions: 3,116 chose the proctored setting while nearly three times as many (9,504) chose the unproctored one. People were measured on six scales (conscientiousness, drive, interpersonal effectiveness, leadership, problem solving, and resilience). Again, the unproctored group tended to have lower mean scores but larger variances and intercorrelations than the proctored group. Apart from a problem-solving scale, DTF effects sizes were small indicating that measurement properties of the scales were similar across conditions. People who chose to have the proctored condition had higher scores on conscientiousness and drive. This could account for the overall higher level of performance of this group. In general the Do, Shepard, and Drasgow (2007) studies suggest that there are some differences in the way people respond across administration conditions, but these do not affect measurement equivalence nor is there any evidence for adverse impact relating to administration condition.

Huff (2007) analyzed data from the Wonderlic Personnel Test (WPT) using the Differential Functioning of Items and Test (DFIT) procedure. He compared data from 325 paper-and-pencil administrations with data from 325 Web-based administrations. The results indicated low levels of DIF though the scale scores were higher for the Web-based version. The DIF effects for certain items could be explained by the fact that these tended to be items where a response had to be typed into the computer rather than by just clicking an option. This is a more complex form of response than writing an answer on a paper answer sheet. Differences in usability between paper and computer versions of a test can be confounding variables when comparisons between proctored and unproctored conditions also involve differences in test media.

4.2 Applicant Reactions and the Effects of Test-Taking Environment

Morrison and Weiner (2007) asked applicants to complete a test environment survey (TES) in which they could rate (from Poor to Excellent) the lighting, temperature, computer system and equipment, noise level, workplace, testing staff, and overall conditions. Participants completed a cognitive and non-cognitive test in one of two conditions: either both were proctored or the non-cognitive test was completed unproctored and the cognitive one only was procotored. No differences were found between conditions for scores on the non-cognitive measures, nor were there any differences in TES ratings. However, there were positive correlations between scores on the non-cognitive test (a sales- and tenure-focused attitudinal measure) and TES ratings. The authors suggest that this could be accounted for by an underlying factor, such as agreeableness or impression management, that is influencing scores on both the non-cognitive scales and the TES ratings.

The move to on-line testing is generally reported as a positive move by organizations. Philo and Green (2007) describe the experience of an organization which hires 10,000 front-line associates every year. They started a pilot on-line application process in 2006 for all of these positions and when this suggested that flow rates, diversity, and pass rates were not going to be affected, began on-line testing for all front-line positions. Applicant flow rates increased (as McCook 2007 and others have also reported) and eligible candidates were willing to take the on-line tests. There were some concerns expressed by the HR and administrators over security, in particular the risk of dishonest applicants and problems associated with applicants for whom English was a problem. However, the overall response from HR and administrators was very positive in that the on-line process saved them time and speeded up the overall selection process. Applicants also found the experience positive: they found the on-line process more efficient and judged the content to be fair and reasonable. It also reflected positively on the image they had of the organization.

Philo and Green's (2007) study is interesting for what it tells us about the choices applicants make. Applicants could choose where they completed the tests. Around 10 percent chose to do the tests at a proctored testing center rather than in an unproctored on-line setting, with fewer white/Caucasian applicants (6 percent) than Latino/Hispanic (12 percent) or black/African American (13 percent). This may reflect differences in access to the Web. Most chose to do the tests at home: 71 percent for white/Caucasian versus 62 percent and 57 percent respectively for Latino/Hispanic and black/African Americans. The other locations used were someone else's home (around 10 percent) and a few percent each for "at work," "at a school," "at a public library," "at a community center" or "other." Applicants' ratings of the usability of the procedure showed very little variation as a function of setting. The proctored setting was rated no better than the other settings for being able to complete the process without distractions or disruptions, for internet connection speeds, and for general environmental conditions.

Wasko, Chawla, and Scott (2007) report a study in which they separated out mode of administration effects on the basis of whether they were proctored, unproctored in a home setting, or unproctored in a public setting (such as a school, library, or community center). Their data were based on 10,648 supervis-ory-level job applicants from eight different client organization selection proced-ures. Of these, 1,114 completed the tests in proctored settings, 890 in public unproctored settings, and the rest (8,644) in unproctored home settings. The measures were part of a leader-oriented selection test and covered situational judgment, personality, and background experience. Situational judgment test scores were slightly but significantly higher for the home than for the other two conditions. For personality scores and background experience scores, the public setting applicants had lower scores than in the other two conditions. Interestingly, applicants reported significantly fewer distractions for the home conditions than either the public or proctored conditions. Detailed analyses showed little evidence of subgroup differences. The results suggest that the generally higher levels of performance associated with the home setting are related to the more positive ratings by applicants of this being an environment where they are in control and where they can minimize distractions.

4.3 Validity of On-line Testing

While there is a growing body of evidence to suggest that tests administered on-line under unproctored conditions retain their psychometric properties in terms of norms and reliabilities, there is far less research to show that this translates into comparable levels of validity.

Burke and Wright (2007) report a meta-analysis of Verify ability test validities. Verify is a system of delivering numerical and verbal reasoning tests, where different tests are generated from an item bank for each applicant and delivered in unproctored mode. Short-listed applicants then receive a "verification test" that checks whether the score level obtained in the unproctored condition was likely to have been produced by a person with the ability level of the one completing the verification test. They report average validities of $r = 0.50$ for verbal and $r = 0.39$ for numerical for samples with total Ns of 548 and 760 and average Ns per study of 91 and 95 for verbal and numerical respectively. Artifacts accounted for all the between-study variance in validities. These validities are comparable to those obtained from full-length traditional proctored versions of these types of test.

Inceoglu and Bartram (2007) looked at the validities of a personality instrument (OPQ32) and showed that validities from unproctored high-stakes administration studies were the same as found in the meta-analysis reported by Bartram (2005) for proctored administration of the instrument. From the earlier meta-analysis the mean uncorrected validity for predicted relationships between personality traits and line manager rated competencies was 0.16 and for unpredicted relationships was 0.02. For the later set of unproctored administration studies (five studies with a total $N = 1,214$), the mean uncorrected validity for the predicted relationships was slightly higher ($r = 0.19$) while that for the unpredicted ones remained at 0.02.

5. MANAGING ISSUES OF TEST SECURITY, TEST TAKER VERIFICATION, AND AUTHENTICATION

The use of cognitive tests in unproctored mode could provide the greatest single advance in test use for recruitment and selection. We know that cognitive ability tests are the single best predictor of future job success and training outcome. We know that the utility of a selection procedure will be maximizing if the highest validity assessment tools are applied as early as possible in the recruitment process. However, the challenge has always been that you cannot do cognitive ability testing until you have short-listed people, because the testing needs to be carried out under supervision.

The need for supervision arises for the reasons noted in Tippins et al. (2006): prevention of piracy and prevention of cheating. Putting a test on-line that exists in only a single form is almost certain to lead to the test being compromised sooner rather than later if it is used in any form of high-stakes assessment. In relation to ability testing and tests with right answers, lack of local supervision raises three key issues for test providers and test users: maintaining the security of test content, verifying the identity of the test taker, preventing cheating. In relation to cheating, you need to control:

- Cheating by proxy. You need to be able to authenticate the identity of the test taker to avoid people getting someone else (of higher ability) to do the test for them.
- Cheating by collusion. You have to ensure people do not collude with other either directly or over the phone.
- Cheating by access to aids. You need to ensure people do not have access to unfair methods of answering questions, such as a list of the correct answers.

The last of these is dependent upon the answers to the test questions being in the public domain and hence is related to the issue of protection of test security. The Web has made access to information much faster than it used to be. A student who captures the items of an ability test can have them up for sale, or for free distribution, on a website within minutes. Protection of test security has been a major problem in the past for paper-based tests, as it has relied on the diligence of test users to keep materials locked away, to ensure people do not take copies of items out of test sessions, and so on.

For all these reasons, we would generally regard cognitive tests as needing to be restricted to supervised conditions of administration, in order to ensure that cheating was not possible and the security of the items was not compromised. Baron, Miles, and Bartram (2001) describe the use of test generation technology as the basis for on-line ability screening instruments that are used in unproctored modes as part of a job recruitment process. A different test is created for each test taker, thus making it difficult for them to cheat. The delivery software is also carefully constructed to make it impossible to interfere with timing or other aspects of the delivery and administration (any such attempts are detected and reported). The use of on-line screening tests like this provide organizations with considerable cost benefits in terms of the overall average cost per hired person, as it enables them to screen out a higher proportion of applicants before they are brought into an assessment center. However, it is also important to understand that the screening test is part of a larger process, a process which is made explicit to the test taker: all applicants need to know in advance that anyone who passes the screen will be reassessed under supervised conditions later, in order to detect any "false positives."

What we have seen in the very recent past is rapid progress in technology towards a form of what can be called "remote supervision." These developments have tackled each of the areas of risk and have resulted in test designs and procedures that are in many ways more secure than the traditional locally supervised modes of administration. The ways in which this has been achieved are exemplified in the system developed by Kryterion for remote proctored assessment (Foster and Maynes 2004; Foster 2007). While this has been developed mainly with educational assessment, professional licensing, and certification assessment fields in mind, it embodies all the principles that are now finding their way into systems for the remote administration of cognitive tests in employment testing.

5.1 Cheat-Resistant Tests

We have already mentioned the move toward using IRT as the basis for test construction. This provides the means by which one can create cheat-resistant tests. It is also possible to make classically constructed tests more cheat resistant. When a test consists of the same set of items always presented in the same order (as in paper-and-pencil testing), memorization of the answer key is relatively easy. This can be made harder by randomizing the order of items for each test taker and randomizing the order of response alternatives within each item. Care needs to be taken to ensure that this does not change the properties of the test. For example if the test is progressive in terms of item difficulty, then it would not be appropriate to randomize the item order, but one could randomize orders of response alternative.

Foster (2007) describes an item type that reduces the degree of exposure item response alternatives have in multiple choice items. In a traditional test all alternatives are shown and the test taker has to pick the one they think is correct. In Foster's item type, alternatives are presented, randomly, one at a time with the test taker responding "Yes" or "No" until they have either responded "Yes" (correctly or incorrectly) or responded "No" incorrectly. On average around half the response alternatives are exposed to each candidate and the reported correlation between the number of correct scores using this method and the traditional method is 0.76.

Some more sophisticated procedures vary item content in ways that are intended only to affect the "incidental" content of the item (i.e. aspects of the item that are unrelated to its difficulty). Item generation has been used to create new items for tests where "incidental" features are randomly generated while the "radicals" (i.e., those aspects directly affecting difficulty) are strictly controlled (Irvine, Dann, and Evans 1987; Irvine 2002). This approach can be carried out for relatively simple item types using classical test theory models.

The main benefit of using IRT is that one can develop banks of calibrated items from which tests can be generated to fit a wide range of specifications or sets of constraints—in terms of content, length, difficulty, and so on. To be a successful cheat, you need to know not just the contents of a test but the contents of a whole item bank—and be able to remember it and then recognize the relevant items when they appear in a test. With sufficiently large item banks, regularly item "refreshment," and monitoring of the stability of item parameters over time this provides a very robust way of making life very difficult for people who want to cheat.

5.2 Web Patrols

When test items have been stolen and put on the Web for other people to have unauthorized access to, it is necessary for the perpetrator to advertise this in some way—otherwise no one will find the content. Web patrols are regular searches of the internet for copyright content, such as test items. If this is carried out on a routine basis, stolen items can be found before they have been widely disseminated. For testing in the employment field, such behavior is relatively rare but it is potentially very damaging for traditional fixed tests if it is not detected quickly. To a large extent, the use of test generation procedures renders pointless attempts to "sell" on-line information about the answers to tests.

5.3 Data Forensics

Using item generation and test generation methods makes it very difficult to cheat. However we now have another tool that can be used to indicate the likelihood of cheating behavior as it happens. Data forensics is a new science that identifies "aberrant" patterns in the responses provided by test takers. For example, we can now time the responses to each item in an ability test and develop norms for these. These norms can be used to see whether a person is taking the test much too quickly (in which case they could be working from a scoring key) or too slowly (in which case they might be working in collusion with others). Add to this the pattern of correct and error responses in relation to the difficulty of the items and one can identify patterns typical of "item harvesters" (people who are busy photographing items rather than taking the test) or other forms of aberrance. Data forensics also provide the opportunity for looking at geographical and temporal patterns of responding that can flag up possible collusion.

5.4 Remote Proctoring

The strongest form of control over remote administration is remote proctoring or remote supervision. Test takers can be required to use a computer that has a web-cam attached and which can provide an authentication method, such as fingerprint recognition. Test takers will register with the system providing a fingerprint and web-cam photo. When they logon to take a test these can be verified and the web-cam will continuously monitor the test session. A remote proctor can

potentially supervise many hundreds of test takers and can be altered by the data forensics analyses to check out any aberrant responding. The proctor can then view the test taker; step back through their session; and on the basis of this and the aberrance report decided whether to interrupt or stop the test.

5.5 Verification Testing

One of the key issues raised in the discussion presented in Tippens et al. (2006) is the need for some form of verification assessment in high-stakes situations where decisions have been wholly or partly based on the results of an unproctored ability test. This had already been flagged as an approach to managing this risk by Segall (2001) and Baron, Miles, and Bartram (2001). The ITC Guidelines on Computer Based Testing and Internet Delivered Testing (2006, Guideline 45.3) specifically address this issue:

- *For moderate and high stakes assessment (e.g., job recruitment and selection), where individuals are permitted to take a test in controlled mode (i.e., at their convenience in non-secure locations), those obtaining qualifying scores should be required to take a supervised test to confirm their scores.*
  - > *Procedures should be used to check whether the test taker's original responses are consistent with the responses from the confirmation test.*
  - > *Test-takers should be informed in advance of these procedures and asked to confirm that they will complete the tests according to instructions given (e.g., not seek assistance, not collude with others, etc.).*
  - > *This agreement may be represented in the form of an explicit honesty policy which the test taker is required to accept.*

It is important to note that this guideline pulls together the need for verification testing with the need to make clear to test takers what the procedure will be well in advance. This provides those who might be weighing up the risks of being caught out if they cheat with the information necessary for them to know that those risks are very high. The SHL Verify tests have adopted this approach with a full-length test being given in unproctored mode and then short-listed candidate being given a shorter verification test to confirm whether the original score "fits" them (Burke and Wright 2007). Using IRT it is possible to make both of these tests quite short, with the verification test being only a few items long.

While the verification test concept provides a guard against cheating, it is also important to ensure that people who might have cheated and got short-listed do not push out people who did not cheat but who had sufficient scores for short-listing. It is important, therefore, to use a select-out rather than select-in strategy when basing decisions on measures that could be subject to faking or cheating.

5.6 Psychological Contracts

The need to be open with test takers is paramount. Consider the factors that might lead people to cheat or fake on job applications: people need to have

- The disposition to cheat. Some people are more likely to cheat than others.
- The motivation to cheat. This will tend to relate to the importance of the outcome and how much it matters to the individual to "pass the test".
- The means to cheat. For example, access to the answer key.
- The opportunity to cheat. Situations where cheating behaviors have a very low probability of being detected.

Presenting job applicants with a clear statement about what the procedure is, what is expected of them, the verification procedures that are in place, and so on is likely to affect their perception of the opportunity to cheat and may reduce their motivation if the penalty they pay for detection can be made clear. Data forensics, variable test content, and other techniques all reduce the means to cheat. Ultimately the assessment designer's task is to make it very difficult to cheat, to make cheating a high-risk strategy (in that detection is highly probable), and to make the costs not worth the effort.

By making clear to job applicants and other test takers the nature of the expectations that the organization has and its responsibilities to the test takers, the organization enters into a psychological contract. Surveys have indicated that one of the main concerns the majority of test takers have in on-line assessment is that other people may gain an unfair advantage through cheating. By making clear the steps that have been taken to prevent this, not only is cheating deterred, but the majority of test takers are also reassured about the equity of the process.

6. THE CHANGING RELATIONSHIP BETWEEN PUBLISHER AND TEST USER

The Internet has opened up a whole new set of opportunities for advancing the science of psychometrics and the technology of testing. It has also created some new challenges for those involved in test design and testing. In particular, we are seeing changes in the traditional balance of power between test producers, test users, test takers, and the consumers of the results of testing.

Item development and item banking requires an item database, item authoring and prototyping tools and interfaces, and some means of managing content through item inventory control and management. Test assembly and construction requires item selection and quality control procedures and procedures for dealing with the final rendering of the test—whether for on-line delivery or for off-line printing as a paper test. The factory analogy is a useful one as it highlights the way in which we are beginning to apply industrial procedures to what has been a craft process. A "test factory" is a set of systems that bring together a range of technologies and levels of automation associated with: test design, test development and manufacturing, warehousing and inventory control, test assembly, and, finally, delivery of the test to the customer.

The first generation of tests were pre-industrial. In the pre-industrial world, product manufacture was a distributed craft activity. Guilds and other organizations brought produce together from manufacturers and found markets for it. Until relatively recently the development of tests has followed the craft industry approach (and still does in many areas). A test author crafts a new product and then seeks a publisher to sell it.

In the second generation of test production, we see the application of industrialization procedures to tests. The first stage of industrialization was to bring these resources together into factories and to "deskill" the craftsmen. We are seeing that happen now as the larger test producers automate the procedures needed for item design and creation, develop item banks and item warehouses, and automate the quality control procedures needed to ensure that the finished products meet some pre-specified requirements and psychometric standards. However, this first stage of industrialization still follows the traditional manufacturing model in most cases. It is a "push" model that works on the basis of identifying a market need, creating a product that should meet that need, and then pushing that out into the market. Tests are designed and developed, admittedly with far greater efficiency and control over quality, and then made available for delivery, being stored either physically or virtually in a "warehouse" until required.

We are now in the third generation of test production. This involves the application of new industrialization procedures to "just-in-time testing." Here the factory process is a "pull" one rather than a "push" one. The requirements are identified from the market, these requirements are converted into a technical specification and fed into the factory as an "order," and the factory then delivers a test directly back into the market.

This move from craft industry to post-industrial manufacturing process is a major change in testing. Not surprisingly it is in the licensing and certification field and the high-volume educational testing areas that we see these procedures most highly developed. The same industrialization process is taking place in the employment testing field now. For example, SHL now deliver over a million on-line test administrations worldwide each year, mostly in unproctored or controlled mode, and the numbers are growing rapidly. In the past two or three years we have had to radically redesign our test production procedures, developing "industrialized," just-in-time procedures like those discussed above.

6.1 The Impact of Changes in HR on the Role of the "Professional" Test User

For testing in the employment field, the dominant role of the psychologist is changing from the person who is the consummate artist; who uncovers the mysteries of each person's psyche; to the expert craftsperson, who can add value to the results of using standard instruments through his or her expertise as a psychologist; and on to the specialist technologist who can package the expertise in such a way that lay users (e.g., line managers) can get value directly from the results of testing. While all three roles may coexist, there is an increasing demand on the need for packaging the expertise in such a way that lay users can get direct benefit from the use of tests without requiring the intervention of an "expert." It is always important for us to remember who the end user is for psychological testing. In employment testing, it is not the I/O psychologist; it is not even the human resources professional. It is generally a line manager needing to make hiring, succession planning, or other decisions, or an individual needing help with their personal progression and development.

Thus, one of the major factors affecting the impact a test has is how the scores are used and reported. It is, therefore, surprising that score reporting has received such scant attention, in comparison with other aspects of testing. The ITC Guidelines for Test Use (2001) emphasize the importance of providing feedback, of reporting that is unbiased and which does not overinterpret the results of a test. The more recent Guidelines on Computer Based Testing and Internet-Delivered testing (ITC 2006) also place an emphasis on the need for test developers, test distributors, and test users to pay attention to the provision of feedback.

In the traditional employment testing scenario in the UK, results (especially of personality and other self-report inventories) were often fed back to test takers in a face-to-face session that provided opportunities for the feedback provider to address issues, and the recipient of the information to ask questions. While it is still recommended that complex score reporting (such as the feedback of the results of a multi-scale personality inventory) should be supported as much as possible or practical with personal contact, the growth of internet-based testing has tended to make feedback and reporting as "remote" an event as the test administration. The more complex issue of reporting back to non-experts (test takers or line managers in the occupational field) on constructs like personality, intelligence, or motivation needs further attention.

It is because test results tend to impact indirectly on outcomes, because their effects are mediated through reporting processes, assessment policies, and their combination with other information, that the simple psychometric concepts of validity have limited value in applied settings. We should be placing far more emphasis on the consequential validity of test information. This is an issue to which far more attention will have to be paid in the future as on-line testing becomes more and more common.

7. CONCLUSION

Psychological testing probably touches more people more often than any other application of psychology. We are tested from cradle to grave; we are tested as we progress through the educational system; when we are well and when we are failing to cope with life; when we want to get a job, when we are at work, and when we need help in knowing what to do when we leave work; to help us spend our leisure time well and to help us excel at sport. On-line testing has made tests more available and more accessible. That is good insofar as it encourages people to base employment decisions on more objective forms of assessment. However, it is a risk in that it also creates a deregulated space in which it becomes harder for the test user to know good from bad. Just as the internet has made a wealth of information available for all, so it has raised the question: How do you discriminate between well-founded fact and opinion or fiction?

As psychologists we concern ourselves with trying to ensure that psychological tests are used in ways that are equitable, so that we create accurate and valid descriptions of people and make fair discriminations between them. The concept of equity in assessment is a complex one, because it involves competing demands. When assessing someone for a job we need to ensure that we assess all those attributes that are relevant for the job (not just some of them) and do not assess attributes that are not relevant. The way we assess needs to be accurate, valid, and free from irrelevant biases. In addition, the methods of assessment need to be acceptable: not only to be fair but to be seen to be fair and reasonable by all the parties involved (Gilliland 1993; 1994). Finally, they must be practical, in terms of cost, ease of use, user training requirements, and so on.

In practice, ensuring equity always involves compromise: people find short assessments more acceptable than long ones, but we know that, other things being equal, length is related to reliability and hence to validity. So if we want to make tests shorter we have to make them more efficient in measurement terms in order to enhance equity. We know test users want tests to be easy to use, not to require long training courses, and to be inexpensive. But test design, development, and production are costly, time-consuming processes; creating easy to use output from tests is both difficult and also very expensive. So how do we balance the consumer demand for assessments that cover the whole range of attributes that they need to assess, which are acceptable and practical, with the psychometric needs to ensure reliability validity and freedom from bias?

These tensions have always been present, but they have become even more apparent with the advent of on-line testing, which has not only revolutionized the ways tests are used in the employment field, but it has also impacted on the design and production of tests—creating a need for greater efficiency and industrialization. We are just at the beginning of the on-line revolution in testing. Within the next decade we are likely to see all assessment move on-line, including much more diverse forms of assessment (assessment center exercises, interviews, interactive problem-solving tests, and so on). The advantages of using this medium for testing really come down to two key benefits: control and reach. Through the use of software we can choose exactly how much control we want to exercise over test content, its administration, and the feedback of information. Through the use of the internet we can exercise this control at a distance.

REFERENCES

AGR. 2007. The AGR Graduate Recruiter Survey 2007: Summer Review. Warwick, UK: Association of Graduate Recruiters.

ANDERSON, N. 2003. Applicant and recruiter reactions to new technology in selection: a critical review and agenda for future research. *International Journal of Selection and Assessment*, 11 (2–3): 121–36.

BARON, H., MILES, A., and BARTRAM, D. 2001. Using online testing to reduce time to hire. Paper presented at the 16th annual conference of the Society for Industrial and Organizational Psychology, San Diego, April.

BARTRAM, D. 1994. Computer based assessment. *International Review of Industrial and Organizational Psychology*, 9: 31–69.

—— 2000. Internet recruitment and selection: kissing frogs to find princes. *International Journal of Selection and Assessment*, 8 (4): 261–74.

—— 2001. The impact of the Internet on testing for recruitment, selection and development. Keynote paper presented at the Fourth Australian Industrial and Organizational Psychology Conference, Sydney.

—— 2005. The Great Eight Competencies: a criterion-centric approach to validation. *Journal of Applied Psychology*, 90: 1185–203.

—— 2006. Computer-based testing and the Internet. A. Evers, N. Anderson, and O. Voskuijl. Pp. 399–418 in *The Blackwell Handbook of Personnel Selection*, ed. A. Evers, N. Anderson, and O. Smit-Voskuijl. Oxford: Blackwell Publishing.

—— 2007. Global norms? Some guidelines for aggregating personality norms across countries. Paper presented at 22nd Annual Society for Industrial and Organizational Psychology Conference (SIOP), New York, May.

—— and BAYLISS, R. 1984. Automated testing: past, present and future. *Journal of Occupational Psychology*, 57: 221–37.

—— and BROWN, A. 2004. Online testing: mode of administration and the stability of OPQ32i scores. *International Journal of Selection and Assessment*, 12: 278–84.

—— HAMBLETON, R. K. 2006. *Computer-Based Testing and the Internet: Issues and Advances*. Chichester: Wiley.

BEATY, J. C., Jr., FALLON, J. D., and SHEPERD, W. 2002. Proctored versus unproctored web-based administration of a cognitive ability test. In F. L. Oswald and J. M. Stanton (Chairs), Being Virtually Hired: Implications of Web Testing for Personnel Selection.

Symposium presented at the 17th Annual Conference of the Society for Industrial and Organizational Psychology, Toronto, April.

BERNERS-LEE, T. 1999. *Weaving the Web: The Original Design and Ultimate Destiny of the World Wide Web by its Inventor.* New York: Harper Collins.

BROWN, A., BARTRAM, D., HOLZHAUSEN, G., MYLONAS, G., and CARSTAIRS, J. 2005. Online personality and motivation testing: is unsupervised administration an issue? Paper presented at the 20th Annual Society for Industrial and Organizational Psychology Conference (SIOP) Conference, Los Angeles, April.

BURKE, E., and WRIGHT, D. 2007. Addressing the issues of cheating and online unsupervised ability testing. Paper presented at the 13th European Congress of Work and Organizational Psychology, Stockholm, May.

CIPD. 2006. *Recruitment, Retention and Turnover.* Annual Survey Report. London: Chartered Institute of Personnel and Development.

DO, B.-R., SHEPARD, W., and DRASGOW, F. 2007. Measurement equivalence across proctored and unproctored administration modes of web-based measures. Paper presented at 22nd Annual Society for Industrial and Organizational Psychology Conference (SIOP), New York, May.

FOSTER, D. 2007. Maximizing security for high-stakes internet exams using the ITC guidelines. Paper presented at the 10th European Congress of Psychology, Prague, July.

—— and MAYNES, D. 2004. Detecting test security problems using item response times and patterns. In D. Foster and R. Hambleton (Chairs), Solve Testing Security Problems Using Technology and Statistics. Symposium presented at the Association of Test Publishers Conference, Palm Springs, CA, February.

GIBSON, W. M., and WEINER, J. A. 1997. Equivalence of computer-based and paper-pencil cognitive ability tests. Paper presented at the 12th annual conference of the Society for Industrial and Organizational Psychology, St Louis, April.

GILLILAND, S. W. 1993. The perceived fairness of selection systems: an organizational justice perspective. *Academy of Management Review,* 18: 694–734.

—— 1994. Effects of procedural and distributive justice on reactions to a selection system. *Journal of Applied Psychology,* 79: 691–701.

HUFF, K. 2007. DFIT analysis of web-based and paper-based versions of the WPT. Paper presented at 22nd Annual Society for Industrial and Organizational Psychology Conference (SIOP), New York, May.

INCEOGLU, I., and BARTRAM, D. 2007. Does unsupervised assessment lower validity? Paper presented at the 13th European Congress of Work and Organizational Psychology, Stockholm.

INTERNATIONAL TEST COMMISSION. 2001. International guidelines for test use. *International Journal of Testing,* 1: 93–114.

—— 2006. Guidelines on computer based testing and internet-delivered testing. *International Journal of Testing,* 6: 143–72.

IRVINE, S. H. 2002. The foundation of item generation. In *Item Generation for Test Development,* ed. S. H. Irvine and P. Kyllonen. Mahwah, NJ: Lawrence Erlbaum.

—— DANN, P. L., and EVANS, J. ST. B. T. 1987. Item generative approaches for computer based testing: A prospectus for research. Report for the Army Personnel Research Establishment. Human Assessment Laboratory, University of Plymouth.

KING, W. C., and MILES, E. W. 1995. A quasi-experimental assessment of the effects of computerized non cognitive paper-and-pencil measurements: a test of measurement equivalence. *Journal of Applied Psychology*, 80: 643–51.

LIEVENS, F., and HARRIS, M. M. 2003. Research on internet recruitment and testing: current status and future directions. Pp. 131–65 in *International Review of Industrial and Organizational Psychology*, vol. 18, ed. C. L. Cooper and I. T. Robertson. Chichester: John Wiley and Sons.

McCOOK, K. 2007. Comparison of proctored vs. unproctored response data trends on personality and basic ability assessments. Paper presented at 22nd Annual Society for Industrial and Organizational Psychology Conference (SIOP), New York, May.

MEAD, A. D., and DRASGOW, F. 1993. Equivalence of computerized and paper-and-pencil cognitive ability tests: a meta-analysis. *Psychological Bulletin*, 114: 449–58.

MORRISON, J., and WEINER, J. 2007. The environmental trade-offs of unproctored pre-employment assessment. Paper presented in the symposium J. Weiner (Chair), The Impact of Testing Conditions on Online Assessment at the 22nd Annual Society for Industrial and Organizational Psychology Conference (SIOP), New York, May.

OSWALD, F. L., CARR, J. Z., and SCHMIDT, A. M. 2001. The medium and the message: dual effects of supervision and web-testing on measurement equivalence for ability and personality measures. In F. L. Oswald (Chair), Computers-Good? How Test-User and Test-Taker Perceptions Affect Technology-Based Employment Testing. Symposium presented at the 16th Annual Conference of the Society for Industrial and Organizational Psychology, San Diego, CA, April.

PHILO, J., and GREEN, A. 2007. Is online testing the right move for your organization? Paper presented at 22nd Annual Society for Industrial and Organizational Psychology Conference (SIOP), New York, May.

SEGALL, D. O. 2001. Detecting test compromise in high-stakes computerized adaptive testing: A verification testing approach. Paper presented at the Annual General Meeting of the National Council on Measurement in Education, Seattle, April.

TIPPINS, N. T., BEATY, J., DRASGOW, F., GIBSON, W. M., PEARLMAN, K., SEGALL, D. O., and SHEPERD, W. 2006. Unproctored internet testing in employment setting. *Personnel Psychology*, 59: 189–225.

WASKO, L. E., CHAWLA, A., and SCOTT, D. 2007. An examination of the opportunities and challenges presented by proctored vs. unproctored testing. Paper presented in the symposium J. Weiner (Chair), The Impact of Testing Conditions on Online Assessment at the 22nd Annual Society for Industrial and Organizational Psychology Conference (SIOP), New York, May.

WATERS, S. D., and POMMERICH, M. 2006. Context effects in internet testing: a literature review. HumRRO Report prepared for Defense Manpower Data Center, M67004-05-D-0009, June 12.

PART III

METHODOLOGICAL ISSUES

MODELS AND METHODS FOR EVALUATING RELIABILITY AND VALIDITY

KEVIN R. MURPHY

1. INTRODUCTION

TESTS and structured assessments are used to make inferences and decisions about individuals and groups. In personnel selection, these can range from assessments of the knowledge, skills, and abilities thought to be necessary for successful job performance to evaluations of current and past job performance. Assessments of these measures usually concentrate on two broad questions—i.e., evaluating whether they measure what they claim to measure and evaluating whether (as in personnel selection) measures of one construct (e.g., ability) can be used to predict standing on another construct (e.g., job performance; Murphy and Davidshofer 2005).[1] Investigations of the reliability and validity of the tests and assessments

---

[1] The term "construct" is used to refer to properties of individuals that cannot be directly observed (e.g., intelligence, achievement motivation) or to broad categories of behavior (e.g., performance) that are measured by tests, assessments, judgments, etc.

used in personnel psychology are central to the claim that scientific methods can be usefully applied to understanding and predicting human behavior in the workplace. Without good measurement, it is hard to see how it is possible to make good decisions about individuals or to formulate and test useful theories and hypotheses about behavior in organization.

In this chapter, I will discuss assessments that range from paper-and-pencil tests of work-related abilities and skills to measures based on the judgments of an interviewer or a supervisor. Many of the principles of psychometrics were first developed in the context of multi-item written tests of abilities or other enduring characteristics of individuals, and my descriptions of the main models and methods of psychometrics will often be framed in terms of specific characteristics of these tests (e.g., the use of multiple test items, in which all items are designed to measure the same characteristic of individuals).

2. RELIABILITY

Scores on tests and assessments are never perfectly stable. The same individual might take two similar tests and receive different scores on each. Someone might take the same test on two different occasions and receive different scores. Because many of the tests and assessments used in personnel selection are designed to measure relatively stable characteristics of individuals (e.g., abilities, personality traits), this instability in test scores is a significant concern, and a great deal of attention has been given to developing models and methods for estimating the reliability of tests and other assessments.

2.1 Conceptual and Statistical Models of Reliability

The concept of reliability can be traced back to an influential set of papers by Spearman early in the 1900s, in which he laid the foundations for what is now referred to as classical test theory (CTT). Spearman's early papers pointed the way toward the development of both the concept of test reliability and the method of factor analysis (Thorndike and Lohman 1990).

The starting point for CTT is the realization that measures obtained in real-world settings will be affected by a number of attributes of the persons measured, the test itself, and the situations in which measures are obtained. The simplest breakdown of test scores partitions the observed score (X) on a test into two general components, true score (T) and error (e). That is:

$$X = T + e. \tag{1}$$

In CTT, errors of measurement are assumed to reflect the combined effects of testing procedures, idiosyncrasies of the particular test or measurement method, unpredictable fluctuations in the examinee's state, errors in marking answers on a response sheet, and a litany of other variables that are not substantively related to the construct the test is designed to measure, but that might affect a particular set of test scores. The critical assumption in this theory is that errors are statistically independent of true scores (i.e., $r_{Te} = 0$). As Lord and Novick (1968) showed, the assumption that true scores and errors are independent can be proven to be true, given particular definitions of exactly what "true score" is taken to mean, and is a reasonable one under a wide variety of alternative decisions.

The assumed independence of true scores and errors leads to a number of important conclusions (Lord and Novick 1968). First, if true scores and errors are independent, the variance in observed scores can be defined as the simple sum of the variance due to true scores and variance due to errors of measurement. That is,

$$\sigma_X^2 = \sigma_T^2 + \sigma_e^2. \tag{2}$$

If we partition the variance of observed scores into that which is explained by true score variance and that which is explained by error, a natural question arises about what proportion is due to true scores vs. errors. In CTT, the *reliability coefficient* is defined as the proportion of the observed score variance that is explained by true scores, or equivalently, as the squared correlation between true scores and observed scores. That is,

$$\text{Reliability coefficient} = \sigma_T^2/(\sigma_T^2 + \sigma_e^2) = \sigma_T^2/\sigma_X^2 = \rho_{XT}^2. \tag{3}$$

Therefore, saying that the reliability of a test is equal to .85 is equivalent to saying that 85 percent of the variance in test scores is due to true scores, and 15 percent is due to measurement error. Since one of the principal goals of measurement theory is to define and control measurement error, the reliability coefficient (often symbolized as ρ_{XX}) is understandably one of the more important indices used in CTT to evaluate tests.

This simple breakdown of observed scores into independent true score and error components has a number of profound consequences. First, in this theory measurement errors are assumed to be independent of true scores *and* independent of errors in other measures. If this assumption is true, it follows that the correlations between two different tests or measures *must* be due to the true score components of each test. It is also easy to show that measurement errors can obscure, or at least diminish, the correlations among various tests and measures. One of Spearman's early insights was that it is possible to estimate, and perhaps even correct for, the effects of measurement errors on the correlations among observed scores. The *correction for attenuation*, which is a direct result of Spearman's earliest work in this area, can be defined as:

$$\text{Corrected } r_{xy} = \text{observed } r_{xy}/(\text{sqrt}(\rho_{XX}) * \text{sqrt}(\rho_{YY})). \qquad (4)$$

For example, assume that you knew that the reliabilities of X and Y were .90 and .80, respectively, and that $r_{xy} = .30$. The correction for attenuation suggests that if you could remove the effects of error, you would expect to find a correlation of about .35 between X and Y. It may not be possible to completely remove the effects of measurement errors, but famous and widely used correction does give some indication of the results that might reasonably be expected if highly reliable measures were used.

Classical test theory has had substantial effects on both research and practice. In particular, corrections for the effects of measurement error are a common part of meta-analysis and analyses of the generalizability of test validities (Schmidt and Hunter 1977). While CTT can provide useful and interesting results, Spearman's formulation has long been recognized as a rough approximation, and serious questions have sometimes been raised about the usefulness of results derived from CTT. In particular, CTT poses some very difficult questions about the definition and meaning of true scores.

2.1.1 *Meaning of true scores*

There are two ways of building a model of true scores and errors that can yield very different interpretations of the meaning of test scores. One possibility is to start with a substantive definition of what "true score" means, which by implication defines errors in measurement as all other sources of variation in test scores. That is, if we define what we mean by "T," then:

$$e = X - T. \qquad (5)$$

Alternatively, we could define measurement errors as the random components of the observed score, which by definition defines the true score as whatever is left over when errors are removed. That is, if we define what we mean by "E," then:

$$T = X - e. \qquad (6)$$

To understand the implications of these two approaches to constructing true score models, consider the case of a test designed to measure three-dimensional spatial visualization. If we defined true scores as the person's true level of spatial visualization ability, measurement errors would not simply reflect the random fluctuations in measures that are at the heart of CTT. Rather, *anything* about the test or the testing situation that was not related to true spatial visualization ability would be lumped into error. So, if some of the variation in test scores was a function of the format of the test (e.g., some people do better on computerized tests and others do better on paper-and-pencil versions), this type of model would treat this systematic difference between individuals as one source of measurement error.

The history of psychometric theory includes many different definitions of true scores. Lord and Novick (1968) provide a detailed critique of the concept of "Platonic true score"—i.e., true score defined in terms of the individual's true standing on the construct being measured. It is common in personnel selection research to treat true scores and constructs as if they were virtually interchangeable (e.g., Viswesvaran, Schmidt, and Ones 2005), but it is clear that this Platonic conception of true scores is unrealistic, and that the traditional breakdown of scores into true scores and random errors does not reflect the reality of most psychological tests and assessments

The most satisfactory definition of a true score is laid out in Lord and Novick (1968), who define true scores in terms of expected values. Suppose an individual was able to take the same test or assessment many times, and we were somehow able to wipe the examinee's memory of the test clean each time, so that each administration of the test was an independent event. The average score over all test administrations would be a good approximation to the expected value of the test score, and this hypothetical average defines that person's true score. Using this definition of a true score, it is easy to show that errors in measurement are independent of true scores. This definition of true scores can be generalized to a variety of situations, for example, when an individual obtains scores on several different tests or assessments designed to measure the same construct. If these tests are thought of as representing a random sample of assessments that might have been used to measure this construct, a true score can be defined as the expected value over multiple tests or assessments, as opposed to an expected value over several independent administrations of the same test.

2.1.2 *Generalizability theory*

Generalizability theory is the most general and most realistic model of test reliability (Brennan 1983; Cronbach et al. 1972; Shavelson, Webb, and Rowley 1989). Generalizability theory starts with the assertion that the goal of measurement is to generalize from the measures one actually obtains to the universe of permissible observations. For example, suppose four teachers evaluate a student's performance in seventh grade. These evaluations can be thought of as a sample of a broader universe of observations that might have been used to evaluate a student's performance (e.g., ratings from other teachers), and the question this theory is designed to address is the extent to which scores obtained in this sample of observations generalize to the broader universe from which they were sampled.

It should be obvious that random measurement error will affect one's ability to make good and accurate generalizations. A test in which a good proportion of the variance in observed scores is due to random measurement error will obviously not allow you to say much about the individuals who take the test. The key insight of generalizability theory is that random errors of measurement are not the only factors that might affect one's ability to make valid generalizations. Rather, this theory starts with the assumption that there might be multiple sources of measurement error, some of which might represent systematic but unwanted sources of variability. Suppose, for example, three different types of measures (e.g., multiple choice, constructed response, video vignettes) are used to assess conscientiousness. Some measures are obtained in group settings, and others in one-on-one interviews. In this setting, variability in test scores that is due to the type of measure would not be thought of as true score variance, but it is certainly not random error. Similarly, variability that is due to group vs. one-on-one assessments is not a source of true score variance, but is also not a source of random measurement errors.

Generalizability theory places a great deal of emphasis on the intended use of test scores. The universe of admissible observations is defined in terms of the range of alternative measures decision makers might accept as appropriate for their purposes. In CTT, true scores are assumed to be fixed values for each individual, and measurement errors are assumed to be a function of the test itself, not of the potential uses or interpretation of the test. Thus, it makes sense in CTT to assert that each test has a certain level of reliability that is essentially independent of the uses and interpretations of test scores. Generalizability theory suggests that the same test might be a member of several different universes of admissible observations, and that the level of reliability of a test might vary considerably across situations, depending on the interpretation and use of test scores and on the effects of various conditions of measurement on scores.

The universe of admissible observations can be described in many different ways, but the most useful is to describe this universe in terms of its various facets. Returning to an earlier example, suppose that three different types of measures (e.g., multiple choice, constructed response, video vignettes), applied in both group settings and one-on-one interviews, are used to assess conscientiousness. An analysis of generalizability would start with an analysis of variance, as illustrated in Table 11.1. First, variance components are estimated. These represent estimates of the population variance that can be attributed to different facets of the universe. People are assumed to vary on the trait or the construct the test is designed to measure; the variance component for persons (σ^2_P) represents true score variability. This variance needs to be interpreted in light of the variability attributable to error, and the sources of error depend substantially on the way tests will be used.

Tests can be used for either *absolute* or *relative* measurement. In the present example, a variety of tests and assessments are used to measure conscientiousness. Different factors will contribute to measurement error depending on whether tests are used to measure each person's level of conscientiousness (absolute) or to determine which people in a sample have higher or lower levels of conscientiousness (relative). In absolute measurement, all of the variance components in the ANOVA model shown in Table 11.1 other than the variance component for persons

Table 11.1 Analysis of variance used to evaluate generalizability

Facet	Variance components	Meaning
Persons (P)	σ_P^2	Variability due to persons—analogous to true score in CTT
Measure (M)	σ_M^2	Variability due to measurement methods
Setting (S)	σ_S^2	Variability due to differences between group and one-on-one measurement settings
$P \times M$	$\sigma_{P \times M}^2$	Variability due to the interaction between persons and measurement methods (e.g., some people may do better with paper and pencil, others with video)
$P \times S$	$\sigma_{P \times S}^2$	Variability due to the interaction between persons and settings methods (e.g., some people may do better with group tests, others with individual interviews)
$M \times S$	$\sigma_{M \times S}^2$	Variability due to the interaction between measurement methods and settings (e.g., the effects of using paper and pencil vs. video might be different in individual and in group settings)
Error	σ_e^2	Error. This includes variability due to the three-way interaction between persons, measurement methods, and settings as well as all other sources of random measurement error

(σ_P^2) represent sources of measurement error. In relative measurement, only σ_e^2 and those facets that represent interactions between persons and conditions of measurement (and thus could affect the rank ordering of people) represent sources of measurement error.

Generalizability theory provides an analog to the reliability coefficient, the *generalizability coefficient* (ρ_{XX}^2). Like the reliability coefficient, this coefficient represents a ratio of true score variance to true score plus relative error variance. Using the variance components presented in Table 11.1, this relative error variance (σ_{REL}^2) is defined as:

$$\sigma_{REL}^2 = \sigma_{PXM}^2 / n_m + \sigma_{PxS}^2 / n_s + \sigma_{error}^2 / n_m n_s \qquad (7)$$

where n_m and n_s represent the number of measurement methods (3) and situations (2), respectively. The generalizability coefficient ($\rho_{XX}2$) is given by:

$$\rho_{XX}^2 = \sigma_P^2 / (\sigma_P^2 + \sigma_{REL}^2). \qquad (8)$$

2.1.3 Comparing CTT and generalizability theory

Classic test theory starts with the assumption that there are two and only two sources of variance in test scores, true scores and random measurement error.

When these assumptions are met, CTT provides an extremely powerful and elegant set of methods for estimating and interpreting reliability. Unfortunately, these assumptions are rarely true, and in fact are rarely even plausible.

Cronbach et al. (1972) note that CTT represents a special case of the more general model provided by generalizability theory. Like CTT, generalizability theory assumes that both true scores and random errors of measurement are important determinants of test scores. However, generalizability theory recognizes that there are often a number of systematic factors that affect test scores that are neither true score nor error (e.g., test formats, conditions of measurement). Generalizability theory provides both a conceptual and an analytic framework for separating these systematic sources of variability from the traditional categories of true score and error. Unless there is a good reason to believe that the more restrictive CTT is a reasonable way of thinking about a particular measure, it is always better to consider how generalizability theory might be applied to provide a more realistic model for understanding test scores.

2.1.4 *IRT*

The method of choice for contemporary psychometric analysis is Item Response Theory (Hulin, Drasgow, and Parsons 1983; Lord 1980). Item response theory is concerned with understanding the relationship between an individual's standing on a particular trait or construct and his or her responses to test items. This relationship is usually depicted in the form of an Item Characteristic Curve (ICC); an ICC for an item on a test of verbal ability is shown in Figure 11.1.

CTT defines reliability as an attribute of test scores. In IRT, the concept of *information* is the closest analog to reliability. IRT suggests that each item conveys a certain amount of information about the individual being measured, and that high reliability translates into a good deal of information. Information functions can be defined for each item in a test and for the overall test score. One key result from IRT is the demonstration that it is possible to get highly reliable information from a small number of items, if items are chosen with difficulties that match the ability level of the applicants (e.g., as in tailored or computerized adaptive testing).

2.2 Estimating the Reliability and Dependability of Test Scores

The concept of reliability in CTT is a relatively straightforward one, but the problem of obtaining good estimates of the reliability of test scores has proved to be a significant challenge, in part because of the frequent disconnect between the conceptual models used to define reliability and the operational procedures used for estimating levels of reliability. Historically, the first attempts to develop workable estimation procedures were built around the *parallel test model* of reliability.

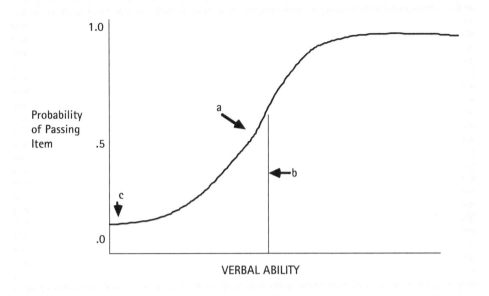

Fig.11.1 Item characteristic curve

Notes:
(a) slope—the extent to which the item discriminates low-ability examinees from high-ability.
(b) difficulty—level of ability needed to have a probability of passing halfway between c and 1.0.
(c) guessing—the probability that a person who has a very low ability level will pass the item.

Two tests are parallel if they measure the same true score, yield the same observed score variance, and measure the true scores with equal levels of precision. The correlation between scores on two parallel tests is equal to the reliability coefficient (Lord and Novick 1968).

2.2.1 *Using alternative forms to estimate reliability*

The parallel test model led to the development of reliability estimates based on alternative forms of the same test. In principle, it might be possible to develop two alternative forms of the same test that are distinct but essentially interchangeable. In the strictest version of the parallel forms model, alternative forms must be developed that would be equally acceptable to and appropriate for individuals across the entire range of test scores. The development of alternative test forms that approach the strict requirements of the parallel test model can be extremely challenging, although algorithms for developing tests of this type have been developed (Beok-kooi-Timminga 1990). Alternative forms exist for many tests, but it is often challenging (and sometimes impossible) to demonstrate that all forms of a particular test measure the same true scores. A number of less restrictive alternatives to the parallel test model have been proposed and identified (e.g., tau-equivalent test model, congeneric test model; Lord and Novick 1968) but all variations of CTT share the same general weakness—i.e., the difficulty of defining and measuring true scores.

2.2.2 *Internal consistency estimates*

Rather than administering two separate tests, most estimates of the reliability of multi-item tests are obtained using internal consistency estimates. The conceptual rationale of internal consistency methods starts with the assumption that each test item is an observation of behavior or responses that contain some information about the construct the test is designed to measure. If it can be shown that each item taps the same construct, pooling together a number of independent pieces of information about that construct should allow one to obtain stable, reliable measures.

Historically, the first internal consistency estimates were obtained using the *split-half* method, in which a test is split into two parts (often using an odd–even split, in which odd-numbered items form one part and even-numbered items form the other), and scores on the two parts are correlated. Conceptually, this correlation between two halves of a test can be interpreted in very much the same way as the correlation between two alternative forms (with an important caveat, noted below). Because the two halves of the same test are likely to be at least roughly parallel, this split-half correlation can be interpreted as a reliability estimate.

There are two problems with split-half methods. First, if you split a 50-item test into two 25-item halves, this method estimates the reliability of a half-length test, not the reliability of the original test. The need to account for the effects of test length in estimating reliability led to the famous *Spearman–Brown correction*. Murphy and Davidshofer (2005) discuss the general form of this correction, which can be used to estimate the reliability of a test if its length is increased by a factor of n:

$$\text{new}r_{xx} = \frac{n \times \text{old}r_{xx}}{1 + (n-1)\,\text{old}r_{xx}}. \tag{9}$$

For example, if the reliability of a 30-item test is .75, tripling the length of the test should yield a reliability of .90.

The more important problem with split-half methods is that there are many ways to split a test in half, and these will not, in general, yield identical split-half correlations. As a result, split-half methods have fallen somewhat out of favor, although they are still useful for estimating the reliability of speeded tests. They have been replaced in large part by *coefficient alpha* (Cronbach 1951), the most widely used internal consistency estimate of reliability (Schmidt, Le, and Iles 2000).

Coefficient alpha is a function of two characteristics of a test, the relationships between test items and the number of items. The general formula for coefficient alpha is:

$$\alpha = k\,(1 - \Sigma\sigma^2_{item}/\sigma^2_{\text{test}})/(k-1) \tag{10}$$

where k is the number of items and the sum of the individual item variances is compared to the variance of the total test score (which reflects both the variances and the covariances of the items). A common variant is the *standardized coefficient alpha*, which is given by:

$$\alpha = \frac{k \; (\text{average } r_{ij})}{1 + (k-1)(average \; r_{ij})} \tag{11}$$

where (average r_{ij}) represents the mean of the inter-item correlations. As both formulas suggest, the higher the intercorrelation among items and/or the larger the number of items, the more reliable the test score is expected to be.

Given its widespread use, there is an extensive literature dealing with coefficient alpha (e.g., Cortina 1993; Rodriquez and Maeda 2006). For unidimensional tests (in which all items measure the same thing) coefficient alpha is generally regarded as a reasonable lower-bound estimate for reliability (Cortina 1993). That is if alpha is equal to .85, psychometric theory suggests that true scores account for at least 85 percent of the variance in observed scores. When alpha is applied to estimate the reliability of tests that measure several different attributes, it can provide reliability estimates that are seriously inaccurate (Cortina 1993).

2.2.3 *Test-retest methods*

Rather than using the correlation between two arguably parallel tests to estimate reliability, one might use the correlation between two separate administrations of the same test. Test-retest methods for estimating reliability are feasible only in situations where there is no carry-over effect—i.e., applications in which taking the first test does not directly affect responses to the second test. Test-retest methods do not require any assumption of unidimensionality, nor do they require an assumption of parallelism (in either its strong or weak form). Test-retest correlations are often referred to as *stability coefficients*.

In general, the magnitude of test-retest reliabilities is not constant over varying intervals, nor is the value likely to be consistent with coefficient alpha (Lord and Novick 1968; Schmidt, Le, and Iles 2000). As Schmidt, Viswesvaran, and Ones (2000) note, there are different sources of measurement error that can have very different implications for tests and assessments. In particular, they describe methods for distinguishing between transient error, random response error, and specific factor errors, and they suggest that most reliability studies ignore transient errors, leading to overestimates of reliability.

This discussion of different types of measurement error points to a critical weakness in CTT—i.e., the failure to define either true scores or measurement errors in entirely consistent terms. The fundamental starting point for CTT is the equation $X = T + e$, but this equation may not be all that useful if the definition of true scores and measurement errors changes, depending on the uses of tests and the circumstances under which reliability studies are conducted. For example, coefficient alpha is usually interpreted as a lower bound for reliability, but test-retest reliabilities might be substantially different (usually smaller than) alpha. This is because "error" depends substantially on the tests, the way tests are administered and used, and the populations in which the test is administered. One lesson that can be drawn from Schmidt and Hunter's (1996) review of the various definitions of true score and error in different research scenarios is that statements such as "the reliability of this test is .85," or "the reliability of this class of measures is .52," cannot be taken seriously.

2.2.4 Interrater reliability

There is a very large literature dealing with the question of whether or not and under what conditions two independent raters are likely to agree in their subjective judgments. Interrater agreement and interrater reliability are not the same (Kozlowski and Hattrup 1992; Shrout and Fleiss 1979); agreement measures reflect absolute differences in ratings whereas reliability measures reflect similarity or difference in the rank ordering of ratees.

There have been extensive debates over the meaning and measurement of interrater reliability, especially in the context of performance rating (Viswesvaran, Ones, and Schmidt 1996). For example, Viswesvaran et al.'s review showed that the average coefficient alpha for supervisory ratings of overall job performance was .86, while the average interrater correlation (which is interpreted as a reliability estimate) for supervisory ratings of overall job performance was .52. If interrater correlations are interpreted as reliability coefficients, this low interrater reliability estimate suggests that 48 percent of the variance in job performance ratings reflects random measurement error. One implication of this conclusion is that the observed correlations between performance ratings and other measures (e.g., selection tests) will be seriously attenuated, and that validity studies that rely on performance ratings as criteria will severely underestimate the validity and usefulness of tests as predictors of job performance (Schmidt and Hunter 1977).

Murphy and DeShon (2000a) argued that interrater correlations are not reliability coefficients, and that the assumption that different raters act as parallel tests (an assumption that is necessary to interpret interrater correlations as reliability estimates) is not plausible, given all we know about the dynamics of performance rating. Their analysis suggests that numerous factors other than true performance and random error influence performance ratings, and that the correlations between raters are not sensible estimates of reliability. Schmidt, Viswesvaran, and Ones (2000) and Murphy and DeShon (2000b) debated the relative merits of the traditional CTT model and more modern models for understanding the reliability and validity of performance ratings.

2.2.5 Estimates based on structural equation modeling

Structural equation modeling (SEM) provides an attractive method for defining and estimating error variance in test scores (Graham 2006; McDonald 2000;

Murphy and DeShon 2000a). First, this method required researchers to develop and articulate a model for understanding the meaning of test scores, rather than assuming that some a priori model (e.g., $T = X + e$) is necessarily appropriate or useful. Second, it requires researchers to determine whether the model actually fits the data. The application of SEM to reliability estimation also highlights one of the themes of the present chapter, that assessments of reliability and assessments of validity are closely linked. In particular, one of the assumptions of SEM is that the meaning of test scores, and the separation of error from systematic variance in test scores, is best done in the context of modeling the relationships among multiple measures.

In CTT, measurement error for a particular test is assumed to be uncorrelated with true scores and with true or error scores on other measures. It is easy to build structural models in which error terms show these exact characteristics. However, SEM does not limit researchers to traditional definitions of error; structural models with correlated error terms are sometimes preferable to the traditional models that treat error as uncorrelated with all other sources of variance (Reddy 1992).

The relationship between CTT, generalizability theory, and SEM is best understood in terms of a hierarchical structure. CTT is a special case of generalizability theory. When the assumptions of CTT can be met, it provides a powerful and elegant solution to a wide range of measurement problems. When these assumptions cannot be met (e.g., in assessments of interrater reliability), generalizability theory provides a more general model for identifying the sources of variance in scores and for deciding which should be treated as errors when making specific generalizations from test scores. SEM represents the most general model, in which models of test scores are generated and tested, and in which the estimation of error is part of a broader process for determining whether particular test score models make sense in light of the available data. When possible, SEM probably provides the best single method of estimating reliability.

2.2.6 *Reliability generalization*

Suppose there have been a dozen studies of the psychometric characteristics of a particular scale. You have just collected data using that scale, and need to assess the reliability of scale scores. Traditionally, assessments of reliability and validity were often done using the data at hand, essentially ignoring the cumulative evidence of test score reliability and validity. Schmidt and Hunter (1977) introduced methods of incorporating validity evidence from existing studies to assess the generalizability of validity (these are discussed in more detail in subsequent sections). Similar methods have been proposed for pulling together evidence about test score reliability and making sense of this evidence (Thompson and Vacha-Haase 2000; Vacha-Haase 1998). Reliability generalization analyses and related meta-analytic approaches for examining the consistency and variability of reliability estimates are increasingly common (e.g., Rodriquez and Maeda 2006), and they have proved useful for determining when and whether the cumulative body of research allows one to draw useful conclusions about the reliability of tests in particular circumstances.

3. VALIDITY

The concept of validity has evolved considerably over the last fifty years. At one time, psychologists spoke of different types of validity and advocated a number of seemingly distinct strategies for defining and estimating the validity of tests (American Psychological Association 1954; Guion 1980; Landy 1986). In personnel selection, it was common to draw substantial distinctions between content-, construct-, and criterion-related validity; this trinitarian view of validity is still central to equal employment law in the US (Guion 1980; Kleiman and Faley 1985). It is now widely accepted that validity is a unitary concept (American Psychological Association 1985; 1999), and that validity is a property of the inferences made on the basis of test scores, not a property of the tests themselves (e.g., Lawshe 1985).

Tests are neither valid nor invalid. However, when tests are used to make inferences about people on the basis of test scores (e.g., Sam received a high score on a Conscientiousness scale, therefore Sam is probably dependable and reliable) these inferences may or may not be valid. Explorations of the meaning of test scores are concerned mainly with the validity of these inferences. There are a variety of strategies for investigating validity, some of which concentrate on content-based evidence, some of which concentrate on the relationships between test scores and other criteria, but the goal of *all* methods of validation is to determine whether particular conclusions one draws about individuals on the basis of test scores are valid ones.

Most of the inferences that are based on test scores fall into two broad categories. First, there are inferences about the construct, domain, or concept one is trying to measure. Murphy and Davidshofer (2005) refer to questions about whether a test really measures what it claims to measure falling under the heading of "validity of measurement." Many of the validation strategies based on examination of test content or on links between test scores and the constructs that underlie test scores fall under this broad heading. Second, there are inferences about things other than what the test is designed to measure. For example, I might use a test of cognitive ability to predict job performance. The test is not a performance measure per se, but these might be ample grounds for inferring that people who do well on this test will also perform well on the job. Assessments of the validity of these inferences fall under broad headings such as "criterion-related validity" or "validity of decisions" (Binning and Barrett 1989; Murphy and Davidshofer 2005).

A range of validation strategies might be used to attack questions about the validity of inferences within either of these broad categories. Examination of test content might be used to help determine what the test measures, but might also be used to determine whether test scores are likely to predict job performance (Goldstein and Zedeck 1996). Examinations of the correlations between test scores and performance measures might be part of a criterion-related validity study, but they might also be part of a broad effort to determine what the test actually measures. Thus, validation strategies are not limited to one of these two categories of inferences. Any data that help in shedding light on the meaning and implications of test scores are potentially useful for validation (Landy 1986).

3.1 Content-Oriented Strategies

One common method of validation involves examination of the content of a test, using expert judgment and/or empirical analyses to assess the relationship between the content of a test and the content domain the test purports to measure or predict. The assumption underlying this method of validation is that if the test is a representative sample of the domain, people who receive high scores on the test are likely to exhibit a high level of the attribute the test is designed to measure.

In the context of personnel selection, the term "content validity" has taken on a unique and special meaning, i.e., using assessments of the content of a test to make inferences about the likelihood that individuals who receive high scores on a selection test will also perform well on the job (Guion 1978a). This definition of content validity is clearly distinct from definitions that focus on the adequacy with which the test samples the domain it is designed to measure. In personnel selection many "content-valid" tests are designed to measure attributes thought to be relevant to performance on the job (e.g., knowledge, skills, and abilities), but these tests are not designed or interpreted as measures of job performance per se, but rather as predictors of job performance.

The most common content validation strategy involves making judgments about whether a test measures knowledge, abilities, and/or skills that are required for successful job performance. Cascio (1998) provides a detailed description of this approach. Content-related validity is evaluated in terms of the extent to which members of a Content Evaluation Panel perceive overlap between the knowledge, skills, and abilities (KSA) the test measures and the KSAs essential for job performance. This process is carried out in several steps: (1) each member of the panel is given a set of test items and independently indicates whether the knowledge or skill measured by the item is essential, useful but not essential, or not necessary to the performance of the job; (2) responses from all panelists are pooled and the number indicating "essential" is determined; (3) a Content Validity Ration (CVR) is determined for each test item [CVR $= (n_e - N/2)/(N/2)$, where n_e is the number of panelists indicating "essential" and N is the total number of panelists]; (4) items are eliminated if the CVR fails to meet statistical significance (which can be determined from a table presented in Lawshe 1975); and (5) the mean CVR value of the retained items (the Content Validity Index; CVI) is then computed. The CVI represents a quantitative estimate of the extent to which perceived overlap exists between capability to function in a job performance domain and performance on the test under investigation.

Linkage methods represent a variation on the performance requirements approach described above, in which subject-matter experts are asked to make judgments about overlaps in the knowledge, skills, and abilities needed to do well on a test and those needed to do well on a job. Goldstein and Zedeck (1996) argue that "when there is congruence between the KSAs required to perform on the job and the KSA required to perform on the testing instrument, then it should be possible to make inferences about how the test scores relate to job behavior" (p. 28; see also Goldstein, Zedeck, and Schneider 1993). This method involves: (1) linking KSAs to specific job elements (i.e., making a judgment that specific KSAs are required for or contribute to performance of specific aspects of a job); (2) linking KSAs to test items or to subtests (these steps are often done by independent groups of experts— Goldstein and Zedeck 1996 refer to this step as retranslation); and (3) assessing the communalities between these KSA lists. If the same KSAs are judged to be required for performing well on the test and for performing well on the job, then the inference is made that people who do well on the test will also do well on the job.

There is a long history of criticism of content validity in the personnel psychology literature, most notably a set of papers by Guion (1977; 1978a; 1978b), who claimed that "there is no such thing as content validity" (1978a, 212). Guion (1978b) went on to note that validity refers to inferences from scores, not to the test themselves, suggesting that an examination of test content might not in principle be sufficient to support an inference that test scores predict performance. His argument is that tests cannot be valid or invalid; even if items are representative of content domain, this does not guarantee that scores obtained when administering a test made up of these items will predict future performance on that domain. For example, bias in scoring could affect validity. Tests might be so easy or so difficult that there is little variance in scores; severe restriction in range will substantially limit the correlations between test scores and performance measures. Test items might be representative of the job, but the responses people make to these items might have little or nothing to do with responses to the same sort of content in a work setting (Guion 1977).

Perhaps more to the point, there is little evidence that the match or mismatch between the content of selection tests and the content of jobs has any real bearing on validity. The only recent study that has directly tested the hypotheses that judgments about content validity are at all related to a test's success in predicting job performance yielded very disappointing results (Carrier, Dalessio, and Brown 1990). They showed that tests and test items that were judged to have good content validity were not better for predicting performance than tests judged to have poor content validity. Although content-oriented strategies are still widely used in personnel selection, these are probably the weakest strategies for validating the inference that people who do well on a selection test will also do well on the job.

3.2 Criterion-Oriented Methods

The central concern of many validity studies in personnel psychology is to determine whether people who do well on selection tests are also likely to perform well on the job. The simplest and most direct strategy for validating inferences of this sort is to correlate test scores (X) with measures of job performance (Y). There are thousands of validity studies examining relationships between various tests and criteria.

Most validity studies reflect one of two basis designs, that are best illustrated in the context of personnel selection, where tests are administered to a set of job applicants, and test scores are correlated with measures of job performance. *Predictive* validity designs involve obtaining test scores from a group of applicants, but not using the test, either directly or indirectly, in making selection decisions. At some later time, performance measures are obtained for those persons hired and are correlated with test scores to obtain the predictive validity coefficient. *Concurrent* validity designs involve obtaining both test scores and criterion scores in some intact, preselected population and computing the correlation between the two. Most concurrent validity studies in the personnel selection literature involve job incumbents, who were selected for the job in part on the basis of their test scores.

The names of these two strategies suggest that it is the timing of measurement that is the most important distinction, but in fact the critical distinction has to do with the samples studied (Guion and Cranny 1982). In predictive designs, people are *not* selected or screened on the basis of their test scores, whereas in a concurrent design, people are typically screened. Consider, for example, a concurrent validity study of scholastic admission tests conducted at a very selective university. The only subjects included in this study would be people who had done very well on these tests; people with low scores would have been screened out. As a result, concurrent validity studies can lead to substantial *range restriction*, which in turn is likely to substantially affect the correlations between test scores and criterion measures.

3.2.1 *Range restriction*

There is a large and robust literature dealing with the effects of range restriction and methods of correcting for these effects (e.g., Sackett and Ostgaard 1994; Schmidt, Oh, and Le 2006). To illustrate the effects of range restriction, consider a widely used formula for direct range restriction,[2] which can be used to estimate the correlation between X and Y that would be obtained if there were no range restriction in the predictor (e.g., no selection):

$$r_c = \frac{r(\sigma u/\sigma res)}{\sqrt{1 - r^2 + r^2(\sigma^2 u/\sigma^2\ res)}} \tag{12}$$

where:

r_c = estimate of the population r, correcting for range restriction

r = sample correlation coefficient

σu = standard deviation of the sample on the predictor before range restriction

$\sigma\ res$ = standard deviation of sample after range restriction.

Suppose, for example, that you found a correlation of .25 between test scores and performance measures in a sample. The standard deviation of the predictor is 10.0, but you know that the company you are working with only hires applicants with high scores, and that in the general applicant population, the standard deviation of the test is 25.0. Formula 12 suggests that the correlation between X and Y in a population that was not selected on the basis of X would be about .54. Schmidt, Oh, and Le (2006) suggest that the corrections used in most validity studies underestimate the effects of range restriction, and that validity estimates obtained from restricted samples might be gross underestimates of test validity.

Research on range restriction would lead you to expect that concurrent validity estimates should be substantially smaller than estimates of the validity of the same tests obtained using a concurrent design. In fact, several reviews have shown that concurrent validity estimates are not much different from estimates obtained in predictive designs (Barrett, Phillips, and Alexander 1981; Guion and Cranny 1982). In part, this is because severe range restriction is fairly rare, and in part it is because correction formulas ignore many of the factors that affect the outcomes of real-world validity study. For example, Murphy (1986) showed that most statistical estimates of the impact of testing on performance ignore decisions made by job candidates (e.g., some people turn down job offers, drop out, quit early, etc.), and as a result greatly overestimate the validity and value of some selection tests.

---

[2] Range restriction is referred to as direct if people are selected for the validity study on the basis of their scores on X or Y. Range restriction is indirect if people are selected on the basis of some other variable that is correlated with X or Y (e.g., people are selected for a job on the basis of interview scores, which turn out to be correlated with scores on the test that is being validated).

3.2.2 *Synthetic validity*

Lawshe (1952) introduced the method of synthetic validity over fifty years ago. He noted that jobs can be broken down into a number of components, and these components (e.g., supervision, obtaining information from gauges and devices) are shared across a number of settings. Jobs differ in terms of their particular mixes of components, but the general building blocks are quite similar across many jobs and organizations. Lawshe realized that if one could obtain estimates of the validity of tests for each of these components, it would be possible to combine these to produce an estimate of the validity of the test or tests for any job, regardless of its specific content (Peterson et al. 2001).

Implementing this method would certainly be a challenge; this method would require you to describe jobs in terms of a relatively universal taxonomy of components, establish the validity of different classes of tests for each component, then build a validity estimate on the basis of what you know about the validities of the tests for each component and the intercorrelations of the tests and the components, all of which might prove challenging. Nevertheless, the method has clear conceptual appeal. However, despite fifty years of research on synthetic validity, this method has not proved completely or particularly successful (Steel, Huffcutt, Kammeyer-Mueller 2006). Advances in meta-analysis have made this method more feasible (Steel et al. 2006), but probably have also suggested that there may be simpler solutions to the problem of estimating validity in a job where no validity studies exist.

3.2.3 *A multivariate model for criterion-related validity*

Murphy and Shiarella (1997) noted that personnel selection is rarely if ever a univariate problem. Organizations use multiple tests and assessments to select employees, and constructs such as performance or effectiveness have multiple dimensions. They proposed a general multivariate model for validity studies, and noted that the validity of selection test batteries would depend not only on the tests and the performance components, but also on the relative weight given to these by the organization. Most critically, two organizations might define performance in quite different terms (e.g., one might give a great deal of weight to task accomplishment, while another gives substantial weight to contextual factors, such as teamwork), and the relative weights given to both performance dimensions and selection tests can substantially affect validity.

Although not cast in terms of synthetic validity, Murphy and Shiarella's (1997) multivariate model provides a framework for synthetic validation. That is, they present a general set of equations for linking scores on a set of tests with measures of a set of performance components, and they allow for differences, across occasions, organizations, etc., in the relative weight attached to both predictor tests and performance dimensions.

3.2.4 *Validity generalization*

In a series of papers, Schmidt, Hunter, and their colleagues have argued that it is often possible to generalize from existing research on test validity to draw conclusions about the validity of tests in a variety of settings. In particular, they have shown that it is often possible to generalize the findings of existing validity research to new findings, thus providing a general solution to the same problem that motivated the synthetic validity model—i.e., the problem of estimating validity in a particular context without doing a new validity study in that context. Personnel psychologists had long assumed that validity estimates were too low and that the results of validity studies were simply too inconsistent from organization to organization or from job to job to permit this sort of generalization. Schmidt and Hunter's critical insight was that statistical artifacts, such as sampling error, range restriction, and unreliability, had led personnel psychologists to underestimate the size and overestimate the variability of validity coefficients.

Schmidt and Hunter (1977) developed a validity generalization model that estimates and corrects for the effects of statistical artifacts, such as limited reliability and range restriction, on the distributions of test validity estimates. The Schmidt–Hunter validity generalization model suggests that in almost every test, true validities are (1) substantially larger; and (2) much less variable than psychologists have traditionally believed (Murphy 2000; 2003; Salgado et al. 2003; Schmidt 1992; Schmidt and Hunter 1977; 1980; 1998).

There is a large body of research examining the criterion-related validity of different selection tests, particularly written tests that measure general or specific facets of cognitive ability. Validity generalization analyses of these studies suggest that measures of cognitive ability are positively correlated with measures of performance in virtually all jobs, and that the results are sufficiently consistent across hundreds of validity studies (after correcting for the effects of sampling error, limited reliability, etc.) to support the inference that ability tests are valid predictors of performance in virtually any job (Hunter 1986; McHenry et al. 1990; Ree and Earles 1992; Schmidt and Hunter 1998). Broad validity generalization has also been claimed for personality traits, such as Conscientiousness (Barrick and Mount 1991).

Over the last thirty years, a number of variations of the basic model first proposed by Schmidt and Hunter (1977) have been proposed. Murphy's (2003) edited volume on validity generalization includes excellent chapters that review the history of validity generalization models (Schmidt, Landy), propose new analytic models based on maximum likelihood estimation (Raju and Drasgow) and Bayesian statistics (Brannick and Hall), and discuss the conceptual and analytic challenges in applying these models to draw inferences about the validity of selection tests (Bobko and Roth, Burke and Landis). Bayesian models for validity generalization appear to have considerable potential for addressing the problem of how to interpret and apply validity generalization results (Newman, Jacobs, and Bartram in press).

3.3 Construct Validation

Most psychological tests are designed to measure constructs—i.e., attributes of individuals that cannot be directly observed, but must be inferred and indirectly assessed (e.g., intelligence, motivation, honesty). Cronbach and Meehl (1955) introduced the idea of construct validity; their ideas form the core of much of our current understanding of validity (see also Cronbach 1988). The current *Standards for Educational and Psychological Testing* (APA 1999) go so far as to argue that virtually all validation efforts fit under the umbrella of construct validation.

The best way of thinking about construct validation is to treat it as an ongoing process of forming and testing hypotheses about the meaning of test scores (Landy 1986; Smith 2005). For example, I might believe that a test provides a good measure of the personality dimension Agreeableness. People who are high on Agreeableness tend to do well in a range of social situations, tend to have more friends, tend to avoid arguments, etc. If my test really measures Agreeableness, this should lead to several hypotheses, such as:

- People who receive high test scores should receive high ratings on measures of social skills
- People who receive high test scores should report having more friends
- In stressful situations, people with low test scores should be more likely to get into arguments than people with high test scores.

If I collect data to test these hypotheses, I will learn about what this test measures. If all of these hypotheses are supported, I might conclude (at least tentatively) that the test really does measure the construct Agreeableness. As with all other types of hypothesis testing, conclusions about construct validity are always tentative, because there may always be some future hypothesis that is not supported. Thus, the task of construct validation is, in a sense, never complete. Virtually any type of data might provide information about the meaning and implication of test scores.

Murphy and Davidshofer (2005) note that virtually any type of data might prove useful in a construct validity study. Examinations of test content can help in developing an understanding of the meaning of test scores. Outcomes of validity studies can be useful; often the best way of knowing what a test does or does not measure is by determining what is and is not correlated with scores on that test. Data from experiments, observational studies, archival records, etc. can all help in assessing construct validity.

Campbell and Fiske (1959) proposes a method for investigating construct validity based on multi-method, multi-trait studies. They showed that if multiple methods were used to assess each of several traits, it would be possible to obtain a range of insights into the meaning of test scores. In particular, they suggested that assessment of convergent and discriminant validity might prove especially useful. Convergent validity refers to the extent to which different methods of measuring the same construct yield consistent results, whereas discriminant validity refers to the extent to which scores on measures of supposedly different traits are in fact distinct. A number of variations of the methods proposed by Campbell and Fiske have been proposed, including those based on Analysis of Variance (Kavanaugh, McKinney, and Wolins 1971) and confirmatory factor analysis (Razmovic and Razmovic 1981).

Because construct validation is by definition an ongoing process, there is no "construct validity coefficient," nor does it make any sense to argue that a particular test is or is not valid. There are, to be sure, differences in the scope and the persuasiveness of the evidence supporting particular interpretations of different tests, but construct validity cannot be easily boiled down to a particular statistic (like a validity coefficient) or metric. It is the accumulation of relevant evidence that helps you to make sense of the meaning of test scores, and this is the heart of construct validity.

3.4 An Integrated Framework for Validation

Binning and Barrett (1989) proposed a general framework for integrating the various questions about validity that might sensibly be asked in evaluating the validity of a selection test; this framework is illustrated in Figure 11.2.

Several features of this framework are likely to be interested in several aspects of validity, including:

- *Measure to Measure Relationships*—how well do scores on the test correlate with performance ratings (criterion-related validity)?

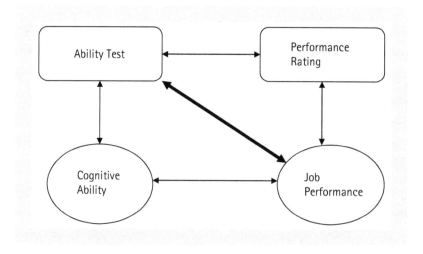

Fig. 11.2 Relationships between constructs and measures
Source: Adapted from Binning and Barrett 1989.

- *Measure to Construct Relationships*—how well do test scores represent cognitive ability? How well do performance ratings represent job performance (construct validity)?
- *Predictor Measure to Criterion Construct Relationships*—do test scores predict job performance (as opposed to performance ratings)?

Typically, criterion-related validity studies start (and sometimes end) with measure-to-measure relationships—e.g., the correlation between test scores and performance ratings. As the Binning and Barrett framework makes clear, these correlations are not really the main focus of a validity study. Validity studies usually start with the assumption that there are strong links between the criterion measure and the construct it is supposed to represent—here, this is equivalent to assuming that performance ratings are good measures of job performance, an assumption that is probably not true (Murphy and Cleveland 1995). If there is strong evidence of the construct validity of criterion measures, the Binning and Barrett (1989) framework suggests that it should be possible to make strong inferences about the link between test scores and the performance construct (this link is shown with a heavy line in Figure 11.2). However, establishing a strong link between the predictor and the criterion construct requires, first and foremost, good criterion measures. Given the long and sorry history of criterion measures used in personnel psychology (Austin and Villanova 1992), it is hard to be optimistic about our ability to make well-founded inferences about links between test scores and poorly measured criteria.

This framework implies that construct validity issues may have different meanings for predictors and criteria. The simplest case is one in which both the test and the criterion show strong evidence of construct validity. In that case, empirical correlations between tests and criterion measures provide convincing evidence that the underlying constructs are related. On the other hand, it is possible that a test that shows poor construct validity could nevertheless show good performance as a predictor. The correlation between test scores and both criterion measures and the criterion constructs they represent does not necessarily depend on the construct validity of the predictor. Poor construct validity on the criterion side, on the other hand, renders empirical evidence of correlations between predictors and criterion measures potentially useless. Nobody really cares if tests are correlated with performance *ratings*; what is important is whether or not test scores are correlated with performance.

4. The Dubious Distinction between Reliability and Validity

Traditionally, reliability and validity have been presented as somewhat separate concepts. It has long been understood that low reliability limits validity, in the sense that a test that is plagued by measurement error is unlikely to be correlated with other measures. However, many if not most personnel psychologists would agree with Schmidt, Le, and Iles's (2000) assertion that "reliability is not validity and validity is not reliability". Murphy and DeShon (2000b) argue that the field of personnel psychology is seriously out of step with modern psychometric thinking. For example, leading researchers in this field still take the parallel test model quite seriously, even in situations where the measures being examined are clearly not parallel (Murphy and DeShon 2000a). More generally, the idea that reliability and validity are fundamentally different concepts represents a throwback to an earlier generation of psychometric research and theory that has largely been abandoned by serious psychometricians.

A number of authors have noted that reliability and validity are closely related concepts, and that the traditional distinction between the two is an issue of style rather than substance (Graham 2006; McDonald 1999; Murphy and DeShon 2000b). The idea that reliability and validity are variations on a common theme is hardly a new one; Cronbach et al. (1972) made this point over thirty-five years ago. Virtually all of the concerns of reliability or generalizability theory can be subsumed under the broad heading of construct validity. McDonald (1999) noted that both traditional factor analysis and structural equation modeling also represent variations on the same set of concepts that underlie construct validity theory, which implies that this distinction is not very useful or important.

The aim of construct validity is to understand the meaning of test scores. One way to do this is to develop and test structural models of test scores, identifying the sources of variance in test scores. When you say that a test shows a high level of construct validity, that is the same as saying that a large portion of the variance in test scores is due to the construct the test is designed to measure. Measurement error, in the classical sense, is one of many things that can cause test scores to imperfectly represent constructs. Generalizability theory suggests that there is often variation in test scores that is due to things other than random measurement error or the construct being measured (e.g., systematic variation attributable to measurement conditions, rater differences, etc.); this theory lays out a number of methods of estimating these various effects.

Reliability assessment represents a very special, and possibly very small, niche within the larger domain of construct validity. CTT deals with random measurement error, which can be dealt with in relatively straightforward ways if the extent of error is known. When the assumptions of CTT are met (e.g., observed scores can be sensibly divided into true scores and random measurement errors), reliability theory can provide elegant and powerful approaches for interpreting data, but the idea that one can or should investigate reliability without at the same time thinking about validity is not a sensible one (Murphy and DeShon 2000b). Several recent studies have discussed or illustrated ways of linking assessments of reliability with assessments of construct validity (Kraiger and Teachout 1990; Murphy and DeShon 2000a).

The goal of virtually all psychometric investigations is the same—i.e., to make sense of test scores. The methods of evaluating reliability described here can all contribute to that goal. Knowing whether or not test scores are stable over time (test-retest reliability), or whether difference evaluators reach similar conclusions (interrater reliability), or whether the different items on a test hand together (coefficient alpha) can help in understanding what tests mean. It is not sensible, and indeed, it is not clear that it is possible, to investigate reliability without learning about validity or to investigate validity without learning about reliability.

REFERENCES

AMERICAN PSYCHOLOGICAL ASSOCIATION. 1954. Technical recommendations for psychological tests and diagnostic techniques. *Psychological Bulletin*, 31: 201–38.

—— 1985. *Standards for Educational and Psychological Testing*. Washington, DC: American Psychological Association.

—— 1999. *Standards for Educational and Psychological Testing*. Washington, DC: American Psychological Association.

AUSTIN, J. T., and VILLANOVA, P. 1992. The criterion problem 1917–1992. *Journal of Applied Psychology*, 77: 836–74.

BARRETT, G. V., PHILLIPS, J. S., and ALEXANDER, R. A. 1981. Concurrent and predictive validity designs: a critical reanalysis. *Journal of Applied Psychology*, 66: 1–6.

BARRICK, M. R., and MOUNT, M. K. 1991. The Big Five personality dimensions and job performance: a meta-analysis. *Personnel Psychology*, 44: 1–26.

BEOKKOOI-TIMMINGA, E. 1990. The construction of parallel tests from IRT-based item banks. *Journal of Educational Statistics*, 15: 129–45.

BINNING, J. F., and BARRETT, G. V. 1989. Validity of personnel decisions: a conceptual analysis of the inferential and evidential bases. *Journal of Applied Psychology*, 74: 478–94.

BRENNAN, R. L. 1983. *Elements of Generalizability Theory*. Iowa City, IA: American College Test Program.

CAMPBELL, D. T., and FISKE, D. W. 1959. Convergent and discriminant validity in the multi-trait multi-method matrix. *Psychological Bulletin*, 56: 81–105.

CARRIER, M. R., DALESSIO, A. T., and BROWN, S. H. 1990. Correspondence between estimates of content and criterion-related validity values. *Personnel Psychology*, 43: 85–100.

CASCIO, W. F. 1998. *Applied Psychology in Human Resource Management* 5th edn. Upper Saddle River, NJ: Prentice-Hall.

CORTINA, J. M. 1993. What is coefficient alpha? An examination of theory and applications. *Journal of Applied Psychology*, 78: 98–104.

CRONBACH, L. J. 1951. Coefficient alpha and the internal structure of tests. *Psychometrika*, 16: 297–334.

—— 1988. Five perspectives on the validity argument. In *Test Validity*, ed. H. Wainer and H. Brown. Hillsdale, NJ: Erlbaum.

—— and MEEHL, P. E. 1955. Construct validity in psychological tests. *Psychological Bulletin*, 52: 281–302.

CRONBACH, L. J., GLESER, G. C., NANDA, H., and RAJARATNAM, N. 1972. *The Dependability of Behavioral Measurements: Theory of Generalizability for Scores and Profiles.* New York: Wiley.

GOLDSTEIN, I. L., and ZEDECK, S. 1996. Content validation. pp. 27–37 in *Fair Employment Strategies in Human Resource Management,* ed. R. Barrett. Westport, CT: Quorum Books.

—— —— and SCHNEIDER, B. 1993. An exploration of the job analysis-content validity process. In *Personnel Selection in Organizations,* ed. N. Schmitt and W. C. Borman. San Francisco: Jossey-Bass.

GRAHAM, J. M. 2006. Congeneric and (essentially) tau-equivalent estimates of score reliability: what they are and how to use them. *Educational and Psychological Measurement,* 66: 930–44.

GUION, R. M. 1977. Content validity, the source of my discontent. *Applied Psychological Measurement,* 1: 1–10.

—— 1978a. "Content validity" in moderation. *Personal Psychology,* 31: 205–13.

—— 1978b. Scoring content domain samples: the problem of fairness. *Journal of Applied Psychology,* 63: 499–506.

—— 1980. On trinitarian doctrines of validity. *Professional Psychology,* 11: 385–98.

—— and CRANNY, C. J. 1982. A note on concurrent and predictive validity designs. *Journal of Applied Psychology,* 67: 239–44.

HULIN, C. L., DRASGOW, F., and PARSONS, C. K. 1983. *Item Response Theory: Application to Psychological Measurement.* Homewood, IL: Dow Jones-Irwin.

HUNTER, J. E. 1986. Cognitive ability, cognitive aptitudes, job knowledge, and job performance. *Journal of Vocational Behavior,* 29: 340–62.

KAVANAUGH, M. J., MacKINNEY, A., and WOLINS, L. 1971. Issues in managerial performance: multitrait–multimethod analysis of ratings. *Psychological Bulletin,* 75: 34–49.

KLEIMAN, L. S., and FALEY, R. H. 1985. The implications of professional and legal guidelines for court decisions involving criterion-related validity: a review and analysis. *Personnel Psychology,* 38: 803–33.

KOZLOWSKI, S. W. J., and HATTRUP, K. 1992. A disagreement about within-group agreement: disentangling issues of consistency versus consensus. *Journal of Applied Psychology,* 77: 161–7.

KRAIGER, K., and TEACHOUT, M. S. 1990. Generalizability theory as construct-related evidence of the validity of job performance ratings. *Human Performance,* 3: 19–36.

LANDY, F. J. 1986. Stamp collecting versus science: validation as hypothesis testing. *American Psychologist,* 41: 1183–92.

LAWSHE, C. H. 1952. What can industrial psychology do for small business? (a symposium). *Personnel Psychology,* 5: 31–4.

—— 1975. A quantitative approach to content validity. *Personnel Psychology,* 28: 563–75.

—— 1985. Inferences from personnel tests and their validities. *Journal of Applied Psychology,* 70: 237–8.

LORD, F. M. 1980. *Applications of Item Response Theory to Practical Testing Problems.* Hillsdale, NJ: Erlbaum.

—— and NOVICK, M. R. 1968. *Statistical Theories of Mental Test Scores.* Menlo Park, CA: Addison-Wesley.

McDONALD, R. P. 1999. *Test Theory: A Unified Treatment.* Mahwah, NJ: Lawrence Erlbaum Associates.

McHenry, J. J, Hough, L. M., Toquam, J. L., Hanson, M. A., and Ashworth, S. 1990. Project A validity results: the relationship between predictor and criterion domains. *Personnel Psychology*, 43: 335–55.

Murphy, K. R. 1986. When your top choice turns you down: effects of rejected offers on selection test utility. *Psychological Bulletin*, 99: 133–8.

—— 2000. Impact of assessment of validity generalization and situational specificity on the science and practice of personnel selection. *International Journal of Selection and Assessment*, 8: 194–206.

—— 2003. *Validity Generalization: A Critical Review*. Mahwah, NJ: Erlbaum.

—— and Cleveland, J. 1995. *Understanding Performance Appraisal: Social, Organizational and Goal-Oriented Perspectives*. Newbury Park, CA: Sage.

—— and Davidshofer, C. O. 2005. *Psychological Testing: Principles and Applications*, 6th edn. Upper Saddle River, NJ: Prentice Hall.

—— and DeShon, R. 2000a. Inter-rater correlations do not estimate the reliability of job performance ratings. *Personnel Psychology*, 53: 873–900.

—— —— 2000b. Progress in psychometrics: can industrial and organizational psychology catch up? *Personnel Psychology*, 53: 913–24.

—— and Shiarella, A. 1997. Implications of the multidimensional nature of job performance for the validity of selection tests: multivariate frameworks for studying test validity. *Personnel Psychology*, 50: 823–54.

Newman, D. A., Jacobs, R. R., and Bartram, D. In press. Choosing the best method for local validity estimation: relative accuracy of meta-analysis vs. a local study vs. Bayes-analysis. *Journal of Applied Psychology*.

Peterson, N. G., Wise, L. L., Arabian, J., and Hoffman, R. G. 2001. Synthetic validation and validity generalization when empirical validation is not possible. Pp. 411–51 in *Exploring the Upper Limits of Personnel Selection and Classification*, ed. J. Campbell and D. Knapp. Mahwah, NJ: Erlbaum.

Razmovic, E. L., and Razmivic, V. 1981. A confirmatory factor analysis approach to construct validation. *Educational and Psychological Measurement*, 41: 61–72.

Reddy, S. K. 1992. Effects of ignoring correlated measurement error in structural equation models. *Educational and Psychological Measurement*, 52: 549–70.

Ree, M. J., and Earles, J. A. 1992. Intelligence is the best predictor of job performance. *Current Directions in Psychological Science*, 1: 86–9.

Rodriquez, M. C., and Maeda, Y. 2006. Meta analysis of coefficient alpha. *Psychological Methods*, 11: 306–22.

Sackett, P. R., and Ostgaard, D. J. 1994. Job-specific applicant pools and national norms for cognitive ability tests: implications for range restriction corrections in validation research. *Journal of Applied Psychology*, 79: 680–4.

Salgado, J. F., Anderson, N., Moscoso, S., Bertua, C., and de Fruyt, F. 2003. International validity generalization of GMA and cognitive abilities: a European Community meta-analysis. *Personnel Psychology*, 56: 573–605.

Shavelson, R. J., Webb, N. M., and Rowley, G. L. 1989. Generalizability theory. *American Psychologist*, 44: 922–32.

Schmidt, F. L. 1992. What do data really mean? Research findings, meta-analysis, and cumulative knowledge in psychology. *American Psychologist*, 47: 1173–81.

—— and Hunter, J. E. 1977. Development of a general solution to the problem of validity generalization. *Journal of Applied Psychology*, 62: 643–61.

SCHMIDT, F. L. 1980. The future of criterion-related validity. *Personnel Psychology*, 33: 41–60.
—— —— 1996. Measurement error in psychological research: lessons from 26 research scenarios. *Psychological Methods*, 1: 199–223.
—— —— 1998. The validity and utility of selection methods in personnel psychology: practical and theoretical implications of 85 years of research findings. *Psychological Bulletin*, 124: 262–74.
—— LE, H., and ILES, R. 2000. Beyond alpha: an empirical examination of the effects of different sources of measurement error on reliability estimates for measures of individual differences constructs. *Psychological Methods*, 2: 206–24.
—— OH, I., and LE, H. 2006. Increasing the accuracy of corrections for range restriction: implications for selection procedure validities and other research results. *Personnel Psychology*, 59: 281–305.
—— VISWESVARAN, C., and ONES, D. S. 2000. Reliability is not validity and validity is not reliability. *Personnel Psychology*, 53: 901–12.
SHROUT, P. E., and FLEISS, J. L. 1979. Intraclass correlations: uses in assessing rater reliability. *Psychological Bulletin*, 86: 420–8.
SMITH, G. T. 2005. On construct validity: issues of method and measurement. *Psychological Assessment*, 17: 396–408.
STEEL, P. G., HUFFCUTT, A. I., and Kammeyer-MUELLER, J. 2006. From the work one knows the worker: a systematic review of challenges, solutions and steps to creating synthetic validity. *International Journal of Selection and Assessment*, 14: 16–36.
THOMPSON, B., and VACHA-HAASE, T. 2000. Psychometrics is datametrics: the test is not reliable. *Educational and Psychological Measurement*, 60: 174–95.
THORNDIKE, R. M., and LOHMAN, D. F. 1990. *A Century of Ability Testing*. Chicago: Riverside.
VACHA-HAASE, T. 1998. Reliability generalization: exploring variance in measurement error affecting score reliability across studies. *Educational and Psychological Measurement*, 58: 6–20.
VISWESVARAN, C., ONES, D. S., and SCHMIDT, F. L. 1996. Comparative analysis of the reliability of job performance ratings. *Journal of Applied Psychology*, 81: 557–74.
—— SCHMIDT, F. L., and ONES, D. 2005. Is there a general factor in ratings of job performance? A meta-analytic framework for disentangling substantive and error influences. *Journal of Applied Psychology*, 90: 108–31.

ADVANCES IN TRAINING EVALUATION RESEARCH

J. KEVIN FORD

RUCHI SINHA

1. INTRODUCTION

TRAINING evaluation is the systematic collection of descriptive and judgmental information necessary to make effective training decisions (Goldstein and Ford 2002). A key characteristic of a systematic approach to training evaluation is the emphasis on the continuous use of feedback. This process, which includes both formative (process) and summative (outcome) evaluation strategies, can aid in identifying, collecting, and providing information to make a variety of instructional decisions. For example, information can be collected by decision makers to determine whether training objectives have been met, whether trainees are applying the knowledge and skills gained in training to the job, and whether the program should be continued or perhaps expanded to other locations or trainees (Kraiger 2002).

This chapter reviews the progress that has been made in evaluation science that has particular relevance to workplace training programs. We first focus on the

implications of the changing nature of work for conducting effective training evaluation. Second, we describe how the field of training evaluation has progressed in terms
of criterion development (e.g., learning and performance constructs), measurement
issues (e.g., the relationships among criterion elements), and methodology (e.g.,
experimental quasi-experimental design) issues. Third, we discuss key challenges
that remain in the field that require additional theory development and research.

1.2 The Changing Nature of Work

There have been at least four major movements that have affected jobs over the last 30
to 40 years (Ilgen and Pulakos 1999; Thayer 1997). First, there has been a rush toward
more highly technical and sophisticated systems in the workplace. For example,
advanced manufacturing techniques now permit the tailoring of products to the
needs of the customer (Wall and Jackson 1995). This shift has placed a great emphasis
on increased knowledge and skill requirements for most jobs. Second, there has been a
shift from manufacturing to service jobs (Howard 1995). These jobs are characterized
by an increase in the importance of people skills as in working with customers and
clients rather than interacting primarily with co-workers and things (Goldstein and
Ford 2002). Third, organizations have become more lean with the dual objectives of
cutting costs while at the same time improving productivity in order to meet
competitive pressures. The move to lean has resulted in broader responsibilities for
workers, and emphasis on teamwork, and an enhanced role for effective leadership
(Cutcher-Gershenfeld and Ford 2005). Finally, there is clearly a movement to a more
global market and society where jobs and organizations need to be increasingly fluid.
The globalization of industry has led to increased importance to project teams that
may span different organizations and workers from different countries to produce a
single final product (Friedman 2006).

Yelon and Ford (1999) discussed the implications for training of this changing
world of work. They conceptualized training needs as consisting of two key
dimensions based on the changing nature of jobs. One dimension deals with the
types of skills being trained. Many jobs have moved from an emphasis on what they
termed "closed skills" to a necessity to train for more "open skills." Closed skills are
those where workers must respond in one particular way according to a set of
rules—done in a precise fashion. On the other end of the scale are highly variable
open skills—there is not one right way to act, there is freedom to perform and
where procedures are based on principles not discrete steps. Salas, Milham, and
Bowers (2003) discuss the challenges for training evaluation in the military as jobs
evolve from physical to cognitive tasks. They argue that not only are the skills more
difficult to train but also that tasks requiring high-level cognitive components go
thorough greater and more rapid decay then the development and retention of
motor skills.

The second dimension focuses on the extent of supervision. With increased emphasis on downsizing (or rightsizing) and empowerment, many jobs have moved from situations where individuals are heavily supervised to situations in which workers have more autonomous jobs (and thus less direct supervision). The issue of autonomy can also be expanded beyond the individual to teams. As noted by Salas et al. (2003), teams are changing from those consisting of small collocated team members to those that are farther apart or distributed which pose challenges for training design and evaluation.

The training field up to the 1970s was typically concerned with jobs that could be considered as having closed skills and being heavily supervised (Kraiger and Ford 2007). Today's changing reality is that more jobs require open skills and are not heavily supervised. This makes it more difficult to determine what to train and what to look for in the job setting after training. It is also more difficult to evaluate job impact given the limited supervision. Yelon and Ford (1999) conclude that the intersection of these two dimensions—the quadrant where skills are open and the individual is autonomous poses challenges for training evaluation. The next section discusses advances in the area of training evaluation that are helping to address these challenges.

2. Advances in Evaluation

Rational decisions related to the selection, adoption, support, and worth of training activities require the collection of data for determining that the instructional program is responsible for whatever changes have occurred. Three key questions for evaluation have stayed the same over the decades: (1) Does an examination of the various criteria indicate that a change has occurred? (2) Can the changes be attributed to the instructional program? (3) is it likely that similar changes would occur for new participants in the same program? (Kraiger 2002).

While the key questions have remained the same, there have been important advances in the development of evaluation models. We focus on three key advances in training evaluation—the expanded understanding of relevant criteria, the building of a nomological network of relationships among criteria, and improvements to techniques for examining change as a function of training.

2.1 Expanded Criteria

It is difficult to discuss training criteria without beginning with Kirkpatrick's (1959) four levels—reaction, learning, behavior, and results. Reactions are defined as the trainee's perceptions about the training program such as how much they liked the program. Learning concerns the degree to which the intended outcomes of instruction (e.g., principles, facts, and techniques) have been acquired. Behavior is defined as a transfer issue—the use of the "learning" on the job. Results are defined as the end goals or the organizational impact of the training such as reduced costs, lower turnover, an increase in quality or improved morale.

This framework is certainly the most influential and the most used approach by training practitioners. As noted by Alliger and Janek (1989), the power of the framework is in its simplicity which provides a common vocabulary to build an understanding of evaluation criteria. A number of researchers have provided useful critiques in order to expand our understanding of criteria relevant for evaluation (Alliger and Janek 1989; Bates 2004; Holton 1996; Kraiger, Ford, and Salas 1993). These critiques have focused on incorporating improvements in our understanding of trainee perceptions, learning outcomes, performance constructs, and strategies for analyzing training impact. Below we define each criterion element and then discuss advances that have been made in our understanding of training criteria.

2.1.1 *Trainee perceptions*

Training practitioners have typically examined trainee perceptions in relation to reactions of whether trainees liked the program and the instructor. Positive reactions are seen as providing a good atmosphere for learning the material. Recent research has expanded the notion of trainee perceptions to include multiple facets. Warr and Bunce (1995) discussed three types of trainee perceptions—enjoyment of the course, the relevance of the course for the job, and the difficulty of the course. Alliger et al. (1997) also distinguished between the more traditional affective reactions to training and perceptions of utility. The utility perceptions focus on how relevant trainees see the training material for gaining needed skills and for improving job performance. Morgan and Casper (2000) examined trainee perception data from over 400 training classes and found support for six key factors including satisfaction with the training, the instructor and the management process, the testing process, the materials used, course structure, and the utility of the program for the trainee. Brown (2005) examined the underlying structure and nomological network of trainee reactions. He argues that these training related perceptions can be conceptualized as being hierarchical and found support for the notion that there are three key facets (enjoyment, perceived relevance, and satisfaction with the technology). Each of these facets loaded on an overall satisfaction with training factor.

2.1.2 *Learning outcomes*

Researchers have long noted the need to understand and measure the learning of facts, principles, and techniques that were specified as training objectives. For example, McGehee and Thayer (1961) stressed that measures of learning during training should be objective and quantifiable through methods such as multiple choice and recall tests as well as through skill-based testing.

Advances have been made in our understanding of what we mean by learning and what learning outcomes could be the focus of training evaluation. Kraiger, Ford, and Salas (1993) examined learning taxonomies from other educational and cognitive science disciplines in order to develop a classification scheme of learning outcomes. They divided learning outcomes into three central types: (1) cognitive outcomes which reflect concepts like verbal knowledge, knowledge organizations, and cognitive strategies; (2) skill-based outcomes such as automaticity; and (3) affective outcomes (attitudinal and motivational constructs) such as self-efficacy and attitude strength. For each type (e.g., cognitive outcomes), they provided a list of relevant learning constructs (e.g., declarative knowledge, mental models, and metacognition) and the appropriate foci for measurement (e.g., amount of knowledge, accuracy of recall, accessibility of knowledge, similarity of knowledge structure to an ideal, and self-regulation). Based on these measurement options, they provided a list of potential training evaluation methods (e.g., recall tests, structural assessments, probed protocol analysis).

Ford, Kraiger, and Merritt (in press) have updated this learning outcome approach. Ford et al. note that training studies have begun to move well beyond the measurement of declarative knowledge to other types of learning outcomes and evaluation methods. For example, Kozlowski and Bell (2006) have focused on distinguishing between what they call basic (declarative) knowledge and strategic (procedural) knowledge. These differences in knowledge capabilities are then linked to basic and strategic task performance.

In other research, the organization of knowledge has been the focus of attention. Mental model quality has also been found to predict outcomes over and above more traditional measures of knowledge acquisition. For example, Davis, Curtis, and Tschetter (2003) found that the quality of a trainee's structural knowledge (closeness to an expert model) provided an incremental prediction of post-training self-efficacy beyond measures of declarative knowledge (see Ford, Kraiger, and Merritt, in press) for an examination of advances to measurement of metacognition and attitude change).

In 2001, Anderson et al. created a revision to the well-known Bloom (1956) taxonomy of educational objectives. The original taxonomy focused on cognitive, psychomotor, and affective objectives. It was ordered from simple knowledge to more complex (and concrete to abstract) with the assumption that the simpler category was a prerequisite for mastery of the next complex level. The structure of the original taxonomy started with knowledge (knowledge of specifics, knowledge of ways and means of dealing with specifics, knowledge of principles), comprehensive, application, analysis, synthesis, and evaluation. The revised taxonomy consists of two dimensions. One dimension is the *structure* of knowledge, skill, or affect. The second dimension is the *process* underlying learning. The new knowledge dimension contains four rather than three main categories. Three of the categories include the substance of the original subcategories of knowledge—factual knowledge, conceptual knowledge, and procedural knowledge. The fourth new category is labeled "metacognitive knowledge" which the researchers reserved for knowledge about cognition and an awareness of one's own cognition.

The revised taxonomy by Anderson et al. (2001) and the updated review by Ford et al. (in press) show that our understanding of what we mean by "learning" continues to expand. The constructs of procedural knowledge, knowledge organization, and metacognition are beginning to be addressed in training evaluation contexts and thus underscore the need for a broader concept of what is meant by "learning." As skill needs become more "open," this broader conception of learning has led to more refined approaches for measuring changes in learning as a function of training.

2.1.3 *Performance constructs*

Regardless of the amount of learning during training, a key outcome is whether individuals transfer their increase in knowledge and skills to the job (Baldwin and Ford 1988). Kirkpatrick focused attention to changes in performance and suggested the need for a systematic appraisal (from multiple sources) of on-the-job performance both before and after training. McGehee and Thayer (1961) noted the problem of trying to determine whether or not the training procedures actually resulted in the modification of the behaviors of the trainees. This early work linking behavior change and work performance has been supported by subsequent research on job performance. As noted by Motowidlo and Schmit (1999), performance needs to be considered as a behavioral construct. They also stress that the performance domain is also behaviorally multidimensional—where different kinds of behavior can affect one's job performance and hence advance or hinder organizational goals.

Researchers have long bemoaned the "criterion problem" in selection and training domains (e.g., see Wallace 1965; Guion 1998). Recent work, though, has expanded our understanding of the performance domain. For example, Campbell (1990) defines performance as behavior that is relevant for the organization's goals and that can be measured in terms of the level of proficiency or contribution to goals that is represented by a particular set of actions. The performance model developed by Campbell and his colleagues includes eight primary factors: job-specific task proficiency, non-job-specific task proficiency, written and oral communication, demonstration of effort, maintenance of personal discipline, facilitation of peer and team performance, supervision/leadership, and management/administration. These factors are intended to be as distinct as possible in terms of the work behaviors that are included in each factor or dimension (Campbell 1999). Campbell makes a clear distinction between performance and the determinants of performance. The learning outcomes discussed above are consistent with Campbell's notion of direct determinants of job performance (declarative knowledge, procedural knowledge and skill, and motivation).

Motowidlo and Schmit also provide a number of different ways of conceptualizing performance including (1) persisting with enthusiasm and extras effort as necessary to completing tasks; (2) volunteering to carry out tasks that are not formally part of one's own job; (3) helping and cooperating with others; (4) following organizational rules and procedures; and (5) endorsing, supporting, and defending organizational objectives. They provide a variety of sources that have identified these key dimensions and provide ways of measuring behaviors relevant to these performance dimensions.

Pulakos et al. (2000) developed a taxonomy of adaptive job performance and examined the implications of the taxonomy for understanding and training for adaptive behavior. They identified and found support for an eight-dimension taxonomy including dimensions of (1) handling emergencies or crisis situations; (2) handling work stress; (3) solving problems creatively; (4) dealing with uncertain and unpredictable work situations; (5) learning work tasks, technologies, and procedures; (6) demonstrating intrapersonal adaptability; (7) demonstrating cultural adaptability; and (8) demonstrating physically oriented adaptability.

Finally, there has been an explosion of interest in multirater or 360-degree feedback systems (e.g., see Bracken, Timmreck, and Church 2001). This interest has led to a number of leadership taxonomies that focus on key leader behaviors. For example, Bracken et al. describe the development of a leadership survey in which thirty-three behavioral statements were identified including dimensions such as coaching/support, commitment to quality and customer satisfaction, communication, creating a team environment, and providing feedback. Traditionally, multirater systems have been used for leader development with feedback being the catalyst for motivating behavioral change. The measurement tools can also be used by training researchers and practitioners to measure or assess changes in behavior on the job as a function of leadership training (see Jellema, Visscher, and Scheerens 2006 for an example of this approach).

In 1961 McGehee and Thayer stressed the need to consider using specific criterion measures of performance that examine changes in the specific behaviors that the training program is targeting versus measuring summary indicators of changes in overall job performance. Since that time, there has been much effort devoted to developing conceptually rigorous models of job performance. These models have led to the identification of job performance dimensions that can help guide choices made by training evaluation researchers and practitioners about the relevant performance criteria. In addition, job performance researchers have created reliable and valid measures that can be applied to measuring specific changes in job performance as a function of training.

2.1.4 *Organizational impact*

As noted by McGehee and Thayer (1961), a careful and critical evaluation should answer the question of whether the dollars being spent on training are producing the results needed by the organization. Organizational impact is characterized as the effects on the business and the work environment that result from the improved performance of trainees. This level of evaluation helps to relate the training program to organizational objectives. In today's lean organizations, it is becoming increasingly important that training specialists provide evidence for the return on investment for training programs.

Training objectives for organizational training programs can be stated in the form of outcomes like increased production, reduced accidents, lower rates of employee turnover and absenteeism. The difficult aspect is to determine whether the training itself influenced these results or whether there were other unrelated factors to training like increased pay, seasonal variations, and market place change (Wexley and Latham 2002). Nevertheless, the field has a number of more powerful methods such as return on investment analysis and utility analysis to assess organizational impact.

Return on Investment (ROI) analysis involves estimating the ratio of total training benefits in terms of dollars divided by the total costs (also expressed in dollars). As the aim of an ROI analysis is to determine the financial impact of training it is important to systematically gather information to make any inferences. One must compute the costs of a training program in terms of program development, hours of training, trainer fee, etc. The next step is to measure the benefits of training and then convert those outcomes into dollar terms. This is especially difficult when training focuses on open skills.

Phillips and Phillips (2005) outlined steps to convert outcomes into monetary benefits. The first step is to identify a unit of improvement (number of grievances, number of promotions, etc). The second step is to determine the value of each unit on an average (cost of having a single grievance on an average). The third step is to determine the change in performance data in terms of the units of focus. Once we have the total change, the fourth step is to multiply that with the value of the unit and calculate the total value of the improvement. Kraiger (2002) shows that an ROI strategy can not only examine short-term gains but also estimate the long-term impact of training as one can calculate and adjust the ROI ratios for every year after the training.

ROI analysis of training can be considered part of a larger methodology for assessing organizational impact known as utility analysis. Schneider and Schmitt (1986) pointed out that utility analysis was originally developed in the selection field in order to translate validity evidence for a test into the "dollar criteria" which might be more meaningful for top management. It is a financial analysis of costs versus benefits that provides bottom line estimates. There have been various formulae for conducting utility analysis that have been recommended (e.g., Boudreau 1983; 1988; Schmidt, Hunter, and Pearlman 1982). Boudreau (1991) provides an extensive discussion of utility analysis for human resource decisions such as recruitment, selection, and retention. He also notes that utility analysis is a special case of a multi-attribute framework that can be applied to any functional area of personnel management.

Cascio (1982) describes the various procedures and issues related to conducting utility analysis within a training context. He also makes a distinction between cost–benefit analysis and cost-effectiveness analysis. Cost–benefit analysis is the comparison between training costs and non-monetary behavioral outcomes like employee behavior, health, and safety. Cost-effectiveness analysis is the comparison between training costs and benefits in monetary units like cost of production waste and increase in sales. Cascio (1989) also developed a step-by-step procedure for applying utility analysis to evaluating training outcomes. In the first step, he recommends using a capital budget methodology to estimate the minimum annual benefit in dollars required from any training program. The next step is to use break-even analysis (introduced by Boudreau 1984; 1991) to estimate the minimum effect size that needs to be produced by a program to get the desired benefits. Finally he recommends using data from multiple studies to determine the actual cost–benefit ratio for a training program.

Utility analysis is always deficient in some way as not all factors can be built into the formula for estimating costs and benefits. As noted by Wexley and Latham (2002) there is a tendency to overemphasize quantitative outcomes and under-represent less tangible outcomes that are not easily quantifiable. There is also the issue of how cost-related results can be influenced by factors outside the control of the training function. In addition, there are certain training programs like the outdoor management training (open skills) that are not designed to necessarily result in bottom line tangible outcomes.

Despite these difficult issues, there are now a number of examples of innovative approaches to examining organizational impact that minimize these disadvantages and thus provide hard evidence for the usefulness of a variety of organizational impact analyses. These studies balance the difficult task of developing expanded and detailed utility analyses with the need to minimize the complexity that makes it difficult to communicate the models and their findings to organizational decision makers.

Mathieu and Leonard (1987) provided one of the first empirical studies that showed how utility analysis can be applied to training—in this case a supervisory training program. Their utility formula to calculate dollar value expanded upon previous selection utility formulae (e.g., Schmidt, Hunter, and Pearlman 1982) by taking into account the potential for diminished effects of training on performance over time and the impact of turnover. Their formula included the number of years over which the utility estimates were calculated, the marginal utility gained in a particular year, the total number of groups trained, the number of trainees per group adjusted for turnover, the standard deviation of job performance in dollar units, the effect size estimate for the training group, and the cost of training per year of training. They employed a quasi-experimental design (with a matched control group—post hoc) to examine training effects on job performance (performance appraisal ratings). They also conducted break-even analysis and an employee flow analysis. The results indicated a substantial dollar benefit to the organization from training the supervisors. Despite the cost of training (over $50,000), the net utility for training sixty-five supervisors was found to be over $34,000 for the first year with increased benefits for a number of years beyond the initial training.

Morrow, Jarrett, and Rupinski (1997) describe a four-year study that investigated the effect and utility of managerial and sales training. The study expanded our understanding of the organizational impact of training by focusing on multiple training programs within one organization. They used a quasi-experimental design, incorporated meta-analytic information to summarize the impact of different types of training, and used a particular type of utility analysis (Raju, Burke, and Normand 1990) to estimate the economic impact of the training. They found great variation in the effectiveness of eighteen training programs within an organization. They also found that a more specific sales training program had a greater impact on job performance and a greater return on investment than the broader managerial training program.

2.2 Building a Nomological Network

Research has improved our understanding of training criteria relevant to evaluation. There is an emerging interest in understanding the nomological network connecting the different training criteria. The most commonly collected criterion measure continues to be the reaction of the participants to the program (Sugrue and Kim 2004). Alliger and Janek (1989) found only twelve research articles on training programs reporting twenty-six correlations between various criteria such as reaction and learning measures. They found that the relationships among reaction measures and the other three criterion levels (learning, behavior, results) were low.

Consistent with the growth in the training literature, a more recent meta-analysis by Alliger et al. (1997) found 34 studies and 115 correlations across various training criteria. They showed that when reactions focused on satisfaction with the trainer or instructor, there was virtually no relationship to learning measures. On the other hand, when the trainee perceptions focused on utility type reactions such as perceived relevance of the material for job performance, there were some modest relationships with immediate learning measures ($r = .26$) and on the job transfer (performance) measures ($r = .18$). Alliger et al. also found that immediate knowledge measures and knowledge retention measures were related ($r = .35$). Relations between knowledge measures and within training skill or behavior measures were less robust ($r = .18$). The relationship between the immediate, retained, and skill/behaviors within training measures and actual on the job transfer measures were quite modest with correlations of .11, .08, and .18. This indicates that the current learning measures obtained in these studies are not very predictive of how well a person actually transfers the learning to the job. Only two studies were found that correlated immediate learning and results type criteria.

Subsequent research has provided additional information as to the interrelationships among criterion elements in training evaluation. Warr, Allan, and Birdi (1999) employed a longitudinal design of three types of training evaluation measures—reactions (enjoyment, usefulness, perceived difficulty of learning, and motivation to learn), learning (confidence, knowledge level, and learning strategy), and behavioral change (frequency of use of equipment). This allowed for the examination of the interrelations of criterion measures of change scores as well as the more traditional post-training attainment scores for the learning and behavior measures. Most reaction measures were found to be predictive of changes in learning outcomes but not to changes in job behavior. On the other hand, the more difficult the trainees perceived the training, the less likely they were to try and use the equipment on the job. The correlation of learning attainment scores (knowledge) and job behavior scores were low ($r = .16$) while the relationship between change scores for learning and behavior were not significant. They found that learning strategies and transfer climate were predictive of job behavior changes. The study demonstrates the importance of examining change scores as well as the typical post-training assessments to understand outcome interrelationships.

The building of an understanding of the nomological network of relationships among criterion elements of training evaluation has improved. Nevertheless, there is still more work to be done. Our understanding of what we mean by learning has advanced but empirical studies examining multiple dimensions of learning are only now becoming more the norm (Ford, Kraiger, and Merritt in press). Research assumes a relatively linear relationship among criterion elements. What is needed are more nuanced studies that examine when we should expect linkages among criterion elements and under what conditions or factors one would expect relationships and when one would not expect them to occur.

2.3 Evaluation Design and Methodologies

More than fifty years back, researchers (e.g., Fleishman 1953) pointed out the need for more experimental evidence regarding training impact. Since then the field has made strong progress in terms of the techniques and designs for carrying out experimental studies on training evaluation. There exists a well-established litera-ture on experimental design and methodologies for training evaluation. Originally, Campbell and Stanley (1963) organized a list of threats to experimental design. We now have extensive discussions of possible threats to internal (e.g., history, testing, instrumentation, regression) and external (e.g., reactive effects of pre-testing) validity and how different quasi-experimental designs can address these threats (Cook, Campbell, and Peracchio 1990). We are also more aware of threats to validity that stem from the decision to evaluate a program. These include things like compensatory equalization of treatment, rivalry and demoralization amongst participants in the control group (Goldstein and Ford 2002). Recently, Shadish, Cook, and Campbell (2002) have updated the list of threats and have emphasized the role values of different stakeholders (trainees, trainers, evaluators, and organ-izational sponsors) play in terms of threats to the validity of the design.

Apart from having a list of threats to validity, we also have a number of research designs that can be employed to control some of the above-mentioned threats (Goldstein and Ford 2002). We now have examples of multiple time series and multiple baseline designs to determine the impact of training. We also know a lot about the advantages of using different statistical techniques like ANCOVA, mul-tiple regression procedures, and hierarchical regression models to determine from experimental data if there has been a change as a result of training intervention.

Goldstein and Ford (2002) expressed the fact that as training evaluators we tend to overemphasize the ideal experimental designs, even when we know the challenges of achieving these ideal conditions. In recent years researchers have put forth a cost-saving perspective that takes into account some of the tradeoffs and provides evalu-ators with options that balance both cost/practicality and validity. Such a cost-saving perspective brings us closer to the reality of today's changing world. Research ex-amples include issues related to statistical power, innovative quasi-experimental designs, and the use of retrospective testing and internal referencing strategies.

As noted by Kraiger (2002), there is a growing understanding that less rigorous research design may still be useful for effective training evaluation. For example, Sackett and Mullen (1993) noted that when one is solely interested in whether training objectives have been achieved by the trained group, an experimental design is not even needed. In addition, Sackett and Mullen show how pre-experimental designs can also be a powerful tool for examining training effects under certain conditions.

Training evaluation research has tended to compare different experimental designs in terms of their advantages and disadvantages in controlling threats to validity. One of the focus areas of comparison has been the relative statistical power of different designs to detect training effects. It has long been known that given a total N of subjects, designs which equally divide the sample into training and control group have the largest statistical power to detect training effects. Although this has been common wisdom, Yang, Sackett, and Arvey (1996) presented a cost-saving perspective to designing training evaluation. They took into account evaluation costs and demonstrated how one can obtain adequate statistical power even when one is using unequal group size design (unequal sample for training and control group). They also demonstrated how the use of a less expensive and less valid proxy criterion measure in a post-test-only control group design can reduce evaluation cost without sacrificing statistical power.

Another area that has received attention and also stems from the cost-saving perspective is the idea of retrospective pretests. Hill and Betz (2005) emphasize how both retrospective pre-tests and traditional pre-tests have certain biases and that there are tradeoffs in using one over the other. They stress that traditional pretests are better at examining program effects and that retrospective pretests are better at evaluating subjective experiences of program-related changes.

Quasi-experimental designs are another innovative way of collecting data so as to control some of the confounding factors to validity. The literature on quasi-experimental research designs has long emphasized the advantages of using time-series design and non-equivalent control group designs. Haccoun and Hamtiaux (1994) introduced the "Internal Referencing Strategy" wherein post-test measures include both items relevant to the training material and items that assess content that was not covered in the training intervention. The impact of the training program is confirmed if the change in the pre-test and post-test scores on the relevant items is greater than that on irrelevant items. Such a design permits the investigators to examine confounding effects of validity threats like history effects and effects of pre-sensitization.

3. FUTURE DIRECTIONS

In this chapter, we have presented the challenges to training evaluation as well as described progress. It is clear that we have improved our ability to determine if change has occurred and if the change can be attributed to training. In this final section, we outline three directions for future research. First, there is a need to apply additional concepts and frameworks to evaluation research. Second, there is a need to expand our repertoire of methodologies used to evaluate training outcomes. Third, there is a need to increase our relevance as evaluators to organizational decision makers.

3.1 Applying Additional Conceptual Frameworks

There are at least three areas in which existing conceptual frameworks and models can be applied to improve research in training evaluation. First, with more training focusing on developing open skills (Yelon and Ford 1999), a critical outcome for training is changing individual mindsets as well as changing individual skill sets (Cutcher-Gershenfeld and Ford 2005). Training evaluation has tended to ignore changes in attitudes and perspectives (e.g., becoming more open to new ideas) as a function of an intervention. Second, the focus on individual-level constructs (reactions, learning) in training evaluation studies ignores higher-level constructs and the issue that group-level effects may be the focus of the training intervention (e.g., training intact teams). This calls for incorporating advances in our understanding of multi-level issues in training evaluation research (Brown and Van Buren 2007; Klein and Kozlowski 2000). Third, while training evaluation is ultimately about changes in attitude, behavior, performance, and/or results, there have been few discussions about the assumptions researchers are making about how individuals (and team level) change. The typical conception is that change is linear and that change is immediate. Other change models may have relevance depending on the type of change envisioned and the type of training intervention.

3.1.1 *Attitudes*

Kraiger, Ford, and Salas (1993) argued that an emphasis on behavioral or cognitive measurement at the expense of attitudinal and motivational issues provides an incomplete profile of learning. They proposed a broader range of motivationally and attitudinally based outcomes that could be measured and used to infer that learning had occurred during training. Change in the affective outcome might be the major goal of the training program (e.g., diversity training), or these changes might indirectly support the acquisition of knowledge and skills and the desire to transfer those skills to the job.

Kraiger, Ford, and Salas (1993) recommended that when attitudinal learning outcomes are of interest, attitude strength should be assessed in addition to the more traditional focus on attitude direction. Strong attitudes are more persistent over time and more resistant to change than are weak attitudes (Bizer and Krosnick 2001). Ford, Kraiger, and Merritt (in press) suggested that individuals who experience an increase in attitude strength throughout the course of training may be more likely to demonstrate behavioral transfer of training than are those who have weaker attitudes. Krosnick et al. (1993) identified multiple dimensions of attitude strength that have been studied including affective intensity, certainty, accessibility, and latitudes of rejection and non-commitment. Empirical evidence has supported the multidimensionality of attitude strength (e.g., Holland and Van Knippenberg 2003). In addition, research indicates that attitude strength may be an important moderator of the attitude direction—behavior link (Crano and Prislin 2006).

3.1.2 *Multilevel effects*

As noted by Klein and Kozlowski (2000), organizational systems are in essence multi-level systems. They observe that "individual level processes can be manifest as a group, subunit, and organizational phenomenon and need to be explicitly incorporated into meaningful models of organizational behavior" (p. 11). Multi-level issues are inherent in training evaluation research.

Kozlowski et al. (2000) have applied a multi-level approach to understanding training effectiveness. They note that the intent of training can be to target higher levels such as groups and subunits. For example, army units are trained together to coordinate their efforts in battle. Medical personnel are formed into teams to deal with patient care. A focus on changes in individual-level knowledge (e.g., an individual's mental model) and skills (how the individual should respond to a particular situation) is a necessary but not sufficient condition for evaluation. Adding up or aggregating individual knowledge and skills in these types of teams will not allow for a complete or accurate assessment of training effects. A key aspect of the evaluation must be to target measuring changes of higher-level constructs such as team knowledge (e.g., shared mental models) and team-level skills such as information dissemination, cooperation, and coordination.

Researchers have begun to investigate team and multi-level issues in training such as the impact of changes in mental models due to training on team perform-ance and/or team process (e.g., Marks, Zaccaro, and Mathieu 2000; Mohammed and Dumville 2001; Smith-Jentsch, Mathieu, and Kraiger 2005). For example, Marks, Zaccaro, and Mathieu (2000) hypothesized and found support that team interaction training (cross-training) led to enhanced levels of mental model simi-larity (sharedness), which led to more effective communication and increased overall team performance.

Kozlowski et al. (2000) emphasize that taking a levels approach to training evaluation presents both conceptual and statistical challenges. It also necessitates a research design that samples multiple teams/units and as well as multiple organizations to study higher-level effects. A recent large-scale educational research study by Zvoch, Letourneau, and Parker (2007) reflects the move to more complex evaluation designs that incorporate multi-level and multi-site approach. They evaluated the impact of an early childhood literacy program for over 1,200 students in 49 classroom sites distributed across a number of schools. Their criterion was changes in literacy performance as assessed by growth curves. A three-level multi-level model was adopted and results analyzed by hierarchical linear modeling (Raudenbush et al. 2004) for estimating growth trajectories. We are in need of similar large-scale training evaluation efforts in the workplace. For example, training research is needed that examines the impact of different amounts or types of training across multiple groups in order to help increase our understanding of team and multi-level effects (Kozlowski et al. 2000).

3.1.3 *Change models*

Training evaluation research has taken a fairly straightforward view of change that a training intervention is seen as having a direct, linear effect on training outcomes such as performance. In many instances (e.g., closed skills such as learning how to do a lockout/tag out procedure on a machine), one can argue that this view of causality (direct impact of a training intervention to performance) is correct. Nevertheless, for more open skills (e.g., how to empower work teams), the impact of training on performance could be more complex.

Mitchell and James (2001) provide eight configurations that are possible to consider when interested in causality between an intervention (X) and an outcome (Y). The traditional assumption of training evaluation of direct linear effects is noted by Mitchell and James as the simplest and most frequently appearing relationship in our literature. In another configuration, the initial effect of training on performance could be minimal. Performance enhancement might only be seen over time when a trainee had a number of opportunities to try out the new skills after training (Ford et al. 1992; Sonnentag 2000). In this case, X does in fact cause Y, but Y changes over time. The change in Y may be a very predictable mean change but in other cases there may be less precision in understanding the rate of change over time.

Mitchell and James (2001) also stress that there can be more complex configurations beyond the eight they describe, including curvilinear relationships, rhythms, and cycles. The organizational change literature also speaks to different conceptualizations of change from clear, ordered, and linear change to change that is discontinuous including delays, reversals, and oscillations (e.g., Amis, Slack, and Hinings 2004; Purser and Petranker 2005). The eight configurations of causality by Mitchell and James and the various theories of change present a challenge to training evaluation research to go beyond the traditional X directly leads to Y perspective.

Training interventions can also be thought of as part of a larger organizational effort to go beyond first-order change (where there is tacit reinforcement of present understandings) to second-order change where there is an effort to modify existing schemas in the organization (e.g., Bartunek and Moch 1987). When second-order change is desired, training evaluation would need to focus on changes in mindsets as well as skillsets. Such an analysis might include changes in the use of linguistic symbols such as stories, myths, and use of language relevant to the change. This type of research calls for expanding our evaluation methodologies.

3.2 Expanding Evaluation Methodologies

Workplace training evaluation research has been dominated by the use of quantitative approaches. Training researchers need to look to educational program evaluation strategies, the approaches to empowerment and social justice evaluation by community psychologists, and to policy analysis studies for ideas on how to expand the repertoire of methodological tools available to determine the impact of various types of interventions (e.g., Cook and Reichardt 1979; Madey 1982; Rossman and Wilson 1985; Smith and Louis 1982). In particular, there have been more extensive efforts in these domains to mix evaluation methodologies and to take into account decision-maker needs for quick and accurate answers to evaluation questions.

Cook (1985) emphasizes "multiplism" or a mixed method design strategy that stresses how validity of results can be enhanced via convergence of results from multiple methods, theoretical orientations, and political or value perspectives. If data sources converge or corroborate with one another, then the validity of enquiry is enhanced while ruling out the question of whether any individually obtained data is an artifact of the method choice. When different methods provide slightly different information, the discrepancies can lead researchers to delve further into the phenomenon of interest and can often result in fresh and insightful explanations (McGrath and Johnson 2003).

Evaluators can utilize information from traditional methods of qualitative research such as participant observation, case studies, in-depth interviews, narrative analysis, and focus groups as well as recent advances in areas such as discourse analysis and visual storytelling (photovoice) (Foster-Fishman et al. 2005; Marecek 2003). These methods can help elicit open-ended responses from trainees, trainers, and managers regarding the impact of the program on performance (Farquhar et al., 2006). It can not only provide information about the trainee's reactions but also the gain in their knowledge and learning and their likelihood of transferring the learning to the work context (Basle 2000). For example, Zhao (2005) used qualitative methods in a study conducted in China to examine how different types of training can help establish a corporate culture. Green and Skinner (2005) provide an example of triangulation of methods regarding the effectiveness of a time management training program. They used qualitative interviews and questionnaires of trainees, trainers, and management personnel to identify observed changes in workplace behavior.

There are many computer programs that exist today which can analyze qualitative data more efficiently and effectively than in the past. Programs like Ethnograph, and Nud.ist allow researchers to feed in transcribed data and the program develops the themes (Wilkinson 2003). Information and themes from qualitative methods can further be used to develop survey-based quantitative measures which can then be used to test hypotheses and clarify other quantitative evaluation findings (Mertens 2005). It has the strength to provide information useful to not only understand whether the training had any impact but also to understand the processes behind observed changes.

In order to aid understanding, the data collected by qualitative methods must meet some criteria for accuracy and usefulness. There are a number of suggestions regarding criteria for evaluating data collected through qualitative methods such as credibility, transferability, confirmability, authenticity, and fairness (e.g., see Guba and Lincoln 1989; Patton 2002). For example, confirmability is defined as the extent to which findings are grounded in the data collected. This can be assessed by reviewing research records to determine if findings can be traced to the data and the data back to the original sources.

3.3 Increasing Relevance to Decision Makers

A systematic approach to training includes assessment, design, and evaluation. Feedback from the evaluation data can then be used to inform decision makers so that training decisions can be made as well as steps taken to continuously improve the training system (Goldstein and Ford 2002). Preskill and Caracelli (1997) reinforce this view as they reported that 99 percent of evaluators surveyed agreed that providing information to decision makers and improving programs were the key purposes for conducting evaluations. Unfortunately, evaluation efforts are often underfunded and once data is collected, the data may not be used by decision makers to improve training effectiveness.

Kraiger (2002) emphasized the need to strengthen the linkage of evaluation and improvement by taking a more decision-based approach to training evaluation. As Kraiger notes, the key is not implementing the perfect evaluation study but to "win the game" by accomplishing the purpose of collecting enough data to answer a practical question about training effectiveness. He provides a useful analysis of three targets of evaluation (training content and design, changes in learners, and organizational payoffs) and how these targets can be the focus of evaluation efforts with the goal of affecting decisions made about training systems.

Henry and Mark (2003) investigated the impact of evaluation reports on organizational decision makers across three levels of analysis: individual, interpersonal, and collective. For example, the process and outcomes of training evaluation as reflected in an evaluation report can lead decision makers to have different attitudes towards a particular type of training (e.g., behavioral modeling approaches "work"), can lead decision makers to reprioritize the importance of a particular training issue (e.g., we need more funding of this type of training), and can lead to behavioral change (e.g., adopting more rigorous methods of evaluation on other types of organizational interventions). They also describe interpersonal-level issues such as using evaluation findings to support (justification) a previously held position or using the data to persuade others about a certain course of action. At the collective level, evaluation findings can lead to a push for diffusion of a training innovation or lead to a policy change. They conclude that there are multiple pathways of evaluation influence and that we have limited understanding of those pathways and the impact of different types of evaluation data on the decision-making process.

A recent study provides one direction for research on evaluation findings and its potential influence on decision making. Christie (2007) used a set of scenarios derived from actual evaluation studies to examine the reported influence of evaluation information on the potential actions taken by decision makers. Educational leaders and program directors of healthcare departments examined nine scenarios and determined the extent to which the information presented in evaluation data within the scenario would influence their decision making. Christie found that decision makers stated they were more influenced by large-scale quantitative data and case-study data but less so by anecdotal evidence in an evaluation report. There was no difference in influence between case-study and large-scale quantitative data. In fact, educators in the sample tended to prefer data from the case study. This points to decision makers desiring broad as well as in-depth information when making decisions about a program. More studies on factors that influence decisions are clearly needed.

Brown and Gerhardt (2002) remind us that formative evaluation can provide critical information for decision makers during the design, development, and implementation of a program. As they note, knowing that trainees failed to gain knowledge from pre-test to post-test helps to identify a problem but does not assess the root causes of the problem. While training professionals believe that formative evaluation is critical to improving training effectiveness (White and Branch 2001), there are few studies that have been conducted examining the impact of different approaches to formative evaluation. Brown and Gerhardt provide an integrative formative evaluation model that includes the training stages of concept, design, prototype, and pilot work. At each stage, they identify what to evaluate, what to measure, who to involve in the evaluation process, when evaluation is most critical, and what problems or challenges may arise. Based on this model, they provide a number of research gaps that need to be filled. For example, efforts at the pilot stage can focus on learner engagement. Data can be gathered at multiple points through experience sampling techniques to determine if and when engagement suffers during the training. Follow-up interviews can then identify key information to improve training effectiveness. A study can then examine the benefits of this enhanced focus on improving learner engagement on valued training outcomes.

At other times, more outcome-oriented (summative evaluation) data serves the need for the feedback required to make timely corrections so the intervention can eventually have its largest possible impact. Large-scale societal interventions such as emergency responses by the UN to a humanitarian crisis or community-based interventions such as AIDS prevention can be very costly. Decision makers want to know while the intervention is ongoing if the effort is succeeding or failing. This need has led to the development of what has been termed rapid evaluation and assessment method (REAM) (e.g., Anker et al. 1993; McNall et al. 2004).

McNall and Foster-Fishman (2007) provide the steps in a typical REAM: (1) real-time evaluations are initiated as a crisis emerges or appears imminent relevant to an intervention; (2) multiple evaluators are organized as a cell to systematically collect and review data as the crisis unfolds; (3) evaluators interact and share their observations and recommendations on an ongoing basis with field staff to allow operational problems to be corrected; and (4) at the conclusion of the REAM, evaluators hold interactive debriefing sessions with staff and other stakeholder groups about what was learned. As noted by McNall and Foster-Fishman, the typical REAM uses a mixed methods approach including semi-structured interviews, focus groups, site visits, a limited number of in-depth interviews, and reviews of secondary documentation. The key is to use different data collection methods to rapidly collect, analyze, and report data on focused or targeted outcomes. They reviewed thirteen field projects regarding the various approaches taken, purpose, target population, research methods, and stakeholder participation in the evaluation. They stress the need for the process to be rapid, participatory (many stakeholder groups), team based (evaluation team working collaboratively on all aspects of the evaluation process), and iterative (data analyzed as it is being collected, preliminary findings guiding decisions about additional data needs, etc.).

As noted by McNall and Foster-Fishman (2007), REAM would seem most appropriate when there is an urgent need for information on the basis of which immediate action needs to be taken (e.g., an organization planning on launching a new sales program worldwide). Rather than contributing to theory per se, this approach provides data of sufficient quality at key decision points to improve the effectiveness of correction actions. For example, a key research issue in I/O Psychology is the enhancement of safety in the workplace. Training on adherence to safety protocols in hospital settings (Hofmann and Mark 2006) or using protective safety equipment at nuclear facilities (Burke et al. 2002) would seem to have consequences for error large enough to warrant consideration of REAM.

References

ALLIGER, G. M., and JANEK, E. A. 1989. Kirkpatrick's levels of training criteria: thirty years later. *Personnel Psychology*, 42: 331–42.

—— TANNENBAUM, S. I., BENNETT, W., TRAVER, H., and SHOTLAND, A. 1997. A meta analysis of the relations among training criteria. *Personnel Psychology*, 50: 341–58.

AMIS J., SLACK, T., and HINNGS, C. 2004. The pace, sequence, and linearity of radical change. *Academy of Management Journal*, 47: 15–39.

ANDERSON, L. W., KRATHWOHL, D. R., AIRASIAN, P. W., CRUIKSHANK, D. A., MAYER, R. E., PINTRICH, P. R., RATHS, J., and WITTROCK, M. C. 2001. *A Taxonomy for Learning and Assessing: A Revision of Bloom's Taxonomy of Educational Objectives*. New York: Longman.

ANKER, M., GUIDOTTI, R., ORZESZYNA, S., SAPIRIE, S., and THURIAX, M. 1993. Rapid evaluation methods (REM) of health services performance: methodological observations. *Bulletin of the World Health Organization*, 71: 15–21.

BALDWIN, T. T., and FORD, J. K. 1988. Transfer of training: a review and directions for future research. *Personnel Psychology*, 41: 63–105.

BARTUNEK, J., and MOCH, M. 1987. First, second, and third order change and organizational development interventions: a cognitive approach. *Journal of Applied Behavioral Science*, 23: 483–500.

BATES, R. 2004. A critical analysis of evaluation practice: the Kirkpatrick model and the principles of beneficence. *Evaluation and Program Planning*, 27: 341–7.

BASLE, M. 2000. Comparative analysis of quantitative and qualitative methods in French non-experimental evaluation of regional and local policies. *Evaluation*, 6: 323–34.

BIZER, G. Y., and KROSNICK, J. A. 2001. Exploring the structure of strength-related features: the relation between attitude importance and attitude accessibility. *Journal of Personality and Social Psychology*, 81: 566–86.

BLOOM, B. 1956. *Taxonomy of Learning Objectives: The Cognitive Domain*. New York: Donald McKay.

BOUDREAU, J. W. 1983. Economic considerations in estimating the utility of human resource productivity improvement programs. *Personnel Psychology*, 36: 551–76.

—— 1984. Decision theory contributions to HRM research and practice. *Industrial Relations*, 23: 198–217.

—— 1988. Utility analysis: a new perspective on human resource management decision making. Pp. 125–86 in *Human Resource Management: Evolving Roles and Responsibilities*, ed. L. Dyer. Washington, DC: Bureau of National Affairs.

—— 1991. Utility analysis for decisions in human resource management. Pp. 621–745 in *Handbook of Industrial and Organizational Psychology*, vol. iii, ed. M. D. Dunnette and L. M. Hough. Palo Alto, CA: Consulting Psychologists Press.

BRACKEN, D. W., TIMMRECK, C. W., and CHURCH, A. H., eds. 2001. *The Handbook of Multisource Feedback*. San Francisco: Jossey-Bass.

BROWN, K. 2005. An examination of the structure and nomological network of trainee reactions: a closer look at the "smile sheets." *Journal of Applied Psychology*, 90: 991–1001.

—— and GERHARDT, M. W. 2002. Formative evaluation: an integrative practice model and case study. *Personnel Psychology*, 55: 951–83.

—— and VAN BUREN, M. E. 2007. Applying a social capital perspective to the evaluation of distance training. In *Toward a Science of Distributed Learning*, ed. S. M. Fiore and E. Salas. Washington, DC: American Psychological Association.

BURKE, M. J., SARPY, S. A., TESLUK, P. E., and SMITH-CROWE, K. 2002. General safety performance: a test of a grounded theoretical model. *Personnel Psychology*, 55: 429–67.

CAMPBELL, D. T., and STANLEY, J. C. 1963. *Experimental and Quasi-experimental Designs for Research*. Chicago: Rand McNally.

CAMPBELL, J. P. 1990. An overview of the army selection and classification project (Project A). *Personnel Psychology*, 43: 231–9.

—— 1999. The definition and measurement of performance in the new age. Pp. 399–429 in *The Changing Nature of Performance*, ed. D. R. Ilgen and E. D. Pulakos. San Francisco: Jossey-Bass.

CASCIO, W. F. 1982. *Costing Human Resources: The Financial Impact of Behavior in Organizations*. Boston: Kent Publishing Co.

—— 1989. Utility analysis as an evaluation tool. Pp. 63–88 in *Training and Development in Organizations*, ed. I. L. Goldstein. San Francisco: Jossey-Bass.

CHRISTIE, C. A. 2007. Reported influence of evaluation data on decision makers' actions. *American Journal of Evaluation*, 28: 8–25.

COOK T. 1985. Postpositivist critical multiplism. Pp. 25–62 in *Social Science and Social Policy*, ed. R. Shotland and M. Mark. Beverly Hills, CA: Sage.

COOK, T. D., and REICHARDT, C. S., eds. 1979. *Qualitative and Quantitative Methods in Evaluation Research*. Beverly Hills, CA: Sage.

—— CAMPBELL, D. T., and PERACCHIO, L. 1990. Quasi-experimentation. Pp. 491–576 in *Handbook of Industrial and Organizational Psychology*, vol. i, ed. M. D. Dunnette and L. M. Hough. Palo Alto, CA: Consulting Psychologist Press.

CRANO, W. D., and PRISLIN, R. 2006. Attitudes and persuasion. *Annual Review of Psychology*, 57: 345–74.

CUTCHER-GERSHENFELD, J., and FORD, J. K. 2005. *Valuable Disconnects in Organizational Learning Systems: Integrating Bold Vision and Harsh Realities*. New York: Oxford University Press.

DAVIS, M. A., CURTIS, M. B., and TSCHETTER, J. D. 2003. Evaluating cognitive training outcomes: validity and utility of structural knowledge assessment. *Journal of Business and Psychology*, 18: 191–206.

FARQUHAR, S. A., PARKER, E. A., SCHULZ, A. J., and ISRAEL, B. A. 2006. Application of qualitative methods in program planning for health promotion interventions. *Health Promotion Practice*, 7: 234–42.

FLEISHMAN, E. A. 1953. The description of supervisory behavior. *Personnel Psychology*, 37: 1–6.

FORD, J. K., KRAIGER, K., and MERRITT, S. in press. An updated review of the multi-dimensionality of training outcomes: new directions for training evaluation research. In *Learning, Training, and Development in Organizations*, ed. S. W. J. Kozlowski and E. Salas. Mahwah, NJ: LEA.

—— QUIÑONES, M. A., SEGO, D. J., and SORRA, J. S. 1992. Factors affecting the opportunity to perform trained tasks on the job. *Personnel Psychology*, 45: 511–27.

FOSTER-FISHMAN, P., NOWELL, B., DEACON, Z., NIEVAR, M. A., and McCANN, P. 2005. Using methods that matter: the impact of reflection, dialogue, and voice. *American Journal of Community Psychology*, 36: 275–91.

FRIEDMAN, T. J. 2005. *The World if Flat*. New York: Farrar, Straus and Giroux.

GOLDSTEIN, I. L., and FORD, J. K. 2002. *Training in Organizations*, 4th edn. Belmont, CA: Wadsworth.

GREEN, P., and SKINNER, D. 2005. Does time management training work? An evaluation. *International Journal of Training and Development*, 9: 124–39.

GUBA, E., and LINCOLN, Y. 1989. *Fourth Generation Evaluation*. Newbury Park, CA: Sage.

GUION, R. M. 1998. *Assessment, Measurement, and Prediction for Personnel Decisions*. Mahwah, NJ: LEA.

HACCOUN, R. R., and HAMTIAUX, T. 1994. Optimizing knowledge tests for inferring learning acquisition levels in single group training evaluation designs: the internal referencing strategy. *Personnel Psychology*, 47: 593–604.

HENRY, G. T., and MARK, M. M. 2003. Beyond use: understanding evaluation's influence on attitudes and actions. *American Journal of Evaluation*, 24: 293–314.

HILL, L., and BETZ, D. 2005. Revisiting the Retrospective Pretest. *American Journal of Evaluation*, 26: 501–17.

HOFMANN, D. A., and MARK, B. 2006. An investigation of the relationship between safety climate and medication errors as well as other nurse and patient outcomes. *Personnel Psychology*, 59: 847–70.

HOLLAND, R. W., and VAN KNIPPENBERG, A. 2003. From repetition to conviction: attitude accessibility as a determinant of attitude certainty. *Journal of Experimental Social Psychology*, 39: 594–601.

HOLTON, E. F. 1996. The flawed four-level evaluation model. *Human Resource Development Quarterly*, 7: 5–21.

HOWARD, A. 1995. Rethinking the psychology of work. Pp. 513–55 in *The Changing Nature of Work*, ed. A. Howard. San Francisco: Jossey-Bass.

ILGEN, D. R., and PULAKOS, E. D. 1999. *The Changing Nature of Performance*. San Francisco: Jossey-Bass.

JELLMA, F., VISSCHER, A., and SCHEERENS, J. 2006. Measuring change in work behavior by means of multisource feedback. *International Journal of Training and Development*, 10: 121–39.

KIRKPATRICK, D. L. 1959. Techniques for evaluating training programs. *Journal of the American Society of Training Directors*, 13: 3–32.

KLEIN, K. J., and KOZLOWSKI, S. W. J. 2000. *Multilevel Theory, Research, and Methods in Organizations*. San Francisco: Jossey-Bass.

KOZLOWSKI, S. W. J., and BELL, B. S. 2006. Disentangling achievement orientation and goal setting: effects on self-regulatory processes. *Journal of Applied Psychology*, 91: 900–16.

—— BROWN, K. G., WEISSBEIN, D. A., CANNON-BOWERS, J. A., and SALAS, E. 2000. A multilevel approach to training effectiveness: enhancing horizontal and vertical transfer. Pp. 157–210 in *Multilevel Theory, Research, and Methods in Organizations*, (ed. K. J. Klein and S. W. J. Kozlowski.). San Francisco: Jossey-Bass.

KRAIGER K. 2002. Decision-based evaluation. Pp. 331–75 in *Creating, Implementing and Maintaining Effective Training and Development: State-of-the-art Lessons for Practice*, ed. K. Kraiger. San Francisco: Jossey-Bass.

—— and FORD, J. K. 2007. The history of training in Industrial/Organizational Psychology. In *The Science and Practice of Industrial and Organizational Psychology: Historical Aspects from the First 100 Years*, ed. L. Koppes. Mahwah, NJ: LEA.

—— FORD, J. K., and SALAS, E. 1993. Application of cognitive, skill-based, and affective theories of learning outcomes to new methods of training evaluation. *Journal of Applied Psychology*, 78: 311–28.

KROSNICK, J. A., BONINGER, D. S., CHUANG, Y. C., BERENT, M. K., and CARNOT, C. G. 1993. Attitude strength: one construct or many related constructs? *Journal of Personality and Social Psychology*, 65: 1132–51.

McGEHEE, W., and THAYER, P. 1961. *Training in Business and Industry*. New York: McGraw Hill.

McGRATH, J. E., and JOHNSON, B. A. 2003. Methodology makes meaning: how both qualitative and quantitative paradigms shape evidence. In *Qualitative Research in Psychology: Expanding Perspectives in Methodology and Design*, ed. P. M. Camic, J. E. Rhodes, and L. Yardley. Washington, DC: American Psychological Association.

McNALL, M. A., and FOSTER-FISHMAN, P. G. 2007. Methods of rapid evaluation, assessment and reappraisal. *American Journal of Evaluation*, 28: 1151–68.

McNALL, M. A., WELCH, V. E., RUH, K. L., MILDNER, C. A., and SOTO, T. 2004. The use of rapid-feedback evaluation methods to improve the retention rates of an HIV/AIDS healthcare intervention. *Evaluation and Program Planning*, 3: 287–94.

MADEY, D. L. 1982. Some benefits of integrating qualitative and quantitative methods in program evaluation, with illustrations. *Educational Evaluation and Policy Analysis*, 4: 223–36.

MARECEK, J. 2003. Dancing through minefields: toward a qualitative stance in psychology. Pp. 49–69 in *Qualitative Perspectives in Methodology and Design*, ed. P. M. Camic, J. E. Rhodes, and L. Yaradley. Washington, DC: American Psychological Association.

MARKS, M. A., ZACCARO, S. J., MATHIEU, J. E. 2000. Performance implications for leader briefings and team-interaction training for team adaptation to novel environments. *Journal of Applied Psychology*, 85: 971–86.

MATHIEU, J. E. and LEONARD R. L., Jr. 1987. Applying utility concepts to a training program in supervisory skills: a time based approach. *Academy of Management Journal*, 30: 316–35.

MERTENS, D. M. 2005. *Research and Evaluation in Education and Psychology*, 2nd edn. Thousand Oaks, CA: Sage.

MITCHELL, T. R., and JAMES, L. R. 2001. Building better theory: time and the specification of when things happen. *Academy of Management Review*, 26: 530–47.

MOHAMMED, S., and DUMVILLE, B. C. 2001. Team mental models in a team knowledge framework: expanding theory and measurement across disciplinary boundaries. *Journal of Organizational Behavior*, 22: 89–106.

MORGAN, R. B., and CASPER, W. 2000. Examining the factor structure of participant reactions to training: a multidimensional approach. *Human Resource Development Quarterly*, 11: 301–17.

MORROW, C. C., JARRETT, M. Q., and RUPINSKI, M. T. 1997. An investigation of the effect and economic utility of corporate-wide training. *Personnel Psychology*, 50: 91–119.

MOTOWIDLO, S. J., and SCHMIT, M. J. 1999. Performance assessment in unique jobs. Pp. 56–86 in *The Changing Nature of Performance*, ed. D. R. Ilgen and E. D. Pulakos. San Francisco: Jossey-Bass.

PATTON, M. 2002. *Qualitative Research and Evaluation Methods*, 3rd edn. Thousand Oaks, CA: Sage.

PURSER, R., and PETRANKER, J. 2005. Unfreezing the future: exploring the dynamic of time in organizational change. *Journal of Applied Behavioral Science*, 41: 182–203.

PHILLIPS, J. J., and PHILLIPS, P. P., eds. 2005. *ROI at Work: Best Practice Case Studies from the Real World*. Alexandria, VA: American Society for Training and Development.

PRESKILL, H., and CARACELLI, V. J. 1997. Current and developing conceptions of use: Evaluation Use Topical Interest Groups survey results. *Evaluation Practice*, 18: 209–25.

PULAKOS, E. D., ARAD, S., DONOVAN, M. A., and PLAMONDON, K. E. 2000. Adaptability in the workplace: development of a taxonomy of adaptive performance. *Journal of Applied Psychology*, 85: 612–24.

RAJU, N. S., BURKE, M. J., and NORMAND, J. 1990. A new approach for utility analysis. *Journal of Applied Psychology*, 75: 3–12.

RAUDENBUSH, S. W., BRYK, A. S., CHEONG, Y. F., and CONGDON, R. T. 2004. *HLM 6: Hierarchical linear and nonlinear modeling*. Chicago: Scientific Software International.

ROSSMAN, G. B., and WILSON, B. L. 1985. Numbers and words: combining quantitative and qualitative methods in a single large-scale evaluation study. *Evaluation Review*, 9: 627–43.

SACKETT, P. R., and MULLEN, E. J. 1993. Beyond formal experimental design: towards an expanded view of the training evaluation process. *Personnel Psychology,* 46: 613–27.

SALAS, E., MILHAM, L. M., and BOWERS, C. A. 2003. Training evaluation in the military: misconceptions, opportunities, and challenges. *Military Psychology,* 15: 3–16.

SCHMIDT, F. L., HUNTER, J. E., and PEARLMAN, K. 1982. Assessing the economic impact of personnel programs on workforce productivity. *Personnel Psychology,* 35: 333–47.

SCHNEIDER, B., and SCHMITT, N. 1986. *Staffing Organizations,* 2nd edn., Glenview, IL: Scott, Foresman.

SHADISH, W. R., COOK, T. D., and CAMPBELL., D. T. 2002. *Experimental and Quasi-Experimental Designs for Generalized Causal Inference.* Boston: Houghton-Mifflin.

SMITH, A. G., and LOUIS, K. S., eds. 1982. Multimethod policy research: issues and applications [Special issue]. *American Behavioral Scientist,* 26.

SMITHER, J. W., LONDON, M., VASILOPOULOS, N., REILLY, R. R., MILLSAP, R. E., and SALVEMINI, N. 1995. An examination of the effects of an upward feedback program over time. *Personnel Psychology,* 48: 1–34.

SMITH-JENTSCH, K., MATHIEU, J., and KRAIGER, K. 2005. Investigating linear and inter-active effects of shared mental models on safety and efficiency in a field setting. *Journal of Applied Psychology,* 90: 523–35.

SONNENTAG, S. 2000. Expertise at work: experience and excellent performance. Pp. 223–64 in *International Review of Industrial and Organizational Psychology,* 15, ed. C. I. Cooper and I. T. Robertson. Chichester: John Wiley and Sons.

SONNICHSEN, R. 2000. *High Impact Internal Evaluation: A Practitioner's Guide to Evaluation and Consulting Inside Organizations.* Thousand Oaks, CA: Sage.

SUGRUE, B., and KIM, K. 2004. *State of the Industry: ASTD's Annual Review of Trends in Workplace Learning and Performance.* Alexandria, VA: American Society of Training and Development.

THAYER, P. W. 1997. A rapidly changing world: some implications for training systems in the Year 2001 and beyond. Pp. 15–30 in *Training for a Rapidly Changing Workplace,* ed. M. A. Quinones and A. Ehrenstein. Washington, DC: APA.

WALL, T. D., and JACKSON, P. R. 1995. New manufacturing initiatives and shopfloor job design. Pp. 139–74 in *The Changing Nature of Work,* ed. A. Howard. San Francisco: Jossey-Bass.

WALLACE, S. R. 1965. Criteria for what? *American Psychologist,* 20: 411–17.

WARR, P., and BUNCE, D. 1995. Trainee characteristics and the outcomes of open learning. *Personnel Psychology,* 48: 347–75.

—— ALLAN, C., and BIRDI, K. 1999. Predicting three levels of training outcome. *Journal of Occupational and Organizational Psychology,* 72: 351–75.

WEXLEY, K., and LATHAM, G. P. 2002. *Developing and Training Human Resources in Organizations,* 3rd edn. Upper Saddle River, NJ: Prentice Hall.

WHITE, B. S., and BRANCH, R. M. 2001. Systematic pilot testing as a step in the instructional design process of corporate training and development. *Performance Improvement Quarterly,* 14: 75–94.

WILKINSON, S. 2003. Focus groups. In *Qualitative Psychology: A Practical Guide to Research Methods,* ed. J. A. Smith. Thousand Oaks, CA: Sage.

YANG, H., SACKETT, P. R., and ARVEY, R. D. 1996. Statistical power and cost in training evaluation: some new considerations. *Personnel Psychology,* 49: 651–68.

YELON, S. L., and FORD, J. K. 1999. Pursuing a multidimensional view of transfer. *Performance Improvement Quarterly*, 12: 58–7.

ZHAO, C. 2005. Management of corporate culture through local managers' training in foreign companies in China: a qualitative analysis. *International Journal of Training and Development*, 9: 232–55.

ZVOCH, K., LETOURNEAU, L. E., and PARKER, R. P. 2007. A multilevel multi-site outcomes-by-implementation evaluation of an early childhood literacy model. *American Journal of Evaluation*, 28: 132–50.

13

JOB PERFORMANCE MEASUREMENT: THE ELUSIVE RELATIONSHIP BETWEEN JOB PERFORMANCE AND JOB SATISFACTION

STEPHEN A. WOODS

1. INTRODUCTION

How can people's performance at work be conceptualized and measured? Think about the colleagues, supervisors, or subordinates you work with. How could you assess and quantify their job performance and how would you know that your measurement was fair and accurate? How could your performance be quantified? It is a common problem in management and human resource practice that many managers tend to know intuitively whether staff are performing well or poorly, but are at a loss about exactly how to quantify performance. The problem of quantifying job performance is also prevalent in research. Job performance is so important in occupational, organizational, I/O, and personnel psychology that it is often referred to simply as "the criterion" (Dalal 2005), and the "criterion problem" refers to the unavailability of robust job performance criteria in applied research (Austin and Villanova 1992). This is of real concern for researchers and practitioners because so many activities rely on job performance measurement: validation of selection systems and individual difference measures, training and development planning, promotion planning, job appraisal, and other performance management activities to list a few. Thayer (1992) summarizes the concern about relying on poor performance measures: "I am concerned with the continuing tendency to accept criteria that are 'lying around', our uncritical acceptance of criteria that management uses for its own decisions, our apparent lack of concern over the reliability of such criteria and the meaning of such criteria" (Thayer 1992, 97). Casting a critical, objective eye over applied research incorporating job performance measures leaves one hard pushed to defend a substantial proportion of it against Thayer's concern. This chapter reviews recent literature on job performance measurement to examine advances in theories of job performance measurement, and their implications for the practice of job performance assessment. The chapter also considers the antecedents of job performance and in particular, revisits the issue of whether happy, satisfied workers are also productive workers.

2. PERFORMANCE MEASUREMENT AND PERFORMANCE CRITERIA

What is job performance measurement? Tannenbaum (2006) concisely describes job performance measurement as the "collection and use of judgements, ratings, perceptions, or more objective sources of information to better understand the performance of a person, team, unit, business, process, program or initiative in order to guide subsequent actions or decisions." The focus in this chapter is on measuring the job performance of individuals and teams, which most commonly involves the use of surveys or rating forms to assess and evaluate employee behavior or job competencies (Viswesvaran, Ones, and Schmidt 1996). Subjective ratings may be provided by supervisors, peers, subordinates, or clients and customers. Performance measurement may also make use of data from archival records (such as productivity or absence data), often referred to as objective data.

The relationship between subjective and objective performance criteria is sometimes misunderstood. The association between objective performance records such as sales figures, production quantity and quality, and subjective performance ratings is around 0.40 (Bommer et al. 1995). From the results of their meta-analysis, Bommer et al. (1995) concluded that objective and subjective measures should not be combined as outcome criteria in validity and other research studies. Others have commented that the distinction is less clear cut. Campbell (1990) argues that determining the boundaries for acceptable versus unacceptable performance is a subjective task, and so many "objective measures" could easily be conceptualized as subjective.

From a psychological perspective, job performance is conceptualized as behavioral (Motowildo, Borman, and Schmit 1997). Behavior represents what people actually do at work. Judgments about job performance are based on the evaluation of behavior as either positive or negative within a given organizational context. Results or performance outcomes represent the contribution that an individual's job performance makes to an organization and its goals. Motowildo, Borman, and Schmit (1997) argue that behavior should be the focus of performance assessment because results and outcomes can be affected by many factors outside the control of individuals. The results achieved by poorly performing employees and managers can be compensated by a buoyant business environment or co-worker support. Conversely, a person who performs all of the desirable behaviors required in their job might achieve poor results because the product or service that he or she is delivering is inadequate, or not in demand, factors that may be outside the employee's control.

The variety of possible performance behaviors that a person may demonstrate logically leads to a multifaceted or multidimensional model of job performance. Multidimensional models allow us to make sense of complex behavioral phenomena. The basic principle underlying such models is that discrete behaviors can be empirically or conceptually clustered into broad homogeneous dimensions. Each dimension is defined according to the common theme among its constituent behaviors. For example, key management performance behaviors include formulating short- and long-term team objectives, and organizing and prioritizing work. These two activities are conceptually related, and might be grouped under a broader heading of planning and organizing (e.g., Borman and Brush 1993). This multidimensional approach has led to a number of different models of job performance.

3. Models of Job Performance

3.1 Military Performance

Possibly the most in-depth studies of job performance criteria are those conducted as part of the US army's job performance measurement project by J. P. Campbell,

C. H. Campbell, and colleagues. The most detailed were conducted within the US army in "Project A." These projects were designed to produce comprehensive models of performance for service personnel and to inform selection and recruitment activities for the military. As a consequence, the studies have provided work psychologists with a wealth of material on the structure and analysis of job performance criteria (Knapp 2006). Campbell et al. (1990) describe the techniques and processes used to develop job performance measures for the broad sample of jobs within the army. Job content was first analyzed using task analysis and critical-incidents analysis. From these job analysis data, an array of work sample tasks, pencil-and-paper tests, and performance rating instruments were constructed, supplemented by archival performance data. Across all the jobs analyzed, more than 200 individual performance indicators were generated.

Cambell, McHenry, and Wise (1990) subjected the performance indicators to a structural analysis based on the data from over 9,000 job holders. The starting point of their analysis was an assumption that there are two general factors of job performance: (1) performance dimensions that relate to a specific job or role; and (2) performance dimensions that are relevant across jobs and roles. In their structural analyses, Campbell, McHenry, and Wise identified five factors that best represented the data. The first was core technical proficiency, representing the performance of tasks central to the specific job role. The second was a general proficiency dimension that represented the performance of tasks that were important in all roles. The remaining three factors also represented aspects of performance that generalized across roles, assessed through performance ratings. These were Effort/Leadership, Maintaining Personal Discipline, and Fitness/Military Bearing.

Although the model was specific to army personnel, the results of these and other US military studies led to the development of the widely cited eight-dimensional model of Campbell et al. (1993). This model extended the five-dimension model to encompass job performance criteria applicable across all jobs. The eight dimensions are: (1) job-specific task proficiency; (2) non-job-specific task proficiency; (3) written and oral communication; (4) demonstrating effort; (5) maintaining personal discipline; (6) maintaining peer and team performance; (7) supervision/leadership; and (8) management/administration. The model may be thought of as a job performance framework applicable to any occupation, with the eight categories populated with job-relevant information and assigned specific weights depending on the nature of the job.

3.2 Viswesvaran, Ones, and Schmidt's (1996) Ten-Dimension Model

In their meta-analysis of the reliabilities of job performance measures, Viswesvaran, Ones, and Schmidt (1996) derived ten job performance dimensions, based around an initial model proposed by Viswesvaran (1993). These dimensions were defined by first extracting 486 separate job performance measures from the research literature, and grouping those that were conceptually similar. The perspective adopted by Viswesvaran and colleagues is informative in understanding the purpose of performance modeling. Whilst most psychologists emphasize the need to conduct thorough job analyses to define the job performance in specific jobs, this does not mean that the basic elements of job performance change across different jobs (Viswesvaran and Ones 2000). The ten-dimensional model is an attempt to identify dimensions of performance that apply across all jobs, again with the relative importance of each changing across different job roles. The model is also important because it has been used in several influential meta-analyses (e.g. Viswesvaran, Ones, and Schmidt 1996; Viswesvaran, Schmidt, and Ones 2002). The ten dimensions are (1) overall job performance; (2) productivity; (3) effort; (4) interpersonal competence; (5) administrative competence; (6) quality; (7) job knowledge; (8) communication; (9) leadership; and (10) compliance or acceptance of authority.

3.3 A General Factor of Job Performance

Is there a general factor of job performance? Viswesvaran, Schmidt, and Ones (2005) present evidence of a general job performance factor based on an examination of the "halo effect." The halo effect is most adequately described as a psychological process affecting how job performance is rated (Viswesvaran, Schmidt, and Ones 2005). Before a rater assesses a person's job performance, they form an impression about that individual's overall merit. This impression influences the way that the rater evaluates the person's performance on a range of performance dimensions.

The shared variance across ratings of different job performance dimensions may be split into two components. The first is halo or measurement error arising from the idiosyncratic impression of the rater. The second component is the part of the impression that overlaps with other raters. This proportion can be considered to be true variance, representing agreement between raters about the general level of performance of a specific target. According to Viswesvaran, Schmidt, and Ones (2005), this component may be considered to be a general factor of job performance (shared "true" variance across performance dimensions). In their analyses, Viswesvaran et al. extracted a large single factor from ratings of job performance dimensions, and reported that this general factor accounted for 60.3 percent of the variance among job performance dimensions. It appears that people who score highly on one job dimension also tend to score highly on others. This finding is important because it justifies the combination of performance dimensions into single job performance indices, and explains why past studies have usually concluded that performance ratings are still highly useful criteria, even when halo is detected (e.g., Jackson and Furnham 2001).

One implication of identifying a general performance dimension is that job performance can be conceptualized as hierarchical (Viswesvaran and Ones 2000). A hierarchical model of job performance would be structured with the general factor at the top, with more specific job dimensions organized underneath, each subsuming a number of actual job performance measures. The existence of a general factor does not rule out the utility of specific dimensions, which may be useful for particular practical purposes or for predicting specific criteria. A complex issue is organizing the space in the job performance hierarchy underneath a general factor. A potentially acceptable solution could be provided for the next level down by differentiating task performance and organizational citizenship behaviors.

3.4 Task versus Organizational Citizenship Behaviors

Probably the most influential advance in job performance modeling in the past twenty years is the differentiation of task performance and organizational citizenship behavior (e.g., Motowildo and Van Scotter 1994; Motowildo, Borman, and Schmit 1997). The traditional view of job performance restricted the domain of interest to aspects of task performance (Dalal 2005). Task performance is defined by Borman and Motowildo (1997, 99) as "the effectiveness with which job incumbents perform activities that relate to the organisation's technical core." Motowildo, Borman, and Schmit (1997) expand this definition to encompass two basic kinds of task performance activities. The first comprises the conversion of raw materials into goods and services that constitute the products of the organization (such as selling merchandise, operating machinery, teaching a class, performing surgical procedures). The second group of activities comprise activities that maintain and service the technical core of the organization (such as the supervision of staff, planning core activities, distributing supplies and products). Task performance therefore has a direct impact on the core function of an organization.

More recently, theories and models of job performance have acknowledged the importance of work behaviors that fall outside the domain of task performance, often referred to as discretionary or extra-role behaviors. In contemporary business environments characterized by flatter structures, international competition, and increased employee autonomy, such behaviors are now considered critical to effective organizational performance (Podsakoff et al. 2000). The most widely used term for these aspects of job performance is organizational citizenship behavior (OCB).

The concept of OCB was proposed by Organ in the late 1980s (e.g., Organ 1988), who observed that, to a varying extent, people tend to contribute to the continued existence of their organization beyond their core task activities. Such contributions include helping and cooperating with others, and general support for the organization and its mission. OCB was initially defined as extra-role behavior, not directly recognized through formal reward systems. Such behavior was therefore considered desirable, but not enforceable (Smith, Organ, and Near 1983). This definition was modified by Borman and Motowildo (1993), who proposed an alternative construct labeled contextual performance. They defined contextual behaviors as those that "supported the organisational, social and psychological environment in which the technical core must function" (p. 74), elaborating this with examples such as helping co-workers, volunteering for extra work, and describing the organization in a positive way. They noted that whilst task behavior is job specific, contextual behaviors were desirable across all jobs.

An important development of the theory was the recognition that such behaviors need not fall outside formal reward systems. Many OCBs would be considered to be central to effective performance, and reward follows from the evaluation of performance rather than from the behaviors directly. Organ (1997) modified his theory of OCB so that the behaviors were not considered to be extra-role, or unrewarded, bringing OCB in line with Borman and Motowildo's definition of contextual performance. The two may be considered interchangeable in contemporary research, but I agree with Organ (1997) that OCB is a better term, because people intuitively know what citizenship is about, whereas "contextual performance" is a colder, more abstract term.

3.4.1 *Dimensions of OCB*

There are several dimensional models of OCB in the research literature. Organ (1988) proposed five dimensions labeled altruism, courtesy, conscientiousness, sportsmanship, and civic virtue. A simpler two-dimensional structure was described by Williams and Anderson (1991), who distinguished between citizenship behaviors directed towards individuals (OCB-I) and organizations (OCB-O). The five dimensions proposed by Organ can be subsumed under these two broader dimensions. The two dimensions are also represented in a model of contextual performance proposed by Coleman and Borman (2000), in the dimensions Personal Support and Organizational Support respectively. Their model incorporated a third dimension labeled Conscientious Initiative. Table 13.1, taken from Hanson and Borman (2006), describes the Coleman and Borman (2000) model. Hanson and Borman provide a fuller discussion of the overlaps and relationships between the various models of OCB. One dimension unaccounted for in these mainstream models of OCB is adaptive performance (specifically dealing with work stress). Johnson (2001) proposes that an ability to deal with stress should be included in OCB models.

In their recent quantitative review of OCB models, Hoffman et al. (2007) derived a single OCB dimension from confirmatory factor analyses. The mean meta-analytic intercorrelation among the five OCB dimensions included in the analysis

Table 13.1 Three dimensions of citizenship performance

Dimension	Definition
Personal Support	Helping others by offering suggestions, teaching them useful knowledge or skills, directly performing some of their tasks, and providing emotional support for their personal problems. Cooperating with others by accepting suggestions, informing them of events they should know about, and putting team objectives ahead of personal interests. Showing consideration, courtesy, and tact in relations with others as well as motivating and showing confidence of them.
Organizational Support	Representing the organization favorably by defending and promoting it, as well as expressing satisfaction and showing loyalty by staying with the organization despite temporary hardships. Supporting the organization's mission and objectives, complying with organizational rules and procedures, and suggesting initiatives.
Conscientious Initiative	Persisting with extra effort despite difficult conditions. Taking the initiative to do all that is necessary to accomplish objectives even if not normally a part of own duties and finding additional productive work to perform when own duties are completed. Developing own knowledge and skills by taking advantage of opportunities within the organization and outside the own organization using own time and resources.

Source: Coleman and Borman (2000).

was 0.52 (range $r = 0.36$–0.66). Differentiating dimensions of OCB may therefore be of practical rather than empirical benefit. Separating OCB into more specific dimensions would give greater depth of detail to applied performance assessments. However, these dimensions are probably best conceptualized as facets of an overall OCB factor, which may be more useful in validation and other research studies.

The assessment of OCB typically utilizes supervisor reports as an assessment methodology. Numerous scales are available for supervisors to use to assess aspects of OCB (e.g., Williams and Anderson 1991). Two important properties of OCB scales are that they are behavioral and frequency based (Hanson and Borman 2006). Supervisors are not asked to make global judgments about the outcomes of work activities, rather they are asked to rate the frequency with which employees engage in particular behaviors.

3.4.2 *Relationship of OCB, task performance, and overall performance*

Theories of OCB propose that performance is different in task and OCB domains (Motowildo and Van Scotter 1994). There is emerging evidence that the empirical distinction between the two is less substantive than might be expected. Hoffman et al. (2007) examined the relationship of task performance and OCB in their meta-analysis. They reported a multiple correlation of 0.74 between task performance and facets of OCB, concluding that OCB was distinct, but highly similar to task performance. A comparison may be drawn with the conclusions of Viswesvaran, Schmidt, and Ones (2005), regarding a general underlying factor of job perform-ance. The overlap of ratings of task performance and OCB is consistent with the idea that all dimensions of job performance are related to an underlying overall performance factor. However, it would be wrong to conclude that the overlap is the same in different kinds of jobs. Conway (1999) examined the relationships between task performance and OCB dimensions in a meta-analysis using only managerial samples. He reported that the interpersonal facilitation facet of OCB was less important for managers than in previous studies of non-managers. This is because there is a strong overlap of the management task dimension of leadership and the OCB dimension of interpersonal facilitation. The extent to which task performance and OCB may be differentiated therefore depends in part on whether elements of OCB are integrated into an individual's job design and are therefore considered to be a core task of their job.

A related issue is the relative importance of judgments about task performance and OCB on overall ratings of job performance. Werner (1994) examined ratings of secretarial performance made by 116 supervisors. He found that for secretaries rated as average or high on task performance, intercorrelations among perform-ance dimensions were stronger for those rated high on OCB-I. OCB may exert a disproportionate influence on overall performance ratings. Johnson (2001) reported a more balanced contribution of task performance and OCB to overall judgments of job performance. By examining the relative weights of task and OCB dimensions regressed onto overall job performance, he determined that (1) the relative importance of task and OCB dimensions varied across job families; (2) task proficiency dimensions were consistently most strongly weighted in judgments of overall performance, although differences were modest; and (3) among the OCB dimensions, job-task conscientiousness was most important (i.e., most strongly related to overall performance ratings).

3.4.3 *Counter-productive work behaviors*

Theories of OCB tell us numerous ways that employees can engage in behaviors that enhance working practices, environments, and relationships. Conversely, employ-ees can engage in behaviors that are damaging to other individuals, to productivity, and to the organization as a whole. Such behaviors fall under the overarching concept of counter-productive work behaviors (CWB). Viswesvaran and Ones (2000) include CWB as a third broad performance dimension next to task per-formance and OCB. They identify several kinds of common CWB: Property damage (including theft and misuse of resources), substance abuse at work, violence (which may also include workplace bullying), lateness, absenteeism, social loafing, and turnover. Viswesvaran and Ones (2000) point out that all of these behaviors are considered by supervisors when they rate the performance of their employees.

If one thinks for a moment about the kinds of things that a bad organizational citizen would be guilty of, some if not all of the behaviors listed above intuitively spring to mind. The implicit perspective on OCB and CWB is therefore that they are at opposite ends of a single continuum. However, this assumption is misguided. In a meta-analysis addressing the question, Dalal (2005) reported an association of −0.32 between the two performance domains. This moderate negative relationship is too small to conclude that they are polar opposites. A better perspective is to view OCB and CWB as separate but related constructs (Kelloway et al. 2002). It appears that employees can be rated as both good citizens and as engaging in counter-productive behaviors.

4. Practical Measurement Issues

4.1 Reliability

Subjective job performance ratings may be conceptualized in exactly the same way as any other psychometric measure, and the principles of psychological assessment can be applied to them. A fundamental property of any assessment is reliability—the extent to which ratings represent true score variance on the construct being measured. The reliability of a given assessment is typically indicated by scale consistency (internal consistency reliability), the stability of ratings over time (test-retest reliability), and interrater agreement (interrater reliability).

These three methods of assessing reliability present interesting applied inter-pretations when applied to job performance measures. Scale consistency can sometimes be interpreted as poor discrimination of performance dimensions by supervisors. Striving for stability in performance ratings goes against our intuitions that performance can change over time. Interrater reliability raises questions about the frame of reference that people apply when they rate job performance. To what extent does one rater's idea of effective performance generalize to other raters? These issues are important because job performance measurement is central to a substantive volume of work psychology research and HRM practice. For example, reliability estimates are critical in meta-analyses, where they are used to correct validity coefficients. Moreover, reliability is important for the practical use of job performance ratings, for example to determine pay, promotion, and training requirements. None of these activities can be adequately carried out if performance measures are unreliable.

Viswesvaran, Ones, and Schmidt (1996) conducted a meta-analysis of the reli-ability of job performance ratings. They reported modest interrater reliabilities for overall job performance assessments for supervisors (0.52) and for peers (0.42). Interestingly, reliabilities across dimensions varied, with the dimensions Quality, Productivity, and Administrative Competence demonstrating the highest reliability and Communication and Interpersonal Competences the lowest. Borman (1979) and Wohlers and London (1989) suggest that such variations reflect the availability of evidence to raters. The implication is that supervisor and peer ratings of job performance are most reliable when there is available evidence upon which to make a judgment.

Coefficient alpha reliabilities tended to be higher than interrater reliabilities in Viswesvaran, Ones, and Schmidt's (1996) analyses: 0.86 for supervisors (range = 0.73–0.86) and 0.85 for peers (range = 0.61–0.85). One confound in this finding is that halo error inflates coefficient alpha reliability in the same way that social desirability creates response sets in surveys. Viswesvaran, Schmidt, and Ones (2005) estimate the inflation effect on coefficient alpha reliabilities to be around 30 percent for supervisory ratings and 60 percent for peer ratings.

Using a small meta-analytic sample, Viswesvaran, Ones, and Schmidt (1996) also calculated test-retest stability for supervisor ratings of overall job performance ($r = 0.81$). A similar finding was reported by Salgado, Moscoso, and Lado (2003), who also found that specific dimensions of job performance demonstrated lower test-retest reliabilities over all job performance. A more in-depth examination of the stability of performance measures over time was presented by Sturman, Cheramie, and Cashen (2005). They differentiate three concepts that should be considered when examining performance over time. The first is stability, which reflects the extent to which true job performance is the same at two different points in time. The second is temporal consistency, reflecting the extent to which performance assessed using a specific scale or measure is the same at two different points in time. The third is test-retest reliability, which indicates the extent to which a measure provides the same performance score at two different times assuming that actual performance is constant. The concepts of stability and temporal consistency represent performance change over time.

Sturman, Cheramie, and Cashen (2005) reported that subjective measures demonstrated higher reliabilities than objective measures, but noted that this may be a result of consistent error variances due to bias in supervisory ratings. They also found that reliability was lower for high-complexity jobs, most likely as a result of more complex parameters for performance measurement in these jobs. They modeled stability and temporal consistency, estimating substantial decreases in the predictability of performance over longer periods of time (in particular periods greater than one year). The message: regular assessments of performance are required in order to be confident about a measure of an employee's job performance.

The comparative reliability of ratings of job performance from a variety of sources was addressed in a meta-analysis conducted by Conway and Huffcutt

(1997). They hypothesized that the reliability of ratings of job performance would vary as a function of rater source, job type, and rating type, and these hypotheses were largely supported. The reliability of supervisor ratings was highest (meta-analytic $r = 0.50$), followed by peer ratings (meta-analytic $r = 0.37$), with subordinate ratings emerging as least reliable (meta-analytic $r = 0.30$). Both supervisors and peers tended to rate performance in non-managerial jobs more reliably than managerial jobs, and composite ratings (ratings derived statistically from dimension scores) were more reliable than overall performance ratings and single dimension scores.

From their results, Viswesvaran, Ones, and Schmidt (1996) argued that interrater reliability was the most adequate index for job performance as this reflects the basic question about whether two equally knowledgeable judges would rate the same individual's job performance similarly. As such, interrater reliability determines the effectiveness of, for example, applying single performance standards across organizations (where different supervisors rate the performance of different employees), or placing team members in new positions or project teams. As a consequence of using coefficient alpha to estimate reliability (which is typically higher), they conclude that corrections applied to validity coefficients in research may lead to underestimations of those validities.

4.2 Assessment Concerns of Scientists and Practitioners

A number of authors note the gap between research and the application of performance measurement in organizations. Austin and Crespin (2006) separate the field into the sub-areas criterion development and performance appraisal methods. They observe that whilst research has progressed in both areas, progress in practice has been much slower. They suggest that this disconnection may be due to a lack of techniques from research that allow performance assessments to produce simple results, and because practitioners are often put off research papers and journals because of the complexity of methods. It is true that the major theoretical contributions in this field rarely communicate explicitly how to apply findings in assessments of job performance.

Part of making findings clearer to understand involves an appreciation of the perspectives of scientists and practitioners about what makes a good performance criterion. Tannenbaum (2006) summarizes the major differences (see Table 13.2). Tannenbaum highlights that whilst scientists concern themselves with questions about validity, reliability, and theoretical underpinning, practitioners are much more concerned that assessments should be understandable, easy, and cost effective to apply, and viewed as credible by others within their organization. To identify one perspective as superior to the other would be a moot point. Researchers must make the application of research findings clearer to have real impact on practice, and

Table 13.2 Criteria for determining the usefulness of a job performance
measure: scientists vs. practitioners

Scientist	Practitioner
Key Question: Is the Measure	
Generalizable?	Relevant to specific setting?
Valid?	Practical/easy to collect?
Reliable?	Accepted/viewed as credible?
Comprehensive?	Cost effective?
Theoretically meaningful?	Understandable/logical/insightful?
Able to predict/account for variance?	Actionable?

Source: Tannenbaum (2006).

practitioners should challenge themselves to invest time to understand ideas that might initially appear complex—effective human resource management is rarely a simple task.

4.3 Multi-source and 360-degree Performance Assessment

Ratings of job performance are most commonly provided by supervisors, but may be provided by a variety of sources. Multi-source performance ratings are valued by organizations because they appear to be more comprehensive than single sources, providing a more thorough assessment of performance across a range of different contexts. Supervisor ratings of performance may be based on limited evidence of employee competence because they may not observe the ratee in interactions with peers or subordinates. Despite practitioner enthusiasm for multi-source systems such as 360-degree appraisal, researchers have remained sceptical. Fletcher (2001) points out that this scepticism often arises because 360-degree systems are sometimes poorly operationalized, and because the information collected is not always used effectively.

Nevertheless, the past ten years have witnessed some important developments in the understanding of multi-source performance ratings. There have been a number of methodological advances that have allowed a detailed examination of construct validity and other psychometric properties of multi-source ratings (Cheung 1999), the most notable being structural equation modeling (SEM). SEM allows the examination of complex relationships between sets of variables, providing an index of fit between a theoretical model and collected performance data. In multi-source performance measurement research, the technique has been used to disentangle the sources of variance in multi-source ratings.

Studies generally support the measurement equivalence of performance ratings across sources (Maurer, Raju, and Collins 1998; Facteau and Craig 2001). Overall, it appears that measures of the same construct provided by different sources are conceptually similar. So, for example, a supervisory rating of leadership skill is likely to represent the same kinds of behaviors as a corresponding peer rating. Borman, White, and Dorsey (1995) examined the factors that influence overall performance ratings and found that supervisors and peers similarly weighted task and OCB performance, and that both groups tended to weight interpersonal factors and core task performance equally. These conclusions may not apply across all performance dimensions, however (Harris and Schaubroeck 1988; Mabe and West 1982). Viswesvaran, Schmidt, and Ones (2002) examined convergence of supervisor and peer ratings on ten performance dimensions. They found that at the construct level (i.e., examining correlations corrected for unreliability), supervisor and peer ratings converged for some dimensions but not others. Supervisors and peers may therefore conceptualize some elements of performance differently. However, Viswesvaran, Schmidt, and Ones (2002) concluded that weak convergence between supervisor and peer ratings of performance is more strongly attributable to rating difficulty—dimensions that are harder to rate (perhaps because of lower availability of observable behavioral evidence) tend to converge less strongly.

In multi-source assessment systems, individuals may also rate their own job performance. Self–other convergence of performance ratings tend to be lower than other–other convergence (Conway and Huffcutt 1997). This may be due to personality influences that inflate or suppress self-ratings of performance (e.g., Goffin and Anderson 2007). Conway and Huffcutt (1997) point out that lower convergence might not necessarily mean that self-ratings are invalid. Indeed, self-assessments of performance might be both valid and unique, but future research is needed to better establish their utility.

One of the most interesting developments in the understanding of multi-source performance ratings is the examination of the effects of unique relationships on rating variance. The premise of these studies is straightforward. When one person judges or perceives the performance of another, their perception is based on two sources of information. The first is actual or "true" performance. This may be thought of as the individual's consistent standard of performance across times and situations. The second is the performance observed or perceived by the specific rater, but no one else. This performance is therefore based on the unique working relationship between the rater and the ratee. Each rating of performance is also affected by measurement error.

Studies of theses effects find that whist multi-source ratings appear to be consistent, substantial variance in ratings may be attributed to the rater–ratee relationship effect. Woehr, Sheehan, and Bennett (2005) found that roughly equal proportions of variance could be attributed to actual differences in the performance dimension being rated and the source of the rating. A person's peer rating is therefore influenced roughly equally by their actual job performance and the fact that it is their peer providing the rating. A more recent study took this further, suggesting that variance attributable to rater source actually outweighed true score variance (Van Hooft, Van der Flier, and Minne 2006). Viswesvaran, Ones, and Schmidt (1996) also considered rater source in their examination of reliability and found that between 20 and 30 percent of rating variance is specific to the rater, rather than the ratee. Overall, these results indicate that a substantial amount of the variance in job performance measurements reflects idiosyncratic perceptions of job performance of the rater.

Although a greater understanding of the psychometric properties of multi-source ratings is emerging, evidence of their impact in appraisal systems and performance management practice is still marginal at best. The application of multi-source systems usually involves multi-source performance feedback to communicate the perceptions of performance from the various raters. Smither, London, and Reilly (2005) found that only small improvements in performance were observed as a result of feedback processes. They speculate that practitioners should not anticipate widespread improvements in performance and specify a number of conditions that facilitate improvement. From a performance management perspective, however, the utility of multi-source feedback is questionable without evidence that it actually improves performance over time.

4.4 Fairness of Job Performance Measures

Job performance measures are critical to a range of personnel decisions such as promotion, tenure, and performance-related pay. Any systematic differences or biases in job performance ratings across demographic groups may therefore result in differential opportunities for career development and access to pay. These are important issues for organizations because they can leave organizations open to potential litigation, and interfere with efforts to increase representation from different demographic groups within the organization (Roth, Huffcutt, and Bobko 2003). Investigations of the fairness of job performance measures typically involve an examination of the differences in mean performance scores for different groups.

Ethnic group differences in performance measures are widely investigated in meta-analyses, which have been periodically updated over the past twenty years as researchers learn more about job performance criteria. Ford, Kraiger, and Schechtman (1986) conducted one of the earliest, comparing white–black differences on objective and subjective performance criteria. They found that black ratees typically scored 0.21 and 0.20 standard deviations (SD) lower than white ratees on objective and subjective performance measures respectively. More recent meta-analyses have introduced a number of moderators into the analyses, and have examined additional ethnic groups. Roth, Huffcutt, and Bobko (2003) reported an overall difference in favor of the white group of 0.35 SD, and 0.40 SD if military samples are excluded. Values in this range were observed regardless of job complexity. Differences between overall ratings of Hispanics and whites were much smaller (0.04 SD), although larger differences were observed on work sample measures and assessments of job knowledge. At time of writing, the most recent meta-analysis is McKay and McDaniel (2006). They report that across all job performance ratings, blacks scored 0.27 SD lower than whites, but that when job performance criteria were operationalized as specifically task performance or OCB, differences were smaller (0.21 SD and 0.13 SD respectively).

Gender differences in job performance are less widely studied. Bowen, Swim, and Jacobs (2000) reported no difference in appraisal ratings for men and women, even within gender stereotypical roles. There were rating biases, however, with men tending to receive higher scores than women from all-male rater groups. This similar-to-me effect is often observed in performance ratings. Varma and Stroh (2001) reported that male and female supervisors tended to rate subordinates of the same sex more highly than subordinates of the opposite sex. Kraiger and Ford (1985) reported a similar effect across ethnic groups with whites receiving higher scores than blacks from white raters, but lower scores from black raters. Biases are not restricted to gender and ethnicity. Miller and Werner (2005) conducted an experiment where a non-disabled confederate performed the same work activity at the same rate, playing roles of having no disability, a physical disability, and a mental disability to three independent samples. The confederate received higher performance ratings in the physical- and mental-disability conditions despite there being no objective difference in their performance. Finally, Waldman and Avolio (1986) report that subjective ratings of performance tend to be lower for older workers than younger workers, even though objective measures tend to increase marginally with age.

The vast majority of studies in this area are from the US and address US-centric questions. For example, in the UK, we have no data on performance measure differences between white employees and employees from black and Asian communities. Moreover, within the European Union, there are no studies comparing the job performance of employees from local and migrant populations, despite this issue receiving considerable political interest. This is critical, because well-conducted research has the potential to make an impact on legislation in this area. Despite all our knowledge about group differences in performance measures and appraisal, court decisions about job appraisals almost exclusively rely on issues of due process and fairness in decision making (i.e., agreement between raters), with issues of accuracy and validity appearing to have no effect on court decisions (Werner and Bolino 1997).

4.5 Team Performance

Human resource practitioners and managers are frequently required to measure the performance of groups or teams to facilitate performance management activities beyond an individual level. Measuring the performance of teams gives rise to an additional set of measurement challenges, which are largely based on the nature of teams and the way that they operate. These issues are important to address as teams become ever more popular as an organizational strategy and diverse in composition and function. Within the scope of this chapter, there are several principles that differentiate measurements of individuals and measurements of teams (Salas, Burke, and Fowlkes 2006; Kendall and Salas 2004). Performance dimensions for teams are different to those for individuals, and performance measurement should be structured around relevant dimensions. For example, Cannon-Bowers et al. (1995) classify performance criteria for individual team members based on their applicability to specific teams or tasks.

Performance dimensions should also reflect team outcomes and processes. Outcomes are critical in team performance assessment because teams are usually set up with a specific purpose or role to fulfil. The objective performance of the team reflects the extent to which the goals are achieved. Process is also important, however, because teams rely on effective relationships and interactions between team members. Teams achieving required outcomes at the expense of future effective working relationships are unlikely to maintain performance over time. Process assessment typically requires observation of team member interaction (Salas, Burke, and Fowlkes 2006). Finally, team performance measurement should reflect various levels of analysis within the team. A common team design is the allocation of individuals to small teams nested within larger work groups. Team performance measurement should address all of these levels: individuals, small sub-teams, and larger work groups. The complexity of team performance measurement is heightened by the emergence of new forms of teams, such as distributed teams (where members may be working in different geographical locations, connected through information and communications technology) and culturally diverse teams (Salas, Burke, and Fowlkes 2006).

5. The Elusive Relationship between Job Performance and Job Satisfaction

The relationship between job performance and job satisfaction has preoccupied managers and work psychologists for more than seventy years, since the publication of the Hawthorne Studies in the 1930s. Ruch, Hershauer, and Wright (1976) describe the issue as the productivity puzzle, describing the "paradoxical notion that although some happy workers are productive, there are also many happy workers who are unproductive" (p. 5). However, when one thinks in more depth about the simple idea that happy employees are productive employees, the lack of a consistent relationship is less surprising. The link between human affective states and behavioral outcomes is rarely straightforward, and this is true of the relationship between job performance on the one hand and job attitudes such as job satisfaction and commitment on the other. However, the plethora of studies of the issue have given rise to several meta-analyses since 2001 that begin to build our understanding of the relationship. Importantly, measures and models of job performance are influential in the results of these studies.

The first step in understanding the relationship is to understand the various forms it may take. Judge et al. (2001) review seven different potential models. The first is that job satisfaction causes job performance. This model represents the typical implicit perspective on satisfaction and performance. The second is that job performance causes job satisfaction. Attaining high levels of performance at work is likely to result in extrinsic and intrinsic rewards, thereby fostering positive job attitudes. Third, satisfaction and performance cause each other. A combination of effects from the first and second models give rise to a reciprocal relationship. Fourth, it is possible that there is no direct link between satisfaction and performance, with any observed correlation reflecting overlap with an unmeasured variable. Fifth, there may be no relationship between satisfaction and performance at all.

The remaining two models outlined by Judge et al. (2001) are more complex. One proposes that the relationship between performance and satisfaction may be moderated by another variable. If an individual is satisfied in their job, but lacks some of the skills required to perform it, he or she is unlikely to be productive. Job knowledge, skills, abilities, and characteristics may moderate the relationship between satisfaction and commitment. Finally, both satisfaction and performance could be reconceptualized to provide a better understanding of the relationship. For example, job attitudes such as satisfaction and commitment might actually reflect affectivity (the predisposition for either positive or negative emotional states). A theme throughout this chapter is that job performance is multidimensional, so perhaps satisfaction relates to some dimensions but not others.

Meta-analyses have offered tests of some, but not all of these models. Judge et al. (2001) tested the relationship between job satisfaction and job performance and tested a number of moderator variables. Based on 312 studies, assessing more than 54,000 participants, they found a moderate overall relationship between job satisfaction and job performance (rho = 0.30). It seems that satisfied workers do tend to be higher-performing workers. When studies in the meta-analysis were separated, there were some notable differences. Satisfaction tended to be more strongly associated with peer and subordinate ratings (rho = 0.36) than with supervisor ratings (rho = 0.30) and objective ratings (rho = 0.26). Global measures of job performance were more strongly associated with satisfaction than composite measures (rho = 0.35 and 0.28 respectively). Longitudinal studies (where satisfaction was measured at time one and performance at time two) reported weaker associations than cross-sectional studies (rho = 0.23 and 0.31 respectively). The strongest association was observed for high-complexity jobs (rho = 0.52).

Job commitment was similarly examined by Riketta (2002). The meta-analyses of 111 studies ($N = 26{,}344$) revealed a weaker relationship with performance than was observed for satisfaction (rho = 0.20). Riketta also controlled for a number of moderators. The relationship was stronger for supervisor ratings of performance than for objective ratings (rho = 0.19 and 0.12 respectively) and was stronger for OCB (extra-role) performance than task (in-role) performance (rho = 0.25 and 0.18 respectively). Meyer et al. (2002) also reported stronger associations of commitment with OCB than with task performance.

The convergence of job satisfaction and commitment has led some investigators to combine the constructs to give an overall job attitudes variable. Harrison, Newman, and Roth (2006) examined the association of these combined job attitudes with task performance, OCB, lateness, absenteeism, and turnover. When performance outcomes were treated as separate measures, absolute meta-analytic associations ranged from 0.27 to 0.42, with the strongest coefficient exhibited for OCB. However, recall that in a hierarchical model of performance, it is possible to conceptualize a single overall performance dimension. When all five individual performance variables were combined in a single factor, the association with job attitudes increased to 0.59, almost double the size of the correlation reported by Judge et al. (2001).

A further contribution of the Harrison, Newman, and Roth (2006) meta-analysis was a more thorough examination of the longitudinal effects of attitudes and performance. Similar correlations were reported between satisfaction and task performance regardless of when they were assessed. Support was therefore found for models in which satisfaction predicts performance and in which performance predicts satisfaction. By contrast, commitment tended to be more strongly associated with future measures of performance than past measures. For satisfaction, no meaningful difference in association was observed for task and OCB criteria, although commitment was more strongly associated with OCB than with task performance. Riketta (2007) highlights a shortcoming of many longitudinal meta-analyses which is that baseline measures of attitudes are not controlled. By restricting the inclusion of studies in meta-analyses to those that control for baseline measures, Riketta found only small associations with job performance (rho = 0.06 across all attitudinal and performance measures).

6. A Case for the Importance of Job Performance Measures and Models

Despite the advances in understanding of the relationship between job attitudes and job performance, there is still no real consensus among researchers in this area, and Judge et al. (2001) identify a range of potentially important, and mostly untested, moderators and mediators. For example, one obvious issue already highlighted in this chapter is the limited potential for individual attitudes and attributes to influence objective productivity criteria. An alternative approach is to examine job attitudes in the context of job performance models and well-established individual difference antecedents of job performance dimensions.

In psychology, the most extensively studied individual differences are the orthogonal (independent) domains of intelligence or cognitive ability and personality traits. Among these individual differences, the most consistent predictors of performance are general cognitive ability and personality traits related to conscientiousness and emotional stability (e.g., Schmidt and Hunter 1998; Salgado 1997; Barrick and Mount 1991; Barrick, Mount, and Judge 2001). Advances in performance measurement and modeling have allowed these relationships to be investigated in more depth.

For example, when ability and personality predictors are examined in relation to specific dimensions of job performance, a clear differential pattern of prediction is observed, with cognitive abilities tending to predict task performance and personality traits tending to predict OCB (Motowildo, Borman, and Schmit 1997). Critically, the same personality dimensions that predict OCB also tend to predict job satisfaction (Judge, Heller, and Mount 2002; Heller, Watson, and Ilies 2004), and to be related to positive and negative affectivity more broadly (the tendency to hold characteristically positive and negative attitudes). Perhaps satisfied workers tend to be better performers because their traits also tend to lead them to be better organizational citizens.

When one considers the complexity of these relationships, it is clear that a complete understanding of the relationship between job attitudes and job performance is dependent, first, on understanding the cognitive, dispositional, and affective antecedents that influence both attitudes and performance and, second, on understanding the structure of job performance represented in diverse measures and assessment techniques. The elusive relationship between job satisfaction and job performance provides one further reason why knowledge of job performance criteria and measurement is so critical to effective work psychology research and practice.

REFERENCES

AUSTIN, J. T., and CRESPIN, T. R. 2006. Problems of criteria in industrial and organizational psychology: progress, problems, and prospects. Pp. 9–48 in *Performance Measurement: Current Perspectives and Future Challenges*, ed. W. Bennet, Jr., C. E. Lance, and D. J. Woehr. Mahwah, NJ: LEA.

—— and VILLANOVA, P. 1992. The criterion problem: 1917–1992. *Journal of Applied Psychology*, 77: 836–74.

BARRICK, M. R., and MOUNT, M. K. 1991. The Big Five personality dimensions and job performance: a meta-analysis. *Personnel Psychology*, 44: 1–26.

—— —— and JUDGE, T. A. 2001. Personality and performance at the beginning of new millenium: what do we know and where do we go next? *International Journal of Selection and Assessment*, 9: 9–30.

BOMMER, W. H., JOHNSON, J. L., RICH, G. A., PODSAKOFF, P. M., and McKENZIE, S. B. 1995. On the interchangeability of objective and subjective measures of employee performance: a meta-analysis. *Personnel Psychology*, 48 (3): 587–605.

BORMAN, W. C. 1979. Format and training effects on rating accuracy and rater errors. *Journal of Applied Psychology*, 64: 410–21.

—— and BRUSH, D. H. 1993. More progress toward a taxonomy of managerial performance requirements. *Human Performance*, 6: 1–21.

—— and MOTOWIDLO, S. J. 1993. Expanding the criterion domain to include elements of contextual performance. In *Personnel Selection in Organisations*, ed. N. Schmitt, W. C. Borman, et al. San Francisco: Jossey-Bass.

—— —— 1997. Task performance and contextual performance: the meaning for personnel selection research. *Human Performance*, 10 (2): 99–109.

—— WHITE, L. A., and DORSEY, D. W. 1995. Effects of ratee task performance and interpersonal factors on supervisor and peer performance ratings. *Journal of Applied Psychology*, 80: 167–77.

BOWEN, C. C., SWIM, J. K., and JACOBS, R. R. 2000. Evaluating gender biases on actual job performance of real people: a meta-analysis. *Journal of Applied Social Psychology*, 30 (10): 2194–215.

CAMPBELL, C. H., FORD, P., RUMSEY, M. G., PULAKOS, E. D., BORMAN, W. C., FELKER, D. B., DeVERA, M. V., and RIEGELHAUPT, B. J. 1990. Development of multiple job performance measures in a representative sample of jobs. *Personnel Psychology*, 43: 277–300.

CAMPBELL, J. P. 1990. Modeling the performance prediction problem in industrial and organizational psychology. Pp. 687–731 in *Handbook of Industrial and Organizational Psychology*, 2nd edn., vol. i, ed. M. D. Dunnette and L. M. Hough. Palo Alto, CA: Consulting Psychologists Press.

—— McHENRY, J., and WISE, L. L. 1990. Modeling job performance in a population of jobs. *Personnel Psychology*, 43: 313–33.

—— McCLOY, R. A., OPPLER, S. H., and SAGER, C. E. 1993. A theory of performance. Pp. 35–70 in *Personnel Selection in Organizations*, ed. N. Schmitt and W. Borman. San Francisco: Jossey Bass.

CANNON-BOWERS, J. A., TANNENBAUM, E. S., VOLPE, C. E. 1995. Understanding the dynamics of diversity in decision-making teams. In *Team Effectiveness and Decision Making in Organizations*, ed. R. A. Guzzo and E. Salas San-Francisco: Jossey-Bass.

CHEUNG, G. W. 1999. Multifaceted conceptions of self–other ratings disagreement. *Personnel Psychology*, 52: 1–36.

COLEMAN, V. I., and BORMAN, W. C. 2000. Investigating the underlying structure of the citizenship performance domain. *Human Resource Management Review*, 10: 25–44.

CONWAY, J. M. 1999. Distinguishing contextual performance from task performance for managerial jobs. *Journal of Applied Psychology*, 84: 3–13.

—— and HUFFCUTT, A. I. 1997. Psychometric properties of multi-source performance ratings: a meta-analysis of subordinate, supervisor, peer, and self-ratings. *Human Performance*, 10: 331–60.

DALAL, R. S. 2005. A meta-analysis of the relationship between organizational citizenship behavior and counterproductive work behavior. *Journal of Applied Psychology*, 90: 1241–55.

FACTEAU, J. D., and CRAIG, S. B. 2001. Are performance appraisal ratings from different rating sources comparable? *Journal of Applied Psychology*, 86: 215–27.

FLETCHER, C. 2001. Performance appraisal and management: the developing research agenda. *Journal of Occupational and Organizational Psychology*, 74 (4): 473–87.

FORD, J. K., KRAIGER, K., and SCHECHTMAN, S. 1986. The study of race effects in objective indices and subjective evaluations of performance: a meta-analysis of performance criteria. *Psychological Bulletin*, 99: 330–7.

GOFFIN, R. D., and ANDERSON, D. W. 2007. The self-rates's personality and self-other disagreement in multi-source performance ratings. *Journal of Managerial Psychology*, 22: 271–89.

HANSON, M. A., and BORMAN, W. C. 2006. Citizenship performance: an integrative review and motivational analysis. Pp. 141–74 in *Performance Measurement: Current Perspectives and Future Challenges*, ed. W. Bennet, Jr., C. E. Lance, and D. J. Woehs. Mahwah, NJ: LEA.

HARRIS, M. M., and SCHAUBROECK, J. 1988. A meta-analysis of self vs. supervisor, self vs. peer, and peer vs. supervisor ratings. *Personnel Psychology*, 41: 43–62.

HARRISON, D. A., NEWMAN, D. A., and ROTH, P. L. 2006. How important are job attitudes? Meta-analytic comparisons of integrative behavioral outcomes and time sequences. *Academy of Management Journal*, 49: 305–25.

HELLER, D., WATSON, D., and ILIES, R. 2004. The role of person versus situation in life satisfaction: a critical examination. *Psychological Bulletin*, 130: 574–600.

HOFFMAN, B. J., BLAIR, C. A., MERIAC, J. P., and WOEHR, D. J. 2007. Expanding the criterion domain? A quantitative review of the OCB literature. *Journal of Applied Psychology*, 92: 555–66.

JACKSON, C. J., and FURNHAM, A. 2001. Appraisal ratings, halo and selection: a study using sales staff. *European Journal of Psychological Assessment*, 17: 17–24.

JOHNSON, J. W. 2001. The relative importance of task and contextual performance dimensions to supervisor judgments of overall performance. *Journal of Applied Psychology*, 86: 984–96.

JUDGE, T. A., HELLER, D., and MOUNT, M. K. 2002. Five-factor model of personality and job satisfaction. *Journal of Applied Psychology*, 87: 530–41.

—— THORESEN, C. J., BONO, J. E., and PATTON, G. K. 2001. The job satisfaction–job performance relationship: a qualitative and quantitative review. *Psychological Bulletin*, 127: 376–407.

KELLOWAY, K., LOUGHLIN, C., BARLING, J., and NAULT, A. 2002. Counterproductive and organizational citizenship behaviors: separate but related constructs. *International Journal of Selection and Assessment*, 10 (1–2): 143–51.

KENDALL, D., and SALAS, E. 2004. Measuring team performance: review of current methods and consideration of future needs. The Science of Simulation and Human Performance. *Advances in Human Performance and Cognitive Engineering Research*, 5: 307–26.

KNAPP, D. J. 2006. The U.S. joint service job performance measurement project. Pp. 113–40 in *Performance Measurement: Current Perspectives and Future Challenges*, ed. W. Bennet, Jr., C. E. Lance, and D. J. Woehr. Mahwah, NJ: LEA.

KRAIGER, K., and FORD, J. 1985. A meta-analysis of ratee race effects in performance ratings. *Journal of Applied Psychology*, 70: 821–3.

MABE, P. A., and WEST, S. G. 1982. Validity of self-evaluation of ability: a review and meta-analysis. *Journal of Applied Psychology*, 67: 280–96.

McKay, P., and McDaniel, M. A. 2006. A re-examination of black–white mean differences in work performance: more data, more moderators. *Journal of Applied Psychology*, 91: 531–54.

Maurer, T. J., Raju, N. S., and Collins, W. C. 1998. Peer and subordinate performance appraisal measurement equivalence. *Journal of Applied Psychology*, 83: 693–702.

Meyer, J. P., Stanley, D. J., Herscovitch, L., and Topolnytsky, L. 2002. Affective, continuance, and normative commitment to the organization: a meta-analysis of antecedents, correlates and consequences. *Journal of Vocational Behavior*, 61 (1): 20–52.

Miles, D. E., Borman, W. E., Spector, P. E., and Fox, S. 2002. Building an integrative model of extra role work behaviors: a comparison of counterproductive work behavior with organizational citizenship behavior. *International Journal of Selection and Assessment*, 10: 51–7.

Miller, B. K., and Werner, S. 2005. Factors influencing the inflation of task performance ratings for workers with disabilities and contextual performance ratings for their co-workers. *Human Performance*, 18 (3): 309–29.

Motowidlo, S. J., Borman, W. C., and Schmit, M. J. 1997. A theory of individual differences in task and contextual performance. *Human Performance*, 10 (2): 71–83.

—— and Van Scotter, J. R. 1994. Evidence that task performance should be distinguished from the contextual performance. *Journal of Applied Psychology*, 79: 475–80.

Organ, D. W. 1988. *Organizational Citizenship Behavior: The Good Soldier Syndrome*. Lexington, MA: Heath.

—— 1997. Organizational citizenship behavior: it's construct clean-up time. *Human Performance*, 10 (2): 85–97.

Podsakoff, P. M., MacKenzie, S. B., Paine, J. B., and Bachrach, D. G. 2000. Organizational citizenship behaviors: a critical review of the theoretical and empirical literature and suggestions for future research. *Journal of Management*, 26: 513–63.

Riketta, M. 2002. Attitudinal organizational commitment and job performance: a meta-analysis. *Journal of Organizational Behavior*, 23: 257–66.

—— 2007. The causal relation between job attitudes and performance: a meta-analysis of panel studies. Unpublished Manuscript.

Roth, P. L., Huffcutt, A. I., and Bobko, P. 2003. Ethnic group differences in measures of job performance: a new meta-analysis. *Journal of Applied Psychology*, 88: 694–706.

Ruch, W. A., Hershauer, J. C., and Wright, R. G. 1976. Toward solving the productivity puzzle: worker correlates to performance. *Human Resource Management*, 15: 2–6.

Salas, E., Burke, C. S., and Fowlkes, J. E. 2006. Measuring team performance "in the wild": challenges and tips. Pp. 245–72 in *Performance Measurement: Current Perspectives and Future Challenges*, ed. W. Bennet, Jr., C. E. Lance, and D. J. Wochr. Mahwah, NJ: LEA.

Salgado, J. F. 1997. The five factor model of personality and job performance in the European Community. *Journal of Applied Psychology*, 82: 30–43.

—— Moscoso, S., and Lado, M. 2003. Test-retest reliability of ratings of job performance in managers. *International Journal of Selection and Assessment*, 11: 98–101.

Schmidt, F., and Hunter, J. E. 1998. The validity and utility of selection methods in personnel psychology: practical and theoretical implications of 85 years of research findings. *Psychological Bulletin*, 124: 262–74.

Smith, C. A., Organ, D. W., and Near, J. P. 1983. Organisational citizenship behavior: its nature and antecedents. *Journal of Applied Psychology*, 68: 653–63.

SMITHER, J., LONDON, M., and REILLY, R. 2005. Does performance improve following multisource feedback? A theoretical model, meta-analysis, and review of empirical findings. *Personnel Psychology*, 58: 33–66.

STURMAN, M. C., CHERAMIE, R. A., and CASHEN, L. H. 2005. The consistency, stability, and test-retest reliability of employee job performance: a meta-analytic review of longitudinal findings. *Journal of Applied Psychology*, 90: 269–83.

TANNENBAUM, S. I. 2006. Applied measurement: practical issues and challenges. Pp. 297–320 in *Performance Measurement: Current Perspectives and Future Challenges*, ed. W. Bennet, Jr., C. E. Lance, and D. J. Woehr. Mahwah, NJ: LEA.

THAYER, P. W. 1992. Construct validation: do we understand our criteria? *Human Performance*, 5: 97–108.

VAN HOOFT, E. A., VAN DER FLIER, H., and MINNE, M. R. 2006. Construct validity of multi-source performance ratings: an examination of the relationship of self-, supervisor-, and peer-ratings with cognitive and personality measures. *International Journal of Selection and Assessment*, 14: 67–81.

VARMA, A., and STROH, L. K. 2001. The impact of same-sex LMX dyads on performance evaluations. *Human Resources Management*, 40 (4): 309–20.

VISWESVARAN, C. 1993. Modeling job performance: is there a general factor? Unpublished doctoral dissertation, University of Iowa, Iowa City.

—— and ONES, D. S. 2000. Perspectives on models of job performance. *International Journal of Selection and Assessment*, 8: 216–26.

—— —— and SCHMIDT, F. L. 1996. Comparative analysis of the reliability of job performance ratings. *Journal of Applied Psychology*, 81: 557–60.

—— SCHMIDT, F. L., and ONES, D. S. 2002. The moderating influence of job performance dimensions on convergence of supervisory and peer ratings of job performance: unconfounding construct-level convergence and rating difficulty. *Journal of Applied Psychology*, 87: 345–54.

—— —— —— 2005. Is there a general factor in ratings of job performance? A meta-analytic framework for disentangling substantive and error influences. *Journal of Applied Psychology*, 90: 108–31.

WALDMAN, D. A., and AVOLIO, B. J. 1986. Meta-analysis of age differences in job performance. *Journal of Applied Psychology*, 71: 33–8.

WERNER, J. M. 1994. Dimensions that make a difference: examining the impact of in-role and extrarole behaviors on supervisory ratings. *Journal of Applied Psychology*, 79: 98–107.

—— and Bolino, M. C. 1997. Explaining U.S. Court of Appeals decisions involving performance appraisal: accuracy, fairness, and validation. *Personnel Psychology*, 50: 1–24.

WILLIAMS, L. J., and ANDERSON, S. E. 1991. Job satisfaction and organizational commitment as predictors of organizational citizenship and in-role behaviors. *Journal of Management*, 17: 418–28.

WOEHR, D. J., SHEEHAN, M. K., and BENNETT, W. 2005. Assessing measurement equivalence across rating sources: a multitrait-multirater approach. *Journal of Applied Psychology*, 90 (3): 592–600.

WOHLERS, A. J., and LONDON, M. 1989. Ratings of managerial characteristics: evaluation difficulty, coworker agreement, and self-awareness. *Personnel Psychology*, 42: 235–61.

PART IV

TRAINING AND DEVELOPMENT

14

CROSS-CULTURAL DIFFERENCES IN PERSONNEL PSYCHOLOGY

PETER B. SMITH

1. INTRODUCTION

In recent decades, substantial advances have been made in the creation of systematic procedures for the conduct of policies relevant to an organization's human resources. At the same time, organizations have experienced a massive increase in their exposure to the processes of globalization. At the individual level, this has occurred through both immigration and emigration. At the organizational level, it has been driven by the globalization of markets, with the consequent pressure on companies to survive by locating production facilities in low-cost locations and by achieving sales in all relevant markets.

These developments present challenges to the validity of personnel practices that have been honed in monocultural settings. Put rather too crudely, companies must either modify their practices to accommodate the increasing diversity of their workforces, or they must find ways to create sufficiently uniform organizational cultures to permit the retention of the procedures developed earlier. An early indication of the difficulties inherent in the second of these options was provided by Hofstede's (1980; 2001) survey of IBM employees. While IBM had a strong reputation as a company that put substantial resources into the creation and maintenance of a supportive and coherent global organizational culture, this study revealed substantial local variation in employees' work motivations and responses to leadership in the company at that time.

Hofstede's project has a continuing importance to the field, because it provided the first conceptual framework that could be used to summarize cultural variations in issues of relevance to personnel psychology. This chapter first discusses the extent to which that framework requires updating, then considers some of the major ways in which cultural variations may affect organizational behavior, and finally considers some implications for practice.

2. THINKING ABOUT CULTURE

The concept of culture has proved singularly helpful in clarifying organizational processes, whether one is thinking in terms of team culture, organization culture, functional cultures, or national cultures. A key aspect of Hofstede's pioneering study was his emphasis on distinguishing between levels of analysis when thinking about culture. At each level of analysis one can discern what is shared between the relevant parties in interpreting what goes on around them. His principal focus was upon identifying the nation-level dimensions that could be used to classify differences in the ways in which IBM employees had responded to the company's survey. Later he demonstrated empirical support for his argument that the same data when aggregated to different levels of analysis will yield different sets of dimensions, each of which has value at the level to which it refers (Hofstede, Bond, and Luk 1993).

Among the five dimensions of national culture identified by Hofstede, individualism–collectivism and power distance have attracted greatest interest. Until recently personnel psychology was a practice undertaken largely within the dozen nations out of the many in the world that Hofstede found to have scored highest on individualism and lowest on power distance. The authors of all chapters in this handbook are based at locations in this same range of nations.

Hofstede's study has been discussed extensively over the years. Some commentators see no value in thinking in terms of dimensions (MacSweeney 2002), while others favour added or redefined dimensions. All agree that we require more recent surveys to determine the current utility of dimensions. Recent surveys find that despite cultural change in all parts of the world (Inglehart and Oyserman 2004), nation-level differences persist that do parallel the earlier line-up in terms of dimensions comparable to individualism–collectivism and power distance

(House et al. 2004; Smith et al. 2002). In addition to differing in terms of prevailing values, there is evidence that nations can be classified in terms of prevailing beliefs (Bond et al. 2004). Some of the dimensions of prevalent beliefs that have been identified have direct relevance to personnel psychology. For instance, consistent differences are found in beliefs as to whether hard work and effort will be rewarded. Thinking less in terms of aggregated beliefs and values and more in terms of organizational processes, it is clear that differences persist in how business is conducted by companies headquartered in different nations. For instance, despite fifty years of globalization, the business systems that function in Western European nations such as Germany, France, and the UK remain distinctively different from one another (Whitley 1999; Redding 2005).

Debate continues as to the optimal way to describe differences in national culture (Hofstede 2006; Javidan et al. 2006). For instance the GLOBE project researchers (House et al. 2004) asked respondents to describe which values they perceived to be endorsed in their society, while Hofstede's analysis was based primarily on respondents' descriptions of their own values. Both approaches may prove useful (Smith 2006). However, much of personnel psychology is concerned with the behavior of individuals rather than whole nations, and Hofstede's nation-level concepts have rather often been misapplied to the study of individuals, without any measurement of those specific individuals that are being studied, or else with measures that derive from Hofstede's concepts but have not been adequately validated for individual-level analyses (Kirkman, Lowe and Gibson 2006). The work of Schwartz (1999; 2004) does provide a clear distinction between differences in the structure of values that characterize nations and those that characterize individuals. Individual-level measures of values (Schwartz et al. 2001) and beliefs (Leung and Bond 2004) provide the best currently available instruments for investigating the relevance of cultural variations to personnel matters. This chapter now draws on both nation-level and individual-level concepts in detailing a cultural perspective on seven key issues relevant to personnel psychology.

3. KEY ISSUES

3.1 What is a Job?

It is accepted good practice that when hiring an employee a job description shall be provided which specifies the duties that the employee is expected to perform. Thus the act of hiring creates a contract between the individual and the organization, which not only includes certain explicit duties but also implicitly excludes other duties. This way of conceptualizing employment makes perfect sense in the context of individualistic cultures and reflects the preference for explicit forms of communication that prevails within them (Hall 1966). However in collectivistic cultures the nature of the preferred bond between individual and organization is rather different and more implicit. A typical member of a collectivistic culture will derive his or her identity from a long-standing commitment to one or more salient groupings, such as family, social caste, or employing organization. Thus, in Japan a graduate trainee will typically not be hired for a specific work role, but as an employee who will be asked to work in a variety of roles in order to become fully cognizant with all aspects of the organization's business. The act of hiring is a commitment to the organization, not to the job.

3.1.1 *The psychological contract*

Researchers in Western nations have devised concepts that acknowledge that even in Western organizations the nature of the contract between employee and organization is not wholly bounded by explicit job descriptions. For instance, there is typically an only partially stated "psychological" contract, which specifies how the employee and the organization expect to relate toward one another (Rousseau 1990). Rousseau and Schalk (2000) reported an interview study of local understandings of the psychological contract in thirteen different nations. Psychological contracts in the more collectivistic nations included in their sample (e.g., Hong Kong, India, Singapore, Japan, and Mexico) were found to be less tangible and less formal but broader in scope, more stable, and more concerned with obligation to one's seniors. Scope refers to the degree to which a boundary is drawn between work life and family life. In a more recent questionnaire survey of employers and employees in six European nations, contracts were found to be broader in Spain and the UK than in Belgium and the Netherlands (Psycones 2005). Perhaps the best way to test the limits of the psychological contract is to ask employees when it has been breached. Kickul, Lester, and Belgio (2004) found that US managers reacted most negatively to breaches of intrinsic aspects of the contract (such as freedom to be creative and receiving honest communication) whereas Hong Kong managers reacted most negatively to breaches of extrinsic aspects (such as training opportunities and healthcare benefits). These findings evidently relate to cultural differences in work motivation, which is discussed in a later section.

3.1.2 *Organizational citizenship*

Western theorists have also sought to look beyond the limitations of formal job contracts by formulating the concept of organizational citizenship, also known as extra-role behavior (Organ, Podsakoff, and MacKenzie 2006). Clearly, it becomes more difficult to define what is or is not extra-role behavior in contexts where job descriptions are less explicit or absent. Different measures will be required in different locations. Farh, Zhong, and Organ (2004) developed a new measure of organizational citizenship in China. Some overlap was found with citizenship as defined in US studies, but there were also specific behaviors that were considered to be an aspect of good citizenship in each nation that were not identified in the other. This study provides an excellent illustration of the need to establish local validity of research measures in new cultural locations, rather than placing reliance on simple translations of measures devised in North America or Western Europe. Farh, Hackett, and Chen (2008) have conducted a detailed review of cross-cultural studies of organization citizenship. They conclude that employees from collectivistic, high power distance nations are more likely to regard good citizenship as part of their work. They also note that individual-level measures related to individualism or collectivism predict aspects of citizenship behavior in differing ways in different cultures. For instance, sales persons in both the Netherlands and the Philippines experienced shame about their performance failures (Bagozzi, Verbeke and Gavino 2003). However, Filipinos coped with shame by enhancing their citizenship behaviors, whereas the Dutch were more likely to withdraw from failure situations to protect their individual self-concept.

3.1.3 *Work–family balance*

As noted above, psychological contracts in collectivist cultures have broader scope, thus incorporating more reference to family issues. Issues of work–family balance are of critical importance in family businesses, and the salience of family businesses in for instance Indian and Chinese ethnic communities is well known. We have some qualitative knowledge of the conduct of Chinese family business (Redding 1990). More extensive questionnaire surveys have underlined that work–family balance is strongly influenced by institutional factors including maternity leave entitlements, childcare arrangements, and provision for part-time working. Within multinational enterprises, these factors interact with company policies. For instance, Lyness and Kropf (2005) surveyed managers in twenty European nations. In nations with institutional policies favouring gender equality, company policies were more supportive of work–family balance, and respondents reported better work–family balance. However, Lyness and Kropf next divided their data between respondents working in the nation where their employer's headquarters was located and those who were in subsidiary locations. Employees' work–family balance was more affected by company policies in headquarters nations, and more affected by nation-level predictors in subsidiaries. This study illustrates some of the conflicting priorities that act upon the implementation of personnel policies within multinational enterprises.

If the relation between one's work and one's family is more distinct in individualistic nations, this implies that long hours of work may be more of a threat to work–family balance in Western nations. Spector et al. (2004) found support for this hypothesis, sampling employees from fifteen nations. They suggested that employees in Western nations feel guilt about working long hours, whereas the lesser distinction between work and family in collectivist nations rests on employees' stronger perception that they are working for the benefit of the family.

3.1.4 *What is a job? Summary*

Jobs are defined in a more diffuse, implicit manner in non-Western nations. This has implications for selection and evaluation procedures, and for expectations as to what will motivate employees' performance.

3.2 Selection Processes

Substantial national differences have been noted in the frequency of use of specific selection procedures (Newell and Tansley 2001). The distinctive reliance on graphological analysis by companies in France and French-speaking Belgium is particularly striking (Shackleton and Newell 1994). More generally, there are substantial differences between reliance of structured interviews, psychometric tests, and assessment centres in some nations and reliance on unstructured interviews and personal recommendations in others. Ryan et al. (1999) surveyed the extent of reliance on eleven selection methods in twenty-two nations and then tested hypotheses predicting the degree to which Hofstede scores would be related to frequent use of particular methods. They found that high uncertainty avoidance nations use more types of test, conduct more interviews, and avoid procedures that are difficult to verify. In higher-power distance nations, greater weight is given to interviews and to selecting graduates from higher-status universities. The popularity of different selection methods with applicants also varies across nations, although interviews are popular everywhere (Steiner and Gilliland 2001).

In this field, there is an evident contrast between the preference of many multinational enterprises to implement a standard set of selection procedures globally and culturally driven preferences for procedures perceived locally as more valid. In evaluating this contrast it is important to bear in mind the contrasting perceptions of employment discussed in the preceding section. If one is hiring a person for a clearly described job, it is relatively simple to design and validate a targeted set of selection procedures focused primarily on relevant skills. If one is hiring a person as a member of an organization, it may be more important to assess the extent to which that person is amenable to subsequent socialization by the organization than to test for job-specific skills. In organizations where responsibility for task achievement is shared collectively, presence of skills in one specific person would be less critical.

3.2.1 *Expatriation*

Current trends toward globalization require an increasing proportion of the workforce to work with persons from cultural backgrounds different from their own. This may entail actual expatriation, but shorter-term visits and day-to-day working in multicultural teams are also increasingly frequent. Selection of expatriates is particularly critical, given the known costs of expatriate failure. Early estimates of frequent expatriate failure have not been replicated by later surveys. Tung (1998) found no more than 7 percent of failed assignments among 174 US expatriates. Despite this apparent improvement in success rates, it appears that selection priorities continue to be driven only by the presence of relevant technical skills, by prior record with the company and by willingness to undertake the assignment, both in the US (Anderson 2005) and in Europe (Harris and Brewster 1999). In establishing more valid selection procedures for expatriates, it will be important not simply to determine success or failure of assignments, but to examine the specific processes that enhance expatriate success. Evidence continues to support the utility of training for expatriates (Morris and Robie 2001; Waxin and Panaccio 2005), but more attention is also required to the circumstances of their placement. For instance, what attributes of expatriates enhance the willingness of local employees to work effectively with them? Varma et al. (2006) found Chinese host country nationals were more responsive to those whom they perceived to hold similar values and were more willing to assist Indians than Americans.

3.2.2 *Cross-cultural skills*

The more general question to investigate is whether there are skills distinctively associated with success in working cross-culturally that could be used in selection of expatriates and others for whom such skills would be critical. The studies listed in the preceding paragraph are notable for making no reference to language skills. Some recent writers have attempted to formulate a concept of cultural intelligence (Earley and Ang 2003; Thomas and Inkson 2004). However, it is unclear to what extent skill in working with others different from oneself can be considered as a trait-like quality. Skill in working with a Chinese co-worker may not generalize to working well with say an Argentinean or an Arab. Nor is it likely that cross-cultural skills can be validly measured by self-report inventory. From a literature survey, Thomas and Fitzsimmons (2008) conclude that cross-cultural effectiveness rests on information skills, interpersonal skills, action skills, and analytic skills. By analytic skills they refer to what they describe as cultural metacognition. This term concerns the capacity to be aware of one's thinking and learning capacities. Thus someone with this skill could access ways of thinking about a particular problematic cross-cultural interaction that would entail understanding why it was occurring, identifying ways of handling it, and learning how to anticipate such situations in future. Skills of this type are of course useful also in monocultural settings.

3.2.3 *Selection processes: summary*

The validity of selection procedures may well vary depending upon the cultural context within which they are employed. Successful work performance is dependent on the organizational context within which work is undertaken as much as on attributes of the individual selected.

3.3 Work Motivation

The study of work motivation has long had a central place in the cross-cultural study of organizational behavior. Indeed, both the cultural dimension of individualism–collectivism and that of masculinity–femininity identified by Hofstede (1980) were defined by answers to questions about work motives. While these dimensions have provided frameworks for cross-cultural analyses, they do not advance our understanding of work motives, which are essentially individual-level phenomena. More recent researchers have used multi-level analyses to overcome this problem. Huang and Van de Vliert (2004) used data from 129,000 employees in 39 nations to test hypotheses derived from Maslow's (1954) hierarchical theory of motivation. They were able to show that white collar workers are more satisfied than blue collar workers in individualistic nations, but that there was no such difference among respondents from collectivistic nations. They reasoned that this effect was obtained because Maslow's "higher" needs such as self-actualization and self-esteem are not valued highly in collectivistic cultures. In a further study with an additional 107,000 respondents, Huang and Van de Vliert (2003) showed that intrinsic job characteristics were positively associated with job satisfaction in nations with high levels of social security or low power distance (or both). However, there was no such link in nations that had both low social security and high power distance. Thus, employees give emphasis to different elements within Maslow's model in ways that are predictable on the basis of both national culture and institutional factors.

Some recent studies appear to qualify this conclusion. For instance, Spector et al. (2001) found that internal work locus of control predicted well-being among employees in each of twenty-four nations. However, it could be that employees use this sense of individual agency to advance individual goals in individualist and collectivist contexts in different ways. As Hui, Au, and Foch (2004) argued, there is a distinction to be made between perceiving oneself to have been given autonomy by the organization (discretionary empowerment) and perceiving oneself to have the freedom to act (psychological empowerment). Locus of control measures focus on psychological empowerment. Sampling data from thirty-three nations, Hui et al. found that discretionary empowerment predicted job satisfaction only in low power distance nations. The contrast between the findings of these studies thus underlines the importance of distinguishing between respondents' reports of their inner states and their perceptions of their organizational context. Both are important if we are to understand the drivers of work performance (Huang 2008).

3.3.1 *Organizational commitment*

Managements in recent times have favoured achievement not simply of employees' job satisfaction but of their commitment to the organization. Most cross-cultural studies of organization commitment have employed measures derived from Meyer and Allen's (1997) distinction between affective commitment, normative commitment, and continuance commitment. This distinction is of particular interest, because it might be expected that within more collectivistic nations normative and continuance commitment would be stronger predictors of outcomes than is the case in individualistic nations. Normative commitment refers to a sense of obligation toward the organization, while continuance commitment refers to a lack of alternatives. There would be fewer alternatives in collectivist contexts because in these contexts one's identity is more tightly bound to one's present employer. Stanley et al. (2007) used the clusters of culturally similar nations identified by the GLOBE researchers (House et al. 2004) to test these expectations in relation to turnover expectations. In the sample as a whole turnover cognition correlated negatively with all three types of commitment. However, the correlation with normative commitment varied from −.34 in the more individualistic Anglo cluster to −.67 in the more collectivist Middle Eastern cluster. Similarly, the correlation with continuance commitment varied from −.21 in Anglo nations to −.55 in the Confucian Asian cluster. The stronger effects in the collectivist clusters supports the predictions.

Studies by Wasti in Turkey underline and extend this conclusion. Wasti (2003) found that the correlation between turnover intention and normative commitment was most strongly negative among respondents with an allocentric (that is, collective) self-construal. Allocentrics also scored higher on continuance commitment (Wasti 2002). Thus these effects are confirmed not just on the basis of a categorization of clusters of nations derived from a separate source, but on the basis of measures provided by the actual respondents sampled.

3.3.2 *Work motivation: summary*

Organizational contexts that are collectivistic and high on power distance foster a range of work motives and bases for commitment to the organization that are distinctively different in strength. To optimize engagement, managements need to address locally salient motives.

3.4 Organizational Justice

There is little doubt that employee performance is affected by perceptions of the fairness with which one has been treated, although there may be more sensitivity to this issue in some cultural contexts than others. Western researchers have made distinctions between distributive justice (fairness of rewards), procedural justice (just allocation procedures), and interactional justice (the way that procedures and rewards are explained). Fischer (2008) reported that these distinctions were upheld among data from respondents in each of eleven nations. There is also an important distinction to be made between studies that focused on preferred justice criteria and those that have examined reactions to actual events.

3.4.1 *Preferred criteria*

Researchers into distributive justice have mostly compared preferences for reward allocations based on equity, equality, or need. A meta-analysis by Fischer and Smith (2003) indicated stronger preference for equity among respondents from high power distance nations. However, Fischer (2008) suggests that the distinction between equity and equality is insufficiently clear. Whether or not an allocation is judged equitable will depend on which inputs and outputs are taken into consideration. Cultural differences may be most apparent in terms of whether factors such as age, seniority, or need are considered as allowable inputs. Indeed, the choice of whom one compares oneself with may outweigh all other criteria. Leung et al. (1996) found that Chinese joint venture hotel managers compared their pay with the much lower pay achieved by managers in Chinese state enterprises and felt equitably paid. Three years later, they felt ready to compare themselves with expatriate managers within the hotels and felt inequitably paid (Leung, Wang and Smith 2001).

Research into procedural justice has for instance compared preference for "voice" (opportunity to influence the decision) and the impartiality of the senior figure across seven nations (Cohn, White, and Sanders 2000). Voice was perceived as fair universally, but impartiality was more strongly favoured in Central and Eastern European nations than in France, Spain, and the US. We have noted earlier that the perceived procedural justice of some selection methods also varies across nations.

3.4.2 *Perceived justice*

Studies of perceived justice have used more sophisticated research designs than those found in some other fields, often including individual-level measures of cultural orientation as well as sampling from different nations. Perhaps for this very reason, they have uncovered a more complex set of findings (Fischer 2008). Some studies (e.g., the study in Taiwan by Farh, Earley, and Lin 1997) have indicated that respondents with more traditional values react less to perceived injustices.

Endorsement of modern values enhanced the link between perceived justice and organizational citizenship behaviors. However, some subsequent studies have suggested that procedural injustice has stronger effects among those endorsing low power distance values and others that it has weaker effects. The explanation may lie in the types of study design that have been employed, with some sampling long-term employees, but others using hypothetical scenarios (Fischer 2008).

3.4.3 *Organizational justice: summary*

Most studies of justice have been conducted within an overly restrictive conceptual framework. We are only beginning to obtain a full view of the cultural determinants of fairness. The evidence suggests that modernity of employees will increase their concerns about being treated equitably.

3.5 Leadership and Influence

Many studies have been reported that sought to establish the cross-cultural validity of the numerous leadership theories that have been formulated within the US. The GLOBE project (House et al. 2004) is perhaps the largest-scale cross-cultural research project to have been undertaken to date, involving 170 investigators, who collected data from managers within three industries in sixty-one nations. A major strength of this project lies in the fact that theory-driven measures were constructed and used to characterize the organizations and nations that were sampled, avoiding the weakness of earlier studies that either assumed that samples could be characterized through use of scores derived from earlier projects such as that of Hofstede (1980), or else simply used US measures in all locations without any attempt to characterize cultural context (e.g., Bass 1997).

Respondents to the GLOBE survey were asked to identify traits that would describe effective leaders. The intent was to determine the extent to which charismatic, value-based leadership based on integrity would be endorsed universally, compared to the emergence of culturally distinctive profiles of effective leadership in different locations. The study yielded evidence in favour of both perspectives. Clusters of traits named as charismatic and team-oriented were universally endorsed. Endorsement of clusters identified as participative, humane, autonomous, and narcissistic each showed significant cultural variation. Cultural contingencies in effective leader styles have also been identified in many other less comprehensive investigations (Aycan 2008).

Despite the positive qualities of the GLOBE project outlined above, the measures of preferred leader attributes used by these researchers share one weakness in common with many of the earlier studies. The listing of desired leader traits imposes a perspective on respondents that is inherently individualistic. Leadership and influence qualities are seen as inherent in the leader, without any reference to his or her context. An alternative perspective would be one that starts from the relatedness that is central to groups and organizations within nations that are more collectivist and higher in power distance. Researchers working in this way have mostly focused on paternalistic leadership.

3.5.1 *Paternalism*

The concept of paternalism has negative connotations in contemporary individualistic nations. It has overtones of outdated leadership practices in which entrepreneurs exploited their juniors by presuming to know better than their juniors what was good for them. In collectivistic nations, paternalistic leadership is posited to comprise the following elements (Aycan 2006): the leader creates a family atmosphere at work, building an individualized relation with each subordinate, and making no distinction between work and non-work life. In response, the subordinate contributes loyalty and deference. These elements are interactive. In other words, the actions of leader and subordinate each contribute to the creation of paternalism. Thus this model differs from those that conceptualize leadership in terms of a one-way process of influence that flows solely from leader to subordinate. Relatively few empirical studies of paternalistic leadership have yet been published, but it has been shown to predict criterion measures in Turkey (Aycan 2006), China (Cheng et al. 2004) and the Philippines (Restubog and Bordia 2006).

3.5.2 *Leadership: summary*

There are universal aspects of leadership that are perceived to be effective. However, no studies have yet provided an estimate of the relative importance of universal and culture-contingent aspects of leadership. Some progress is evident in identifying approaches to leadership other than those that are conceptualized in individualistic ways.

3.6 Teamworking

It is evident that employees in all parts of the world frequently work in teams. The contrast between teamwork in individualist and collectivist nations lies not in its frequency but in the nature of members' commitment to their teams. Earley (1993) compared individual work and teamwork in China, Israel, and the US. In the collectivist nations, team members worked harder than when alone, so long as the team comprised in-group members. In the US, team members worked harder when alone and who was in the team had no effect. Furthermore, an individual-level measure of collectivism predicted working harder in teams within each of the nations sampled. The differing motivational bases of teamwork suggest a stronger need for team development activities in individualistic contexts and a stronger need for attention to team composition in collectivistic contexts. Team performance is also likely to be enhanced by different procedures. Earley

(1994) found that efficacy of individualists was best enhanced by individual feed-back, while collectivists showed a better response to group-focused feedback.

Multinational organizations also frequently propose the creation of self-man-aged teams. The effectiveness of such teams is likely to be problematic in contexts where there is a strong preference for power distance. Kirkman and Shapiro (2001) surveyed self-managed teams within two companies operating in Belgium, Fin-land, the Philippines, and the US. Effectiveness was rated highest in those teams that had a culture of high collectivism but low power distance.

3.6.1 *Multicultural teams*

The studies reviewed above were conducted with culturally homogeneous teams. However an increasingly large number of teams include persons of varied cultural background, whether they are in face-to-face teams or virtual teams. Numerous factors that influence whether heterogeneous teams perform better than homogeneous ones have been identified, including the nature of the task, team duration, and member co-location (Halevy and Sagiv 2008). Teamwork is particularly problematic if a heteroge-neous team contains a "faultline" (Lau and Murnighan 2005) between two clearly marked subgroups. It is substantially easier to create an effective team culture where there is a more varied composition with no group predominating. To date, this literature has emphasized homogeneity versus heterogeneity, and neglected other fundamental issues such as differences in language skills, cultural differences in pre-ferred communication mode, and orientation towards collective working. Chevrier (2003) reported case studies illustrating alternative strategies for handling group process issues in three European multicultural teams. The first team favoured tolerance and self-control in the face of difference. The second favoured getting to know one another personally and discovering through trial and error how much flexibility each party was willing to contribute. The third team built cohesion through identification with their shared professional culture of engineering. None of these strategies was judged wholly satisfactory by the team members, but Chevrier indicated that they hold potential in combination with more explicit attention to cultural differences. It is not necessarily the case that low team conflict will optimize effectiveness. Elron (1997) surveyed twenty-two top management teams within multinational enterprises. The teams whose members spanned a broader range of nations had more conflict and felt less satisfied. However, they were more effective because they had more adequately represented the divergent concerns of their constituencies.

3.6.2 *Teamworking: Summary*

Cultural factors have a major impact on the motives that members bring to teams, on the way that they are likely to structure their work, and on the degree of challenge that they may face in doing so. Attention to these factors can aid team effectiveness.

3.7 Negotiation

The management of difference is also at the forefront of all types of negotiation. Much of the early work in this field was influenced by US studies that distinguished various styles of conflict management. For instance Morris et al. (1998) compared the negotiation styles favoured by business students in India, Hong Kong, the Philippines, and the US. Competitive bargaining was more strongly favoured in the US sample than elsewhere, while avoidance was favoured more in the other samples than in the US. Morris et al. were also able to use Schwartz's (1999) measures to show that these differing preferences could be explained by the varying values endorsed by their respondents. There are practical reasons why these differences are particularly important. US studies have shown that when negotiators are accountable to a group, their behavior becomes more competitive (e.g., Klimoski and Ash 1974). However, when Gelfand and Realo (1999) compared the effect of accountability on negotiations in Estonia and the US, they found that while US negotiators did become more competitive, Estonians became more cooperative. Thus intercultural negotiation accentuates cultural contrasts.

More recent research has used complex scenarios to gain a more vivid indication of the ways in which bargaining is typically conducted (Brett and Crotty 2008). In a series of studies Brett and her colleagues have investigated the ways in which preference for direct or indirect communication (Hall 1966) affects dyadic negotiation behavior. Adair and Brett (2005) showed that negotiators from low-context nations (Sweden, Israel, Germany, and the US) used more direct information exchange by way of questions and answers, and did not make offers until late in the negotiation. Negotiators from high-context nations (Thailand, Hong Kong, Japan, and Russia) were more likely to make early initial offers without revealing the information that lay behind the offers, and to make inferences about the opponent's position from responses to these offers.

Practical interest focuses particularly on intercultural negotiation and Adair and Brett also studied US–Japanese and US–Hong Kong dyads. Here the interchanges included more direct questioning and early offers, but this did not lead to the formulation of offers that were mutually acceptable. Joint gains were lower than in the single-nation dyads. This may be because the making of early offers serves a different function within high- and low-context nations, so that in intercultural dyads they create confusion.

3.7.1 Negotiation: Summary

This field of investigation has particular merit because it is one of the few that has started to move on from the necessary detailing of cultural differences to consideration of cross-national collaboration.

4. MULTICULTURAL ENTERPRISE

The preceding sections have given an overview of some of the more important cultural contrasts that have relevance to the practice of personnel psychology. How can an effective enterprise best take benefit from these forms of diversity, rather than be impeded by them?

4.1 The Global Organization

The discussion in this chapter has followed the convenient and prevailing assumption made by many cross-cultural psychologists that nations can be described as cultures. While the assumption does have its uses, it is also self-evident that nations do not comprise homogeneous cultures. One can readily identify subcultures within nations that are defined by region, by profession, by occupation, and by organization. Consequently, one strategy available to the multinational enterprise is to seek to create and sustain a company culture through selecting employees whose values are compatible with the preferred company culture. Through the processes of attraction, selection, and attrition (Schneider, Goldstein, and Smith 1995), the organization could achieve a focus on its core mission and minimize diversity issues.

Erez and Shokef (2008) propose that this type of procedure does not just characterize a particular strategy for *some* multinational enterprises, but that it is possible to define a range of values that are required for the success of *any* multinational enterprise in the contemporary environment. They identify nine such values: competitive performance orientation, quality, customer orientation, openness to change, interdependence, social responsibility, trust, personal development, and openness to cultural diversity. Erez and Shokef constructed a fifty-two-item survey in which respondents were asked to specify the extent to which their employer stressed each of the nine specified values. Their measure thus resembles the ones used by the GLOBE project researchers (House et al. 2004); it concerns perceptions of the values in one's environment, not one's personal values. The survey was administered to employees of a single multinational enterprise working in Italy, Israel, South Korea, and Singapore. The three values that were found to be endorsed most highly and equally strongly across all samples were customer orientation, competitive performance orientation, and openness to cultural diversity. Endorsement of personal development showed the greatest variation across samples. By focusing on a set of previously formulated company values rather than on personal values, this study comes closer to testing for the existence of a global organization culture than was achieved for instance by Hofstede's (1980) survey. However, the results suggest that at least within the enterprise that was sampled, substantial evidence of diversity remains present.

4.2 The Multinational Organization

Bartlett and Ghoshal (1989) first distinguished between global organizations and multinational organizations. They saw global organizations as those with strong emphasis on centralization and weak local autonomy. Multinational organizations are defined as showing the reverse emphasis on strong local autonomy and less emphasis on central control. They also identified a transnational organization as one that can achieve both central control and local autonomy. Although these concepts were presented as a typology, there are clearly an infinite range of gradations between these differing ideal types of enterprise.

In all of these types of enterprise there will be some degree of tension between uniformity and diversity. This tension is next examined in terms of both policies and practices and at both micro- and macro-levels.

4.2.1 *Role relationships*

Managers in all types of organization experience some degree of role conflict in responding to pressures on them from the members of their role set. Within the multinational organization, country managers are asked to engage in a critically important process of cultural boundary spanning, linking company headquarters and the local organization. Bartlett and Ghoshal identified four aspects of the country manager role: information exchange, coordination, information scanning, and control. The salience of these four aspects of their role will vary dependent upon the degree of centralization sought by the company. Whatever the salience of these aspects, the country manager is likely to be evaluated in quite different ways by headquarters and by local employees, given their differing priorities. He or she will be a key player in continuing consideration of many of the issues identified earlier in this chapter. To what extent shall the company implement uniform policies in respect of selection, appraisal, remuneration, terms of employment, training of leaders, and many other issues? Where the country manager is also an expatriate, the potentialities for role conflict are exacerbated since he or she must take account of the way in which headquarters evaluations will influence subsequent career progress on completion of the placement. While expatriate failure is no longer seen as a major problem, there is continuing evidence that companies fail to utilize the talents of returning expatriates, leading to substantial subsequent returnee turnover (Tung 1998). It appears that country managers that handle their problems most effectively are those that succeed in identifying with both headquarters and the local organization, rather than privileging one over the other (Vora, Kostova, and Roth 2007).

4.2.2 *Knowledge transfer*

Multinational organizations rather frequently seek to transfer forms of organizational knowledge to new locations. Kostova and Roth (2002) proposed that transfers of what they called "strategic organizational practices" are dependent on the degree to which they fit within the norms and meanings provided by their new institutional contexts. Such practices may include systems of vocational training, diversity initiatives, systems of appraisal, or many other aspects of human resource management. For instance, Gooderham, Nordhaug, and Ringdal (2006) compared transfer of the US practices of appraisal and performance-related pay to subsidiaries. The more restrictive institutional contexts of Norway, Denmark, Germany, and Ireland were found to restrict managerial autonomy, through legal protection of individual rights, requirements for co-determination, and the presence of strong unions. Transfer was therefore less successful there than in the liberal economies of the UK and Australia. However, Lervik and Lunnan (2004) note that successful knowledge transfer is not simply dependent on the presence or absence of institutional constraints, but also on the ways in which key persons are able to attach locally relevant meanings to proposed innovations.

4.2.3 *Mergers and acquisitions*

A major component of the contemporary scene is the continuing sequence of mergers and acquisitions, whereby organizations seek to extend both their viability and their entry into additional markets. These activities often entail a much more abrupt collision between contrasting cultural systems than those involved in more specific knowledge transfers. Current meta-analytic evidence indicates mergers and acquisitions frequently do not accomplish their intended financial goals (King et al. 2004). Such failures have often been attributed to cultural differences between the parties. Numerous attempts to predict success by crude comparisons of "distance" indices derived from Hofstede scores for the relevant nations have proved inconclusive. However, a further meta-analysis of forty-six mergers and acquisitions does indicate that by focusing upon the extent of intended integration between the parties and on how closely similar they were initially both at the organizational and at the national level, one can predict the probability of realization of benefit (Stahl and Voigt 2008).

5. CONCLUSION

There is now substantial evidence that many aspects of organization behavior vary across national cultures. The extent of such variation is probably underestimated, because sampling has often been restricted to the cluster of globally most powerful economies. Even those organizations that restrict their activities to a single nation are increasingly likely to employ a multicultural workforce. Large-scale surveys of global value change do suggest similar directional effects among many nations, but also indicate maintenance of existing differences between nations (Inglehart and Oyserman 2004). In a similar way, Mayrhofer, Morley, and Brewster (2004) note some parallel developments in human resource management throughout Europe, but with substantial evidence of continuing divergence. The challenge for the future therefore remains the management of difference.

Cross-cultural research can assist this process in several ways. First, it can develop more sophisticated indicators of cultural difference. Existing measures have often been unduly dependent on those developed in Western economies and may fail to detect effects that are present universally but are less strongly expressed in Western contexts. We know how to develop better measures (Van de Vijver and Leung 1997; Van de Vijver and Hambleton 1996). Second, researchers can survey the consequences of varying ways of handling difference, as has been illustrated in this chapter in fields as varied as work–family balance, teamworking, knowledge transfer, and mergers and acquisitions. Third, researchers can contribute to improved understanding of the distinctive nature of cross-cultural skills, and how they may best be enhanced. Finally, and in the short run perhaps most important of all, cross-culturalists must find ways to persuade their peers in psychology and in human resource management that a continuing awareness of cultural issues is not so much a distinct specialism, but a necessary component of the skills required of any fully competent practitioner.

REFERENCES

ADAIR, W. L., and BRETT, J. M. 2005. The negotiation dance: time, culture, and behavioral sequences in negotiation. *Organizational Science*, 16 (1): 33–51.

ANDERSON, B. A. 2005. Expatriate selection: good management or good luck? *International Journal of Human Resource Management*, 16: 567–83.

AYCAN, Z. 2006. Paternalism: towards conceptual refinement and operationalization. Pp. 445–66 in *Scientific Advances in Indigenous Psychologies: Empirical, Philosophical, and Cultural Contributions*, (ed. K. S. Yang, K. K. Hwang, and U. Kim.). Cambridge: Cambridge University Press.

—— 2008. Cross-cultural approaches to leadership. Pp. 219–38 in *Handbook of Cross-cultural Management Research*, ed. P. B. Smith, M. F. Peterson and D. C. Thomas. Thousand Oaks, CA: Sage.

BAGOZZI, R. P., VERBEKE, W., and GAVINO, J. C., Jr. 2003. Culture moderates the self-regulation of shame and its effects on performance: the case of salespersons in the Netherlands and the Philippines. *Journal of Applied Psychology*, 88: 219–33.

BARTLETT, C. A., and GHOSHAL, S. 1989. *Managing across Borders: The Transnational Solution*. Boston: Harvard Business School Press.

BASS, B. M. 1997. Does the transactional-transformational leadership paradigm transcend organizational and national boundaries? *American Psychologist*, 52: 130–9.

BOND, M. H., LEUNG, K., AU, A., TONG, K.-K., REIMEL DE CARRASQUEL, S., MURAKAMI, F., et al. 2004. Cultural-level dimensions of social axioms and their correlates across 41 cultures. *Journal of Cross-Cultural Psychology*, 35: 548–70.

BRETT, J. M. and CROTTY, S. 2008. Culture and negotiation. Pp. 269–83 in *Handbook of Cross-cultural Management Research*, ed. P. B. Smith, M. F. Peterson and D. C. Thomas. Thousand Oaks, CA: Sage.

CHENG, B. S., CHOU, L. F., WU, T. Y., HUANG, M. P., and FARH, J. L. 2004. Paternalistic leadership and subordinate responses: establishing a leadership model in Chinese organizations. *Asian Journal of Social Psychology*, 7: 89–117.

CHEVRIER, S. 2003. Cross-cultural management in multinational project groups. *Journal of World Business*, 38: 141–9.

COHN, E. S., WHITE, S. O., and SANDERS, J. 2000. Distributive and procedural justice in seven nations. *Law and Human Behavior*, 24: 553–79.

EARLEY, P. C. 1993. East meets west meets mideast: further explorations of collectivistic and individualistic work groups. *Academy of Management Journal*, 36: 319–48.

—— 1994. The individual and collective self: an assessment of self-efficacy and training across cultures. *Administrative Science Quarterly*, 39: 89–117.

—— and ANG, S. 2003. *Cultural intelligence: individual interactions across cultures*. Stanford, CA: Stanford University Press.

ELRON, E. 1997. Top management teams within multinational corporations: effects of cultural heterogeneity. *Leadership Quarterly*, 8: 393–412.

EREZ, M., and SHOKEF, E. 2008. The culture of global organisations. Pp. 285–300 in *Handbook of Cross-cultural Management Research*, ed. P. B. Smith, M. F. Peterson and D. C. Thomas. Thousand Oaks, CA: Sage.

FARH, J., EARLEY, P. C., and LIN, S. 1997. A cultural analysis of justice and organisational citizenship behavior in Chinese society. *Administrative Science Quarterly*, 42: 421–44.

—— HACKETT, R. D, and CHEN, Z. J. 2008. Organizational citizenship behavior in the global context. Pp. 165–84 in *Handbook of Cross-cultural Management Research*, P. B. Smith, M. F. Peterson and D. C. Thomas. Thousand Oaks, CA: Sage.

—— ZHONG, C. B., and ORGAN, D. W. 2004. Organizational citizenship behavior in the People's Republic of China. *Organization Science*, 15: 241–53.

FISCHER, R. 2008. Organisational justice and reward allocation. Pp. 135–50 in *Handbook of Cross-cultural Management Research*, ed. P. B. Smith, M. F. Peterson and D. C. Thomas. Thousand Oaks, CA: Sage.

—— and SMITH, P. B. 2003. Reward allocation and culture: a meta-analysis. *Journal of Cross-Cultural Psychology*, 34: 251–68.

GELFAND, M., and REALO, A. 1999. Individualism-collectivism and accountability in intergroup negotiations. *Journal of Applied Psychology*, 84: 721–36.

GOODERHAM, P. N., NORDHAUG, O., and RINGDAL, K. 2006. National embeddedness and calculative human resource management in US subsidiaries in Europe and Australia. *Human Relations*, 59: 1491–513.

HALEVY, N., and SAGIV, L. 2008. Teams within and across cultures. Pp. 253–68 in *Handbook of Cross-cultural Management Research*, ed. P. B. Smith, M. F. Peterson and D. C. Thomas. Thousand Oaks, CA: Sage.

HALL, E. T. 1966. *The Hidden Dimension*. New York: Doubleday.

HARRIS, H., and BREWSTER, C. 1999. The coffee-machine system: how international selection really works. *International Journal of Human Resource Management*, 10: 488–500.

Hofstede, G. 1980. *Culture's Consequences: International Differences in Work-Related Values.* Beverly Hills, CA: Sage.

—— 2001. *Culture's Consequences: Comparing Values, Behaviors, Institutions, and Organizations across Nations.* Thousand Oaks, CA: Sage.

—— 2006. What did GLOBE really measure? Researchers' minds versus respondents' minds. *Journal of International Business Studies,* 37: 882–96.

—— Bond, M. H., and Luk, C. L. 1993. Individual perceptions of organizational cultures: a methodological treatise on levels of analysis. *Organizational Studies,* 14: 483–503.

House, R. J., Hanges, P. J., Javidan, M., Dorfman, P. W., Gupta, V. and GLOBE Associates 2004. *Culture, Leadership, and Organizations: The GLOBE Study of 62 Societies.* Thousand Oaks, CA: Sage.

Huang, X. 2008. Motivation and job satisfaction across nations: how much do we really know? Pp. 77–93 in *Handbook of Cross-cultural Management Research,* ed. P. B. Smith, M. F. Peterson and D. C. Thomas. Thousand Oaks, CA: Sage.

—— and Van de Vliert, E. 2003. Where intrinsic motivation fails to work: national moderators of intrinsic motivation. *Journal of Organizational Behavior,* 24: 159–79.

—— —— 2004. Job level and national culture as joint roots of job satisfaction: challenging jobs worldwide. *Applied Psychology: An International Review,* 53: 329–48.

Hui, M., Au, K., and Fock, H. 2004. Empowerment effects across cultures. *Journal of International Business Studies,* 35: 46–60.

Inglehart, R., and Oyserman, D. 2004. Individualism, autonomy and self-expression: the human development syndrome. Pp. 74–96 in *Comparing Cultures: Dimensions of Culture in a Comparative Perspective,* ed. H. Vinken, J. Soeters, and P. Ester. Leiden: Brill.

Javidan, M., House, R. J., Dorfman, P. W., Hanges, P. J., and Sully de Luque, M. S. 2006. Conceptualizing and measuring cultures and their consequences: a comparative review of GLOBE's and Hofstede's approaches. *Journal of International Business Studies,* 37: 897–914.

Kickul, J., Lester, S. W., and Belgio, E. 2004. Attitudinal and behavioral outcomes of psychological contract breach: a cross-cultural comparison of the United States and Hong Kong Chinese. *International Journal of Cross-Cultural Management.* 4: 229–52.

King, D. R., Dalton, D. R., Daily, C. M., and Covin, J. G. 2004. Meta-analyses of post-acquisition performance: indications of unidentified moderators. *Strategic Management Journal,* 25: 187–200.

Kirkman, B. L., and Shapiro, D. L. 2001. The impact of team members' cultural values on productivity, cooperation, and empowerment in self-managing work teams. *Journal of Cross-Cultural Psychology,* 32: 597–617.

—— Lowe, K. B., and Gibson, C. B. 2006. A quarter century of Culture's Consequences: a review of empirical research incorporating Hofstede's cultural values framework. *Journal of International Business Studies,* 37: 285–320.

Klimoski, R. J., and Ash, R. A. 1974. Accountability and negotiation behavior. *Organizational Behavior and Human Performance,* 11: 409–25.

Kostova, T., and Roth, K. 2002. Adoption of an organizational practice by subsidiaries of multinational corporations: institutional and relational effects. *Academy of Management Journal,* 45: 215–33.

Lau, D. C., and Murnighan, J. K. 2005. Interactions within groups and sub-groups: the effects of demographic faultlines. *Academy of Management Journal,* 48: 645–59.

LERVIK, J. E., and LUNNAN, R. 2004. Contrasting perspectives on the diffusion of management knowledge: performance management in a Norwegian multinational. *Management Learning*, 35: 287–302.

LEUNG, K., and BOND, M. H. 2004. Social axioms: a model for social beliefs in multicultural perspective. Pp. 119–97 in *Advances in Experimental Social Psychology*, vol. 36, ed. M. Zanna. Orlando, FL: Academic Press.

—— SMITH, P. B., WANG, Z. M., and SUN, H. 1996. Job satisfaction in joint venture hotels in China: an organizational justice analysis. *Journal of International Business Studies*, 27: 947–63.

—— WANG, Z. M., and SMITH, P. B. 2001. Job attitudes and organizational justice in joint venture hotels in China: the role of expatriate managers. *International Journal of Human Resource Management*, 12: 926–45.

LYNESS, K. S., and KROPF, M. B. 2005. The relationships of national gender equality and organizational support with work-family balance: a study of European managers. *Human Relations*, 58: 33–60.

MACSWEENEY, B. 2002. Hofstede's model of national cultural differences: a triumph of faith—a failure of analysis. *Human Relations*, 55: 89–118.

MASLOW, A. H. 1954. *Motivation and Personality*. New York: Harper and Row.

MAYRHOFER, W., MORLEY, M., and BREWSTER, C. 2004. Convergence, stasis, or divergence? Pp. 417–36 in *Human Resource Management in Europe: Evidence of Convergence?*, C. Brewster, W. Mayrhofer, and M. Morley. ed. London: Elsevier/Butterworth-Heinemann.

MEYER, J. P. and ALLEN, N. J. 1997. *Commitment in the Workplace: Theory, Research and Application*. Thousand Oaks, CA: Sage.

MORRIS, M., and ROBIE, C. 2001. A meta-analysis of the effects of cross-cultural training on expatriate performance and adjustment. *International Journal of Training and Development*, 5 (2): 112–25.

—— WILLIAMS, K., LEUNG, K., LARRICK, R., MENDOZA, T., BHATNAGAR, D., LI, J., KONDO, M., LUO, J., and HU, J. 1998. Conflict management style: accounting for cross-national differences. *Journal of International Business Studies*, 29: 729–47.

NEWELL, S., and TANSLEY, C. 2001. International uses of selection methods. *International Review of Industrial/Organizational Psychology*, Pp. 195–213 in vol. 16, ed. C. L. Cooper and I. T. Robertson. Chichester: Wiley.

ORGAN, D. W., PODSAKOFF, P. M., and MACKENZIE, S. B. 2006. *Organizational Citizenship behavior: Its Nature, Antecedents, and Consequences*. Thousand Oaks, CA: Sage.

PSYCONES 2005. *Final Scientific Report: Psychological Contracts across Employment Situations*. <www.uv.es/~psycon/>, accessed June 1, 2007.

REDDING, S. G. 1990. *The Spirit of Chinese Capitalism*. Berlin: De Gruyter.

—— 2005. The thick description and comparison of societal systems of capitalism. *Journal of International Business Studies*, 36: 123–55.

RESTUBOG, S. L. D., and BORDIA, P. 2006. Workplace familism and psychological contract breach in the Philippines. *Applied Psychology: An International Review*, 55: 563–85.

ROUSSEAU, D. M. 1990. New hire perceptions of their own and their employer's obligations: a study of psychological contracts. *Journal of Organizational Behavior*, 11: 389–400.

—— nd SCHALK, R. 2000. *Psychological Contracts in Employment: Cross-national Perspec-*, CA: Sage.

RYAN, A. M., MCFARLAND, L., BARON, H., and PAGE, R. 1999. An international look at selection practices: nation and culture as explanation for variability in practice. *Personnel Psychology*, 52: 359–91.

SCHNEIDER, B., GOLDSTEIN, H. W., and SMITH, D. B. 1995. The ASA framework: an update. *Personnel Psychology*, 48: 747–73.

SCHWARTZ, S. H. 1999. A theory of cultural values and some implications for work. *Applied Psychology: An International Review*, 48: 23–47.

—— 2004. Mapping and interpreting cultural differences around the world. Pp. 43–73 in *Comparing Cultures: Dimensions of Culture in a Comparative Perspective*, ed. H. Vinken, J. Soeters, and P. Ester. Leiden: Brill.

—— MELECH, G., LEHMANN, A., BURGESS, S., HARRIS, M., and OWENS, V. 2001. Extending the cross-cultural validity of the theory of basic human values with a different method of measurement. *Journal of Cross-Cultural Psychology*, 32: 519–42.

SHACKLETON, V., and NEWELL, S. 1994. European management selection methods: a comparison of five countries. *International Journal of Selection and Assessment*, 2: 91–102.

SMITH, P. B. 2006. When elephants fight, the grass gets trampled: The GLOBE and Hofstede projects. *Journal of International Business Studies*, 37: 915–21.

—— PETERSON, M. F., SCHWARTZ, S. H., et al. 2002. Cultural values, sources of guidance and their relevance to managerial behavior: a 47 nation study. *Journal of Cross-Cultural Psychology*, 33: 188–208.

SPECTOR, P. E., COOPER, C. L., POELMANS, S., et al. 2004. A cross-national comparative study of work-family stressors, working hours, and well-being: China and Latin America versus the Anglo world. *Personnel Psychology*, 57: 119–42.

—— —— SANCHEZ, J., O'DRISCOLL, M., SPARKS, K., BERNIN, P., et al. 2001. Do national levels of individualism and internal locus of control relate to well-being: an ecological-level international study. *Journal of Organizational Behavior*, 22: 815–32.

STAHL, G. K., and VOIGT, A. 2008. Do cultural differences matter in mergers and acquisitions? A tentative model and meta-analytic examination. *Organization Science*, 19: 160–76.

STANLEY, D. J., MEYER, J. P., JACKSON, T. A., et al. 2007. *Cross-cultural Generalizability of the Three-Component Model of commitment*. Poster presented at the 22nd annual conference of the Society for Industrial and Organizational Psychology, New York.

STEINER, D. D., and GILLILAND, S. W. 2001. Procedural justice in personnel selection: International and cross-cultural perspectives. *International Journal of Selection and Assessment*, 9: 134–7.

THOMAS, D. C., and FITZSIMMONS, S. R. 2008. Cross-cultural skills and abilities: from communication competence to cultural intelligence. Pp. 201–15 in *Handbook of Cross-cultural Management Research*, ed. P. B. Smith, M. F. Peterson and D. C. Thomas. Thousand Oaks, CA: Sage.

—— and INKSON, K. 2004. *Cultural Intelligence: People Skills for Global Business*. San Francisco, CA: Berrett-Koehler.

TUNG, R. L. 1998. American expatriates abroad: from neophytes to cosmopolitans. *Journal of World Business*, 33: 125–44.

VAN DE VIJVER, F. J. R., and HAMBLETON, R. K. 1996. Translating tests: some practical guidelines. *European Psychologist*, 1: 89–99.

—— and LEUNG, K. 1997. *Methods and Data Analysis for Cross-cultural Research*. Thousand Oaks, CA: Sage.

VARMA, A., BUDHWAR, P., BISWAS, S., and TOH, S. M. 2006. A quasi-experimental field study of Chinese HCNs' willingness to help expatriates. Paper presented at the Academy of Management Conference, Atlanta, GA.

VORA, D., KOSTOVA, T., and ROTH, K. 2007. Roles of subsidiary managers in multinational corporations: the effect of dual organizational identification. *Management International Review*, 47: 1–26.

WASTI, S. A. 2002. Affective and continuance commitment to the organization: test of an integrated model in the Turkish context. *International Journal of Intercultural Relations*, 26: 525–50.

—— 2003. Organizational commitment, turnover intentions and the influence of cultural values. *Journal of Occupational and Organizational Psychology*, 76: 303–21.

WAXIN, M. F., and PANACCIO, A. 2005. Cross-cultural training to facilitate expatriate adjustment: it works! *Personnel Review*, 34: 51–67.

WHITLEY, R. 1999. *Divergent capitalisms: The Social Structuring and Change of Business Systems*. Oxford: Oxford University Press.

15

SELECTION AND TRAINING FOR WORK ADJUSTMENT AND ADAPTABILITY

BERYL HESKETH

BARBARA GRIFFIN

1. INTRODUCTION

THIS chapter outlines a conceptual framework for integrating recent developments in understanding the individual difference variables that directly influence and interact with situational variables in optimizing work adjustment and adaptive performance. A particular focus of the framework will be on the dynamic attainment of achievement goals and the role that information and communication technology (ICT) can play when there is a turbulent and changing set of situational factors and job requirements. The chapter will take a futuristic approach and challenge readers to consider implications of the rapidly developing field of ICT for traditional models of selection and training.

2. CONTEXT AND DEFINITIONS

Much has been written about the need for adaptability in today's workplace, with changes being driven by technology, globalization, mergers and acquisitions, and, perhaps more recently, global warming. Change, however, is not new, and in this chapter we draw on a well-established conceptual framework for addressing change and adjustment, the Minnesota Theory of Work Adjustment (TWA) (Lofquist and Dawis 1969; Dawis and Lofquist 1984), but include an overlay that gives it a more contemporary slant.

Throughout the centuries, technological developments have been a key driver of change, and ongoing developments in information and communication technologies (ICT) continue to have a major impact on the way we live, socialize, commute, and of course work. Understanding the interface between ICT and human performance at work will become core business for anyone engaged in selecting, training, developing, managing, and optimizing people and organizations for work in the future. It is our contention that industrial and organizational psychology models have not kept pace with the need for more refined theorizing and research at this interface, and we use an updated approach to TWA to address this need.

The primary manner in which we are using the term *adaptability* in this chapter positions it as an individual difference variable, one that has both trait (relatively stable) and state (malleable) features, and hence is an attribute that can be the focus of both selection and training. However, there is also a secondary manner in which we use the term, namely to apply to the adaptability of the environment or organization in which the person will be working. Environments can be strong or weak, to draw on the terms used by Mischel (1976) and others (Dickson, Resick, and Hanges 2006; Schneider, Salvaggio, and Subirats 2002), but better terms might be rigid and flexible in the context of the dynamic process of work adjustment. The mutual responsiveness of people and their work environments gives rise to desired work outcomes, with criteria that typically include productivity, performance, satisfaction, and turnover, all of which can be considered indicators of work adjustment. In the latter part of the chapter we focus on the particular contribution of ICT directly, indirectly, and interactively to the adaptability of people and their work environments, and hence to productivity, performance, and other work adjustment indicators.

We begin the chapter by outlining the components of the Theory of Work Adjustment, including an explanation of the dynamic aspects of the theory. We then discuss how the theory might be adapted and utilized to enhance selection and training for adaptability. In this section we also suggest how the TWA can be extended to include information and communication technologies. Technology is ubiquitous in all spheres of work and life, and traditional models of selection and training need to be updated to take account of the interaction between people and their technology-based work contexts. The chapter concludes with a discussion of how these issues need to be included in future research agendas.

3. Updated Version of the Theory of Work Adjustment (Dawis 2005; Hesketh and Griffin 2005)

The history of the Theory of Work Adjustment is well documented elsewhere (Dawis and Lofquist 1984; Dawis 2005; Hesketh and Griffin 2005). It received primary attention within the vocational psychology literature for many decades, where it was positioned incorrectly as a static "fit" theory, and frequently lumped in with Holland's (1973: 1985) framework. Dawis (2005) highlights the importance of both components of TWA, namely *fit*, which is the correspondence of the person and the environment and *interaction*, which is the action on and reaction to the environment by the person and vice versa. Hesketh and Dawis (1991) repositioned the framework, highlighting its role as a general structure within which selection, training, career decision making, and ergonomic interventions could be understood. It is the repositioned TWA that provides the backbone on which we graft newer ideas drawn from recent literature in I/O psychology and the interface between psychology and ICT.

When defining the person and the work environment in this chapter, we restrict ourselves to a Person or individual employee on the one hand, and on the other variously to the Job, Group, Organization, or Environment. This ensures a focus on the individual and the relationship of the individual to the environment, group, and organization, and mirrors the growing literatures in I/O psychology under the umbrella of Person–Environment Fit (P–E Fit) that includes Person–Job Fit (P–J Fit), Person–Group Fit (P–G Fit), and Person–Organization Fit (P–O Fit). Conceptually, one might substitute group or team for the person, but that adds a layer of complexity that we reserve for another discussion. An important component of TWA, and of any fit model, is the commensurate measurement of the constructs used to assess both the person and the environment. In TWA, commensurate measurement goes beyond just the measures of fit to the process variables used by each party in acting on or reacting to the other.

In additional to the different levels of fit, a number of different types of fit have been identified. TWA focuses on *demands–abilities fit*, which describes the situation when the person's knowledge, skills, abilities, and other characteristics (KSAOs) match the demands or requirements of the organization, and *needs– supplies fit*, which occurs when the person's needs are fulfilled by the organization.

However, others have identified two further ways that fit can be operationalized. *Supplementary fit* is defined as the type of fit that occurs when the person and the environment possess similar characteristics. For example, a highly creative person working with similarly gifted others in an R and D company with high requirements for innovation. In contrast, *complementary fit* is when the person fills a gap in the organization or provides characteristics that are currently missing.

Fit can be measured in two very different ways. First, subjective measures of fit seek for a direct assessment from individuals or organizations as to the degree of fit between the two components, without reference to the individual contributions. Second, each component can be measured individually and these two sources of measurement combined to provide a range of possible indices of fit. In using the former, one purportedly overcomes the problem associated with combining the sources of fit or whether there are any direct relationships between the component parts and fit. However, it does not allow for an analysis of the types of fit, such as described in the above paragraph (supplementary fit, complementary fit, etc.). Measuring components individually allows for the control of direct effects on outcome measures before assessing the contribution of fit (Edwards 1991), but these analyses can become very complex where multi-attributes are used to describe people and environments.

A recent article by Piasentin and Chapman (2006) provides a conceptual analysis of subjective P–O Fit, highlighting the problems of aligning the conceptual component with measurement. They provide an analysis of forty-six studies, and code these in terms of the type of fit (needs–supplies, demands–abilities, supplementary or complementary), the operational definition of organization, and the content domain (e.g., personality, KSAs, values, goals, etc.). Their analysis does raise doubt about the classification of the different types of fit, as no studies examine all simultaneously, so the extent of overlap cannot be assessed. Piasentin and Chapman (2006) note that little work has been done on how individuals differ in the ways in which they evaluate fit. We would argue that the Theory of Work Adjustment (TWA) framework used in this chapter provides an attempt at this through its personality and adjustment style variables.

TWA is best illustrated and recalled diagrammatically. Figure 15.1 provides an updated version of the model, based on that outlined in Hesketh and Dawis (1991). Working from right to left, we discuss each constellation of constructs and how they have evolved in meaning over the past decade.

4. TENURE AND TURNOVER

The original view of tenure in TWA (Fig. 15.1, Box 1) represented the ultimate criterion conceptually, or the actual criterion when measured, namely the extent to which a

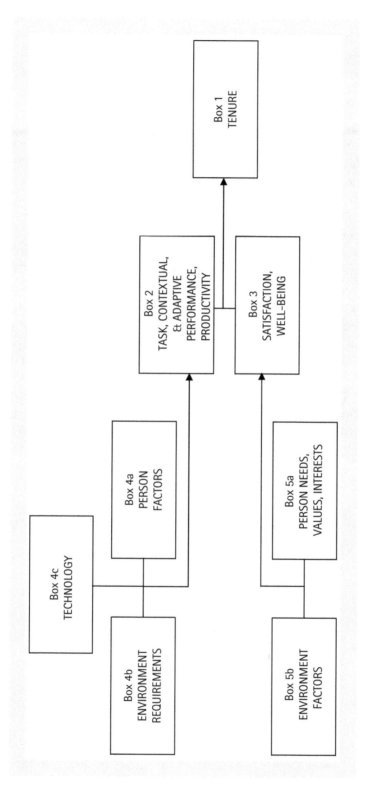

Fig. 15.1 The Minnesota Theory of Work Adjustment (TWA)

Source: Used with permission Hesketh and Griffin, 2005.

relationship between the person and the work environment continues. Although there are limits and constraints that both people and employers (representing the group, environment, or organization) face, in principle individuals are free to leave a job if it no longer meets their needs, and an employer is free to terminate the relationship if the employee is no longer delivering what is required. This simple notion needs to be treated in a stylized manner, given the increasing flexibility and diversity of employment arrangements such as contracting, casual work, and even volunteerism.

Tenure (length of time two parties have interacted) is different from turnover, which is the aggregated count of terminations and departures. Length of tenure, per se, is not necessarily a "good" outcome, as in many instances parties may only have agreed on a fixed term of appointment. It will always be necessary to understand the context of an agreed optimum tenure, and also to clarify the reasons for turnover. There is a rich literature upon which researchers can draw in defining and measures these (e.g., Johns 2002).

Tenure can be thought of as a lag indicator of the extent to which a work relationship is functioning in a mutually responsive manner, but the breakdown of the relationship (turnover) and the lead indicators are more useful in managing relationships. Within TWA two broad categories of lead indicators are used, satisfactory performance and satisfaction, and these are represented in Boxes 2 and 3 in Figure 15.1.

5. Satisfactory Performance

In most I/O Psychology fields of research the performance domain (Fig. 15.1, Box 2) is treated as a major outcome variable, and models of performance are now well developed. The earlier division of performance into task and contextual performance (Borman and Motowidlo 1993) has been extended to include adaptive performance (Allworth and Hesketh 1999; Griffin, Neal, and Parker 2007; Pulakos et al. 2000). Task performance refers to the performance of duties generally listed in a job description that fall within the domain of formal organizational reward systems, while contextual performance relates to discretionary work behaviors such as altruism and generalized compliance. In today's less hierarchical work environments where employees are given increasing degrees of autonomy and responsibility, contextual performance is seen as essential for organizational functioning (Podsakoff et al. 2000). Likewise adaptive performance, or the extent to which an individual deals with changing job requirements and novel or unusual situations, is recognized as critical in modern workplaces that are typically characterized by frequent change and uncertainty.

The rapid change in technology is one factor contributing to the salience of adaptive performance, where assessment must take into account people's capacity not just to adapt to technology but to use it to enhance their performance. Traditionally, technology has been viewed as a moderator of performance rather than a direct determinant, with the corollary that assessments of performance should be restricted to behaviors that are under the complete control of the individual (Campbell, McHenry, and Wise 1990). However, Hesketh and Neal (1999), while accepting the conceptual purity of this view for an ultimate criterion, debate whether it is possible to ever obtain a pure measure of actual performance unconfounded by technology or other aids.

As mentioned earlier and discussed in more detail below, TWA proposes that outcomes such as satisfactory performance can arise from the mutual responsiveness of the individual to the environment and vice versa. Adaptive performance captures this responsiveness in the context of change. Using TWA concepts, Hesketh and Griffin (2005) suggest that adaptive performance can be described as being either reactive, when the person responds by changing their behavior, or proactive, when the person responds by effecting change in the environment.

The focus on performance (or satisfactoriness from the perspective of the employer) has been almost exclusively on productive behavior. It is only recently that attention has turned to the wide spectrum of disruptive, antisocial, and deviant behaviors that employees can engage in, known collectively as counter-productive work behavior (CWB). Specific actions within this domain include physical violence, sexual harassment, theft, absenteeism, rudeness, and social undermining. Technology offers a vehicle through which employees can enact counter-productive behaviors in a potentially more covert manner, for example bullying via SMS, IT sabotage, and theft. Performance of a counter-productive nature could be conceptualized as a form of *maladaptive* performance, where a person responds to changing and stressful conditions in a reactive manner (e.g., yelling at a colleague) or with a proactive effort to alter the conditions (e.g., undermining the work of another person).

Decades of selection research have provided a thorough understanding of the person factors that contribute to satisfactory performance (Fig. 15.1, Box 4a). In particular, they have shown that cognitive ability has a strong relationship with performance, with correlations of .51 to .53 (Schmidt and Hunter 1998). Cognitive ability also predicts related constructs such as acquisition of job knowledge (Hough and Oswald 2000), occupational level attained (Schmidt and Hunter 2004), and general career success in terms of pay and promotions (Judge et al. 1999). More specific ability and job knowledge tests have an overall correlation of .48 with global job performance (Schmidt and Hunter 1998) but tend to be used less often. Personality has also received much attention in selection research. Although TWA did not include personality factors within the original theory of person attributes related to performance, the introduction of meta-analytic techniques and the Big Five theory of personality have highlighted the utility of personality in predicting job performance. In particular, conscientiousness and neuroticism (emotional stability) appear to generalize as predictors of performance across job contexts (Barrick and Mount 1991; Tett, Jackson, and Rothstein 1991).

More recently, the selection literature has advocated adopting a construct-oriented approach where person factors and criterion constructs are conceptually matched. This strategy parallels one of the cornerstones of TWA, that is, the need for commensurate measurement. As a result, researchers have shown that cognitive ability is a better predictor of task performance, whereas conscientiousness is a better predictor of contextual performance (Borman and Motowidlo 1997), and counter-productive performance is related to agreeableness and emotional stability (Berry, Ones, and Sackett 2007). We discuss the specific predictors of adaptive performance later in this chapter.

Few have considered the direct contribution that jobs/environments (Fig. 15.1, Box 4b) may make to performance. For example, technology-rich environments can create opportunities for individuals to demonstrate enhanced performance while others working on older technologies may not be able to demonstrate the same level of performance. Also, recent investigations of counter-productive performance suggest that a characteristic of the work culture, fairness or justice, has direct effects on the extent that people engage in this type of behavior (Berry, Ones, and Sackett 2007).

Surprisingly little research has seriously looked at the interaction between individuals and job requirements in predicting performance, although this is implicit in the common approach that suggests job analysis as the first task in selection, and only after this has been done should one select appropriate predictors that correspond with the job requirements. However, the importance of interaction between the environment and person is demonstrated in research that shows that cognitive ability is more predictive of performance in complex jobs than in simple jobs (Murphy 1989). The findings that extroversion is important for successful performance in sales positions and agreeableness for good performance in team settings (Barrick, Mount, and Judge 2001) are further examples of demands–ability fit.

Earlier in the chapter we drew attention to how the characteristics typical of work today place new demands for different types of employee performance. High levels of autonomy and responsibility require high levels of contextual performance; and dynamic, uncertain environments require greater levels of adaptive performance. We further suggest that the extent that such demands are present in a work environment will also determine the opportunity for individual difference expression. For example, conscientiousness is more predictive of performance in environments high in autonomy than those low in autonomy (Barrick and Mount 1993). The concept of *strong* and *weak* environments (Mischel 1976) is used to explain this result. Strong environments are very prescriptive of behavior, allowing little room for expression of individual differences. In contrast, weak environments give employees greater latitude in their choice of behaviors, and therefore provide conscientious people with the opportunity to act in prosocial ways. The extent that an organization is flexible or inflexible is another factor that might be an alternative to the strong/weak dimension category. Although never investigated, it is possible that flexibility in an organization could moderate the extent that adaptable individuals are able to act in proactive ways to change the environment.

6. SATISFACTION, MENTAL HEALTH, AND WELL-BEING

A cluster of variables has been studied within this domain (Fig. 15.1, Box 3). Although the broad field of health psychology highlights the many different factors that contribute to well-being and health, the focus in TWA is on the contribution of work in general, and the interaction of the individual and the work environment to job satisfaction and well-being.

Hulin and Judge (2003) define job satisfaction as a person's psychological response to his or her job, which includes cognitive, affective, and behavioral components. More simply, it can be thought of as the degree to which people enjoy their jobs (Fritzsche and Parrish 2005). However, this is but one of a number of conceptually distinct work attitudes that might be considered as alternative outcomes, such as job involvement, organizational commitment, career commitment, and career satisfaction, all subject to considerable research within I/O psychology (Bowling, Beehr, and Lepisto 2006; Tziner and Meir 1997). In terms of well-being constructs, job-related stress is an important adjustment criterion, given the enormous and increasing cost of the physical and psychological consequences of stress for both individuals and organizations (Cooper, Dewe, and O'Driscoll 2001).

Traditionally, the person factors in TWA (Fig. 15.1, Box 5a) that relate to satisfaction are needs, values, and interests, and the environmental factors (Fig. 15.1, Box 5b) are rewards and reinforcers. The measures that Dawis and Lofquist (1984) suggested for assessing these environments provide a basis for commensurate measurement. Conceptually it is possible to link the higher-order needs of the individual (safety, comfort, status altruism, achievement, and autonomy) with the three sources of reinforcement from an environment (the external environment or job itself, the social or people element of the environment, and from the self; Alderfer 1972).

Higher-Order Needs   *Source of Reinforcement*

Safety
Comfort   } The physical environment

Status
Altruism   } The social environment

Autonomy
Achievement   } Self

In terms of social-cognitive theories, needs and motivation are operationalized as goals. Although not usually considered in PE fit theories, Lent and Brown (2006) highlight the importance of individual goal-setting behavior and the extent that people can set their own goals for achieving satisfaction at work and in general life domains. There is a rich history of research on goal setting that can be drawn upon to further enhance our understanding of adjustment at work (Locke and Latham 2002). In addition, we have previously argued that personality could also be included here (Hesketh and Griffin 2005), supported by recent findings that the Big Five factors of extroversion, neuroticism, and conscientiousness together explain 17 percent of the variance in job satisfaction (Judge, Heller, and Mount 2002).

Direct effects of the environment and the person on satisfaction were demonstrated in a longitudinal study by Bowling, Beehr, and Lepisto (2006). They found that both stable individual dispositions and temporal stability (remaining in an organization) predicted a range of affective work outcomes, including job satisfaction and organizational commitment, but that changing environments (moving to a different organization) altered these outcomes. Similarly, while environmental factors can affect levels of stress, for example Tytherleigh, Webb, and Cooper (2005) showed that those working in the higher-education sector had significantly more stress than those in other jobs; person variables such as negative affectivity can also have a direct effect on job stress (Spector, Zapf, and Chen 2000). Commensurate measurement facilitates an understanding of the direct contribution of the individual difference variables to satisfaction and well-being, the extent to which some environments result in better outcomes on average, and how individuals and environments interact.

The concept of fit in TWA comes into play in understanding how individual differences interact with the rewards and reinforcers that are available within a work environment. The ability of fit in relation to needs, values, and interests to explain adjustment outcomes has substantial support (e.g., Kristof-Brown, Zimmerman, and Johnson 2005). Nevertheless, methodological issues are critical in gaining an appropriate understanding of the complexity in what on the face appears a simple matter of fit. Edwards (1991), Evans (1991), and others have written extensively on this, yet many studies continue to ignore the danger of examining fit without controlling for the direct effects of the component parts.

Alternative approaches such as subgroup analysis may be useful where sample size permits (Clegg and Wall 1990).

7. Dynamic Component of the Theory of Work Adjustment

Dawis (2005) provides an updated version of the dynamic component of TWA, which includes two groups of style variables. The behavioral flavor underlying the theory points to the need to describe typical patterns of behavior that take on trait-like features (*personality style* variables) as well as direct behavioral responses to situations described as *adjustment style* variables. A review of the personality and adjustment style variables in TWA is essential in understanding this process component.

Personality style variables represent patterns of responding over longer periods of time and include: (1) *Celerity*, the typical quickness of response; (2) *Pace*, the typical intensity of a response; (3) *Rhythm*, the general pattern of responding; and (4) *Endurance*, the past pattern of persistence in responding that will influence the length of time that the response continues. These style variables can be applied to the responses of the individual or the environment.

Adjustment style variables, found more typically in relation to circumstances, or arising when mismatch reaches a trigger point, include: (1) *Flexibility*, the degree of misfit that can be tolerated by either the person or the environment before initiating efforts to make a change; (2) *Activeness*, efforts made to change another party (person or environment) in the adjustment process; (3) *Reactiveness*, efforts by the person or the environment to make internal changes in order to respond more appropriately to the other; and (4) *Perseverance*, how long one or other party continues to make the efforts to adjust either actively or reactively during an adjustment phase.

Within this general structure provided by the original TWA we argue that it is possible to measure different levels of flexibility in an environment. Flexible environments would tolerate more misfit than rigid environments. Parker (2000) suggests that some environments provide more diversity of opportunity for individuals to express their interests and use their skills and abilities and those with greater *flexible role orientation* have more potential for performing well in such environments.

Although an artificial separation, it is conceptually useful to think about TWA in two different states, namely a steady state and an adjustment state. In the steady state, reinforcers in the work environment are sufficient to satisfy the needs of the individual and the individual's supply of skills and abilities is sufficient to meet the job or environment requirements, resulting in tolerable satisfaction and perform-ance, and a continued interaction, as illustrated through tenure. Flexibility on the part of the individual and the organization is critical to understanding the degree of misfit that is tolerable in maintaining the steady state. In the adjustment state, either the individual's level of dissatisfaction, or the employer's level of dissatisfac-tion with performance will trigger active and reactive efforts to return to whatever "set point" is acceptable to both parties. The adjustment style variable of perse-verance should determine how long the parties will continue efforts to regain acceptable fit.

Given the growing importance of ICT in work contexts, we devote a later part of the chapter to exploring how technology can be used to enhance the supply of skills and abilities of the individual or equally change or reduce the job requirements on the individual. Similarly, ICT has made possible increased levels of telecommuting which has a major impact on the needs of an individual, and the capacity of employers to provide environments where these needs are met.

8. Variables Related to Adaptability

8.1 Selection

The TWA framework provides a structure for managing selection in contexts of change and uncertainty. In this section we review work that focuses on identifying individuals who can naturally adjust and adapt to change, as well as those with the capacity to benefit from training.

Just as cognitive ability is a good predictor of routine task performance, it also appears to be vital for adaptive performance (Allworth and Hesketh 1999; LePine, Colquitt, and Erez 2000; Pulakos et al. 2002). This is unsurprising given that cognitive ability is more predictive of complex than simple jobs and relates most strongly to performance early in one's appointment (Murphy 1989). Applicants with high levels of cognitive ability are more likely to manage the demands for rapid learning and transfer of skills required in dynamic environments (Hunter and Hunter 1984). Griffin and Hesketh (2003) suggest that a more specific ability in the cognitive domain that will predict adaptive performance is cognitive flexibility, or the capacity to inhibit a previously learned response in favor of a new and more appropriate response. This involves being able to generate a variety of possible responses to a new situation and choosing the best option.

It is less clear which personality factors relate well to adaptive performance. Despite the strong relationship between conscientiousness and task and contextual performance (Barrick and Mount 1993), there is growing evidence that it may be less effective in predicting performance in changing environments. Murphy (1996) suggested that because highly conscientious workers are likely to be conservative and rule bound they may find it difficult to function in a rapidly changing work environment. Recent research supports this argument, particularly in relation to some aspects of conscientiousness, such as dependability and orderliness (Griffin and Hesketh 2005). These findings alert us to the need to consider personality at a lower order than the Big Five for effective selection when the outcome of interest is also more specific than "overall job performance" (Ashton 1998). This may be particularly relevant when selecting for adaptive performance, given the unique demands of dynamic environments. Another of the Big Five personality factors, openness to experience, has attracted attention in relation to adaptability. Open individuals are described as being flexible and tolerant of change and different viewpoints (McCrae and Costa 1997), and they were more able to cope with organizational change (Judge et al. 1999) and perform adaptively in a complex laboratory task (LePine, Colquitt, and Erez 2000). There has also been a consistent relationship between openness and training performance suggesting that it can be used to identify those who are willing and able to participate in learning new tasks and technologies. However, consideration of openness at a facet, or lower-order level, may also be important (Griffin and Hesketh 2005). The usefulness of using more specific personality traits is further illustrated by research showing adaptive performance is associated with change receptiveness (Parker 2000), tolerance of ambiguity (Judge et al. 1999), proactive personality (Bateman and Crant 1993), and personal initiative (Frese et al. 1996).

Traditionally, measures of the individual factors related to needs and values (Fig. 15.1, Box 5a) have not been used as selection tools. Nevertheless, there are several motivation style factors that have been shown to be valid predictors of performance in the midst of change. For example, those who value lifelong learning and who are self-directed learners are likely to be particularly valuable (London and Mone 1999). Self-efficacy, which is the extent that one feels capable of performing certain behaviors (Parker 1998), has a reasonably strong relationship with adaptable outcomes such as coping with the introduction of new technology (Hill, Smith, and Mann 1987), adjustment to organizational settings (Saks 1995), change acceptance in the face of major restructuring (Wanberg and Banas 2000), and finding re-employment after job loss (Caplan et al. 1989). Parker (1998) argues that having the confidence to carry out a wider range of activities than would be expected in a traditional role is important in jobs that require competence across a number of areas. She termed this *role breadth self-efficacy* and showed that selection should focus on factors such as self-esteem, proactive personality, cognitive ability, and intrinsic motivation in order to identify those who are likely to develop high role breadth self-efficacy. A related construct, *flexible role orientation* (Parker 2000), describes people who are prepared to take on broader responsibilities and solve problems that relate to the wider organization's function. Those who had high levels of flexibility in this area were more likely to perform well in team roles.

Well-planned fit can quickly change (Furnham 2001) and selection that just focuses on optimizing fit for a job's current requirements risks hiring people with limited capacity to adjust to future demands. Consideration of the cognitive, personality, and motivational factors listed above will assist organizations in identifying those who can adapt quickly to changing job requirements in both the existing and aspirational work culture, who can tolerate potential misfit, and who are most likely to engage in reactive and proactive strategies to improve fit.

8.2 Training

In the past, training programs focused on teaching a person to perform a skill with little consideration of the complexities involved in transferring that learning to different contexts or to different tasks. Transfer of training becomes increasingly important in organizations that have rapidly changing skill requirements and where complex or novel problems and situations place high demands for adaptability on employees. Karaevli and Hall (2006) argue that managers in particular must develop adaptive expertise, which includes the ability to consider multiple interpretations of events, then differentiate and integrate these when making decisions. Much of the recent training literature has therefore focused attention on identifying training designs that maximize the development of adaptive expertise.

Training that engages the trainee in active processing is more effective in promoting adaptive transfer (Hesketh and Ivancic 2002). This requires careful thought in designing the learning environment so that trainees are provided with at least some structure to ensure that they know what the task is, but where there is sufficient uncertainty to ensure that they have to expend mental effort in identifying the problems and asking the questions as well as answering them. Getting the right balance between allowing trainees to flounder and providing excessively detailed information about what is to be learned is important, and suggests that consideration of motivational aspects is also necessary to increase the proactivity of the individual in their own training to ensure the active processing needed for adaptability.

Using errors in training is one way of engaging trainees in active processing. Error training focuses on using errors to aid learning (Dormann and Frese 1994). In addition to encouraging active processing, it is thought to be effective because errors are salient and memorable, provide immediate feedback, and assist in the development of accurate mental models (Hesketh 1997).

Exposure to multiple examples or problem types during training also helps trainees to abstract underlying principles and thereby develop accurate mental models of the problem domain (Hesketh 1997). Outside of formal training contexts, a similar effect might be obtained from providing employees with a variety of experiences. Norburn (1989) for example, showed that experience of a wide range of organizational contexts distinguished successful CEOs from their less successful subordinates. Similarly, Caligiuri (2006) reports that expatriates who are given rotational assignments in several different countries develop skills that enhance their leadership in both international and domestic contexts.

In higher education, where a purported aim is to develop lifelong learners, there has been a change in approach from the traditional lecture and tutorial/laboratory sessions to forms of problem-based learning where knowledge is discovered as part of solving a problem rather than being taught in discrete subject areas. Developments in many medical programs typify this, although the early pure problem-based approaches are being replaced with a mix of problem-based learning and structured content. Within training research studies conducted to explore the best way of combining rules and examples (Neal et al. 2006), there is support for combining structured content (if we liken this to rules) with problem-based approaches (examples).

Higher education teaching and learning approaches are trending toward the use of a variety of approaches that involve more active learning and effort on the part of learners. However, courses that require effortful learning (known to foster transfer; Hesketh 1997; Bjork 1995) are often rated as somewhat less enjoyable and may elicit less favorable feedback immediately after training, although participants often look back after a delay and recognize the value of these approaches. Although it is obviously important to provide courses that students rate positively, there are dangers in responding too readily to student feedback. Peer assessment, based on an evidenced approach to learning and transfer, will be a welcome supplement to the current focus on student feedback.

In any learning or staff development context in organizations "stretch assignments" are valuable as they enhance motivation, and provide opportunities for performance and creative decision making (Thompson, Hochwarter, and Mathys 1997).

The discussion above highlights the need to take motivational aspects of training into account when developing programs. Recent research suggests that the effectiveness of different types of training is also impacted by a Trainee by Training Design interaction. For example, Gully et al. (2002) found that encouraging highly conscientious individuals to make errors reduced their self-efficacy whereas discouraging error making for those high in openness to experience actually nullified the normal positive effects of openness on training outcomes. Loh et al. (2007) extended these results to show that those high in both cognitive ability and extroversion performed better in error encouragement conditions than in error avoidance conditions.

Opportunities exist to use technology to assist in targeting training and instructional content. Well-designed quizzes, answered through mobile phones, blackberries, or other IT tools, with software that integrates results immediately can inform a lecturer or trainer of the level of understanding of the audience, and allow them to adapt the material accordingly, or to target particular individuals who need support. It can also help identify those who need "stretch assignments." Advances in IT should help us tailor and adapt interventions to optimize the capabilities of individuals. This is where the future opportunities for enhanced productivity lie.

9. Information and Communication Technologies

Technology is ubiquitous in all spheres of work and life. Many technologies aim to adapt to user requirements and situational demands. In this section of the chapter we suggest that the TWA framework could be extended to take account of interactive adaptivity among people- and technology-based work contexts (Box 4c), and consider the implications of this for more traditional models of selection and training.

The issue can be highlighted through a discussion on the differences between performance and productivity. Performance is used extensively as one of the major criterion or outcome constructs in organizational psychology. We select to improve performance, train to improve performance, and, as discussed earlier, improvement in "fit" is evidenced by improvements in performance. Performance measures can be either subjective (peer, supervisory, and sometimes self-ratings, although the last mentioned is not recommended for many areas) or objective (sales, documents produced, items manufactured, etc.). If performance is to be used as a way of evaluating training, selection, ergonomic, or career interventions, it is important that the measure be uncontaminated by technology or the environment, and that it represent input from the person only. Hesketh and Neal (1999) have argued that this ideal is very difficult to achieve in the modern workplace where outputs are often an indistinguishable mix of the interaction between people, technology, and their work environment. It is an almost impossible task for any supervisor or even peer to provide a rating of performance that removes any input from technology. Rather, these judgments tend to be holistic, influenced by many factors other than pure performance, including the extent to which the individual may have benefited relative to others from more advanced technology.

Productivity tends to be used at an organizational or even national level as a descriptor for the output obtained from the interaction between people and their work environments. At its simplest, if one can reduce the workforce but continue the same level of output, then productivity has increased. More constructively, increases in productivity can come from clever work design, improved internal and external communications, advances in supply chain management, and of course, specific improvements in a range of technologies. The term productivity allows the confounding of people, their environments, and technology in a way that performance does not. We would argue that in terms of selection and training, the focus now should be on increasing the individual difference capacity to stretch the technology and get the most out of it, or to work most effectively with the environment to achieve enhanced performance and productivity. The focus is on both the direct contribution from the individual as well as the interaction between the individual and the technology or environment that is available. This highlights the importance of conceptual clarity in understanding the various components of fit raised earlier in the chapter.

In TWA tradition, one should also consider environments that are able to adapt to individuals to increase performance and productivity. Most common examples can be found in motor vehicle design research where the use of eye monitors to detect sleepy drivers coupled with an appropriate intervention are being trialed. One might also conceptualize vehicles that learn typical errors of their drivers and provide adequate compensatory action or warning. More commonly, we have all experienced the unfortunate consequence of some of the word processing software's attempts to second guess what we need! In high-stakes environments (nuclear power plants, etc.), having both the individual and the technology in the environment on adaptive alert, as it were, will become important.

In a technologically rich environment, it may not be sufficient to select staff using traditional testing approaches alone, even though there is a high probability that higher-ability employees are more likely to also extract more productivity from technology. Selection may need to include an adaptive (or stretch) component, such as outlined in the section above. Once selected, quite specific training may be needed to help all staff recognize their own capability level, and also the capacity of the technologies with which they work to stretch that capability to enhance their own performance and productivity generally.

10. FUTURE DIRECTIONS

Industrial and organizational psychology has made enormous advances over the past 100 years. As is often the case these advances arise from increased and important specialization and incremental research, but this is sometimes at the expense of the bigger picture of people and their work organizations. We would argue that there is value in broader frameworks that require researchers to keep asking about context, and to understand that the specific issue they are examining always exists in a broader context, including the context of what is happening in allied fields such as technology and biotechnology. People work in work groups, but work groups are part of larger organizations, and organizations exist in society. Technology has had and will continue to have a pervasive influence at every level. We hope that the updated TWA framework, and its potential to accommodate further changes, will assist researchers in considering contexts.

Specifically, we suggest that future research should address the ways in which technology interacts with individual differences to enhance performance and productivity, and in increasing adaptability. We think that an important aim of future training research will be in exploring how best to exploit individual differences and technology enhancements to increase performance and productivity. Research will need to be specific, and may require a rethinking of some of the more traditional models used in organizational research. Different components of individual variability may become important as we learn how technology can enhance capacity. There may need to be a degree of adaptability in organizational psychology models and approaches to permit this invasion by technology into the domain, but in ways that retain important ethical standards. Although this chapter does not address the implications for organizational psychology of the biotechnology and genetic advances, the issues for adaptability are the same. Already there is discussion about using genetic profiles as part of selection, which may, in some cases be ethically justifiable, but in others not. Unless organizational psychologists are abreast of these developments and issues, and unless we have appropriate research to inform comment, it will be difficult to contribute evidence-based approaches to the debate in future. These are issues that need research.

REFERENCES

ALDERFER, C. P. 1972. *Existence, Relatedness, and Growth: Human Needs in Organizational Settings.* New York: Free Press.

ALLWORTH, E. A., and HESKETH, B. 1999. Construct-oriented biodata: capturing change-related and contextually relevant future performance. *International Journal of Selection and Assessment,* 7: 97–111.

ASHTON, M. C. 1998. Personality and job performance: the importance of narrow traits. *Journal of Organizational Behavior,* 19: 289–303.

BARRICK, M. R., and MOUNT, M. K. 1991. The big five personality dimensions and job performance: a meta-analysis. *Personnel Psychology,* 44: 1–25.

BARRICK, M. R., and MOUNT, M. K. 1993. Autonomy as a moderator of the relationships between the big five personality dimensions and job performance. *Journal of Applied Psychology*, 78 (1): 111–18.

——— and JUDGE, T. A. 2001. Personality and performance at the beginning of the new millennium: what do we know and where do we go next? *International Journal of Selection and Assessment*, 9 (1/2): 9–30.

BATEMAN, T. S., and CRANT, J. M. 1993. The proactive component of organizational behavior: a measure and correlates. *Journal of Organizational Behavior*, 14: 103–18.

BERRY, C. M., ONES, D. S., and SACKETT, P. R. 2007. Interpersonal deviance, organizational deviance, and their common correlates: a review and meta-analysis. *Journal of Applied Psychology*, 92 (2): 410–24.

BJORK, R. A. 1995. Memory and meta-memory considerations in the training of human beings. Pp. 185–285 in *Metacognition: Knowing about knowing*, ed. J. Metcalfe and A. P. Shimamura. Cambridge, MA: MIT Press.

BORMAN, W. C., and MOTOWIDLO, S. J. 1993. Expanding the criterion domain to include elements of contextual performance. In *Personnel Selection in Organizations*, ed. N. Schmitt, W. C. Borman, et al. San Francisco: Jossey-Bass Publishers.

——— ——— 1997. Task performance and contextual performance: the meaning for personnel selection research. *Human Performance*, 10 (2): 99–109.

BOWLING, N. A., BEEHR, T. A., and LEPISTO, L. R. 2006. Beyond job satisfaction: a five year prospective analysis of the dispositional approach to work adjustment. *Journal of Vocational Behavior*, 69: 315–30.

CALIGIURI, P. 2006. Developing global leaders. *Human Resource Management Review*, 16 (2): 219–28.

CAMPBELL, J. P., McHENRY, J. J., and WISE, L. L. 1990. Modeling job performance in a population of jobs. Special issue: Project A: The US Army Selection and Classification Project. *Personnel Psychology*, 43 (2): 313–33.

CAPLAN, R. D., VINOKUR, A. D., PRICE, R. H., and van RYN, M. 1989. Job seeking, reemployment, and mental health: a randomized field experiment in coping with job loss. *Journal of Applied Psychology*, 74: 759–69.

CLEGG, C., and WALL, T. 1990. The relationship between simplified jobs and mental health: a replication study. *Journal of Occupational Psychology*, 63: 289–96.

COOPER, C. L., DEWE, P. J., and O'DRISCOLL, M. P. 2001. *Organizational Stress: A Review and Critique of Theory, Research, and Applications*. Thousand Oaks, CA: Sage.

DAWIS, R. V. 2005. The Minnesota Theory of Work Adjustment. In *Career Development and Counseling: Putting Theory and Research to Work*, ed. S. D. Brown and R. W. Lent. New York: Wiley.

——— and LOFQUIST, L. H. 1984. *A Psychological Theory of Work Adjustment*. Minneapolis: University of Minnesota Press.

DICKSON, M. W., RESICK, C. J., and HANGES, P. J. 2006. When organizational climate is unambiguous, it is also strong. *Journal of Applied Psychology*, 91: 351–64.

DORMANN, T., and FRESE, M. 1994. Error training: replication and the function of exploratory behavior. *International Journal of Human-Computer Interaction*, 6 (4): 365–72.

EDWARDS, J. 1991. Person–job fit. In *International Review of Industrial and Organizational Psychology 1991*, ed. C. Cooper and I. Robertson. Chichester: Wiley.

EVANS, M. G. 1991. The problem of analysing multiplicative composites: interactions revisited. *American Psychologist*, 46: 6–15.

FRESE, M., KRING, W., SOOSE, A., and ZEMPEL, J. 1996. Personal initiative at work: differences between East and West Germany. *Academy of Management Journal*, 39 (1): 37–64.

FRITZSCHE, B. A., and PARRISH, T. J. 2005. Theories and research on job satisfaction. Pp. 180–202 in *Career Development and Counseling: Putting Theory and Research to Work*, ed. S. D. Brown and R. W. Lent. Hoboken, NJ: John Wiley and Sons Inc.

FURNHAM, A. 2001. Vocational preference and P–O fit: reflections on Holland's theory of vocational choice. Special issue: Person–Organisation Fit. *Applied Psychology: An International Review*, 50 (1): 5–29.

GRIFFIN, B. and HESKETH, B. 2003. Adaptable behaviours for successful work and career adjustment. *Australian Journal of Psychology*, 55 (2): 65–73.

—— —— 2004. Why openness to experience is not a good predictor of job performance. *International Journal of Selection and Assessment*, 12 (3): 243–51.

—— —— 2005. Are conscientious workers adaptable? *Australian Journal of Management*, 30 (2): 1–15.

—— NEAL, A., and PARKER, S. K. 2007. A new model of work role performance: positive behavior in uncertain and interdependent contexts. *Academy of Management Journal*, 50 (2): 327–47.

GULLY, S. M., PAYNE, S. C., KOLES, K. L. K., and WHITEMAN, J. K. 2002. The impact of error training and individual differences on training outcomes: an attribute-treatment interaction perspective. *Journal of Applied Psychology*, 87: 143–55.

HESKETH, B. 1997. Dilemmas in training for transfer and retention. *Applied Psychology: An International Review*, 46: 317–39.

—— and DAWIS, R. 1991. The Minnesota Theory of Work Adjustment: a conceptual framework. In *Psychological Perspectives on Occupational Health and Rehabilitation*, ed. B. Hesketh and A. Adams. Marrickville, NSW: Harcourt Brace Jovanovich.

—— and GRIFFIN, B. 2005. Work adjustment. In *Handbook of Vocational Psychology, vol. iii*, ed. W. B. Walsh and M. L. Savickas. Hillsdale, NJ: Lawrence Erlbaum Associates.

—— and IVANCIC, K. 2002. Enhancing performance through training. In *Psychological Measurement of Individual Performance*, ed. S. Sonnentag. London: John Wiley and Sons, Ltd.

—— and NEAL, A. 1999. Technology and performance. In Pp. 21–55 in *The Changing Nature of Work Performance: Implications for Staffing, Motivation and Development*, ed. D. Ilgen and E. D. Pulakos. Society for Industrial and Organizational Psychology New Frontiers Series. San Francisco: Jossey Bass.

HILL, T., SMITH, N. D., and MANN, M. F. 1987. Role of efficacy expectations in predicting the decision to use advanced technologies. *Journal of Applied Psychology*, 72: 307–14.

HOLLAND, J. L. 1973. *Making Vocational Choices: A Theory of Careers*. Englewood Cliffs, NJ: Prentice Hall.

—— 1985. *Making Vocational Choices: A Theory of Vocational Personalities and Work Environments*. Englewood Cliffs, NJ: Prentice Hall.

HOUGH, L. M., and OSWALD, F. L. 2000. Personnel selection: looking toward the future— remembering the past. *Annual Review of Psychology*, 51: 631–64.

HULIN, C. L., and JUDGE, T. A. 2003. Job attitudes. Pp. 255–76 in *Handbook of Psychology: Industrial and Organizational Psychology, vol. xii*, ed. W. C. Borman, D. R. Ilgen, and R. Klimoski. New York: Wiley.

HUNTER, J. E., and HUNTER, R. F. 1984. Validity and utility of alternative predictors of job performance. *Psychological Bulletin*, 96 (1): 72–98.

JOHNS, G. 2002. The psychology of lateness, absenteeism, and turnover. Pp. 232–52 in *Handbook of Industrial, Work and Organizational Psychology*, ii: *Organizational Psychology*, ed. N. Anderson, D. S. Ones, H. K. Sinangil, and C. Viswesvaran. Thousand Oaks, CA: Sage Publications, Inc.

JUDGE, T. A., HELLER, D., and MOUNT, M. K. 2002. Five-factor model of personality and job satisfaction: a meta-analysis. *Journal of Applied Psychology*, 87: 530–41.

—— THORESEN, C. J., PUCIK, V., and WELBOURNE, T. M. 1999. Managerial coping with organizational change: a dispositional perspective. *Journal of Applied Psychology*, 84 (1): 107–22.

KARAEVLI, A., and HALL, D. T. T. 2006. How career variety promotes the adaptability of managers: a theoretical model. *Journal of Vocational Behavior*, 69: 359–73.

KRISTOF-BROWN, A. L., ZIMMERMAN, R. D., and JOHNSON, E. C. 2005. Consequences of individuals' fit at work: a meta-analysis of person–job, person–organisation, person–group, and person–supervisor fit. *Personnel Psychology*, 58: 281–342.

LENT, R. W., and BROWN, S. D. 2006. Integrating person and situation perspectives on work satisfaction: a social-cognitive view. *Journal of Vocational Behavior*, 69: 236–47.

LEPINE, J. A., COLQUITT, J. A., and EREZ, A. 2000. Adaptability to changing task contexts: effects of general cognitive ability, conscientiousness, and openness to experience. *Personnel Psychology*, 53 (3): 563–93.

LOCKE, E. A., and LATHAM, G. P. 2002. Building a practically useful theory of goal setting and task motivation: a 35-year odyssey. *American Psychologist*, 57 (9): 705–17.

LOFQUIST, L. H., and DAWIS, R. V. 1969. *Adjustment to Work*. New York: Appleton-Century Crofts.

LOH, V., ANDREWS, S., HESKETH, B., and GRIFFIN, B. 2007. Person attributes in error training: who learns from their mistakes? Paper presented at the 22nd Annual Conference of the Society for Industrial and Organizational Psychology, New York.

LONDON, M., and MONE, E. M. 1999. Continuous learning. In *The Changing Nature of Performance*, ed. D. R. Ilgen and E. D. Pulakos. San Francisco: Jossey-Bass Publishers.

MCCRAE, R. R., and COSTA, P. T. 1997. Conceptions and correlates of openness to experience. Pp. 825–47 in *Handbook of Personality Psychology*, ed. R. Hogan, R. Johnson, and S. Briggs. San Diego: Academic Press, Inc.

MISCHEL, W. 1976. Towards a cognitive social model of learning reconceptualization of personality. Pp. 166–207 in *Interactional Psychology and Personality*, ed. N. S. Endler and D. Magnusson. New York: Wiley.

MURPHY, K. R. 1989. Is the relationship between cognitive ability and job performance stable over time? *Human Performance*, 2: 183–200.

—— 1996. Individual differences and behaviour in organizations: much more than g. Pp. 3–29 in *Individual Differences and Behaviour in Organizations*, ed. K. R. Murphy. San Francisco: Jossey-Bass Publishers.

NEAL, A., GODLEY, S. T., KIRKPATRICK, T., DEWSNAP, G., JOUNG, W., and HESKETH, B. 2006. An examination of learning processes during critical incident training: implications for the development of adaptable trainees. *Journal of Applied Psychology*, 91 (6): 1276–91.

NORBURN, D. 1989. The chief executive: a breed apart. *Strategic Management Journal*, 10: 1–15.

PARKER, S. K. 1998. Enhancing role breadth self-efficacy: the roles of job enrichment and other organizational interventions. *Journal of Applied Psychology*, 83 (6): 835–52.

—— 2000. From passive to proactive motivation: the importance of Flexible Role Orientations and Role Breadth Self-Efficacy. *Applied Psychology: An International Review*, 49 (3): 447–69.

PIASENTIN, K. A., and CHAPMAN, D. S. 2006. Subjective person–organization fit: bridging the gap between conceptualization and measurement. *Journal of Vocational Behavior*, 69: 202–21.

PODSAKOFF, P. M., MACKENZIE, S. B., PAINE, J. B., and BACHRACH, D. G. 2000. Organizational citizenship behaviors: a critical review of the theoretical and empirical literature and suggestions for future research. *Journal of Management*, 26: 513–63.

PULAKOS, E. D., ARAD, S., DONOVAN, M. A., and PLAMONDON, K. E. 2000. Adaptability in the workplace: development of a taxonomy of adaptive performance. *Journal of Applied Psychology*, 85 (4): 612–24.

—— SCHMITT, N., DORSEY, D. W., ARAD, S., HEDGE, J. W., and BORMAN, W. C. 2002. Predicting adaptive performance: further tests of a model of adaptability. *Human Performance*, 15 (4): 299–323.

SAKS, A. M. 1995. Longitudinal field investigation of the moderating and mediating effects of self-efficacy on the relationship between training and newcomer adjustment. *Journal of Applied Psychology*, 80 (2): 211–25.

SCHMIDT, F. L., and HUNTER, J. E. 1998. The validity and utility of selection methods in personnel psychology: practical and theoretical implications of 85 years of research findings. *Psychological Bulletin*, 124 (2): 262–74.

—— —— 2004. General mental ability in the world of work: occupational attainment and job performance. *Journal of Personality and Social Psychology*, 86 (1): 162–73.

SCHNEIDER, B., SALVAGGIO, A. N., and SUBIRATS, M. 2002. Climate strength: a new direction for climate research. *Journal of Applied Psychology*, 87: 220–9.

SPECTOR, P. E., ZAPF, D., and CHEN, P. Y. 2000. Why negative affectivity should not be controlled in job stress research: don't throw out the baby with the bath water. *Journal of Organizational Behavior*, 21 (1): 79–95.

TETT, R. P., JACKSON, D. N., and ROTHSTEIN, M. 1991. Personality measures as predictors of job performance: a meta-analytic review. *Personnel Psychology*, 44: 703–42.

THOMPSON, K. R., HOCHWARTER, W. A., and MATHYS, N. J. 1997. Stretch targets: what makes them effective? *Academy of Management Executive*, 11 (3): 48–60.

TYTHERLEIGH, M. Y., WEBB, C., and COOPER, C. L. 2005. Occupational stress in UK higher education institutions: a comparative study of all staff categories. *Higher Education Research and Development*, 24 (1): 41–61.

TZINER, A., and MEIR, E. I. 1997. Work adjustment: extension of the theoretical framework. In *International Review of Industrial and Organizational Psychology*, vol. xii, ed. C. I Cooper and I. T. Robertson. London: John Wiley and Sons Ltd.

WANBERG, C. R., and BANAS, J. T. 2000. Predictors and outcomer of openness to changes in a reorganized workplace. *Journal of Applied Psychology*, 85 (1): 132–42.

—— and KAMMEYER-MUELLER, J. D. 2000. Predictors and outcomes of proactivity in the socialization process. *Journal of Applied Psychology*, 85 (3): 373–85.

THE INFLUENCE OF ORGANIZATIONAL POLITICS ON PERFORMANCE APPRAISAL

GARY P. LATHAM

SILVIA DELLO RUSSO

1. INTRODUCTION

THE fact that the politics inherent in organizational behavior affect an employee's appraisal was noted more than a quarter of a century ago by behavioral scientists (e.g., Gandz and Murray 1980). Nevertheless, there is a paucity of systematic research on this subject. Thus the purpose of the present chapter is fourfold. First, the phenomenon of organizational politics is described. Second, studies on the relationship between political behavior and appraising employees are reviewed. Third, steps to minimizing its adverse effects on the appraisal of employees are outlined. Finally, a research agenda is suggested.

Preparation of this chapter was supported in part by a grant to the first author from the Social Sciences and Humanities Research Council, Canada.

2. ORGANIZATIONAL POLITICS

Political behaviors in organizations consist of self-serving actions taken by an individual or group (Mintzberg 1983). They are directed toward the goal of furthering one's own self-interest without regard for the well-being of others in the organization (Kacmar and Baron 1999). Such actions are informal and, as part of an organization's culture, regulate interpersonal relationships. As Mayes and Allen (1977) noted, the actions imply a dynamic power of influence. When this influence is exercised within organizational sanctioned boundaries, the behaviors are not considered political.

Examples of political behavior in the workplace include self-promotion and ingratiation (Godfrey, Jones, and Lord 1986). Self-promotion behaviors are typically proactive. Their purpose is to gain attention, to create an image of oneself as a competent committed employee. Ingratiation behaviors are less proactive. They focus on "attention giving" to a target person or persons relative to "attention getting" from others. A recent study found that politically skilled employees who engage in ingratiatory behavior toward their supervisors were not only viewed positively by them, they were subsequently rewarded for doing so (Treadway et al. 2007). In fact, career success is typically affected by an ability to convince others that one has the requisite skills to perform higher-level jobs effectively (Rafaeli et al. 1997). Self-promotion is one way to do this.

A dramatic illustration of non-sanctioned action was provided in *The Times*:

> Deep down we all suspect that it is the brutal, simple ugly stuff that really gets us to the top of the tribal tree. You can work hard, network nicely, and try to merit everything you told the performance-appraisal team, but all the time your dark side is wheedling to get ahead. (Naish 2005)

Despite its hyperbolic overtone, this quote resonates with what has been reported in the academic literature. Wortman and Linsenmeier (1977) argued that employees engage in impression management to advance their personal interests, often at the expense of the organization. Moreover, political behavior appears to be pervasive in the workplace (Longenecker 1989). And this behavior is not confined to the employee. The employee's supervisor may also engage in this process.

Longenecker, Sims, and Gioia (1987) conducted in-depth interviews with upper-level executives employed by well-known corporations. The authors obtained an admission from these executives that they consciously manipulate their performance ratings of the people who report to them. Moreover, these executives argued that an appraisal instrument that permits discretion and flexibility was more important to them than one that facilitates accuracy. When organizational earnings were down, they frequently lowered their rating of a high-performing subordinate so as to justify a lower than deserved compensation decision. Hence, Folger, Konovsky, and

Cropanzano (1992) concluded that a performance appraisal is essentially a political process involving two or more parties with different interests regarding the allocation of resources.

Maier (1955) argued that performance is a function of ability and motivation. Similarly, Mintzberg (1983) argued that a person's political behavior is a function of political skill, namely, the ability to successfully execute political actions, and a person's political will, namely, the motivation to do so.

2.1 Measurement

Ferris and his colleagues developed and validated an instrument for assessing organizational politics, Perceptions of Organizational Politics or POPs (Kacmar and Ferris 1991). The construct and discriminant validity of the scale has been shown to be adequate. With regard to the construct, Kacmar and Carlson (1997) found that it is multi rather than unidimensional. The first dimension they labeled "general political behavior," namely, self-serving actions taken by people to attain their own goals. The second dimension, "go along to get ahead," refers to the lack of action people take (e.g., withholding needed information) in order to realize the attainment of one or more of their goals. The third dimension, "pay and promotion politics," refers to organizational practices that result in a culture in which political activity becomes commonplace.

With regard to discriminant validity, Andrews and Kacmar (2001) found that organizational politics is different from, yet negatively related to, perceptions of distributive and procedural justice (Cropanzano and Greenberg 1997), as well as perceptions of organizational support (Eisenberger et al. 1986). Although the correlation between perceptions of politics and organizational support was negative ($r = -.72$) as were the correlations between engaging in political behavior and distributive and procedural justice ($r = -.43, -.48$ respectively), a confirmatory factor analysis revealed four different concepts each having different predictors.

2.2 Predictors of Political Behaviors

Ferris, Russ, and Fandt (1989) proposed a model of predictors of organizational political behavior. In the above study, Andrews and Kacmar (2001) tested the model. They found empirical evidence that the following variables correlate with organizational politics: external locus of control ($r = .54$), co-worker cooperation ($r = -.29$), centralization ($r = .29$), formalization ($r = -.16$), and leader member exchange or LMX ($r = .11$). The latter correlation was contrary to the researcher's hypothesis. It is likely that LMX enhances perceptions of organizational politics because it makes salient to all parties the difference in treatment employees in in-versus out-groups receive from their supervisor. Mohrman and Lawler (1983) reported that managers are more likely to exercise discretion in their performance appraisals of employees with whom they have a close relationship than they are for those with whom they are distant.

Mintzberg's (1983) assumption that political will is an antecedent of political behavior was tested by Treadway et al. (2005b). They operationalized political will as need for achievement and intrinsic motivation because, they said, the willingness to pursue one's self-interest is likely consistent with the need to excel. The results from two questionnaires administered at two points in time revealed that 33 percent of the variance associated with political behavior was explained by a person's intrinsic motivation and need for achievement.

2.3 Outcomes

The outcomes of perceptions of an organization rife with internal political behavior are for the most part negative.

(a) Cropanzano et al. (1997) found that organizational politics correlated with turnover intentions in two studies, one with full-time employees and the other with part-time workers (.49 and .29, respectively).

(b) Using a sample from a cross-section of organizational data, Ferris and Kacmar (1992) found that organizational politics correlated negatively with job satisfaction ($r = -.29$) as well as job involvement ($r = -.19$). Moreover, in a second investigation with a sample of nurses, they found that co-workers and cliques' political behavior correlated negatively and significantly with job satisfaction ($r = -.60$).

(c) Vigoda-Gadot (2000) found that perceptions of organizational politics predicted both in-role and OCB performance six months later. Employees with lower perceptions of organizational politics tended to perform better than those with high perceptions. Higher perceptions of organizational politics are associated with strain and low morale (Vigoda-Gadot 2002). It appears that these employees feel they have to expend cognitive resources on ways to cope with the issues that arise from the self-serving behaviors of others.

(d) In a study involving two different public sector organizations, Vigoda-Gadot, Vinarski-Peretz, and Ben-Zion (2003) found that organizational politics is a precondition for the formation of a negative organizational image. Employee perceptions of politics correlated negatively with job satisfaction and organizational commitment which in turn mediated the relationship with the image employees have of their employer.

(e) Turnover intentions and counter-productive work behavior are distal outcomes of organizational politics (Rosen, Levy, and Johnson 2007).

An arguably positive outcome of perceptions of organizational politics was suggested by Harrell-Cook, Ferris, and Dulebohn (1999). They hypothesized that an upside of this behavior is that it gives employees a tacit understanding of how the organization truly works versus the way it says it works regarding its processes and procedures for obtaining hard-to-acquire resources. They reported a positive interaction between perceived organizational politics and political behaviors (ingratiation, self-promotion) on the part of nurses that appears to mitigate the negative effects on job satisfaction and intention to leave the organization.

2.4 Mediators

Given the negative consequences of engaging in political behavior, why does it occur? The explanation is at least twofold. First, perceived organizational support, or the lack thereof, has been found to fully mediate the relationship between perceived political behavior at the highest level of the organization and an employee's negative affective organizational commitment, job tension, job satisfaction, and performance (Hochwarter et al. 2003). This explanation is congruent with a second inference that can be drawn from correlational studies regarding employee perceptions of having little or no control over their job environment. Harrell-Cook, Ferris, and Dulebohn (1999) found that employees engage in political behaviors as a coping mechanism. That is, they engage in ingratiatory behavior. Giving attention to their superiors is seen as instrumental for goal attainment. If this political behavior on their part is not effective, they are likely to quit their job.

2.5 Moderators

What environmental and individual difference variables increase or decrease the likelihood of organizational politics?

2.5.1 Environmental

Ferris et al. (1989) developed a conceptual model that asserts that perceptions of control over one's environment buffer the effects of organizational politics. A subsequent study suggests that this is indeed the case. Ferris et al. (1996) found that perceived control moderated the relationship between perceptions of politics and job anxiety, general job satisfaction, and satisfaction with one's supervisor.

Harris and Kacmar (2005) found that a supportive supervisor acts as a buffer against the stress employees experience from organizational politics. Likewise, goal congruence between a supervisor and an employee reduces the negative consequences of organizational politics on job performance. Explaining relevant issues, and clarifying instructions increase an employee's understanding and sense of control over the workplace (Witt 1998).

Organizational structure, in terms of centralization and formalization, is related to perceptions of political behavior. Andrews and Kacmar (2001) reported that the degree of centralization correlates positively ($r = .56$, $p < .05$) with organizational politics. Several studies support the argument that politics emerges in an environment where procedures are ill defined (e.g., Mayes and Allen 1977). These procedures include interdepartmental coordination, delegation of authority, promotion, and transfers; on the other hand, outcomes such as hiring and disciplining employees are seen as less politically motivated (Gandz and Murray 1980). Formalization correlates negatively with perceptions of politics. When there is high role ambiguity, employees often engage in organizational citizenship behaviors directed toward the organization, but not toward fellow employees. They do so to impress their respective bosses (Yun, Takeuchi, and Liu 2007). Whether their motivation to do so is a benefit to the employing organization in the same ways as are OCBs stemming from actual concern for the organization as well as one's social values is debatable.

Given these early findings, it is not surprising that perceptions of organizational justice are related to perceptions of political behavior. Implicit in the construct of organizational politics are employee perceptions that the work environment is unfair, it is unjust.

Where one is in the organizational hierarchy moderates justice perceptions (Bengley, Lee, and Hui 2006). People in higher-level jobs believe that distributive justice is more important than procedural justice because they need adequate resources for their organizational unit's effectiveness. Moreover, receiving adequate resources means having power in the organization. People in lower-level jobs believe that procedural justice is more important than distributive justice because the extent to which they are treated fairly affects their self-identity and self-esteem as important members of the organization.

Employees perceive more political behavior at higher rather than lower managerial levels. Gandz and Murray (1980) reported that lower-level employees see themselves as the victims of organizational politics.

Finally, organizational politics have been shown to be expressions and reflections of an organization's culture (Ferris et al. 1989). The "organizational context" perceived at a given point in time is the result of previous "political games" (Frost 1987). A major way that culture is communicated to employees is through its human resource procedures, including performance appraisals (Tichy 1983).

2.5.2 *Individual differences*

An external locus of control correlates positively with perceptions of politics (Andrews and Kacmar 2001; Moberg 1978). Conscientiousness has been shown to be related to job performance for only those employees who perceive a high level of organizational politics; no relationship was found for those people who perceived little or no political behavior (Hochwarter, Witt, and Kacmar 2000). Bozeman et al. (2001) found that people with high self-efficacy regarding their job performance experience job dissatisfaction and low organizational commitment when they perceive that their peers are rewarded on the basis of political skill rather than merit. The interaction effect between perceived self-efficacy and a perceived political environment explained an additional 4 percent of the variance in the measure of job satisfaction and 5 percent of the variance in the measure of organizational commitment.

People with negative affectivity appear to be adversely affected by their perceptions of politics ($r = -.77$), relative to their peers who score high on a measure of positive affectivity ($r = -.44$). This was true, however, for job satisfaction rather than performance (Hochwarter and Treadway 2003). People who score high on negativity (negative affectivity) are predisposed to see the downsides in almost everything, including their job. Performance, on the other hand, was worse for those who scored high on positive rather than negative affect. Because of their predisposition to see that which is good in their organization, these employees expect fair and equal treatment based on merit. When events prove otherwise, they may experience dissonance and their performance drops.

Using two sets of questionnaires at two different points in time, Treadway et al. (2005a) found that age moderates the effect of perceived politics on a person's job performance. They interpreted this finding as suggesting that older people feel they have fewer resources than their younger colleagues to cope with the stress induced by a politically charged climate. Older employees often lack resiliency from their over-exposure to this source of job stress. It is also likely that older employees who have not been promoted to upper management positions are disillusioned because of their perception of having been adversely affected by organizational politics.

In a study of office and technical employees, as well as managers, Hochwarter et al. (1999) examined the moderating effect of affective organizational commitment. Their results indicate that highly committed lower-level employees experienced less job tension from organizational politics than their less committed peers. Moreover, the job tension of middle and upper-level managers who were highly committed to their organization actually decreased when they perceived an increase in organizational politics. This may be because these people have more control over their environment than do lower-level employees. This in turn may enable them to act politically to attain their desired goals. In doing so, they create and perpetuate a culture that embraces organizational politics by modeling this behavior for their subordinates. Acting politically to gain desired outcomes becomes "accepted" practice. Kacmar, Collins, and Harris (2007) examined the moderating effects of the person and the environment on political behavior. Using correlational data, involving state government employees, they found that individuals who scored high on core self-evaluation (Judge, Locke, and Durham 1997) engaged in more ingratiatory behavior than those who scored low, when they viewed their environment as more rather than less political. This suggests that in a highly political environment, employees shift their attention from the job to less productive behaviors.

Rosen, Chang, and Levy (2006) using a person-based, interactionist approach concluded that organizational politics do not lead to negative outcomes for everyone. Some people respond in more positive ways than others to perceptions of politics. Their correlational data suggest that high self-monitors and those who score high on agreeableness see the political environment as an opportunity to enhance their image with supervisors; and do so by engaging in OCBs.

2.6 Summary

A gap in this literature is the lack of knowledge on the effect of different pay plans on the prevalence of organizational politics. Is political behavior affected differentially by pay plans that reward the individual, the team, or both the individual and the team? The answer awaits further research.

A further limitation of the extant research is that it consists for the most part of correlational studies. Hence, the direction of causality is not known. A third limitation of studies in organizational politics that all but screams at the reader is the problem of common method variance and its concomitant, percept-percept correlations. Hence, the correlations reported in many of these studies are likely inflated. Arguably, it is difficult to conduct experiments on this phenomenon where one or more independent variables are manipulated to see the effect on one or more dependent variables. Yet, two or more methods could be used in future studies (e.g., questionnaire and an interview) where data are collected at different points in time from samples from two or more populations (e.g., boss, peers, subordinates). Experiments could also be conducted using simulations similar, if not identical, to those used at the Center for Creative Leadership[1] as well as those typically used in an assessment center.

Despite the methodological limitations of many of the above studies, the consistency of the findings, collected for the most part in organizational settings, are impressive, and the expertise of the researchers (e.g., Ferris) in interpreting the data is beyond question. Organizational politics appears to be pervasive and for the most part pernicious. It is negatively related to job performance, OCB, job satisfaction, intention to remain in the organization, etc. It appears to occur for at least two reasons, a desire to gain control over one's environment and as a way to cope in an environment where organizational support is seen as lacking, an environment that lacks codified procedures. It is also likely to be found when the organization is centralized and informal, and where people have concluded they are not part of the

---

[1] The Center for Creative Leadership is a non-profit educational/research organization headquartered in Greensboro, NC, with branch offices in Brussels, Colorado Springs, San Diego, and Singapore.

in-group. It is moderated by where one is in the hierarchy, one's relationship with one's supervisor, and one's age. All of these factors are likely to be relevant to the process of appraising employees. Yet to date there is a paucity of studies that have systematically examined the effect of organizational politics on the conduct of performance appraisals and the subsequent behavior of the employees.

3. PERFORMANCE APPRAISAL AND ORGANIZATIONAL POLITICS

Research on performance appraisal has been ongoing since the outset of the twentieth century (Farr and Levy 2007; Patterson 1922; 1923). The focus has been on improving the appraisal scale, the accuracy of the rater, the rater's cognitive processes, and feedback to the employee (Latham and Mann 2006; Latham, Sulsky, and MacDonald 2007). This may be because performance appraisals are currently used in 90 percent of organizations for making administrative decisions regarding an organization's employees (Bernthal et al. 1997).

In an enumerative review of the performance appraisal literature, Latham and Mann (2006) found studies that indicated that appraisals were a stronger reflection of a rater's overall biases than of an employee's job performance, that a person's knowledge and skill accounted for only a small amount of the variance in an appraisal decision, and that a woman's appraisal is affected by her gender, especially when the appraiser is male. In a field study of over 1,000 managerial employees, Landau (1995) reported that females were rated lower than males, and blacks and Asians were rated lower than whites even after controlling for an employee's age, education, tenure, salary grade, functional area, and satisfaction with support for one's career. Politics per se was not examined in these studies.

The role that organizational politics plays in the appraisal process is only now beginning to be studied. Identifying the social context in which a performance appraisal occurs is important for both theory and practice. The social context of a performance appraisal is typically conceptualized as the social-psychological processes operating in the relationship between a rater and a ratee (Murphy and Cleveland 1991). Because of this relationship, the procedures inherent in a performance appraisal cannot be improved solely through the development and application of appraisal scales, let alone training initiatives to minimize a rater's cognitive biases. Moreover, as discussed above, performance appraisals are affected by an organization's culture, and at the same time contribute to this culture. For this reason, a performance appraisal is an activity where organizational politics are likely to take place, yet it has been a relatively neglected area of study.

As noted earlier, Kacmar and Carlson (1997) emphasized three features of organizational politics: (1) It is a process through which individuals exercise social influence; (2) aimed at obtaining scarce resources; and (3) through social interactions involving at least two parties. On the basis of these features, the process of conducting performance appraisals would appear to be a "hot-bed" for organizational politics in that:

- It always involves at least two parties.
- One party has more power than the other in that the rater (usually the supervisor) influences important outcomes for an employee.
- This influence is expressed through the possibility of giving an employee an increase in visibility, office size, promotion, transfer, pay increase, termination, etc. These outcomes typically represent scarce resources in an organization.

In the next section, we review the few studies that have investigated this social phenomenon within the context of employee appraisals.

3.1 Appraisal Process and Outcomes

The performance appraisal is a process for making administrative decisions as well as developmental plans that affect an organization's employees (Latham and Wexley 1994). Several studies (e.g., Bjerke et al. 1987; Gandz and Murray 1980; Mohrman and Lawler 1983; Prince, Lawler, and Mohrman 1991) reported results similar to those obtained by Longenecker, Sims, and Gioia (1987). In brief, these studies suggest that politics are common in organizations and this is especially true in the conduct of performance appraisals. For example, Gandz and Murray (1980) collected incidents describing examples of workplace politics. The incidents most frequently reported were those involving an employee being bypassed for a promotion. The second most common theme in the incidents was the unfair assessment of one's work performance (e.g., perceptions of being evaluated on either "hidden" criteria, or criteria beyond a person's control).

Managers frequently review their ratings of an employee with their boss prior to giving feedback to a subordinate. They consciously utilize this prefeedback review as a way of legitimizing their appraisal to an employee (Mohrman and Lawler 1983, 183). As a result, subordinates often view such appraisals as "locked in." They do not believe that they can express their voice during the feedback process even if they believe that pertinent data regarding their performance had been omitted in the evaluation. Voice is key to perceptions of procedural justice (Greenberg 2000).

Navy officers admitted that they inflated their ratings of subordinates. This is done to improve their promotion prospects (Bjerke et al. 1987).

3.2 Measurement

All of the above findings were obtained through qualitative methodology, namely, open-ended interviews. In order to quantitatively address the incidence of political behavior influencing an appraisal, Tziner et al. (1996) developed a 25-item questionnaire (i.e., Questionnaire of Political Considerations in Performance Appraisal, QPCPA) that measures employees' perceptions of the extent to which supervisors in their organization engage in specific political considerations in performance evaluations. These considerations include: (a) acquiring personal benefits; (b) exercising control; (c) avoiding confrontation with the employees over low performance ratings; (d) motivating employees; and (e) maintaining a positive climate.

The results of this study showed that the QPCPA consists of a one-factor structure that explains 59.7 percent of variance. Its internal consistency was .97 and .98 on two administrations, respectively. The test-retest reliability between the two administrations of the questionnaire, conducted one week apart, was .86. Convergent validity was assessed with regard to measures of Need for Power and Machiavellianism, two constructs related to political considerations. The correlations with these two constructs were .23 and .33 ($p < .01$), respectively. Discriminant validity was assessed with regard to measures of organizational commitment and state-trait anxiety. The results showed a negative correlation with organizational commitment ($r = -.27$, $p < .01$). The correlation with state-trait anxiety was not significant. In a subsequent study, using confirmatory factor analysis, Tziner (1999) again obtained support for the unidimensionality of the QPCPA. The internal consistency was high (alpha = .94).

Poon (2004) explored the link between "performance appraisal politics" and the reactions of employees. Using fifteen items from the QPCPA, he found a two-factor structure. The first factor he labeled "motivational motive." This factor encompasses items regarding the supervisor's purpose for rewarding employees and maintaining a positive climate in the workgroup. The second factor he labeled "personal bias and punishment motive." This factor encompasses items related to supervisors' penchant for engaging in favoritism and using punishment tactics. The criteria in this study were job satisfaction and turnover intentions. The motivational factor did not correlate with either outcome. The personal bias and punishment factor, however, significantly and negatively predicted job satisfaction, and positively predicted turnover intentions. Moreover, the relationship between perceived politics and turnover intentions was fully mediated by job satisfaction.

Salimäki and Jämsén (2007), in a study of employees in three agencies of the Finnish government, also obtained a two-factor solution for QPCPA. The first factor, labeled "conflict avoidance," consisted of three items having to do with giving an inflated rating to avoid negative or uncomfortable feedback sessions with a subordinate. The second factor they called "interpersonal relationship."

It consisted of four items that assessed a supervisor's liking for or disliking of an employee. Unfortunately, these studies have not been followed by systematic research on the ways organizational politics are manifested in the performance appraisal process. The few studies that have measured the incidence of political considerations in a performance appraisal, however, have yielded interesting results.

3.3 Predictors, Moderators, and Causal Variables

As noted earlier, Tziner et al. (1996) and Tziner, Prince, and Murphy (1997) found that Need for Power and Machiavellianism correlate with a measure of perceptions of politics in performance appraisal. Tziner (1999) investigated whether and when political considerations distort performance appraisal evaluations. Among the personal variables he considered was raters' self-efficacy in conducting perform-ance appraisals. Among the contextual variables he considered were perceived organizational climate, the quality of rater–ratee relationships, affective and con-tinuance commitment. Two of these variables had a significant relationship with political behavior. Specifically, self-efficacy as a rater negatively predicted political considerations in a performance appraisal ($-.27$, $p < .01$), whereas continuance commitment positively predicted political distortions ($.15$, $p < .05$). Thus, it ap-pears that raters with low self-efficacy may handle uncomfortable situations (such as giving negative feedback to their subordinates) by engaging in political distor-tions of their evaluations. In short, they inflate their ratings of performance. Raters with high self-efficacy are more confident of their capabilities to deal with negative appraisals, and hence give lower ratings than their colleagues who have low self-efficacy for doing so. On the other hand, raters who are committed to their organization for personal reasons (e.g., maximizing their own benefits) are more likely to use performance appraisal as a means to obtain additional personal returns. In summary, Tziner's finding is consistent with earlier studies that found that managers willfully inflate ratings so as to avoid potentially damaging inter-personal relationships (e.g., Harris 1994; Villanova et al. 1993). Other studies (Harris 1994; Villanova and Bernardin 1989) suggest that managers give employees high ratings when it is self-enhancing for them to do so (e.g., make themselves look competent as leaders, gain resources, enhance their group's prestige).

Rosen, Levy, and Hall (2006) obtained findings similar to those reported earlier (e.g., Harris and Kacmar 2005) on the important role a supervisor can play in mitigating the effects of organizational politics on an employee. In a study involv-ing 150 supervisor–subordinate dyads, they found that feedback quality, delivery, and availability correlated negatively ($r = -.65$) with employee perceptions of politics. Similar to the conclusion reached by both Witt (1998) and Harris and Kacmar (2005), discussed earlier in this chapter, Rosen et al. likewise concluded that when supervisors clarify with their employees the behaviors that are expected and will be subsequently rewarded, the process is no longer viewed by employees as politically driven.

Using a cross-section of organizations in Barbados, Nurse (2005) found that there is a positive correlation between employee perceptions of the fairness of the appraisal process and their expectations of career advancement. Where formal performance appraisal procedures did not exist, supervisors did not engage in interactional justice. This lends support to the earlier argument by Gandz and Murray (1980) that in the absence of codified systems and procedures, politically motivated behavior is likely.

As is the case with studies of organizational politics, a limitation of the above studies is that the data come from correlational studies that are cross-sectional rather than longitudinal. Mero and Motowidlo (1995), in a laboratory experiment involving college students, found that raters are sensitive to being held accountable to pressures on them to achieve certain outcomes. Those who knew that they would be required to justify their appraisal took more and better notes than those who were not given this information. Moreover, those given equity information regarding women who historically received lower appraisals than men, or were told that their subordinates had historically received lower ratings, typically increased them. Curtis, Harvey, and Ravden (2005) also conducted one of the few experiments in this research domain. They obtained evidence in a laboratory setting for two contextual factors that influence political distortions in the ratings of others, namely appraisal purpose and rater accountability. Administrative decisions were found to be more subject to political distortions than those that are developmental. Therefore, using the same rating for multiple purposes may not be appropriate. Additionally, the experimental group which was held downwardly accountable (i.e., the rater had to justify a rating to a ratee) had significantly more lenient ratings than the group which was upwardly accountable (i.e., the rater had to justify a rating to the researcher). The third group, which was held accountable both downwardly and upwardly, had the least lenient ratings, although the difference in ratings from those of the second group was not significant. The interesting implication for practice is the finding that "upward" accountability in this experiment was not represented by the participant's supervisor, but rather by the researchers. This suggests that simply holding raters accountable to a third party may be sufficient to reduce rating leniency.

Salimäki and Jämsén (2007) examined the effect of pay on the employee's political behavior in Finnish government agencies. The correlational findings suggest that highly paid individuals, in an environment that they perceive to be politically charged, do not feel comfortable speaking freely. They think twice about expressing their thoughts and feelings. The researchers concluded that these employees are motivated to preserve their interests by maintaining silence. However, a moderator variable is the type of compensation. A weaker relationship was obtained with performance-based pay. This may be because employees knew they were being evaluated on relatively objective criteria.

4. Recommendations for Minimizing Organizational Politics in Performance Appraisal

Suggestions for minimizing organizational politics in the performance appraisal process can be inferred from the extant studies. Longenecker (1989), for instance, provided suggestions about how to manage the politics of a performance appraisal. His recommendations take into account the manager's behavior ("re-think his/her purpose of the appraisal;" "rethink his/her approach to the appraisal process;" "be sure to set the stage for subordinate performance;" "make appraisal an ongoing activity;" "use long-term strategy in writing appraisals;" "base the appraisal interview on trust") as well as the organization's leaders ("lead by example"); and the organization's practices ("performance appraisal training that addresses the topic of political behavior;" "create an open and positive appraisal environment;" "do not make organizational policy a political stumbling block for the rater;" "provide managers with feedback on their appraisal performance"). None of these suggestions is tied directly to theory.

Another atheoretical approach that may prove to be effective in mitigating politics from entering the appraisal process is the use of 360-degree feedback. This may be especially likely if supervisors are made aware that their assessments will be examined by their boss and their employee in light of the assessments an employee receives from others. Specifically, evidence would exist in the court of public opinion as to how an employee's performance is viewed by peers, subordinates, and customers in addition to one's boss. This evidence would make it more difficult for a supervisor to politicize an appraisal than is the case where the supervisor is the lone source of an appraisal.

Three theoretical frameworks suggest additional solutions: (a) Greenberg's (2000) conceptualizations of organizational justice; (b) Bandura's social cognitive theory (1986); and (c) Locke and Latham's (1990) goal-setting theory. If there is a panacea to the problems related to organizational politics, it is likely to be found in the adoption of and adherence to the principles of organizational justice, distributive as well as procedural (Greenberg 1986). Greenberg (1987) proposed a taxonomy of studies regarding principles of organizational justice. He classified these studies using two independent axes: content/process and reactive/proactive. The content/process axis refers to the perception of fairness regarding the distribution of outcomes, and the process adopted to distribute the outcomes (i.e., distributive versus procedural justice). The second axis refers to employees' reactions to perceptions of unfairness (e.g., unequal balances as well as unjust decision-making procedures) versus the actions taken that tend to increase perceptions of justice.

A similar taxonomy should be applied to the studies of the phenomenon of organizational politics. This topic is directly related to perceptions of organizational justice, as described earlier, and hence can be considered its conceptual antonym. Studies of organizational politics can be classified using the reactive/proactive dimension. Both scientists and practitioners are interested in understanding how people react to their perceptions of workplace politics, its negative effects, and how this phenomenon can be minimized. The majority of studies on organizational politics have focused on the reactive pole. The extant research suggests the negative effects of organizational politics on employees' outcomes. With the exception of the study discussed earlier by Vigoda-Gadot, Vinarski-Peretz, and Ben-Zion (2003), little is known about the detrimental consequences that this can have at the organizational level, and also in the way an organization is seen in the external environment. Hence there is a need to conceptualize perceptions of organizational politics in a proactive framework.

Inherent in this step toward minimizing the occurrence of organizational politics entering into appraisals is to codify the procedures. This step is consistent with findings obtained by Mayes and Allen (1977) and Gandz and Murray (1980), discussed earlier. Included in this step are the establishment of an appeal process and the appointment of an ongoing champion for an employee. Extreme formalization, however, can lead to rigid bureaucracy that in turn can result in an "iron cage" (Weber 1946). Hence the principles of organizational justice must be implemented with caution. People frequently engage in strategies to avoid the excessive constraints imposed by rules. With regard to performance appraisals, Mohrman and Lawler (1983, 177) found that managers "may create informal systems to communicate such data." A formal system that uses the same performance data for all purposes (i.e., administrative, developmental, and career advancement) may not allow raters to differentiate among the data relevant for each purpose. Another caveat regarding the adoption of an adherence to procedural justice principles by managers is that employee trust in managers moderates the effect these principles have on their cooperation (De Cremer and Tyler 2007). Over time, however, managerial adherence to those principles is likely to engender trust in management.

Social cognitive theory suggests the importance of enhancing a supervisor's ability and motivation to minimize the extent to which organizational politics enters into a performance appraisal. Steps should be taken to increase a supervisor's self-efficacy in conducting appraisals particularly on how to give negative yet constructive feedback to employees. Failure to take this step will likely lead to political manipulations of employee ratings (Tziner 1999). In addition to self-efficacy, the outcome expectancies of raters must be taken into account. They must see the relationship between conducting apolitical appraisals and the attainment of desired outcomes.

Napier and Latham (1986) showed that a rater's outcome expectancies play a critical role in shaping their behaviors in appraising employees above and beyond self-efficacy to do so. In their two-study investigation of a newsprint facility and a bank, the authors found that appraisers reported few, if any, positive outcomes for them to conduct performance appraisals. Despite the fact the appraisers had high self-efficacy that they could conduct performance appraisals, they seldom did so. This is because they did not see a positive or negative performance appraisal as having any effect on an employee's job status. Moreover, they themselves were neither rewarded for conducting performance appraisals, nor were they punished for failing to do so. Low outcome expectancies resulted in supervisors abandoning behaviors they were confident they could do well.

Changing outcome expectancies can change behavior. A practical way to do so is to use an "empathy box" (Latham 2001). The box consists of a 2×2 table for collecting data on the positive and negative outcomes people expect with regard to organizationally desired and undesired behavior. Latham interviewed employees about the "upsides and downsides" of engaging in honest versus dishonest behavior. Based on their responses, management developed an intervention to bring about honest behavior by changing the outcomes the employees expected from theft. Similarly, the empathy box should be useful for identifying what positive and negative outcomes appraisers expect from taking political considerations into account when conducting and feeding back an appraisal to their employees, as well as the positive and negative outcomes they expect from making evaluations of employees that are "fair." Understanding the outcomes appraisers expect should facilitate an understanding of their appraisal behavior. It would yield clues as to ways of changing the positive outcomes they expect from undesirable political behavior to desired apolitical behavior when appraising their direct reports.

Setting specific high goals not only leads to high performance, it makes both parties aware of what is going to be evaluated (Latham and Locke 2007). Goal setting allows for transparency and hence facilitates trust between supervisor and subordinate. Supervisors are less able to manipulate their ratings of subordinates when measurable objective standards are made known a priori to all parties involved in the appraisal process. Subordinates know exactly which behaviors are expected of them. Supervisors know what they should be looking at (Wherry and Bartlett 1982). This reduces uncertainty around the appraisal process. Hence, employees are more likely to perceive appraisal decisions as less political. This recommendation is consistent with findings reported earlier by Rosen, Levy, and Hall (2006).

Borgogni and Pettita (2003) stressed an additional benefit of goal setting. It teaches supervisors the importance of setting priorities, and of helping subordinates overcome obstacles to goal attainment. To do this effectively, they recommended that supervisors receive formal training in ways to behave as a coach of the members of their respective teams.

It is well known that feedback in the absence of goal setting has no effect on behavior unless it leads to the setting of and commitment to one or more specific high goals (Locke and Latham 1990). A novel methodology that has yet to be empirically investigated is feedforward, an intervention developed by Kluger and Nir (2006). Qualitative data from organizations in Israel suggest that employees do not haggle over an appraisal of their performance when feedforward precedes a traditional appraisal. This intervention includes the following steps: (1) An employee is asked to tell a story about when he/she was at his/her "best." Included in the story are the circumstances (personal/contextual) that made this event possible. This procedure has parallels with Herzberg's (Herzberg, Mausner, and Snyderman 1959) use of Flanagan's (1954) critical incident technique. (2) The employee describes the emotions experienced. (3) The person is asked to describe plans (i.e., goals) to recreate similar incidents in the immediate future. Kluger and Nir argued that the effectiveness of their intervention is based on the positive emotions it creates within the person. These emotions elicit action to re-experience them. Hence the focus by employees to reduce the discrepancy between the future goal and the current state, positive self-talk for creating that future, and the positive bond that is ultimately created between a supervisor who initiates "feedforward" and the employee who engages in it. This last aspect, the positive bond, may mitigate a desire by a supervisor and/or an employee to politicize the appraisal process. Kluger and Nir's findings are consistent with the correlational findings obtained by Rosen, Levy, and Hall (2006) discussed earlier. A high-quality feedback environment appears to diminish an environment conducive to political behaviors.

Engaging in a feedforward intervention should be investigated in concert with setting specific high learning rather than performance outcome goals (Winters and Latham 1996; Latham, Seijts, and Crim 2006). A learning goal focuses attention on the strategies/ processes necessary to attain a desired end state rather than the end state itself.

5. A RESEARCH AGENDA

From the vantage point of a practitioner, the primary value of a review of the literature is its suggestions on "what to do;" hence the previous section will hopefully prove helpful to practitioners. From a scientist's point of view, the value is the path forward a review provides for future research. This is the goal of the closing section of this chapter.

1. As noted earlier, many of the correlational studies should be replicated in ways that are not susceptible to common method variance. In addition, lagged effects should be examined. For example, it would be interesting to study the lagged effects of organizational commitment and organizational politics on one another over time. Commitment is likely to moderate the adverse effect of perceived politics, but it is also likely affected by it (Maslyn and Fedor 1998). As noted earlier, employees who are highly committed to their organization respond less negatively to political behavior than their peers who are less committed. But, over time their identification with their organization may dissipate (see Mayer and Schoorman 1998).

2. Using the Perception of Organizational Politics questionnaire (Kacmar and Ferris 1991) and/or the Questionnaire of Political Considerations in Performance Appraisal (Tziner et al. 1996) as mediators or dependent variables, conduct simulated or actual field experiments, that include control groups, which examine the effects of training supervisors:

   (a) on the principles of organizational justice;
   (b) on feedforward with and without learning goals;
   (c) to be supportive coaches with emphasis on increasing their self-efficacy for doing so and strengthening outcome expectancies for desirable end states.

3. Determine the underlying factor structure of the Questionnaire of Political Considerations in Performance Appraisal. Is it uni- or multidimensional?

4. Examine whether employees in an out-group, such as women in historically male-dominated jobs, receive higher appraisal ratings of their performance than their counterparts in a control group after being trained in impression management techniques.

5. Examine the effect of organizational design and job enrichment interventions on responses to the Perceptions of Organizational Politics Questionnaire and the Questionnaire of Political Considerations in Performance Appraisal.

6. Examine organizational culture/climate as a moderator of the effects of the above suggestions.

7. In addition, examine societal culture as a moderator of the above effects as the purpose of and the reaction to an appraisal varies across societies (Fletcher and Perry 2001).

As Tichy (1983, 269) once said: "having diagnosed the state of the current corporate culture, the next step is proactive." It is the authors' hope that this section and the one that preceded it will lead to steps being taken to minimize the adverse effects of organizational politics in general, and those in performance appraisals in particular.

REFERENCES

ANDREWS, N. J., and KACMAR, J. P. 2001. The measurement and antecedents of affective, continuance and normative commitment to the organization. *Journal of Occupational Psychology*, 63: 1–18.

BANDURA, A. 1986. *Social Foundations of Thought and Action: A Social Cognitive Theory.* Englewood Cliffs, NJ: Prentice Hall.

BENGLEY, T. M., LEE, C., and HUI, C. 2006. Organizational level as a moderator of the relationship between justice perceptions and work-related reactions. *Journal of Organizational Behavior*, 27: 705–21.

BERNTHAL, P., SUMBIN, R., DAVIS, P., and ROGERS, B. 1997. *Performance Management Practices Survey Report.* Pittsburgh: Developmental Dimensions International.

BJERKE, D. G., CLEVELAND, J. N., MORRISON, R. R., and WILSON, W. C. 1987. Officer fitness report evaluation study. *Navy Personnel Research and Development Center Report*, TR 88–4.

BORGOGNI, L., and PETTITA, L. 2003. *Lo sviluppo delle persone nelle organizzazioni (People's Development in Organizations).* Rome: Carocci.

BOZEMAN, D. P., PERREWÉ, P. L., HOCHWARTER, W. A., and BRYMER, R. A. 2001. Organizational politics, perceived control, and work outcomes: boundary conditions on the effects of politics. *Journal of Applied Social Psychology*, 31: 486–503.

CROPANZANO, R., and GREENBERG, J. 1997. Progress in organizational justice: tunneling through the maze. Pp. 317–72 in *International Review of Industrial and Organizational Psychology*, ed. C. L. Cooper and I. T. Robertson. New York: Wiley.

—— HOWES, J. C., GRANDEY, A. A., and TOTH, P. 1997. The relationship of organizational politics and support to work behaviors, attitudes, and stress. *Journal of Organizational Behavior*, 18: 159–80.

CURTIS, A. B., HARVEY, R. D., and RAVDEN, D. 2005. Sources of political distortions in performance appraisals. *Group and Organization Management*, 30: 42–60.

DE CREMER, D., and TYLER, T. R. 2007. The effects of trust in authority and procedural fairness on cooperation. *Journal of Applied Psychology*, 92: 639–49.

EISENBERGER, R., HUNTINGTON, R., HUTCHISON, S., and SOWA, D. 1986. Perceived organizational support. *Journal of Applied Psychology*, 71: 500–7.

FARR, J. L., and LEVY, P. E. 2007. Performance appraisal. Pp. 311–30 in *Historical Perspectives in Industrial and Organizational Psychology*, ed. L. L. Koppes. Mahwah, NJ: Lawrence Erlbaum.

FERRIS, G. R., and KACMAR, K. M. 1992. Perceptions of organizational politics. *Journal of Management*, 18: 93–116.

—— RUSS, G. S., and FANDT, P. M. 1989. Politics in organizations. Pp. 143–70 in *Impression Management in the Organization*, ed. R. A. Giancalone and P. Rosenfield. Hillsdale, NJ: Erlbaum.

—— FEDOR, D. B., CHACHERE, J. G., and PONDY, L. R. 1989. Myths and politics in organizational contexts. *Group and Organization Studies*, 14: 83–103.

—— FRINK, D. D., BHAWUK-DHARM, P. S., ZHOU, J., and GILMORE, D. C. 1996. Reactions of diverse groups to politics in the workplace. *Journal of Management*, 22: 23–44.

FLANAGAN, J. C. 1954. The critical incident technique. *Psychological Bulletin*, 51: 327–58.

FLETCHER, C., and PERRY, E. L. 2001. Performance appraisal and feedback: a consideration of national culture and a review of contemporary research and future trends. In

Handbook of Industrial, Work, and Organizational Psychology, ed. N. Anderson, D. S. Ones, K. Sinangil, and C. Viswesvaran. Thousand Oaks, CA: Sage Publications.

FOLGER, R., KONOVSKY, M., and CROPANZANO, R. 1992. A due process metaphor for performance appraisal. Pp. 129–77 in *Research in Organizational Behavior*, xiv, ed. B. M. Staw and L. L. Cummings. Greenwich, CT: JAI Press.

FROST, P. 1987. Power, politics, and influence. Pp. 503–48 in *Handbook of Organizational Communication*, ed. F. Jablin, L. Putnam, K. Roberts, and L. Porter. Newbury Park, CA: Sage.

GANDZ, J., and MURRAY, V. V. 1980. The experience of workplace politics. *Academy of Management Journal*, 23: 237–51.

GODFREY, D. K., JONES, E. E., and LORD, C. C. 1986. Self-promotion is not ingratiating. *Journal of Personality and Social Psychology*, 50: 106–15.

GREENBERG, J. 1986. Determinants of perceived fairness of performance evaluations. *Journal of Applied Psychology*, 71: 340–2.

—— 1987. A taxonomy of organizational justice theories. *Academy of Management Review*, 12: 9–22.

—— 2000. Promote procedure justice to enhance acceptance of outcomes. Pp. 181–95 in *Handbook of Principles of Organizational Behavior*, ed. E. A. Locke. Malden, MA: Blackwell.

HARRELL-COOK, G., FERRIS, G. R., and DULEBOHN, J. H. 1999. Political behaviors as moderators of the perceptions of organizational politics–work outcomes relationships. *Journal of Organizational Behavior*, 20: 1093–105.

HARRIS, K. J., and KACMAR, K. M. 2005. Easing the strain: the buffer role of supervisors in the perceptions of politics–strain relationship. *Journal of Occupational and Organizational Psychology*, 78: 337–54.

HARRIS, M. 1994. Rater motivation in the performance appraisal context: a theoretical framework. *Journal of Management*, 20: 737–56.

HERZBERG, F., MAUSNER, B., and SNYDERMAN, B. B. 1959. *The Motivation to Work*, 2nd edn. New York: John Wiley and Sons.

HOCHWARTER, W. A., and TREADWAY, D. C. 2003. The interactive effects of negative and positive affect on the politics perceptions–job satisfaction relationship. *Journal of Management*, 29: 551–67.

—— WITT, L. A., and KACMAR, K. M. 2000. Perceptions of organizational politics as a moderator of the relationship between conscientiousness and job performance. *Journal of Applied Psychology*, 85: 472–78.

—— PERREWÉ, P., FERRIS, G. R., and GUERCIO, R. 1999. Commitment as an antidote to the tension and turnover consequences of organizational politics. *Journal of Vocational Behavior*, 55: 277–97.

—— KACMAR, C., PERREWÉ, P., and JOHNSON, D. 2003. Perceived organizational support as a mediator of the relationship between politics perceptions and work outcomes: a multi-level analysis. *Journal of Vocational Behavior*, 63: 438–56.

JUDGE, T. A., LOCKE, E. A., and DUNHAM, C. C. 1997. The dispositional causes of job satisfaction: a core evaluation approach. *Research in Organizational Behavior*, 19: 151–88.

KACMAR, K. M., and BARON, R. A. 1999. Organizational politics: the state of the field, links to related processes, and an agenda for future research. Pp. 1–39 in *Research in Human Resource Management*, 17, ed. G. R. Ferris. Greenwich, CT: JAI Press.

—— and CARLSON, D. S. 1997. Further validation of the perceptions of politics scale (POPS): a multiple sample investigation. *Journal of Management*, 23: 627–58.

KACMAR, K. M., and BARON, R. A., and COLLINS, B. S., and HARRIS, K. J. 2007. Moderating effect of political environments on the core self evaluation–ingratiation relationship. In J. Greenberg and G. P. Latham (Chairs), Political Influences on Human Resource Management Practices. Symposium presented at the annual meeting of the Academy of Management, Philadelphia, August.

—— and FERRIS, G. R. 1991. Perceptions of organizational politics scale (POPS): development and construct validation. *Educational and Psychological Measurement*, 51: 193–205.

KLUGER, A., and NIR, D. 2006. Feedforward first, feedback later. Invited address. International Congress of Applied Psychology, Athens, July.

LANDAU, J. 1995. The relationship of race and gender to managers' ratings of promotion potential. *Journal of Organizational Behavior*, 16: 391–400.

LATHAM, G. P. 2001. The importance of understanding and changing employee outcome expectancies for gaining commitment to an organizational goal. *Personnel Psychology*, 54: 707–16.

—— and LOCKE, E. A. 2007. New developments in and directions for goal setting. *European Psychologist*, 12 (4): 290–300.

—— and MANN, S. 2006. Advances in the science of performance appraisal: implications for practice. Pp. 295–337 in *International Review of Industrial and Organizational Psychology*, 21, ed. G. P. Hodgkinson, and J. K. Ford. Hoboken, NJ: Wiley Publishing.

—— and WEXLEY, K. N. 1994. *Increasing Productivity through Performance Appraisal*, 2nd edn. Reading, MA: Wesley Publishing Co.

—— SEIJTS, H., and CRIM, D. 2006. The effects of learning goal difficulty level and cognitive ability on strategies and performance. Paper presented at the annual meeting of the Academy of Management, Atlanta, August.

—— SULSKY, L. M., and MacDONALD, H. 2007. Performance management: answers and questions. In *The Oxford Handbook of Human Resource Management*, ed. P. Boxall, P. Wright, and J. Purcell. New York: Oxford University Press.

LOCKE, E. A., and LATHAM, G. P. 1990. *A Theory of Goal Setting and Task Performance*. Englewood Cliffs, NJ: Prentice Hall.

LONGENECKER, C. O. 1989. Truth or consequences: politics and performance appraisals. *Business Horizons*, 32: 76–82.

—— SIMS, H., and GIOIA, D. A. 1987. Behind the mask: the politics of employee appraisal. *Academy of Management Executive*, 1: 183–93.

MAIER, N. R. F. 1955. *Psychology in Industry*, 2nd edn. Boston: Houghton Mifflin.

MASLYN, J. M., and FEDOR, D. B. 1998. Differentiating antecedents of organizational commitment: a test of March and Simon's model. *Journal of Organizational Behavior*, 19: 15–28.

MAYER, R. C., and SCHOORMAN, F. D. 1998. Perceptions of politics: does measuring different foci matter? *Journal of Applied Psychology*, 84: 645–53.

MAYES, B. T., and ALLEN, R. W. 1977. Toward a definition of organizational politics. *Academy of Management Review*, 2: 672–78.

MERO, N., and MOTOWIDLO, S. 1995. Effects of rater accountability on the accuracy and the favorability of performance ratings. *Journal of Applied Psychology*, 80: 517–24.

MINTZBERG, H. 1983. *Power in and around Organizations*. Englewood Cliffs, NJ: Prentice Hall.

MOBERG, D. J. 1978. Factors which determine the perception and use of organizational politics. Paper presented at the National Meeting of the Academy of Management, San Francisco.

MOHRMAN, A. M., and LAWLER, E. E., III. 1983. Motivation and performance appraisal behavior. Pp. 173–89 in *Performance Measurement and Theory*, ed. F. Landry, S. Zedeck, and J. Cleveland. Hillsdale, NJ: Erlbaum.

MURPHY, K. R., and CLEVELAND, J. N. 1991. *Performance Appraisal: An Organizational Perspective* (Human Resource Management Series). Needham Heights, MA: Allyn and Bacon.

NAISH, J. 2005. The office psychologist. Office politics. *The Times*. Retrieved March 17, 2005, from <http://www.timesonline.co.uk/tol/life_and_style/career_and_jobs/graduate_ma nagement/article428515.ece>.

NAPIER, N. K., and LATHAM, G. P. 1986. Outcome expectancies of people who conduct performance appraisals. *Personnel Psychology*, 39: 827–37.

NURSE, L. 2005. Performance appraisal, employee development and organizational justice: exploring the linkages. *International Journal of Human Resource Management*, 16: 1176–94.

PATTERSON, D. G. 1922. The Scott Company graphic rating scale. *Journal of Personnel Research*, 361–76.

—— 1923. Methods of rating human qualities. *Annual of the American Academy of Politics and Social Science*, 81–93.

POON, J. M. L. 2004. Effects of performance appraisal politics on job satisfaction and turnover intentions. *Personnel Review*, 33: 322–34.

PRINCE, J. B., LAWLER, E. E., and MOHRMAN, A. M. 1991. Manager–subordinate divergence in performance. Unpublished manuscript, Concordia University.

RAFAELI, A., DUTTON, J., HARQUAIL, C. V., and MACKIE-LEWIS, S. 1997. Navigating by attire: the use of dress by female administrative employees. *Academy of Management Journal*, 40: 9–37.

ROSEN, C. C., CHANG, C.-H., and LEVY, P. E. 2006. Personality and politics perceptions: a new conceptualization and illustration using OCBs. Pp. 29–52 in *Handbook of Organizational Politics*, ed. E. Vigoda-Gadot, A. Drory, and Ben-Gurion. Cheltenham: Edward Elgar Publishing.

—— LEVY, P. E., and HALL, R. J. 2006. Placing perceptions of politics in the context of the feedback environment, employee attitudes, and job performance. *Journal of Applied Psychology*, 91: 211–20.

—— —— and JOHNSON, R. E. 2007. Coping with strains and breaches: consequences of organizational politics. In J. Greenberg and G. P. Latham (Chairs), Political Influences on Human Resource Management Practices. Symposium presented at the annual meeting of the Academy of Management, Philadelphia, August.

SALIMÄKI, A., and JÅMSÉN, S. 2007. Perceptions of organizational politics in performance-based systems. In J. Greenberg and G. P. Latham (Chairs), Political Influences on Human Resource Management Practices. Symposium presented at the annual meeting of the Academy of Management, Philadelphia, August.

TICHY, N. M. 1983. *Managing Culture Strategically: Technical, Political, and Cultural Dynamics*. New York: Wiley.

TREADWAY, D. C., FERRIS, G. R., HOCHWARTER, W. A., PERREWÉ, P., WITT, L. A., and GOODMAN, J. M. (2005a). The role of age in perceptions of politics- job performance relationship: A three study constructive replication. *Journal of Applied Psychology*, 90: 872–81.

—— HOCHWARTER, W. A., KACMAR, C. J., and FERRIS, G. R. (2005b). Political will, political skill, and political behavior. *Journal of Organizational Behavior*, 26: 229–45.

TREADWAY, D. C., FERRIS, G. R., DUKE, A. B., ADAMS, G. L., and THATCHER, J. B. 2007. The moderating role of subordinate political skill on supervisors' impressions of subordinate ingratiation and ratings of subordinates' interpersonal facilitation. *Journal of Applied Psychology*, 92: 848–55.

TZINER, A. 1999. The relationship between distal and proximal factors and the use of political considerations in performance appraisal. *Journal of Business and Psychology*, 14: 217–31.

—— PRINCE, J. B., and MURPHY, K. R. 1997. PCPAQ—the questionnaire for measuring perceived political considerations in performance appraisal: some new evidence regarding its psychometric qualities. *Journal of Social Behavior and Personality*, 12: 189–99.

—— LATHAM, G. P., PRICE, B. S., and HACCOUN, R. 1996. Development and validation of a questionnaire for measuring perceived and political considerations in performance appraisal. *Journal of Organizational Behavior*, 17: 179–90.

VIGODA-GADOT, E. 2000. Internal politics in public administration systems: an empirical examination of its relationship with job congruence, organizational citizenship behavior, and in-role performance. *Public Personnel Management*, 29: 185–210.

—— 2002. Stress related aftermaths of workplace politics: the relationship among politics, job distress, and aggressive behaviors in organizations. *Organizational Behavior*, 23: 571–91.

—— VINARSKI-PERETZ, H., and BEN-ZION, E. 2003. Politics and image in the organizational landscape: an empirical examination among public sector employees. *Journal of Managerial Psychology*, 18: 764–87.

VILLANOVA, P., and BERNARDIN, J. 1989. Impression management in the context of performance appraisals. Pp. 299–314 in *Impression Management in the Organization*, ed. R. Giacalone and P. Rosenfeld. Mahwah, NJ: Lawrence Erlbaum.

—— BERNARDIN, J., DAHMUS, S., and SIMS, R. 1993. Rater leniency and performance appraisal discomfort. *Educational and Psychological Measurement*, 53: 789–99.

WEBER, M. 1946. *Essay in Sociology*, ed. and trans. H. H. Gerth and C. Wright Mills. New York: Oxford University Press.

WHERRY, R. J., Sr., and BARTLETT, C. J. 1982. The control of bias in ratings: a theory of rating. *Personnel Psychology*, 35: 521–51.

WINTERS, D., and LATHAM, G. P. 1996. The effects of learning versus outcome goals on a simple versus complex task. *Group and Organization Management*, 21: 236–50.

WITT, L. A. 1998. Enhancing organizational goal congruence: a solution to organizational politics. *Journal of Applied Psychology*, 83: 666–74.

WORTMAN, C. B., and LINSENMEIER, J. A. 1977. Interpersonal attraction and techniques of ingratiation in organizational settings. Pp. 133–78 in *New Directions in Organizational Behavior*, ed. M. B. Staw and G. R. Salancik. Chicago: Krieger Pub Co.

YUN, S., TAKEUCHI, R., and LIU, W. 2007. Employee self-enhancement motives and job performance behaviors: investigating the moderating effects of employee role ambiguity and managerial perceptions of employee commitment. *Journal of Applied Psychology*, 92: 745–56.

PART V

POLICIES AND PRACTICES

17

FLEXIBLE WORKING ARRANGEMENTS: FROM WORK–LIFE TO GENDER EQUITY POLICIES

SUZAN LEWIS

IAN ROPER

1. INTRODUCTION

WITHIN personnel psychology, "work–life" policies are often conceptualized as an offshoot of equal opportunities (EO) polices, although in practice the connection can be tenuous. For a start, a discourse of equal opportunities implies that men and women should be treated the same. In practice this is often interpreted as giving women the "equal opportunity" to act like men—for example to work long hours—rather than changing the cultures, structures, and working practices to benefit both men and women. Work–life policies on the other hand have developed from what used to be called "family friendly" policies and are widely interpreted as being policies for women, focusing on difference rather than sameness, despite usually officially being articulated as policies for both women and men. In practice, there are rarely equal opportunities for men to use work–life or flexible working policies to the same extent as women. As a result, these policies often act to marginalize those workers—mainly women—who take up opportunities to work non-standard working time; the "non-standard" worker invariably finds themselves penalized in career terms for not behaving like (traditional) men who continue to be regarded as ideal workers (Lewis 2001; Judiesch and Lyness 1999; Fried 1998; Rapoport et al. 2002). In response to the issue of "sameness" a more recent focus on "diversity" emphasizes the different needs and circumstances of diverse groups, thus resolving the dilemma, in EO, of women "levelling down" to male workplace cultural practice, as discussed above. With diversity, however, there has been an equal but opposite danger of reifying difference. In the case of "work–life" policies such an overemphasis could serve to trivialize structural disadvantage faced by women in the labor market by emphasizing the notion of "lifestyle choices;" and can also underlie a neglect of men's work and family needs. In practice, however, as is pointed out by a number of writers (Kirton and Green 2000; Liff and Dickens 2000), recognizing both similarities and differences as an integrated approach is quite possible without undermining the principles of either equal opportunities or of diversity.

The dilemma in relation to work–life or work–family policies, then, is that currently women tend to take on more family responsibilities than men, suggesting the need for "special treatment" for women. However, as long as initiatives to support the integration of work and personal life are directed primarily at women they will not be mainstreamed into organizations and they will perpetuate gender inequities. In view of the tensions in approaches taken to equality, we refer in this chapter to policies and practices to promote *gender equity*. Gender equity refers to a goal of fair or equitable division of opportunities and constraints among men and women. This implies the need to change work to enable all employees to integrate their work and family or personal lives (Rapoport et al. 2002; Williams 2000). We also prefer to avoid, where possible the terms work–life policies and especially work–life balance policies, with the implications that work is not part of life and which tend to focus on individual "choices" rather than organizational issues (Gambles, Lewis, and Rapoport 2006; Lewis, Gambles, and Rapoport 2007). Instead we discuss policies and practices that aim to support men and women integrating or harmonizing their paid work and personal lives in gender equitable ways. The goal is that such policies should enable women and men to make optimum contributions at work and in their lives beyond work. The term "work–life policies" is generally used to incorporate flexible working arrangements (FWAs) and dependent care initiatives. We focus predominantly here on FWAs, as these shift the focus from individual needs and non-work obligations, to the nature of work (though we also refer to dependent care arrangements from time to time when appropriate).

In this chapter we first discuss the social and psychological cases for gender equity and for policies and practices to support the integration of work and non-work life.

As the implementation of FWAs (and dependent care initiatives) is influenced by public policy provisions we then consider the regulatory background from a European/UK perspective before going on to consider the types of "work–life" policies or flexible working arrangements introduced in organizations. The impact and effectiveness of these policies and residual barriers to their success are then discussed, drawing on psychological concepts and theories at the individual and organizational levels. Such outcomes include well-being and perceived organizational justice, as well as organizational learning and other organizational issues. We demonstrate the interrelationships between individual and workplace outcomes, emphasizing the limitations of policy alone and the importance of implementation and practice.

2. THE SOCIAL CASE FOR GENDER EQUITY AT WORK

The need to consider the wider "social case" for gender equity stems from it forming the basis of the "external" forces influencing regulatory pressures, industrial/sectoral practices, company-level practices, and values-based influences on individual preferences for "work–life balance". Demands for gender equity do not merely arise on aggregate from individual employees; nor do they arise neutrally as some sort of human resource strategy in the face of competitive pressures. They arise as a result of the interaction between social forces within and outside organizations. Sayer (2007), making a more general point, puts this very succinctly:

We...cannot afford to ignore the special character of organisations as hierarchical and instrumental institutions pursuing highly specific goals. We also need to take account of the embedding of both employees and organisations in a wider field of social relations among equals and unequals. (Sayer 2007, 21)

The wider social influence on workplace gender equity is that of gendered labor market segmentation; itself a product of a wider (gendered) division of labor in society. At the core of the feminist critique of political economy is how the structure of the family is reproduced at societal level and how this creates structural disadvantage for women (Barratt-Brown 1995; Kirton and Green 2000). At the highest level, humankind requires reproduction as a prerequisite for survival; and the economic interests of capital requires future workers to be nurtured. The notion that women should bear a disproportionate burden of responsibility for this activity while men are able to fulfill their aspirations in the wider labor market has been termed "the myth of separate spheres" whereby the public sphere of work is regarded as primarily the domain of men while family and personal life are regarded as primarily the domain of women. This dualism impacts on workplaces by reinforcing gender inequity at work. It leads to the overvaluing of certain types of behavior, incorporated in gendered organizational cultures. In particular there is often an assumption that traditional male patterns of continuous full-time work is the norm and that stereotypically masculine characteristics such as rationality and competitiveness (rather than, for example, interpersonal skills) are necessary to be effective in the workplace (Rapoport et al. 2002)

The moral basis for the equitable treatment of women in the labor market has been supplemented by more instrumental pressures. Two developments are of particular importance, both of which relate to the most consistent demographic trend in every developed economy in the world; that of the rise in female participation in the labor market. Female participation in the labor market has grown from low absolute levels, marginalized within peripheral occupations, to almost parity in numbers and a presence in all occupations at the turn of the twenty-first century. Indeed, trends show that increased female participation has continued across the majority of OECD countries even since 1981 (OECD 2004). The first consequence of this demographic shift has been the growth in equality legislation arising, politically, from the women's movement and, industrially, from women's influence within the labor movement. The second consequence has been the increased bargaining power of (particularly) professional women in the labor market in recent decades. Thus, the growth in equality legislation acts as a negative incentive for employers to adjust inequitable practices affecting all employees so as to avoid litigation, while the enhanced labor market position (for some women) creates a more positive incentive for employers to adjust practices to appeal to those women whose skills and expertise are valued and who could be considered expensive to recruit, train, and therefore replace. In recent years the second of these factors has become particularly influential in creating a "business case" argument to make greater recognition of the domestic responsibilities of employees.

In short, then, social practices and social attitudes have shifted markedly in recent decades on the assumed roles of men and women within the workplace and in (although perhaps less so) the domestic sphere; in turn these changed assumptions and practices have shaped individual expectations, as we shall now discuss.

3. THE PSYCHOLOGICAL CASE FOR FLEXIBLE WORK TO SUPPORT GENDER EQUITY AT WORK

In terms of gender equity, most of the discussion from the organizational psychology literature has been based around the need to enhance employee choices in work patterns through the greater adoption of flexible working arrangements (FWAs). FWAs can support the integration of work and personal life which also addresses, to varying extents, the issue of gender equity at work. There are four main, interrelated psychological arguments for this. The argument that has received the most research attention rests on the case that multiple roles (particularly in work and family) have the potential to affect well-being negatively and create stress, unless policies are introduced to increase flexibility and autonomy in managing the work and family interface. In this approach the focus is very much on family responsibilities as the form of non-work roles under consideration and there is a large literature on the relationships between work, family, and well-being. This research originally stemmed from studies of the impact of maternal employment and hence a focus on women and difference. However it is increasingly recognized that both men and women have multiple roles in work and family.

The core concept in this perspective on the work–family interface is that of work–family conflict; a form of inter-role conflict in which the role pressures from the work and family domains are mutually incompatible in some respect (Greenhaus and Beutell 1985). There are different forms of conflict but that which has received most attention is time-based conflict.[1] This involves competing demands on time such as when a business meeting and a child's doctor's appointment coincide. Research on time-based work–family conflict stresses the importance of policies to help employees to manage their work and family time demands, although it does not always consider the gendered use of time. Although the concept of work–family conflict has been refined since the 1980s, for example distinguishing between work conflicting or interfering with family and family interfering with work, which have different antecedents and consequences (Frone, Russell, and Cooper 1992; O'Driscoll et al. 2003; Mesmer-Magnus and Viswesvaran 2006), work–family conflict remains the most widely researched concept in the psychology of work and family. It is argued that multiple roles can be a source of role overload, which in turn can be associated with stress, burnout, job dissatisfaction, and other negative consequences for individuals and organizations (see Bellavia and Frone 2005; MacDermid 2005; Tetrick and Buffardi 2006 for reviews). For instance, role overload has been linked to individual outcomes such as increased levels of anxiety, fatigue, burnout, depression, and emotional and physiological stress and to decreased satisfaction with family and work (Guelzow et al. 1991). Work–family conflict is also linked to a number of organizational outcomes including higher rates of absenteeism, lower levels of organizational commitment, and increased thoughts of quitting (Duxbury, Lyons, and Higgins in press).

This approach is based on a scarcity hypothesis; that is, the belief that individuals have a finite amount of time and energy, and that work and family compete for these finite resources. It implies that this is a problem of individual employees (who

---

[1] Other forms of conflict are strain based and behavior based (Greenhaus and Beurell 1985).

by implication are "different" from the norm) and views the role of organizations as being to introduce policies such as childcare support or flexible working policies to help individual employees to manage their complex demands and to avoid or reduce individual stress, absenteeism, and other negative outcomes. The focus on individuals, especially women in most cases, means that wider organizational systems remain largely unchallenged and gender inequities persist.

An alternative perspective is based on the role expansion hypothesis. This recognizes that multiple roles can create multiple sources of satisfaction and even protect against stress in some circumstances (Lewis, Kagan, and Heaton 2000). The positive side of the work–family interface—or the idea that work and family may actually be mutually beneficial—has begun to receive more attention (Frone, Russell, and Cooper 1992; see Carlson and Grzywacz in press, for review) supported by the growing interest in positive psychology more generally. Concepts from the positive perspective include positive spillover, enrichment, or facilitation (Carlson and Grzywacz in press). Positive spillover refers to the transfer of positive affect, skills, behaviors, and values from one domain to the other, having overall beneficial effects (Hanson, Hammer, and Colton 2006), while work–family enrichment refers to the extent to which experiences in one role improve performance or the quality of life in the other role (Greenhaus and Powell 2006; Wayne, Randel, and Stevens 2006). Work–family facilitation focuses on the synergies or complementarities that occur between an individual's work and family life (Frone 2003; Wayne, Randel, and Stevens 2006) or more recently the extent to which an individual's engagement in one social system (e.g., work or family) contributes to growth in another social system (family or work) (Carlson and Grzywacz in press). Another positive approach is work–family boundary theory (Campbell Clark 2000) which views people as active boundary crossers, developing active strategies for crossing boundaries between work and family rather than passive recipients of work–family pressures

These approaches are helpful in moving beyond a deficit view of those who have multiple roles in work and family to an acknowledgment of the potential positive outcomes of multiple roles, if workplace policies and practices support work–family boundary management. This has the potential to encourage a focus on workplace systems: cultures, structures, and working practices that might enable members of the workforce and the organization itself to benefit from the synergies between work and non-work lives. In practical terms it involves going beyond policies designed to mitigate stress (which are necessary but not sufficient) to seek win-win solutions to benefit both employees (men and women) and the organization as a whole.

A third perspective focuses on the life course. Work–family conflict and related stress appears to be greatest during the phase where employees have young children (Lewis and Cooper 1987; Barnett and Gareis 2006), although this may change in the context of ageing populations and explosion of eldercare issues which are also associated with work–family conflict (Townsend, Maline, and Druley 2001). Taking the role expansion approach it can be argued that experiences of caring at home during some periods in the life course can facilitate valuable workplace skills, particularly interpersonal skills. Problems arise because most organizations still adhere to traditional images of careers, whereby career progression has to take place at the same time as the family building phase and anyone who takes time out for family reasons, or who does not wish to work long hours while they have young children, risk losing their places on a career track. This view is short-sighted for two reasons. First, this model of career is no longer normative in the post jobs-for-life era. And second, organizations risk losing the skills of trained employees or of only promoting those who do not gain the potential advantages associated with participation in family as well as occupational life. The implication of this approach therefore is that gender equity and work–life/FWA approaches include a need to find ways of valuing diverse career shapes to take account of the sequencing of work and family events and to recognize that men as well as women are (or want to be) able to derive satisfaction from multiple domains.

A fourth approach which integrates aspects of both the positive and negative approaches focuses on the challenges of contemporary twenty-first century workplaces, rather than individual non-work commitments, taking account of changes and turbulence associated with technological developments, the changing nature of work, and the shifting nature of work/non-work boundaries in the global economy (Lewis and Cooper 1999). This includes a focus on the increased time in work, shifting cultural expectations; that is, organizational norms that reward long hours at the workplace rather than performance, the blurring of work/non-work boundaries, growing intensity of workloads, and faster pace of work demands (Bailyn 1993; Gambles, Lewis, and Rapoport 2006; Lewis and Smithson 2006; Lewis 2003a; Fried 1998; Wharton and Blair-Loy 2002; Duxbury, Lyons, and Higgins in press; Andreassi and Thompson in press; Hyman et al. 2003). All of these appear to be growing globally (Gambles, Lewis, and Rapoport 2006; Lewis and Smithson 2006; Duxbury, et al. Lyons, and Higgins in press). These trends tend to reinforce gendered organizational cultures. There are many opportunities for satisfaction and personal involvement in contemporary knowledge work (Lewis 2003a; Hochschild 1997). Among white collar and professional workers it often appears that long working hours are freely chosen, but in fact these "choices" are made within the constraints of lean workforces, high targets, and organizational cultures that often value willingness to work long hours and presenteeism for their own sake (Lewis 2003a; Perlow 1998). Research suggests that when job demands require "too much" effort and time (i.e., deadlines are too tight, resources are insufficient to allow the employee to fulfill their responsibilities at work during regular hours), energy and time resources are depleted and the effects of work overload, noted in the negative perspective, undermine the potential positive outcomes of the changing nature of much work, especially in the knowledge economy (Duxbury, Lyons, and Higgins in press).

This approach has also been reflected in research that looks beyond work and family boundaries to examine the impact of what has been termed the "time squeeze" on other aspects of life affecting men and women and reinforces the need to focus on organizations and gender equity rather than individuals and accommodations for individual problems. One example is the need for time and energy for leisure. Both work and leisure are essential for well-being (Bryce and Haworth 2003; Iso-Ahala and Mannell 1997) but time for leisure is increasingly squeezed out by contemporary workplace demands (Haworth and Lewis 2005). Moreover this is gendered, with men more likely to make time for leisure pursuits and women for family (Kay 2001) which increases gender inequities. Other aspects of personal life that are squeezed out by many contemporary work patterns include time for friendships, which again has implications for well-being (Gambles, Lewis, and Rapoport 2006; Parris, Vickers, and Wilkes, in press).

The implications of this approach for FWAs is that there is a need to examine more fundamental aspects of contemporary ways of working, taking a long-term perspective and considering the impact on gender equity, the sustainability of workforces, and broader social sustainability (Lewis, Gambles, and Rapoport 2007).

The psychological case therefore plays into the business case (which is discussed further, below); that is, it supports a case to redesign working practices to gain greater efficiency and to more successfully retain workers by reducing stress and sickness absence and thereby increasing organizational commitment. However, psychological arguments also suggest the need to look beyond fragmented policies to more systemic workplace changes, to take a life-course perspective, and to monitor the impact of contemporary ways of working which can undermine work–life and gender equity policies, and ultimately affect workforce and organizational well-being.

Before discussing workplace policies and practices to support the integration of work and personal life we consider the impact of macro-level context, particularly the role of regulation.

4. REGULATORY BACKGROUND TO THE IMPLEMENTATION OF GENDER EQUITY POLICIES

What determines the minimum standards of work–life policies in organizations is the regulatory environment at national level and on this there is a surprisingly high degree of divergence between countries. Broadly the division falls between those countries whose employment system could be categorized as liberal market economies and those characterized as coordinated market economies (Soskice 2005). Broadly speaking the coordinated market economies—where a "social dimension" is seen to require intervention to temper the excesses of the market—have tended to provide for a generous regulatory environment concerning maternity and childcare. This is best exemplified by the Nordic countries. In contrast, liberal market economies—where labor markets are assumed to be self-regulating and require no intervention—have tended to allow little in the way of regulatory protection at all. The exemplary case, here, is the US, where even paid maternity is not a statutory obligation for employers. A few hybrids exist here. The UK is usually characterized as falling within the liberal market economy type, yet in this area of employment policy, the UK regulatory approach has been tempered by its adoption of EU employment regulation—the Parental Leave Directive being a particularly recent relevant policy, here. Moreover, the UK had also already adopted the principle of paid maternity leave—as a contrast to the example of US practice, above—prior to its dramatic shift into the liberal market camp in the 1980s.

Of course, the regulations laid down, in themselves, are a product of arguments and interests played out over a longer period of time, incorporating a constantly changing consensus in the wider socio-political sphere, the demographic sphere (in relation to the changing gender composition in the workplace); within the family and what is known about the psychological well-being of the individual. In the UK—as in the EU more generally—the trajectory of regulatory change over the latter decades of the twentieth century and early twenty-first century has been tilted towards the enhancement of equality—even if unevenly at times (Dickens 2007). The expansion from "anti-discrimination" into a more positive promotion of equality—recognizing non-market and unpaid domestic work as part of the overall work environment—has been even more recent (Dickens 2007). Thus, paid maternity leave for mothers has been incrementally extended and supplemented with tentative steps towards normalizing minimal levels of paid paternity leave for fathers.

While the case for enhancing statutory work–life entitlements at work has been driven by "external" factors such as supranational regulation (in the case of EU member states), political pressure, and demographics, the regulatory shift has also often been made through a perceived need to convince business interests of the instrumental benefits of adopting such approaches—the so-called "business case." The business case is broadly based on the transaction costs associated with losing skilled and talented staff unable to commit to a traditional "nine-to-five" "presentee-ist" work culture. This has been—particularly in the UK—a largely successful approach inasmuch as business hostility to such incremental enhancements to work–life entitlements has been relatively low. There is, however, a noted danger in appealing to such instrumental values in that it does provide for a quite rational opposition to such enhancements where the benefits are clearly not there for the employer (Dickens and

Hall 2006; Roper, Cunningham, and James 2003)—for example, where margins are low and where high skills are not fundamental to the business model in question.

If we were to consider a continuum of regulations that could legitimately be said to cover the "work–life balance agenda" we would begin with appropriate employment protection for maternity leave, moving through to adequate pay for maternity leave, and to more general protections for parental leave and recognition of the responsibilities parents may have outside of work. This could further extend to appropriate recognition of (paid) paternity/parental leave aimed at equalizing the assumed responsibilities involved in both childcare and paid work. Regulations supporting work–life choices could also be considered important even where not directly aimed at childcare responsibilities; for example, guaranteeing equitable treatment of employees not working the standard working time (either in terms of the working week or the working year) ensuring that choices made are genuine choices and not choices that involve a (pro-rata) financial sacrifice or a substantial loss of job security. Finally, it could extend into a more proactive attempt to encourage fathers to take more time out of work to take more responsibility for childcare; the most notable example of this being the so-called "daddy-month" introduced—and then extended—in Sweden in 1995 and 2002 (Eriksson 2005).

5. Organizational Policies for Integrating Work and Non-work Life

Workplace policies developed to support the integration of work and personal life include dependent care supports and FWAs. Dependent care policies include support for childcare and/or eldercare such as workplace nurseries or funded places in a childcare or eldercare facility, childcare or eldercare vouchers, and out of school schemes. These are more important in contexts where there is limited or no public provision or childcare or other forms of care, or when public provision is limited in some way, so that there is scope for employers to improve provisions. These policies do not change the nature of work, but enable workers with family commitments to sustain employment. They can be regarded as equal opportunities provisions in that they enable women to work in the same ways that men do.

Family related leaves, discussed above, also enable people with family commitments to carry on working, but unlike dependent care provisions they have some impact on working practices as these must be adapted to facilitate temporary absences. Arrangements for dealing with family emergencies are particularly crucial.

Furthermore some forms of leaves, such as the Swedish "daddy leaves", mentioned above, have an explicit goal of supporting gender equity—a fair sharing of rewards and constraints by men and women.

Flexible working arrangements (FWAs) potentially change the nature of work, recognizing that work can be accomplished in different ways and, ideally, that outcomes are more important than input of hours in the workplace. Flexible working arrangements refer to any arrangements that enable workers to vary when and where they work (Lewis 2003b). They include flexitime systems, annualized hours, working from home for all or part of the week, and other forms of flexibility such as compressed working weeks (working full-time hours over a shorter number of days). FWAs also include various forms of part-time or reduced hours such as job sharing or term-time-only working. Ideally, flexible working arrangements provide opportunities for managers to respond to employees' changing needs which might for example be for short periods of part-time work interspersed with full-time flexitime. Flexible working arrangements can be introduced by HR in response to individual requests from staff, or by collective agreement.

Some forms of flexible working schedules such as part-time work, compressed working weeks, annualized hours, and flexitime have a long history and have traditionally been introduced largely to meet employer needs for flexibility or to keep costs down, though they may also have met employee needs and demands (Krausz, Sagie, and Biderman 2000). These and other flexible arrangements are also introduced ostensibly to meet employee needs for flexibility to integrate work and family demands under the banner of so-called family-friendly or work–life employment policies (Lewis and Cooper 1996) where, often, a business case argument has been used to support their adoption (Bevan et al. 1999). Other contemporary drivers of change include increased emphasis on high-trust working practices, the thrust towards gender equity and greater opportunities for working at home because of new technology (Evans 2000). Nevertheless, despite much rhetoric about the importance of challenging outmoded forms of work and the gradual association of FWAs with leading-edge employment practice (Friedman and Greenhaus 2000; Evans 2000; Lee, MacDermid, and Buck 2000), the implementation of these policies remains patchy across organizations (Hogarth et al. 2000).

6. THE IMPACT AND EFFECTIVENESS OF FWAS

How effective are FWAs? The answer varies according to the criteria used for effectiveness of polices and practices, which, in turn, reflect different conceptual/theoretical frameworks within which initiatives are embedded. At the most basic level, evaluation draws on work–family conflict theory (or less commonly, work–family enrichment theory) and consequences for individual well-being and organizational outcomes as discussed above. Research on the low take-up of policies and backlash against policies targeted at particular groups of employees has prompted evaluation in terms of equity and perceived organizational justice. Additionally, some research evaluates the impact on wider organizational culture and learning.

6.1 Impacts on Work–Family Conflict, Individual Well-Being, and Organizational Outcomes

Most research evaluating FWA policies and practices examines work–family conflict as a mediator between policies and organizational outcomes such as absenteeism, organizational commitment, and intention to quit (Kossek and Ozeki 1999; Kossek and Van Dyne in press). The impact of policies on more positive outcomes such as enrichment or facilitation and the implications for workplace outcomes has received less attention, although it is beginning to attract some more research (Wayne et al. 2006). Hence, currently the predominantly implicit focus is on reducing the potential negative effects of managing multiple roles rather than on enabling employees to use their non-work roles and experiences to enrich and facilitate their work. Moreover, evidence of the effectiveness of flexible working policies (and dependent care provisions) on work–family conflict and organizational outcomes is mixed (Kossek and Ozeki 1999; Kossek and Van Dyne in press; Sutton and Noe 2005). First, much depends on the outcomes studied. Second, the impacts of FWAs on work–family conflict and subsequent work-related outcomes also appear to vary for different groups of workers. Gender is a crucial variable (Greenhaus and Parasuraman 1999) and, in particular, the gender composition of workplaces (Holt and Thauow 1996; Maume and Houston 2001). For example, it is generally easier to take up FWAs in a female-dominated workplace than it is in a male-dominated workplace (Holt and Thaulow 1996). Age, life-course phase, and generation also appear to be relevant factors. There is evidence that younger workers—both men and women—are more likely than older workers to want FWAs. For example, in a study of chartered accountants in the UK, the link between work–family conflict and intention to leave was particularly strong among the younger generation who were also the most likely to say they would use FWAs. There is also emerging evidence that older workers, including those who would like to work beyond statutory retirement age, desire FWAs, so that they can integrate work with both family concerns such as eldercare and leisure and other activities (Irving, Steele, and Hall 2005).

FWAs appear to work best where employees are encouraged to participate in designing their own work routines in a way that does not damage output (Lewis and

Cooper 2005: Rapoport et al. 2002). One crucial factor influencing the outcomes of FWAs is the extent to which initiatives are perceived by employees as providing control and autonomy over working hours (Thomas and Ganster 1995; Krausz, Sagie, and Biderman 2000; Tausig and Fenwick 2001). Thomas and Ganster (1995) distinguish between family supportive policies and family supportive managers, both of which they found relate to perceived control over work and family demands, which in turn, are associated with lower scores on a number of indicators of stress among a sample of healthcare professionals. This implies that the more flexibility there is, the better. For example if someone works a fixed compressed working week and is unable to work one day he or she may not be able to make up the time, whereas if that person had complete flexitime they would be able to make up the time— hence absenteeism is lowest where there is most flexibility (Baltes et al. 1999).

However flexibility can also be double-edged in its effects. A theme in much current research is that those workers who have opportunities to work flexibly and have autonomy to manage their own work schedules often use this to work longer rather than shorter hours (Perlow 1998; Holt and Thaulow 1996). This is particularly apparent in the context of intensification of work (Burchell, Lapido, and Wilkinson 2001; Green and McIntosh 2001). Thus, although flexible working arrangements, such as working from home, can be regarded as a positive practice for employees with multiple roles, reducing work–family conflict and its consequences, it can also have negative consequences, such as "allowing" employees to work longer hours to manage intense workloads. Whilst this may seem to be mutually advantageous in the short term, its impact on long-term sustainability is questionable.

Overall, evidence in this tradition indicates that flexible working arrangements can be successful up to a point, but much depends on how they are implemented and managed (Lewis and Cooper 2005). Perceptions of fairness, management support, organizational culture, and learning are particularly crucial in this respect.

6.2 Perceived Organizational Justice

The impact of flexible working policies depends on how they are implemented and, more particularly, how equitable they are perceived to be. Perceived procedural and distributive justice as well as an individual sense of entitlement and equity are both important here.

In terms of perceived procedural justice, interventions in which employees have been able to participate in the design of work schedules appear to have the potential to achieve highly workable flexible arrangements and be associated with positive work-related attitudes (Smith and Wedderburn 1998; Rapoport et al. 2002). Conversely, a lack of consultation by senior managers about the development of FWAs can contribute to feelings of unfairness which may undermine implementation. Front-line managers can feel alienated if they are compelled to introduce policies on which they have not been consulted (Dex and Schriebl 2001), and their subsequent resistance can—and often does—undermine the experiences of FWAs among those whom they manage (Lewis 1997).

Perceived fairness of outcomes (distributive justice) is also important. Although FWAs can potentially benefit all employees and their employing organizations, they are often directed mainly at employees with family commitments—especially parents; and mostly mothers of young children (Young 1999). This can result in what has been termed work–family backlash among employees without children, particularly if they feel that they have to do extra work to cover for colleagues working more flexibly (Young 1999; Lewis and Smithson 2006). This raises the possibility of negative organizational outcomes of FWAs. Such situations could be exacerbated by the framing of regulation. For example, from 2002 employees in the UK were granted the right to request flexible working arrangements in the UK—but only for parents of children up to the age of 6. On the other hand there is some evidence that making FWAs normative and available to all—with rights matched by responsibilities for work being accomplished can be very effective (Rapoport et al. 2002; Lewis and Cooper 2005) which is an argument for extending the right to request to all workers.

Even if FWAs are, in theory, available to all, they are often implemented in a way that privileges management discretion, based on perceived operational needs. This reduces the need for managers to find innovative ways of reorganizing work to accommodate and benefit from flexible working arrangements (Rapoport et al. 2002; Lewis and Cooper 2005). While management discretion may be necessary in some circumstances, if this discretion is perceived to be used inconsistently or some managers are perceived as more supportive than others, this can cause feelings of inequity, job dissatisfaction, and higher intention to quit rates (Lewis and Smithson 2006). Management discretion appears to work best in a context of trust and mutual understanding.

Perceived procedural and distributive justice at the organizational level impact on individual sense of entitlement to take up flexible working arrangements. Sense of entitlement is a concept used to denote a set of beliefs and feelings about rights and entitlements, or legitimate expectations, based on what is perceived to be fair and equitable (Major 1993; Lewis and Smithson 2001; Lewis and Haas 2005). It is different from, albeit influenced by, actual legal or workplace entitlements (Lewis and Lewis 1996). A limited subjective sense of entitlement to be able to work in ways which are compatible with family demands can create low expectations of support and reluctance to request the flexibility that is needed to fulfill work and other obligations (Lewis and Lewis 1997). One criterion for the effectiveness of policies, therefore, is whether or not policies—and the ways in which they are implemented—enhance employees' sense of entitlement to modify work for non-work reasons.

Sense of entitlement is theorized as determined by social comparison processes (Lerner 1987), influenced by social context and ideology, and constructed on the basis of social, normative, and feasibility comparisons (Major 1987; 1993; Lewis and Lewis 1997). Judgments about what is fair or equitable are made on the basis of normative comparisons with others who are assumed to be similar to oneself (Major 1993). Gender appears to be particularly significant in influencing what is perceived as normative, appropriate, and feasible (Reichle 1996; Hochschild 1997). For example, if policies are mostly taken up by women, men are less likely to feel entitled to such support. Regulation can play an important role in enhancing sense of entitlement to use FWAs. A study of young European workers' expectations of employer support (Lewis and Smithson 2001) found that participants in Sweden and Norway—where welfare states are based on an equality gender contract, and a part of parental leave is reserved for fathers—demonstrated a higher sense of entitlement to support from the state and for employer flexibility in terms of working hours than those in Ireland, Portugal, and the UK, who emphasized self or family reliance. Sense of entitlement to work and family support was gendered among all these young adults, but less so in Sweden and Norway where there is strong state support for men as well as women to combine work and family roles. Hence regulation and the assumptions on which it is based can send out strong messages to employees about what is feasible, normative, and equitable.

Regulations such as the right to request flexibility play directly into redefining sense of entitlement. There is some evidence that right to ask for flexibility in the UK has increased requests, especially from women but also men, though with some variation based on organizational size, sector, and degree of unionization (Kersley et al. 2006).

Again however, the outcomes of regulation depend upon how this is implemented in practice. Sense of entitlement to take up public or workplace policies on flexible working can be limited by a culture in which ideal workers are not expected to work flexibly, undermining the potential positive impact of such policies. Moreover, in circumstances where FWAs are directed primarily at parents, perceived inequity by employees without children can also reduce the sense of entitlement to take up provisions among parents themselves (Lewis 1997; Lewis and Smithson 2001), reducing the take-up and therefore outcomes of FWAs.

7. Appropriate Organizational Support Mechanisms and Residual Barriers

It is increasingly recognized, as discussed above, that the impact of both government regulations and organizational FWAs depend on how they are implemented.

However, despite some evidence of positive outcomes (e.g., Goff, Mount, and Jamison 1990), there is now accumulating evidence that the impact of such initiatives depends on a range of factors, particularly organizational climate and support (e.g., Anderson, Coffey, and Byerly 2002; Allen 2001; O'Driscoll et al. 2003; Mauno, Kinnunen, and Piitulainen 2005; Mauno, Kinnunen, and Pyykkö 2005). For example, opportunities for flexible working are not always well communicated (Bond, Hyman, and Wise 2002) and employees with most need for flexibility are often unaware of the possibilities (Lewis, Kagan, and Heaton 2000).

Organizational culture and normative practices are particularly crucial in determining the outcomes of FWAs (Lewis 1997; 2001; Bailyn 1993; Hochschild 1997; Fried 1998). Aspects of culture such as the assumption that long hours of face time in the workplace are necessary to demonstrate commitment and productivity, especially among professional and managerial workers, can coexist with more surface manifestations of work–life support (Perlow 1998; Lewis 1997; 2001; Bailyn 1993; 2006; Rapoport et al. 2002). Drawing on Schein's (1985) model of organizational culture, flexible working arrangements or work–family policies can be regarded as surface-level artifacts which are underpinned and often undermined by values and assumptions (Lewis 1997). For example reduced hours or part-time working policies may be undermined by assumptions that these policies are only for women and that long hours are necessary to be committed or productive and therefore an undervaluing of those who work shorter hours. More recently constructs such as perceived work–family culture, perceptions of family-supportive organizations (Allan 2001), and perceived organizational family support (Jahn, Thompson, and Kopelman 2003) have been developed and operationalized (see Andreassi and Thompson in press for a review). Research consistently shows that these measures better predict positive individual and organizational outcomes than just the existence of work–family policies or FWAs (Andreassi and Thompson in press; Sahibzida et al. 2005; Dikkers et al. 2005; Mauno, Kinnunen, and Pyykkö 2005; Thompson and Prottas 2006).

Work–family culture in its various forms is usually considered to be multidimensional. Important dimensions include organizational time demands and perceived career consequences of using FWAs (Andreassi and Thompson in press). Other research distinguishes between a climate for sharing concerns or for sacrifices (Kossek, Colquitt, and Noe 2001). Given the prevailing focus on women, a more radical definition provided by Haas, Alard, and Hwang (2002) distinguishes different aspects of culture in terms of how far men are supported in taking leaves. In all these approaches supervisory and management support is considered a critical aspect of wider organizational culture and practice which is essential for policies to be effective in practice (Thomas and Ganster 1995; Goff, Mount, and Jamison 1990; Mesmer-Magnus and Viswesvaran 2006).

It is clear from both qualitative and quantitative research that management attitudes, values, and decisions are crucial to the effectiveness of FWAs (Lewis

1997; 2001; Hochschild, 1997; Dex and Schreibl 2001; Perlow 1998; Thomas and Ganster 1995; Goff, Mount, and Jamison 1990; Lee et al. 2000; Rapoport et al. 2002; Bond, Hyman, and Wise 2002). Managers must communicate, implement, and manage FWAs within organizational cultures which they both influence and are influenced by. Managers can increase the effectiveness of FWAs by their support-iveness (Allen 2001; Thompson et al. 1999; Thomas and Ganster 1995) or can undermine them by communicating, in a variety of ways, implicit assumptions about the value of more traditional ways of working (Lewis 1997; 2001; Perlow 1998). Managers also influence flexible working by their response to requests for non-standard work, by the ways in which they manage flexible workers on a day-to-day basis, and by their own flexibility and work–life integration.

Some recent research has begun to focus on other changes at the organizational level of analysis, for example examining contribution of FWAs to organizational learning and change (Lee, MacDermid, and Buck 2000; Rapoport et al. 2002) and demonstrating that FWAs can be a catalyst to positive and transformational workplace change. For example, Lee, MacDermid, and Buck (2000) examined responses to managerial and professional workers' requests for reduced hours in terms of the organizational learning that takes place. They found three different paradigms of organizational learning in this situation: accommodation, elabor-ation, and transformation. *Accommodation* involves making individual adaptations to meet the needs of specific employees, usually as a retention measure but not involving any broader changes. Indeed, efforts are made to contain and limit this different way of working, rather than using it as an opportunity for developing policies or broader changes in working practices. In other organizations with formal policies on FWAs backed up by a well-articulated view of the advantages to the organization, *elaboration* takes place. This goes beyond random individual responses to request for flexibility but full-time employees are still the most valued and employers make efforts to contain and systematize procedures for experiment-ing with FWAs. In the *transformation* paradigm of organizational learning FWAs are viewed as an opportunity to learn how to adapt managerial and professional jobs to the changing conditions of the global market place. The concern of employers is not to limit flexible working arrangements, but to use them to experiment and learn.

The notion that FWAs can be a positive strategy for responding to key business issues implicit in the transformational paradigm is also highlighted in studies that have employed action research to bring about organizational change to meet a *dual agenda* of organizational effectiveness, on the one hand, and work–personal life integration and gender equity, on the other hand, with both afforded equal import-ance (Rapoport et al. 2002). Organizational learning can be deliberately helped along, using a process termed collaborative interactive action research (CIAR). This involves collaboration between researchers and employees to explore the assump-tions underpinning taken-for-granted norms and ways of working that make it difficult to integrate work and non-work activities in gender equitable ways and then to develop collaboratively innovative interventions to address the dual agenda (Rapoport et al. 2002). This method can engender new FWAs implemented in gender equitable ways and elements of job redesign that support the integration on work and family as well as enhancing—or at least sustaining—workplace effectiveness.

Flexible working arrangements developed in this way and implemented in the context of wider systemic change, have the potential to reduce work–family conflict and enhance opportunities for work/non-work synergies in ways that are perceived as equitable by employees involved in the process. However change is ongoing in contemporary organizations and transformational or "win-win" solutions need to be continually monitored for their applicability in shifting contexts. For example, self-managing teams and self-rostering can be very effective ways of engaging workers in the design of work to support work/non-work integration and equity as well as effectiveness. However, recent research involving eleven case studies of private sector (finance) and public sector (social services) organizations in seven European states shows how this could be undermined in current contexts. With intensified workload and lean staffing, workers in self-managed groups were reluctant to work in flexible ways and especially to take off time for family reasons because they know that their colleagues, who would have to cover for them, were already overworked. In this context colleagues rather than managers became agents of control, and work–family conflicts were intensified rather than managed or reduced (Lewis and Smithson 2006). This points to the importance of realistic workloads for FWAs to be really effective.

Despite the possibilities for improvement, residual barriers remain. Many of these have already been mentioned. At the workplace level, this could be a macho culture influencing individual choices or the effects of work intensification creating a peer-generated fear of taking time off. Also, it could be managerial reluctance to challenge presenteeist working culture or a lack of willingness to trust employees to participate in decision-making about their own working arrangements. At the national level, it includes an approach to regulation constrained by the endorsement of representatives of business and, more generally, influenced by dominant ideas of what is possible and desirable within the relevant national business system (particularly if the system fits to the liberal market economy type).

Combine these factors and difficult scenarios become apparent. In liberal-market economies, the lower levels of employment protection and lower exit costs for—in particular—multinational companies and their subsidiaries, create a harsh environment to level up gender equity policies. Within the often maligned but descriptively useful "flexible firm" organizational type (Pollert 1991), the scenario in even the more enlightened employers' strategy, would be for a polarization of gender equity in different labor market subcategories (Blyton and

Turnbull 2004). Thus, men and women working in the "core"—highly skilled and educated, working at the organization at the apex of the supply chain in a professional capacity in a vital function—could expect that the business case for FWA will enable them to experience enlightened management attitudes. In contrast, those on the "periphery"—subcontracted, labor-intensive functions subject to cost-based competition (often, now aided by off-shoring)—will not find their employers able to make the same business case.

8. CONCLUDING COMMENTS

In this chapter the authors propose the use of the term gender equity as a means of integrating the principles of a range of approaches to enhancing the relationship between work and non-work life, without damaging relations between employees in the workplace. An integrated approach is quite possible without undermining the principles of either equal opportunities or of diversity. The dilemma in relation to work–life or work–family policies is that, currently, women tend to take on more family responsibilities than men (although this is changing, slowly). Therefore introducing policies aimed at enhancing family-friendly employment practices, while welcome in reducing work–family conflict, risk reinforcing these wider gender stereotypes by suggesting the need for "special treatment" for women. As long as initiatives to support the integration of work and personal life are directed primarily at women, they will not be mainstreamed into organizations and they will perpetuate gender inequities.

Any changes in workplace practice would ultimately require workplace culture change. However, such culture change will not happen without supportive policy shifts (both regulatory and organizational). The approach to organizational implementation is crucial, including the recognition and challenging of the gendered nature of most organizational cultures. Systemic change—rather than piecemeal change—is therefore crucial and this cannot be aimed at enhancing "choice"—as choice in certain presenteeist workplace cultures can lead to an intensification of work, rather than the opposite.

In many ways the cause of "work–life balance" could be said to have received some notable boosts in recent years. It is an area, in Britain for example, where employment regulation has moved consistently in the direction of improving the rights of employees over recent years—unlike in other areas of employment policy. However, in addition to criticism that such policy initiatives often intervene "on behalf of mothers"—thereby reinforcing traditional gender roles within the family—such policy moves have taken place in a dialogue dominated by the discourse of the "business case." Business case arguments for enhancing gender equity at work are useful, but long term it is not clear how well this could coexist with the broader "social justice" case in an increasingly fragmented employment scenario dominated with outsourcing and off-shoring issues.

On this final point, the role of regulation as a driver for organization change returns. Whilst most point to the importance of culture change as the key to embed practices that could enhance gender equity at work, it is clear that this cannot be assumed to be something that will take place by organizations voluntarily in the cases where it is—arguably—likely to be most needed (the peripheral labor markets). Future research will need to focus on these dilemmas addressing the importance of a multi-layered research approach, taking account of macro, meso, and micro contexts including, for example, the interaction between regulation, workplace policy and practice, and individual sense of entitlement to support for integrating work and family in gender equitable ways.

REFERENCES

ALLEN, T. 2001. Family-supportive work environments: the role of organizational perceptions. *Journal of Vocational Behavior*, 58: 414–35.

ANDERSON, S., COFFEY, B. S., and BYERLY, R. T. 2002. Formal organizational initiatives and informal workplace practices: links to work–family conflict and job-related outcomes. *Journal of Management*, 28 (6): 787–810.

ANDREASSI, J., and THOMPSON, C. In press. Work–family culture: current research and future directions. In *Handbook of Work–Family Integration: Theories, Perspectives and Best Practices*, ed. K. Korabik, D. S. Lero and D. L. Whitehead. New York: Elsevier.

BAILYN, L. 1993. *Breaking the Mold: Women, Men and Time in the New Corporate World*. New York: Free Press.

—— 2006. *Breaking the Mold: Redesigning Work for Productive and Satisfying Lives*, 2nd edn. Ithaca, NY: ILR Press.

BALTES, B. B., BRIGGS, T. E, HUFF, J. W, WRIGHT, J. A., and NEUMAN, G. A. 1999. Flexible and compressed workweek schedules: a meta-analysis of their effects on work-related criteria. *Journal of Applied Psychology*, 84 (4): 496–513.

BARNETT, R. C., and GAREIS, K. C. 2006. Antecedents and correlates of parental after-school concern: exploring a newly identified work–family stressor. *American Behavioral Scientist*, 49: 1382–400.

BARRATT-BROWN, M. 1995. *Models in Political Economy*. Harmondsworth: Penguin.

BELLAVIA. G., and FRONE, M. 2005. Work–family conflict. Pp. 113–47 in *Handbook of Work Stress*, ed. J. Barling, E. K. Kelloway, and M. Frone. London: Sage.

BEVAN, S., DENCH, S, TAMKIN, P., and CUMMINGS, J. 1999. *Family Friendly Employment: The Business Case*. London: DfEE Research Report RR136.

BLYTON, P., and TURNBULL, P. 2004. *The Dynamics of Employee Relations*. 3rd edn. Basingstoke: Palgrave.

BOND, S., HYMAN, J. and WISE, S. 2002. *Family Friendly Working? Putting Policy into Practice*. York: Joseph Rowntree Foundation.

BRYCE, J., and HAWORTH, J. 2003. Psychological well-being in a sample of male and female office workers. *Journal of Applied Social Psychology*, 33 (3): 565–85.

BURCHELL, B., LAPIDO, D., and WILKINSON, F. 2001. *Job Insecurity and Work Intensification*. London: Routledge.

CAMPBELL CLARK, S. 2000. Work/family border theory: a new theory of work/family balance. *Human Relations*, 53 (6): 747–70.

CARLSON, D., and GRZYWACZ, J. In press. Reflections and future directions on measurement in work–family research. In *Handbook of Work–Family Integration: Theories, Perspectives and Best Practices*, ed. K. Korabik, D. S. Lero, and D. L. Whitehead. New York: Elsevier.

DEX, S., and SCHREIBL, F. 2001. Flexible and family friendly working arrangements in SMEs: Business Case 2001. *British Journal of Industrial Relations*, 38 (3): 411–31.

DICKENS, L. 2007. The road is long: thirty years of equality legislation in Britain. *British Journal of Industrial Relations*, 45 (3).

—— and HALL, M. 2006. Fairness—up to a point: assessing the impact of New Labor's employment legislation. *Human Resource Management Journal*, 16 (4): 338–56.

DIKKERS, J., DEN DULK, L., GEURTS, S., and PEPER, B. 2005. Work-nonwork culture, utilization of work-nonwork arrangements, and employee-related outcomes in two Dutch organizations. In *Work and Family: An International Perspective*, ed. S. A. Y. Poelmans. Mahwah, NJ: LEA.

DUXBURY, L., LYONS, S., and HIGGINS, C. In press. Too much to do, and not enough time: an examination of role overload. In *Handbook of Work–Family Integration: Theories, Perspectives and Best Practices*, ed. K. Korabik, D. S. Lero, and D. L. Whitehead. New York: Elsevier.

ERIKSSON, R. 2005. Parental leave in Sweden: the effects of the Second Daddy Month. Swedish Institute for Social Research Working Paper 9/2005, Stockholm University.

EVANS, J. 2000. *Firms' Contributions to the Reconciliation of Work and Family Life*. Paris: OECD.

FRIED, M. 1998. *Taking Time: Parental Leave Policy and Corporate Culture*. Philadelphia: Temple University Press.

FRIEDMAN, S., and GREENHAUS, J. 2000. *Work and Family–Allies or Enemies? What Happens When Business Professionals Confront Life Choices*. Oxford: Oxford University Press.

FRONE, M. R., RUSSELL, M., and COOPER, M. L. 1992. Antecedents and outcomes of work–family conflict: testing a model of the work–family interface. *Journal of Applied Psychology*, 77 (1): 65–78.

GAMBLES, R. LEWIS, S., and RAPOPORT, R. 2006. *The Myth of Work–Life Balance: The Challenge of our Time for Men, Women and Societies*. Chichester: Wiley.

GREEN, F., and MCINTOSH, S. 2001. The intensification of work in Europe. *Labor Economics* 8 (2): 291–308.

GOFF, S. J., MOUNT, M. K., JAMISON, R. L. 1990. Employer supported child care, work/family conflict and absenteeism: a field study. *Personnel Psychology*, 43: 793–809.

GREENHAUS, J. H., and BEUTELL, N. J. 1985. Sources and conflict between work and family roles. *Academy of Management Review*, 10 (1): 76–88.

—— and PARASURAMAN, S. 1999. Research on work, family and gender: current status and future directions. In *Handbook of Gender and Work*, ed. G. Powell. Thousand Oaks, CA: Sage.

GREENHAUS, J. H., and POWELL, G. N. 2006. When work and family are allies: a theory of work–family enrichment. *Academy of Management Review*, 31: 72–92.

GUELZOW, M. G., BIRD, G. W., and KOBALL, E. H. 1991. An explanatory path analysis of the stress process for dual-career men and women. *Journal of Marriage and the Family*, 5: 151–64.

HAAS, L., ALLARD, K., HWANG, P. 2002. The impact of organizational culture on men's use of parental leave in Sweden. *Community, Work and Family*, 5: 319–42.

HANSON, G. C., HAMMER, L. B, and COLTON, C. L. 2006. Development and validation of a multidimensional scale of perceived work–family positive spillover. *Journal of Occupational Health Psychology*, 11: 249–65.

HAWORTH, J., and LEWIS, S. 2005. Work, leisure and well-being. *British Journal of Guidance and Counselling*, 33 (1): 67–79.

HOCHSCHILD, A. 1997. *The Time Bind: When Work Becomes Home and Home Becomes Work*. New York: Henry Holt.

HOGARTH, T., HASLUCK, C., PIERRE, G., WINTERBOTHAM, M., and VIVIAN, D. 2000. *Work-Life Balance 2000: Baseline Study of Work-Life Balance Practices in Great Britain*. London: DfEE.

HOLT, H., and THAULOW, I. 1996. Formal and informal flexibility in the workplace. In *The Work Family Challenge: Rethinking Employment*, ed. S. Lewis and J. Lewis. London: Sage.

HYMAN, J., BALDRY, C., SCHOLARIOS, D., and BUNZEL, D. 2003. Work-life imbalance in call centers and software development. *British Journal of Industrial Relations*, 41 (2): 215–39.

IRVING, P., STEELE, J., and HALL, N. 2005. *Factors Affecting the Labor Force Participation of Older Workers*. London: Department of Work and Pensions, Research Report 281.

ISO-AHOLA, S. 1997. A psychological analysis of leisure and health. In *Work, Leisure and Well Being*, ed. J. T. Haworth. London: Routledge.

—— and MANTELL, R. 1997. A psychological analysis of leisure and health. In *Work, Leisure and Well Being*, ed. J. T. Haworth. London: Routledge.

JAHN, E. W., THOMPSON, C. A., and KOPELMAN, R. E. 2003. Rationale and construct validity evidence for a measure of perceived organizational family support (POFS): because purported practices may not reflect reality. *Community, Work and Family*, 6: 123–40.

JUDIESCH, M., and LYNESS, K. 1999. Left behind? The impact of leaves of absence on managers' career success. *Academy of Management Journal*, 42: 641–51.

KAY, T. 2001. Leisure, gender and family: challenges for work–life integration. ESRC seminar series "Wellbeing: situational and individual determinants" 2001–2 <www.wellbeing-esrc.com> Work, employment, leisure and wellbeing.

KERSLEY, B., ALPIN, C., FORTH, J., BRYSON, A., BEWLEY, H., DIX, J., and OXENBRIDGE, S. 2006. *Inside the Workplace: Findings from the 2004 Workplace Employment Relations Survey*. London: Routledge.

KIRTON, J., and GREEN, A. 2000. *The Dynamics of Managing Diversity*. Oxford: Butterworth-Heinemann.

KOSSEK, E. E., and OZEKI, C. 1999. Bridging the work–family policy and productivity gap: a literature review. *Community, Work and Family*, 2(1): 7–32.

—— and VAN DYNE, L. E. (in press). Face-time matters. A cross-level model of how work–life flexibility influences work performance of individuals and groups. In *Handbook of Work–Family Integration: Theories, Perspectives and Best Practices*, ed. K. Korabik, D. S. Lero and D. L. Whitehead. New York: Elsevier.

—— COLQUITT, J. A., and NOE, J. A. 2001. Caregiving decisions, well-being, and performance: the effects of place and provider as a function of dependent type and work–family
climates. *Academy of Management Journal*, 44 (1): 29–44.

KRAUSZ, M., SAGIE, A., and BIDERMAN, Y. 2000. Actual and preferred work scheduling
control as determinants of job related attitudes. *Journal of Vocational Behavior*, 56: 1–11.

LEE, M., MACDERMID, S., and BUCK, M. 2000 Organizational paradigms of reduced load
work; accommodations, elaboration and transformation. *Academy of Management Journal*, 43 (6): 1211–36.

LERNER, M. J. 1987. Integrating societal and psychological rules of entitlement: implications
for comparable worth. *Social Justice Research*, 1: 107–25.

LEWIS, S. 1997. Family friendly policies: organisational change or playing about at the
margins? *Gender, Work and Organisations*, 4: 13–23.

—— 2001. Restructuring workplace cultures: the ultimate work–family challenge? *Women
in Management Review*, 16 (1): 21–9.

—— 2003a. The integration of work and personal life. Is post industrial work the new
leisure? *Leisure Studies*, 22: 343–55.

—— 2003b. Flexible working arrangements: implementation, outcomes and management.
In *International Review of Industrial and Organisational Psychology*, vol. xviii, ed. C. L.
Cooper and I. Robertson. New York: Wiley.

—— and COOPER, C. L. 1987 Stress in two earner couples and stage in the life cycle. *Journal
of Occupational Psychology*, 60: 289–303.

—— —— 1996. Balancing the work family interface: a European perspective. *Human
Resource Management Review*, 5: 289–305.

—— —— 1999. The work–family research agenda in changing contexts. *Journal of Occupational Health Psychology*, 4 (4): 382–93.

—— —— 2005. *Work–Life Integration: Case Studies of Organisational Change*. New York:
Wiley.

—— and LEWIS, J. 1997. Work family conflict: can the law help? *Legal and Criminological
Psychology*, 2: 155–167.

—— and HAAS, L. 2005. Work-life integration and social policy: a social justice theory and
gender equity approach to work and family. In *Work and Life Integration: Organisational,
Cultural and Individual Perspectives*, ed. E. Kossek and S. Lambert. Mahwah, NJ: LEA.

—— and SMITHSON, J. 2001. Sense of entitlement to support for the reconciliation of
employment and family life. *Human Relations*, 55 (11): 1455–81.

—— —— 2006. Final Report of the Transitions Project for the EU Framework 5 funded
study "Gender, parenthood and the changing European workplace." Manchester: RIHSC,
Manchester Metropolitan University.

—— GAMBLES, R., and RAPOPORT, R. 2007. The constraints of a work–life balance approach: an international perspective. *International Journal of Human Resource Management*, 18 (3): 360–73.

—— KAGAN, C., and HEATON, P. 2000. Dual earner parents with disabled children.
Patterns for working and caring. *Journal of Family Issues*, 21 (8): 1031–60.

LIFF, S., and DICKENS, L. 2000. Ethics and equality: reconciling false dilemmas. In *Ethical
Issues in Contemporary Human Resource Management*, ed. D. Winstanley and J. Woodall.
Basingstoke: MacMillan.

MacDermid, S. 2005. (Re)considering conflict between work and family. In *Work and Life Integration: Organisational, Cultural and Individual Perspectives*, ed. E. Kossek and S. Lambert. Mahwah, NJ: LEA.

Major, B. 1993. Gender entitlement and the distribution of family labor. *Journal of Social Issues*, 493: 141–59.

Major, J. 1987. Gender, justice and the psychology of entitlement. Pp. 124–48 in *Review of Personality and Social Psychology*, vol. vii, ed. P. Shaver and C. Hendrick. Newbury Park, CA: Sage.

Maume, D., and Houston, P. 2001. Job segregation and gender differences in work–family spillover among white collar workers. *Journal of Family and Economic Issues*, 22 (2): 171–89.

Mauno, S., Kinnunen, U., and Piitulainen, S. 2005. Work–family culture in four organizations in Finland: examining antecedents and outcomes. *Community, Work and Family*, 8: 115–41.

—— —— and Pyykkö, M. 2005. Does work–family conflict mediate the relationship between work–family culture and self-reported distress? Evidence from five Finnish organizations. *Journal of Occupational and Organizational Psychology*, 78: 509–31.

Mesmer-Magnus, J. R., and Viswesvaran, C. 2006. How family-friendly work environments affect work/family conflict: a meta-analytic examination. *Journal of Labor Research*, 27: 555.

O'Driscoll, M., Poelmans, S., Spector, P., Kalliath, T., Allen, T., Cooper, C., and Sanchez, J. 2003. Family-responsive interventions, perceived organizational and supervisor support, work–family conflict, and psychological strain. *International Journal of Stress Management*, 10 (4): 326–44.

OECD. 2004. *Female Labor Force Participation: Past Trends and main Determinants in OECD Countries*. Organisation for Economic Cooperation and Development, May.

Parris, M., Vickers, M., and Wilkes, L. In press. Fitting friendship into the equation: middle managers and the work/life balance. *Community, Work and Family*.

Perlow, L. A. 1995. Putting the work back into work/family. *Group and Organization Management*, 20: 227–39.

—— 1998 Boundary control: the social ordering of work and family time in a high tech organisation. *Administrative Science Quarterly*, 43: 328–57.

Pollert, A. 1991. The orthodoxy of flexibility. In *Farewell to Flexibility*, ed. A. Pollert. Oxford: Blackwell.

Rapoport, R. Bailyn, L., Fletcher, J., and Pruitt, B. 2002. *Beyond Work–Family Balance: Advancing Gender Equity and Work Performance*. Chichester: Wiley.

Reichle, B. 1996. From is to ought and the kitchen sink: on the justice of distributions in close relationships. In *Current Societal Concerns about Justice*, ed. L. Montado and M. Lerner. Critical Issues in Social Justice. New York: Plenum.

Roper, I., Cunningham, I., and James, P. 2003. Promoting family-friendly policies: is the basis of the Government's ethical standpoint viable? *Personnel Review*, 32 (2): 211–32.

Sahibzada, K., Hammer, L. B., Neal, M. B., and Kuang, D. C. 2005. The moderating effects of work–family role combinations and work–family organizational culture on the relationship between family-friendly workplace supports and job satisfaction. *Journal of Family Issues*, 26: 1–20.

Sayer, A. 2007. Moral economy and employment. Pp. 21–40 in *Searching for the Human in Human Resource Management*, ed. S. Bolton and M. Houlihan. Basingstoke: Palgrave.

SCHEIN, E. 1985. *Organizational Culture and Leadership*. San Francisco: Jossey-Bass.

SMITH, P. A., and WEDDERBURN, A. A. 1998. Flexibility and long shifts. *Employee Relations*, 20 (5): 483–9.

SOSKICE, D. 2005. Varieties of capitalism and cross-national gender differences. *Social Politics*, 12 (2): 170–9.

SUTTON, K., and NOE, R. 2005. Family friendly programs and work–life integration: more myth than magic? In *Work and Life Integration: Organizational, Cultural and Individual Perspectives*, ed. E. Kossek and S. Lambert. Mahwah, NJ: LEA.

TAUSIG, M., and FENWICK, R. 2001. Unbinding time: alternate work schedules and work–life balance. *Journal of Family and Economic Issues*, 22 (2): 101–19.

TETRICK, L. E., and BUFFARDI, L. C. 2006. Measurement issues in research on the work–home interface. Pp. 90–114 in *Work-Life Balance: A Psychological Perspective*, ed. F. Jones, R. J. Burke, and M. Westman. Hove: Psychology Press.

THOMAS, L. T., and GANSTER, D. C. 1995. Impact of family-supportive work variables on work–family conflict and strain: a control perspective. *Journal of Applied Psychology*, 80: 6–15.

THOMPSON, C. A., and PROTTAS, D. J. 2006. Relationships among organizational family support, job autonomy, perceived control, and employee well-being. *Journal of Occupational Health Psychology*, 11 (1): 100–18.

—— BEAUVAIS, L. L., and LYNESS, K. S. 1999. When work–family benefits are not enough: the influence of work–family culture on benefit utilization, organizational attachment, and work–family conflict. *Journal of Vocational Behavior*, 54 (3): 392–415.

TOWNSEND, A., MALINE, L., and DRULEY, J. 2001. Balancing parent care with other roles: interrole conflict of adult daughter caregivers. *Journal of Gerontology*, 56 (1): 24–34.

WAYNE, J. H., RANDEL, A. E., and STEVENS, J. 2006. The role of identity and work–family support in work–family enrichment and its work-related consequences. *Journal of Vocational Behavior*, 69: 445–67.

WHARTON, A. S., and BLAIR-LOY, M. 2002. The "overtime culture" in a global corporation: a cross-national study of finance professionals' interest in working part-time. *Work and Occupations*, 29: 32–64.

WILLIAMS, J. 2000. *Unbending Gender: Why Work and Family Conflict and What to Do about it*. NY: Oxford University Press.

YOUNG, M. 1999. Work–family backlash: begging the question, what's fair? *Annals of the American Academy of Political Science*, 562: 32–46.

18

SEX AND RACE DISCRIMINATION IN PERSONNEL DECISIONS

LAURA M. GRAVES

GARY N. POWELL

1. INTRODUCTION

DESPITE the passage of employment equity laws, women and people of color continue to be disadvantaged in today's workplace. The global labor force remains sharply segregated on the basis of sex and race such that women and people of color are over-represented in lower-paying occupations and under-represented in higher-paying occupations (Powell and Graves 2003). Moreover, top management continues to be the exclusive domain of white males in most countries (Catalyst 2006; Wirth 2001).

The disadvantaged workplace status of women and people of color is due to a complex set of historical, social, economic, and organizational factors. In this chapter, we focus on the role of personnel decision-making processes within organizations in perpetuating the disadvantaged status of women and people of color. Personnel decisions, which include judgments about who to hire, promote, and develop, and what to pay them, determine whether women and people of color have access to jobs, financial rewards, and advancement opportunities. Discrimination in these decisions plays a critical role in maintaining the disadvantaged status of women and people of color, who have less favorable career outcomes (e.g., promotions, organizational level, pay) than men and whites even after accounting for human capital variables such as education and experience (Dreher and Cox 2000; Hurley and Giannantonio 1999; James 2000; Landau 1995; Stroh, Brett, and Riley 1992).

Social scientists have offered numerous theoretical explanations for sex and race discrimination. In this chapter, we review the key explanations and discuss how they apply to organizational personnel decisions, citing relevant research findings. We then attempt to make sense of the multiplicity of theories, identifying similarities and contradictions in their arguments and the predictions that follow from them. We also consider the role of organizational factors in the occurrence of sex and race discrimination. We conclude by offering implications for research and practice.

2. EXPLANATIONS FOR DISCRIMINATION

In this section, we review prominent theories of the psychological processes underlying sex and race discrimination in personnel decisions, including stereotyping, prejudice, status characteristics theory, social role theory, prototype matching, the similarity-attraction paradigm, social identity theory, and group composition theories. Most of these theories are based, at least in part, on the premise that people categorize others based on social categories (e.g., sex, race, age, religion, profession). Categorization is a fundamental aspect of interpersonal perception; it brings order to our complex social worlds, helping us to understand others, predict their behavior, and determine how to react to them (Ashforth and Mael 1989; Stangor and Lange 1994; Tajfel 1981; Taylor et al. 1978). Since manifestations of sex and race are visible and highly salient, categorization on the basis of these factors is typically automatic (Fiske and Neuberg 1990; Ito and Urland 2003; Norton, Vandello, and Darley 2004). Sex and race categorization unleashes psychological processes that set the stage for discrimination. These psychological processes are not necessarily mutually exclusive, but may operate simultaneously.

2.1 Stereotyping

Sex and race categorization is likely to activate gender and race stereotypes (Stangor and Lange 1994). Stereotypes are "beliefs about the characteristics, attributes, and behaviors of members of certain groups" (Hilton and Von Hippel 1996,

240). Commonly held gender stereotypes depict the typical woman as communal (e.g., gentle, kind, expressive, affectionate, and tactful) and the typical man as agentic (e.g., dominant, competent, daring, competitive, and courageous) (Carli and Eagly 1999; Deaux and Kite 1993; Williams and Best 1990). Research on race stereotypes has focused primarily on Anglos's general stereotypes of other groups (Fiske 1998). These stereotypes portray blacks as lazy, ignorant, athletic, rhythmic, low in intelligence, poor, criminal, hostile, and loud (Devine and Elliot 1995; Plous and Williams 1995) and Latinos as lazy, dirty, aggressive, traditional, and proud (Stangor and Lange 1994). In addition to general gender and race stereotypes, decision makers are likely to possess stereotypes for subtypes based on sex (e.g., housewife, career woman, macho man), race (e.g., black political activist, black athlete), or combinations of sex, race, and/or other factors (e.g., white blue-collar man, Asian professional woman) (Deaux 1995; Fiske 1998; Stangor et al. 1992).

Recent research suggests that stereotypes of social groups reflect two core dimensions, competence and interpersonal warmth, each of which varies from low to high (Fiske et al. 2002; Fiske, Xu, and Cuddy 1999). Stereotypes of the dominant societal in-group (e.g., white males) consist of positive attributes associated with high competence and high warmth. In contrast, most stereotypes of social out-groups (e.g., women, people of color) are a mix of positive and negative attributes and portray out-group members as lacking in either competence or warmth.

One type of out-group stereotype, the paternalistic stereotype, portrays group members as low in competence and high in warmth. Paternalistic stereotypes are reserved for low-status out-groups (e.g., elderly, disadvantaged blacks, housewives) that are believed to possess no intent to harm the in-group (high warmth) and no ability to do so (low competence) (Fiske et al. 2002; Fiske, Xu, and Cuddy 1999). Members of these out-groups are seen as incompetent, subservient, and perhaps deserving of sympathy (Fiske et al. 2002). The general stereotype of women as high in communal qualities and low in agency is consistent with the paternalistic stereotype. Paternalistic stereotypes, with their assumption of low competence, are clearly inconsistent with high levels of performance in organizational settings.

A second type of out-group stereotype, the envious stereotype, portrays group members as high in competence and low in warmth (Fiske et al. 2002; Fiske, Xu, and Cuddy 1999). Envious stereotypes reflect an underlying belief that members of the out-group pose a competitive threat to the in-group's power and resources (Fiske et al. 2002; Fiske, Xu, and Cuddy 1999). Although out-group members are viewed as performing well (high competence), their goals are believed to be incompatible with the goals of the in-group (low warmth). Envious stereotypes are typically applied to groups that are successful but threatening to the in-group's power and resources. For instance, Asians may be stereotyped as being competent (particularly in quantitative domains), intelligent, and industrious, but lacking warmth (e.g., aloof, not interacting much with others, calculating) (Fiske et al.

2002; Fiske, Xu, and Cuddy 1999; Pittinsky, Shih, and Ambady 2000; Stangor and Lange 1994). Similarly, career women may be stereotyped as competent, but not socially skilled or warm (Fiske et al. 2002; Rudman and Glick 1999). Envious stereotypes are problematic because they imply that group members lack interpersonal skills or cannot be trusted to pursue organizational goals.

Although some out-groups (e.g., welfare recipients, the homeless) are stereotyped as low in both competence and warmth, the paternalistic and envious stereotypes are most common (Fiske et al. 2002). Regardless of the specific stereotype that is activated, decision makers will process information about an individual's qualifications, performance, or future potential in a manner that is consistent with the stereotype (Fiske 1998; Ilgen and Youtz 1986; Stangor and Lange 1994). Decision makers seek, attend to, and more readily accept information that is stereotype consistent (Biernat and Ma 2005; Fiske 1998). In contrast, information that is ambiguous or disconfirms stereotypes is unlikely to be sought, attended to, or accepted.

Decision makers may ask questions of job applicants that confirm rather than disconfirm the activated stereotypes (Snyder and Swann 1978). Decision makers evaluating applicants or employees may also see and recall characteristics and behaviors that are stereotype consistent (Biernat and Ma 2005; Ilgen and Youtz 1986; Pittinsky, Shih, and Ambady 2000). For instance, a study of simulated hiring decisions found that white decision makers recalled black applicants as offering less intelligent interview responses than white applicants, despite the fact that applicants' responses did not vary by race (Frazer and Wiersma 2001). Ultimately, decision makers will see what they expect to see and are unlikely to reject the activated stereotypes unless the available information about the candidate or employee is profoundly inconsistent with the stereotypes (Fiske 1998; Fiske and Neuberg 1990). Given that stereotypes of women and people of color portray them as deficient in some way and that decision makers are likely to process information in a stereotype-consistent manner, the activation of gender and race stereotypes is likely to lead to biased personnel decision making and reduced opportunities and rewards for women and people of color.

2.2 Prejudice

Prejudice is defined as negative affect or attitudes toward members of a certain demographic group (Fiske 1998). Sexism consists of prejudice based on sex, and racism consists of prejudice directed by one racial group towards another.

Scholars have identified various subtypes of sexism and racism (Powell and Graves 2003). Swim et al. (1995) distinguished between old-fashioned and modern sexism. Old-fashioned sexism is blatant; it is associated with endorsement of traditional gender roles in the workplace, differential treatment of women and men, and perceptions of lower female competence. In contrast, modern sexism is associated with the denial of workplace sex discrimination, antagonism toward women's demands that alleged sex discrimination be discontinued, and lack of support for programs designed to help women in the workplace. The modern sexist, thus, expresses disdain toward women who claim that there are barriers to performing non-traditional roles at work.

In the same vein, Glick and colleagues distinguished between hostile and benevolent sexism (Glick and Fiske 1996; 2001; Glick et al. 2000). Hostile sexism entails antagonism toward women who are viewed as challenging or usurping men's power (e.g., feminists, career women, seductresses). Benevolent sexism puts women on pedestals; it characterizes women as "pure creatures who ought to be protected, supported, and adored and whose love is necessary to make a man complete" (Glick and Fiske 2001, 109). Benevolent sexism implies that women are weak and best suited to conventional feminine roles, and offers protection, affection, and rewards to women who endorse these roles (e.g., wives, mothers, romantic objects) (Glick and Fiske 2001). Benevolent sexism is not benign; it assumes women's inferiority and is used to justify women's subordination to men.

Sexism leads to negative outcomes for women in organizations, particularly those who pursue occupations that are associated with men. For instance, modern sexists exaggerate women's representation in male-intensive occupations, reject sex discrimination as a cause of the gender segregation of occupations, and have negative attitudes towards affirmative action programs designed to assist women (Swim et al. 1995; Tougas et al. 1995). Ironically, modern sexists seem to personally benefit from their sexist attitudes; they rely more on men for work-related advice, and, in turn, may gain more access to resources and receive more promotions (Watkins et al. 2006). Both hostile and benevolent sexism among men pose barriers to women's representation in the economy, particularly in non-traditional roles (Glick et al. 2000; 1997). Hostile sexists of both sexes prefer male authority figures over female authority figures, evaluate male candidates for managerial positions more highly than female candidates, and are more tolerant of sexual harassment toward women (Masser and Abrams 2004; Rudman and Kilanski 2000; Russell and Trigg 2004).

Racism may be categorized as old-fashioned or modern (McConahay 1986). Old-fashioned racism entails overt expressions of hostility and antagonism. These overt expressions of prejudice appear to have declined as a result of civil rights legislation and socially dictated egalitarian values (Dovidio and Gaertner 2000). Modern racism, which is also called "aversive" (Gaertner and Dovidio 1986) or "symbolic" (Sears 1988) racism, is a more subtle form of prejudice. Modern racists endorse racial equality and avoid obvious acts of discrimination to maintain their self-images as fair and just individuals. However, they still harbor unconscious negative feelings and beliefs about low-status racial groups. These feelings and beliefs result in subtle bias, particularly when such bias is not obvious or can be rationalized based on factors other than race. Like modern sexists, some modern racists deny the existence of racial discrimination, express antagonism towards the demands of people of color, and resent programs that support people of color (McConahay 1986; Sears 1988). Despite its subtle nature, modern racism is extremely detrimental to people of color (Deitch et al. 2003; Gaertner and Dovidio 1986). It may lead whites to display acts of "microaggression" toward people of color (Pettigrew and Martin 1987), including avoidance, closed and unfriendly verbal and non-verbal communication, and failure to help, all of which lead people of color to feel devalued and discriminated against (Deitch et al. 2003).

Consistent with the concept of modern racism, white decision makers prefer white applicants over black applicants when applicants' qualifications are ambiguous, organizational authorities provide a business rationale for selecting white applicants, or unobtrusive measures are used (e.g., recall of applicant's interview comments, confidence in hiring decisions) (Brief et al. 2000; Dovidio and Gaertner 2000; Frazer and Wiersma 2001; Stewart and Perlow 2001). Further, compared to whites, people of color experience everyday mistreatment at work that is consistent with modern racism (e.g., not provided information needed to do job, unfair performance evaluations, not given assignments needed to advance; Deitch et al. 2003). Such mistreatment not only compromises job attitudes and well-being, but is likely to jeopardize performance and rewards.

2.3 Status Characteristics Theory

According to status characteristics theory (Berger, Fiske, and Norman 1998; Berger, Wagner, and Zelditch 1985; Ridgeway 1991), individuals are assigned social status or esteem based on the demographic groups to which they belong. Judgments of individuals' task competence are based, in part, on the status assigned to members of their demographic group. Individuals who belong to high-status groups are viewed as more competent and able than those of low-status groups; positions of authority are generally reserved for presumably competent high-status individuals (Rudman and Kilanski 2000).

In Western societies, race and sex are demographic characteristics with clearly established status value, and whites and men are held in higher honor and esteem than people of color and women. Because females and people of color are typically ascribed less status, decision makers may believe that they are less competent and able than men and whites. These beliefs apply both to general competence and to various specific skills (Foschi, Lai, and Sigerson 1994). As a result of the perceived inferior competence of women and people of color, organizational decision makers may be reluctant to provide them with opportunities and may require additional evidence of their competence before granting such opportunities (Biernat 2003; Biernat and Fuegen 2001; Biernat and Kobrynowicz 1997; Foschi 1996).

Decision makers' tendency to hold women and people of color in low esteem and to view their ability as suspect leads to discrimination. For instance, lower esteem for women than men is associated with discrimination against women in hiring decisions, even after removing the effects of gender stereotyping (Jackson, Esses, and Burris 2001). Successful performance by women and people of color is less likely to be interpreted as evidence of ability than successful performance by men and whites (Foschi 1996; Foschi, Lai, and Sigerson 1994; Greenhaus and Parasuraman 1993). Further, women and people of color must provide more evidence of their capabilities and possess more human capital (e.g., job-specific and overall work experience) before decision makers are willing to hire or promote them (Baldi and McBrier 1997; Biernat and Kobrynowicz 1997; Smith 2005).

2.4 Social Role Theory

Social role theory (Eagly, Wood, and Diekman 2000) suggests that discrimination, particularly discrimination based on sex, results from social roles. According to the theory, men and women differ in their occupational and family roles. Generally, the resource provider role is assigned to men and the homemaker role is assigned to women. Moreover, when women are employed outside of the home, as is often the case in industrialized countries, they typically hold different types of jobs than men (Eagly, Wood, and Diekman 2000). Consistent with gender stereotypes, women's jobs require more expressive and subordinate behaviors (e.g., nurturing, caretaking), and men's jobs require more agentic, dominant behaviors (e.g., leading, directing). As a result of this distinction between women's and men's roles, women and men often develop different skills and modify their behaviors to be consistent with gender roles. Moreover, people expect, or even demand, that women and men behave in a manner consistent with their assigned social roles.

Sex differences in social roles may lead decision makers to possess very different expectations regarding the roles of men and women at work (Powell and Graves 2003; Pratto et al. 1997; Eagly, Wood, and Diekman 2000). Given men's breadwinner or resource provider role, decision makers are likely to view men's presence in the workplace as normal. Men are also likely to be assigned to high-status jobs that require male-stereotypical agentic and dominant behaviors. In contrast, decision makers may question women's presence in the workplace because it violates the homemaker role. When women are accepted in organizations, they are likely to be assigned to low-status jobs that require female-stereotypic expressive and subordinate behaviors (Eagly, Wood, and Diekman 2000). Moreover, women who violate social roles by displaying agentic and dominant behaviors or seeking roles that are associated with these behaviors are likely to be rated unfavorably (Heilman et al. 2004; Rudman 1998).

Consistent with social role theory, women are viewed as less qualified and are less likely to be hired than men for jobs that are typically held by men, or are perceived to require male-stereotypic agentic and dominant behaviors (Cohen, Broshchak, and Haveman 1998; Davison and Burke 2000; Jawahar and Mattsson 2005; Konrad and Pfeffer 1991; McRae 1994; Pratto et al. 1997; Rudman and Kilanski 2000). Women who hold jobs associated with men or engage in male-stereotypic agentic behaviors receive lower performance ratings than their male counterparts, and are disliked and derogated when they do achieve success (Bartol 1999; Heilman et al. 2004; Robbins and DeNisi, 1993; Rudman 1998; Sackett, DuBois, and Noe 1991).

2.5 Prototype Matching

Sex and race discrimination may also derive from the prototype-matching process that decision makers use to assess applicants and employees (Powell and Graves 2003; Heilman 1983; Perry 1994; Perry, Davis-Blake, and Kulik 1994). During prototype matching, decision makers unconsciously form mental prototypes, or images of the ideal job holder, which define the traits and behaviors that are required for success in a particular job. As decision makers evaluate potential or current employees, they favor individuals whose perceived traits and behaviors come closest to matching these prototypes. Discrimination may occur when decision makers' ideal job holder prototypes incorporate sex (a sex-based prototype) or race (a race-based prototype) in some way (Heilman 1983; Perry, Davis-Blake, and Kulik 1994; Powell and Butterfield 2002).

Prototypes of the ideal job holder may incorporate sex or race by including traits and behaviors that are stereotypically linked to a particular sex or race; individuals who belong to groups that are believed to possess the desired attributes are viewed as more suitable than those who belong to groups that are viewed as lacking those attributes (Glick, Zion, and Nelson 1988; Perry, Davis-Blake, and Kulik 1994; Stewart and Perlow 2001). For example, if the prototype for a particular job (e.g., manager) emphasizes stereotypically masculine traits (e.g., dominant, competent), males may be seen as better qualified (Schein et al. 1996). If the prototype for the job (e.g., day care worker, nurse) includes stereotypically feminine traits (e.g., nurturing, caring), females will be seen as more suitable (Davison and Burke 2000; Glick, Zion, and Nelson 1988). Similarly, if a particular job is deemed to require scientific and quantitative skills, Asians, who are stereotyped as possessing those skills, may be seen as suitable (Leong and Hayes 1990).

Prototypes of the ideal job holder may also incorporate sex or race when job incumbents or applicants are predominantly from one sex or race; individuals typically believe that the demographic group that occupies a job in greater numbers performs best (Davison and Burke 2000, Glick 1981; Konrad and Pfeffer 1991; Perry, Davis-Blake, and Kulik 1994). Thus, for female-intensive jobs (e.g., day care worker, counselor, receptionist/secretary), females are likely to be rated as more qualified, hired more often, offered higher starting salaries and more challenging job assignments (Glick 1981; Heilman 1980). In contrast, males are likely to be favored over females for male-intensive jobs (e.g., firefighter, surgeon, finance officer). Asians, who are highly represented among engineers, mathematicians, and computer scientists, may be seen as possessing the qualities for such jobs (Leong and Hayes 1990). White men, who hold the majority of top management positions, are likely to be seen as possessing the personal qualities necessary for performance as successful executives (Powell and Butterfield 2002).

Sex and race are also incorporated into decision makers' prototypes through their connections with the status differences described earlier. Because men and whites are generally held in high esteem, decision makers may associate men and whites with high-status positions in organizations (Pratto et al. 1997; Rudman and Kilanski 2000; Stewart and Perlow 2001). In contrast, the low societal status of women and people of color may cause them to be linked to low-status positions.

Prototype matching is unlikely to lead decision makers to hire blatantly unqualified applicants of the "correct" sex or race over qualified applicants of the "wrong" sex or race (Powell and Graves 2003). However, they may select moderately qualified applicants of the correct group over slightly more qualified applicants of the other group, perhaps rationalizing their decisions by interpreting the relative importance of the selection criteria in a way that makes the applicant of the correct group appear more qualified (Norton, Vandello, and Darley 2004).

Consistent with the idea of sex-based prototypes (as well as social role theory), a large body of evidence indicates that women experience more discrimination when jobs are associated with masculine traits, men, or high status (Cohen, Broschak, and Haveman 1998; Davison and Burke 2000; Jawahar and Mattsson 2005; Konrad and Pfeffer 1991; McRae 1994; Pratto et al. 1997; Rudman and Kilanski 2000). Race-based prototypes may be less prevalent than sex-based prototypes because race is less strongly linked to particular jobs than is sex (Ilgen and Youtz 1986; Sackett, DuBois, and Noe 1991). Nonetheless, hiring decisions are influenced by the match between the racial composition of job incumbents and the race of the candidate, as well as the similarity between the attributes and status associated with the job and the attributes and status associated with the candidate's racial category (Konrad and Pfeffer 1991; Leong and Hayes 1990; Stewart and Perlow 2001). Also, consistent with the use of race-based prototypes, black, Asian and Latino managers receive lower performance ratings and have lower likelihood of promotion than white managers (Greenhaus, Parasuraman, and Wormley 1990; Hurley and Giannantonio 1999; Landau 1995).

2.6 Similarity-Attraction Paradigm

The similarity-attraction paradigm (Byrne 1971; Byrne and Neuman 1992) suggests that people are attracted to, prefer to interact with, and exhibit a positive bias toward people whom they see as similar to themselves. Demographic character-istics such as sex and race are among the factors that determine perceptions of similarity (Graves and Powell 1995).

Applying the similarity-attraction paradigm to personnel decisions, sex or race similarity between the decision maker and an applicant or employee may lead to perceived similarity in attitudes and values, which in turn leads to interpersonal attraction or liking. This interpersonal attraction will lead to more extensive and favorable interactions and to positively biased personnel decisions (Graves and Powell 1995; 1996; Powell and Graves 2003). For instance, sex or race similarity between an employment interviewer and job applicant might increase interviewer-applicant attraction, enhancing rapport between the two parties and improving the quantity and quality of communication in the interview (Graves and Powell 1996). The interviewer's attraction to a demographically similar candidate may also lead to more positive questioning strategies and to positively biased information stor-age, retrieval, and synthesis (Dipboye and Macan 1988; Graves and Powell 1995). In the end, judgments may be influenced by the sex or race similarity between the interviewer and the applicant.

The implications of the similarity-attraction paradigm go well beyond interview judgments. Similarity-attraction processes may lead to what Kanter (1977a) termed "homosocial reproduction," in which decision makers associate with and sponsor individuals who are similar to themselves in highly visible and immutable demo-graphic characteristics such as race and sex. Since organizational decision makers are often male and white, homosocial reproduction may lead to more opportunities for males and whites than women and people of color (Baldi and McBrier 1997; Green-haus, Parasuraman, and Warmley 1990; Kanter 1977a).

Researchers have found some evidence of same-sex favoritism in interviewers' ratings of applicants and supervisors' ratings of employee performance (e.g., Gallois, Callan, and Palmer 1992; Graves and Powell 1996; Tsui and O'Reilly 1989; Varma and Stroh 2001). Also, mentors appear to prefer to establish relationships with protégés of the same sex rather than the opposite sex (Dreher and Cox 1996). This preference for same-sex mentoring relationships makes it difficult for women to establish mentoring relationships with white men, and, given white men's dominance in organizations, restricts women's compensation attainment (Dreher and Cox 1996; Ragins and Cotton 1999).

Same-race favoritism has been documented in supervisors' evaluations of sub-ordinate performance (Mount et al. 1997; Tsui and O'Reilly 1989) and interviewers' evaluations of job applicants (McFarland et al. 2004; Stoll, Raphael, and Holzer 2004). Race similarity may also affect the formation of supervisor–subordinate and mentor–protégé relationships; supervisors and mentors are likely to prefer same-race relationships (Dreher and Cox 1996; Ensher and Murphy 1997; Lefkowitz 1994; Thomas 1993).

2.7 Social Identity Theory

Social identity theory (Ashforth and Mael 1989; Capozza and Brown 2000; Tajfel and Turner 1986) and self-categorization theory (Turner 1985) suggest that people develop social identities based on the social categories to which they belong. After categorizing themselves and others based on social categories, people seek to build and maintain positive identities by making positively biased comparisons between members of their own group and members of other groups. Accordingly, people generally identify with and favor individuals who share their category memberships, including same-sex and same-race others (Brewer and Miller 1984; Williams and O'Reilly 1998). Such favoritism is presumed to occur even in the absence of interpersonal interaction (Tsui, Egan, and O'Reilly 1992).

Individuals are most likely to identify with and favor same-sex and same-race others when sex and race are salient components of their social identities (Powell and Butterfield 2002). Salience may be heightened by personal factors such as experiences with sexism and/or racism, and situational factors such as a low proportion of women and/or people of color in a role (Ashforth 2001; Wharton 1992). The status associated with an individual's sex and race is also posited to affect the social identification process. Members of low-status social groups, typically women and people of color, may sometimes maintain positive social identities by distancing themselves from their own groups and identifying with high-status groups, typically males and whites (Chattopadhyay, Tluchowska, and George 2004; Ely 1994; Graves and Powell 1995; Tajfel and Turner 1986).

This theoretical perspective implies that personnel decision makers will favor same-sex and same-race others, and that favoritism may occur without interpersonal interaction, such as when recruiters evaluate résumés. The degree to which favoritism occurs depends on the salience of sex and race to the decision maker. Favoritism for opposite-sex and opposite-race others may sometimes be exhibited by decision makers from low-status sex and race categories. To the extent that whites and males are highly represented among decision makers or ascribed high status in the organization, these dynamics are likely to disadvantage women and people of color.

As noted in our discussion of the similarity-attraction paradigm, there is some support for the idea that same-sex and same-race favoritism occurs in personnel decisions. Further, such favoritism appears to be a function of the salience of sex and race. Several studies have found that women are more likely to engage in same-sex favoritism than men, and blacks are more likely to engage in same-race favoritism than whites; due to past experiences with discrimination, sex may be more salient to women than men and race may be more salient to blacks than whites (Gallois, Callan, and Palmer 1992; Graves and Powell 1996; McFarland et al. 2004; Tsui and O'Reilly 1989). There is also evidence, albeit limited, that decision makers from low-status groups identify with high-status groups and devalue members of their own group (Graves and Powell 1995; Powell and Butterfield 2002).

2.8 Group Composition Theories

Group composition theories (e.g., Blau 1974; Gutek 1985; Kanter, 1977b) focus on the effects of the relative numbers of people from different social categories in a work unit or group (Konrad, Winter, and Gutek 1992; Powell and Graves 2003). Such theories suggest that discrimination is likely to occur when a work unit is comprised of a clear numerical majority of a particular sex and/or race. Under these circumstances, members of the numerical majority have few interactions with the numerical minority; members of the minority are highly conspicuous and subject to prejudice and discrimination. In contrast, when a work unit is made up of a more equal representation of the sexes and/or races, the majority find it difficult to avoid interacting with the minority. Social interaction and communication between members of the different social categories decrease their use of these categories in their evaluations of each other. The majority begins to view members of the minority as individuals rather than simply as representatives of their social categories, resulting in a reduction of prejudice and discrimination.

Kanter (1977a; 1977b) theorized that discrimination by the numerical majority against the numerical minority is most problematic in skewed groups, i.e., groups in which the ratio of the majority to the minority ranges from about 85:15 to almost 100:0. Members of the numerical majority in skewed groups are "dominants," because they control the group and its culture. Members of the other category are "tokens," because they are viewed as representatives of their group rather than as individuals.

According to Kanter (1977a; 1977b), tokens receive special treatment that is detrimental to their performance in several ways. First, tokens face performance pressures. Because they are highly visible, they get attention that dominants do not. This does not necessarily lead to recognition of their competence. Tokens may have to work harder to get their accomplishments recognized. Second, differences between tokens and dominants tend to be exaggerated. Dominants then emphasize their own commonalities and exclude tokens from social activities. Third, the characteristics of tokens are often distorted or misperceived because of the dominants' tendency to stereotype them. Tokens are expected to behave in a manner consistent with the stereotype of their group or risk rejection by the majority.

Early theorists (e.g., Blau 1974; Kanter 1977b) assumed that the effects of being in the minority or being a token were identical, regardless of which sex and/or race was in the minority. However, recent literature suggests that the processes described earlier (e.g., stereotypes, status assignments, and social roles) exacerbate the effects of minority status for women and people of color (Gutek 1985; Konrad, Winter, and Gutek 1992; Yoder 1991; Zimmer 1988). In support of this argument, women (Elvira and Cohen 2001; Konrad, Winter, and Gutek 1992;

Lyness and Thompson 2000) and people of color (Zatzick, Elvira, and Cohen 2003) who are numerically under-represented are especially likely to experience discrimination or leave their jobs. For instance, females who are in the minority or tokens are excluded from social networks, and receive lower performance ratings and fewer promotion opportunities. In contrast, men who are in the minority or tokens are unlikely to experience discrimination, and may even derive advantages (e.g., higher performance ratings, more promotions) from their token or minority status (Heikes 1991; Kirchmeyer 1995; Lyness and Thompson 2000; Pazy and Oron 2001).

Some scholars (e.g., Blalock 1967; Tolbert, Graham, and Andrews 1999) have theorized that women and people of color are likely to suffer discrimination, not when their representation in a work unit is very small, but as it grows. Men and whites generally control organizational resources and generally feel little threat to their power when the proportions of women and people of color are small. However, when the proportion of women or people of color increases, men and whites may feel threatened, leading to antagonism between the sexes or races, and discrimination. Discrimination may diminish when the representation of women or people of color increases to the extent (e.g., 40 percent) that they are able to exercise some power. Research focusing on the turnover of women and people of color provide some support for these notions (e.g., Tolbert et al. 1995; Zatzick, Elvira, and Cohen 2003).

In addition, the exact number and nature of the demographic subgroups in a work unit, not just the proportions of the two sexes and various races, may be important to understanding discrimination (Lau and Murnighan 1998; 2005). When there are many possible subgroups and these subgroups are demographically heterogeneous, sex- and race-related effects are unlikely to occur (Brewer 2000; Lau and Murnighan 1998). For example, a work unit comprised of a 40-year-old white male engineer, a 65-year-old black female engineer, a 45-year-old Asian male sales representative, and a 20-year-old white female sales representative could form coalitions based on age, race, occupation, or sex. Because forming a coalition based on any one category would lead to differences within the coalition on other categories, coalition formation is unlikely and sex- or race-related effects should not occur. However, in a unit composed of two middle-aged white male engineers and two young black female sales representatives, there are only two possible subgroups, one composed of white men and one composed of black women. Because this grouping of individuals increases the emphasis on sex and race, sex- and race-related effects are likely to occur (Powell and Graves 2003).

Although the various perspectives on group composition effects offer somewhat different predictions regarding the exact effects of being in numerical minority, they generally suggest that women and people of color are vulnerable to discrimination when their representation is small and there are few possible demographic subgroups in the work unit.

3. COMPARISON OF EXPLANATIONS

The explanations for discrimination described above differ in a number of ways. Three of the explanations, stereotypes, prejudice, and status characteristics theory, imply that discrimination can be predicted directly from decision makers' beliefs about and feelings toward women and people of color. These beliefs and feelings may characterize women and people of color as incompetent, unlikable, and/or unworthy of respect.

The social role theory and prototype matching explanations suggest that the likelihood of discrimination against women and people of color will depend on the nature of the job; women and people of color will be subjected to discrimination when jobs are not typically held by individuals of their sex and race or are believed to require attributes that are not stereotypically associated with their sex and race. Because high-status, high-compensation jobs are often held by men and whites or associated with the characteristics of men and whites (e.g., dominance), these theories suggest that women and people of color will have limited opportunities to obtain such jobs.

The similarity-attraction and social identity theory perspectives suggest that the sex and race of the decision maker will be important in determining whether discrimination occurs. Both of these perspectives suggest that decision makers typically favor individuals from their own race/gender group. The predictions derived from the two theories differ slightly. The similarity-attraction explanation suggests that decision makers will uniformly favor those of their own race and sex. Social identity theory suggests that decision makers will favor others who belong to social groups with which they identify, typically, but not always, members of their own race and sex. Both explanations imply that women and people of color are likely to be discriminated against when there are few women and people of color among organizational decision makers.

Group composition theories propose that discrimination is a function of the relative numbers of men, women, and various racial groups in a work unit, as well as the composition of demographic subgroups in that unit. Women and people of color are likely to experience discrimination when they make up a small proportion of individuals or when demographic subgroups are easily formed on the basis of sex and race.

As noted earlier, the various explanations for discrimination are not mutually exclusive; the psychological processes posited by the various perspectives may co-occur. Thus, discrimination may be a function of the decision maker's beliefs and feelings about women and people of color, the nature of the job and its perceived appropriateness for women and people of color, the decision maker's own sex and race (and his or her similarity to and identification with the applicant/employee), and the demographic characteristics of the members of the work unit. Thus, discrimination against women and people of color is the result of a complex set of processes, making it difficult to understand and prevent.

4. ORGANIZATIONAL FACTORS

Because categorization by sex and race plays a critical role in evoking the psychological processes that create discrimination, it would seem that such discrimination is likely to vary according to whether the organizational context emphasizes or de-emphasizes sex and race (Brewer and Miller 1984; Deaux and Major 1987). When organization factors de-emphasize the importance of sex and race as a component of members' identities or create equality between the sexes and races, categorization should be reduced and negative outcomes may be averted. However, when these factors emphasize the importance of sex and race or discourage equality, discrimination is more likely to occur. Several situational factors appear to be important, including the demographic composition of the organization and its senior officials, the organizational culture, and the nature of personnel decision-making processes.

The sex and race composition of the larger organization is likely to affect the emphasis on sex and race (Milliken and Martins 1996; Powell and Graves 2003). Sex and race differences may be less important in settings where there is a great deal of sex and race diversity than in organizations where there is little. In organizations with a more balanced sex and race composition, individuals should be accustomed to differences in sex and race and should not use these characteristics as the basis for categorization.

The sex and race composition of the organization's senior management may also affect the likelihood of discrimination by influencing the relative status of women and men and of various racial groups (Burke and McKeen 1996; Elvira and Cohen 2001; Ely 1995). In organizations where there are few women and people of color in key roles, membership in various sex and race categories is associated with differences in organizational status and power. This correspondence between sex and race categories on the one hand and status and power on the other hand accentuates attention to sex and race, thereby increasing the likelihood of sex- and race-based psychological processes and discrimination. In contrast, when women and people of color are adequately represented at the top of the organization, there is little correspondence between social category membership and organizational status and power, thereby reducing sex- and race-based categorization and decreasing the likelihood of discrimination. Consistent with this argument, evidence (Burke and McKeen 1996; Ely 1994; 1995; Mellor 1995) suggests that the sex composition of top officials influences the social construction of gender in organizations, as well as women's peer relationships and intentions to remain with their organizations.

The organization's culture, especially its values regarding diversity, may have a strong influence on the emphasis placed on sex and race (Powell and Graves 2003). Organizations with positive diversity cultures reduce the likelihood of categorization and discrimination (Ely and Thomas 2001; Kossek and Zonia 1993). In a positive diversity culture, organizational members value efforts to increase the representation of women and people of color and view members of these groups as qualified. Equality is stressed and differences in status based on sex and race are reduced. Further, employees acknowledge differences among each sex and race, which allows organizational members to view individuals as distinct persons, not just as representatives of their social categories. Moreover, organizations that regard the insights, skills, and experiences of individuals from different backgrounds as valuable business resources create an environment where all employees are valued and respected (Ely and Thomas 2001).

The nature of the organization's personnel decision-making procedures, particularly whether decisions are standardized and structured and decision makers are held accountable, affects the degree of attention to sex and race. Standardized, structured procedures (e.g., structured employment interviews, behaviorally anchored performance appraisal rating scales) force decision makers to obtain and to process information about individuals' qualifications or performance in a systematic and detailed manner, thereby reducing attention to sex and race (Campion, Palmer, and Campion 1997; Powell and Butterfield 1994; Powell and Graves 2003; Williamson et al. 1997). In contrast, procedures that are unstandardized and unstructured are likely to be highly subjective, and, as a result, are susceptible to bias. Of course not all standardized, structured personnel decision-making procedures reduce attention to social categories; the content of such procedures is important. For instance, the US army's official standards for evaluating performance and assigning jobs actually increases the focus on sex by specifying differing standards for the two sexes (e.g., lower fitness requirements for women, no combat eligibility) (Biernat et al. 1998).

The likelihood of discrimination may also be reduced when decision makers are held accountable for their decisions (Powell and Graves 2003). Decision makers who believe that their decisions will be monitored for bias by others (e.g., superiors, human resources department) may be motivated to make fair decisions, increasing the likelihood that they will consciously attend to job-related rather than demographic factors in the decision-making process (Graves 1993). Decision makers' motivation to make bias-free decisions may be especially high when their performance appraisals and rewards are dependent on the quality of their decisions.

In summary, the demographic composition of the organization and its senior management, the diversity culture, and the nature of personnel decision-making procedures are likely to affect attention to sex and race in personnel decision making. Although research on the influence of these factors is limited, it seems that sex and race are less likely to affect decisions when the organization and its senior management are diverse with respect to sex and race, when the organization's diversity culture is positive, and when decision makers use standardized, structured decision-making procedures and are held accountable for their decisions.

5. IMPLICATIONS FOR RESEARCH AND PRACTICE

Our discussion of sex and race discrimination in personnel decisions contains several key themes, each of which has important implications for research and practice. First, sex and race discrimination is extremely complex; it involves a variety of potentially co-occurring psychological processes and may be influenced by several organizational factors. Researchers must acknowledge this complexity by adopting a systematic approach that recognizes the multitude of psychological processes and organizational factors involved. Although no single study can incorporate all of the variables we described in this chapter, integrating several theoretical explanations in a single study with one or two of the organizational factors would be helpful. Studies typically focus on one or two theoretical explanations (e.g., stereotyping and status judgments, similarity-attraction paradigm and social identity theory), and sometimes merely assess sex or race differences in outcomes rather than testing the mechanisms posited by the theories. Ignoring the numerous processes and factors that contribute to discrimination yields conflicting results across studies and does not advance our understanding of discrimination or our ability to prevent it.

Organizational attempts to prevent discrimination must also recognize its complexity. Our review implies that preventing discrimination demands a multifaceted approach and suggests several strategies that might be helpful, including (but certainly not limited to) selecting unbiased decision makers, altering decision makers' beliefs and attitudes through training, ensuring that some decision makers are women and people of color, examining and perhaps modifying the sex and race composition of work units, organizations, and top management, creating a positive diversity culture, and modifying personnel procedures. Although focusing on one or two of these strategies may provide some benefits, fully addressing discrimination demands a more comprehensive approach.

Another theme woven throughout our discussion is the importance of categorization. Categorization by sex and race appears to trigger the psychological processes that lead to sex and race discrimination; eliminating categorization may be a key factor in preventing discrimination. Researchers should test the role of categorization in evoking each of the psychological processes outlined in the chapter. For instance, does reducing categorization reduce the influence of prejudice in personnel decisions or do prejudiced decision makers always exhibit bias? Are sex- and race-based similarity-attraction and social identification processes less likely to occur when sex- and race-based categorization are reduced? It would also be useful to identify specific strategies for reducing categorization and to test their relative effectiveness. Our discussion of organizational factors offers several suggestions regarding strategies that might be tested including altering the demographic composition of the unit, organization, and top management, creating a positive diversity culture, and improving personnel decision-making procedures.

Organizations that wish to reduce discrimination might find it fruitful to focus on techniques that reduce categorization. As noted above, organizational factors such as the demographic composition of the unit, organization, and top management, the diversity culture, and personnel decision-making procedures deserve close attention. It may also be desirable to provide decision makers and employees with alternative (non-demographic) sources of identity such as a team, work unit, or larger organization (Elsass and Graves 1997; Brewer and Miller 1984). For instance, structuring work such that tasks and outcomes are interdependent and individuals must work together to achieve mutual goals may lead individuals to identify themselves as part of a larger group; the collective identity may supplant identities based on demographic characteristics (Brewer and Miller 1984; Elsass and Graves 1997; Fiske 2000).

6. CONCLUSION

Sex and race discrimination in personnel decision making plays a key role in perpetuating the disadvantaged workplace status of women and people of color. Discrimination against women and people of color appears to be triggered by sex and race categorization, which unleashes a multitude of potentially damaging psychological processes. These processes include stereotyping, prejudice, status judgments, social role prescriptions, prototype-matching processes, similarity-attraction dynamics, social identification, and group composition effects. The characteristics of the organization, particularly the extent to which they draw attention to sex and race, influence whether categorization and the associated psychological processes occur. Overall, our discussion underscores the complexity of discrimination and the difficulty of understanding and preventing it. Both research and organizational practice must mirror this complexity if we are to be successful in eradicating discrimination.

References

ASHFORTH, B. E. 2001. *Role Transitions in Organizational Life: An Identity-Based Perspective.* Mahwah, NJ: Erlbaum.

ASHFORTH, B. E., and MAEL, F. 1989. Social identity theory and the organization. *Academy of Management Review,* 14: 20–39.

BALDI, S., and McBRIER, D. B. 1997. Do the determinants of promotions differ for blacks and whites? *Work and Occupations,* 24: 478–97.

BARTOL, K. M. 1999. Gender influences on performance evaluations. Pp. 165–78 in *Handbook of Gender and Work,* ed. G. N. Powell. Thousand Oaks, CA: Sage.

BERGER, J., FISKE, M. H., and NORMAN, R. Z. 1998. The evolution of status expectations: a theoretical extension. Pp. 175–205 in *Status, Power and Legitimacy: Strategies and Theories,* ed. J. Berger and M. F. Zelditch. New Brunswick, NJ: Transaction.

—— WAGNER, D. G., and ZELDITCH, M., Jr. 1985. Introduction: expectations states theory: review and assessment. Pp. 1–72 in *Status, Rewards, and Influence,* ed. J. Berger and M. Zelditch Jr. San Francisco: Jossey-Bass.

BIERNAT, M. 2003. Toward a broader view of social stereotyping. *American Psychologist,* 58: 1019–27.

—— and FUEGEN, K. 2001. Shifting standards and the evaluation of competence: complexity in gender-based judgment and decision making. *Journal of Social Issues,* 57: 707–24.

—— and KOBRYNOWICZ, D. 1997. Gender- and race-based standards of competence: lower minimum standards but higher ability standards for devalued groups. *Journal of Personality and Social Psychology,* 72: 544–57.

—— and MA, J. E. 2005. Stereotypes and the confirmability of trait concepts. *Personality and Social Psychology Bulletin,* 31: 483–95.

—— CRANDALL, C. S., YOUNG, L. V., KOBRYNOWICZ, D., and HALPIN, S. M. 1998. All that you can be: stereotyping of self and others in a military context. *Journal of Personality and Social Psychology,* 75: 301–17.

BLALOCK, H. M. 1967. *Toward a Theory of Minority Group Relations.* New York: Wiley.

BLAU, P. M. 1974. Presidential address: parameters of social structure. *American Sociological Review,* 39: 615–35.

BREWER, M. B. 2000. Reducing prejudice through cross-categorization: effects of multiple social identities. Pp. 165–83 in *Reducing Prejudice and Discrimination,* ed. S. Oskamp Mahwah, NJ: Lawrence Erlbaum.

—— and MILLER, N. 1984. Beyond the contact hypothesis: theoretical perspectives on desegregation. Pp. 281–302 in *Groups in Contact: The Psychology of Desegregation*, ed. N. Miller and M. B. Brewer. Orlando, FL: Academic Press.

BRIEF, A. P., DEITZ, J., COHEN, R. R., PUGH, S. D., and VASLOW, J. B. 2000. Just doing business: modern racism and obedience to authority as explanations for employment discrimination. *Organizational Behavior and Human Decision Processes*, 81: 72–97.

BURKE, R. J., and MCKEEN, C. A. 1996. Do women at the top make a difference? Gender proportions and the experiences of managerial and professional women. *Human Relations*, 49: 1093–104.

BYRNE, D. 1971. *The Attraction Paradigm*. New York: Academic Press.

—— and NEUMAN, J. H. 1992. The implications of attraction research for organizational issues. Pp. 29–70 in *Issues, Theory, and Research in Industrial and Organizational Psychology*, ed. K. Kelley. New York: Elsevier.

CAMPION, M. A., PALMER, D. K., and CAMPION, J. E. 1997. A review of structure in the selection interview. *Personnel Psychology*, 50: 655–702.

CAPOZZA, D., and BROWN, R. 2000. *Social Identity Processes: Trends in Theory and Research*. London: Sage.

CARLI, L. L., and EAGLY, A. H. 1999. Gender effects on social influence and emergent leadership. Pp. 203–21 in *Handbook of Gender and Work*, ed. G. N. Powell. Thousand Oaks, CA: Sage.

CATALYST. 2006. *Census of Women Corporate Officers and Earners*. New York: Catalyst.

CHATTOPADHYAY, P., TLUCHOWSKA, M. and GEORGE, E. 2004. Identifying the ingroup: a closer look at the influence of demographic dissimilarity on employee social identity. *Academy of Management Review*, 29: 180–202.

COHEN, L. E., BROSCHAK, J. P., and HAVEMAN, H. A. 1998. And then there were more? The effect of organizational sex composition on the hiring and promotion of managers. *American Sociological Review*, 63: 711–27.

DAVISON, H. K., and BURKE, M. J. 2000. Sex discrimination in simulated employment context: a meta-analytic investigation. *Journal of Vocational Behavior*, 56: 225–48.

DEAUX, K. 1995. How basic can you be? The evolution of research on gender stereotypes. *Journal of Social Issues*, 51: 11–20.

—— and KITE, M. 1993. Gender stereotypes. Pp. 107–39 in *Psychology of Women: A Handbook of Issues*, ed. F. L. Denmark and M. A. Paludi. Westport, CT: Greenwood.

—— and MAJOR, B. 1987. Putting gender into context: an interactive model of gender-related behavior. *Psychological Review*, 94: 369–89.

DEITCH, E. A., BARSKY, A., BUTZ, R. M., CHAN, S., BRIEF, A. P., and BRADLEY, J. C. 2003. Subtle yet significant: the existence and impact of everyday discrimination in the workplace. *Human Relations*, 56: 1299–324.

DEVINE, P. G., and ELLIOT, A. J. 1995. Are racial stereotypes *really* fading? The Princeton trilogy revisited. *Personality and Social Psychology Bulletin*, 21: 1139–50.

DIPBOYE, R. L., and MACAN, T. M. 1988. A process view of the selection/recruitment interview. Pp. 217–32 in *Readings in Personnel and Human Resource Management*, ed. R. S. Shuler, S. A. Youngblood, and V. L. Huber. St Paul, MN: West.

DOVIDIO, J. F., and GAERTNER, S. L. 2000. Aversive racism and selection decisions: 1989 and 1999. *Psychological Science*, 11: 315–19.

DREHER, G. F., and COX, T. H. 1996. Race, gender, and opportunity: a study of compensation attainment and the establishment of mentoring relationships. *Journal of Applied Psychology*, 81: 297–308.

—— —— 2000. Labor market mobility and cash compensation: the moderating effects of race and gender. *Academy of Management Journal*, 43: 890–900.

EAGLY, A. H., WOOD, W., and DIEKMAN, A. B. 2000. Social role theory of sex differences and similarities: a current appraisal. Pp. 123–47 in *The Developmental Social Psychology of Gender*, ed. T. Eckes and H. M. Trautner. Mahwah, NJ: Erlbaum.

ELSASS, P. M., and GRAVES, L. M. 1997. Demographic diversity in decision-making groups: the experiences of women and people of color. *Academy of Management Review*, 22: 946–73.

ELVIRA, M. M., and COHEN, L. E. 2001. Location matters: a cross-level analysis of the effects of organizational sex composition on turnover. *Academy of Management Journal*, 44: 591–605.

ELY, R. J. 1994. The effects of organizational demographics and social identity on relationships among professional women. *Administrative Science Quarterly*, 39: 203–38.

—— 1995. The power in demography: women's social construction of gender identity at work. *Academy of Management Journal*, 38: 589–634.

—— and THOMAS, D. A. 2001. Cultural diversity at work: the effects of diversity perspectives on work group processes and outcomes. *Administrative Science Quarterly*, 46: 229–73.

ENSHER, E. A., and MURPHY, S. E. 1997. Effects of race, gender, perceived similarity and contact on mentor relationships. *Journal of Vocational Behavior*, 50: 460–81.

FISKE, S. T. 1998. Stereotyping, prejudice, and discrimination. Pp. 357–411 in *The Handbook of Social Psychology*, vol. ii, 4th edn., ed. D. T. Gilbert, S. T. Fiske, and G. Linzey. Boston: McGraw-Hill.

—— 2000. Interdependence and the reduction of prejudice. Pp. 115–35 in *Reducing Prejudice and Discrimination*, ed. S. Oskamp. Mahwah, NJ: Lawrence Erlbaum.

—— and NEUBERG, S. L. 1990. A continuum model of impression formation from category-based to individuating processes: influences of information and motivation on attention and interpretation. Pp. 1–74 in *Advances in Experimental Social Psychology*, vol. xxiii, ed. M. P. Zanna. San Diego: Academic Press.

—— XU, J., and CUDDY, A. C. 1999. (Dis)respecting versus (dis)liking: status and interdependence predict ambivalent stereotypes of competence and warmth. *Journal of Social Issues*, 55: 473–89.

—— CUDDY, A. J. C., GLICK, P., and XU, J. 2002. A model of (often mixed) stereotype content: competence and warmth respectively follow from perceived status and competition. *Journal of Personality and Social Psychology*, 82: 878–902.

FOSCHI, M. 1996. Double standards in the evaluation of men and women. *Social Psychology Quarterly*, 59: 237–54.

—— LAI, L., and SIGERSON, K. 1994. Gender and double standards in the assessment of job applicants. *Social Psychology Quarterly*, 57: 326–39.

FRAZER, R. A., and WIERSMA, U. J. 2001. Prejudice versus discrimination in the interview: we may hire equally but our memories harbor prejudice. *Human Relations*, 54: 173–91.

GAERTNER, S. L., and DOVIDIO, J. F. 1986. The aversive form of racism. Pp. 61–89 in *Prejudice, Discrimination, and Racism*, ed. J. F. Dovidio and S. L. Gaertner. Orlando, FL: Academic Press.

GALLOIS, C., CALLAN, V. J., and PALMER, J. M. 1992. The influence of applicant communication style and interviewer characteristics on hiring decisions. *Journal of Applied Social Psychology*, 22: 1041–60.

GLICK, P. 1981. Trait-based and sex-based discrimination in occupational prestige, occupational salary, and hiring. *Sex Roles*, 25: 351–78.

—— and FISKE, S. T. 1996. The Ambivalent Sexism Inventory: differentiating hostile and benevolent sexism. *Journal of Personality and Social Psychology*, 70: 491–512.

—— —— 2001. An ambivalent alliance: hostile and ambivalent sexism as complementary justifications for gender equality. *American Psychologist*, 56 (2): 109–18.

—— ZION, C., and NELSON, C. 1988. What mediates sex discrimination in hiring decisions? *Journal of Personality and Social Psychology*, 35: 178–86.

—— DIEBOLD, J., BAILEY-WERNER, B., and ZHU, L. 1997. The two faces of Adam: ambivalent sexism and polarized attitudes toward women. *Personality and Social Psychology Bulletin*, 23: 1323–34.

—— FISKE, S. T., MLADINIC, A., SAIZ, J. L., ABRAMS, D., MASSER, B., et al. 2000. Beyond prejudice and antipathy: hostile and benevolent sexism across cultures. *Journal of Personality and Social Psychology*, 79: 793–75.

GRAVES, L. M. 1993. Sources of individual differences in interviewer effectiveness: a model and implications for future research. *Journal of Organizational Behavior*, 14: 349–70.

—— and POWELL, G. N. 1995. The effect of sex-similarity on recruiters' evaluations of actual applicants: a test of the similarity-attraction paradigm. *Personnel Psychology*, 48: 85–98.

—— —— 1996. Sex similarity, quality of the employment interview and recruiters' evaluation of actual applicants. *Journal of Occupational and Organizational Psychology*, 69: 243–61.

GREENHAUS, J. H., and PARASURAMAN, S. 1993. Job performance attributions and career advancement prospects: an examination of gender and race effects. *Organizational Behavior and Human Decision Processes*, 55: 273–97.

—— —— and WORMLEY, W. M. 1990. Effects of race on organizational experiences, job performance evaluations, and career outcomes. *Academy of Management Journal*, 33: 64–86.

GUTEK, B. A. 1985. *Sex and the Workplace*. San Francisco: Jossey-Bass.

HEIKES, E. J. 1991. When men are in the minority: the case of men in nursing. *Sociological Quarterly*, 32: 389–401.

HEILMAN, M. E. 1980. The impact of situational factors on personnel decisions concerning women: varying the sex composition of the applicant pool. *Organizational Behavior and Human Performance*, 26: 386–95.

—— 1983. Sex bias in work settings: the lack of fit model. Pp. 269–98 in *Research in Organizational Behavior*, vol. v, ed. L. L. Cummings and B. M. Staw. Greenwich, CT: JAI.

—— WALLEN, A. S., FUCHS, D., and TAMKINS, M. M. 2004. Penalties for success: reactions to women who succeed at male gender-typed tasks. *Journal of Applied Psychology*, 89: 416–27.

HILTON, J. L., and VON HIPPEL, W. 1996. Stereotypes. Pp. 237–71 in *Annual Review of Psychology*, vol. 47, ed. J. T. Spence, J. M. Darley, and D. J. Foss. Palo Alto, CA: Annual Reviews.

HURLEY, A. E., and GIANNANTONIO, C. M. 1999. Career attainment for women and minorities: the interactive effects of age, gender, and race. *Women in Management Review*, 14: 4–14.

ILGEN, D. R., and YOUTZ, M. A. 1986. Factors affecting the evaluation and development of minorities in organizations. Pp. 307–37 in *Research in Personnel and Human Resources Management*, vol. iv, ed. K. M. Rowland and G. R. Ferris. Greenwich, CT: JAI Press.

ITO, T. A., and URLAND, G. R. 2003. Race and gender on the brain: electrocortical measure of attention to the race and gender of multiply categorizable individuals. *Journal of Personality and Social Psychology*, 85: 616–26.

JACKSON, L. M., ESSES, V. M., and BURRIS, C. T. 2001. Contemporary sexism and discrimination: the importance of respect for men and women. *Personality and Social Psychology Bulletin*, 27: 48–61.

JAMES, E. H. 2000. Race-related differences in promotions and support: underlying effects of human and social capital. *Organizational Science*, 11: 493–508.

JAWAHAR, I. M., and MATTSSON, J. 2005. Sexism and beautyism in selection as a function of self-monitoring level of the decision maker. *Journal of Applied Psychology*, 90: 563–73.

KANTER, R. M. 1977a. *Men and Women of the Corporation.* New York: Basic.

—— 1977b. Some effects of group proportions on group life: skewed sex ratios and responses to token women. *American Journal of Sociology*, 82: 965–90.

KIRCHMEYER, C. 1995. Demographic similarity to the work group: a longitudinal study of managers at the early career stage. *Journal of Organizational Behavior*, 16: 67–83.

KONRAD, A. M., and PFEFFER, J. 1991. Understanding the hiring of women and minorities in educational institutions. *Sociology of Education*, 64: 141–57.

—— WINTER, S., and GUTEK, B. A. 1992. Diversity in work group sex composition: implications for majority and minority members. Pp. 115–40 in *Research in the Sociology of Organizations*, vol. x, ed. P. S. Tolbert and S. B. Bacharach. Greenwich, CT: JAI.

KOSSEK, E. E., and ZONIA, S. C. 1993. Assessing diversity climate: a field study of reactions to employer efforts to promote diversity. *Journal of Organizational Behavior*, 14: 61–81.

LANDAU, J. 1995. The relationship of race and gender to managers' ratings of promotion potential. *Journal of Organizational Behavior*, 16: 391–400.

LAU, D. C., and MURNIGHAN, J. K. 1998. Demographic diversity and faultlines: the compositional dynamics of organizational groups. *Academy of Management Review*, 23: 325–40.

—— —— 2005. Interactions within groups and subgroups: the effects of demographic faultlines. *Academy of Management Journal*, 48: 645–59.

LEFKOWITZ, J. 1994. Race as a factor in job placement: serendipitous findings of "ethnic drift." *Personnel Psychology*, 47: 497–513.

LEONG, F. T., and HAYES, T. J. 1990. Occupational stereotyping of Asian Americans. *Career Development Quarterly*, 39: 143–54.

LYNESS, K. S., and THOMPSON, D. E. 2000. Climbing the corporate ladder: do female and male executives follow the same route? *Journal of Applied Psychology*, 85: 86–101.

MCCONAHAY, J. B. 1986. Modern racism, ambivalence, and the modern racism scale. Pp. 91–125 in *Prejudice, Discrimination, and Racism*, ed. J. F. Dovidio and S. L. Gaertner. Orlando, FL: Academic Press.

MCFARLAND, L. A., RYAN, A. M., SACCO, J. M., and KRISKA, S. D. 2004. Examination of structured interview ratings across time: the effects of applicant race, rater race, and panel composition. *Journal of Management*, 30: 435–52.

MCRAE, M. B. 1994. Influence of sex role stereotypes on personnel decisions of black managers. *Journal of Applied Psychology*, 79: 306–9.

MASSER, B. M., and ABRAMS, D. 2004. Reinforcing the glass ceiling: the consequences of hostile sexism for female managerial candidates. *Sex Roles*, 51: 609–15.

MELLOR, S. 1995. Gender composition and gender representation in local unions: relationships between women's participation in local office and women's participation in local activities. *Journal of Applied Psychology*, 80: 706–20.

MILLIKEN, F. J., and MARTINS, L. L. 1996. Searching for common threads: understanding the multiple effects of diversity on occupational groups. *Academy of Management Review*, 21: 402–33.

MOUNT, M. K., SYTSMA, M. R., HAZUCHA, J. F., and HOLT, K. E. 1997. Rater–ratee race effects in developmental performance ratings of managers. *Personnel Psychology*, 50: 51–69.

NORTON, M. I., VANDELLO, J. A., and DARLEY, J. M. 2004. Casuistry and social category bias. *Journal of Personality and Social Psychology*, 87: 817–31.

PAZY, A., and ORON, I. 2001. Sex proportion and performance evaluation among high-ranking military officers. *Journal of Organizational Behavior*, 22: 689–702.

PERRY, E. 1994. A prototype matching approach to understanding the role of applicant gender and age in the evaluation of job applicants. *Journal of Applied Social Psychology*, 24: 1433–73.

—— DAVIS-BLAKE, A., and KULIK, C. T. 1994. Examining gender-based selection decisions: a synthesis of contextual and cognitive processes. *Academy of Management Review*, 19: 786–820.

PETTIGREW, T. F., and MARTIN, J. 1987. Shaping the organizational context for Black American inclusion. *Journal of Social Issues*, 43: 41–78.

PITTINSKY, T. L., SHIH, M., and AMBADY, N. 2000. Will a category cue affect you? Category cues, positive stereotypes and reviewer recall for applicants. *Social Psychology of Education*, 4: 53–65.

PLOUS, S., and WILLIAMS, T. 1995. Racial stereotypes from the days of American slavery: a continuing legacy. *Journal of Applied Social Psychology*, 25: 795–817.

POWELL, G. N., and BUTTERFIELD, D. A. 1994. Investigating the "glass ceiling" phenomenon: an empirical study of actual promotions to top management. *Academy of Management Journal*, 37: 68–86.

—— —— 2002. Exploring the influence of decision makers' race and gender on actual promotions to top management. *Personnel Psychology*, 55: 397–428.

—— and GRAVES, L. M. 2003. *Women and Men in Management*, 3rd edn. Thousand Oaks, CA: Sage.

PRATTO, F., STALLWORTH, L. M., SIDANIUS, J., and SIERS, B. 1997. The gender gap in occupational role attainment: a social dominance approach. *Journal of Personality and Social Psychology*, 72: 37–53.

RAGINS, B. R., and COTTON, J. L. 1999. Mentor functions and outcomes: a comparison of men and women in formal and informal mentoring relationships. *Journal of Applied Psychology*, 84: 529–50.

RIDGEWAY, C. L. 1991. The social construction of status value: gender and other nominal characteristics. *Social Forces*, 70: 367–86.

ROBBINS, T. L., and DENISI, A. S. 1993. Moderators of sex bias in the appraisal process: a cognitive analysis. *Journal of Management*, 19: 113–26.

RUDMAN, L. A. 1998. Self-promotion as a risk factor for women: the costs and benefits of counterstereotypical impression management. *Journal of Personality and Social Psychology*, 74: 629–45.

RUDMAN, L. A. and GLICK, P. 1999. Feminized management and backlash toward agentic women: the hidden costs to women of a kinder, gentler image of middle managers. *Journal of Personality and Social Psychology*, 77: 1004–10.

—— and KILANSKI, S. E. 2000. Implicit and explicit attitudes toward female authority. *Personality and Social Psychology Bulletin*, 26: 1315–28.

RUSSELL, B. L., and TRIGG, K. Y. 2004. Tolerance of sexual harassment: an examination of gender differences, ambivalent sexism, social dominance and gender roles. *Sex Roles*, 50: 565–73.

SACKETT, P. R., DuBois, C. L. Z., and NOE, A. W. 1991. Tokenism in performance evaluation: the effects of work group representation on male–female and white–black differences in performance ratings. *Journal of Applied Psychology*, 76: 263–7.

SCHEIN, V. E ., MUELLER, R., LITUCHY, T., and LIU, J. 1996. Think manager—think male: a global phenomenon? *Journal of Organizational Behavior*, 17: 33–41.

SEARS, D. O. 1988. Symbolic racism. Pp. 53–84 in *Eliminating Racism: Profiles in Controversy*, ed. P. A. Katz and D. A. Taylor. New York: Plenum.

SMITH, R. A. 2005. Do the determinants of promotions differ for White men versus women and minorities? *American Behavioral Scientist*, 48: 1157–81.

SNYDER, M., and SWANN, W. B., Jr. 1978. Hypothesis-testing processes in social interaction. *Journal of Personality and Social Psychology*, 36: 1202–12.

STANGOR, C., and LANGE, J. E. 1994. Mental representations of social groups: advances in understanding stereotypes and stereotyping. Pp. 357–416 in *Advances in Experimental Social Psychology*, vol. xxvi, ed. M. Zanna. San Diego: Academic Press.

—— LYNCH, L., DUAN, C., and GLASS, B. 1992. Categorization of individuals based on multiple social features. *Journal of Personality and Social Psychology*, 62: 207–18.

STEWART, L. D., and PERLOW, R. 2001. Applicant race, job status, and racial attitude as predictors of employment discrimination. *Journal of Business and Psychology*, 16: 259–75.

STOLL, M. A., RAPHAEL, S., and HOLZER, H. J. 2004. Black job applicants and the hiring officer's race. *Industrial and Labor Relations Review*, 57: 267–87.

STROH, L. K., BRETT, J. M., and REILLY, A. H. 1992. All the right stuff: a comparison of female and male managers' career progression. *Journal of Applied Psychology*, 77: 251–60.

SWIM, J. K., AIKIN, K. J., HALL, W. S., and HUNTER, B. A. 1995. Sexism and racism: old-fashioned and modern prejudices. *Journal of Personality and Social Psychology*, 68: 199–214.

TAJFEL, H. 1981. *Human Groups and Social Categories*. London: Cambridge University Press.

—— and TURNER, J. C. 1986. The social identity theory of intergroup behavior. Pp. 7–24 in *Psychology of Intergroup Relations*, 2nd edn., ed. S. Worchel and W. G. Austin. Chicago: Nelson-Hall.

TAYLOR, S. E., FISKE, S. T., ETCOFF, N. L., and RUDERMAN, A. J. 1978. Categorical and contextual bases of person memory and stereotyping. *Journal of Personality and Social Psychology*, 36: 778–93.

THOMAS, D. A. 1993. Racial dynamics in cross-race developmental relationships. *Administrative Science Quarterly*, 38: 169–94.

TOLBERT, P. S., GRAHAM, M. E., and ANDREWS, A. O. 1999. Group gender composition and work group relations: theories, evidence, and issues. Pp. 179–202 in *Handbook of Gender and Work*, ed. G. N. Powell. Thousand Oaks, CA: Sage.

—— Simons, T., Andrews, A., and Rhee, J. 1995. The effects of gender composition in academic departments on faculty turnover. *Industrial and Labor Relations Review*, 48: 562–79.

Tougas, F., Brown, R., Beaton, A. M., and Joly, S. 1995. Neosexism: plus ça change, plus c'est pareil. *Personality and Social Psychology Bulletin*, 21: 842–9.

Tsui, A. S., and O'Reilly, C. A., III 1989. Beyond simple demographic effects: the importance of relational demography in superior–subordinate dyads. *Academy of Management Journal*, 32: 402–23.

—— Egan, T. D., and O'Reilly, C. A., III 1992. Being different: relational demography and organizational attachment. *Administrative Science Quarterly*, 37: 549–79.

Turner, J. C. 1985. Social categorization and the self-concept: a social cognitive theory of group behavior. Pp. 77–122 in *Advances in Group Processes: A Research Annual*, vol. ii, ed. E. J. Lawler. Greenwich, CT: JAI Press.

Varma, A., and Stroh, L. K. 2001. The impact of same-sex LMX dyads on performance evaluations. *Human Resource Management*, 40: 309–20.

Watkins, M. B., Kaplan, S., Brief, A. P., Shull, A., Dietz, J., Mansfield, M., et al. 2006. Does it pay to be a sexist? The relationship between modern sexism and career outcomes. *Journal of Vocational Behavior*, 69: 524–37.

Wharton, A. S. 1992. The social construction of gender and race in organizations: a social identity and group mobilization perspective. Pp. 55–84 in *Research in the Sociology of Organizations*, vol. x, ed. P. S. Tolbert and S. B. Bacharach. Greenwich, CT: JAI Press.

Williams, J. E., and Best, D. L. 1990. *Measuring Sex Stereotypes: A Multination Study*, rev. edn. Newbury Park, CA: Sage.

Williams, K. Y., and O'Reilly, C. A., III. 1998. Demography and diversity in organizations: a review of 40 years of research. Pp. 77–140 in *Research in Organizational Behavior*, vol. xx, ed. B. M. Staw and L. L. Cummings. Greenwich, CT: JAI Press.

Williamson, L. G., Campion, J. E., Malos, S. B., Roehling, M. B., and Campion, M. A. 1997. Employment interview on trial: linking interview structure with litigation outcomes. *Journal of Applied Psychology*, 82: 900–12.

Wirth, L. 2001. *Breaking through the Glass Ceiling: Women in Management*. Geneva: International Labour Office.

Yoder, J. D. 1991. Rethinking tokenism: looking beyond numbers. *Gender and Society*, 5: 178–92.

Zatzick, C. D., Elvira, M. M., and Cohen, L. E. 2003. When is more better? The effects of racial composition on voluntary turnover. *Organizational Science*, 14: 483–96.

Zimmer, L. 1988. Tokenism and women in the workplace: the limits of gender-neutral theory. *Social Problems*, 35: 64–77.

19

BULLYING AND HARASSMENT AT WORK

STÅLE EINARSEN

STIG BERGE MATTHIESEN

LARS JOHAN HAUGE

1. INTRODUCTION

IN 1976, an American psychiatrist, Carroll M. Brodsky, published an intriguing book called *The Harassed Worker*, describing how workers on all organizational levels were systematically mistreated and abused by their superiors or co-workers while at work. Inspired by thousands of years of literature on the cruelty and brutality human beings may show towards both enemies and foes, sometimes for no apparent reason, Brodsky investigated more than 1,000 cases where employees complained to have been injured, mistreated, or crippled while at work. Among these cases, Brodsky discovered a group of patients who suffered from severe stress reactions and ill health without being exposed to injuries or physical damage, but with severe psychological scars caused by the intentional or unintentional cruelty of other organizational members through harassment of a sexual or in most cases generic kind. The mistreatment was often conducted by psychological means and by rather subtle and discreet actions, yet causing severe and traumatic effects on the targets by being repeatedly and persistently aimed at someone who felt unable to retaliate in kind. The effects on the targets were devastating.

Unaware of this book, as Brodsky's pioneering work did not receive much attention at the time, Heinz Leymann, a German-born Swedish psychiatrist and psychologist, came across a similar phenomenon in the Swedish working life, as he found employees being victimized at work by a systematic and stigmatizing exposure to hostility and psychological violence from superiors or co-workers often for no apparent reason or at least not in any way justifiable. Leymann soon became convinced that this problem had less to do with those involved, but was deeply rooted in organizational factors and qualities of the psychosocial work environment. Inspired by Leymann and much public interest and debate, as well as legal changes securing workers the right to a work environment free of harassment, large research projects were initiated in both Norway (Einarsen et al. 1994; Matthiesen, Raknes, and Røkkum 1989), Sweden (Leymann 1990; 1996), and Finland (Vartia 1991; 1996), documenting the existence and gross negative effects such treatment and these experiences had on both targets as well as observers (see Einarsen and Mikkelsen 2003 for a review).

Seemingly parallel with this development, UK journalist Andrea Adams in cooperation with the psychologist Neil Crawford, put the issue of bullying at work firmly on the UK agenda through radio shows and a popular book (Adams 1992). In the US, similar efforts and discoveries have happened later on (Bassman 1992; Keashly 1998; Keashly, Trott, and MacLean 1994). Again, the very same phenomenon is described, and again, the message is the same: (1) many employees suffer from severe mistreatment at work by superiors or co-workers in the form of systematic exposure to sometimes flagrant and subtle forms of aggression, mainly characterized by its persistency and long term duration; (2) the effects on the targets are devastating and traumatic, with negative effects also found in the health, motivation, and well-being of its observers, with potential gross costs for employers; and (3) managers and employers, sometimes even authorities and legal bodies, are often unwilling to accept the very existence of the problem, much less prevent it and fairly manage those cases that come to the front.

Yet, from this situation, many countries have now enforced specific legal remedies to help employers and employees to intervene correctly in specific cases, as well as to create safe working environment also in a psychosocial sense, free of hostility, harassment, abuse and mistreatment (see also Yamada 2003). The present chapter reviews the literature and research findings in this field, which has blossomed during the last ten years.

2. THE NATURE OF BULLYING AT WORK

2.1 A Plethora of Terms

The issue handled in this chapter is a complex one. It may come in many shapes and shades, with multiple causes on many levels, and with diverging views on its very nature. No wonder that different terms and concepts have been used. Leymann used the terms "psychological terror" and "mobbing" (Leymann 1990), while Brodsky (1976) used "harassment," and Adams (1992) "bullying." Others again have used terms such as "emotional abuse" (Bassman 1992; Keashly 1998) and "victimization" (Aquino and Lamertz 2004). In addition, concepts such as "workplace aggression," "incivility," "workplace deviance," and "mistreatment" have been used to describe more single occurrences of interpersonal and psychological violence at work (see also Keashly and Jagatic 2003). The construct of social undermining also bears close resemblance to bullying and harassment, involving behavior over time that is intended to hinder someone in their ability to establish and maintain positive interpersonal relationships, as well as damage their work-related success or favorable reputation (Duffy, Ganster, and Pagon 2002).

Terms of a more metaphorical kind have also been used, such as "spitting" used in a Japanese book (Tokunga, Crawford, and Tanaka 1998; see also Tokunga and Tanaka 1998) and "corporate hyenas" in a South African one (Marais and Herman 1997). However, while "mobbing" seems to be the preferred term in Europe (Zapf, Knorz, and Kulla 1996), "bullying" or harassment seems to be the preferred terms in the UK and the US (Namie and Namie 2000). In practice, only minor differences exist between the two concepts (Zapf and Einarsen 2005). Yet, the term bully more easily lends itself to descriptions of the perpetrator who behave aggressively in many situations and possibly towards more than one target. The concept of mobbing, on the other hand, normally refers to the experiences of targets who are systematically exposed to harassment by one or more perpetrators and who over time become severely victimized by this treatment. Hence, the concepts seem to look at the two different sides of the same phenomenon, the perpetrators and the targets. According to Leymann (1996), the choice of the term "mobbing" in preference to "bullying" was a conscious decision, reflecting the fact that the phenomena among adults often refer to subtle, less direct forms of aggression as opposed to more physical forms of aggression that may be associated with the term "bullying." Yet, even among those who uses the term bullying and even more so those who uses the terms "victimization" and "emotional abuse", empirical evidence suggest that the behaviors involved are more often of a verbal, passive, and indirect nature (Einarsen et al. 2003; Keashly and Harvey 2005). The acting-out bully, behaving in a rude and dominant manner, loudly speaking or demanding, the stereotype of the perpetrator expressing overt tyrannical behavior, is probably not typical for many bullying cases, at least as seen in most European countries. Hence, in the present chapter the terms "harassment" and "bullying" will be used interchangeably to refer to both these phenomena, namely as the systematic exhibition of aggressive behavior at work directed towards a subordinate, a superior or a co-worker, as well as the perception of being systematically exposed to such mistreatment while at work.

2.2 Bullying Defined

Brodsky (1976) described harassment at work as repeated and persistent attempts by an individual to torment, wear down, frustrate, or get a reaction from another individual, and as treatment that persistently provokes, pressures, frightens, intimidates, or otherwise causes discomfort in an individual at work. It may take the form of open verbal or physical attacks, but may also be more discreet and subtle such as excluding or isolating the target from one's peer group (Einarsen, Raknes, and Matthiesen 1994; Leymann 1996; Zapf, Knorz, and Kulla 1996). Yet studies have clearly shown that the most frequent forms of hostility in workplaces are not of a violent or physical kind, but rather come as verbal, indirect, and passive kinds of aggression (Baron and Neuman 1998). Furthermore, bullying may either take a direct form, like verbal abuse, or be indirect (e.g., libel and slander, withholding of information). It can also be distinguished between work-related actions that make it difficult for victims to carry out their work or involve taking away some or all of their responsibilities, and actions that are primarily person related (Einarsen 1999). Social exclusion, spreading rumors, libels, ignoring opinions, teasing/insolence, and undesired sexual approaches are all examples of the latter. Based upon empirical and theoretical evidence, Zapf (1999) broadens the categorization of bullying to five types. These five are (1) work-related bullying (work tasks are changed or difficult to manage); (2) social isolation (exclusion from daily communication, or from daily events); (3) personal attacks (ridicule, insulting remarks); (4) verbal threats (criticism, telling-off, humiliation in front of others); and (5) spreading rumours (social reputation is attacked).

Following Hadjifotiou (1983), bullying has also been defined as all those repeated actions and practices that are directed to one or more workers, which are unwanted by the victim, which may be done deliberately or unconsciously, but clearly cause humiliation, offence, and distress, and that may interfere with job performance and/or cause an unpleasant working environment (Einarsen and Raknes 1997).

2.2.1 Frequent and repeated

This definition emphasizes the two main features of most definitions of bullying at work: repeated and enduring aggressive behaviors that are intended to be hostile and/or perceived as hostile by the recipient, and from which the persons affected find it difficult to protect themselves. Thus, bullying is normally not about single and isolated events, but rather about behaviors that are repeated and persistently directed towards one or more individuals by one individual or by a group. Isolated episodes of being given work below one's level of competence, or isolated incidents of being laughed at or not being asked to join colleagues for lunch, may be seen as ordinary features of working life and therefore not as bullying. However, such acts may become acts of bullying when they are used in a systematic manner over a period of time, resulting in an unpleasant and hostile work situation for the recipient (Salin 2003b). Although single acts of aggression and harassment may occur fairly often in everyday interaction at workplaces, a strong relationship with reduced well-being and job satisfaction exist if these behaviors are experienced on a regular basis (Einarsen et al. 2005).

2.2.2 *A power imbalance*

Another central feature of many bullying definitions is the imbalance of power between the parties. Typically, targets of bullying find it difficult to defend or protect themselves against the behavior, as their opportunity for retaliation is more or less ruled out (Zapf and Einarsen 2005). Power differences may have many origins such as greater physical size, a more powerful position in the organization, or even the number of colleagues considered to be on one's side (Bowling and Beehr 2006). Knowledge about another individual's "weak point" may also become a strong source of power, and may help a perpetrator to exploit perceived inequalities and power deficits in the target's personality or work performance (Einarsen 1999). Many cases also involve a supervisor in the role as the perpetrator and subordinates in the role of the target, again indicating the imbalance of power between the individuals involved (Einarsen et al. 1994; Leymann 1996; Zapf, Knorz, and Kulla 1996). Imbalance of power in the context of bullying means that the person concerned has little control or few possibilities to retaliate in kind. A work situation characterized by low control combined with high strain has been found to be particularly stressful (Karasek and Theorell 1990), and may thus explain the severe health damage often observed in victims (Zapf and Einarsen 2005).

Based upon clinical contacts with bullying victims (e.g., Matthiesen et al. 2003), we would also suggest some additional facets to the aforementioned definitional criteria in that the exposed individual typically: (a) perceives the bullying to be intentional and/or directed against them; (b) lacks opportunities to evade it; (c) lacks adequate social support that could act as a "buffer"; (d) experiences the bullying sanctions as unfair or out of place (over-dimensioned); (e) is personally or socially vulnerable; and (f) feels extremely insulted, humiliated, or ashamed by the treatment. In a study of experienced emotions in leader–subordinate relationships, Glasø and Einarsen (2006) found that feelings of violation, including specific feelings such as resentment and humiliation, were one of four basic emotional dimensions in such work-related relationships. Hence, such feelings are at the cornerstone of abusive relationships, as well as being a potential part of all relationships at work where some person is in a stronger position than another.

2.2.3 *An escalating process*

Many authors have pinpointed that bullying is not necessarily an "either/or" phenomenon, but exists on a continuum and therefore also may be a gradually evolving process. Einarsen (1999) classified the bullying process into four stages as aggressive behaviors, bullying, stigmatization, and severe trauma. Aggressive behaviors may in the beginning be subtle and indirect, and thus hard to recognize and confront. Later on the target may be subjected to more direct negative behavior in which the target becomes increasingly more humiliated, ridiculed, and isolated. The following stigmatization makes it ever more difficult for the target to defend himself, as an image of a "difficult person" may have been established among peers and superiors. At the end of the bullying process the target often suffers from a range of severe stress symptoms where long periods of sickness absenteeism are necessary to cope with the situation (Einarsen et al. 1994). In later stages neither management nor colleagues are likely to interfere in the bullying process in support of the target, but are more likely to question the target's own role in the ongoing situation, blaming the target for their own misfortune (Leymann 1996). The unsupportiveness of such work environments is reinforced by the finding that targets of bullying often advise other targets to leave their organization and rather seek support elsewhere (Zapf and Gross 2001).

2.2.4 *A definition*

In line with this we define victimization from bullying (as in mobbing) as follows:

> Bullying at work means harassing, offending, socially excluding someone or negatively affecting someone's work tasks. In order for the label bullying (or mobbing) to be applied to a particular activity, interaction or process, it has to occur repeatedly and regularly (e.g. weekly) and over a period of time (e.g. about six months). Bullying is an escalating process in the course of which the person confronted ends up in an inferior position and becomes the target of systematic negative social acts. A conflict cannot be called bullying if the incident is an isolated event or if two parties of approximately equal "strength" are in conflict. (Einarsen et al. 2003, 15)

2.2.5 *What about intent?*

Bullying and harassment may of course be seen as a kind of repeated aggression at work. However, while a cornerstone in definitions of workplace aggression is that the behaviors must be intended to cause harm (cf. Baron 1997), intent is generally not considered an essential element in bullying research (Zapf and Einarsen 2005). First of all, it is normally impossible to verify the presence of intent (Björkqvist, Österman, and Hjelt-Bäck 1994; Hoel, Rayner, and Cooper 1999), as indicated by research in the sexual harassment field (Pryor and Fitzgerald 2003). Furthermore, a distinction between (1) the intent to act, (2) the intent to cause harm, (3) the intent to victimize, and (4) the intent to be systematic and repeated, may explain why definitions of bullying exclude intent. While the former is probably present in most situations, the latter kinds of intent are probably seldom present in actual bullying cases. The behaviors of the perpetrator may be done consciously and deliberately. Still, the perpetrator may not necessarily have a clear intent to become systematic, nor even to cause harm (Hoel 2002). However, the behavior involved may still be considered as instrumental in the sense that it is perpetrated in order to achieve certain goals or objectives. These may, however, be, or be claimed to be, different from that perceived by others. Situations where someone offends, provokes, or otherwise angers another person may be perceived and interpreted quite differently by the two participants (Baumeister, Stillwell, and Wotman 1990). Thus, a more important question to ask than the one about intent would be, to what extent the bully is aware of his or her behavior? How does the bully interpret and justify this behavior? And not least, has the behavior actually happened, and if so, is it reasonable that the target objects to it and suffers from it? Yet, as mentioned earlier, perceptions of intent are probably crucial to the subjective perceptions made by the targets.

2.2.6 Subjective versus objective bullying

The concepts of "subjective" and "objective" bullying have been proposed in order to solve the difficulty of deciding when something is and is not bullying, which in cases may be difficult (see also Einarsen et al. 2003). For instance, Niedl (1995) argues that the definitional core of bullying at work must rest on the subjective perception made by the victim that these repeated acts are hostile, humiliating, and intimidating and that they are directed at himself/herself. Hence, Niedl argues for bullying to be defined as a subjective construct where the focus is on the perceptions of the bullying. "Objective bullying" on the other hand, refers to situations where there is observable evidence or statements from third parties that bullying is taking place (Brodsky 1976). From a legal perspective, such evidence is of course important, especially if sanctions are to be given to a perpetrator. Einarsen and colleagues (2003) argue that the stigmatization processes involved in bullying, the often subtle nature of the negative acts, and the fact that power differences are more visible from the point of view of those experiencing it may make "objective bullying" difficult to detect in many cases. Hence, proper investigation methods must be used when an employer handles the most severe allegations of bullying. In less severe cases, where more informal solutions may be possible, subjective bullying may be far enough evidence for a manager to intervene using low key informal method.

3. Different Kinds of Harassment and Bullying Situations

Bullying may occur in a range of different situations and settings and may come in many shades and forms (see also Matthiesen 2006; Einarsen et al. 2003), with many different origins and precursors. Yet, situations of bullying mainly come in two broad categories; cases that are dispute-related and cases that are predatory in kind (Einarsen 1999).

3.1 Dispute-Related Bullying

Dispute-related bullying develops from an interpersonal conflict, often involving social control reactions to perceived wrongdoing. Such bullying cases are typically triggered by a work-related conflict, where the social climate between the conflicting parties has gone sour, escalating into harsh personified conflict, where the total destruction of the opponent is seen as a legitimate action by the parties (Leymann 1990; Zapf and Gross 2001). In highly escalated conflicts both parties may deny the opponent's human value, thus clearing the way for manipulation, retaliation, elimination, and destruction (van de Vliert 1998). If one of the parties has or acquires a disadvantaged position in this struggle, he or she may become a target of bullying (Björkqvist, Österman, and Hjelt-Bäck 1994). It may also be true that claiming to be a victim of bullying may be used as a strategy in interpersonal conflicts, and in some cases even used by both parties. In highly intense interpersonal conflicts, aggressive outlets may come from both parties, making the situation rather complex (Einarsen et al. 1994). Hence, in some cases it may in practice actually be rather difficult to differentiate between what is bullying and what is not to be regarded as a case of bullying, as the conflicting parties as well as non-involved third parties may perceive and label the situation quite differently. Typical for these cases is also that while the target has a strong sense of being a victim of bullying and being on the receiving end of a host of highly unfair behaviors and sanctions, the alleged offenders as well as many colleagues refuse to acknowledge the perceptions of the target and rather explain the situation as being one where a highly difficult and neurotic person is misperceiving the situation or even just "gets what they deserved".

From a conceptual point of view, the difference between bullying and interpersonal conflicts is not necessarily found in what is done and how it is done (cf. Einarsen et al. 2003), but rather in the frequency and duration of what is done and the ability that the parties possess to defend themselves and their reputation in the actual situations. As opposed to interpersonal conflicts, bullying is not a mutual and reciprocal process where both parties have the same opportunity to be aggressive and where the effects of the different parties on the opponent's actions must be seen to be equal. Bullying is about having unequal power and about being exposed to negative acts over and over again without being able to defend oneself in the actual situation.

Many authors have related bullying to the broader concept of conflicts (e.g. Zapf and Gross 2001), viewing bullying as a certain subset of conflicts. Following Evert van de Vliert (1998, 351) who defines conflict as "Two individuals, an individual and a group, or two groups, are said to be in conflict when and to the extent that at least one of the parties feels it is being obstructed or irritated by the other," bullying would clearly fall under such a rubric. Van de Vliert contends that important aspects covered in this definition are: (a) conflicts are subjective experiences (they do not necessarily have an objective basis); (b) the frustration may be cognitive or affective, or both (e.g., blocked goals, feelings of hostility); (c) the frustration is blamed on another individual or group; (d) the magnitude of the frustration may vary (conflicts escalate or de-escalate across a time dimension); (e) the frustration is not necessarily coupled with particular conflict behavior towards the other party; and (f) the conflict can be one-sided (e.g., when only one party feels frustrated or attributes the frustration to the other).

Yet Keashly and Jagatic (2003) warns against seeing bullying as only a kind of conflict, as this may de-emphasize the seriousness, unethical, and counterproductive aspects of the bullying. The distinction between single incidents and enduring hostile interaction is also important when workplace bullying is compared with interpersonal conflicts in general (Keashly 1998). While conflict may be seen as inherent in social interaction, bullying must been seen as deviant and unacceptable behavior, never to be minimized or normalized. Secondly, labelling bullying as a conflict may create a sense of shared responsibility and accountability among the parties, and a sense that it is something that the target must be able to manage. Hence, to label bullying as a conflict without important qualifications may indeed be disastrous for the target, potentially causing even more distress, shame, and a diminished sense of self-esteem and competence. Yet a conflict perspective may still have much to offer in the understanding of processes involved in and in the management of bullying (Keashly and Jagatic 2003).

3.2 Predatory Bullying

In cases of predatory bullying, the target has personally done nothing provocative
that may reasonably justify the behavior of the bully, but is more or less acciden-
tally in a situation where a predator demonstrates power or exploits an accidental
victim into compliance. These cases may for instance involve a manager or a
particular employee with a consistent aggressive repertoire or a general destructive
leadership style lording it over accidental subordinates. In other cases, subordinates
become isolated, ostracized, or in other ways mistreated by the organization due to
a leader's neglect and lack of proper leadership initiatives, often called laissez-faire
leadership (Skogstad et al. 2007). Using the concept of "petty tyrants," Ashforth
(1994) described abusive managers as people who lord it over others through
arbitrariness and self-aggrandizement, by the belittling of subordinates, by the
lack of consideration and the use of an authoritarian style of conflict management.
These leaders shout and scream at subordinates, they criticize, complain, and
demean them, and they lie and manipulate others in order to have their way.
Hornstein (1996) describes such an abusive leader as one whose primary objective
is the control of others, and such control is achieved through methods that create
fear and intimidation. The paradox of such tyrannical leadership is however that
these leaders may be quite efficient in other realms of their job (see also Einarsen,
Aasland, and Skogstad 2007). Other kinds of predatory kinds of bullying are
described in the following.

3.2.1 *Scapegoating*

Two early works in this field (Brodsky 1976; Thylefors 1987) point out that
scapegoating is a particular type of work harassment, where frustration is
displaced on to an available and "deserving" target who is bullied by being an
easy target of vented frustration and stress. In situations where stress and
frustration are caused by a source that either is indefinable, inaccessible, too
respected, or too powerful to be attacked, the group may turn its hostility
towards a person who is less powerful than themselves, using this person as a
scapegoat. Displaced aggression refers to the tendency to aggress against someone
other than the actual source of provocation (Marcus-Newhall et al. 2000).
Perpetrators of bullying generally seek behavior that are effective in harming
the target while incurring as little damage to themselves as possible through
retaliation or other consequences. The effect–danger ratio refers to aggressors
estimates of these two components (Björkqvist, Österman, and Lagerspetz 1994).
Because aggressing against the source itself may be too dangerous, individuals
willing to aggress against conditions within their workplaces often select targets
that are relatively weak and defenceless, use disguised forms of aggression making
it difficult to identify them as the actual source of such harm, and thus a pattern
of bullying behavior may arise (Neuman and Baron 2003). If the provocateur is

one's manager, aggressing might result in the employee losing a favored position or even their job, although evidence for aggressing against managers has also been found (Baron, Neuman, and Geddes 1999). Thus, a less powerful target may be chosen for venting one's frustration (Bushman et al. 2005; Marcus-Newhall et al. 2000; Neuman and Baron 2003). Typical behavior that may contribute to attaining the status of a scapegoat includes being too honest, unwillingness to compromise, and behavior that does not keep pace with the development within the work group or the organization (Thylefors 1987).

3.2.2 *Sexual harassment*

Although a field of research in itself, it may also be argued that sexual harassment (see Pryor and Fitzgerald 2003 for a review) may be seen as a subtype of work harassment, where a target, in many cases a younger female worker, is exposed to repeated and unwanted sexual attention by a more powerful and often older co-worker or superior. This attention may also be combined with threats about future job prospects, in order to coerce the target to subjugation, or may in itself act to create a hostile work environment. Brodsky (1976), as one of the first writers on sexual harassment, saw this as one of many kinds of harassment. Interestingly, while sexual harassment saw a boost of research efforts during the 1980s, general harassment only received its due interest much later.

3.2.3 *The destructiveness of humor*

In many workplaces, person-oriented joking or humor may be widespread. Rough humour played out between equals, i.e., work colleagues within the same in-group, may indicate job satisfaction or work commitment. Humor can be symmetrical, so that employees tease one another. However, if the person-oriented humor is directed towards someone in an out-group, or at a person unable to retaliate, the individual may eventually come to experience it as bullying. Here, the jokes or humorous behavior may be imbalanced or asymmetrical, with the real or perceived intent to be aggressive through hostile forms of teasing. Being repeatedly made the laughing stock of the department is reported by many targets of bullying.

3.2.4 *Stalking*

Work-related stalking such as sending letters or gifts, making telephone calls, or waiting outside a person's home or workplace, may be another form of bullying, again involving behaviors that if considered individually may seem inoffensive and not particularly threatening to the uninvolved observer (Purcel, Pathe, and Mullen 2004). Stalking can be defined as a course of conduct in which one individual inflicts upon another repeated unwanted intrusions and communications, to such an extent that victims fear for their safety (Pathe and Mullen 1997), in this case against an employee or another organizational member. Most episodes of stalking covered by the media seem to consist of rejected ex-partners, after separation or divorce, bombarding or terrorizing their former wives or husbands with telephone calls, SMS messages, or e-mails. Yet celebrities, e.g., pop stars or sports heroes, may also be exposed to stalking because of their fame and role in working life, as may ordinary workers. In Norway, a tourist bus driver was stalked for years by one of the accompanying female tourists he met in his job. The male driver was terrorized with thousands of letters and telephone calls and stalked day and night. The stalker was finally imprisoned due to the vast number of bullying episodes that she initiated, despite several warnings.

3.2.5 *Rite de passage*

Bullying of workplace newcomers, or *rite de passage* bullying, comprises an old type of workplace bullying, known for centuries, especially occurring in male dominating workplaces such as shipping and military alike institutions (Archer 1999; Brodsky 1976). In such cases, newcomers in the workplace are met with intimidating behavior as a kind of hazing. This conduct can of course be regarded as a cultural tradition, in which the new person is "tested." Yet, the rites may be so intense or so long-lasting that they may qualify to be perceived as bullying. An old sailor once told us a story about a young colleague who on his first voyage was unable to cope with or endure the humiliating and frequent *rites de passages* he was faced with. The outcome in this case was fatal; he ended up drowning himself.

3.2.6 *Shooting the messenger*

The last kind of bullying we have come across arises as retaliatory acts after whistle-blowing. Near and Miceli (1996) define whistle-blowing as an act that takes place when an employee is witnessing wrongdoing at the workplace (e.g., unethical conduct, corruption, criminal acts, violence or bullying against others) from a fellow employee or a superior (or a group of employees or superiors). The whistle-blower then tries to stop the wrongdoing by informing someone who is in a position to stop it. Whistle-blowers may voice their concern internally (e.g., to a superior within the company), but may also do it externally (e.g., informing the authorities or a local nature conservation association to give but a few examples). Sometimes such whistle-blowing leads to a victimization process where the organization or its members "shoots the messenger," that is retaliation or bullying of the person that did not keep quiet. Whistle-blowing turned out to be the second most frequent reason for workplace bullying as reported in a Norwegian survey conducted among a group of targets of bullying ($n = 221$, own unpublished data), when they were asked to rank reasons for why they were targeted for bullying (Matthiesen 2004). "Don't kill the messenger" is a rule quite often ignored. A typical mode of punishing or sanctioning whistle-blowers is to meet them with tough ostracism, to completely isolate the person from others or from work tasks. Many whistle-blowers are simply sacked from their jobs, or their work contracts are not renewed. They may even experience that rumours about this "disloyal" worker are spread around widely, including other companies, thus making it difficult to obtain other jobs.

4. PREVALENCE AND RISK GROUPS OF WORKPLACE BULLYING

4.1 Prevalence of Bullying

Findings on the prevalence of exposure to bullying vary greatly, with figures ranging from 1 percent at the lowest level to above 50 percent at the highest level, dependent upon the applied measurement strategy, occupation, or sector, as well as country (Di Martino, Hoel, and Cooper 2003). A meta-study undertaken in Norway, in which fourteen subsamples were summarized to encompass 7,118 subjects in total, demonstrated that 8.6 percent had been bullied during the last six months (Einarsen 1996). Specifically, 1.2 percent were bullied weekly, 3.4 percent "now and then," and 4 percent once or twice. Quine (1999) in a 1,100-person study of UK National Health Service employees, revealed a prevalence rate of 38 percent. O'Moore (ref. in Di Martino, Hoel, and Cooper 2003) in a 1,009-person random national Irish sample found a prevalence rate of 17 percent, whereas a 2,410 representative Spanish sample revealed an occurrence of 16 per cent (Piñual and Zabala 2002, ref. in Di Martino, Hoel, and Cooper 2003). A study of the general working population in South-east France in a sample of 3,132 men and 4,562 women, showed that the point prevalence of bullying on the survey day was 7.6 percent, varying from 3 to 18 percent in different sectors. The twelve-month prevalence was 9 percent among men and 11 percent among women (Niedhammer, David, and Degioanni 2006). Correspondingly, a study in a representative British sample of 5,288 employees, revealed a six-month prevalence rate of 10.6 percent bullying according to self-labeling (Hoel, Cooper, and Faragher 2001).

However, the observed prevalence rates of bullying seem to be highly influenced by the research strategy applied. Where bullying is measured by means of a precise definition and refer to a regular experience on a weekly basis for a period of at least six months, less than 5 percent of the population are normally found to be bullied (Di Martino, Hoel, and Cooper 2003; Zapf et al. 2003). Also, when using a single-item methodology where respondents are asked to self-label as a victim after being presented with a strict definition, a prevalence of 3 to 7 percent is most typical (Mikkelsen and Einarsen 2001; Salin 2001; Zapf et al. 2003). In a study of 745

Norwegian assistant nurses employing such a method, 3 percent reported to being bullied at present, whereas 8 percent had previous experiences as victims (Einarsen, Matthiesen, and Skogstad 1998). Yet, when bullying is measured by exposure to specific behaviors typically involved in bullying with less strict criteria and cut-off points, the findings show higher numbers (cf. Mikkelsen and Einarsen 2001; Salin 2001). Hence, Keashly and Jagatic (2003) conclude that the lack of common terminology and well-developed methodology makes it difficult to determine the exact prevalence of workplace bullying. However, Notelaers et al. (2006) paint a nuanced picture of the prevalence of exposure to bullying that may tie these diverse findings more closely together. Employing Latent Class Cluster Analysis as a statistical technique to scrutinize the prevalence on bullying, Notelaers and colleagues showed bullying not to be an either/or phenomenon. In their study of 6,175 Belgian workers who had responded to an eighteen-item version of the Negative Acts Questionnaire, altogether six main clusters of respondents were identified, each with a specific kind of exposure to bullying behaviors. Only some 35 percent did not experience any kind of such behaviors at all. Another group of respondents (28 percent) experienced some negative work-related behavior now and then, while another group of 16 percent experienced some more personal-related bullying behavior now and then during the previous six months. Hence, some 80 percent reported no or only marginal exposure to bullying. However, three other groups of respondents reported a much higher and more systematic exposure to these behaviors. One group, labeled latent victims, comprising 9 percent of the total sample, reported exposure to many different kinds of bullying behaviors, although each type of behavior occurred only now and then. Taken together, however, their exposure was quite substantial and with clearly lowered well-being and job satisfaction. A second group, comprising 8 percent of the total sample, reported high exposure to a few kinds of behaviors; their job situation was manipulated in a negative way combined with social exclusion from the work group. This group was labelled "work-related bullying." The last group, however, comprising 3 percent of the respondents, reported a high exposure to all kinds of bullying behaviors, with severely deteriorated health and well-being, and was therefore labeled the victims. Following this study, some 20 percent may be exposed to varying kinds of bullying at work, while the very severely affected targets are in the arca of 3 percent.

4.2 Duration and Demographical Risk Factors

Theoretically, bullying is a long lasting process, or at least something that repeats itself over a period of time. Large representative samples in Sweden (Leymann 1996) and Norway (Einarsen and Skogstad 1996) have also found the average duration of bullying cases to be rather long, varying between fifteen to eighteen months. British findings have found 67 percent of victims to be bullied for more than one year (Hoel, Cooper, and Faragher 2001) and 39 percent to be bullied for more than two years (Hoel and Cooper 2000). A Finnish study found a mean duration of 2.7 years (Salin 2001).

In most studies, targets of bullying are about one-third men and two-thirds women (Zapf et al. 2003). Gender differences in the Scandinavian countries regarding prevalence of bullying have generally found to be only minor (Einarsen and Skogstad 1996; Nielsen et al. 2008). However, in a random sample of Norwegian assistant nurses, 10.2 percent of the men and 4.3 percent of the women reported that they had been exposed to bullying at work during the previous six months after adjustments for a series of background factors (Eriksen and Einarsen 2004). In this sample men comprised no more than 3 percent of the workforce, indicating that gender minority may be a particular risk factor. Still, in most studies the women/men ratios of targets fairly corresponds to their respective overall ratios, and thus higher prevalence rates for either gender may be due to an over-representation of the specific gender in that sample (Zapf et al. 2003).

Relatively little is known about the organizational status of targets, as bullying and harassment seem to affect both high and low in the hierarchy, with females in managerial positions as one possible risk group (Hoel, Cooper, and Faragher 2001). Hence, this points at powerlessness as a relative factor, again stressing that power imbalance between two parties may arise independently of each party's personal strength or objective position.

About perpetrators little is known. Men seem to be overrepresented, as are managers who are reported as the main perpetrator in between 30 and 80 percent of cases. Multiple perpetrators are found in the majority of cases, while in between 20 and 40 percent of cases there is only one alleged bully involved (see Zapf et al. 2003 for an overview of empirical findings).

5. ANTECEDENTS OF WORKPLACE BULLYING

Bullying and harassment have been claimed to be an inherent characteristic and a basic mechanism in all human interaction (Brodsky 1976), used both to punish others, to gain advantages and evade contesters in the ever ongoing micro-political play at work, or to exploit others for personal gains, sometimes just for the "fun of it." As seen above, the origin of such situations may also be many, making any exhaustive list of antecedents impossible. A variety of factors ranging from personality traits to organizational factors have been presented as possible antecedents of bullying at work (e.g., Coyne, Seigne, and Randall 2000; Einarsen et al. 1994; Hoel, Zapf, and Cooper 2002).

5.1 Individual Antecedents of Bullying

5.1.1 *Targets' personality*

To look for antecedents of bullying in targets has been a controversial issue in bullying research, as victim blaming or "devil hunting" may easily follow such an approach (Zapf and Einarsen 2003; 2005). To state that anxiety and low self-esteem are predominant personality characteristics of many targets of workplace bullying is probably uncontroversial. The controversy lies in whether and to what extent these characteristics actually should be considered causes of bullying or whether they are the result of the bullying process (O'Moore et al. 1998). Leymann (1996) strongly opposed the notion that the personality of an individual predisposes who becomes targets of workplace bullying. The neurotic and often obsessive behavior of many targets should rather be understood as a normal response to an abnormal situation, and the observed changes in personality traits in targets may just be seen as a consequence of their traumatic experience of being exposed to bullying (Leymann and Gustafsson 1996). Yet, the debate concerning personality traits as antecedents of bullying are likely to continue until longitudinal research into this issue has been undertaken (Coyne, Seigne, and Randall 2000).

With these cautions in mind, individuals who are introverted, conscientious, neurotic, and submissive have also been found more likely to become targets of bullying and subsequently victimized (Coyne, Seigne, and Randall 2000). Based on interviews and case studies, Brodsky (1976) described targets as literal-minded and as overachievers with an unrealistic view of both their own abilities and recourses, as well as the demands of their work tasks. A view of oneself as more accurate or punctual than one's colleagues may be perceived by others in the work environment as patronizing (Einarsen 1999). Individuals who violate expectations, annoy others, and violate social norms may elicit aggressive behavior in others, and thus more likely be subjected to aggression from others (Felson 1992).

However, a Norwegian study among 72 targets of bullying matched with a control group of 72 non-exposed respondents using cluster analyses revealed two groups of targets. The first cluster comprising 64 percent ($n = 46$) of the target sample, did not differ from the control group. The second cluster, comprising 36 percent ($n = 26$) of the targets, were less extrovert, agreeable, and conscientious than both the victims in cluster one and the control group. They also scored lower on emotional stability and on openness to experience, indicating that these targets are more neurotic and less mentally flexible and creative. Hence, the majority of targets were quite like non-targets as far as personality is concerned (Glasø et al. 2007). Similarly, a Norwegian study among 85 former and current targets using the MMPI-2 revealed an elevated personality profile among these targets, indicating a range of deviances in terms of personality and psychiatric distress. Again, the study indicated that the targets could be divided into distinct subgroups with different personalities: "The seriously affected," "The disappointed and depressed," and "The common group." The latter group did not portray any particular personality profile, thereby questioning the existence of a general victim profile (Matthiesen and Einarsen 2001). Zapf (1999) found that although targets generally saw themselves as being different from their co-workers, results also showed heterogeneous groups of targets, where one group was characterized by low social competencies, bad conflict management skills, and as unassertive and neurotic personalities, whereas another group was characterized as more achievement-oriented and more conscientious than their colleagues. For the latter group, one explanation may be that their behavior clashes with the norms of the rest of the group characterized by rigidity and low tolerance for diversity. Targets may be viewed with annoyance or even as threats to their work group, and thus aggressive behavior may take place directed against these individuals in an attempt to enforce conformity or even to get rid of them (Zapf and Einarsen 2005). Long-term unresolved interpersonal conflicts may then escalate into bullying if no effective conflict management strategies and interventions are implemented (Einarsen 2000).

5.1.2 *Perpetrators*

Not much in-depth information on the characteristics of perpetrators yet exists and most available information has so far been provided by targets of bullying. In summarizing the empirical findings on perpetrators, Zapf and Einarsen (2003) suggest three types of explanations, namely bullying due to protection of self-esteem, bullying due to lack of social competencies, and bullying due to micro-political behavior, where the first two are considered individual antecedents. Protecting and enhancing one's self-esteem is considered a basic motive in individuals and would thus influence and control one's behavior. When individuals feel respected and recognized there is agreement between external and self-evaluation, and interactions with others will probably proceed well. When this is not the case, conflicts may arise, especially when one's positive self-evaluation is questioned or denied by others. Aggression is thus related to high rather than low self-esteem, since individuals low in self-esteem may show depressive reactions and withdrawal rather than aggression towards others (Baumeister, Smart, and Boden 1996). Bullying due to protection of self-esteem is hypothesized to occur more often if the perpetrator is a manager, because being dominant, having high self-esteem, and protecting this self-esteem is expected from this group (Zapf and Einarsen 2003). Lack of social competencies may be another characteristic of the perpetrator. To be high on social and emotional competence would require the ability to detect, understand, and respond appropriately to others' feelings (Frey, Hirschstein, and Guzzo 2000). Supervisors yelling at their subordinates due to frustration or anger may indicate lack of emotional control. Perpetrators may also not be fully aware of what they are doing and how their behavior may affect the targets, implying a lack of self-reflection and perspective taking (Zapf and Einarsen 2003).

5.2 Organizational Factors

5.2.1 *Psychosocial work environment*

The work environment hypothesis, stating that a poor psychosocial work environment will create conditions that may lead up to and encourage bullying in the work group, has traditionally been a favored model of explaining workplace bullying, especially in Scandinavia (Agervold and Mikkelsen 2004; Einarsen, Raknes, and Matthiesen 1994; Leymann 1996). The basis of the work environment hypothesis first put forward by Leymann (1990; 1993) is that the stress and frustration caused by a negative psychosocial environment may lead to bullying of an exposed target, especially if management do not handle the situation in a firm and just way. Zapf (1999) provided support for this view that bullying is associated with a negative work environment, comparing targets of bullying with a control group of non-victimized individuals. Targets assessed their environment more negatively than the control group on all features related to the quality of the work environment, including the work environment quality that existed prior to the onset of bullying. Based on interviews with victims, Leymann (1993) claimed that four factors are prominent in eliciting bullying at work. These were (1) deficiencies in work design; (2) deficiencies in leadership behavior; (3) a socially exposed position of the victim; and (4) a low moral standard in the department.

A range of studies have shown workplace bullying to be correlated with role conflicts and role ambiguity, work control, a heavy workload, organizational restructuring, change of management, "negative management" styles, organizational climate, and conflicts in general (Baron and Neuman 1996; Björkqvist, Österman, and Hjelt-Bäck 1994; Einarsen, Raknes, and Matthiesen 1994; Hauge, Skogstad, and Einarsen 2007; Vartia 1996; Zapf 1999). A study among thirty Irish victims of bullying found their workplaces to be highly stressful and competitive, troubled with interpersonal conflicts and a lack of a friendly and supportive atmosphere, undergoing organizational changes managed under a general authoritarian leadership style (O'Moore et al. 1998). Having a weak superior, competition for tasks, status or advancement, or competition for the supervisor's favor are other perceived reasons for bullying among targets (Einarsen 2000; Zapf and Einarsen 2005). A low-quality work environment and increased role conflicts, as well as dissatisfaction with the social climate and leadership at the workplace, have also been reported by observers of bullying (Einarsen, Raknes, and Matthiesen 1994). In work groups where the need for cooperative efforts is high or the work is based on group performance, bullying may be a way of punishing members of the group that do not perform as expected by the rest of the group (Agervold and Mikkelsen 2004). Further, "weak", "inadequate", and a laissez-faire leadership style also seems to be conducive to workplace bullying (Einarsen, Raknes, and Matthiesen 1994; Hauge, Skogstad, and Einarsen 2007). In a random sample of some 2,300 Norwegian employees, a laissez-faire leadership style was found to positively correlate with role conflict, role ambiguity, and conflicts with co-workers (Skogstad et al. 2007). Furthermore, these stressors mediated the effects of laissez-faire leadership on bullying. Hence, the findings showed that laissez-faire leadership is not a type of zero-leadership, but rather a destructive form of leadership creating a stressful milieu with elevated risks for bullying to prosper.

5.2.2 *Organizational culture*

Brodsky (1976) argues that for harassment to occur, the elements behind such behavior must exist within an organizational culture that either permits or rewards such harassment, and thus includes the direct or indirect agreement and permission from management. What behavior is to be tolerated or accepted is decided by the dominant coalition within an organization who decides when to sanction and when to reward behavior (Bennet et al. 2005). In his qualitative study of bullying in the fire service, characterized by a white male majority, Archer (1999) explores how bullying may become institutionalized and passed on as an organizational culture to ensure the continuation of a white male culture. Hence, both females and non-white males were at risk of being singled out as targets. Perpetrators were found to often have been exposed to a similar experience sometime in their career. Further, in an autocratic leadership culture where superiors have been brought up within the same tradition, it is difficult to break out of the vicious cycle. The fact that many targets of bullying considered complaining to be an act of disloyalty further emphasizes the strength and impact of such socialization processes at work (Archer 1999).

5.2.3 *Theoretical explanations of relationships between bullying and the work environment*

Theoretically, at least three distinct arguments may be put forward as explanations for the relationships found between work environment factors and bullying. First, the revised frustration-aggression hypothesis (Berkowitz 1989) states that highly stressful working situations may lead to aggressive behavior through production of negative affect in employees. Bullying will then flourish in ill-conditioned working environments due to environmental effects on aggressive behavior in alleged perpetrators (Einarsen 2000). Second, according to the social interactionist approach (e.g., Felson 1992; Neuman and Baron 2003), stressful situations may also affect aggression indirectly through their effect on targets' behavior and reactions. Anxious, depressive, and obsessive behavior from distressed workers may cause an unpleasant working environment, and thus lead to a negative reaction in the work group which may end in escalated interpersonal conflicts and eventually bullying (Zapf and Einarsen 2003). Distressed individuals may also violate expectations in the work environment, perform less competently and efficiently, annoy other colleagues, and thus elicit aggressive responses in others (Felson 1992). Bullying can thus be seen as an interactional response to norm violations and as an instrument for social control (Hoel, Rayner, and Cooper 1999). Third, a stressful working environment may also increase the likelihood of interpersonal conflicts which, if unresolved, might escalate into bullying behavior (Zapf and Einarsen 2005). These experiences may be caused by factors such as high levels of role conflict, lack of self-monitoring possibilities, and poorly performing supervisors. Role conflict and lack of control may lead to elevated tension, stress, and frustration in work groups. In turn, such situations may act as antecedents of conflict and deteriorated inter-worker relationships, and thus be related to bullying through its negative impact on individuals' relationships with other co-workers (Einarsen 2000).

Salin (2003b) classifies organizational conditions and processes associated with workplace bullying into three factors, namely enabling structures or necessary antecedents, motivating structures or incentives, and precipitating processes or triggering circumstances. Hence, conditions related to the work environment may not in themselves lead to bullying, but may act as enabling factors if there are additional motivational or triggering conditions present. Similarly, motivating and precipitating factors do not result in workplace bullying unless the conditions for such behaviors are right. The enabling factors may provide fertile soil for bullying to take place, i.e., making the environment conducive to bullying. When motivating and precipitating structures and processes are present, the existence or lack of enabling conditions in the organization will affect whether workplace bullying is possible or not. Enabling factors include a perceived power imbalance between the possible target and the perpetrator, low perceived costs for the perpetrator, and a general dissatisfaction and frustration with the work environment. Examples of motivating factors may include high internal competition, certain forms of reward systems, and expected benefits for the perpetrator of the bullying behavior. The enabling factors explain why certain situations and organizations are prone to bullying and the motivating factors explain why it might be rewarding to engage in such behavior. Yet there are still additional factors that may act as the actual triggers of bullying. Precipitating processes are typically related to changes in an organization such as downsizing, other organizational changes, or changes in the composition of the work group (Salin 2003b). Internal competition and rivalry in order to improve own interests may lead employees to engage in bullying behaviors in order to eliminate other competitors (Matthiesen and Einarsen 2007; Salin 2003a). Although this model may be a useful tool in structuring and characterizing different steps and antecedents in a bullying process, the usefulness of this theoretical framework in relation to bullying is still uncertain as no empirical study has yet tested the model.

5.3 Societal Factors as Antecedents of Bullying at Work

A review of the antecedents of workplace bullying would be incomplete without also acknowledging the possible impact of societal factors. Researchers show increasingly more attention to the effects of globalization, liberalization of markets, an increasing struggle for efficiency, and work intensification, arguing that these changes affecting most organizations may lead to an increase in bullying and abusive behavior by managers and co-workers (Lee 2000; McCarthy 1996). In order to stay competitive, organizations are forced to engage in significant organizational and technological changes, often including restructuring and downsizing (Burke and Nelson 1998; Hoel and Cooper 2001). As a result of such processes, employees at all levels of the organization may find themselves in situations of increasing workloads and uncertainty with regard to future employment (Hellgren, Sverke, and Isaksson 1999). With greater job insecurity in many sectors, employees may become less resistant to pressure and more unlikely to challenge unfair and aggressive treatment from their management. Simultaneously, managers are given greater opportunity to use their power (Hoel and Cooper 2001). A compression of career structures resulting from restructuring and de-layering processes may force many managers, even if involuntarily, to use more authoritarian and even abusive behavior to carry out their work (McCarthy 1996). Organizations are likely to exert increased pressure on managers, and with less time and resources available, managers may employ bullying tactics in order to reach their goals. Managers may apply such tactics because they know their behavior will go unchallenged due to power differences between the parties involved (Sheehan 1999). Further, even more employees on all levels in organizations may more likely employ bullying tactics, possibly as a matter of survival in situations appearing unsolvable by other means (Hoel and Cooper 2001).

However, the literature on the societal effects on bullying is to a large extent anecdotal in nature and to our knowledge, only a few studies have thus far been published showing relationships between the effects of the changing nature of work on workplace bullying or workplace aggression. In a study of among some 450 US employees, Baron and Neuman (1998) found support for relationships between change factors such as cost cutting, organizational change, social change, and job insecurity, and three forms of workplace aggression, namely verbal aggression, obstructionism (i.e. passive forms of aggression impeding the target's ability to perform their work), and workplace violence. Further, Hoel and Cooper (2000) found in a national survey in Great Britain that targets of bullying reported significantly more organizational changes during the previous six months compared to non-targets. In a study of 2,400 Norwegian employees, organizational changes were found to be associated with bullying and exposure to several changes in the organization increased the likelihood of being exposed (Skogstad, Matthiesen, and Einarsen 2007). The relationship was however not strong, and conflicts with supervisors were a more important antecedent of bullying than were organizational changes. These conflicts with supervisors were not related to organizational changes, but rather reside elsewhere. Hence, more research is definitely needed on the relationships between changes and bullying, but also on other factors on a societal level, such as economical welfare and national culture. The latter, especially related to differences in power distance and masculinity, has been proposed as an important cultural antecedent of bullying (Einarsen 2000).

6. CONSEQUENCES OF BULLYING AT WORK

6.1 Individual Consequences

When working with victims of long-term bullying, what strikes one most is the intense and pervasive health problems they display. Exposure to systematic bullying at work causes a host of negative health effects in targets (see Einarsen and Mikkelsen 2003 for a review). A range of studies have also shown that victimization from bullying may lead to pervasive emotional, psychosomatic, and psychiatric problems in targets (e.g., Einarsen, Matthiesen, and Skogstad 1998; Mikkelsen and Einarsen 2002), and among the effects most frequently reported are stress symptoms (Vartia 2001), impaired mental health (Zapf, Knorz, and Kulla 1996), depression (Mikkelsen and Einarsen 2001), irritability and anxiety (Niedl 1996). A "ripple effect" have also been observed in bullying (Hoel, Cooper, and Faragher 2001), as several studies have found that observers of bullying reported higher levels of generalized stress and lower job satisfaction than those who had not observed bullying take place (Einarsen, Raknes, and Matthiesen 1994; Hauge et al. 2007; Vartia 2001). In a study of male industrial workers, a significant negative association between exposure to bullying at work and measurements of psychological health and well-being were found (Einarsen and Raknes 1997). In fact, exposure to bullying explained 23 percent of the variance in psychological health and well-being. The strongest relationships existed between experienced personal derogation and psychological well-being. A random sample of Norwegian assistant nurses (Einarsen, Matthiesen, and Skogstad 1998) showed that nurses reporting exposure to bullying portrayed significantly higher levels of burnout, lowered job satisfaction, and lowered psychological well-being compared to their non-bullied colleagues. In view of the particular symptom constellation found in many studies, it has been argued that many victims of long-term bullying at work may in fact suffer from post-traumatic stress disorder (Björkqvist, Österman, and Hjelt-Bäck 1994; Leymann and Gustafsson 1996). The diagnosis PTSD refers to a constellation of stress symptoms following a traumatic event, where the trauma is relived through return-ing, insistent, and painful memories of the event, recurring nightmares, or by intense psychological discomfort at reminders, where the person avoids situations associated with the trauma, and may lack the ability to react emotionally adequately, for instance by having reduced interests in activities that used to bring joy, by showing limited affect, or by the feeling of having no future. An early Swedish study among sixty-four victims of bullying at work attending a rehabilitation program concluded that 65 percent of the patients suffered from PTSD (Leymann and Gustafsson 1996). In a study conducted among 102 victims of long-term bullying at work recruited among members of two Norwegian national associations against bullying, 75 percent of victims portrayed stress symptoms indicating a post-traumatic stress disorder (Matthiesen and Einarsen 2004). A total of 76 percent scored above a level on the Hopkins Symptom Check List indicating psychiatric pathology as opposed to 21 percent for females and 12 percent for males in a control group. The level of post-traumatic symptoms was highly related to the intensity of the reported aggressive behaviors, and were especially salient if the aggressive behavior was perceived as being of a personally degrading nature.

Interview studies show that the victims typically report being normal and healthy prior to their victimization and that as a result of exposure to bullying they have subsequently developed severe health problems. In fact, many victims claim that their health has been ruined due to the bullying. However, given the retrospective design of most studies in this field and the use of self-reports, we do not know if victims are particularly vulnerable prior to being subjected to bullying, or perhaps due to exposure to other distressing life events. Such exposure might account for the symptoms reported. Indeed, results of a study of 118 Danish victims of bullying (Mikkelsen and Einarsen 2002) showed that many victims had experi-enced other distressing life events such as accidents, divorce, or bereavements. However, 80 percent of the victims in this study stated that none of these events affected them more negatively than the bullying they had suffered.

6.2 Organizational Effects

Less attention has been paid to the potential organizational outcomes, although the costs of such behavior are hypothesized to be related to increased absenteeism and turnover, as well as reduced productivity for both targets and work groups (Hoel, Einarsen, and Cooper 2003). In studies exploring the association between bullying and sickness absenteeism, relationships have normally been found to be relatively weak (Hoel and Cooper 2000; Vartia 2001). However, a study among some 5,500 Finnish hospital staff showed that targets of bullying had a 1.5 times higher risk of being medically certified sickness absent the year following their bullying exposure, than did their colleagues (Kivimäki, Elovainio, and Vahtera 2000). Increased health problems resulting from exposure to bullying may also demotivate employees with gradually reduced job satisfaction as a consequence and with increased absence and lowered productivity as possible results (Hoel, Einarsen, and Cooper 2003).

Turnover has to date been the organizational outcome that has received most attention in research, with studies revealing greater intention to leave the organization for both targets and observers of bullying (Hoel and Cooper 2000), and with reports of a considerable number of targets who actually have left their jobs (Rayner 1997). To leave the organization may be a coping strategy as it removes exposed individuals from the source of the problem (Zapf and Gross 2001). Others may quit their employment in despair or as a result of prolonged health problems (Einarsen et al. 1994). Others again may be expelled or forced out of their organization against their will (Leymann 1996; Zapf and Gross 2001), possibly as a tactic to get rid of employees considered unproductive or unsuitable, or to avoid paying redundancy cost (Einarsen, Raknes, and Matthiesen 1994; Lee 2000). Personal reasons for staying on, such as a desire for revenge, or a hope for justice and a belief that the problem may go away one day (Kile 1990), may be a reason why the relationship between bullying and turnover is not even stronger (Hoel, Einarsen, and Cooper 2003). Moreover, labor market considerations, lack of mobility, and difficulties in finding new employment may prevent targets to leave their current positions (Tepper 2000).

The observed reduction in job satisfaction, work motivation, and organizational commitment may also result in a reduction in employees' job performance and productivity. Although information on the relationship between bullying and productivity to a large extent is anecdotal in nature, probably due to the difficulties in measuring productivity (Hoel, Einarsen, and Cooper 2003), some empirical studies have however been conducted. In a Norwegian study, 27 percent of the respondents agreed to the statement "bullying at my workplace reduces our efficiency" (Einarsen, Raknes, and Matthiesen 1994), while a UK study later found a percentage of 32.5 for the same measure (Hoel and Cooper 2000). Assuming that bullying can go on for years, with the employee getting paid without having any real work to do combined with long periods of sick leave, Leymann (1990) estimated the annual costs to be between 30,000 and 100,000 US dollars per case. While not forgetting the human costs involved, there is reason to believe that in financial terms it would make good sense to combat workplace bullying in most organizations (Hoel, Einarsen, and Cooper 2003).

7. CONCLUSION

Bullying is a complex and multi-causal phenomenon seldom sufficiently explained by one factor alone. A wide range of factors at different explanatory levels may influence why bullying develops and who will be targeted. It is our experience that bullying is neither the product of chance nor of destiny, but should instead be understood as an interplay between individuals where neither contextual, situational, nor personal factors entirely suffice as explanations (Einarsen 2000). However, from an employer and management perspective, the more important issues are those that are influenced or controlled by the organization. In this respect many of the factors associated with individual predisposition and personality, albeit in some cases central to the development of bullying, are normally beyond the control and influence of the organization. While choosing a strategy where one tries to restrict the employment of potential bullies and targets may seem tempting, bullying must rather be seen as an inherent organizational problem which should be met by organizational measures. In this respect, approaches which aim at identifying, minimizing, and controlling organizational factors which might contribute to bullying would be a more productive strategy (Einarsen et al. 2005). The main focus must be on the acceptance and management of diversity in the workforce, on leadership quality and leadership culture, including a rise in basic conflict management skills combined with a strong focus on improving the work organization and the social work environment quality in the departments. A strong focus must also be on organizations' culture and how it potentially may permit or even reward negative behavior, especially supporting those who may have personal characteristics or values that are not at the heart of the traditional organizational culture.

Solid research-based information on the causes and consequences of bullying are needed to develop sound interventions and preventive strategies. However, not all possible causes of bullying may easily be altered, and information regarding possible interventions and action steps, as well as the cost-benefit of different strategies, is sorely needed. Intervention programs on bullying among schoolchildren have been developed with focus on the school and the classroom as social systems and have involved all children, teachers, and parents belonging to the particular school, even if research has shown that personality plays a role in who becomes a target and who becomes a perpetrator (Olweus 2003). Probably this is how we need to proceed in relation to preventing and handling bullying among adults as well. After all, the protection of employee health, safety, dignity, and respect is at the heart of any employer's responsibility in a democratic society. Therefore, it is also the employer's task to ensure that any case of bullying or mistreatment emerging within the organization is treated in a flexible, fair, ethical, and legally responsible way, ensuring the rights of targets as well as alleged perpetrators; to "respond quickly to bullying, when emotions and discussion run high and when every party tries to rally support to their cause, is by no means an easy task, either for managers, or for involved parties or colleagues who may be bystanders or observers of the behavior in question" (Einarsen and Hoel 2008). Hence, a well-developed anti-bullying policy is necessary (cf. Richards and Daley

2003), including both informal systems for support and guidance of targets, as well as a fair system for the management of formal complaints. The process of developing such a policy through active participation and involvement of a broad cross-section of organizational members at different levels and functions may in itself also have a preventive effect (see Einarsen and Hoel 2008 for more details). Although Brodsky initially thought workplaces rather easily could be made cruelty and harassment proof, his experiences over his research project made him far less convinced that this was the case. Leymann and Adams were also rather pessimistic in their view on employees and managers in these cases. Let's prove them wrong!

REFERENCES

ADAMS, A. 1992. *Bullying at Work: How to Confront and Overcome it.* London: Virago Press.

AGERVOLD, M., and MIKKELSEN, E. G. 2004. Relationships between bullying, psychosocial work environment and individual stress reactions. *Work and Stress,* 18 (4): 336–51.

AQUINO, K., and LAMERTZ, K. 2004. A relational model of workplace victimization: social roles and patterns of victimization in dyadic relationships. *Journal of Applied Pscyhology,* 89 (6): 1023–34.

ARCHER, D. 1999. Exploring "bullying" culture in the para-military organisation. *International Journal of Manpower,* 20 (1/2): 94–105.

ASHFORTH, B. 1994. Petty tyranny in organizations. *Human Relations,* 47 (7): 755–78.

BARON, R. A. 1997. *Human Aggression.* New York: Plenum Press.

—— and NEUMAN, J. H. 1996. Workplace violence and workplace aggression: evidence on their relative frequency and potential causes. *Aggressive Behavior,* 22 (3): 161–73.

—— —— 1998. Workplace aggression: the iceberg beneath the tip of workplace violence: evidence on its forms, frequency, and targets. *Public Administration Quarterly,* 21 (4): 446–64.

—— —— and GEDDES, D. 1999. Social and personal determinants of workplace aggression: evidence for the impact of perceived injustice and the Type A behavior pattern. *Aggressive Behavior,* 25 (4): 281–96.

BASSMAN, E. S. 1992. *Abuse in the Workplace: Management Remedies and Bottom Line Impact.* Westport, CT: Quorum Books.

BAUMEISTER, R. F., SMART, L., and BODEN, J. M. 1996. Relation of threatened egotism to violence and aggression: the dark side of high self-esteem. *Psychological Review,* 103 (1): 5–33.

—— STILLWELL, A., and WOTMAN, S. R. 1990. Victim and perpetrator accounts of interpersonal conflict: autobiographical narratives about anger. *Journal of Personality and Social Psychology,* 59 (5): 994–1005.

BENNET, R. J., AQUINO, K., REED II, A., and THAU, S. 2005. The normative nature of employee deviance and the impact of moral identity. In *Counterproductive Behavior: Investigations of Actors and Targets,* ed. S. Fox and P. E. Spector. Washington, DC: American Psychological Association.

BERKOWITZ, L. 1989. Frustration-Aggression hypothesis: examination and reformulation. *Psychological Bulletin*, 106 (1): 59–73.

BJÖRKQVIST, K., ÖSTERMAN, K., and HJELT-BÄCK, M. 1994. Aggression among university employees. *Aggressive Behavior*, 20: 173–84.

—— —— and LAGERSPETZ, K. M. J. 1994. Sex differences in covert aggression among adults. *Aggressive Behavior*, 20 (1): 27–33.

BOWLING, N. A., and BEEHR, T. A. 2006. Workplace harassment from the victim's perspective: a theoretical model and meta-analysis. *Journal of Applied Psychology*, 91 (5): 998–1012.

BRODSKY, C. M. 1976. *The Harassed Worker.* Toronto: Lexington Books.

BURKE, R. J., and NELSON, D. 1998. Mergers and acquisitions, downsizing, and privatization: a North American perspective. Pp. 21–54 in *The New Organizational Reality: Downsizing, Restructuring, and Revitalization*, ed. M. K. Gowing, J. D. Kraft, and J. C. Quick. Washington, D.C.: American Psychological Association.

BUSHMAN, B. J., BONACCI, A. M., PEDERSEN, W. C., VASQUEZ, E. A., and MILLER, N. 2005. Chewing on it can chew you up: effects of rumination on triggered displaced aggression. *Journal of Personality and Social Psychology*, 88 (6): 969–83.

COYNE, I., SEIGNE, E., and RANDALL, P. 2000. Predicting workplace victim status from personality. *European Journal of Work and Organizational Psychology*, 9 (3): 335–49.

DI MARTINO, V., HOEL, H., and COOPER, C. L. 2003. *Preventing Violence and Harassment in the Workplace.* Dublin: European Foundation for the Improvement of Living and Working Conditions.

DUFFY, M. K., GANSTER, D., and PAGON, M. 2002. Social undermining in the workplace. *Academy of Management Journal*, 45 (2): 331–51.

EINARSEN, S. 1996. Bullying and harassment at work: epidemiological and psychosocial aspects. Unpublished doctoral dissertation, University of Bergen.

—— 1999. The nature and causes of bullying at work. *International Journal of Manpower*, 20 (1/2): 16–27.

—— 2000. Harassment and bullying at work: a review of the Scandinavian approach. *Aggression and Violent Behavior*, 5 (4): 379–401.

—— and HOEL, H. 2008. Bullying and mistreatment at work: how managers may prevent and manage such problems. In *Employee Well-Being Support: A Workplace Resource*, ed. A. Kinder, R. Hughes, and C. L. Cooper. London: John Wiley and Sons.

—— and MIKKELSEN, E. G. 2003. Individual effects of exposure to bullying at work. Pp. 127–44 in *Bullying and Emotional Abuse in the Workplace: International Perspectives in Research and Practice*, ed. S. Einarsen, H. Hoel, D. Zapf, and C. L. Cooper. London: Taylor and Francis.

—— and RAKNES, B. I. 1997. Harassment in the workplace and the victimization of men. *Violence and Victims*, 12: 247–63.

—— and SKOGSTAD, A. 1996. Bullying at work: epidemiological findings in public and private organizations. *European Journal of Work and Organizational Psychology*, 5: 185–201.

—— AASLAND, M. S., and SKOGSTAD, A. 2007. Destructive leadership behavior: a definition and conceptual model. *Leadership Quarterly*, 18 (3): 207–16.

—— MATTHIESEN, S. B., and SKOGSTAD, A. 1998. Bullying, burnout and well-being among assistant nurses. *Journal of Occupational Health and Safety: Australia and New Zealand*, 14 (6): 563–8.

—— S. Raknes, B. I., and Matthiesen, S. B. 1994. Bullying and harassment at work and their relationship to work environment quality: an exploratory study. *European Work and Organizational Psychologist*, 4 (4): 381–401.

—— Raknes, B. I., Matthiesen, S. B., and Hellesøy, O. H. 1990. Mobbing i arbeidslivet: utbredelse—ytringsformer—konsekvenser: en prosjektbeskrivelse [Bullying at work: prevalence—modes of expressions—consequences: description of a project]. *Nordisk Psykologi*, 42 (2): 294–8.

—— Hoel, H., Zapf, D., and Cooper, C. L. 2003. The concept of bullying at work: the European tradition. In Pp. 3–30 in *Bullying and Emotional Abuse in the Workplace: International Perspectives in Research and Practice*, ed. S. Einarsen, H. Hoel, D. Zapf, and C. L. Cooper. London: Taylor and Francis.

—— —— —— —— 2005. Workplace bullying: individual pathology or organizational culture? In Pp. 229–47 in *Workplace Violence: Issues, Trends, Strategies*, ed. V. Bowie, B. S. Fisher, and C. L. Cooper. Cullompton: Willan.

Eriksen, W., and Einarsen, S. 2004. Gender minority as a risk factor of exposure to bullying at work: the case of male assistant nurses. *European Journal of Work and Organizational Psychology*, 13 (4): 473–92.

Felson, R. B. 1992. "Kick 'em when they're down": explanations of the relationship between stress and interpersonal aggression and violence. *Sociological Quarterly*, 33 (1): 1–16.

Frey, K. S., Hirschstein, M. K., and Guzzo, B. A. 2000. Second step: preventing aggression by promoting social competence. *Journal of Emotional and Behavioral Disorders*, 8 (2): 102–12.

Glasø, L., and Einarsen, S. 2006. Experienced affects in leader-subordinate relationships. *Scandinavian Journal of Management*, 22 (1): 49–73.

—— Matthiesen, S. B., Nielsen, M. B., and Einarsen, S. 2007. Do targets of workplace bullying portray a general victim personality profile? *Scandinavian Journal of Psychology*, 48 (4): 313–19.

Hadjifotiou, N. 1983. *Women and Harassment at Work*. London: Pluto Press.

Hauge, L. J., Skogstad, A., and Einarsen, S. 2007. Relationships between stressful work environments and bullying: results of a large representative study. *Work and Stress*, 21 (3): 220–42.

Hellgren, J., Sverke, M., and Isaksson, K. 1999. A two-dimensional approach to job insecurity: consequences for employee attitudes and well-being. *European Journal of Work and Organizational Psychology*, 8 (2): 179–95.

Hoel, H. 2002. *Bullying at Work in Great Britain*. Manchester: University of Manchester, Institute of Science and Technology.

—— and Cooper, C. L. 2000. *Destructive Conflict and Bullying at Work*. Manchester: Manchester School of Management, University of Manchester Institute Science and Technology.

—— —— 2001. Origins of bullying: theoretical frameworks for explaining workplace bullying. In Pp. 3–19 in *Building a Culture of Respect: Managing Bullying at Work*, ed. N. Tehrani. London: Taylor and Francis.

—— —— and Faragher, B. 2001. The experience of bullying in Great Britain: the impact of organizational status. *European Journal of Work and Organizational Psychology*, 10: 443–65.

—— Einarsen, S., and Cooper, C. L. 2003. Organisational effects of bullying. Pp. 145–62 in *Bullying and Emotional Abuse in the Workplace: International Perspectives in Research and Practice*, ed. S. Einarsen, H. Hoel, D. Zapf, and C. L. Cooper. London: Taylor and Francis.

HOEL, H. RAYNER, C., and COOPER, C. L. 1999. Workplace bullying. Pp. 195–230 in *International Review of Industrial and Organizational Psychology*, ed. C. L. Cooper and I. T. Robertson. Chichester: John Wiley and Sons.

—— ZAPF, D., and COOPER, C. L. 2002. Workplace bullying and stress. Pp. 293–333 in *Historical and Current Perspectives on Stress and Health*, ed. P. L. Perrewe and D. C. Ganster, vol. ii. Amsterdam: Jai.

HORNSTEIN, H. A. 1996. *Brutal Bosses and their Prey*. New York: Riverhead Books.

KARASEK, R. A., and THEORELL, T. 1990. *Healthy Work: Stress, Productivity, and the Reconstruction of Working Life*. New York: Basic Books.

KEASHLY, L. 1998. Emotional abuse in the workplace: conceptual and empirical issues. *Journal of Emotional Abuse*, 1 (1): 85–117.

—— and HARVEY, S. 2005. Emotional abuse in the workplace. Pp. 201–35 in *Counterproductive Behavior: Investigations of Actors and Targets*, ed. S. Fox and P. E. Spector. Washington, DC: American Psychological Association.

—— and JAGATIC, K. 2003. By another name: American perspectives on workplace bullying. Pp. 31–61 in *Bullying and Emotional Abuse in the Workplace: International Perspectives in Research and Practice*, ed. S. Einarsen, H. Hoel, D. Zapf, and C. L. Cooper. London: Taylor and Francis.

—— TROTT, V., and MACLEAN, L. M. 1994. Abusive behavior in the workplace: a preliminary investigation. *Violence and Victims*, 9 (4): 341–57.

KILE, S. M. 1990. *Helsefarleg leierskap: ein eksplorerande studie (Health Endangering Leadership: An Exploratory Study)*. University of Bergen: Department of Psychosocial Science.

KIVIMÄKI, M., ELOVAINIO, M., and VAHTERA, J. 2000. Workplace bullying and sickness absence in hospital staff. *Occupational and Environmental Medicine*, 57 (10): 656–60.

LEE, D. (2000). An analysis of workplace bullying in the UK. *Personnel Review*, 29 (5): 593–612.

LEYMANN, H. 1990. Mobbing and psychological terror at workplaces. *Violence and Victims*, 5 (2): 119–26.

—— 1993. *Mobbing: Psychoterror am Arbeitsplatz und wie man sich dagegen wehren kann*. Hamburg: Rowohlt Reinbeck.

—— 1996. The content and development of mobbing at work. *European Journal of Work and Organizational Psychology*, 5 (2): 165–84.

—— and GUSTAFSSON, A. 1996. Mobbing at work and the development of post-traumatic stress disorders. *European Journal of Work and Organizational Psychology*, 5 (2): 251–75.

MCCARTHY, P. (1996). When the mask slips: inappropriate coercion in organisations undergoing restructuring. Pp. 47–65 in *Bullying: From Backyard to Boardroom*, ed. P. McCarthy, M. Sheehan, and W. Wilkie. Alexandria, NSW: Millennium Books.

MARAIS, S., and HERMAN, M. 1997. *Corporate Hyenas at Work: How to Spot and Outwit Them by Being Hyenawise*. Pretoria: Kagiso Publishers.

MARCUS-NEWHALL, A., PEDERSEN, W. C., CARLSON, M., and MILLER, N. 2000. Displaced aggression is alive and well: a meta-analytic review. *Journal of Personality and Social Psychology*, 78 (4): 670–89.

MATTHIESEN, S. B. 2004. When whistleblowing leads to bullying at work. *Occupational Health Psychologist*, 1 (1): 3.

—— 2006. Bullying at work: antecedents and outcomes. Ph.D. thesis, University of Bergen.

—— and EINARSEN, S. 2001. MMPI-2 configurations among victims of bullying at work. *European Journal of Work and Organizational Psychology*, 10 (4): 467–84.

MATTHIESEN, S. B. 2004. Psychiatric distress and symptoms of PTSD among victims of bullying at work. *British Journal of Guidance and Counselling*, 32 (3): 335–56.

—— —— 2007. Perpetrators and targets of bullying at work: role stress and individual differences. *Violence and Victims*, 22 (6): 735–53.

—— RAKNES, B. I., and RØKKUM, O. 1989. Mobbing på arbeidsplassen [Bullying at work]. *Tidsskrift for Norsk Psykologforening*, 26: 761–74.

—— AASEN, E., HOLST, G., WIE, K., and EINARSEN, S. 2003. The escalation of conflict: a case study of bullying at work. *International Journal of Management and Decision Making*, 4 (1): 96–112.

MIKKELSEN, E. G., and EINARSEN, S. 2001. Bullying in Danish work-life: prevalence and health correlates. *European Journal of Work and Organizational Psychology*, 10 (4): 393–413.

—— —— 2002. Basic assumptions and symptoms of post-traumatic stress among victims of bullying at work. *European Journal of Work and Organizational Psychology*, 11: 87–11.

NAMIE, G., and NAMIE, R. 2000. *The Bully at Work: What you can Do to Stop the Hurt and Reclaim the Dignity on the Job*. Naperville,IL: Sourcebooks, Inc.

NEAR, J. P., and MICELI, M. P. 1996. Whistle-blowing: myth and reality. *Journal of Management*, 22 (3): 507–26.

NEUMAN, J. H., and BARON, R. A. 2003. Social antecedents of bullying: a social interactionist perspective. Pp. 185–202 in *Bullying and Emotional Abuse in the Workplace: International Perspectives in Research and Practice*, ed. S. Einarsen, H. Hoel, D. Zapf, and C. L. Cooper. London: Taylor and Francis.

NIEDHAMMER, I., DAVID, S., and DEGIOANNI, S. 2006. Association between workplace bullying and depressive symptoms in the French working population. *Journal of Psychosomatic Research*, 61 (2): 251–9.

NIEDL, K. 1995. *Mobbing/Bullying am arbeitsplatz*. Munich: Rainer Hampp Verlag.

—— 1996. Mobbing and well-being: economic and personnel development implications. *European Journal of Work and Organizational Psychology*, 5 (2): 239–49.

NIELSEN, M. B., SKOGSTAD, A., MATTHIESEN, S. B., GLASØ, L., AASLAND, M. S., NOTELAERS, G., and EINARSEN, S. 2008. Prevalence of workplace bullying in Norway: comparisons across time and estimation methods. *European Journal of Work and Organisational Psychology*. In press.

NOTELAERS, G., EINARSEN, S., DE WITTE, H., and VERMUNT, J. K. 2006. Measuring exposure to bullying at work: the validity and advantages of the latent class cluster approach. *Work and Stress*, 20 (4): 288–301.

OLWEUS, D. 2003. Bully/victim problems in school: basic facts and an effective intervention programme. Pp. 62–78 in *Bullying and Emotional Abuse in the Workplace: International Perspectives in Research and Practice*, S. Einarsen, H. Hoel, D. Zapf and C. L. Cooper. London: Taylor and Francis.

O'MOORE, M., SEIGNE, E., McGUIRE, L., and SMITH, M. 1998. Victims of bullying at work in Ireland. *Journal of Occupational Health and Safety: Australia and New Zealand*, 14 (6): 569–74.

PATHE, M., and MULLEN, P. E. 1997. The impact of stalkers on their victims. *British Journal of Psychiatry*, 170: 12–17.

PRYOR, J. B., and FITZGERALD, L. F. 2003. Sexual harassment research in the United States. Pp. 79–100 in *Bullying and Emotional Abuse in the Workplace: International Perspectives in*

Research and Practice, ed. S. Einarsen, H. Hoel, D. Zapf, and C. L. Cooper. London: Taylor and Francis.

PURCEL, R., PATHE, M., and MULLEN, P. E. 2004. Stalking: defining and prosecuting a new category of offending. *International Journal of Law and Psychiatry*, 27 (2): 157–69.

QUINE, L. 1999. Workplace bullying in NHS community trust: staff questionnaire survey. *British Medical Journal*, 318: 228–32.

RAYNER, C. 1997. The incidence of workplace bullying. *Journal of Community and Applied Social Psychology*, 7: 199–208.

RICHARDS, J., and DALEY, H. 2003. Bullying policy: development, implementation and monitoring. Pp. 247–58 in *Bullying and Emotional Abuse in the Workplace: International Perspectives in Research and Practice*, ed. S. Einarsen, H. Hoel, D. Zapf, and C. L. Cooper. London: Taylor and Francis.

SALIN, D. 2001. Prevalence and forms of bullying among business professionals: a comparison of two different strategies for measuring bullying. *European Journal of Work and Organizational Psychology*, 10 (4): 425–41.

—— 2003a. Bullying and organisational politics in competitive and rapidly changing work environments. *International Journal of Management and Decision Making*, 4 (1): 35–46.

—— 2003b. Ways of explaining workplace bullying: a review of enabling, motivation and precipitating structures and processes in the work environment. *Human Relations*, 56 (10): 1213–32.

SHEEHAN, M. 1999. Workplace bullying: responding with some emotional intelligence. *International Journal of Manpower*, 20 (1/2): 57–69.

SKOGSTAD, A., MATTHIESEN, S. B., and EINARSEN, S. 2007. Organizational changes: a precursor of bullying at work? *International Journal of Organization Theory and Behavior*, 10 (1): 58–94.

—— EINARSEN, S., TORSHEIM, T., AASLAND, M. S., and HETLAND, H. 2007. The destructiveness of Laissez-Faire leadership behavior. *Journal of Occupational Health Psychology*, 12 (1): 80–92.

TEPPER, B. J. 2000. Consequences of abusive supervision. *Academy of Management Journal*, 43 (2): 178–90.

THYLEFORS, I. 1987. *Syndabockar: om utstötning och mobbning i arbetslivet [Scapegoats: About Expulsion and Bullying in Working Life]*. Stockholm: Natur och Kultur.

TOKUNGA, T., and TANAKA, R. 1998. Bullying at work in Japan. In *Bullying at Work 1998: Research Update Conference Proceedings*, ed. C. Rayner, M. Sheehan, and M. Barker. Stafford: Staffordshire University/Brighton: The Andrea Adams Trust.

—— CRAWFORD, N., and TANAKA, R. 1998. *Spitting*. Japan: NHK.

VAN DE VLIERT, E. 1998. Conflict and conflict management. Pp. 351–76 in *Handbook of Work and Organizational Psychology*, iii: *Personnel Psychology*, 2nd edn., ed. P. J. D. Drenth, H. Thierry, and C. J. de Wolff. Hove: Psychology Press.

VARTIA, M. 1991. Bullying at workplaces. Paper presented at the Towards the 21st century: work in the 1990s International Symposium on Future Trends in the Changing Working Life, Helsinki.

—— 1996. The sources of bullying: psychological work environment and organizational climate. *European Journal of Work and Organizational Psychology*, 5 (2): 203–14.

—— 2001. Consequences of workplace bullying with respect to the well-being of its targets and the observers of bullying. *Scandinavian Journal of Work, Environment and Health*, 27 (1): 63–9.

YAMADA, D. C. 2003. Workplace bullying and the law: towards a transnational consensus. Pp. 399–411 in *Bullying and emotional abuse in the Workplace: International Perspectives in Research and Practice*, ed. S. Einarsen, H. Hoel, D. Zapf, and C. L. Cooper. London: Taylor and Francis.

ZAPF, D. 1999. Organisational, work group related and personal causes of mobbing/bullying at work. *International Journal of Manpower*, 20 (1/2): 70–85.

—— and EINARSEN, S. 2003. Individual antecedents of bullying: victims and perpetrators. Pp. 165–84 in *Bullying and Emotional Abuse in the Workplace: International Perspectives in Research and Practice*, ed. S. Einarsen, H. Hoel, D. Zapf, and C. L. Cooper. London: Taylor and Francis.

—— —— 2005. Mobbing at work: escalated conflicts in organizations. Pp. 237–70 in *Counterproductive Work Behavior: Investigations of Actors and Targets*, ed. S. Fox and P. E. Spector. Washington, DC: American Psychological Association.

—— and GROSS, C. 2001. Conflict escalation and coping with workplace bullying: a replication and extension. *European Journal of Work and Organizational Psychology*, 10 (4): 497–522.

—— KNORZ, C., and KULLA, M. 1996. On the relationship between mobbing factors, and job content, the social work environment and health outcomes. *European Journal of Work and Organizational Psychology*, 5 (2): 215–37.

—— EINARSEN, S., HOEL, H., and VARTIA, M. 2003. Empirical findings on bullying in the workplace. Pp. 103–26 in *Bullying and Emotional Abuse in the Workplace: International Perspectives in Research and Practice*, ed. S. Einarsen, H. Hoel, D. Zapf, and C. L. Cooper. London: Taylor and Francis.

LABOR RELATIONS

E. KEVIN KELLOWAY

C. GAIL HEPBURN

LORI FRANCIS

1. INTRODUCTION

ALTHOUGH the extent of unionization may have declined in some jurisdictions, the practice of labor relations continues to have considerable impact on both individuals and organizations. On the organizational front, labor relations practice has implications for the implementation of human resource practices in organizations (for a review see Barling, Fullagar, and Kelloway 1992; Kochan 1980) as well as for organizational performance (e.g., Deery and Iverson 2005). For individuals, the dynamic of labor relations has been characterized as involving both conflict and change—a dynamic that brings with it the potential for considerable stress (e.g., Bluen and Barling 1987; 1988; Francis and Kelloway 2005) and, indeed, violence (Francis, Cameron, and Kelloway 2006).

In this chapter we review research on labor relations highlighting its impact on individuals and organizations. We begin by considering the extent and nature of unionization in various jurisdictions. We then consider the major "events" characterizing labor relations; from an individual's decision to join a union, through the negotiation of collective agreements and related strike action, to the administration and enforcement of agreement provisions via member grievances. We

Preparation of this chapter was supported by grants from the Social Sciences and Humanities Research Council of Canada.

conclude with a review of other research assessing consequences of labor relations that are of critical importance for human resource management.

2. EXTENT AND NATURE OF UNIONIZATION

Although unionization has declined in many jurisdictions (Visser 2006), a substantial percentage of the workforce continues to work under, or be influenced by, negotiated collective agreements. In the European Union, unionization rates range from 11 to 84 percent (Schabel and Wagner 2005). In the United States overall union density is 12 percent (Bureau of Labor Statistics 2007), yet in Canada over 30 percent of the workforce belongs to a union (Akyeampong 2003). Australia reports union density rates of 22.9 percent, while Japan's union density rate is approximately 19.7 percent of the working population (Visser 2006).

However, such overall unionization rates may present a misleading picture of the nature of unionization. First, there can be considerable variation within a country attributable to jurisdictional or regional differences. Within the US, there is considerable variation by state. In 2001, the state unionization rates ranged from approximately 4 percent in North and South Carolina to 26 percent in New York (Hirsch, MacPherson, and Vroman 2001). Sectoral differences may also play a role with the public sector typically reporting higher unionization rates than the private sector (Akyeampong 2003; Bureau of Labor Statistics 2007). Similarly, shifts in the economy, in particular the decline in the manufacturing sector and the growth in the service sector, have also affected unionization rates (Kelloway, Barling, and Harvey 1998).

Further, changes in the nature of the workforce have affected the composition of unions. First, with the growing number of women entering the labor force, the number of women in trade unions has dramatically increased (Kelloway, Barling, and Harvey 1998) and in many countries the unionization rate among women is equal to, or greater than, that of men (Visser 2006). Second, the ageing population, coupled with the fact that unionization rates are declining among young workers, has resulted in a graying of the unionized workforce (Kelloway, Barling, and Harvey 1998; Visser 2006). Finally, it should be noted that unionization rates fluctuate over time. For example, there has been a general decrease in the unionization rate in Canada in recent years (Human Resources and Social Development Canada 2006). However, the number of unionized workers in Canada increased by 60,000 workers between 2005 and 2006 (Human Resources and Social Development Canada 2006). A recent increase in the popularity and number of unionization drives in both the US and other jurisdictions (Blader 2007) may add further to the instability in unionization rates. This increase is part of a more global "renewal" strategy in which labor unions worldwide are expending effort and allocating resources toward increasing membership density (for a review of the union renewal literature see Kumar and Schenk 2006). Certainly, recruitment challenges are associated with the increasing diversity of the workforce, and, largely due to the growth in the service sector, the acceptance and use of part-time, contract, and contingent work arrangements. However, union leaders are devising innovative strategies to attract the attention of the changing workforce and those with more precarious work arrangements. Specifically, they target the effectiveness of labor unions in addressing issues related to respectful treatment in the workplace and participation in decision making, thereby moving beyond the more traditional bread and butter economic concerns. In light of this activity it is important to consider the reasons individuals have for deciding to join a union or vote in a union certification campaign and it is to these reasons that we now turn our attention.

3. LABOR RELATIONS EVENTS

3.1 Union Joining

Why individuals choose to join a union is the single most researched topic relating to unions (Barling, Fullagar, and Kelloway 1992). Despite the existence of "closed shop" agreements in some jurisdictions that mean that many workers join a union as a condition of employment in a particular organization, both unions wishing to increase union membership and employers wishing to prevent unionization have a strong vested interest in the answer to this question.

Three theoretical frameworks have guided union joining research; frustration-aggression, social context and identity, and rational choice (Buttigieg, Deery, and Iverson 2007). According to these models individuals join unions as a result of dissatisfaction with their workplace (i.e., frustration), their identification with the union movement (i.e., social context), or as a result of the perceptions that union-ization would be instrumental in improving their workplace (i.e., rational choice). As noted by Kelloway et al. (2007a) there is great similarity between the themes of these models and those themes appearing in the models explaining participation in other forms of social protest (e.g., Klandermans 1997; 2002; Opp 1998).

Certainly, a great deal of research confirms the importance of negative job attitudes (e.g., Friedman, Abraham, and Thomas 2006) and, in particular, job dissatisfaction (see Barling, Fullagar, and Kelloway 1992; Davy and Shipper 1993;

Fiorito and Gallagher 1986) as "triggers" (Brett 1980) for pro-union voting in certification elections. Perceptions of procedural injustice (i.e., the perceived fairness of important procedures, Cropanzano and Greenberg 1997; Leventhal, Karuza, and Fry 1980; Thibaut and Walker 1975), also predict union joining and union-related protest (e.g., Blader 2007; Buttigieg, Deery, and Iversen 2007; Kelloway et al. 2007a).

With respect to social context and identification, research guided by social identity theory finds that group identification is a determinant of a collective response to injustice (DeWeerd and Klandermans 1999). Regarding unions specifically, Brett (1980) focused on belief in collective action as an important predictor of pro-union voting. These beliefs are most often operationalized as identification with the union or positive general attitudes toward unions (Kelloway, Barling, and Catano 1997). Elaborating on this basic conceptualization, LaHuis and Mellor (2001) suggested that pro-union attitudes are associated with a greater willingness to join the union and anti-union attitudes are associated with a resistance to union joining.

Finally, the rational choice model emphasizes the instrumental nature of unionization. The perception that a union will be instrumental in resolving job dissatisfactions or injustice is frequently identified as a predictor of union joining (e.g., Barling, Fullagar, and Kelloway 1992; Buttigieg, Deery, and Iversen 2007; Charlwood 2002; Visser 2002). For example, Mellor, Holzworth, and Conway (2003) found that the perceived costs and benefits of unionization were important predictors of individual voting decisions in a union representation election.

Further, there is evidence to suggest that innovative recruitment strategies targeting a union's ability to be instrumental in non-traditional areas, such as respectful treatment at work and participation in decision making, may be essential for recruitment success among those individuals in more precarious types of employment. In Hepburn and Barling's (2001) vignette study, graduate student research and teaching assistants' intent to vote in a union representation election required not only union support of traditional economic issues, but also their support of emerging issues related to respect, discrimination, and participation in decision making. In a case study of a successful union campaign in a call center, a workplace largely populated by women, young workers, and recent immigrants engaged in part-time employment, the union's attention to issues of respect and dignity were deemed critical to the campaign's success. Indeed, interviews with campaign staff, activists, and rank and file members emphasized that issues related to respect, fairness, and stress reduction were more important than increases in wages (Guard et al. 2006).

Of the three models, the balance of empirical evidence supports the rational choice model (e.g., Charlwood 2002; Visser 2002). That said, it is highly likely that these models complement rather than exclude each other. For example, Brett (1980) proposed that the path to unionization is the combined result of job dissatisfaction (i.e., frustration), belief in the value of collective action (identification), and the perception that joining a union would be instrumental in resolving the dissatisfaction (rational choice).

Empirical support for the notion of model complementarity is accumulating. In two studies, Blader (2007) demonstrated that perceived injustice, union identification, and perceptions of instrumentality contributed significantly to graduate students' support for unionization and their union voting behavior. Importantly, these three factors significantly predicted student support for union certification, while controlling for economic concerns and the potential economic instrumentality of the union.

As further support for the value of potential model integration, Blader's (2007) work suggests that the categories of predictors (i.e., injustice, identification, and instrumentality) of union joining may be related. He found support for a mediational model suggesting that perceptions of injustice led to identification with the organizing group. Given the cross-sectional nature of his data, however, the possibility that identification leads to perceptions of injustice could not be ruled out. Coupled with the view that union attitudes (i.e., identification) may serve as a "perceptual filter" through which issues and events are seen and interpreted (Kelloway and Barling 1994), these findings suggest that researchers need to continue to examine how these three central predictors interact and influence each other in order to understand fully their influence on the decision to join a union.

Park, McHugh, and Bodha's (2005) survey of non-unionized professional employees illustrates one manner in which the various predictors may work together to predict union joining. Both general union attitudes and specific instrumentality perceptions affected union voting intentions in a hypothetical representation election. However, in this case general union attitudes influenced instrumentality perceptions, but the converse was not so. Thus, professional employees evaluated the instrumentality of joining a union at least partially through their attitudes to labor organizations in general.

Cregan's (2005) qualitative analysis of open-ended survey responses further demonstrates the interplay of these three factors. She asked union members and non-members to explain their membership status. Consistent with previous quantitative research, Cregan's thematic analysis focused around themes of instrumentality, identification/belief in collective action, and injustice and pointed to the dangers of focusing on one theme to the exclusion of the others as a "strategy that merely develops an awareness of injustice in workers is insufficient; for many workers, the union must still 'deliver' " (Cregan 2005, 300–1).

3.2 Collective Bargaining

After a union is certified or recognized in a workplace, the next step is to negotiate the contract or collective agreement that will govern union–management relations in the workplace. Although negotiations will occur at regular intervals over the life of the relationship, the first set of negotiations is likely to be the most protracted and controversial due to pressures on both sides and the fact that the initial agreement sets the baseline and expectations for future agreements. Chaison (2006, 104–5) points to this wide range of negotiation experiences when he notes:

Sometimes, unions negotiate their first agreements at workplaces after certification, meeting with employers for months or even years and fashioning contracts with hundreds of clauses. In other cases, the unions and employers meet for only a few sessions to tweak old agreements by revising wages and benefits clauses or changing a word here and there in some vague clause.

From the union's perspective, in a first agreement there is considerable pressure to secure the conditions necessary for continued security (i.e., recognition as the sole bargaining agent) as well as to demonstrate their instrumentality to members by achieving gains on both economic and non-economic issues. On the management side, there is considerable concern with maintaining managerial autonomy and "holding the line" on items that would restrict managerial decision making or add to the costs of doing business.

3.3 Process

Given the ongoing pressures on both sides, it is not at all surprising that conflict is frequently identified as one of the primary underlying dynamics of labor relations (e.g., Bluen and Barling 1988; Francis and Kelloway 2005). At a broad level, bargaining can be characterized as distributive or integrative (Chaison 2006). Distributive bargaining is characterized as win-lose or zero-sum bargaining. In contrast, integrative bargaining is sometimes termed win-win or mutual gains bargaining. The development of integrative bargaining techniques for handling conflicts in bargaining has been identified as one of the most visible innovations in the labor relations process (Cutcher-Gershenfeld and Kochan 2004).

These integrative (e.g., Walton and McKersie 1965) or "interest-based" (Fisher, Ury, and Patton 1991) bargaining techniques are designed to achieve collaborative solutions at the bargaining table and appear to be a key element influencing the labor relations climate (Deery and Iverson 2005). Indeed, in their analysis of two case studies, Caverly, Cunningham, and Mitchell (2006) suggested that the process of implementing an integrative approach may be as important to enhancing the management labor relationship as the actual issues at hand. Collective agreement clauses related to joint governance and organizational innovation seem to be particularly affected by the implementation of interest-based bargaining (Paquet, Gaetan, and Bergeron 2000). Certainly, the development of a cooperative labor relations climate is typically seen as having beneficial effects on firm performance (e.g., Deery and Iverson 2005; Gittell 2003). Indeed, in their study of the airline industry, Hoffer-Gittell, von Nordenflycht, and Kochan (2004) found that reduced conflict and workplace culture had a stronger impact on organizational performance than did traditional structural factors (e.g., unionization per se, wages). Cutcher-Gershenfeld and Kochan (2004) reported that by 1999, over 80 percent of union representatives and 65 percent of management representatives were familiar with interest-based bargaining techniques, and that a majority of both union and management representatives had used these techniques in bargaining. Although both union and management representatives rated these techniques as being effective, management representatives seemed to favour these techniques while union members tended to prefer traditional collective bargaining over interest-based bargaining.

3.4 Content

Collective bargaining can focus on numerous issues related to the operation of the workplace, the administration of the agreement itself, wages, benefits, working conditions, and the relationship between union and management (Chaison 2006). Consistent with attention being paid to union renewal strategies, bargaining provisions directed toward such things as employee participation in decision making appear to be on the rise (Akeampong 2005). Despite this change, arguably the most interesting and influential of these issues are those related to the traditional "bread and butter" issues of pay and working conditions. Regardless, there is little doubt that these issues have been a central focus for unions (Barling, Fullagar, and Kelloway 1992).

Perhaps the most obvious and well-documented effect of unionization is the increase in wages and benefits that comes with unionization (e.g., Booth, Francesconi, and Zoega 2003). In fact, virtually all aspects of compensation are enhanced through unionization (Dwayne, Gunderson, and Riddell 2002). For example, union members are more likely than are non-members to have fringe benefits including health plans and pension plans (Marshall 2003).

The wage premium attributable to unionization can be substantial—in Canada data from 2005 suggested that union members earned on average 18 percent more than their non-unionized counterparts. These effects can be pronounced for some employees. Part-time workers who are unionized earn almost twice the amount earned by non-unionized part-timers as a result of both increased wages and increased work hours (Anonymous 2006). However, there are also data suggesting a decline in the union wage effect (e.g., Belman and Voos 2004; Blanchflower and Bryson 2004). For example, Booth, Francesconi, and Zoega (2003) reported that union members earned only 4 percent more than non-members. Although this still reflects a wage premium, it is a much smaller premium than the 10–20 percent that has characterized research on the union wage effect. A similarly negligible union wage premium has been noted in Britain (Goddard 2007).

The union wage effect is typically related to union power to enforce contract demands (e.g., Forth and Milward 2002) and manifests both directly and indirectly. Direct effects emerge from simply bargaining for higher wages. More indirectly, Booth, Francesconi, and Zoega (2003) showed that unionized male workers in Britain received both (a) more work-related training than their non-union counterparts; and (b) higher wage differentials as a result of training and that these factors contribute to the union wage effect.

In addition to the absolute amount of wages, unions also have an effect on compensation policies in the workplace. Unions have typically advocated salary structures based on job classification and seniority (Barling, Fullagar, and Kelloway 1992) and opposed performance based salary structures (e.g., Hanley and Nguyen 2005). Although seniority-based models are currently the norm within unionized settings, there is some evidence that this preference does not preclude alternative structures. For example, Mericle and Kim (1999) provided evidence that it is possible to transition to skill-based pay schemes in unionized environments and that such schemes need not be inconsistent with the principle of seniority that is enshrined in virtually all union contracts (Gordon and Johnson 1982).

Such influence on wages has its consequences. Consistent with the importance of instrumentality to union joining, the union wage effect results in enhanced member satisfaction with the union (Currall et al. 2005). However, perhaps not surprisingly, demands for higher wages also lead to more adversarial relationships with management (Bryson 2005) although they appear to be unrelated to the decline in unionization rates in the US (Belman and Voos 2006).

Beyond wages, unions also directly bargain for improvements in a variety of working conditions. As previously noted, union members are more likely to receive workplace training than are non-members (Booth, Francesconi, and Zoega 2003). Unions have also negotiated for some forms of family-friendly policies designed to assist members to handle work and family conflict. Budd and Mumford (2004) found that unions enhanced the likelihood that members had access to parental leave, paid leave, and job sharing. Interestingly, unionization was negatively associated with flexible work hours and work-at-home arrangements indicating that unions, or the individuals and occupations that they represent, may have specific preferences as to how workplace issues are addressed. Thus, unions have appeared to focus on the reduction of work demands rather than the enhancement of worker control as a means of reducing workplace conflict (Kelloway and Gottlieb 1998).

The enhancement of health and safety in the workforce has long been a primary focus of union bargaining (Kelloway 2003). As is the case with other issues (e.g., Budd and Mumford 2004) the union role in this area is complex. Certainly unions engage in adversarial collective bargaining around issues of health and safety (Gray, Myers, and Myers 1998) although the data do not indicate that safety issues are used as "weapons" in bargaining (Hebdon and Hyatt 1998). Beyond their bargaining role, unions may also collaborate with management to promote health and safety in the workplace, thus the union-management relationship around health and safety might be best described as one of conflict and cooperation (Kelloway 2003).

As a result of the complexity of interaction, it is difficult to reach a simple conclusion about the effects of unionization on issues such as health and safety. For example, the available data suggest that unionized workers are more likely to suffer injuries and file for workers' compensation (Hirsch, McPherson, and Dumond 1997; Meng and Smith 1993). It is unclear whether this increased incidence reflects the fact that unions may disproportionately organize unsafe organizations or whether unionized workers become more aware of their rights to compensation when injuries are experienced. Paradoxically, when they do receive compensation, some studies show that unionized workers return to work quicker than do non-union workers (Campolieti 2005)—an effect typically attributed to information and support provided by the union (e.g., Cunningham and James 1997). As Krause et al. (2001) note, the data regarding the effect of unionization on return to work are by no means consistent, perhaps reflecting that research into the impact of organizational variables is still in its infancy.

3.5 Strikes

Strikes can emerge from a breakdown in the process of negotiating a collective agreement. Although any discussion of labor relations should consider the issues of strikes and lockouts, it needs to be emphasized at the outset that such events are extraordinarily rare (Bluen 1994) and typically occur only under extreme provocation. For example, Soya (2006) presented data on work stoppages between 1995 and 2005 in Canada noting that strikes accounted for less than 0.10 percent of work time with a further 0.01 percent of time being lost during lockouts. Moreover, the significant strikes were uniformly concentrated in organizations and industries facing fundamental structural change—not the "normal" bargaining issues of wages, benefits, and working conditions. The Canadian experience is typical of that of other developed economies (International Labor Office, n.d.).

Although strikes are rare events (Bluen 1994), they can have extreme consequences for those involved including the employing organizations, managers who have to cross a picket line, the striking workers, and members of the public. Taking the issue of picket line violence as an example (Francis, Cameron, and Kelloway 2006), the organization may experience violence in the form of stealing and sabotaging equipment and buildings, replacement workers and managers may suffer threats and injury as they cross picket lines (Grant and Wallace 1991), and the striking workers themselves may be subject to threats from individuals crossing or policing the picket line and may experience vandalism to their homes and vehicles.

Members of third parties may also experience consequences of strikes (Amos, Day, and Power 1993; Day et al. 2006; Grayson 1999; Greenglass et al. 2002). For instance, university students expected considerable disruptions as a result of a faculty strike, and these expected disruptions contributed to strain (Day et al. 2006). Customers are another example of third parties who may be negatively affected during a strike and their displeasure may ultimately influence firm performance. Postulating a so-called "anger effect," Block and Silver (2002) found that potential customers evidenced a negative intent to purchase based on strikes at both General Motors and Northwest Airlines. They suggested that substitution of alternative suppliers is more likely the more commoditized the goods or services in question are. Indeed the adverse consequences of striking for unions and employing organizations are perhaps best illustrated with the observation that having been on strike once, a union is unlikely to engage in a second strike—an observation that Campolieti, Hebdon, and Hyatt (2005) term the "teetotaler" effect.

Given the potential negative impact of strikes, some research has focused on the features that lead to longer or shorter strike durations. The size of the union is one such predictor (Campolieti, Hebdon, and Hyatt 2005); longer strikes are typically associated with smaller unions who are, perhaps, less able to disrupt the economic activity of the firm to a degree that forces an early settlement. The use of replacement workers also appears to be associated with longer (Singh, Zinni, and Jain 2005) and perhaps more volatile (Francis, Cameron, and Kelloway 2006) strikes.

The ability of the union to garner support from members of the public is also critical to determining the length of a strike. To the extent that members of the public can be persuaded to respect the picket line, or show public support for the union such as blowing the car horn when driving by a picket, public pressure can be brought to bear and this may be especially efficacious in resolving public sector strikes (Leung, Chiu, and Au 1993; see also Mellor, Paley, and Holzworth 1999). Recent research (Kelloway et al. in press) illustrates that such third party support is predicted by perceptions that the union is being treated unfairly by the employer (injustice), general union attitudes (identification), and the perception that showing support would be effective in bringing the strike to an end (instrumentality).

3.6 Grievances

A grievance is an allegation that one party to the agreement, most typically the employer, has violated a provision of an existing agreement (Francis and Kelloway 2005). Grievance systems are typically seen as part of the workplace justice system and tied to outcomes for both unions and employers. Gordon and Fryxell (1993, 251) spoke to the importance of grievance systems for union–member relationships when they noted "a union's relations with its constituents is tied more closely to the procedural and distributive justice afforded by its representation in the grievance system than by any other type of benefit provided in the collective bargaining agreement." This assertion has been empirically validated with perceptions of organizational justice being linked to union outcomes such as citizenship and turnover intent (Aryee and Chay 2001) as well as members' satisfaction with the union (Fryxell and Gordon 1989).

Grievance systems also have implications for outcomes of interest to the employing organization. For example, the provision of grievance systems may predict employees' attitudinal commitment to the organization (Fiorito et al. 2007) and intent to stay with the firm (Olson-Buchanan 1996). Indeed, at least one set of reviewers has suggested that human resource practitioners might consider a union-grievance system as a form of high involvement work practice (Peterson and Lewin 2000).

4. Consequences of Labor Relations

Throughout the chapter we have introduced a number of consequences of labor relations for both the organization and the individual worker. For example, firm performance may be enhanced if new integrative bargaining techniques improve the labor relations climate, but an organization's bottom line may suffer due to strike action. Unionized workers may benefit from the increase in wages, benefits, and working conditions associated with unionization, but demands for higher wages may negatively impact a union's relationship with management. We now move to detail other consequences of labor relations that are of importance for human resource management.

4.1 Individual Consequences of Labor Relations

4.1.1 *Labor relations stress*

As implied throughout the foregoing review, the dynamics of the labor relations process are fundamentally rooted in conflict, change (Bluen and Barling 1987; 1988; Fried 1993), and perceptions of injustice (Francis and Kelloway 2005). It is not at all surprising that the practice of labor relations has been characterized as being intrinsically stressful with adverse individual consequences associated with being a union member (Shirom and Kirmeyer 1988), being active in the union (Kelloway and Barling 1994; Nandram and Klandermans 1993), assuming a leadership role within the union (e.g., shop stewards; Martin and Berthiaume 1993), striking (e.g., Barling and Milligan 1987; Milburn, Schuler, and Watman 1983), and engaging in collective bargaining (e.g., Bluen and Jubiler-Lurie 1990).

The stress associated with labor relations practice and events can manifest as several forms of strain (Pratt and Barling 1988). Symptoms of strain such as increased blood pressure, (Bluen and Jubiler-Lurie 1990), heightened anxiety and decreased psychological well-being (Bluen and Jubiler-Lurie 1990), and emotional exhaustion (Nandram and Klandermans 1993) have all been associated with involvement in various aspects of labor relations practice. Intense labor relations events, such as strikes, can be characterized as acute stressors (Pratt and Barling 1988) and carry a number of long term stress-related consequences. Psychological distress, decreased perceptions of health, and exhaustion have all been linked to striking (MacBride, Lancee, and Freeman 1981; Milburn, Schuler, and Watman 1983). Some of these symptoms may in fact persist for months after the labor dispute has been resolved (Barling and Milligan 1987).

There is, of course, also evidence that unions can mitigate the effects of stressors in the workplace. Support from shop stewards (e.g., Fried and Tiegs 1993) or the union in general (Shore et al. 1994) can help individuals deal with both labor relations and other stressors. For instance, in the context of occupational health and safety, the union can be a valuable source of support for and help to mitigate the stress of workers who experience workplace trauma (Bluen and Edelstein 1993).

4.1.2 *Labor relations violence*

Given a burgeoning literature focused on issues of workplace violence and aggression (Kelloway, Barling, and Hurrell 2006), it is not at all surprising that there is now increased interest in the phenomenon of violence associated with labor relations. In particular, there have been detailed reviews and case analyses of historical events of violence on the picket line (e.g., Baker 2002; Francis, Cameron, and Kelloway 2006; Snyder and Kelly 1976). Picket line violence includes both *physical* altercations as well as *psychologically* aggressive acts (Thieblot and Haggard 1983). Such violence can be either *confrontational* (i.e., heat of the moment) or *purposeful* (i.e., planned and deliberate) and directed at varied targets (Francis, Cameron, and Kelloway 2006). Analyses of data from the US National Institute for Labor Relations Research, indicates that 30 percent of the strike-related violence is directed at the *organization* (e.g., equipment sabotage), while 43 percent of incidents involve *interpersonal* attacks, often on those who cross the picket line (Francis et al. 2006). In one study 100 percent of picket line crossers, reported that they experienced verbal assaults, 40 percent indicated that their vehicles were damaged and 11 percent had gunshots fired at their vehicle or their property (Stennett-Brewer 1997).

Unlike other forms of workplace violence, which are typically rejected as unacceptable, the picket line setting may provide an air of legitimacy to strike-related violent acts. In fact, aggression and violence are often treated as "par for the course" on the picket line and it is not uncommon for negotiated back to work agreements to indemnify individuals who had committed illegal or violent acts during a strike (Thieblot, Haggard, and Northrup 1999).

Most accounts of picket line violence have focused on union members as perpetrators (Francis, Cameron, and Kelloway 2006). However, it is equally common for picketers to be victims of picket line violence. Customers, managers, and replacement employees have been known to force their way through a picket line by speeding toward the line in an automobile. Managers who had experienced a bitter four-month strike reported that they felt a growing sense of anger as they experienced attacks and insults from individuals who were formerly their colleagues (Scales, Kelloway, and Francis 2007). Perhaps it is predictable that individuals who have to cross a hostile picket line each day as a condition of their employment may eventually retaliate against those who they increasingly see as the enemy.

4.2 Organizational Consequences of Labor Relations

4.2.1 *Job dissatisfaction*

One of the most paradoxical effects of unionization is that union members are more dissatisfied with their jobs than are non-union members (e.g., Berger, Olson and Boudreau 1983; Bluen and VanZwam, 1987; Guest and Conway 2004; Hammer and Avgar 2005; Pfeffer and Davis-Blake 1990), but are concurrently more likely to indicate that they intend to stay with their present employer (e.g., Spencer 1986). This phenomenon is often attributed to the voice that unions provide for their members. That is, unions provide members with the potential to voice their dissatisfaction rather than to quit (Abraham, Friedman, and Thomas 2005; Guest and Conway 2004; Iverson and Currivan 2003).

Unfortunately, methodological difficulties make it difficult to interpret this paradoxical effect. Most of the research that established a union effect on job satisfaction was based on large individual surveys (e.g., nationally representative samples) wherein each individual respondent may represent a different organization. When researchers have teased apart this confound, the effect disappears. Gordon and DeNisi (1995), for example, showed that unionized workers were more dissatisfied with their job than were non-unionized workers, a result in keeping with the literature (for a review see Barling, Fullagar, and Kelloway 1992). However, when they examined union–non-union differences within a workplace, the differences in job satisfaction disappeared. In a similar vein, Renaud (2002) observed that when statistically controlling for job quality, as unionized workers often work in lower-quality jobs, the association between unionization and job dissatisfaction disappeared. Similarly, Bryson, Cappellari, and Lucifora

(2004) found that the initial relationship between unionization and job dissatisfaction disappeared after implementing statistical controls for endogeneity.[1]

4.2.2 *Absenteeism*

The relationship between unionization and absenteeism is equally complex. Although unionization is generally associated with greater absenteeism, presumably as a result of negotiated paid sick leave (Barling, Fullagar, and Kelloway 1992), some recent research points to a more complex conclusion. Deery, Erwin, and Iverson (1999) found the relationship between unionization and absenteeism is moderated by the quality of the union–management climate. It seems that union members are more motivated to help the firm by reducing absenteeism when the union–management climate is positive than when it is negative (see also Deery and Iverson 2005). More recently, Iverson, Buttigieg, and Magquire (2003) replicated these results and suggested that homogeneity in union member status within organizations may lead to a lowered absence culture. Thus, while much of the earlier research focused on unionization as the independent variable in studying absenteeism, more recent investigations suggest that the quality of union–management relations is also critical to determining the nature and extent of any secondary effects of unionization.

5. SUMMARY AND CONCLUSION

In our review of the labor relations literature the impact of labor relations at both the individual and organizational levels was very apparent. A positive labor relations climate has beneficial impacts on issues critical to organizations such as absenteeism and firm performance. Further, in all likelihood, a positive climate will be associated with health and safety in workplaces. Certainly, unionized workers benefit from the negotiation of collective agreements affording them higher wages, the availability of fringe benefits, and better working conditions. However, labor relations processes are characterized by conflict and change and therefore are inherently stressful for all involved—union members, managers, and third parties alike. During strikes both union members and managers may suffer violence on the picket line, and organizations may experience sabotage and lose customers frustrated with delays. Although union rates worldwide have declined in recent years, unionization drives are on the rise. Unionization will only continue

---

[1] In regression, endogeneity refers to a statistical problem whereby a predictor is, in itself, an outcome of other predictors. This gives rise to correlated error terms and violates a fundamental assumption of regression.

while there are dissatisfied workers who believe in the union movement and to whom unions can provide support that is instrumental in improving their workplaces. The importance of labor relations in today's and future workplaces should not be underestimated.

References

ABRAHAM, S. E., FRIEDMAN, B. A., and THOMAS, R. K. 2005. The impact of unions on intent to leave: additional evidence on the voice face of unions. *Employee Responsibilities and Rights Journal*, 17: 201–13.

AKYEAMPONG, E. B. 2003. Fact sheet on unionization. *Perspectives on Labor and Income*, 4 (8): 1–25.

—— 2005. Collective bargaining priorities. *Perspectives on Labor and Income*, 6 (5): 5–10.

AMOS, M., DAY, V., and POWER, E. 1993. Students' reactions to a faculty strike. *Canadian Journal of Higher Education*, 26: 86–103.

ANONYMOUS. 2006. Unionization. *Perspectives on Labor and Income*, 18: 64–70.

ARYEE, S. and CHAY, W. Y. 2001. Workplace justice, citizenship behavior, and turnover intentions in a union context: examining the mediating role of perceived union support and union instrumentality. *Journal of Applied Psychology*, 86: 154–60.

BAKER, D. 2002. "You dirty bastards, are you fair dinkum?" Police and union confrontation on the wharf. *New Zealand Journal of Industrial Relations*, 27: 33–47.

BARLING, J., and MILLIGAN, J. 1987. Some psychological consequences of striking: a six month, longitudinal study. *Journal of Occupational Behavior*, 8: 127–38.

—— FULLAGAR, C., and KELLOWAY, E. K. 1992. *The union and its members: a psychological approach*. New York: Oxford University Press.

BELMAN, D., and VOOS, P. 2004. Changes in union wage effects by industry: a fresh look at the evidence. *Industrial Relations*, 43: 491–520.

—— —— 2006. Union wages and union decline: evidence from the construction industry. *Industrial and Labor Relations Review*, 60: 67–87.

BERGER, C. J., OLSON, C. A., and BOUDREAU, J. W. 1983. Effects of unions on job satisfaction: the role of work-related and perceived rewards. *Organizational Behavior and Human Performance*, 32: 289–324.

BLADER, S. L. 2007. What leads organizational members to collectivize? Injustice and identification as precursors of union certification. *Organization Science*, 18: 108–26.

BLANCHFLOWER, D. G., and BRYSON, A. 2004. What effect do unions have on wages now and would Freeman and Medoff be surprised? *Journal of Labor Research*, 25: 383–414.

BLOCK, R. N., and SILVER, B. D. 2002. *Post-strike Effects of Labor Conflict on Retail Consumers: Preliminary Evidence from the 1998 Northwest Airlines and General Motors Strikes*. Report for Institute for Public Policy and Social Research, Michigan State University.

BLUEN, S. D. 1994. The psychology of strikes. Pp. 113–35 in *International Review of Industrial and Organizational Psychology*, vol. ix, ed. C. L. Cooper and I. T. Robertson. London: John Wiley and Sons.

—— and BARLING, J. 1987. Stress and the industrial relations process: development of the Industrial Relations Events Scale. *South African Journal of Psychology*, 17: 150–9.

—— —— 1988. Psychological stressors associated with industrial relations. Pp. 175–205 in *Causes, Coping and Consequences of Stress at Work*, ed. C. L. Cooper and R. Payne. London: John Wiley and Sons.

—— and EDELSTEIN, I. 1993. Trade union support following an underground explosion. *Journal of Organizational Behavior*, 14: 473–80.

—— and JUBILER-LURIE, V. G. 1990. Some consequences of labor-management negotiations: laboratory and field studies. *Journal of Organizational Behavior*, 11: 105–18.

—— and VAN ZWAM, C. 1987. Trade union membership and job satisfaction. *South African Journal of Psychology*, 17: 160–4.

BOOTH, A. L., FRANCESCONI, M., and ZOEGA, G. 2003. Unions, work-related training and wages: evidence for British men. *Industrial and Labor Relations Review*, 57: 68–91.

BRETT, J. M. 1980. Why employees want unions. *Organizational Dynamics*, 8: 47–59.

BRYSON, A. 2005. Union effects on employee relations in Britain. *Human Relations*, 58: 1111–40.

—— CAPPELLARI, L., and LUCIFORA, C. 2004 Does union membership really reduce job satisfaction? *British Journal of Industrial Relations*, 42 (3): 439–59.

BUDD, J. W., and MUMFORD, K. 2004. Trade unions and family friendly policies in Britain. *Industrial and Labor Relations Review*, 57: 204–22.

BUREAU OF LABOR STATISTICS. 2007. *Union Members Summary.*(USDL No. 07-0113). Retrieved August 27, 2007, from <http://www.bls.gov/news.release/pdf/union2.pdf>.

BUTTIGIEG, D. M., DEERY, S. J., and IVERSON, R. D. 2007. An event history analysis of union joining and leaving. *Journal of Applied Psychology*, 92: 829–39.

CAMPOLIETI, M. 2005. Unions and the duration of workers compensation claims. *Industrial Relations*, 44: 625–53.

—— HEBDON, R., and HYATT, D. 2005. Strike incidence and strike duration: some new evidence from Ontario. *Industrial and Labor Relations Review*, 58: 610–30.

CAVERLY, N., CUNNINGHAM, B., and MITCHELL, L. 2006. Reflections on public sector-based integrative collective bargaining: conditions affecting cooperation within the negotiation process. *Employee Relations*, 28: 62–75.

CHAISON, G. 2006. *Unions in America*, Thousand Oaks, CA: Sage.

CHARLWOOD, A. 2002. Why do non-union employees want to unionize? Evidence from Britain. *British Journal of Industrial Relations*, 40: 463–91.

CREGAN, C. 2005. Can organizing work? An inductive analysis of individual attitudes toward labor unions. *Industrial and Labor Relations Review*, 58: 282–304.

CROPANZANO, R., and GREENBERG, J. 1997. Progress in organizational justice: tunneling through the maze. Pp. 317–72 in *International Review of Industrial and Organizational Psychology*, vol. xii, ed. C. L. Cooper and I. T. Robertson. London: John Wiley and Sons.

CUNNINGHAM, I., and JAMES, P. 1997. Absence and return to work: toward a research agenda. *Personnel Review*, 29: 33–47.

CURRALL, S. C., TOWLER, A. J., JUDGE. T. A., and KOHN, L. 2005. Pay satisfaction and organizational outcomes. *Personnel Psychology*, 58: 613–51.

CUTCHER-GERSHENFELD, J., and KOCHAN, T. 2004. Taking stock: collective bargaining at the turn of the century. *Industrial and Labor Relations Review*, 58: 3–26.

DAVY, J. A., and SHIPPER, F. 1993. Voter behavior in union certification elections: a longitudinal study. *Academy of Management Journal*, 36: 187–99.

DAY, A. L., STINSON, V., CATANO, V. M., and KELLOWAY, E. K. 2006. Third party reactions to the threat of a labor strike. *Journal of Occupational Health Psychology*, 11: 3–12.

DEERY, S. J., and IVERSON, R. D. 2005. Labor-management cooperation: antecedents and impact on organizational performance. *Industrial and Labor Relations Review*, 58: 588–609.

—— ERWIN, P. J., and IVERSON, R. D. 1999. Industrial relations climate, attendance behaviour and the role of trade unions. *British Journal of Industrial Relations*, 37: 533–58.

DEWEERD, M., and KLANDERMANS, B. 1999. Group identification and political protest: farmers' protest in the Netherlands. *European Journal of Social Psychology*, 29: 1073–95.

DWAYNE, B., GUNDERSON, M., and RIDDELL, C. 2002. *Labor Market Economics*. Toronto: McGraw-Hill Ryerson.

FIORITO, J., and GALLAGHER, D. G. 1986. Job content, job status, and unionism. Pp. 261–316 in *Advances in Industrial and Labor Relations*, vol. iii, ed. D. Lipsky and D. Lewin. Greenwich, CT: JAI Press.

—— BOZEMAN, D. P., YOUNG, A., and MEUR, J. A. 2007. Organizational commitment, human resources practices and organizational characteristics. *Journal of Managerial Issues*, 19: 186–207.

FISHER, R., URY, W., and PATTON, B. 1991. *Getting to YES!*, 2nd edn. New York: Penguin.

FORTH, J., and MILLWARD, N. 2002. Union effects on pay levels in Britain. *Labor Economics*, 9: 547–61.

FRANCIS, L., and KELLOWAY, E. K. 2005. Industrial relations. Pp. 325–52 in *Handbook of Work Stress*, ed. J. Barling, E. K. Kelloway and M. R. Frone. Thousand Oaks, CA: Sage.

—— CAMERON, J. E., and KELLOWAY, E. K. 2006. Crossing the line: violence on the picket line. Pp. 231–60 in *Handbook of Workplace Violence*, ed. E. K. Kelloway, J. Barling, and J. J. Hurrell, Jr. Thousand Oaks, CA: Sage.

FRIED, Y. 1993. Integrating domains of work stress and industrial relations: introduction and overview. *Journal of Organizational Behavior*, 14: 397–9.

—— and TIEGS, R. B. 1993. The main effect model versus the buffering model of shop steward social support: a study of rank-and-file auto workers in the U.S.A. *Journal of Organizational Behavior*, 14: 481–93.

FRIEDMAN, B. A., ABRAHAM, S. E., and THOMAS, R. K. 2006. Factors related to employees' desire to join and leave unions. *Industrial Relations*, 45: 102–10.

FRYXELL, G. E, and GORDON, M. E. 1989. Workplace justice and job satisfaction as predictors of satisfaction with union and management. *Academy of Management Journal*, 32: 851–66.

GITTELL, J. H. 2003. *The Southwest Airlines Way: Using the Power of Relationships to Achieve High Performance*. New York: McGraw-Hill.

GODDARD, J. 2007. Unions, work practices and wages under different institutional environments: the case of Canada and England. *Industrial and Labor Relations Review*, 60: 457–76.

GORDON, M. E., and DENISI, A. S. 1995. A re-examination of the relationship between union membership and job satisfaction. *Industrial and Labor Relations Review*, 48: 222–36.

—— and FRYXELL, G. 1993. The role of interpersonal justice in organizational grievance systems. Pp. 231–55 in *Justice in the workplace: Approaching Fairness in Human Resource Management*, ed. R. Cropanzano. Hillsdale, NJ: Erlbaum.

—— and JOHNSON, W. A. 1982. Seniority: a review of its legal and scientific standing. *Personnel Psychology*, 35: 255–80.

GRANT, D. S., II, and WALLACE, M. 1991. Why do strikes turn violent? *American Journal of Sociology*, 96: 1117–50.

GRAY, G. R., MYERS, D. W., and MYERS, P. S. 1998. Collective bargaining agreements: safety and health provisions. *Monthly Labor Review* (May): 13–35.

GRAYSON, J. P. 1999. Student hardship and support for a faculty strike. *Research in Higher Education*, 40: 589–611.

GREENGLASS, E. R., FIKSENBAUM, L., GOLDSTEIN, L., and DESIATO, C. 2002. Stressful effects of a university faculty strike on students: implications for coping. *Interchange*, 33: 261–79.

GUARD, J., GARCIA-ORGALES, J., STEEDMAN, M., and MARTIN, D. 2006. Organizing call centers: the Steelworkers' experience. Pp. 277–92 in *Paths to Union Renewal: Canadian Experiences*, ed. P. Kumar and C. Schenk Peterborough, Ont: Broadview Press.

GUEST, D. E., and CONWAY, N. 2004. Exploring the paradox of unionized workers' dissatisfaction. *Industrial Relations Journal*, 35: 102–21.

HAMMER, T. H., and AVGAR, A. 2005. The impact of unions on job satisfaction, organizational commitment and turnover. *Journal of Labor Research*, 26: 241–66.

HANLEY, G., and NGUYEN, L. 2005. Right on the money: what do Australian unions think of performance related pay? *Employee Relations*, 27: 141–60.

HEBDON, R., and HYATT, D. 1998. The effects of industrial relations factors on health and safety conflict. *Industrial and Labor Relations Review*, 51: 579–93.

HEPBURN, C. G., and BARLING, J. 2001. To vote or not to vote: abstaining in union representation elections. *Journal of Organizational Behavior*, 22: 569–91.

HIRSCH, B. T., MACPHERSON, D. A., and DUMOND, J. M. 1997. Workers' compensation recipiency in union and nonunion workplaces. *Industrial and Labor Relations Review*, 50: 213–36.

—— —— and VROMAN, W. G. 2001. Estimates of union density by state. *Monthly Labor Review*, 124: 51–5.

HOFFER-GITTELL, J., von NORDENFLYCHT, A., and KOCHAN, T. A. 2004. Mutual gains or zero sum? Labor relations and firm performance in the airline industry. *Industrial and Labor Relations Review*, 57: 163–80.

HUMAN RESOURCES AND SOCIAL DEVELOPMENT CANADA. 2006. *Union Membership in Canada—January 1, 2006*. Retrieved August 27, 2007, from <http://www.hrsdc.gc.ca/en/lp/wid/info.shtml>.

INTERNATIONAL LABOR OFFICE. n.d. Yearbook of labor statistics. In Statistics Canada (2003). *Strikes and lockouts, workers involved and workdays not worked*. Retrieved July 25, 2003, from <http://www.statscan.ca/english/Pgdb/labor30a.htm>.

IVERSON, R. D., and CURRIVAN, D. B. 2003. Union participation, job satisfaction, and employee turnover: an event history analysis of the exit-voice hypothesis. *Industrial Relations*, 42: 101–5.

—— BUTTIGIEG, D., and MAGUIRE, C. 2003. Absence culture, the effects of union member status and union management climate. *Relations Industrielles*, 58: 483–514.

KELLOWAY, E. K. 2003. Labor unions and safety: conflict and cooperation. Pp. 249–64 in *Psychology of Occupational Safety*, ed. J. Barling, and M. Frone. Washington, DC: APA Books.

—— and BARLING, J. 1994. Industrial relations stress and union activism: costs and benefits of participation. *Proceedings of the 46th Annual Meeting of the Industrial Relations Research Association*, 442–51.

KELLOWAY, E. K. and CATANO, V. M. 1997. Union attitudes as a perceptual filter. Pp. 225–34 in *The Future of Trade Unionism: International Perspectives on Emerging Union Structures*, ed. M. Sverke. London: Avebury.

—— —— and HARVEY, S. 1998. Changing employment relations: what can unions do? *Canadian Psychology*, 39: 124–32.

—— —— and HURRELL, J., Jr. 2006. *Handbook of Workplace Violence*. Thousand Oaks, CA: Sage.

—— and GOTTLIEB, B. H. 1998. The effect of alternative work arrangements on women's well-being. *Women's Health: Research on Gender, Behavior, and Policy*, 4: 1–18.

—— FRANCIS, L., CATANO, V. M., and TEED, M. 2007a. Predicting protest. *Basic and Applied Social Psychology*, 29: 13–22.

—— —— —— and DUPRE, K. In press. Third party support strike action. Revised manuscript resubmitted for publication.

KLANDERMANS, B. 1997. *The Social Psychology of Protest*. Oxford: Blackwell.

—— 2002. How group identification helps to overcome the dilemma of collective action. *American Behavioral Scientist*, 45: 887–900.

KOCHAN, T. A. 1980. *Collective Bargaining and Industrial Relations: From Theory to Policy and Practice*. Homewood, IL: Richard D. Irwin.

KRAUSE, N., FRANK, J. W., DASINGER, L. K., SULLIVAN, T. J., and SINCLAIR, S. J. 2001. Determinants of duration of disability and return-to-work after work-related injury and illness: challenges for future research. *American Journal of Industrial Medicine*, 40: 464–84.

KUMAR, P., and SCHENK, C. 2006. Union renewal and organizational change: a review of the literature. Pp. 29–60 in *Paths to Union Renewal: Canadian Experiences*, ed. P. Kumar and C. Schenk. Peterborough, Onta.: Broadview Press.

LaHUIS, D. M., and MELLOR, S. 2001. Antiunion and prounion attitudes as predictors of college students' willingness to join a union. *Journal of Psychology*, 135: 661–81.

LEUNG, K. CHIU, W., and AU, Y. 1993. Sympathy and support for industrial actions: a justice analysis. *Journal of Applied Psychology*, 78: 781–7.

LEVENTHAL, G. S., KARUZA, J., and FRY, W. R. 1980. Beyond fairness: a theory of allocation preferences. Pp. 167–218 in *Justice and Social Interaction*, ed. G. Mikula. New York: Springer-Verlag.

MACBRIDE, A., LANCEE, W., and FREEMAN, S. J. J. 1981. The psychosocial impact of a labor dispute. *Journal of Occupational Psychology*, 54: 125–33.

MARSHALL, K. 2003. Benefits of the job. *Perspectives on Labor and Income*, 4(5): 5–12.

MARTIN, J. E., and BERTHIAUME, R. D. 1993. Stress and the union steward's role. *Journal of Organizational Behavior*, 14: 433–66.

MELLOR, S., HOLZWORTH, R. J. and CONWAY, J. M. 2003. Individual unionization decisions: a multilevel model of cost-benefit influences. *Experimental Psychology*, 50 (2): 142–54.

—— PALEY, M. J., and HOLZWORTH, R. J. 1999. Fans' judgments about the 1994–95 Major League Baseball players' strike. *Multivariate Behavioral Research*, 34: 59–87.

MENG, R., and SMITH, D. 1993. Union impacts on the receipt of workers' compensation benefits. *Relations Industrielles*, 48: 503–18.

MERICLE, K., and KIM, D. 1999. From job-based pay to skill-based pay in unionized establishments: a three-plant comparative analysis. *Relations Industrielles*, 54: 549–80.

MILBURN, T. W., SCHULER, R. S., and WATMAN, K. H. 1983. Organizational crisis. Part II: strategies and responses. *Human Relations*, 36: 1161–80.

NANDRAM, S. S., and KLANDERMANS, B. 1993. Stress experienced by active members of trade unions. *Journal of Organizational Behavior*, 14: 415–31.

OLSON-BUCHANAN, J. B. 1996. Voicing discontent: what happens to the grievance filer after the grievance? *Journal of Applied Psychology*, 81: 52–63.

OPP, K. D. 1998. Does antiregime action under communist rule affect political protest after the fall? Results of a panel study in East Germany. *Sociological Quarterly*, 39: 189–213.

PAQUET, R., GAETAN, I. and BERGERON, J. G. 2000. Does interest-based bargaining (IBB) really make a difference in collective bargaining outcomes? *Negotiation Journal*, 16: 281–96.

PARK, H., McHUGH, P. P., and BODAH, M. M. 2005. Revisiting general and specific union beliefs: the union voting intentions of professionals. *Industrial Relations*, 45: 270–89.

PETERSON, R. B. and LEWIN, D. 2000. Research on unionized grievance procedures: management issues and implications. *Human Resource Management*, 39: 395–406.

PFEFFER, J., and DAVIS-BLAKE, A. 1990. Unions and job satisfaction: an alternative view. *Work and Occupations*, 17: 259–83.

PRATT, L. I., and BARLING, J. 1988. Differentiating between daily events, acute and chronic stressors: a framework and its implications. In *Occupational Stress: Issues and Developments in Research*, ed. J. J. Hurell, Jr., L. R. Murphy, S. L Sauter, and C. L. Cooper. New York: Taylor and Francis.

RENAUD, S. 2002. Rethinking the union membership/job satisfaction relationship: some empirical evidence from Canada. *International Journal of Manpower*, 2: 137–51.

SCALES, A., KELLOWAY, E. K. and FRANCIS, L. 2007. *Crossing the Line: Managers' Experiences During a Strike*. Manuscript in preparation.

SCHABEL, C., and WAGNER, J. 2005. Determinants of unionization in 18 European Union countries: evidence from micro-data, 2002/2003. Discussion paper No. 1464. Bonn: Institute for Study of Labor.

SHIROM, A., and KIRMEYER, S. 1988. The effects of unions on blue collar role stresses and somatic strains. *Journal of Organizational Behavior*, 9: 29–42.

SHORE, L. M., TETRICK, L. E., SINCLAIR, R. R., and NEWTON, L. A. 1994. Validation of a measure of perceived union support. *Journal of Applied Psychology*, 79: 971–7.

SINGH, P., ZINNI, D. A., and JAIN, H. C. 2005. The effects of the use of striker replacement workers in Canada: an analysis of four cases. *Labor Studies Journal*, 30: 61–86.

SNYDER, D., and KELLY, W. R. 1976. Industrial violence in Italy, 1878–1903. *American Journal of Sociology*, 82: 131–63.

SOYA, G. 2006. Industrial relations: strikes and lockouts. What do the data tell us? *Canadian HR Reporter*, 9, February 27.

SPENCER, D. G. 1986. Employee voice and employee retention. *Academy of Management Journal*, 29: 488–502.

STENNETT-BREWER, L. 1997. *Trauma in the Workplace: The Book about Chronic Work Trauma*. Mount ZION, IL: Nepenthe Publications.

TETRICK, L. E., and FRIED, Y. 1993. Industrial relations: stress induction or stress reduction? *Journal of Organizational Behavior*, 14: 511–14.

THIBAULT, J., and WALKER, L. 1975. *Procedural Justice: A Psychological Analysis*. HILLSDALE, NJ: Erlbaum.

THIEBLOT, A. J., and HAGGARD, T. R. 1983. *Union Violence: The Record and the Response by the Courts, Legislatures, and the NLRB*. Philadelphia: Industrial Research Unit, Wharton School, University of Pennsylvania.

THIEBLOT, A. J., and HAGGARD, T. R. and NORTHRUP, H. R. 1999. *Union Violence: The Record and the Response by the Courts, Legislatures, and the NLRB*, rev. edn. Fairfax, VA: George Mason University, John M. Olin Institute of Employment Practice and Policy.

VISSER, J. 2002. Why fewer workers join unions in Europe: a social custom explanation of membership trends. *British Journal of Industrial Relations*, 40: 403–30.

—— 2006. Union membership statistics in 24 countries, *Monthly Labor Review*, 129: 38–49.

WALTON, R., and MCKERSIE, R. 1965. *A Behavioral Theory of Labor Negotiations*. Ithaca, NY: ILR Press.

FAIRNESS IN SELECTION AND RECRUITMENT: A STIGMA THEORY PERSPECTIVE

ANN MARIE RYAN

JENNIFER WESSEL

1. INTRODUCTION

IN recent years, there has been a strong research focus on understanding the applicant's perspective in selection and recruitment (see Hausknecht, Day, and Thomas 2004; Ryan and Ployhart 2000, for reviews). Many studies of applicant perceptions of selection processes use an organizational justice lens (e.g., Bauer et al. 2001; Gilliland 1993; Truxillo et al. 2002). While this has advanced our understanding, there may be value in applying additional theoretical perspectives, and specifically when examining the perceptions of applicants who may face discrimination in hiring. That is, while more narrow topics such as applicant perceptions of affirmative action programs in the US have received a fair amount of attention (see Harrison et al. 2006, for a meta-analytic review) and there are numerous reviews (including some in this volume) on discriminatory hiring practices (e.g., Goldman et al. 2006; Landy 2005), there has not been a more comprehensive consideration of how individuals that belong to stigmatized groups approach the selection process. That is, this burgeoning body of literature on the perspective of the applicant has not fully addressed what may be unique about the perceptions of applicants from traditionally stigmatized groups. In this chapter, we plan to explore how concepts from research on stigmatization can inform and enhance our understanding of applicant reactions to selection procedures.

It is important to emphasize that this chapter is not about what might lead an organization's representatives to engage in discriminatory practices or about the adverse impact of different selection tools; it is about the perceptions and behaviors of those applicants who are members of stigmatized groups. Crocker and Major (1989) defined stigmatized individuals as those who belong to social categories about which others hold negative attitudes, stereotypes, and beliefs. They note that what constitutes a stigmatized group is culturally determined, as these are social categories devalued by a particular society or culture. However, across cultural boundaries, groups that tend to be devalued by many societies include ethnic or cultural minorities, women, the disabled, homosexuals, the unattractive, immigrants, the obese, and the mentally ill (Crocker and Major 1989).

We begin the chapter with a very brief, general review of the literature on applicant perceptions where we discuss the importance of studying in particular the reactions of individuals who might be considered members of stigmatized groups in any given society. Next, we introduce some core concepts from the literature on stigmatization (e.g., perceived controllability of stigma, group identification). We discuss how these concepts might inform understanding how individuals react to recruitment and selection processes beyond what has been established in the literature on applicant reactions.

2. APPLICANT PERCEPTIONS LITERATURE

Research on applicant reactions to selection procedures has found that aspects of selection processes (e.g., interpersonal treatment, opportunity to perform) do affect applicant perceptions of the process (e.g., justice perceptions) and these affect performance in the process, organizational attractiveness and job pursuit intentions, and self-perceptions (see Hausknecht, Day, and Thomas 2004 for a meta-analytic review). Thus, we know that applicant perceptions of fairness of the process and the outcome can affect attitudes and behavior in ways that may affect an organization's ability to recruit top candidates and avoid complaints (Smither et al. 1993).

Within this literature some attention has been paid to whether membership in common out-groups (e.g., ethnic/racial minorities and women) relates to perceptions. As noted earlier, there are ethnic and gender differences in perceptions of some organizational policies related to selection (e.g., affirmative action; Harrison et al. 2006). However, in their meta-analytic review, Hausknecht, Day, and Thomas (2004) did not find differences across ethnic or gender groups in perceptions of the procedural and distributive justice of selection processes (i.e., whether the process and outcome are seen as fair). A conclusion of no differences should be viewed with caution, however, as the meta-analysis was based on a small number of studies and the authors were unable to consider contextual moderators along with examinations of demographic group. The authors conclude that there is a need to elucidate the conditions under which different groups might react differently to the same process.

It is our view that a closer examination of the research on stigmatization can provide a means for developing that understanding. The need to ascertain whether and when stigmatized groups might react differently to a selection process than individuals without a given stigma is important for several reasons. First, in many countries and for a number of stigmas, applicants who feel they have been treated unfairly may pursue legal recourse (Chao and Nguyen 2005). Second, many organizations may be seeking to enhance the diversity of their workforce and targeting members of traditionally stigmatized groups in their recruiting (Avery and McKay 2006); unfavorable reactions to a hiring process would negate any efforts made to increase workforce diversity as individuals may turn down offers, withdraw from job pursuit, and not recommend the employer to others. Finally, while negative effects of hiring processes on self-perceptions of all applicants are important to study, effects on the well-being of members of stigmatized groups seem particularly important in light of the body of research demonstrating negative mental and physical health consequences from discrimination (e.g., Dambrun 2007; James, Lovato, and Khoo 1994; Krieger and Sidney 1996).

3. Stigmatization in the Selection Context

The literature on stigmatization can inform several key questions: when will belonging to a stigmatized group play a role in applicant perceptions, and what will the effects of belonging to such a group be on those perceptions. In this section, we will discuss the complex answers to those questions by discussing factors affecting whether an individual with a stigma will feel he/she has been treated unfairly or received an unfair outcome in a selection process. We organize these factors into three areas: the hiring process itself (the treatment of the applicant, the procedures used, the outcome received), the characteristics of the individual applicant (group identification, expectations, stigma concealability, stigma controllability, stereotype vulnerability, endorsement of status legitimizing ideologies), and the selection context (occupational stereotyping, relational demography).

3.1 The Hiring Process

3.1.1 *Treatment*

It is perhaps obvious that applicant perceptions will be affected by whether any discriminatory or differential treatment related to a stigma occurs during the selection process. Stigmatization can be overt and/or subtle (Dovidio and Gaertner 2000). Subtle discrimination may not be illegal or against organizational policy but may consist of behaviors that convey a desire not to interact with a stigmatized individual (e.g., smiling less during the interview, terminating interactions sooner, keeping the applicant waiting longer; Dovidio, Kawakami, and Gaertner 2002; Hebl et al. 2002; Turner, Fix, and Struyk 1991). Whether stigmatized individuals notice such subtle treatment has been debated in the literature, with many researchers finding chronically stigmatized individuals deny they were treated differentially or underestimate the level of discrimination (e.g., Crocker, Major, and Steele 1998; Crosby 1994). Indeed, when confronted with blatant discrimination, often stigmatized individuals do not publicly acknowledge it (Kaiser and Miller 2004; Stangor et al. 2002; Swim and Hyers 1999).

Whether a particular act is seen as one of bias on the basis of one's membership in a stigmatized group is a complex judgment. When the discrimination is blatant and overt (e.g., stating a candidate's stigma disqualifies him/her from consideration), applicants will see this as discrimination (see Major, Quinton, and Schmader 2003). More subtle and ambiguous acts however, are interpreted differently by members of stigmatized groups based on a number of factors, such as what one views as the motive of the perpetrator (Crocker, Major, and Steele 1998) and whether one sees the treatment as justified (Major et al. 2002). For example, an applicant may see a short, unfriendly interaction with a recruiter as reflecting a naturally curt individual or an overworked employee rather than as subtle stigmatization. Or, the applicant may attribute the recruiter's behavior as a reaction to the applicant's own social ineptitude or lack of qualifications, rather than as connected to a stigma.

In terms of applicant perceptions, this literature suggests that direct differential treatment will be viewed as unfair, but subtle differential treatment may or may not be viewed as unfair. For certain stigmas in certain societies, direct differential treatment in employment contexts may not be unusual (e.g., in the US it is not illegal to discriminate against homosexuals in hiring in a number of jurisdictions; in South Africa the law provides for preferential treatment of certain ethnic groups). However, for many stigmas the more frequent occurrence will be subtle differentiations; hence, it is harder to predict how stigmatized applicants will react to those contexts. Further, in many selection processes, an applicant does not have clear information on how other candidates were treated that can provide cues to whether one was treated differently (e.g., one does not know how long other interviews lasted or whether a particular interviewer avoided eye contact with all candidates).

Note also that some members of a stigmatized group may be more likely to experience discriminatory treatment. For example, Hodson, Dovidio, and Gaertner (2002) demonstrated that discrimination did not occur when the credentials of an individual were consistently strong or weak, but mixed credentials afforded an opportunity for high prejudice individuals to rationalize discriminatory treatment. Thus, stigmatized individuals who are highly qualified for a given position may experience less differentiated treatment than a member of the same stigmatized group that has a more mixed profile of credentials for the position. Derous and colleagues (Derous, Nguyen, and Ryan 2006; Derous et al. 2007) found some evidence that those presenting a more ethnically identified profile (i.e., ethnic sounding name and affiliations with ethnic related organizations) may be evaluated more negatively than those seen as less ethnically identified. These studies suggest we would not expect all individuals who are members of a given stigmatized group to receive the same treatment by an employer; hence it is no surprise that a coarse meta-analysis (Hausknecht, Day, and Thomas 2004) finds fairness perceptions of applicants from stigmatized groups are not necessarily more negative than those belonging to non-stigmatized groups.

3.1.2 *Procedures*

Membership in stigmatized groups may affect reactions to certain selection tools (Chan 1997; Hayes et al. 1995). For example, researchers have hypothesized that US ethnic minority groups will react more negatively to cognitive ability tests because of group differences on such tools (e.g., Chan 1997; Chan et al. 1997). The stigmatization literature would suggest that less favorable reactions to certain tools will occur, as the selective devaluation of domains by members of stigmatized groups to protect self-esteem is well documented (Crocker, Major, and Steele 1998). One might expect then to see differences in job relevance perceptions for certain tools based on group membership (e.g., gender differences in views of math and mechanical ability tests, those with speech impediments and physical disfigurements viewing the interview less favorably), yet this body of research is not well integrated nor is it conclusive.

While Hausknecht, Day, and Thomas (2004) reported mean differences in perceptions across various types of selection tools, they did not examine demographic differences in these perceptions. Smither et al. (1993) did not find ethnic differences in perceptions of fourteen different selection methods, although they did find some gender and race differences in perceptions of a specific process. Others have found group differences in the perceptions of different media (Chan and Schmitt 1997; Truxillo and Hunthausen 1999). In general, this research has not been systematic in articulating theoretical rationales as to why differences might be expected (although stereotype threat theory, reviewed later, does provide such a rationale), nor in investigating varied stigmatized groups.

Note that the stigmatization research on selective devaluing focuses on the context where the individual does not have any individual performance or outcome information (Crocker and Major 1989). In a selection context, where personal outcome information must be provided (i.e., hired or not hired), the devaluing of particular selection tools may be influenced more by individual outcomes than by stereotypes connected to performance of members of a group on a given tool (e.g., women who do well in math are less likely to devalue math tests as selection tools).

3.1.3 *Outcomes*

It is well established in the applicant reactions literature that a key driver of perceptions is the outcome one receives, labeled the self-interest effect (see Chan et al. 1998; Ployhart and Ryan 1997). However, while being rejected for a job may result in less favorable perceptions of the selection process itself (i.e., procedural fairness, job relevance) in many instances, research suggests some complexity in effects on self-perceptions (e.g., Ployhart, Ryan, and Bennett 1999). Applicant perceptions researchers have shown that attributions of outcomes to internal, stable or external, unstable causes have different consequences for subsequent reactions and behavior (Arvey et al. 1990; Ployhart and Ryan 1997).

Multiple studies in the stigmatization literature have focused on attributional ambiguity in stigmatization contexts, supporting the notion that when there is some ambiguity about the reason for a negative consequence (e.g., not being hired) an individual with a stigma can attribute the negative decision to prejudice as a means of self-protection of one's self-esteem (Crocker et al. 1991). Hence, we might expect that members of stigmatized groups may attribute negative outcomes in selection contexts to bias or prejudice on the part of the organization or interviewer, rather than conclude that they are less qualified for the position. Research exploring the interactive effects of stigma status and outcome on self-views may yield insights into self-protective activities of applicants.

Stigmatization research has also clearly established that positive feedback can be attributed to one's stigmatizing condition (Crocker, Major, and Steele 1998), resulting in lowered self-perceptions. In those cases, an applicant who advances through the selection process but feels that the advancement is due to group membership, will have more negative self-perceptions. This has been well established with regard to applicant perceptions in the work of Madeline Heilman and colleagues (Heilman and Alcott 2001; Heilman et al. 1993; Heilman, McCullough, and Gilbert 1996), who have demonstrated lowered self-perceptions of those who believe their hiring was due to group membership rather than to personal merit. These researchers have demonstrated that women who believe they have benefited from a hiring process that gives preference to their stigmatized group are more likely to feel incompetent and have negative self-perceptions. Hence, in contrast to the effects of selection outcome on perceptions of non-stigmatized individuals which generally suggests a self-interest effect, we can see that for stigmatized individuals an important consideration may be whether they attribute the outcome, positive or negative, to something to do with their stigma.

Further, the nature of feedback provided by the hiring organization may also factor into stigmatized individuals' reactions. Ployhart, Ryan, and Bennett (1999) demonstrated that specific reasons for rejections that do not allow a self-protective mechanism of attributions to external causes will lead to lower self-perceptions. For an individual with a stigma, specific feedback may disallow an attribution of a rejection to one's stigmatized status, preventing that path of self-protection (Schinkel, van Dierendonck, and Anderson 2004). The applicant with a stigma who is given a specific test score as feedback when rejected may feel less favorably about the fairness of the process and outcome than one given a more vague rejection letter that allows for self-esteem protective mechanisms. Note this is not specific to applicants belonging to stigmatized groups but would hold true of all applicants.

More generally, research on providing explanations for decisions suggests that providing some form of explanation results in more favorable perceptions of the fairness of the decision (Shaw, Wild, and Colquitt 2003), particularly among those receiving a less favorable outcome. Further, the type of explanation (e.g., ideological, referential) has been established as influencing perceptions (Bobocel and Farrell 1996; Horvath, Ryan, and Stierwalt 2000; Ployhart, Ryan, and Bennett 1999). For stigmatized individuals in selection contexts, we know little about how explanations might affect fairness perceptions (i.e., while Horvath, Ryan, and Stierwalt (2000) found a three-way interaction between race, outcome favorability, and type of explanation, they lacked sufficient power to fully explore possible interpretations). Given what is known in stigmatization research about attributions to discrimination and effects on the individual, explanations that either heighten or reduce perceptions of differential treatment are likely to have effects on stigmatized group members (e.g., Heilman and Alcott 2001; Heilman et al. 1993; Heilman, McCullough, and Gilbert 1996).

3.2 Applicant Characteristics

3.2.1 *Identification*

The effects of membership in a particular stigmatized group on individual attitudes and behavior varies depending upon the extent to which that particular social identity is of importance to the individual and the extent to which that identity is made salient in a particular context (e.g., Hogg, Terry, and White 1995). For example, Operario and Fiske (2001) demonstrated that highly identified individuals are likely to interpret ambiguous cues as discrimination (see also Branscombe, Schmitt, and Harvey 1999; Major, Quinton, and Schmader 2003). Whether an applicant's stigmatized group membership will play a role in his/her reactions to selection processes will depend on both that applicant's own level of identification with the stigmatized group as well as the extent to which that particular identity is salient in the selection context. Of note, researchers in the stereotype threat area have demonstrated that simply asking demographic questions of test takers may make a stereotype salient (Schmader and Johns 2003; Steele and Aronson 1995); hence, it may be that gender and ethnic/racial group membership are very typically made quite salient in selection contexts where demographic questions are asked as part of routine tracking. Expectations of "best professional appearance" during interviews may heighten the salience of appearance-based stigmas. Other stigmas may not be as salient and therefore may be less likely to play a role in applicant reactions to the selection process.

Individuals belong to multiple groups and have multiple identities (Crisp and Hewstone 1999). Research has focused on the possibility that "multiple minority status" might have exacerbated effects on stigmatization (Nelson and Probst 2004). For example, minority women are affected by stereotypes regarding both gender and ethnicity (Buchanan 2004; Buchanan and Ormerod 2002) and some evidence suggests that the combination of minority race and minority sexual orientation may lead to greater experiences of sexual orientation discrimination (Crow, Fok, and Hartman 1995; Friskopp and Silverstein 1995). However, other research on ethnicity and gender shows ethnic minority women as advantaged over ethnic minority men (Bendick et al. 1991; Hosoda, Stone-Romero, and Coats 2003), suggesting complexity in how multiple stigmas might be viewed. The fairness perceptions of an applicant who belongs to multiple stigmatized groups could be influenced by subtle differential treatment based on one or more groups, identification levels with each group, identity salience of each group in a given selection context, attributions for the treatment and attributions for the outcome he/she receives (e.g., it was my ethnicity not my gender that played a role).

3.2.2 *Expectations*

Some research has established that those who are members of stigmatized groups have greater expectations of being treated unfairly (Levin et al. 2002). Bell, Ryan, and Wiechmann (2004) discuss how expectations of a selection process are influenced by applicant past experiences with selection processes, indirect experiences from significant others, and enduring beliefs about justice. For individuals in stigmatized groups, past personal experiences of differential treatment and knowledge of family/friend experiences can lead to expectations that a process will not be fair. While many stigmatized individuals may enter the process with greater expectations of unfairness, variability in expectations is quite likely, leading to variability in process perceptions.

3.2.3 *Concealability*

Research has established that while those with concealed stigmas may face less prejudice, they cannot attribute negative outcomes to prejudice in situations where others are unaware of their stigma (Crocker, Major, and Steele 1998; Jones et al. 1984). Hence, while we might expect applicants with concealable stigmas (orientation, certain mental and physical illnesses) to face less direct discriminatory treatment, we might also expect rejections to have a stronger effect on self-perceptions than for those with stigma that are not concealable. While a concealed stigma does not necessarily affect short-term social interactions (e.g., an interview), it may create long-term consequences in self-perceptions and health (Cole et al. 1996; Frable, Platt, and Hoey 1998; Herek, Gillis, and Cogan 1999; Major and Gramzow 1999; Meyer 2003).

It is useful to consider cases where individual applicants may mask cues to their stigmatized status. For example, individuals with disabilities may be reluctant to ask for accommodations in selection contexts so as not to reveal or call attention to one's stigma (Baldridge and Veiga 2001; 2006) or candidates of multi-ethnic backgrounds may "pass" as members of a majority group (Clair, Beatty, and Maclean 2005). Research on identity management strategies of homosexuals has indicated that individuals employ counterfeiting (constructing a false heterosexual identity), avoiding (reveal nothing about one's identity), and integrating strategies (revealing one's true identity) in the workplace to varying degrees with different co-workers (Chrobot-Mason, Button, and DiClementi 2001; Woods 1994); similar differences in applicant identity management strategies for those with other concealable stigmas are likely.

For many individuals, the decision to disclose a stigmatized identity during a selection process may be a difficult one. Ragins (2008) proposed that individuals will reveal a stigmatized identity when it is a central part of their identity, when they do not fear negative consequences from the disclosure, and when the environment is supportive of disclosure. For many, the selection context may not be one perceived as supportive and without negative consequences of disclosure, and this may affect an individual with an invisible stigma's reactions to the selection process. For example, an employer may be unaware of an individual's stigma and it may play no role in his/her hiring decision, yet the applicant may view the selection process in a negative light because he/she was unable to disclose information important to his/her self-concept.

3.2.4 Controllability

Stigmas vary in the degree to which the stigmatized individual is believed to be personally responsible for his/her stigma (Crocker, Major, and Steele 1998). Those perceived to have more controllable stigmas are treated more harshly and rejected more often than those with what are perceived to be uncontrollable stigmas (Crandall 1994; Kurzban and Leary 2001; Weiner, Perry, and Magnusson 1988). In the context of applicant reactions, we may expect more negative reactions then from individuals with stigmas that others tend to see as controllable such as obesity, mental illness, and homosexuality.

A related issue is how "prior stigmas" are viewed. That is, Rodin and Price (1995) found less harsh judgments of those described as previously having a stigma that they removed through their own initiative and determination (e.g., obesity, physical unattractiveness). This follows from other research that suggests more positive judgments of those who are perceived to be coping with their stigmas (Schwarzer and Weiner 1991). At first blush, one might suggest applicants with stigmas that are perceived to be controllable should consider ways to lessen discriminatory treatment by providing information on how attempts are being made to control or remove a stigma (King et al. 2006). However, this is highly problematic because views differ greatly as to what is seen as controllable and individuals may have no desire to change their identity even if they agree the stigma is controllable.

Finally, the concept of "stickiness" has been defined as the extent to which a taint from a mark remains after a stigma has been removed (Bergman and Gaulke 2004). For example, being previously employed in a work role that would be considered "dirty work" (e.g., exotic dancer) or employed by a dubious employer (e.g., Enron), having previously been treated for a mental illness, or having been exonerated of an accusation (e.g., theft from an employer, harassment)—all might be cases where a prior stigmatizing characteristic does not currently apply, yet there is some stickiness to the stigma. Individuals may work toward concealing prior stigmatizing events and characteristics lest they "stick" (Bergman and Gualke 2004)

3.2.5 Stereotype vulnerability

Researchers have established that individuals in stigmatized groups tend to mistrust performance feedback in stereotyped domains (e.g., Cohen and Steele 2002), and this tendency to discount feedback is especially true for those higher in stereotype vulnerability or rejection sensitivity (Mendoza-Denton et al. 2002), defined as a tendency to expect and be affected by negative stereotypes about one's social group (Aronson 2002; Steele and Aronson 2004). Chronic awareness of one's stigmatized status and the perception that it regularly affects social inter-actions has been labeled as stigma consciousness or sensitivity to stigmatization (Mendoza-Denton et al. 2002; Pinel 1999; 2002). Aronson and Inzlicht (2004) found that stereotype vulnerability leads individuals to be less self-aware of their actual ability levels, creating more unstable levels of self-efficacy. We might expect those high in stereotype vulnerability to be more aware of subtle differential treatment, to have more negative expectations of fairness, and to be more mis-trusting of feedback received in the hiring process. In particular, those high in stereotype vulnerability will have less of a sense of their qualifications for various jobs that require performance in stereotyped domains (e.g., women in jobs requir-ing mathematical skill) and may therefore experience greater difficulty in ascer-taining job fit.

3.2.6 *Status-legitimizing ideologies*

Stigmatized individuals who endorse legitimizing ideologies believe that the exist-ing social order is justified, and hence will not see negative outcomes as due to bias but as justified (Jost, Pelham, and Carvallo 2002; Major et al. 2002). These individuals will therefore be more likely to exhibit more negative self-perceptions after rejections than stigmatized individuals who do not endorse legitimizing ideologies and who have available to them the option of attributing a rejection decision to bias and maintaining self-esteem.

3.3 Selection Context

3.3.1 *Occupational stereotypes*

Employers may have a certain image of the ideal job holder, which can affect selection decisions (King et al. 2006). Occupational stereotyping, or preconceived notions about the types of people suitable for certain jobs (Avery, Hernandez, and Hebl 2004; Lipton et al. 1991), can have several origins, such as the stereotypical nature of the tasks or the demographic characteristics of the usual job holder (Lyness and Heilman 2006). For example, individuals still seem to view Caucasian males as more similar to the prototypical image of a successful manager, as compared to females and ethnic minorities (Chung-Herrera and Lankau 2005; Dodge, Gilroy, and Fenzel 1995; Duehr and Bono 2006; Maume 1999). Stigmatized applicants are often pigeon-holed into certain fields (e.g., women into staff rather than line jobs; Lyness and Heilman 2006; ethnic minorities in low-skill occupa-tions; Huffman and Cohen 2004; Kulis and Shaw 1996; Shih 2002), even receiving a boost in selection preference for low-skilled occupations that are seen as more "suitable" for their social status (King et al. 2006; Shih 2002; Terpstra and Larsen 1980). Outz (2005) notes that in addition to the "glass ceiling," a term coined to refer to artificial barriers to upward mobility of stigmatized groups, there are "glass walls" where stigmatized group members are channeled into jobs outside the business mainstream. Indeed, Chao and Nguyen (2005) note that in some countries there are "brick walls," where clearly discriminatory barriers are set in place to keep members of stigmatized groups from employment in certain occupations (e.g., ads in China with specific gender requirements).

While the above research shows the effects of occupational stereotyping on the evaluation of stigmatized applicants, it says very little regarding how occupation stereotyping affects the reactions of the stigmatized in a selection context. Literature on *stereotype threat* (Steele and Aronson 1995) may provide a lens for understanding potential outcomes of occupational stereotyping for the stigmatized applicant. Stereotype threat is defined as the "social-psychological threat that arises when one is in a situation or doing something for which a negative stereotype about one's group applies" (Steele 1997; Steele and Aronson 1995). While most of this research has looked more specifically about how stereotype threat affects performance on tests, one can examine the occupational stereotype as a source of the threat.

Stigmatized individuals may feel ambivalent towards certain occupations when they feel there is little chance of obtaining the position, as might occur when there is a stereotype regarding the occupation and the group(s) they identify with (Pettigrew and Martin 1987). Furthermore, according to Steele (1997), higher achieving, more confident individuals may feel they have more to lose in confirming a negative stereotype, and thus are more susceptible to stereotype threat. As high-achieving individuals likely have options in occupational choices, they may avoid application to jobs considered *occupationally deviant* in terms of a stereotype.

Further, as noted earlier, the salience of group identity has effects on whether an individual considers stigmatization as occurring in a hiring context (Branscombe, Schmitt, and Harvey 1999; Operario and Fiske 2001). Identity would be more salient to a stigmatized applicant when applying to positions that are occupationally deviant (e.g., female applicants for physically demanding jobs, an obese individual applying to be a TV anchorperson). When the occupation of interest suggests a stereotype related to a group to which the applicant belongs, he/she will have greater expectations of being treated unfairly and may be more likely to attribute outcomes to discrimination.

3.3.2 *Relational demography*

The basic tenets of relational demography research in organizational psychology are rooted in the attraction-selection-attrition model (Schneider 1987) and social identity theory (Turner, Brown, and Tajfel 1979), both of which emphasize identification of personal characteristics and comparison of those characteristics to the characteristics of others or an organization. These theories suggest that demographic similarity may enhance the likelihood of an applicant applying to a certain organization.

While there is considerable research on whether demographic similarity affects interview ratings (e.g., McFarland et al. 2004; Prewett-Livingston et al. 1996; Sacco et al. 2003), this research does not address how stigmatized applicants may react to the interview process. Studies examining recruiter characteristics do point tentatively to a positive relationship between recruiter-applicant racial similarity and applicant perceptions of organizational attractiveness, particularly for those belonging to stigmatized groups (Goldberg 2003; Thomas and Wise 1999).

Low minority representation in an organization may affect stigmatized applicants' perceptions of the hiring process. According to Kanter's (1977) theory of tokenism, a stigmatized individual may be more visible due to their out-group status, and thus be observed more closely than other employees (e.g., MacCorquodale and Jensen 1993; Yoder and Berendsen 2001). The increased attention to stigmatized employees is thought to lead to higher performance pressure from the organization, supervisors, and other employees (Crocker and McGraw 1984; Spangler, Gordon, and Pipkin 1978). In a selection context, one might also expect stigmatized employees to experience greater performance pressure for this reason. Note that there are mixed findings as to whether this pressure translates into actual performance decrements (Inzlicht and Ben-Zeev 2000; Karakowsky and Siegel 1999; Sekaquaptewa and Thompson 2002), which would lead to more unfavorable perceptions of the selection process. Also, Young and James (2001) found that employees of token status had lower self-esteem and lower perceptions of job fit, suggesting representativeness may affect applicant self-perceptions. Researchers have shown that social isolation of minority employees leads to less sharing of important, informal information which could increase job performance (Heikes 1991). During the application process, stigmatized individuals may fail to receive beneficial tips and guidance shared among other applicants or between recruiters and applicants, which may also negatively affect perceptions of the procedural fairness of the process.

In many selection contexts (e.g., Web-based testing, individually scheduled interviews), an applicant is unlikely to know the group identities of other applicants so one might argue that effects of this sort are unlikely to occur. However, Avery and colleagues (Avery, Hernandez, and Hebl 2004; Avery and McKay 2006) provide strong arguments as to why stigmatized candidates are likely to attend to any cues as to workforce composition during the recruitment process. For example, Avery and McKay (2006) suggest that applicants will be affected by diversity impression management tactics (e.g., pictoral diversity in recruiting materials, advertising in publications targeted toward stigmatized groups, attending diversity job fairs). Thus, even without direct knowledge of fellow applicant identities, stigmatized individuals can still draw conclusions as to organizational acceptance of their stigma that will affect their perceptions of the hiring process and attractiveness to the organization.

4. SUMMARY OF STIGMATIZATION
EFFECTS ON APPLICANT PERCEPTIONS

The net effect of the processes outlined in this chapter on data such as that in Hausknecht's meta-analysis is to produce "muddy waters"—some stigmatized individuals who receive negative outcomes will view the process as unfair, but not all; some stigmatized individuals who receive positive outcomes may also view the process as unfair. The current state of research has not adequately incorporated measurement of the attribution for the selection decision, which may be key to predicting the reactions of stigmatized individuals. We echo the admonitions of many stigma scholars: one should not ignore group membership but one should certainly not assume uniformity of attitudes and behaviors due to group membership.

The literature on stigma-related coping suggests that stigmatized applicants will employ multiple strategies as they approach the selection process. Table 21.1 is based on Miller's (2006) summary of different types of coping strategies that stigmatized individuals might engage in; specific derivations related to applicant perceptions and behaviors have been added based on the discussion in this chapter. Note that we are not advocating that stigmatized applicants adopt any particular set of strategies but simply describing the ways stigmatized applicants might react in a selection context.

Some recent research has been directed specifically at what strategies stigmatized individuals might adopt in the selection process, in particular acknowledgment and providing individuating information (Hebl and Dovidio 2005; Singletary and Hebl 2007). For example, Hebl and Kleck (2002) examined reactions to an individual acknowledging his/her possession of a stigma (e.g., acknowledging the existence of a physical disability or obesity) and concluded that acknowledgment may have negative effects for those with certain stigmas, and in particular, for those with stigma perceived as controllable (e.g., obesity). Of interest would be research on when individuals decide to acknowledge a stigma (e.g., Hebl and Kleck 2002 give the example of an answer to an interview question regarding overcoming adversity) and what the consequences of that acknowledgment are for the applicant (e.g., on favorability of the outcome, self-perceptions, attributions for the decision). For example, Barreto et al. (2003) demonstrated that individuals engage in strategic self-presentation of identities in that individuals will not express identities thought to conflict with an audience's norms. Hence applicants are likely to be reluctant to acknowledge stigmatized statuses (even if visible, such as race or gender) if they do not sense openness to that discussion on the part of the organization's representatives.

Table 21.1 Coping strategies of applicants from stigmatized groups

Engagement coping (approach stressor)				Disengagement coping (avoid stressor)	
Primary control strategies (problem solving)	Examples	Secondary control strategies (Change feelings and thinking)	Examples	Strategy	Examples
Confront prejudice	▪ Speak directly to recruiter regarding treatment ▪ Pursue legal action	*Cognitively restructure by blaming prejudice for outcome*	▪ Blame rejection on bias ▪ View preferential treatment as a reason for acceptance	*Avoid interactions with prejudiced people*	▪ Attend to company diversity reputation ▪ Withdraw from processes if encounter ambiguous treatment
Self-stereotype or provided stereotype-consistent self-presentation	▪ Act in stereotypic ways ▪ Choose occupations consistent with stereotypes	*Cognitively restructure to justify treatment*	▪ Attribute negative outcomes to internal, stable characteristics (e.g., qualifications) ▪ Attribute to perpetrator motives other than bias ▪ View treatment as justified	*Psychologically disengage from situation*	▪ Show less motivation in pursuit of job ▪ Engage in less assertive job hunting behaviors ▪ Frame job as less desirable

(continued)

Table 21.1 (continued)

Engagement coping (approach stressor)				Disengagement coping (avoid stressor)	
Primary control strategies (problem solving)	Examples	Secondary control strategies (Change feelings and thinking)	Examples	Strategy	Examples
Disconfirm stereotype	▪ Provide individuating in-formation	*Engage in positive thinking and self-talk*	▪ Think about prior successes ▪ Show optimism about job search	*Conceal stigma*	▪ Do not acknowledge stigmatized status ▪ Avoid discussions that relate to stigma ▪ Lessen cues to status (e.g., leave affiliations off résumé). ▪ Fabrication of information to avoid disclosure
Seek out support	▪ Network with groups related to one's stigma ▪ Discuss job search with others	*Devalue the domain*	▪ Devalue certain types of selection procedures as not job relevant or not predictive	*Disidentify*	▪ View self as not part of stigmatized group ▪ Focus on other aspects of identity
Provide information on stigma	▪ Acknowledge stigma dir-ectly ▪ Signal invisible stigma through hints and cues ▪ Self-disclose efforts at control of stigma (e.g., medication, treatment, rehab)				

Stigmatized individuals might lessen decision-maker reliance on stereotypes by presenting individuating information so as to differentiate oneself from the stereotype (Neuberg and Fiske 1987; Locksley et al. 1980). However, depending on the nature of the selection process, this might be challenging to undertake. That is, a highly structured, consistently administered process might not allow for additional information to be provided. Processes that allow individuals to "add any other relevant information" may be viewed more favorably by stigmatized individuals.

Several researchers have examined what factors affect decisions to pursue legal action against an organization in relation to a discrimination claim (e.g., Goldman 2001). While this research has focused more on termination than hiring contexts, it does provide some insight into the reactions of individuals to stigmatization in the employment process. Specifically, Goldman (2001) has found that social guidance, or receiving advice from friends and family that encourages one to pursue a claim, plays a key role in whether individuals actually do pursue legal action.

Note that stigmatized individuals may be reluctant to complain about differential treatment because those who do complain tend to be disliked and reprimanded (Kaiser and Miller 2001; 2003; Shelton and Stewart 2004). A dilemma arises for an applicant: identifying prejudice is interpersonally costly (Kaiser 2006) but not confronting prejudice is intrapersonally costly (Shelton et al. 2006) in terms of feelings of guilt and regret. Shelton et al. (2006, 80) suggest that targets of prejudice should not confront perpetrators when the "consequences of perpetrator's evaluations are serious," which would imply not confronting prejudice in selection contexts; however, not calling a recruiter on his/her actions may not be acceptable to the stigmatized individual. As Shelton et al. note, each individual applicant will have to weight the interpersonal costs of confrontation with the intrapersonal costs of non-confrontation in a given situation.

One obvious way to reduce negative perceptions on the part of stigmatized individuals is to stop stigmatizing them. Organizations can and should design processes that are consistent, do not afford for differential treatment, and have less adverse impact against stigmatized groups. Further, organizations can attempt to curtail subtle differential treatment on the part of organizational representatives. Individuals may be motivated to suppress prejudice by egalitarian motives but also by attempts to conform to social norms regarding how appropriate it is to express prejudice (Crandall, Eshleman, and O'Brien 2002), norms that the organization can proscribe and encourage. Further, research has been supportive of the effectiveness of training in reducing intergroup bias (e.g., Kawakami, Dovidio, and van Kamp 2005). Thus, it is clear that employers can do a lot in terms of making certain that individuals who are doing the hiring are both internally motivated and externally motivated to suppress prejudice (e.g., through selection of recruiters, through training, through normative expressions of policy, through enforcement of policy).

Note, however, that organizational attempts to design a fair system do not necessarily mean that stigmatized individuals will see it as such. Bell, Ryan, and Weichmann (2004) noted that groups who enter a process with low expectations of being treated fairly will tend to engage in cognitive and behavioral activities to confirm their negative expectations (Olson, Roese, and Zanna 1996). They suggest designing orientations to selection processes that directly challenge negative expectations through providing multiple credible sources of information to support that the process is a fair one.

Further, organizations can work to counteract expectations of stigmatization through impression management, at least for some stigmas. Avery and McKay (2006) presented a model of tactics organizations might use in targeted recruitment of under-represented groups that could be applied to enhancing the perceptions of stigmatized individuals. These strategies include ingratiation tactics with under-represented job seekers (e.g., demographic composition of ads, placement of ads in targeted media, providing inclusiveness statements in advertising, participating in targeted job fairs and recruitment efforts) and presenting evidence of effective diversity management (e.g., winning awards) and corporate social responsibility with respect to diversity (e.g., sponsorship of causes).

While the applicant perception literature has provided a number of proscriptions regarding how to enhance applicant fairness perceptions (e.g., Ryan and Ployhart 2000), there are further factors to consider with regard to fairness perceptions of individuals who possess a stigmatizing characteristic. As the literature reviewed in this chapter illustrates, consideration of such factors by selection system administrators and designers can advance the fair treatment of all applicants.

References

ARONSON, J. 2002. Stereotype threat: contending and coping with unnerving expectations. Pp. 279–301 in *Improving Academic Achievement: Impact of Psychological Factors on Education*, ed. J. Aronson. San Francisco: Elsevier.

—— and INZLICHT, M. 2004. The ups and downs of attributional ambiguity: stereotype vulnerability and the academic self-knowledge of African American college students. *Psychological Science*, 15 (12): 829–36.

ARVEY, R. D., STRICKLAND, W., DRAUDEN, G., and MARTIN, C. 1990. Motivational components of test-taking. *Personnel Psychology*, 43: 695–716.

AVERY, D. R., and MCKAY, P. F. 2006. Target practice: an organizational impression management approach to attracting minority and female job applicants. *Personnel Psychology*, 59: 157–87.

—— HERNANDEZ, M., and HEBL, M. R. 2004. Who's watching the race? Racial salience in recruitment advertising. *Journal of Applied Social Psychology*, 34: 146–61.

BALDRIDGE, D. C., and VEIGA, J. F. 2001. Toward greater understanding of the willingness to request an accommodation: can requesters' beliefs disable the ADA? *Academy of Management Review*, 26: 85–99.

—— —— 2006. The impact of anticipated social consequences on recurring disability accommodation requests. *Journal of Management*, 32: 158–79.

BARRETO, M., SPEARS, R., ELLEMERS, N., and SHAHINPER, K. 2003. Who wants to know? The effect of audience on identity expression among minority group members. *British Journal of Social Psychology*, 42: 299–318.

BAUER, T. N., TRUXILLO, D. M., SANCHEZ, R. J., CRAIG, J., FERRARA, P., and CAMPION, M. A. 2001. Applicant reactions to selection: development of the Selection Procedural Justice Scale (SPJS). *Personnel Psychology*, 54: 387–419.

BELL, B. S., RYAN, A. M., and WIECHMANN, D. 2004. Justice expectations and applicant perceptions. *International Journal of Selection and Assessment*, 12: 24–38.

BENDICK, M., JACKSON, C., REINOSO, V., and HODGES, L. 1991. Discrimination against Latino job applicants: a controlled experiment. *Human Resource Management*, 30: 469–84.

BERGMAN, M. E., and GAULKE, K. M. 2004. "Ex" marks a spot: the stickiness of removed stigmas. In E. E. Umphress (Chair), The Causes and Consequences of Prejudice and Discrimination: Innovative Theoretical Development and Empirical Investigations. Presented at the Academy of Management Conference, New Orleans, LA, August.

BOBOCEL, D. R, and FARRELL, A. C. 1996. Sex-based promotion decisions and interactional fairness: investigating the influence of managerial accounts. *Journal of Applied Psychology*, 81: 22–35.

BRANSCOMBE, N. R., SCHMITT, M. T., and HARVEY, R. D. 1999. Perceiving pervasive discrimination among African Americans: implications for group identification and well-being. *Journal of Personality and Social Psychology*, 77: 135–49.

BUCHANAN, N. T. 2004. The nexus of race and gender domination: the racialized sexual harassment of African American women. Pp. 294–320 in *In the Company of Men: Rediscovering the Links between Sexual Harassment and Male Domination*, ed. P. Morgan and J. Gruber. Boston: Northeastern University Press.

—— and ORMEROD, A. J. 2002. Racialized sexual harassment in the lives of African American women. *Women and Therapy*, 25: 107–24.

CHAN, D. 1997. Racial subgroup differences in predictive validity perceptions on personality and cognitive ability tests. *Journal of Applied Psychology*, 82: 311–20.

—— and SCHMITT, N. 1997. Video-based versus paper-and-pencil method of assessment in situational judgment tests: subgroup differences in test performance and face validity perceptions. *Journal of Applied Psychology*, 82: 142–59.

—— —— DESHON, R. P., CLAUSE, C., and DELBRIDGE, K. 1997. Reactions to cognitive ability tests: the relationships between race, test performance, face validity perceptions, and test-taking motivation. *Journal of Applied Psychology*, 82: 300–10.

—— —— JENNINGS, D., CLAUSE, C. S., and DELBRIDGE, K. 1998. Applicant perceptions of test fairness integrating justice and self-serving bias perspectives. *International Journal of Selection and Assessment*, 6: 232–9.

CHAO, G. T., and NGUYEN, H. D. 2005. International employment discrimination: a review of legal issues, human impacts and organizational implications. Pp. 379–408 in *Discrimination at Work: The Psychological and Organizational Bases*, ed. R. Dipboye and A. Colella (SIOP Frontiers Series). Mahwah, NJ: Erlbaum.

CHROBOT-MASON, D., BUTTON, S. B., and DiCLEMENTI, J. D. 2001. Sexual identity management strategies: an exploration of antecedents and consequences. *Sex Roles*, 45: 321–36.

CHUNG-HERRERA, B. G., and LANKAU, M. J. 2005. Are we there yet? An assessment of fit between stereotypes of minority managers and the successful-manager prototype. *Journal of Applied Social Psychology*, 35: 2029–56.

CLAIR, J. A., BEATTY, J. E., and MACLEAN, T. L. 2005. Out of sight but not out of mind: managing invisible social identities in the workplace. *Academy of Management Review*, 30: 78–95.

COHEN, G. L., and STEELE, C. M. 2002. A barrier of mistrust: how stereotypes affect cross-race mentoring. Pp. 303–27 in *Improving Academic Achievement: Impact of Psychological Factors on Education*, ed. J. Anderson. San Diego: Academic Press.

COLE, S. W., KEMENY, M. E., TAYLOR, S. E., and VISSCHER, B. R. 1996. Elevated physical health risk among gay men who conceal their homosexual identity. *Health Psychology*, 15: 243–51.

CRANDALL, C. S. 1994. Prejudice against fat people: ideology and self-interest. *Journal of Personality and Social Psychology*, 66: 882–94.

—— ESHLEMAN, A., and O'BRIEN, L. 2002. Social norms and the expression and suppression of prejudice: the struggle for internalization. *Journal of Personality and Social Psychology*, 82: 359–78.

CRISP, R. J., and HEWSTONE, M. 1999. Differential evaluation of crossed category groups: patterns, processes, and reducing intergroup bias. *Group Processes and Intergroup Relations*, 2: 1–27.

CROCKER, J., and MAJOR, B. 1989. Social stigma and self-esteem: the self-protective properties of stigma. *Psychological Review*, 96: 608–30.

—— and MCGRAW, K. M. 1984. What's good for the goose is not good for the gander: solo status as an obstacle to occupational achievement for males and females. *American Behavioral Scientist*, 27: 357–69.

—— MAJOR, B., and STEELE, C. 1998. Social stigma. Pp. 504–53 in *Handbook of Social Psychology*, 4th edn., ed. D. Gilbert, S.T. Fiske, and G. Lindzey. Boston: McGraw-Hill.

—— VOELKL, K., TESTA, M., and MAJOR, B. 1991. Social stigma: the affective consequences of attributional ambiguity. *Journal of Personality and Social Psychology*, 60: 218–28.

CROSBY, F. J. 1994. Understanding affirmative action. *Basic and Applied Social Psychology*, 15: 13–41.

CROW, S. M., FOK, L. Y., and HARTMAN, S. J. 1995. Who is at greatest risk of work-related discrimination—women, blacks or homosexuals? *Employee Responsibilities and Rights Journal*, 11: 15–26.

DAMBRUN, M. 2007. Gender differences in mental health: the mediating role of perceived personal discrimination. *Journal of Applied Social Psychology*, 37: 1118–29.

DEROUS, E., NGUYEN, H. H., and RYAN, A. M. 2006. Identifiers of ethnicity and discrimination against Arabs. Paper presented at the 21st annual conference of the Society for Industrial and Organizational Psychology, Dallas, May.

—— ORI, I. N., NGUYEN, H. H. D., and RYAN, A. M. 2007. Employment discrimination against Arab minorities in a large Dutch metropolitan area: results from a correspondence and experimental lab study. Paper presented at the 22nd annual conference of the Society for Industrial and Organizational Psychology, New York, April.

DODGE, K. A., GILROY, F. D., and FENZEL, L. M. 1995. Requisite management characteristics revisited: two decades later. *Journal of Social Behavior and Personality Gender in the Workplace*, 10: 253–64.

DOVIDIO, J. F., and GAERTNER, S. L. 2000. Aversive racism and selection decisions: 1989 and 1999. *Psychological Science*, 11: 315–19.

—— KAWAKAMI, K., GAERTNER, S. L. 2002. Implicit and explicit prejudice and interracial interaction. *Journal of Personality and Social Psychology*, 81: 62–8.

DUEHR, E. E., and BONO, J. E. 2006. MEN, women, and managers: are stereotypes finally changing? *Personnel Psychology*, 59: 815–46.

FRABLE, D. E. S., PLATT, L., and HOEY, S. 1998. Concealable stigmas and positive self-perceptions: feeling better around similar others. *Journal of Personality and Social Psychology*, 74: 909–22.

FRISKOPP, A., and SILVERSTEIN, S. 1995. *Straight Jobs, Gay Lives: Gay and Lesbian Professionals, the Harvard Business School, and the American Workplace*. New York: Scribner.

GILLILAND, S. W. 1993. The perceived fairness of selection systems: an organizational justice perspective. *Academy of Management Review*, 18: 694–734.

GOLDBERG, C. B. 2003. Applicant reactions to the employment interview: a look at demographic similarity and social identity theory. *Journal of Business Research*, 56: 561–71.

GOLDMAN, B. M. 2001. Toward an understanding of employment discrimination claiming: an integration of organizational justice and social information processing theories. *Personnel Psychology*, 54: 361–86.

—— GUTEK, B. A., STEIN, J. H., and LEWIS, K. 2006. Employment discrimination in organization: antecedents and consequences. *Journal of Management*, 32: 786–830.

HARRISON, D. A., KRAVITZ, D. A., MAYER, D. M., LESLIE, L. M., and LEV-AREY, D. 2006. Understanding attitudes toward affirmative action programs in employment: summary and meta-analysis of 35 years of research. *Journal of Applied Psychology*, 91: 1013–26.

HAUSKNECHT, J. P., DAY, D. V., THOMAS, S. C. 2004. Applicant reactions to selection procedures: an updated model and meta-analysis. *Personnel Psychology*, 57: 639–83.

HAYES, T. L., CITERA, M., BRADY, L. M., and JENKINS, N. M. 1995. Staffing for persons with disabilities: what is "fair" and "job related"? *Public Personnel Management*, 24: 413–27.

HEBL, M. R., and DOVIDIO, J. F. 2005. Promoting the "social" in the examination of social stigmas. *Personality and Social Psychology Review*, 9: 156–82.

—— and KLECK, R. E. 2002. Acknowledging one's stigma in the interview setting: Effective strategy or liability? *Journal of Applied Psychology*, 32: 223–49.

—— FOSTER, J. B., MANNIX, L. M., and DOVIDIO, J. F. 2002. Formal and interpersonal discrimination: a field study of bias toward homosexual applicants. *Personality and Social Psychology Bulletin*, 28: 815–25.

HEIKES, E. J. U. 1991. When men are the minority: the case of men in nursing. *Sociological Quarterly*, 32: 389–401.

HEILMAN, M. E., and ALCOTT, V. B. 2001. What I think you think of me: women's reactions to being viewed as beneficiaries of preferential selection. *Journal of Applied Psychology*, 86: 574–82.

—— McCULLOUGH, W. F., and GILBERT, D. 1996. The other side of affirmative action: reactions of non-beneficiaries to sex-base preferential selection. *Journal of Applied Psychology*, 81: 346–57.

HEILMAN, M. E., and ALCOTT, V. B., KAPLOW, S. R., AMATO, M. A., and STATHATOS, P. 1993. When similarity is a liability: effects of sex-based preferential selection on reactions to like-sex and different-sex others. *Journal of Applied Psychology*, 78: 917–27.

HEREK, G. M., GILLIS, J. R., and COGAN, J. C. 1999. Psychological sequelae of hate-crime victimization among lesbian, gay, and bisexual adults. *Journal of Consulting and Clinical Psychology*, 67: 945–51.

HODSON, G., DOVIDIO, J. F., and GAERTNER, S. L. 2002. Processes in racial discrimination: differential weighting of conflicting information. *Personality and Social Psychology Bulletin*, 28: 460–71.

HOGG, M. A., TERRY, D. J., and WHITE, K. M. 1995. A tale of two theories: a critical comparison of identity theory with social identity theory. *Social Psychology Quarterly*, 58: 255–69.

HORVATH, M., RYAN, A. M., and STIERWALT, S. 2000. The influence of explanations for selection test use, outcome favorability and self-efficacy on test-taker perceptions. *Organizational Behavior and Human Decision Processes*, 83: 310–30.

HOSODA, M., STONE-ROMERO, E. F., and COATS, G. 2003. The effects of physical attractiveness on job-related outcomes: a meta-analysis of experimental studies. *Personnel Psychology*, 56: 431–62.

HUFFMAN, M. L., and COHEN, P. N. 2004. Racial wage inequality: job segregation and devaluation across U.S. labor markets. *American Journal of Sociology*, 109: 902–36.

INZLICHT, M., and BEN-ZEEV, T. 2000. A threatening intellectual environment: why females are unsusceptible to experiencing problem-solving deficits in the presence of males. *Psychological Science*, 1: 365–71.

JAMES, K., LOVATO, C., and KHOO, G. 1994. Social identity correlates of minority workers' health. *Academy of Management Journal*, 37: 383–96.

JONES, E. E., FARINA, A., HOSTORF, A. H., MARKUS, H., MILLER, D. T., and SCOTT, R. A. 1984. *Social Stigma: The Psychology of Marked Relationships*. New York: Freeman.

JOST, J. T., PELHAM, B. W., and CARVALLO, M. R. 2002. Non-conscious forms of system justification: implicit and behavioral preferences for higher status. *Journal of Experimental Social Psychology*, 38: 586–602.

KAISER, C. R. 2006. Dominant ideology threat and the interpersonal consequences of attributions to discrimination. Pp. 45–64 in *Stigma and Group Inequality*, ed. S. Levin and C. van Laar. MAHWAH, NJ: Erlbaum.

—— and MILLER, C. T. 2001. Stop complaining! The social costs of making attributions to discrimination. *Personality and Social Psychology Bulletin*, 27: 254–63.

—— —— 2003. Derogating the victim: the interpersonal consequences of blaming events on discrimination. *Group Processes and Intergroup Relations*, 6: 223–37.

—— —— 2004. A stress and coping perspective on confronting sexism. *Psychology of Women Quarterly*, 28: 168–78.

KANTER, R. M. 1977. *Men and Women of the Corporation*. New York: Basics BOOKS, Inc.

KARAKOWSKY, L., and SIEGEL, J. P. 1999. The effects of proportional representation and gender orientation of the task on emergent leadership behavior in mixed-gender work groups. *Journal of Applied Psychology*, 84: 620–31.

KAWAKAMI, K., DOVIDIO, J. F., and VAN KAMP, S. 2005. Kicking the habit: effects of nonstereotypic association training and correction processes on hiring decisions. *Journal of Experimental Social Psychology*, 41: 68–75.

KING, E. B., MADERA, J. M., HEBL, M. R., KNIGHT, J. L., and MENDOZA, S. A. 2006. What's in a name? A multiracial investigation of the role of occupational stereotypes in selection decisions. *Journal of Applied Social Psychology*, 36: 1145–59.

KRIEGER, N., and SIDNEY, S. 1996. Racial discrimination and blood pressure: The CARDIA study of young Balck and White adults. *American Journal of Public Health*, 86: 1370–8.

KULIS, S. S., and SHAW, H. E. 1996. Racial segregation among postsecondary workers. *Social Forces*, 75: 575–91.

KURZBAN, R., and LEARY, M. R. 2001. Evolutionary origins of stigmatization: the functions of social exclusion. *Psychological Bulletin*, 127: 187–208.

LANDY, F. J., ed. 2005. *Employment Discrimination Litigation: BEHAVIORAL, QUANTITATIVE, and Legal Perspectives*. San Francisco: Jossey-Bass.

LEVIN, S., SINCLAIR, S., VENIEGAS, R. C., and TAYLOR, P. L. 2002. Perceived discrimination in the context of multiple group memberships. *Psychological Science*, 13: 557–60.

LIPTON, J. P., O'CONNOR, M., TERRY, C., and BELLAMY, E. 1991. Neutral job titles and occupational stereotypes: when legal and psychological realities conflict. *Journal of Psychology*, 125: 129–51.

LOCKSLEY, A., BORGIDA, E., BREKKE, N., and HEPBURN, C. 1980. Sex stereotypes and social judgment. *Journal of Personality and Social Psychology*, 39: 821–31.

LYNESS, K. S., and HEILMAN, M. E. 2006. When fit is fundamental: performance evaluations and promotions of upper-level female and male managers. *Journal of Applied Psychology*, 91: 777–85.

MacCORQUODALE, P., and JENSEN, G. 1993. Women in the law: partners or tokens? *Gender and Society*, 7: 582–93.

McFARLAND, L. A., RYAN, A. M., SACCO, J. M., and KRISKA, S. D. 2004. Examination of structured interview ratings across time: the effects of applicant race, rater race, and panel composition. *Journal of Management*, 30: 435–52.

MAJOR, B., and GRAMZOW, R. H. 1999. Abortion as stigma: cognitive and emotional implications of concealment. *Journal of Personality and Social Psychology*, 77: 735–45.

—— QUINTON, W. J., and SCHMADER, T. 2003. Attributions to discrimination and self-esteem: impact of group identification and situational ambiguity. *Journal of Experimental Social Psychology*, 39: 220–31.

—— GRAMZOW, R. H., McCOY, S. K., LEVIN, S., SCHMADER, T., and SIDANIUS, J. 2002. Perceiving personal discrimination: the role of group status and legitimizing ideology. *Journal of Personality and Social Psychology*, 82: 269–82.

MAUME, D. J. 1999. Glass ceilings and glass escalators: occupational segregation and race and sex differences in managerial promotions. *Work and Occupations*, 26: 483–509.

MENDOZA-DENTON, R., DOWNEY, G., PURDIE, V., DAVIS, A., and PIETRAZAK, J. 2002. Sensitivity to status-based rejection: implications for African American students' college experience. *Journal of Personality and Social Psychology*, 83: 896–918.

MEYER, I. H. 2003. Minority stress and mental health in gay men. Pp. 699–731 in *Psychological Perspectives on Lesbian, Gay, and Bisexual Experiences*, 2nd edn., ed. L. D. Garnets and D. C. Kimmel. New York: Columbia University Press.

MILLER, C. T. 2006. Social psychological perspectives on coping with stressors related to stigma. Pp. 21–44 in *Stigma and Group Inequality: Social Psychological Perspectives*, ed. S. Levin and C. van Laar. Mahwah, NJ: Erlbaum.

NELSON, N. L., and PROBST, T. M. 2004. Multiple minority individuals: multiplying the risk of workplace harassment and discrimination. Pp. 193–217 in *The Psychology of Prejudice and Discrimination: Ethnicity and Multiracial Identity*, ed. J. L. Chin. Westport, CT: Praeger Publishers.

NEUBERG, S. L., and FISKE, S. T. 1987. Motivational influences on impression formation: outcome dependency, accuracy-driven attention, and individuating processes. *Journal of Personality and Social Psychology*, 53: 431–44.

OLSON, J. M., ROESE, N. J., and ZANNA, M. P. 1996. Expectancies. Pp. 231–8 in *Social Psychology: Handbook of Basic Principles*, ed. E. T. Higgins and A. W. Kruglanski. New York: Guilford Press.

OPERARIO, D., and FISKE, S. T. 2001. Ethnic identity moderates perceptions of prejudice: judgments of personal versus group discrimination and subtle versus blatant bias. *Personality and Social Psychology Bulletin*, 27: 550–61.

OUTZ, J. L. 2005. Race discrimination cases: common themes. Pp. 201–28 in *Employment Discrimination Litigation: Behavioral, Quantitative, and Legal Perspectives*, ed. F. J. Landy. San Francisco: Jossey-Bass.

PETTIGREW, T. F., and MARTIN, J. 1987. Shaping the organizational context for Black American inclusion. *Journal of Social Issues*, 43: 41–78.

PINEL, E. C. 1999. Stigma consciousness: the psychological legacy of social stereotypes. *Journal of Personality and Social Psychology*, 76: 114–28.

—— 2002. Stigma consciousness in intergroup contexts: the power of conviction. *Journal of Experimental Social Psychology*, 38: 178–85.

PLOYHART, R. E., and RYAN, A. M. 1997. Toward an explanation of applicant reactions: an examination of organizational justice and attribution frameworks. *Organizational Behavior and Human Decision Processes*, 72: 308–35.

—— —— and BENNETT, M. 1999. Explanations for selection decisions: applicants' reactions to informational and sensitivity features of explanations. *Journal of Applied Psychology*, 84: 87–106.

PREWETT-LIVINGSTON, A. J., FEILD, H. S., VERES, J. G., III., and LEWIS, P. M. 1996. Effects of race on interview ratings in a situational panel interview. *Journal of Applied Psychology*, 81: 178–86.

RAGINS, B. R. 2008. Disclosure disconnects: antecedents and consequences of disclosing invisible stigmas across life domains. *Academy of Management Review*, 33: 194–215.

RODIN, M., and PRICE, J. 1995. Overcoming stigma: credit for self-improvement or discredit for needing to improve? *Personality and Social Psychology Bulletin*, 21: 172–81.

RYAN, A. M., and PLOYHART, R. E. 2000. Applicants' perceptions of selection procedures and decisions: a critical review and agenda for the future. *Journal of Management*, 26: 565–606.

SACCO, J. M., SCHEU, C. R., RYAN, A. M., and SCHMITT, N. 2003. An investigation of race and sex similarity effects in interviews: a multilevel approach to relational demography. *Journal of Applied Psychology*, 88: 852–65.

SCHINKEL, S., van DIERENDONCK, D., and ANDERSON, N. 2004. The impact of selection encounters on applicants: an experimental study into feedback effects after a negative selection decision. *International Journal of Selection and Assessment*, 12: 197–205.

SCHMADER, T., and JOHNS, M. 2003. Converging evidence that stereotype threat reduces working memory capacity. *Journal of Personality and Social Psychology*, 85: 440–52.

SCHNEIDER, B. 1987. The people make the place. *Personnel Psychology*, 40: 437–53.

SCHWARZER, R., and WEINER, B. 1991. Stigma controllability and coping as predictors of emotions and social support. *Journal of Social and Personal Relationships*, 8: 133–40.

SEGREST PURKISS, S. L., PERREWE, P. L., GILLESPIE, T. L., MAYES, B. T., and FERRIS, G. R. 2006. Implicit sources of bias in employment interview judgments and decisions. *Organizational Behavior and Human Decision Processes*, 101: 152–67.

SEKAQUAPTEWA, D., and THOMPSON, M. 2002. The differential effects of solo status on members of high-and low-status groups. *Personality and Social Psychology Bulletin*, 28: 694–707.

SHAW, J. C., WILD, E., and COLQUITT, J. A. 2003. To justify or excuse? A meta-analytic review of the effects of explanations. *Journal of Applied Psychology*, 88: 444–58.

SHELTON J. N., and STEWART, B. 2004. Confronting perpetrators of prejudice: the inhibitory effects of social costs. *Psychology of Women Quarterly*, 28: 215–23.

—— RICHESON, J. A., SALVATORE, J., and HILL, D. M. 2006. Silence is not golden: the intrapersonal consequences of not confronting prejudice. Pp. 65–82 in *Stigma and Group Inequality*, ed. S. Levin and C. van Laar. Mahwah, NJ: Erlbaum.

SHIH, J. U. 2002. "Yeah, I could hire this one, but I know it's gonna be a problem": How race, nativity, and gender affect employers' perceptions of the employability of job seekers. *Ethnic and Racial Studies*, 25: 99–119.

SINGLETARY, S., and HEBL, M. 2007. Strategies for remediating discrimination in a job applicant context. Presented at the annual conference of Society for Industrial and Organizational Psychology, New York.

SMITHER, J. W., REILLY, R. R., MILLSAP, R. E., PEARLMAN, K., and STOFFEY, R. W. 1993. Applicant reactions to selection procedures. *Personnel Psychology*, 46: 49–76.

SPANGLER, E., GORDON, M. A., and PIPKIN, R. M. 1978. Token women: an empirical test of Kanter's hypothesis. *American Journal of Sociology*, 84: 160–9.

STANGOR, C., SWIM, J. K., VAN ALLEN, K. L., and SECHRIST, G. B. 2002. Reporting discrimination in public and private contexts. *Journal of Personality and Social Psychology*, 82: 69–74.

STEELE, C. M. 1997. A threat in the air: how stereotypes shape intellectual identity and performance. *American Psychologist*, 52: 613–29.

—— and ARONSON, J. 1995. Stereotype threat and the intellectual test performance of African Americans. *Journal of Personality and Social Psychology*, 69: 797–811.

—— —— 2004. Stereotype threat does not live by Steele and Aronson alone. *American Psychologist*, 59: 47–8.

SWIM, J. K., and HYERS, L. L. 1999. Excuse me—what did you say?! Women's public and private responses to sexist remarks. *Journal of Experimental Social Psychology*, 35: 68–88.

TERPSTRA, D. E., and LARSEN, J. M. 1980. A note on job type and applicant race as determinants of hiring decisions. *Journal of Occupational Psychology*, 53: 117–19.

THOMAS, K. M., and WISE, P. G. 1999. Organizational attractiveness and individual differences: are diverse applicants attracted by different factors? *Journal of Business and Psychology*, 13: 375–90.

TRUXILLO, D. M., and HUNTHAUSEN, J. M. 1999. Reactions of African-American and White applicants to written and video-based police selection tests. *Journal of Social Behavior and Personality*, 14: 101–12.

—— BAUER, T. N., CAMPION, M. A., and PARONTO, M. E. 2002. Multiple dimensions of procedural justice: longitudinal effects on selection system fairness and test-taking self-efficacy. *International Journal of Selection and Assessment*, 9: 336–49.

TURNER, J. C., BROWN, R. J., and TAJFEL, H. 1979. Social comparison and group interest in ingroup favouritism. *European Journal of Social Psychology*, 9 (2): 187–204.

TURNER, M., FIX, M., and STRUYK, R. 1991. *Opportunities Denied, Opportunities Diminished: Racial Discrimination in Hiring.* Washington, DC: Urban Institute Press.

WEINER, B., PERRY, R. P., and MAGNUSSON, J. 1988. An attributional analysis of reactions to stigmas. *Journal of Personality and Social Psychology,* 55: 738–48.

WOODS, R. L. 1994. *The Corporate Closet: The Professional Lives of Gay Men in America.* New York: Free Press.

YODER, J. D., and BERENDSEN, L. L. 2001. "Outsider within" the firehouse: African American and White women firefighters. *Psychology of Women Quarterly,* 25: 27–36.

YOUNG, J. L., and JAMES, E. H. 2001. Token majority: the work attitudes of male flight attendants. *Sex Roles,* 45: 299–319.

PART VI

FUTURE CHALLENGES

THE BOUNDARYLESS CAREER

KERR INKSON

1. INTRODUCTION

A term which is used with increasing frequency in the careers field is "boundaryless career." The originators of the term (Arthur and Rousseau 1996) mention six specific meanings for the boundaryless career:

- movement across the boundaries of separate employers;
- drawing validation from outside the present employer;
- sustained by networks or information that are external to the current employer;
- breaking traditional organizational career boundaries;
- rejection of traditional career opportunities for personal or family reasons;
- perceiving a boundaryless future regardless of structural constraints.

Thus, the boundaryless career is "the opposite of the organizational career" (Arthur and Rousseau 1996, 5), i.e., in terms of potential and often actual employee mobility it is *extra*-organizational and *inter*-organizational. People in boundaryless careers have career goals, expertise, and networks that go beyond their current

The author wishes to thank Professor Michael Arthur for helpful comments on an earlier draft of this chapter.

employer, so that their careers are "sequences of opportunities that go beyond the boundaries of single employment settings" (DeFillippi and Arthur 1996, 116).

The central idea behind the boundaryless career is not new. Fifty years ago Gouldner (1957) made the distinction between boundaryless and organizational individuals and career paths in his discussion of organizational "locals" and boundaryless "cosmopolitans." But fifty years on, in changed economic conditions, the distinction has attained a new relevance.

The argument for the growing prevalence and importance of boundaryless careers is that as society and its organizations pursue ever-increasing flexibility, careers must also become more flexible. When organizations breach employees' psychological contract expectations that they will enjoy traditional organizational careers with guaranteed security, commitment to organizations is reduced, and employees more frequently adopt boundaryless career attitudes as well as increased mobility, across boundaries and barriers that seem increasingly permeable (Ackah and Heaton 2004; Granrose and Baccili 2006). In a changed environment, boundaryless careers may offer better prospects of career success (Eby, Butts, and Lockwood 2003). The boundaryless career appears a particularly appropriate way of understanding careers in industries such as film production and software development that are based on temporary projects rather than permanent structures (DeFillippi, Arthur, and Lindsay 2006), but these industries may be merely extreme examples of a wider loosening and crossing of boundaries in the world of work. The organizational career, we are told, is dead or dying (Hall 1996), and boundaryless careers are representative not just of a creative elite of workers, but of the mainstream.

This phenomenon, implying as it does a diminution in commitment to current employing organizations, must clearly be of concern to organizational psychologists, HRM practitioners, and others who seek to develop organizations with strong workforce commitment.

2. THE GENESIS OF BOUNDARYLESS CAREERS

The concept of the boundaryless career arose essentially as a reaction against the supposed dominance of the organizational career. Organizational careers were first articulated by Weber (1947), who believed that the classic bureaucratic organization could be supported by a career system in which individuals climb upwards in an organizational hierarchy, acquiring organizational expertise that equips them for more responsible positions vacated as their superiors are promoted or retire. The desirability of organizational careers is implicit in many influential prescriptions for effective management, from Fayol's (1949) administrative management and Drucker's (1954) *The Practice of Management,* to Peters and Waterman's (1982) *In Search of Excellence* (notably, however, both Drucker (1994) and Peters (1988) subsequently changed their minds and became advocates of much less organizationally dominated careers). In practice, the organizational career reached its apotheosis in the lifetime-employment practices of Japanese monoliths (Ouchi 1981), until it was weakened by the unravelling of the Japanese economic miracle (Hirakubo 1999).

In academia, careers, being an individual rather than an organizational preoccupation, were for many years studied intensively by educationalists and psychologists in the context of "vocational guidance," but were ignored or taken for granted in management studies. However, the recognition by Hall (1976) and Schein (1978) that the study of careers provides an important lens for understanding the functioning and management of organizations became the basis of a growing interest. These early works were mainly about the effective management of managers and other staff by means of organizational support for their organizational careers. However, Hall (1976) sounded a cautionary note with his recognition of a variant form, the so-called "protean career," that is managed more by the individual than by the organization.

In recent years, interest in the relationship of careers to organizations, and the specific promotion of new forms of career, including protean and boundaryless careers, has been given impetus by sweeping changes in the economic, business, and cultural conditions in which people are employed. These changes, which are continuing to develop in the new millennium, include, but are not limited to:

- globalization and increased competitive pressures on organizations;
- increased employer demands for flexibility in employment arrangements;
- the restructuring, downsizing, outsourcing, and workforce casualization with which many organizations have responded;
- the decline in Keynesian protection of employment;
- the move from manual and manufacturing work to the provision of services;
- the growth of knowledge work;
- the feminization of the workforce, the partial breaking of gendered occupational stereotypes, and the call for new patterns of career for women;
- increasing societal tolerance for, and encouragement of, individual autonomy and idiosyncrasies;
- a better-educated workforce, whose members are more capable of directing their own careers;
- increased incidence of alternatives to full-time permanent employment: part-time, temporary, contract, casual and project work; telecommuting; moonlighting; multiple job holding; self-employment; and "black economy" work.

Thus, in recent literature, organizational careers have increasingly been thought of as part of a historical employment system based on organizational hierarchies and internal labor markets. These systems are contrasted with a current environment that is dynamic, even turbulent, and involves external and even international labor markets. As the context for careers changes, careers change too.

The late twentieth-century destabilization of many careers, particularly managerial and professional careers, has been well documented. Dogged by layoffs, transfers, demotions, and career blockages, many employees who had previously had predictable careers lost control of them and drifted sideways or downwards in their organizations, or out of them altogether to inferior positions elsewhere (Inkson 1995). By the middle 1990s many felt demoralized and betrayed by the organizations in which they had hoped to build long-term hierarchical careers (Goffee and Scase 1992; Heckscher 1995).

In the wider scheme of things, few careers seem organizational. For example, one longitudinal study in the US that looked at workers between the ages of 18 and 38 concluded that in a twenty-year period, men made an average of 10.4 new job starts and women 9.9 (US Department of Labor 2006). And in a study conducted by Arthur, Inkson, and; Pringle (1999), a random sample of a national workforce had worked in an average of 2.8 organizations each in a ten-year period, and only 16 percent were with the same employer at the end of the period as they had been at the beginning. Both studies, however, showed a marked diminution of mobility as employees age.

Organizational careers may always have been largely confined to a relatively small number of large-scale corporations and public-service departments. Perhaps it is organizational careers that are deviant, their supposed frequency a piece of wishful thinking by managers who seek greater workforce predictability and compliance through the promise of long-term security. It may be that this kind of control is possible only in favorable environments: large, stable, steadily growing bureaucracies. But how many organizations can maintain such a pattern for the forty-year period of a typical career?

The development of the boundaryless career concept paralleled—a little later—critiques of formal organization structure that were fashionable in the late twentieth century. Specifically, the concept was born in 1993 as a response to the Academy of Management's sponsorship of its annual meeting under the theme, "The boundaryless organization"—a term coined by the redoubtable Jack Welch, CEO of General Electric, to promote new, less bureaucratic forms of organization (Ashkenas et al. 1995). At that meeting, a symposium of papers under the rubric *The Boundaryless Career* was organized by Robert DeFillippi and Michael Arthur of Suffolk University, with Arthur subsequently becoming the primary authority on boundaryless careers. The symposium became a Special Issue of the *Journal of Organizational Behavior* (Arthur 1994), which was then expanded into the edited book *The Boundaryless Career: A New Employment Principle for a New*

Organizational Era (Arthur and Rousseau 1996). Since the publication of *The Boundaryless Career,* interest in, and publication about, the concept has grown steadily, to the point where it now almost represents the mainstream in business-school career thinking (e.g., Baruch 2004).

The term "boundaryless career" is a product of chance in that it was coined not as the best label for the phenomena involved, but as a response to a specific conference theme. And indeed, "boundaryless career" may be a misnomer. In recent times many boundaries may indeed have become more permeable and more permeated. But they still exist, and for that reason the term "boundary-*crossing* career" might be more suitable (Inkson 2006).

In the tradition that it represents, the boundaryless career concept does not stand alone. Closely related to the boundaryless career is Hall's (1976; 2002; Hall and Associates 1996) concept of the *protean* career, i.e., a career that is "based upon individually defined goals, encompassing the whole life space, as well as being driven by psychological success rather than objective success such as pay, rank, or power" (Briscoe and Hall 2006, 6). Like the boundaryless career, the protean career is conceptualized as the direct antithesis of the traditional, or organizational, career. Thus, Briscoe and Hall (2006, 6) say that the protean career is managed "by the person, not the organization."

Other related forms of career have also been proposed. Handy (1989), for example, suggested that new forms of organization involving temporary and part-time staff might be supported by "portfolio careers" where workers cultivated ever-changing portfolios of full-time employment, part-time employment, casual employment, self-employment, and multiple job holdings. Arthur, Inkson, and Pringle (1999) used the phrase *The New Careers* to summarize their finding that people migrate their careers between institutions—industries and occupations as well as organizations—much more frequently than commonly supposed. Peiperl and Baruch (1997) noted the trend of disillusioned corporate staff to develop their careers in small firms, entrepreneurial ventures, and consultant roles, and coined the term "post-corporate careers." Colorful metaphorical renditions of new forms of career have also become popular, for example the "chameleon career" (Ituma and Simpson 2005), the "butterfly career" (McCabe and Savery 2007), and the "kaleidoscopic career" (Mainiero and Sullivan 2005).

Boundaryless and protean careers marginalize employing organizations as the managers of careers. Instead, careers are controlled by their owners. This poses problems for both individuals and organizations, placing much responsibility on individual career actors' shoulders which they may or may not be able to handle; and compelling organizations, which cannot rely on long-term career commitment by employees, to look for new ways of harnessing their career energies.

3. BOUNDARYLESS CAREERS AND MAINSTREAM CAREER THEORY

How does the boundaryless career relate, as a concept, to wider theories of career and career development? Here, we may divide approaches to the study of careers into three main categories.

1. Mainstream career theories developed mainly in schools of psychology, education, and counseling (e.g., Brown and Associates 2002) take an individual psychology perspective (e.g., "how should employees develop and manage their own careers so as to achieve long-term personal success and satisfaction?").
2. The HRM/organizational careers approach prevalent in business schools and some business organizations (e.g., Baruch 2004) takes a management perspective (e.g., "how should managers intervene in the careers of their subordinates so as to maximise their contribution to the organization?").
3. A third, sociological, approach (e.g., Johnson and Mortimer 2002), takes a social structure perspective, seeing careers as forms of social reproduction that are largely determined by variables such as economic development, social class, education, and gender, so that influences on careers by both individuals and organizations are relatively constrained.

It is the first of these three approaches, the psychological, that is dominant within career theory and research, perhaps because it is in accord with the popular view that individual people own, and should determine, their own careers. These mainstream theories—effectively summarized by Brown and Associates (2002)—focus on career *decision making*, (e.g., decisions as to which occupation to choose, whether to leave the current job or stay). Two dominant paradigms view the career as an ongoing cycle of personal development and change (e.g., Super 1990), and as an expression of goodness of fit between individual and occupation (e.g., Holland 1997). One outcome of this theorizing and related research is a substantial technology of assessment devices for measuring the characteristics of individuals (e.g., vocational interest inventories) and to some extent jobs, with the aim of providing information to individuals and their advisors to enable them to make better career decisions.

In this literature, the boundaries and categories considered to be fundamental to careers are not organizational but occupational. Organizations are considered merely background aspects of the locations in which individuals enact their careers, and the "traditional" career is one that is confined not to a single organization but to a single profession. These theories are therefore relatively indifferent as to whether that career is conducted within one organization or many. And indeed individuals talking about their careers seldom mention their employing organizations as having more than marginal significance (Arthur, Inkson, and Pringle 1999).

For this reason, the organizational career–boundaryless career contrast, although it may be critical to organizations and their managers, is largely irrelevant or incidental to mainstream career theory and practice, whose proponents would argue that *all* careers are, and should be, managed by the individual, and that the individual normally has points of reference outside the current organization and normally crosses boundaries during his or her career.

Mainstream career theories are relatively strong in understanding the minutiae of individual career decision making, but weak in looking beyond the individual and the job or occupation to understand career *patterns*, the multiple forces which shape them, and the relationship of careers to other social phenomena. Recently, though, recognition has increased that the recent changes and trends in employment practice mentioned above have altered structures of career opportunities; and that career protagonists need to understand these forces, and to anticipate them and take them into account in career planning (Reardon et al. 2006). One of the benefits of the research so far conducted on boundaryless careers has been the willingness of researchers and theorists to look beyond the narrow individual focus of mainstream career theory and the narrow management focus of the business-school approach, and to consider how careers are interwoven and integrated, like threads in a tapestry, with wider conceptualizations of social phenomena and institutions (e.g., Dany, Mallon, and Arthur 2003; Peiperl, Arthur and Anand 2002). There is, however, a considerable need for rapprochement between the psychological "career development," organizationally oriented "career management," and the sociology of careers, to facilitate the development of a suitably broad and integrated "career studies" (Inkson 2007).

4. BOUNDARYLESS CAREERS: THEORETICAL ISSUES

4.1 Objective and Subjective Careers

Some commentators and researchers on boundaryless careers appear to make boundarylessness synonymous with interorganizational mobility (e.g., Becker and Haunschild 2003; Currie, Tempest, and Starkey 2006; Eby, Butts, and Lockwood 2003; Granrose and Baccili 2006; Mao 2004; Van Buren 2003). Likewise, as Arthur, Khapova, and Wilderom (2005) report, research on career success has tended to focus on objective organizational definitions of success. But a boundaryless career is subjective as well as objective (Sullivan and Arthur 2006). For example, without leaving one's current organization one can—echoing four of the six criteria of boundaryless careers mentioned earlier—draw validation from outside the present employer; sustain one's career by networks or information that are external to the current employer; reject traditional career opportunities for personal reasons; and perceive oneself to have a boundaryless future regardless of structural constraints. Sullivan and Arthur (2006) show that boundaryless careers involve psychological as well as physical mobility and that the two are not necessarily closely related. For example, some individuals are geographically mobile between similar opportunities in different organizations but are not attuned to external opportunities and allow their career-relevant knowledge to become exhausted; others, apparently immobile, benefit their employers by utilizing expertise gained in outside networks, thus maintaining a boundaryless career within their current organization. Sullivan and Arthur recommend a research agenda in which both objective and subjective aspects of boundaryless career are considered, while Arthur et al. (2005) similarly advocate conceptualizations of career success that are oriented better towards subjective definitions of success and boundaryless careers.

4.2 Non-organizational Boundaries

The salient boundaries referred to in the boundaryless-career literature are those around organizations. But a boundaryless career may cross other boundaries as well—often without leaving the current employer. For example:

- geographical (for example, moving to a new branch in a new city);
- occupational (for example, a mechanic becoming a salesperson);
- industry (for example, moving from a job in the heavy engineering industry to one in financial services);
- employment status (for example, leaving permanent employment and becoming a temporary contractor);
- work–home (for example, giving up employment, or reducing hours, to be a house-husband).

Sullivan and Arthur (2006, 21) note that the mobility inherent in boundaryless careers may take place between "jobs, firms, occupations, countries," yet the definition of a boundaryless career as the "opposite of the organizational career" privileges organizational boundary-crossing as having special significance. Such a formulation is supported by Tams and Arthur's (2006) treatment of boundaryless careers as necessarily involving physical or psychological movement away from the current employer.

In organizations where different types of employee flexibility are increasingly valued, it may be that interorganizational boundary crossing—focused by managers because it raises the specter of "labor turnover" and "lost resources"—should no longer be considered of pre-eminent importance, and that wider conceptualizations of boundary crossing should be encouraged and the dynamics of career relationships to non-organizational communities should be more carefully examined (Parker, Arthur, and Inkson 2004). Feldman and Ng (2007) usefully survey the literature on career mobility. They note that mobility can occur between jobs, organizations, and occupations; and that the antecedents of mobility are complex and multi-level, including structural and occupational labor market forces, organizational policies and procedures, work-group factors, personal life factors such as family, and individual personality characteristics. For any given individual in a specific situation, the likelihood and likely direction of mobility can therefore be deduced. This approach deals with several co-existing forms of boundaryless career behavior, but covers only objective and not subjective boundarylessness.

Is the crossing of organizational boundaries related to the crossing of non-organizational boundaries such as occupational, industry, social, and work–family ones? Every career stays within some boundaries, and it may even be that the more one crosses one type of boundary, such as organizational, the more one is constrained by others, such as occupational (Bagdadli et al. 2003; Yamashita and Uenoyama 2006). Alternatively, if one conceptualizes boundary crossing as, in part, a psychological predisposition such as the "Big Five" dimension Openness to Experience (Costa and MacRae 1992), then presumably the crossing of one boundary makes the crossing of another *more* likely. The self-generating or self-inhibiting nature of boundaryless career behavior raises intriguing research possibilities.

4.3 Boundaryless International Careers

The recent development of the idea of "boundaryless global careers" (Banai and Harry 2004; Granrose and; Chua 1996) provides an enlightening microcosmic view of the moves, in recent years, from organizational to boundaryless careers thinking. For twenty-five years from its beginnings in the 1970s, consideration of international managerial careers was dominated by the notion of "expatriate assignment" of managers by international organizations (O'Connell 2005). The emphasis in the literature has therefore been on the corporate management of expatriate assignees, for example, their selection, training, support, and succession planning. However, this approach considers only the organizational management of assignees, and not their own motivation; and only short-term rather than long-term boundarylessness. Assignees typically undertake, or accept, expatriation voluntarily for personal and self-development reasons (Osland 1995), and many of them find their careers seriously destabilized by the expatriation and subsequently become more boundaryless (Stahl, Miller, and Tung 2002). Only by considering the perspective of career actors themselves can one understand the subjective and long-term aspects of their careers. Many career actors—for example tourists, migrants, and young people on working sojourns intent on "seeing the world"—travel across international boundaries in pursuit of their careers but are ignored in the organizationally oriented literature (Inkson et al. 1997; Vance 2005).

In recent years, therefore, the focus has moved steadily from approaches emphasizing the corporate management of expatriate assignments (Tung 1987) to the notion of managers who pursue itinerant international careers (Suutari 2003), and thereby become cosmopolitan "global managers" who self-manage their careers, who may work for different organizations that are independent of each other (Banai and Harry 2004), and who even develops a unique and powerful "internationalism career anchor" (Suutari and Taka 2004). Cappellen and Janssens (2005) consider global career paths as being determined by the intersection of three domains: organizational, individual, and global environment. Studies of international global managers and their careers are increasing.

4.4 Boundaryless Careers and Social Structure

Another misconception of boundaryless careers is that in contrast to careers mediated by bureaucratic organizations they are an expression of pure, unconstrained, individual agency. However, the original book (Arthur and Rousseau 1996) included chapters by, for example, sociologists Howard Aldrich and Charles Perrow, economists Michael Best and Anna Lee Saxenian, and organizational theorists Ray Miles and Karl Weick, whose interests were much very wider than careers, and who drew attention to intriguing interactions between careers and wider aspects of social and economic life. This has enabled the boundaryless career concept to help to illuminate theories of organization and society (e.g. Peiperl, Arthur, and Anand 2002).

Tams and Arthur (2006, 45) noted that: "The reality of boundaryless careers is neither unconstrained by social structure nor exclusively regulated by market principles.... Boundaryless careers are embedded within social networks, institutional environments and communities." Thus, individuals rendered boundaryless by changes in conventional employment structures may utilize aspects of the environment to manufacture their own boundaries for self-protection. For example, Currie, Tempest, and Starkey (2006) noted that television industry employees had responded to restructuring and marginalization in their industry by grouping together in specialist supplying organizations as a form of self-protection, while in a large retail bureaucracy, massive middle management layoffs had caused the survivors to develop such a strong *occupational* commitment as to hinder organizational teamwork, flexibility, and competitiveness.

While organization theory has tended to see careers as *outcomes* of organizational functioning (Nystrom and; MacArthur 1989), boundaryless careers thinking lends itself to novel understandings of how careers might be *causes* of organizational phenomena and even industries (e.g., Peterson and Anand 2002; Higgins 2006). Theories of structuration (Giddens 1979) that enable boundaryless careers to be linked to wider institutions in two-way systems of cause and effect have been propounded by Arthur, Inkson, and Pringle (1999), Barley (1989), Duberley, Mallon, and Cohen (2006), and Peiperl, Arthur, and Anand (2002).

There is a growing interest in the relationship of boundaryless careers to careerists' social networks. Parker and Arthur (2000) noted the existence, for most individuals, of many communities additional to the employing organization, that they can use for job contacts and career support: these include professional, occupational, industry, alumni, and religious groups. Whereas "political" views of organizational careers suggest that ambitious careerists should cultivate relationships with powerful people within their organization, boundaryless careerists are likely to seek, and utilize, more diverse connections (Raider and Burt 1996). King, Burke, and Pemberton (2005) found that candidates' prior history with their job placement agencies was more important than their experience and qualifications in enabling them to access vacancies.

5. CRITIQUE OF BOUNDARYLESS CAREERS

Criticisms of the boundaryless career tend to be criticisms not of the concept as originally developed but of the way it has been interpreted and proselytized.

In some popular renditions, boundaryless careers have been over-promoted as an ideal. A "rhetoric of boundaryless careers" (Hirsch and Shanley 1996) has to some extent replaced the rhetoric of organizational careers (Gowler and Legge 1989) as a compelling image for the new millennium. The connotations of boundaryless career are of free individual choice and purposive, self-bettering boundary crossing. The rhetoric presents images of talented men and women, liberated from the constraints of organizational life, moving autonomously to exciting opportunities and developing ever more interesting and prosperous careers. While this may be the reality for some, for many boundarylessness simply means insecurity (Hirsch and Shanley 1996). Managers who change jobs too frequently may find that this creates obstacles to salary attainment (Mao 2004) and access to permanent vacancies (King, Burke, and Pemberton 2005).

A focus on boundaryless careers may also mask the deprivation and marginalization of a large section of the workforce—those with low status in terms of background, gender, and skills (Pringle and Mallon 2003). These people may *seem* boundaryless, and uncommitted to organizations, in their career behavior; but they may be bounded instead by crushing structural constraints. Unskilled people are often mobile not by choice but because they are at the mercy of the labor market, and must keep moving—for example between different short-term contracts or casual situations—to find any work at all. By making the individual totally responsible for his or her career and by applying market forces logic at the level of the individual, boundaryless careers arguably assist those with skills in demand only at the expense of those on the margins of the workforce (Pringle and Mallon 2003). Groups such as unskilled workers, women, ethnic minorities, and long-service middle-aged managers may lack organizational and institutional protection and thus require and deserve the protection of employer patronage. Fenwick (2006) suggests that workers who develop portfolio careers increase their liberation and their exploitation simultaneously, and need to protect themselves from the latter by educating their clients. And according to Van Buren (2003), boundaryless careers create an ethical responsibility for managers to ensure their employees remain employable elsewhere.

6. Implications for Individuals

The promise—and threat—of boundaryless careers to individuals is that they cannot rely on employing organizations to look after their careers. For example, employer support for an employee to complete a professional qualification or MBA may be a good corporate investment if that employee remains loyal for thirty years, but a poor use of resources if he or she immediately progresses elsewhere. But when boundaryless careers force individuals to take responsibility for their own careers in a fluid and insecure environment, the investment rules change. Members of the workforce are no longer the beneficiaries of corporate investments, but must rather choose what investments of their own time and energy to make in the organization.

DeFillippi and Arthur (1996) promulgated a competency-based framework for individual responses to boundaryless careers, arguing that career actors accumulate competencies through their experience, and utilize these both as markers of their development and as "capital" to invest in career opportunities. "Knowing-why" competencies are expressions of individual motivation, values, and identity, which can guide individuals in their choices of occupation, organization, or project. "Knowing-how" competencies are skills and expertise derived from education, training, prior experience, and non-work sources that act as a reservoir of resources to do specific jobs. "Knowing-whom" competencies are based on personal networks through which the individual can access career-relevant opportunities, learning, and support. Each type of competency provides opportunities for the individual to develop the other types. Understanding one's own competencies, their relationship to opportunities in the wider economic environment, and their likely development in future jobs, is the basis of career success in a boundaryless world.

The competency-based model is in keeping with that proposed 100 years ago in the world's first career theory: understand yourself—understand the world of work—use "true reason" to find a match between the two (Parsons 1909). But the competency-based model enhances Parsons' basic formula by explicitly delineating three key types of competency, including knowing-whom, or social capital, which has been shown to be critical to career development (Granovetter 1974) but which gets little mention in the mainstream careers literature. The competency-based model also conceptualizes both self and world-of-work as dynamic and changing (for example, the future as well as the present world of work must be studied), and adds the notion of personal investment and return. In the derived practice of "career capitalism," the individual consciously views each potential project or job as an opportunity to invest, with a view to building an improved stock of knowing-why, knowing-how, and knowing-whom capital (Inkson and Arthur 2001).

Compared with traditional careers advice—for example about initial vocational choice—the new careers principles emphasize coping with transience and insecurity. For example, among the ideas advocated by Arthur, Inkson, and Pringle (1999) for young people are: experimenting with options deliberately chosen for their discontinuity; the self-designed apprenticeship (sacrificing earning for learning, finding one's own mentors, and tailoring learning experiences to one's inclinations); and working holidays around the world (to develop versatility, self-confidence, and cross-cultural skills in contexts that mirror the uncertainties of the wider economic scene).

To coming generations, career improvization may be as important as career planning. Individuals may seek to source careers advice not just from organizational mentors but from wide "developmental networks" including both intra organizational and extra-organizational supporters (Higgins and Kram 2001). Organizational support for career—for example, through personal development opportunities and performance evaluation—will continue to be important, but will be seen not so much as a means for the organization to improve its stock of human resources, but rather as an opportunity for the individual to acquire new career competencies.

7. BOUNDARYLESS CAREERS AND ORGANIZATIONAL MANAGEMENT

In essence, organizational careers are an outcome of bureaucracy. The organization's work is compartmentalized into a set of job descriptions, and a hierarchy of positions enables the individual to develop a career while simultaneously acquiring knowledge of the organization and commitment to its goals. Individual career competencies are thus subordinated to, and developed in accordance with, company goals. In contrast, today's and tomorrow's organizations must recognize the validity of, and continuing change in, employee aspirations, the likelihood that these may be best met in a succession of different organizations, and the labor market power that many employees possess. The essence of the solution is to move from the management of careers as *resources* to the management of career-relevant *relationships*. Employers must cede to employees the right to a personal careers perspective that may include other work partners.

Some careers remain organizational. Some boundaryless careers contain periods, particularly in mid-career and late career, when the individual, for reasons of family cycle or personal energy, seeks to maintain stability in his/her career. So boundaryless careers are not a reason for any organization to give up its normal practices supporting its members' careers. The main practices are job postings (advertising vacancies internally first), support/reimbursement for tuition, performance appraisal, counseling by either manager or HR specialist, job rotation, succession planning, formal mentoring, and systematic career paths (Baruch and Peiperl 2000). These are likely to continue to present desirable options for many employees. And of course, organizations can continue to promulgate high-commitment HR practices (Pfeffer 1998).

But organizations also need to recognize the benefits available to them from new boundaryless employees and contractors who have elsewhere gained experience that potentially provides the organization with novel assets. Careers are repositories of knowledge (Bird 1996), and a smart organization can benefit from the knowledge and contacts brought in through the career mobility of even its short-term members. Instead of merely worrying about the loss of institutional knowledge by departing staff, organizations need to learn how to secure short-term commitment and teamwork from mobile professionals, contractors, and contingent workers and how to identify and institutionalize these workers' special expertise within the organization before they move on. They need to know how to adjust organizational form and purpose to utilize talented recruits' career energies rather than trying to force them to conform to some corporate plan, and how to utilize external project and occupational communities in place of corporate communities and culture. Also, organizations and their employees need to be able openly to discuss the latter's possibly boundaryless careers, and not simply to consider such individuals disloyal (Ito and Brotheridge 2005). Open discussion about such matters may paradoxically lead to greater long-term loyalty (Parker and Inkson 1999).

8. CONCLUSION

The boundaryless career type provides us with a model of career development which appears to have some advantages over traditional occupational or organizational models. In a changing environment, it encourages mobility, flexibility, the development of knowledge and networks, and the taking of responsibility for one's own career. It also resonates effectively with the temporary organization structures and "knowledge workers" (DeFillippi, Arthur, and Lindsay 2006) becoming characteristic of the new century. And there is evidence that it is associated with career success and "marketability" both inside and outside the organization (Eby, Butts, and Lockwood 2003).

In relation to future development and research it may no longer be appropriate to try to define the boundaryless career concept to death, but rather to think more broadly of a boundaryless career *perspective* (Michael Arthur, personal communication, May 2007). In that light, the six meanings from Arthur and Rousseau (1996) outlined at the beginning of this chapter, map out a range of overlapping issues, each with a common core that encourages us to think in wider terms than a simple organizational-versus-boundaryless duality. The boundaryless careers perspective shows great potential to facilitate major developments in integrative theories not just of careers but of wider aspects of economic and business life, as well as improved careers-related practices by both individuals and organizations. It is to be hoped that in coming years, all those challenges will be taken up.

REFERENCES

ACKAH, C., and HEATON, N. 2004. The reality of the "new careers" for men and women. *Journal of European Industrial Training*, 2 (4): 141–58.

ARTHUR, M. B., ed. (1994). *The Boundaryless Career*. Special Issue, *Journal of Organizational Behaviour*, 15(4).

—— and ROUSSEAU, D., eds. 1996. *The Boundaryless Career: A New Employment Principle for a New Organizational Era*. New York: Oxford University Press.

ARTHUR, M. B., INKSON, K., and PRINGLE, J. K. 1999. *The New Careers: Individual Action and Economic Change*. London, UK: Sage.

—— KHAPOVA, S. N., and WILDEROM, C. P. M. 2005. Career success in a boundaryless career world. *Journal of Organizational Behavior*, 26 (2): 177–202.

ASHKENAS, R., ULRICH, D., JICK, T., and KERR, S. 1995. *The Boundaryless Organization: Breaking the Chains of Organizational Structure*. San Francisco: Jossey-Bass.

BAGDADLI, S., SOLARI, L., USAI, A., and GRANDORI, A. 2003. The emergence of career boundaries in unbounded industries: career odysseys in the Italian new economy. *International Journal of Human Resource Management*, 14 (5): 788–808.

BANAI, M., and HARRY, W. 2004. Boundaryless global careers. *International Studies of Management and Organization*, 34 (3): 96–120.

BARLEY, S. R. 1989. Careers, identities and institutions: the legacy of the Chicago School of Sociology. Pp. 41–65 in *Handbook of Career Theory*, ed. M. B. Arthur, D. T. Hall, and B. S. Lawrence. Cambridge: Cambridge University Press.

BARUCH, Y. 2004. *Managing Careers: Theory and practice*. Harlow: FT-Prentice Hall/Pearson.

—— and; PEIPERL, M. A. 2000. Career management practices: an empirical survey and theoretical implications. *Human Resource Management*, 39 (4): 347–66.

BECKER, K. H., and HAUNSCHILD, A. 2003. The impact of boundaryless careers on organizational decision making: an analysis from the perspective of Luhmann's theory of social systems. *International Journal of Human Resource Management*, 14 (5): 713–27.

BIRD, A. 1996. Careers as repositories of knowledge: considerations for boundaryless careers. Pp. 150–68 in *The Boundaryless Career: A New Employment Principle for a New Organizational Era*, ed. M. B. Arthur and D. M. Rousseau. New York: Oxford University Press.

BRISCOE, J. P., and HALL, D. T. 2006. The interplay of boundaryless and protean careers: combinations and implications. *Journal of Vocational Behavior*, 69: 4–18.

BROWN, D., and; Associates. 2002. *Career Choice and Development*, 4th edn. San Francisco: Jossey-Bass.

CAPPELLEN, T., and JANSSENS, M. 2005. Career paths of global managers: towards future research. *Journal of World Business*, 40: 348–60.

COSTA, P. T., and McCRAE, R. R. 1992. Normal personality assessment in clinical practice: the NEO Personality Inventory. *Psychological Assessment*, 4: 5–13, 20–2.

CURRIE, G., TEMPEST, S., and STARKEY, K. 2006. New careers for old? Organizational and individual responses to changing boundaries. *International Journal of Human Resource Management*, 17 (4): 755–74.

DANY, F., MALLON, M., and ARTHUR, M. B., eds. 2003. *Careers and Human Resource Management*. Special Issue, *International Journal of Human Resource Management*, 14 (5).

DEFILLIPPI, R. J., and ARTHUR, M. B. 1996. Boundaryless contexts and career: a competency-based perspective. Pp. 116–31 in *The Boundaryless Career: A New Employment Principle for a New Organizational Era*, ed. M. B. Arthur and D. M. Rousseau. New York: Oxford University Press.

—— —— and LINDSAY, V. J. 2006. *Knowledge at Work: Creative Collaboration in the Global Economy*. Oxford: Blackwell.

DRUCKER, P. F. 1954. *The Practice of Management*. New York: Harper.

—— 1994. The age of social transformation. *The Atlantic Monthly* (Nov.): 53–80.

DUBERLEY, J., MALLON, M., and COHEN, L. 2006. Exploring career transitions: accounting for structure and agency. *Personnel Review*, 35 (3): 281–96.

EBY, L. T., BUTTS, M., and LOCKWOOD, A. 2003. Predictors of success in the era of the boundaryless career. *Journal of Organizational Behavior*, 24 (6): 689–708.

FAYOL, H. 1949. *General and Industrial Management*. London: Pitman. (Originally published in 1916.)

FELDMAN, D. C., and NG, T. W. H. 2007. Careers: mobility, embeddedness and success. *Journal of Management*, 33: 350–77.

FENWICK, T. J. 2006. Contradictions in portfolio careers: work design and client relations. *Career Development International*, 11 (1): 65–79.

GIDDENS, A. 1979. *Central Problems in Social Theory*. Berkeley, CA: University of California Press.

GOFFEE, R., and SCASE, R. 1992. Organizational change and the corporate career: the restructuring of managers' aspirations. *Human Relations*, 45: 363–85.

GOULDNER, A. W. 1957. Cosmopolitans and locals: towards an analysis of latent social roles. *Administrative Science Quarterly*, 2 (3): 281–306.

GOWLER, D., and LEGGE, K. 1989. Rhetoric and bureaucratic careers: managing the meaning of management success. Pp. 437–53 in *Handbook of Career Theory*, ed. M. B. Arthur, D. T. Hall, and B. S. Lawrence. Cambridge: Cambridge University Press.

GRANOVETTER, M. 1974. *Getting a Job: A Study of Contacts and Careers*. Cambridge, MA: Harvard University Press.

GRANROSE, C. S., and BACCILI, P. A. 2006. Do psychological contracts include boundaryless and protean careers? *Career Development International*, 11 (2): 163–82.

—— and CHUA, B. L. 1996. Global boundaryless careers: lessons from Chinese family businesses. Pp. 201–17 in *The Boundaryless Career: A New Employment Principle for a New Organizational Era*, ed. M. B. Arthur, and D. M. Rousseau. New York: Oxford University Press.

HALL, D. T. 1976. *Careers in Organizations*. Glenview, IL: Scott Foresman.

—— 2002. *Careers in and out of Organizations*. Thousand Oaks, CA: Sage.

—— and; Associates. 1996. *The Career is Dead: Long Live the Career*. San Francisco: Jossey-Bass.

HANDY, C. 1989. *The Age of Unreason*. Boston: Harvard Business School Press.

HECKSCHER, C. 1995. *White Collar Blues: Management Loyalties in an Age of Corporate Restructuring*. New York: Basic Books.

HIGGINS, M. C. 2006. *Career Imprints: Creating Leaders across an Industry*. San Francisco: Wiley.

—— and KRAM, K. E. 2001. Reconceptualizing mentoring at work: a developmental network perspective. *Academy of Management Review*, 26: 264–88.

HIRAKUBO, N. 1999. The end of lifetime employment. *Business Horizons*, 42 (Nov.–Dec.): 41–6.

HIRSCH, P. M., and SHANLEY, M. 1996. The rhetoric of boundaryless: or, how the newly empowered managerial class bought into its own marginalization. Pp. 218–33 in *The Boundaryless Career: A New Employment Principle for a New Organizational Era*, ed. M. B. Arthur and D. M. Rousseau. New York: Oxford University Press.

HOLLAND, J. E. 1997. *Making Vocational Choices: A Theory of Vocational Personalities and Work Environments*, 2nd edn. Odessa, FL: Psychological Assessment Resources.

INKSON, K. 1995. The effects of changing economic conditions on managerial job change and careers. *British Journal of Management*, 6: 183–94.

—— 2006. Protean and boundaryless careers as metaphors. *Journal of Vocational Behavior*, 69 (1): 48–63.

INKSON, K. 2007. *Understanding Careers: The Metaphors of Working Lives.* Thousand Oaks, CA: Sage Publications.

—— and ARTHUR, M. B. 2001. How to be a successful career capitalist. *Organizational Dynamics*, 31 (3): 48–61.

—— —— PRINGLE, J., and BARRY S. 1997. Expatriate assignment versus overseas experience: contrasting models of human resource development. *Journal of World Business*, 14 (4): 151–68.

ITO, J. K., and BROTHERIDGE, C. M. 2005. Does supporting employees' career adaptability lead to commitment, turnover, or both? *Human Resource Management*, 44 (1): 5–19.

ITUMA, A., and SIMPSON, R. 2005. The chameleon career: an exploratory study of the work biography of information technology workers in Nigeria. *Career Development International*, 11 (1): 48–65.

JOHNSON, M. K., and MORTIMER, J. T. 2002. Career choice and development from a sociological perspective. Pp. 37–81 in *Career Choice and Development*, 4th edn., D. Brown and; Associates. San Francisco: Jossey-Bass.

KING, Z., BURKE, S., and PEMBERTON, J. 2005. The "bounded" career: an empirical study of human capital, career mobility and outcomes in a mediated labour market. *Human Relations*, 58: 981–1007.

MCCABE, V. S., and SAVERY, L. K. 2007. "Butterflying", a new career pattern for Australia: empirical evidence. *Journal of Management Development*, 26 (2): 103–16.

MAINIERO, L. A., and SULLIVAN, S. E. 2005. *The Opt-out Revolt: Why People are Leaving Companies to Create Kaleidoscopic Careers.* Palo Alto, CA: Davies-Black Publishing.

MAO, H.-Y. 2004. Voluntary employer changes and salary attainment of managers. *International Journal of Human Resource Management*, 15 (1): 180–95.

NYSTROM, P. C., and MACARTHUR, A. W. 1989. Propositions linking organizations and careers. In *Handbook of Career Theory*, ed. M. B. Arthur, D. T. Hall, and B. A. Lawrence. Cambridge: Cambridge University Press.

O'CONNELL, J. 2005. Expatriate assignment. *Blackwell Encyclopaedic Dictionary of International Management.* London: Blackwell.

OSLAND, J. S. 1995. *The Adventure of Working Abroad: Hero Tales from the Global Frontier.* San Francisco: Jossey-Bass.

OUCHI, W. 1981. *Theory Z: How American Business can Meet the Japanese Challenge.* Reading, MA: Addison-Wesley.

PARKER, P., and ARTHUR, M. B. 2000. Careers, organizing and Community. Pp. 99–121 in *Career Frontiers: New Conceptions of Working Lives*, ed. M. A. Peiperl, M. B. Arthur, R. Goffee, and T. Morris. Oxford: Oxford University Press.

—— and INKSON, K. 1999. New forms of career: the challenge to human resource management. *Asia-Pacific Journal of Human Resources*, 37 (1): 67–76.

—— ARTHUR, M. B., and INKSON, K. 2004. Career communities: a preliminary exploration of member-defined career support structures. *Journal of Organizational Behavior*, 27: 489–514.

PARSONS, F. 1909. *Choosing a Vocation.* Boston: Houghton Mifflin.

PEIPERL, M. A., and BARUCH, Y. 1997. Back to square zero: the post-corporate career. *Organizational Dynamics*, 25 (4): 7–22.

—— ARTHUR, M. B., and ANAND, N., eds. 2002. *Career Creativity: Explorations in the Remaking of Work.* Oxford: Oxford University Press.

PETERS, T. J. 1988. *Thriving on Chaos: A Handbook for Management Revolution.* London: Macmillan.

—— and WATERMAN, R. H. 1982. *In Search of Excellence: Lessons from America's Best-Run Companies.* New York: Harper and Row.

PETERSON, R. A., and ANAND, N. 2002. How chaotic careers create orderly fields. In *Career Creativity: Explorations in the Re-making of Work*, ed. M. A. Peiperl, M. B. Arthur, and N. Anand. Oxford: Oxford University Press.

PFEFFER, J. 1998. *The Human Equation: Building Profits by Putting People First.* Boston: Harvard Business School Press.

PRINGLE, J. K., and MALLON, M. 2003. Challenges to the Boundaryless Career Odyssey. *International Journal of Human Resource Management*, 14 (5): 839–53.

RAIDER, H. J., and BURT, R. S. 1996. Boundaryless carers and social capital. Pp. 187–200 in *The Boundaryless Career: A New Employment Principle for a New Organizational Era*, ed. M. B. Arthur and D. M. Rousseau. New York: Oxford University Press.

REARDON, R. C., LENZ, J. G., SAMPSON, J. P., and PETERSON, G. W. 2006. *Career Planning and Development: A Comprehensive Approach*, 2nd edn. Mason, OH: Thomson.

SCHEIN, E. H. 1978. *Career Dynamics: Matching Individual and Organizational Needs.* Reading, MA: Addison-Wesley.

STAHL, G. K., MILLER, E. L., and TUNG, R. L. 2002. Toward the boundaryless career: a closer look at the expatriate career concept and the perceived implications of an international assignment. *Journal of World Business*, 37: 216–27.

SULLIVAN, S. E., and ARTHUR, M. B. 2006. The evolution of the boundaryless career concept: examining physical and psychological mobility. *Journal of Vocational Behavior*, 69: 19–29.

SUPER, D. E. 1990. A life-span, life-space approach to career development. Pp. 197–261 in *Career Choice and Development*, 2nd edn., ed. D. Brown, L. Brooks, and Associates. San Francisco: Jossey-Bass.

SUUTARI, V. 2003. Global managers: career orientation, career tracks, life-style implications and career commitment. *Journal of Managerial Psychology*, 18: 185–207.

—— and TAKA, M. 2004. Career anchors of managers with global careers. *Journal of Management Development*, 23 (9): 833–47.

TAMS, S., and ARTHUR, M. B. 2006. Boundaryless careers. Pp. 44–9 in *Encyclopaedia of Career Development*, vol. 1, i, ed. J. H. Greenhaus and G. A. Callanan. Thousand Oaks, CA: Sage.

TUNG, R. L. 1987. Expatriate assignments: enhancing success and minimizing failure. *Academy of Management Executive*, 1 (2): 117–25.

US DEPARTMENT OF LABOR. 2006. *National Longitudinal Survey of Youth 1979.* Bureau of Labor Statistics. <www.bls.gov/nls/>, accessed May 5, 2007.

VAN BUREN V., III. 2003. Boundaryless careers and employability obligations. *Business Ethics Quarterly*, 13 (2): 131–49.

VANCE, C. M. 2005. The personal quest for building global competence: a taxonomy of self-initiating career path strategies for gaining business experience abroad. *Journal of World Business*, 40 (4): 374–85.

WEBER, M. 1947. *The Theory of Social and Economic Organization.* New York: Free Press. Originally published in 1922.

YAMASHITA, M., and UENOYAMA, T. 2006. Boundaryless career and adaptive HR practices in Japan's hotel industry. *Career Development International*, 11 (3): 230–42.

THE CHALLENGE
OF REMOTE
WORKING

DONALD HISLOP

CAROLYN AXTELL

KEVIN DANIELS

1. INTRODUCTION

REMOTE working has many synonyms—such as teleworking, telecommuting, or virtual working. It is often considered to be enabled by advanced information and communications technologies (ICTs) that allow the electronic transfer of information so that workers can communicate and coordinate tasks in multiple locations and asynchronously. It is the purpose of this chapter to explore the nature, consequences, and management of remote working. We start by examining the incidence of remote working, the major aspects of remote work, and why this form of working is attractive. We then move on to explore workers' experience of remote work. The next section examines issues in the coordination of remote teams and communication between remote workers. In the final section, we will examine the management of remote workers.

2. BACKGROUND: WHO WORKS REMOTELY AND WHAT IS REMOTE WORKING?

Although estimates of remote working have to be assembled by considering a variety of sources (e.g., Felstead, Jewson, and Walters 2005), the various sources converge on the conclusion that remote workers are a significant and growing segment of the labor force in industrial economies.

In 1998, European Commission estimates put the figure at up to 4 million teleworkers in the European Union (EU), representing 3.1 percent of the EU workforce. In 2000, estimates of the number of teleworkers in the EU had risen to around 5 percent engaged in some form of teleworking (Paoli and Merllié 2001). By 2002, 3.79 million UK workers were estimated to work from home at least one day per week, representing an increase of nearly 27 percent from 1997 (Felstead et al. 2005). Felstead et al. also estimated an increase of over 230 percent in the UK between 1981 and 2002 in workers using their home as a base but working mainly at other locations. In the US, according to some sources, there were over 28 million teleworkers in 2001 (Mokhtarian, Salomon, and Choo 2005). At the same time, in Eastern European transitional economies, some 8 percent of the Polish and Slovenian and 9 percent of the Czech labor forces were estimated to engage in teleworking at least some of the time (Paoli and Parent-Thirion 2003).

Some of the variation between countries can be attributed to the extent to which information technology is used in a country and therefore the range of IT skills prevalent in a country's labor force (Tregaskis 2000). However, other factors may also influence the degree of teleworking in a country, including the availability of knowledge workers in a labor market, the geographical dispersion of the labor force, societal attitudes towards work as communal activity, and the vulnerability of commuters to extreme weather conditions (e.g., Daniels, Lamond, and Standen 2001).

The opinions of key stakeholders, such as managers, may be critical in influencing the adoption of remote working, and the communication of the benefits of remote working may sway these opinions (Daniels et al. 2001). Potential benefits of remote working can be discerned for individuals and organizations (see Daniels et al. 2001). At the individual level, benefits might include reduced commuting, greater work autonomy, more flexible working hours, and better work/life balance. Organizations may benefit from, for example, improved employee retention, greater staffing flexibility, and reduced facilities costs. However, such benefits may not be realized or make up merely part of a rhetorical case for remote working.

Importantly, the benefits and costs of remote working seem to be tied closely to the nature of remote working. Ways of conceptualizing remote working have increased in sophistication since early definitions of telework characterized it as work at a location other than a traditional office plus the use of ICTs (e.g., Gray, Hodson, and Gordon 1993). Daniels et al. (2001) considered that teleworking consists of at least five major aspects: the location of work; the extent to which work involves the use of ICTs; the extent of communication with others external to the organization; the extent of communication with others in the same organization; and the knowledge intensity of the work. These aspects are considered to be dynamic with, for example, teleworkers changing the location of their work. Daniels et al. also considered *teleworkers* to be characterized by at least some use of ICTs in their work. However, a more inclusive view of *remote workers* can be obtained by also considering those workers who do not make use of ICTs, but do work from non-traditional industrial work locations, such as the home.

In terms of location, remote workers can then be characterized as: working from home; working from remote work premises including remote office sites, "satellite offices" (controlled by the employer) or other rented facilities; working nomadically, where travel is required to perform some tasks and other tasks might be carried out during travel; or some combination of the above alongside working in a traditional organizational location, such as a main office. Remote workers can also be distinguished by the extent to which they use ICTs, both in terms of hardware (e.g., laptop, PDA, mobile telephone) and software (e.g., Bluetooth, remote access intranets, e-mail), as well as by the extent work entails communication with others in and outside of the organization. Here communication refers both to the frequency of contacts and the range of contacts. Software engineers working at home may use a broader array of hardware and software in order to communicate with members of the same small team, resolve problems, and compile programs than a management consultant working on a report at home, who may use a telephone to communicate with many clients.

Remote workers can also be distinguished by the knowledge intensity of the work. The worker assembling goods at home would be distinguished from the home-based software engineer, the call centre worker at a satellite office from the civil engineer in an on-site office, and the car mechanic with a Bluetooth mobile phone, computer, and satellite navigation on-board a work van from the management consultant also with Bluetooth connectivity, satellite navigation, and a laptop. It is likely that knowledge-intensive remote work is associated with high salaries, high levels of educational attainment, high trust from management, entitlements from work such as training opportunities, and significant latitude over both working processes and the location of work (Felstead, Jewson, and Phizakalea 2002).

So different forms of remote work can be considered to vary as a matter of degree across multiple dimensions. Such complexity makes it difficult to derive clear conclusions concerning remote workers per se, but does go some way to explaining the variation between studies in worker reactions to remote work.

3. THE EXPERIENCE OF BEING A REMOTE TELEWORKER

This section focuses on the experience of what it is like to be a remote worker. It begins by looking at the employment relationship of remote workers. It then compares the rhetoric and reality of the claims that remote working, and home-based working in particular, is a family-friendly form of work. The section then looks at the topics of stress and well-being, before concluding by examining how the experiences of male and female remote workers vary.

Although remote workers are a heterogeneous group with different work patterns, levels of technology use, occupations and employment conditions, academic work on the experience of remote working has not examined all types of remote worker equally. This literature has largely focused on employed, managerial/professional remote workers who spend some time working in their offices and homes.

3.1 Employment Relationship

Few studies have examined how the employment relationship of remote workers affects their experiences of remote working. One important study on the introduction of home-based working found that staff that became homeworkers felt that their employer had let them down badly in how they both managed the transition into teleworking and the lack of ongoing support provided (Harris 2003). As a consequence of their experiences, these workers felt their employer had ruptured their employment relationship, with turnover levels trebling in the year following the implementation of the home teleworking scheme. Thus, managing the transition into remote working and providing adequate ongoing support for remote workers appears to be key to sustaining loyalty and commitment.

3.2 Work–Life Balance/Boundary: Rhetoric and Reality

Much of the early literature on remote working, and particularly that focused on home-based teleworking, suggested that one advantage of this form of work was that it made achieving and sustaining an effective work–life balance easier than for workers who worked purely at their employer's premises (Bryant 2000; Felstead et al. 2002). As will be seen, the experience of remote working is not as clear cut as this rhetoric suggests.

Before examining the topic of work–life balance, it is useful to examine the nature of the work–life boundary of remote workers. For workers who work at their employers' sites, such as offices and factories, there is typically a discrete spatial and temporal boundary between work and non-work domains: work occurs in a particular location, during particular hours, with non-work activities occurring at other times in other locations. The spatial and temporal separation of work and life with remote workers who regularly work off site, and particularly with home-based teleworking, is much more blurred (Tietze and Musson 2005). However, the nature of the spatio-temporal boundary is shaped by the behavior, actions, and preferences of individual homeworkers. So for example, Kossek, Lautsch, and Eaton (2006) identified two different types of work–life boundary management strategy used by teleworkers, one concerned with integrating work and non-work time and the other with maintaining a clear separation between them.

Effectively achieving and sustaining a satisfactory boundary between work and home is not always straightforward, and can be a source of conflict and stress. For example, Harris (2003) found that two-thirds of the forty home teleworkers she studied experienced tensions in managing the boundary between work and non-work time. Similarly, it seems that whatever spatial arrangements teleworkers adopt, conflicts and tensions still exist, with both domestic factors intruding upon work (for example young children at home making noise) and work intruding upon domestic factors (for example with spouses being concerned about who to bring home) (Felstead et al. 2005).

Notwithstanding such conflicts, a number of comparative studies do indicate that home-based workers are generally able to achieve a better work–life balance compared to office-based workers (Collins 2005; Golden 2006a). Hill, Ferris, and Märtinson (2003) surveyed office-based, home-based, and mobile (or nomadic) workers in terms of how happy they were with the work–life balance they had. Their findings agreed with other comparative studies, that home workers are able to achieve a better work–life balance than office-based workers, but they found that it was mobile workers who had the poorest level of work–life balance.

A number of qualitative studies of home-based working also confirm these findings, and provide some explanations for why working at home can allow an effective work–life balance to be achieved. For example, Baines (2002) found that for some of the self-employed media workers she interviewed, their work did closely resemble the positive image of home teleworking advocates. Bryant (2000) found that home teleworking provided workers with significant levels of temporal flexibility, which allowed greater scope than was available to office-based workers to manage work and domestic commitments. Similarly, Baruch (2000) found that while family-related stresses increased for the home teleworkers, overall the teleworkers interviewed felt that working at home had both improved their family relationships and reduced the amount of work-related stress they experienced. Finally, Tremblay (2002) found that home teleworking was attractive to workers as it eliminated travel time and allowed them to be at home during important times of the day, such as when children were departing for, and returning from, school.

However, while home teleworkers generally appear to find it easier to achieve a positive work–life balance than workplace-based workers, this does not mean they experience no work–life conflict. One relatively common source of conflict is over the use of phone and computer equipment in the home. For example, Baines (2002) found this to be a common source of conflict, with for example one female worker trying to do work on the home computer in the evening when her husband wanted to use it for leisure purposes. Another common source of conflict for home teleworkers is over the use of space in the home. Tietze and Musson (2005) found that home teleworking that involved the use of non-specific, shared domestic space could cause resentment among family members, due to perceptions that work was taking over the domestic environment.

Golden, Veiga, and Simsek (2006) separated out directionality in work–life conflict and examined both the extent to which work intruded on domestic matters and vice-versa. Golden et al. concluded that the greater the amount of time teleworkers spent working in the home, the less work was found to interfere with domestic issues, but the more domestic issues intruded upon work time. This finding about domestic matters intruding upon work being a common source of work–life conflict is reinforced by other studies (Lapierre and Allen 2006; Mann and Holdsworth 2003).

Finally, a number of studies suggest that work–life conflict caused by domestic intrusions on work was not experienced equally by all types of teleworker. Bryant's (2000) study of telework in Canada, found a gendered pattern with this type of domestic intrusion on work. While a significant number of the women she studied had to frequently delay some work tasks until the evening due to domestic and childcare responsibilities encroaching on their working day, this was not the case for any of the men studied. Kossek et al. (2006) found that the type of work–life boundary management strategy used by workers influenced how likely work–life conflict would be. Those adopting an integrationist strategy were found to have higher levels of work–life conflict than those adopting a separation-based strategy.

3.3 Health and Well-Being

Another important question regarding the experience of teleworking is the impact it has on health and well-being. Some recent reviews conclude that there is insufficient strong evidence to indicate that teleworking influences psychological or physical well-being (Bailey and Kurland 2002; De Croon et al. 2005). Some primary empirical studies indicate no differences in measures of well-being between teleworkers and traditional office workers (Lapierre and Allen 2006; Mann and Holdsworth 2003) or even between different kinds of teleworkers (Garrett and Danzinger 2007). On the other hand, there are studies that indicate that teleworking is associated with better well-being at work across a range of indicators such as job satisfaction and work exhaustion, as well as being associated with higher levels of organizational commitment and motivation (Collins 2005; Golden 2006a; Montreuil and Lippel 2003). There is also some suggestion that teleworking is associated with shorter spells of sickness absence for home-based teleworkers (Montreuil and Lippel 2003).

A number of explanations for these discrepancies are examined below. First, there may be an optimal level of teleworking. In one survey, the optimal level of teleworking away from the office, as evidenced by the highest level of job satisfaction, was found at around 14–15 hours per week (Golden 2006b). However, whilst there was a rapid increase in satisfaction between low levels of teleworking and 14–15 hours per week, the decline in job satisfaction beyond 14–15 hours was generally very slight. However, it is unknown whether such a conclusion is applicable to all forms of telework or just home-based telework.

Another explanation is that teleworking has a range of influences on work conditions thought to influence well-being (Golden 2006b). In his literature review, Daniels (2000) suggested that many kinds of teleworker may be at risk from experiencing low clarity, low participation in work decisions, high work demands, poor physical work conditions, low support and social isolation from co-workers and have their work attributed as having low social value. More recent evidence supports these suggestions with respect to low participation in decision making (Montreuil and Lippel 2003) and work demands. Such demands might come through an increase in working hours for home-based teleworkers (Dimitrova 2003; Montreuil and Lippel 2003) and especially mobile teleworkers (Garrett and Danzinger 2007). Another source of demands is problems with ICTs (Mann and Holdsworth 2003; Montreuil and Lippel 2003). There is also evidence that teleworkers perceive that complex ICT systems, with their greater propensity for faults and unintentional misuse, can limit productivity (Belanger, Collins, and Cheney 2001).

With respect to reduced support, increased isolation, and reduced social value, evidence is contradictory. Two studies indicate teleworkers have reduced social opportunities (Cooper and Kurland 2002; Mann and Holdsworth 2003), whilst other research indicates that teleworkers do not report any special problems with social issues (Montreuil and Lippel 2003). Moreover, teleworkers in the Mann and Holdsworth study reported social advantages in being removed from office politics. There is also evidence that provision of better communications technology is related to higher teleworker satisfaction (Belanger et al. 2001).

The way in which an organization implements teleworking and the characteristics of teleworkers themselves might also be influential. For example, Donnelly (2004) reported an increase in autonomy, a reduction in working hours, and greater job satisfaction amongst teleworkers choosing this form of working as part of a formalized flexible working package. In respect of teleworker characteristics, self-efficacy and prior experience of teleworking have been found to be related to higher satisfaction with teleworking (Ragurham, Wiesenfeld, and Garud 2003).

3.4 Gender

The final focus in this section is on the extent to which male and female teleworkers have different experiences of home-based teleworking. Primarily, research that has used gender as an analytical lens has typically identified significant differences in the types of work that male and female teleworkers do. Felstead et al. (2001) distinguish between different types of telework based on the amount of time spent working in the home. Felstead et al.'s analysis revealed significant differences between the types of teleworking working done by men and women. They found that women outnumber men in those who mainly worked at home (64 percent compared to 36 percent), while the opposite was true for those who partially worked at home (37 percent women and 63 percent men).

In a separate paper, Felstead et al. (2002) develop another distinction, between those with the option to work at home, and those who have to work at home where a gendered pattern also emerges. Those with the option to work at home were typically privileged workers high up in the organizational hierarchy, were educated to degree level, were employed, worked in managerial/professional occupations, and worked in the private sector. Those with the option to work at home were also more likely to be men than women (60 percent male, 40 percent female). In contrast, those who mainly worked at home, who were more likely to be in routine clerical jobs, were much more likely to be women (75 percent female and 25 percent male). Tremblay's (2002) study of teleworking in Quebec, Canada found patterns of employment that were remarkably similar to Felstead et al.'s (2001; 2002) data: female teleworkers were much more likely than male teleworkers to be full-time, home-based teleworkers, and while female teleworkers typically did routine clerical work, male teleworkers were typically employed in professional/managerial occupations.

4. SOCIAL PROCESSES

This section focuses on the social processes involved in remote working. It starts by outlining some of the differences between part-time and full-time teleworking and goes on to discuss the development of relationships and trust. Finally, it explores the issue of knowledge sharing in remote work.

Whilst there may be few differences between part-time teleworkers and trad-itional office workers in their social processes and intra-organizational communi-cations (e.g., Duxbury and Neufield 1999), full-time teleworkers are likely to experience more disruption, particularly if their work requires collaboration with remote others. For instance, one might expect that the more teleworkers have to interact with distant colleagues (and the greater the number of such links), the more difficult teleworking is (e.g., Belanger et al. 2001).

Thus, the social processes within full-time teleworking relationships are likely to be different and more challenging than the social processes that occur within more traditional co-located work situations or part-time teleworking arrangements, due to physical distance from colleagues and reliance on ICTs. Physical distance between collaborators means there is a lack of face-to-face contact (and so less non-verbal communication, chance encounters, and chats at the water cooler, etc.), and there is often a lack of knowledge about the context in which remote collab-orators are working. Being remote also means there is often a greater reliance on "less rich" ICTs for collaboration (which can be more impoverished than face-to-face, lacking in the social cues that can aid understanding). These issues can have important implications for social processes amongst remote colleagues.

Whilst many experimental studies support the view that computer-mediated communication is more impersonal and that computer-mediated groups are less cohesive than face-to-face groups, many of these were short-term, ad-hoc groups without enough time for stronger relations to develop (Walther 2002). Other experimental studies have found that building relations and trust with a remote colleague may be slower but can develop to equivalent levels as face-to-face collaborations over time (Walther 1992; Wilson, Straus, and McEvily 2006) and that allowing computer-mediated groups longer interaction periods to exchange the same amount of information as face-to-face groups can bring trust up to equivalent levels (Krebs, Hobman, and Bordia 2006).

Other literature, however, suggests that relationship development or attraction to remote colleagues may be immediate and very strong (e.g., Lea, Spears, and De Groot 2001) and so does not necessarily need more time to develop. Some authors argue that this is due to the lack of personal and individuating cues in such circumstances which shifts attention away from individual differences and towards a common group identity based on the social cues that are available (e.g., Spears and Lea 1994). Thus, diversity may be less of a problem in dispersed teams (compared to co-located teams) as the lack of social cues makes such differences less salient. Indeed, Krebs et al. (2006) found partial support for this argument with age differences being negatively related to trust in face-to-face groups but not in computer-mediated groups. However, within dispersed collaborations, even if some individual differences are less observable, location may prove to be a salient cue for self-other categorization (Polzer et al. 2006). People at the same site tend to share a range of attributes (e.g., organizational culture, nationality) which may distinguish them from those at another location, and this can lay down hypothetical dividing lines between subgroups, referred to as "faultlines" by Lau and Murnighan (1998). Stronger faultlines are likely where there are more differences between locations, and these in turn may lead to attenuated performance due to conflict between subgroups, particularly if the subgroups are homogeneous and equal in size (Polzer et al. 2006). Polzer et al. (2006) found that the least strong faultlines occurred in teams where members were each at different sites as there were no location-based subgroups for those individuals to identify with.

For the lone teleworker located away from team members at the main office, there may be an accentuated need for affiliation and identity with the larger organization as it may create feelings of being isolated and different (Thatcher and Zhu 2006). However, their distance might make it harder to create a common identity, in part due to reliance on less rich ICTs for conveying identity information, but also because those at the main site may react negatively to remote teleworkers, questioning their credibility, efficiency, etc. (Thatcher and Zhu 2006). Interestingly, Golden (2006a) found that, although higher levels of teleworking were associated with poorer relationships with colleagues, the relationship with managers improved. He suggested this might be due to greater prioritization of this relationship and compensating for lack of face-to-face contact with regular communications. Of course, it may also be related to the managers' strategy to monitor their remote employees.

Indeed, lack of trust in remote teleworkers has been identified as a key reason why managers do not adopt telework within their workforce (Bailey and Kurland 2002). However, the presence of trust in dispersed collaborations has been related to higher performance (e.g., Jarvenpaa and Leidner 1999) and has been shown to have an impact on members' intentions to exchange information in virtual communities (Ridings, Gefen, and Arinze 2002).

Some theories of trust have emphasized that immediately high trust can occur within new collaborative relationships ("initial trust"—McKnight, Cummings, and Chervany, 1998; and "swift trust"—Meyerson, Weick, and Kramer 1996) and these theories can also be applied to remote relationships. Immediately high trust is argued to be due to a personal disposition to trust, institution-based trust levels and assurances, stereotypic impressions, and adopting a shared identity. However, such positive relations are based on assumptions and only exist in the absence of contraindicating evidence. Thus, trust may reduce over time as negative and more realistic evidence comes to light. In their study of virtual teams, Jarvenpaa and Leidner (1999) found that trust was fragile and reduced (along with performance) for a third of teams who started out with initially high trust. Teams with high trust early on exhibited greater exchange of social information. However, teams who sustained high trust tended to integrate social information into task-oriented messages, so they maintained both social and task performance. Only four of the twenty-nine teams in their sample exhibited a pattern where low trust developed into high trust later on. Most that exhibited low trust early on remained low in trust.

As well as altering the relational dynamics of workgroups, teleworking can also result in a loss of knowledge from the main office. For instance Felstead, Jewson, and Walters (2003) found that in organizations it is often feared that teleworking will impede the sharing of expertise, particularly tacit knowledge. Gaining knowledge remotely may not be straightforward. However, it is likely to be very important for success. For instance, a study of globally distributed systems development teams found that knowledge sharing was associated with successful collaboration (Kotlarsky and Oshri 2005). A shared understanding is typically seen as a precondition for successful collaboration and coordination (Weick and Bougon 1986). Without it, remote colleagues are likely to interpret messages differently based on their different knowledge and understanding, and may falsely assume that they have understood the message in the same way (cf., Krauss and Fussell 1990).

For remote colleagues located at different sites, site differences may also be influential. For instance, Sole and Edmondson (2002) found that misunderstandings were more likely to occur across sites than across functions, due to knowledge that was taken for granted within sites. When face to face, it is easier to share information informally and inadvertently without verbalizing it, as one can see the conditions under which others are working and whether they are conducting certain activities (Hinds and Weisband 2003). However, such implicit processes are not easily available when at a distance and communicating via ICTs.

There may be some advantages to exchanging knowledge and information via asynchronous text-based media, like e-mail, as collaborators have time to think about their answer before replying (Warkentin, Sayeed, and Hightower 1997). However, there are also likely to be some problems. Asynchronous communications like e-mail, as well containing less information than face-to-face communications, can have sequencing problems and lack immediate feedback, which can result in miscommunications that are difficult to resolve (Finholt and Sproull 1990). Different parties may interpret different parts of the same message as salient, and non-response to a message may also be interpreted differently by different people (Cramton 2002). Moreover, lack of trust in the technology as an appropriate medium for sensitive knowledge sharing may be a significant barrier to information exchange (Breu and Hemingway 2004).

Another problem for knowledge sharing is that co-located team members tend to focus on commonly held information (e.g., Stasser and Titus 1985), although they may be more likely to take on board unique information from "out-group" members who are expected to have different perspectives from the "in-group" (Thomas-Hunt, Ogden, and Neale 2003). However, a remote partner's knowledge might be devalued if it deviates from expectations, especially from those of lower status (Sheldon et al. 2006). Moreover, remote collaborators may be even less likely to realize that they hold unique information and may have more difficulty knowing each others' expertise when at a distance and unfamiliar with each other. Assumptions about each other's knowledge may be made based on the stereotypes associated with a person's profession, status or location (Krauss and Fussell 1990) that may not be accurate. People who are more familiar with each other tend to have a better common understanding of each other's expertise (Hollingshead 1998). Therefore, within dispersed collaborations, there is a need to make the different expertise within the team explicit, so that members can be aware of it, as otherwise their knowledge is less visible (Griffith and Neale 2001).

However, much of the above is based on experimental or student-based studies and there may be limitations to applying this knowledge to dispersed teams in work organizations, particularly those that cross significant value boundaries (such as national culture). For instance, Baba et al. (2004) found in a Fortune 500 company that sharing knowledge actually led to greater conflict as the different parties did not consider each other's knowledge as acceptable or valid. This led to reduced contact between the different factions and reduced knowledge sharing. Thus, knowledge sharing is not enough on its own, there is also a need to understand and be open to the reasoning behind these different views. For example, in another study of dispersed work teams, a psychologically safe communication climate (which involves support, openness, trust, mutual respect, and risk taking, where people suspend judgment and remain open to new ideas and perspectives) was found to mitigate the negative impact of geographic dispersion, national diversity, and ICT use (Gibson and Gibbs 2006). This was thought to be due, in part, to psychological safety enabling collaborators to coordinate their work, collect resources across contexts, raise their differences and expectations, admit lack of understanding, ask questions, voice opinions, and resolve conflict. This fostered innovation by allowing different perspectives and viewpoints to be heard, ideas to be merged and differences to be bridged.

5. ORGANIZING REMOTE WORK

The issues and problems identified above raise questions regarding how best to manage remote workers. The chapter thus concludes by examining some of the most important managerial issues.

5.1 Leadership and Management

Hertel, Geister, and Konradt (2005) identified a temporal model of remote/virtual team management and leadership with five key phases. The first phase, "preparation," involves developing a mission statement for the team, personnel selection, task design, development of reward systems, and selection of appropriate technology. Second, "launch" involves activities at the start of the team's life (e.g., kick off workshop, getting to know each other, goal clarification, and development of team protocols and rules). The third phase involves "performance management" and ongoing maintenance of motivation, communication, knowledge management. The fourth phase "team development" includes assessment, training, and evaluation. These last two phases are relevant throughout the team's life. Finally, "disbanding" at the end of the team's life requires proper recognition of the team's achievements.

Certain leadership styles and behaviors have also been identified as suitable within a teleworking/virtual environment. For instance, Kayworth and Leidner (2001) found that the most successful leaders were those who displayed a combination of task-and relationship-oriented behaviors. So, those who were more effective were simultaneously able to provide role clarity, regular, detailed, and prompt communication, be assertive and authoritative at the same time as being understanding, empathic, and providing mentoring for team members. Thus, although relationship building has been identified as a critically important aspect of a leader's role within teleworking environments (e.g., Pauleen 2003), there is still a requirement for task-related leadership.

Other "remote" leadership competencies required include the ability to prevent conflict, promote knowledge sharing, team cohesion and identity, and manage emotional and motivational processes (e.g., Hertel et al. 2005). For instance, as seen earlier, promoting a psychologically safe environment for communication and knowledge sharing would seem to be key to combating the problems of distance (Gibson and Gibbs 2006). Managers need to promote knowledge sharing about team members' individual environments (e.g., through common experiences and mutual training), as well as ensuring equal distribution of information, encouraging the processing of unshared information, and documenting existing knowledge in the team (Hertel et al. 2005). Moreover, managers and leaders need to provide support and advice on issues of work–life balance and managing the boundary between work and home, especially for home-based teleworkers (Harris 2003).

One of the most prevalent debates within the literature is whether remote workers should be managed by trust or control. Although physical distance means that managers cannot observe employees in the traditional manner, modern technology does offer the possibility to monitor employees electronically (e.g., their log on/log off times, work pace, degree of accuracy, e-mail use, phone calls). Such monitoring of teleworkers might be more prevalent in industries that already use such technology, such as call centers (see, for example, Valsecchi 2006), but only allows a narrow range of behaviors to be observed. Moreover, Hertel et al.'s (2005) review suggests that it can be difficult to employ such methods without negative effects on employee stress and satisfaction. Felstead et al. (2003) found that organizations tended to use existing managerial devices like telephone calls and meetings rather than electronic surveillance technologies to gain information about employee plans, practices, and activities. However, these devices also have limitations. For instance, managers may not have the time to telephone each teleworker every day. Moreover, as Piccoli and Ives (2003) found, having process controls within dispersed teams (e.g., having regularly to report on team plans and progress, specifying rules and procedures) can reduce trust because it increases the salience of broken obligations. Thus, managers may be unwise to overuse or rely solely on such devices. Felstead et al. (2003) found that social controls were also used by managers, such as trying to engender greater commitment and a shared identity through induction and socialization, and by emphasizing trust. Such social controls aim to enhance intrinsic motivation towards company goals, which should reduce the need for monitoring.

Managing by "trust" involves devolving responsibility to individuals (or teams) so that they are effectively managing themselves (Bell and Kozlowski 2002). The management function then becomes one of managing outputs (with targets and deadlines) rather than processes. However, management by "outputs" can also have its limitations. Felstead et al. (2003) found that it is not always easy to clearly define relevant targets for some jobs (e.g., in some service organizations) and that sometimes teleworkers ended up diverting their efforts towards measurable (but secondary) outputs that did not relate to overall company objectives. Nevertheless, managing by trust might still form a useful strategy for "remote" managers. Felstead et al. (2003) found that trust operated as a form of control because it was a "moral obligation" whereby in exchange for rewards, employees were expected to manage themselves and be productive in the absence of managerial intervention or scrutiny.

Controls and rules that are designed to reduce uncertainty rather than to control others are likely to be most successful. For instance, Walther and Bunz (2005) found that by following rules based on counteracting the limitations of working remotely and using ICTs (e.g., communicating frequently, overtly acknowledging reading others' messages, being explicit about thoughts and actions, and sticking to set deadlines) was related to greater trust and perceived quality of work (Walther and Bunz 2005). Thus, a balance may be required between trust and control when it comes to managing remote workers. Managers need to build relations and trust as well as provide a framework to guide employee action. Involving employees in setting these controls is likely to help reduce any negative impact they can have (Axtell, Fleck, and Turner 2004).

5.2 Job/Task Design

A particularly pertinent job characteristic for teleworkers is performance feedback. In a "virtual" environment where social cues are reduced, it may be especially important to ensure that performance-related feedback is frequent, concrete, and timely (Hertel et al. 2005). Such feedback might typically focus on performance outcomes with an intention to motivate performance towards a goal. However, team process feedback may also be useful in virtual settings as this is exactly the sort of feedback that is missing when there is little face-to-face contact. Indeed, Geister, Konradt, and Hertel (2006) found that on-line team process feedback which consisted of the team's average ratings of motivation, task aspects (e.g., participation in planning) and relationship aspects (e.g., team identity, conflict management) had a positive impact on motivation, satisfaction, and performance of the team. Those who were initially less motivated seemed to benefit most.

Another key aspect of task design for telework is the level of interdependence with remote colleagues. Much of the literature assumes that due to the limitations of communicating via ICTs at a distance, the tasks that are best suited to teleworking or virtual teams are those that can be separated into subtasks and distributed across locations, thus reducing the level of interdependence and coordination requirements across sites (Hertel et al. 2005). Interdependence with distant colleagues is related to lower perceived productivity amongst teleworkers (Watson-Manheim, Piramuthu, and Narasimhan 2000). However, reducing interdependence may hamper team cohesion and even foster subgroup development and so, in some ways, may be harmful. High task interdependence may be beneficial early on in the development of virtual teams to increase team cohesion and trust, but the relationship between task interdependence and team effectiveness may diminish for older teams (Hertel, Konradt, and Orlikowski 2004). Other work has shown that once a common understanding has been developed, then ICTs can be used more successfully for complex interdependent work (Majchrzak et al. 2000). Thus, managers need to promote interdependence at least at first, if they are to develop strong relationships remotely and need to develop common understandings to reduce some of the process losses that occur when coordinating tasks via ICTs.

5.3 Selection

One advantage of remote working is that it expands the geographical scope of a labor market and can also increase the attractiveness of organizations to those who would benefit from more flexible working locations (Rau and Hyland 2002), so enabling organizations to recruit from a larger pool of individuals. However, because remote working implies less scope for direct supervision, selection becomes more important.

One area that has attracted discussion is the role of personality in the selection process. Lamond, Daniels, and Standen (2004) emphasize the importance of trait conscientiousness and intelligence for all forms of remote working, because of the need for good self-management skills and ability to deal with complex ICTs. They also note that extraversion, openness-to-experience, conscientiousness, and emotional stability are important for predicting performance on training courses and/or good communication skills, which suggests such traits might be useful in remote working where communications and training can be dominated by use of ICTs. However, the role of personality in predicting teleworkers performance remains largely unexplored.

In terms of specific competencies to be assessed during selection, several authors have produced generic listings. For example, Lamond et al.'s review organized competencies into four major areas: personal competencies, such as self-direction; interpersonal competencies, such as good verbal and written communication skills; generic task competencies, such as time management skills; and technical competencies, such as ICT literacy. Duarte and Snyder (2006) outline competencies in six main areas: project management, networking, use of technology, self-management, spanning boundaries, and interpersonal awareness.

As well as selecting on the basis of personality and generic remote working competencies, Lamond et al. (2004) have indicated the selection process should also address the likely impact of remote working on the home/work interface, job characteristics, and the psychological facets of work, in order to establish whether remote working will be beneficial or harmful for the individual.

5.4 Socialization

Socialization during the initial period of remote working is argued to be important as traditional patterns of socialization may break down in remote work (Lipnack and Stamps 2000). Indeed, because distance and "impoverished" communications through ICTs may create obstacles to creating a common organizational identity, it has been suggested that regular face-to-face meetings and minimum requirements for office attendance, at least for newcomers, may help socialization processes (Lamond et al. 2004). To ease the process of socialization further, it has also been suggested that selection of remote workers should include those most likely to assimilate organizational culture, because their values are already consonant with the organizational culture (Billsberry 2000).

5.5 Training

As well as job-specific training, Cascio (2000) considers that remote workers should receive generic training in virtual-collaborative, virtual coordination, and virtual-communication skills plus project management skills for managers where teams consist of freelance teleworkers.

Open/distance learning is an attractive means of training remote workers. Salmon, Allen, and Giles (2000) suggest ICT mediated open/distance learning, through provision of CDs, web, books, and simulations, is an effective means of training. This is partly because the ICT environment mimics the remote working environment, allowing greater situational congruence between training and work, enabling better transfer of learning. It also allows teleworkers to practice on the kinds of ICTs they will use in their jobs. However, unless generic training packages are available, open/distance learning can be an expensive option because of the high start-up costs. However, where there is high volume, such as in large organizations with dispersed virtual teams, then open/distance learning, perhaps through partnering with external suppliers, could be effective and cost efficient (Lipnack and Stamps 2000).

5.6 Career Development

A common perception and concern among remote workers is that if remote working reduces their visibility in their organization this form of work may damage their career prospects. However, it need not be the case that remote workers suffer for limited career opportunities (Hill et al. 2003). It can be the case that organizations can be proactive in career management: remote working can be used to move people through different project teams as a means of developing competencies (Hiltrop 2000). It is felt that both remote workers and managers need to take responsibility for the careers of remote workers, with managers ensuring regular discussions over careers and passing information on the competencies acquired by remote workers onto the next project (Duarte and Snyder 2006).

6. FUTURE DIRECTIONS

To conclude, a number of observations can be made about the literature on this topic. First, while the topic of remote working has been the subject of an enormous amount of writing and research, a number of topics remain relatively neglected, including performance appraisal processes, the role of personality in people's experiences of remote working, and the nature of the employment relationship of remote workers. Methodologically, much research on virtual teams continues to be conducted using student-based group experiments rather than the analysis of real organizational situations, while the narrow focus of the telework literature on part-time, professional teleworkers leads to a limited understanding of the experiences of other types of teleworker. Finally, while this chapter deliberately drew upon both the telework and virtual team literatures in understanding the character of remote working, the vast majority of work on this subject remains narrowly entrenched within either the virtual team or teleworking literatures and does not seek to utilize both. Arguably, therefore, our understanding of the challenges of remote working can be developed through future work not only building from the findings of existing studies, but also through addressing some of these points.

REFERENCES

Axtell, C. M., Fleck, S. J., and Turner, N. 2004. Virtual teams: collaborating across distance. In *International Review of Industrial and Organisational Psychology*, vol. 19, ed. C. Cooper and I. Robertson. Chichester: Wiley.

Baba, M. L., Gluesing, J., Ratner, H., and Wagner, K. H. 2004. The contexts of knowing: natural history of a globally distributed team. *Journal of Organizational Behavior*, 25: 547–87.

Bailey, D., and Kurland, N. 2002. A review of telework research: findings, new directions, and lessons from the study of modern work. *Journal of Organizational Behaviour*, 23: 383–400.

Baines, S. 2002. New technologies and old ways of working in the home of the self-employed teleworker. *New Technology, Work and Employment*, 17: 89–101.

——and Gelder, U. 2003. What is family friendly about the workplace in the home? The case of self-employed parents and their children. *New Technology, Work and Employment*, 18: 223–34.

Baruch, Y. 2000. Teleworking benefits and pitfalls as perceived by professionals. *New Technology, Work and Employment*, 15: 34–49.

Belanger, F., Collis, R.W., and Cheney, P. H. 2001. Technology requirements and work group communication for telecommuters. *Information Systems Research*, 12: 155–76.

Bell, B. S., and Kozlowski, S. W. J. 2002. A typology of virtual teams: implications for effective leadership. *Group and Organization Management*, 27: 14–49.

Billsberry, J. 2000. Socializing teleworkers into the organization. In *Managing Telework: Perspectives from Human Resource Management and Work Psychology*, ed. K. Daniels, D. Lamond, and P. Standen. London: Thomson Learning.

Breu, K., and Hemingway, C. J. 2004. Making organisations virtual: the hidden cost of distributed teams. *Journal of Information Technology*, 19: 191–202.

Bryant, S. 2000. At home on the electronic frontier: work, gender, and the information highway. *New Technology, Work and Employment*, 15: 19–33.

Cascio, W. F. 2000. Managing a virtual workplace. *Academy of Management Executive*, 14: 81–90.

Collins, M. 2005. The (not so simple) case for teleworking: a study of Lloyd's of London. *New Technology, Work and Employment*, 20: 115–32.

Cooper, C. D., and Kurland, N. B. 2002. Telecommuting, professional isolation, and employee development in public and private organizations. *Journal of Organizational Behavior*, 23: 511–32.

CRAMTON, C. D. 2002. Finding common ground in dispersed collaboration. *Organizational Dynamics*, 30: 356–67.

DANIELS, K. 2000. Job features and well-being. In *Managing Telework: Perspectives from Human Resource Management and Work Psychology*, ed. K. Daniels, D. Lamond, and P. Standen. London: Thomson Learning.

——LAMOND, D., and STANDEN, P. 2001. Teleworking: frameworks for organizational research. *Journal of Management Studies*, 38: 1151–86.

DE CROON, E. M., SLUITER, J., KJUIJER, P. P. F. M., and FRINGS-DRESEN, M. W. H. 2005. The effect of office concepts on worker health and performance: a systematic review of the literature. *Ergonomics*, 48: 119–34.

DIMITROVA, D. 2003. Controlling teleworkers: supervision and flexibility revisited. *New Technology, Work and Employment*, 18: 181–95.

DONNELLY, R. 2004. How "free" is the free worker? An investigation into the working arrangements available to knowledge workers. *Personnel Review*, 35: 78–97.

DUARTE, D. L., and SNYDER, N. T. 2006. *Mastering Virtual Teams: Strategies, Tools, and Techniques that Succeed*. New York: Wiley.

DUXBURY, L., and NEUFIELD, D. 1999. An empirical evaluation of the impacts of telecommuting on intra-organisational communication. *Journal of Engineering and Technology Management*, 16: 1–28.

EUROPEAN COMMISSION. 1998. *Status Report on European Telework*. Luxembourg: Office for Official Publications of the European Communities.

FELSTEAD, A., JEWSON, N., and WALTERS, S. 2003. Managerial control of employees working at home. *British Journal of Industrial Relations*, 41: 241–64.

————— 2005. *Changing Places of Work*, Basingstoke: Palgrave Macmillan.

————PHIZACKLEA, A., and WALTERS, S. 2001. Working at home: statistical evidence for seven hypotheses. *Work, Employment and Society*, 15: 215–31.

————————— 2002. The option to work at home: another privilege for the favoured few. *New Technology, Work and Employment*, 17: 204–23.

FINHOLT, T. A., and SPROULL, L. 1990. Electronic groups at work. *Organization Science*, 1: 41–64.

GARRETT, R. K., and DANZINGER, J. N. 2007. Which telework: defining and testing a taxonomy of technology-mediated work at a distance. *Social Science Computer Review*, 25: 27–47.

GEISTER, S., KONRADT, U., and HERTEL, G. 2006. Effects of process feedback on motivation, satisfaction and performance in virtual teams. *Small Group Research*, 37: 459–89.

GIBSON, C. B., and GIBBS, J. L. 2006. Unpacking the concept of virtuality: the effects of geographic dispersion, electronic dependence and national diversity on team innovation. *Administrative Science Quarterly*, 51: 451–95.

GOLDEN, T. D. 2006a. The role of relationships in understanding telecommuter satisfaction. *Journal of Organizational Behavior*, 27: 319–40.

—— 2006b. Avoiding depletion in virtual work: telework and the intervening impact of work exhaustion on commitment and turnover intentions. *Journal of Vocational Behavior*, 69: 176–87.

——VEIGA, J. F., and SIMSEK, Z. 2006. Telecommuting's differential impact on work-family conflict: is there no place like home? *Journal of Applied Psychology*, 91: 1340–50.

GRAY, M., HODSON, N., and GORDON, G. 1993. *Teleworking Explained*. Chichester: Wiley.

GRIFFITH, T. L., and NEALE, M. A. 2001. Information processing in traditional hybrid and virtual teams: from nascent knowledge to transactive memory. *Research in Organizational Behavior*, 23: 379–421.

HARRIS, L. 2003. Home-based teleworking and the employment relationship: managerial challenges and dilemmas. *Personnel Review*, 32: 422–37.

HERTEL, G., GEISTER, S., and KONRADT, U. 2005. Managing virtual teams: a review of current empirical research. *Human Resource Management Review*, 15: 69–95.

——— KONRADT, U., and ORLIKOWSKI, B. 2004. Managing distance by interdependence: goal setting, task interdependence and team-based rewards in virtual teams. *European Journal of Work and Organizational Psychology*, 13: 1–28.

HILL, E., FERRIS, M., and MÄRTINSON, V. 2003. Does it matter where you work? A comparison of how three work venues (traditional office, virtual office, and home office) influence aspects of work and personal/family life. *Journal of Vocational Behaviour*, 62: 220–41.

HILTROP, J. M. 2000. Preparing people and organizations for teleworking. In *Managing Telework: Perspectives from Human Resource Management and Work Psychology*, ed. K. Daniels, D. Lamond, and P. Standen. London: Thomson Learning.

HINDS, P., and WEISBAND, S. 2003. Knowledge sharing and shared understanding in virtual teams. In *Virtual Teams that Work: Creating Conditions for Virtual Team Effectiveness*, ed. C. B. Gibson and S. G. Cohen. San Francisco: Jossey-Bass.

HOLLINGSHEAD, A. B. 1998. Communication, learning and retrieval in transactive memory systems. *Journal of Experimental Social Psychology*, 34: 423–42.

JARVENPAA, S. L., and LEIDNER, D. E. 1999. Communication and trust in global virtual teams. *Organization Science*, 9: 791–815.

KOSSEK, E. E., LAUTSCH, B. A., and EATON, S. C. 2006. Telecommuting, control, and boundary management: correlates of policy use and practice, job control, and work-family effectiveness. *Journal of Vocational Behavior*, 68: 347–67.

KOTLARSKY, J., and OSHRI, I. 2005. Social ties, knowledge sharing and successful collaboration in globally distributed system development projects. *European Journal of Information Systems*, 14: 37–48.

KRAUSS, R., and FUSSELL, S. R. 1990. Mutual knowledge and communicative effectiveness. In *Intellectual Teamwork: Social and Technological Foundations of Cooperative Work*, ed. J. Galegher, R. Kraut, and C. Egido. Hillsdale, NJ: Lawrence Erlbaum Associates.

KREBS, S. A., HOBMAN, E. V., and BORDIA, P. 2006. Virtual teams and group member dissimilarity: consequences for the development of trust. *Small Group Research*, 37: 721–41.

LAMOND, D., DANIELS, K., and STANDEN, P. 2004. Managing virtual organisations and virtual workers. In *The New Workplace: A Guide to the Human Impact of Modern Working Practices*, ed. D. Holman, T. D. Wall, C. W. Clegg, P. R. Sparrow, and A. Howard. Chichester: Wiley.

LAPIERRE, L. M., and ALLEN, T. D. 2006. Work-supportive family, family-supportive supervision, use of organizational benefits, and problem-focused coping: implications for work-family conflict and employee well-being. *Journal of Occupational Health Psychology*, 11: 169–81.

LAU, D. C., and MURNIGHAN, J. K. 1998. Demographic diversity and faultlines: the compositional dynamics of organizational groups. *Academy of Management Review*, 23: 325–40.

LEA, M., SPEARS, R., and DE GROOT, D. 2001. Knowing me, knowing you: anonymity effects on social identity processes within groups. *Personality and Social Psychology Bulletin*, 27: 384–93.

LIPNACK, J., and STAMPS, J. 2000. *Virtual Teams: People Working across Boundaries with Technology*, 2nd edn. New York: Wiley.

MCKNIGHT, D. H., CUMMINGS, L. L., and CHERVANY, N. L. 1998. Initial trust formation in new organizational relationships. *Academy of Management Review*, 23: 473–90.

MAJCHRZAK, A., RICE, R. E., KING, N., MALHOTRA, A., and BA, S. L. 2000. Computer mediated inter-organisational knowledge sharing: insights from a virtual team innovating using a collaborative tool. *Information Resources Management Journal*, 13: 44–53.

MANN, S., and HOLDSWORTH, L. 2003. The psychological impact of teleworking: stress, emotions and health. *New Technology, Work and Employment*, 18: 196–211.

MEYERSON, D., WEICK, K. E., and KRAMER, R. M. 1996. Swift trust and temporary groups. In *Trust in Organizations: Frontiers of Theory and Research*, ed. R. M. Kramer and T. R. Tyler. Thousand Oaks, CA: Sage.

MOKHTARIAN, P., SALOMON, I., and CHOO, S. 2005. Measuring the measurable: why can't we agree on the number of telecommuters in the US? *Quality and Quantity*, 39: 423–52.

MONTREUIL, S., and LIPPEL, K. 2003. Telework and occupational health: a Quebec empirical study and regulatory implications. *Safety Science*, 41: 339–58.

PAOLI, P., and MERLLIE, D. 2001. *Third European Survey of Working Conditions*. Dublin: European Foundation for the Improvement of Living and Working Conditions.

——and PARENT-THIRION, A. 2003. *Working Conditions in the Acceding and Candidate Countries*. Dublin: European Foundation for the Improvement of Living and Working Conditions.

PAULEEN, D. J. 2003. An inductively derived model of leader-initiated relationship building with virtual team members. *Journal of Management Information Systems*, 20: 227–56.

PICCOLI, G., and IVES, B. 2003. Trust and the unintended consequences of behavior control in virtual teams. *MIS Quarterly*, 27: 365–95.

POLZER, J. T., CRISP, D. B., JARVENPAA, S. L., and KIM, J. W. 2006. Extending the faultline model to geographically dispersed teams: how collocated subgroups can impair group functioning. *Academy of Management Journal*, 49: 679–92.

RAGURHAM, S., WIESENFELD, B., and GARUD, R. 2003. Technology enabled work: the role of self-efficacy in determining telecommuter adjustment and structuring behavior. *Journal of Vocational Behavior*, 63: 180–98.

RAU, B. L., and HYLAND, M. M. 2002. Role conflict and flexible work arrangements: the effects of attraction. *Personnel Psychology*, 55: 111–36.

RIDINGS, C. M., GEFEN, D., and ARINZE, B. 2002. Some antecedents and effects of trust in virtual communities. *Journal of Strategic Information Systems*, 11: 271–95.

SALMON, G., ALLEN J., and GILES, K. 2000. Training and development for on-line working. In *Managing Telework: Perspectives from Human Resource Management and Work Psychology*, ed. K. Daniels, D. Lamond, and P. Standen. London: Thomson Learning.

SHELDON, O. J., THOMAS-HUNT, M. C., and PROELL, C. A. 2006. When timeliness matters: the effect of status on reactions to perceived time delay within distributed collaboration. *Journal of Applied Psychology*, 91: 1385–95.

SOLE, D., and EDMONDSON, A. C. 2002. Situated knowledge and learning in dispersed teams. *British Journal of Management*, 13: 17–34.

SPEARS, R., and LEA, M. 1994. Panacea or panopticon—the hidden power in computer-mediated communication. *Communication Research*, 21: 427–59.

STASSER, G., and TITUS, W. 1985. Pooling of unshared information in group decision making: biased information sampling during discussion. *Journal of Personality and Social Psychology*, 48: 1467–78.

THATCHER, S. M. B. and ZHU, X. M. 2006. Changing identities in a changing workplace: identification, identity enactment, self-verification and telecommuting. *Academy of Management Review*, 31: 1076–88.

THOMAS-HUNT, M. C., OGDEN, T. Y., and NEALE, M. A. 2003. Who's really sharing? Effects of social and expert status on knowledge exchange within groups. *Management Science*, 49: 464–77.

TIETZE, S., and MUSSON, G. 2005. Recasting the home-work relationship: a case of mutual adjustment? *Organization Studies*, 26: 1331–52.

TREGASKIS, O. 2000. Telework in its national context. In *Managing Telework: Perspectives from Human Resource Management and Work Psychology*, ed. K. Daniels, D. Lamond, and P. Standen. London: Thomson Learning.

TREMBLAY, D. 2002. Balancing work and family with telework? Organizational issues and challenges for women and managers. *Women in Management Review*, 17: 157–70.

VALSECCHI, R. 2006. Visible moves and invisible bodies: the case of teleworking in an Italian call centre. *New Technology, Work and Employment*, 21: 123–38.

WALTHER, J. B. 1992. Interpersonal effects in computer-mediated interaction: a relational perspective. *Communication Research*, 19: 52–90.

——2002. Time effects in computer-mediated groups: past, present, and future. In *Distributed Work*, ed. P. Hinds and S. Kiesler. Cambridge, MA: MIT Press.

WALTHER, J. B., and BUNZ, U. 2005. The rules of virtual groups: trust, liking, and performance in computer-mediated communication. *Journal of Communication*, 55: 828–46.

WARKENTIN, M. E., SAYEED, L., and HIGHTOWER, R. 1997. Virtual teams versus face-to-face teams: an exploratory study of a web-based conference system. *Decision Sciences*, 28: 975–96.

WATSON-MANHEIM, M. B., PIRAMUTHU, S., and NARASIMHAN, S. 2000. Exploratory analysis of factors influencing performance dynamics of telecommuters and traditional office workers. *IEEE Transactions on SYSTEMS, Man and Cybernetics—Part C: Applications and Reviews*, 30: 239–51.

WEICK, K. E., and BOUGON, M. G. 1986. Organizations as cognitive maps: charting ways to success and failure. In *The Thinking Organization: Dynamics of Organizational Social Cognition*, ed. H. P. Simms and D. A. Gioia. San Francisco: Jossey-Bass.

WILSON, J. M., STRAUS, S. G., and McEVILY, B. 2006. All in due time: the development of trust in electronic and face-to-face groups. *Organizational Behavior and Human Decision Processes*, 99: 16–33.

MOTIVATION AND JOB DESIGN IN THE NEW WORLD OF WORK

YITZHAK FRIED

ARIEL S. LEVI

GREGORY LAURENCE

1. INTRODUCTION

THE area of job design has generated substantial theoretical and empirical interest in the twentieth century as a key contributor to individual motivation and performance at work (e.g., Hackman and Oldham 1976; 1980; Campion 1988). These theories and related research have helped us better understand the attitudes and behaviors of employees at work (e.g., Humphrey, Nahrgang, and Morgeson 2007; Fried and Ferris 1987; Morgeson and Campion 2003; Parker, Wall, and Cordery 2001). A key conclusion from the job design literature is the need to take into account the changing contingencies in the work environment, in order to more

We are indebted to Adam Grant for his helpful comments and suggestions on an earlier version of this article.

fully understand the effect of job design in this changing environment (e.g., Parker, Wall, and Cordery 2001; Fried, Levi, and Laurence 2007). Although job design has been shown to have an important effect on employee motivation, attitudes, and behavior, the rapid and dramatic changes in the work environment during the latter decades of the twentieth century raise a timely question about the role of job design in the twenty-first century. In this chapter we will discuss how the major changes in the work environment that we have been witnessing could affect the role and characteristics of job design in the twenty-first century.

2. JOB DESIGN IN HISTORICAL PERSPECTIVE: AN OVERVIEW

Fredrick W. Taylor, who was the first to focus on job design for individuals, developed the "scientific management" approach in 1911 (Taylor 1911). Taylor's approach focused on specialization and simplification of jobs as mechanisms to enhance efficiency and control performance. However, research has revealed that the routine and standardized tasks associated with the "scientific management" approach have led to a number of unintended adverse consequences, such as higher tardiness, lower motivation and productivity, and sabotage of work equipment. This meant that the gains of the industrial engineering approach were often over-shadowed by its negative effects (Fried, Oldham, and Cummings 1998). The problems associated with the industrial engineering approach produced alternative approaches to job design. These new approaches focused on the motivation of employees at work as a key determinant of job attitudes and performance (Hackman and Oldham 1980; Fried, Oldham and Cummings 1998; Fried et al. 2006). Two theories that have particularly affected the area of job design are the Motivator-Hygiene Theory (MHT), which was developed by Frederick Herzberg and his colleagues in the 1960s, and the Job Characteristics Model (JCM), which was developed by Hackman and Oldham (1976; 1980) on the basis of earlier conceptual development by Turner and Lawrence (1965) and later Hackman and Lawler (1971). The central theme of the MHT is the distinction between *motivator factors*, which are intrinsic to the job itself (and include responsibility, achievement, recognition, and personal growth in competence), and *hygiene factors*, which are associated with the job context or work setting (and include relationships with peers and subordinates, quality of supervision, base wage or salary, benefits, and job security). According to MHT, while hygiene factors merely prevent job dissatisfaction, motivator factors increase workers' motivation and satisfaction on the job. The theory in essence suggests that enriching employees' jobs, by adding responsibility, complexity, and personal growth, is essential to increasing employee motivation and performance. Herzberg's theory has inspired both research and several successful job redesign projects that provide evidence for the positive effect of motivator factors on individual and organizational outcomes. The theory, however, suffers from some weaknesses. These include the lack of clear differentiation between factors, such as pay raises, that can serve as both hygiene and motivator factors; the lack of a suitable measurement instrument to assess the motivator and hygiene factors; and the failure of the theory to consider the effect of individual or cultural differences on motivator and hygiene factors.

The job characteristics model was developed by Hackman and Oldham in the 1970s and 1980s as an attempt to overcome some of the shortcomings of MHT. Specifically, the JCM focuses on five core job characteristics: skill variety, task identity, task significance, autonomy, and job feedback. Briefly, skill variety refers to the number of different skills needed to accomplish a job. Task identity focuses on whether the job requires completion of a whole, identifiable piece of work. Task significance refers to the job's impact on the lives of other people in the organization or on society at large. Autonomy refers to the employee's level of freedom, independence, and discretion in determining how and when to do his or her job. Finally, job feedback refers to the degree to which work activities provide the employee with direct and clear information about his or her job performance (Hackman and Oldham 1976; 1980).

According to the model, these five core job characteristics affect three critical psychological states: experienced meaningfulness of work, experienced responsibility for work outcomes, and knowledge of work results. Skill variety, task identity, and task significance are related to experienced meaningfulness, autonomy is related to experienced responsibility, and job feedback is related to knowledge of results. These three psychological states, in turn, positively affect individual psychological and behavioral outcomes, namely high intrinsic work motivation, job performance, job satisfaction, and reduced absenteeism and turnover. Finally, individual difference variables, which include growth need strength (GNS; the desire for learning and personal accomplishment at work), knowledge and skills, and context satisfaction (satisfaction with supervisors, co-workers, income, and job security), moderate the relationships among job characteristics, psychological states, and the psychological and behavioral work outcomes. Specifically, according to the model, when individuals have high GNS (they strive to be involved in challenging jobs), high knowledge and skills (they have the capabilities needed to accomplish the jobs successfully), and a high level of satisfaction with their supervisor, co-workers, pay, and job security, they will respond well to enriched (challenging) jobs, because they can pursue such jobs without distractions. On the other hand, if GNS and knowledge and skills are low, individuals will lack the motivation and ability to focus on and complete challenging jobs. In addition, if their level of satisfaction with their supervisors, co-workers, pay, and job security is low, they will be distracted and unable to focus on the job (Hackman and Oldham 1980). To measure the model's variables and assess its validity, Hackman and Oldham developed the Job Diagnostic Survey (JDS), which has subsequently been widely used. In fact, most of the contemporary research on job design has drawn on the JCM (Fried and Ferris 1987; Fried, Oldham, and Cumming, 1998; Fried et al., 2006; Fried, Levi, and Laurence 2007; Hackman and Oldham 1980; Parker, Wall, and Cordery 2001; Humphrey, Nahrgang, and Morgeson 2007). The results have provided support for the major premises of the model. However, not all of the theory's hypotheses have been equally supported. Specifically, there is strong support, based on field experiments and cross-sectional and longitudinal field surveys, for the relationships between job characteristics and employee affective reactions (job satisfaction, growth satisfaction, and internal motivation) (e.g., Fried and Ferris 1987; Griffin 1983; 1991; Oldham 1996; Orpen 1979). Research results also support the expected relationships between job characteristics and behavioral outcomes (performance and absenteeism). However, the magnitude of these associations is relatively weak (e.g., Humphrey, Nahrgang, and Morgeson 2007; Fried and Ferris 1987; Kopelman 1985; Oldham 1996; Parker, Wall, and Cordery 2001). Research has also supported the mediating role of the psychological states, though questions remain about the precise relationships between the particular job characteristics and the corresponding psychological states (see, e.g., Fried and Ferris 1987; Humphrey, Nahrgang, and Morgeson 2007; Parker, Wall, and Cordery 2001; Fried, Levi, and Laurence 2007). Further, among the hypothesized moderators, GNS has been investigated the most, and the results are partially supportive. A comprehensive study by Tiegs, Tetrick, and Fried (1992), on a sample of nearly 7,000 individuals across different jobs and occupations, failed to provide such support for the moderating effect of GNS (as well as context satisfaction).

However, reviews of the research evidence by Fried and Ferris (1987), Loher et al. (1985), Oldham (1996), and Spector (1985), provide support for the moderating effect of GNS on the relationship between job characteristics and job satisfaction and performance. In addition, there is little support for the moderating effect of context satisfaction (De Varo, Li, and Brookshire 2007; Fried, Levi, and Laurence 2007; Oldham 1996; Tiegs, Tetrick, and Fried 1992), and there is little research on the moderating role of indicators of knowledge and skills (Fried, Levi, and Laurence 2007).

3. Future Directions of Job Design

While the importance of job design to employee motivation and performance is well established, significant changes in the work environment raise new challenges and questions concerning the role of job design in the twenty-first century. We will first discuss some major changes that have occurred in the context of work, and then analyze how these changes may relate to potential changes in the role of job design as a contributor to employee reactions.

Over the past few decades, there has been a steady increase in the contextual diversity of the work environment (e.g., Parker, Wall, and Cordery 2001; Rousseau and Fried 2001). Perhaps the most important such change has been the dramatic growth of knowledge-based operations and the increased demand for "knowledge employees." The use of technology (e.g., computers) has enabled organizations to better compete in the competitive global economy by utilizing employees' skills and labor from non-traditional work sites (e.g., working from home), and by the use of outsourcing, much of it to organizations and employees in different societies and cultures across the globe. Similarly, organizations have increased their global (multinational) operations, resulting in a greater reliance on virtual operations (e.g., Kirkman and Shapiro 1997; Parker, Wall, and Cordery 2001). There has also been a steady increase in organizational use of autonomous work teams as a mechanism for coping with high technical interdependence, and to promote learning of new skills and strategies needed to deal with uncertain environments and changing requirements (Batt 1999; Parker, Wall, and Cordery 2001; Wall and Jackson 1995). As technology improves and the global economy expands, these trends are likely to become even more prevalent.

In addition, while manufacturing is in decline (although manufacturing jobs are still important in some sectors), the service sector has grown dramatically. More-over, the current workforce is characterized by a significant increase in gender and ethnic diversity, and the presence of more educated and older employees. We will now discuss how these changes affect job design.

3.1 Job Design in the Twenty-First Century: A Contingency Approach

The dramatic changes in the work environment described above have generated some important changes in the area of job design, particularly in the meaning and roles of the job characteristics. We will discuss the most important of these changes with reference to the JCM and its components. We will first focus on changes in the core job characteristics.

An important job dimension in the JCM is *skill variety*, which is defined as "the degree to which a job requires a variety of different activities in carrying out the work, involving the use of a number of different skills and talents of the person" (Hackman and Oldham 1980, 78). However, while traditional theories of job design such as the JCM focus on the job as the key focus of the individual's attention and identification, the increasing need to compete in an uncertain and changing environment has caused organizations and individuals to move to skill or competency-based approaches, which focus on the development of more general skills needed in a particular work domain (cf. Lawler 1994; Feldman and Bolino 1996). As a result, one can expect that employees will experience meaningfulness at work not only because of their contribution to a particular job, but primarily because of their experience of contributing to their team or organization (Lawler 1994; Parker 1998). Moreover, the competency-based approach also means that in the twenty-first century, careers will consist of relatively short learning stages to assure employability in a labor market that increasingly rewards learn-how rather than know-how (Hall 1996). This increased emphasis on competency learning, associated with transitional learning periods, will serve as an important tool for individuals to better compete in the challenging global economy by preparing themselves to work in multiple organizations and positions, as the market dictates (Sitkin 1992; Wrzesniewski and Dutton 2001).

A second dimension discussed by the JCM is *task identity*, which is defined as "the degree to which a job requires completion of a 'whole' and identifiable piece of work, that is, doing a job from beginning to end with a visible outcome" (Hackman and Oldham 1980, 78). This definition of task identity may fall short in explaining the experience of identity and meaningfulness in knowledge-based work environments. In such work environments, neither the final outcome of work effort nor its degree of success will be clearly identifiable. For example, what scientists invent at the end of a development process may depart substantially from the original plan, and frequently, exploration and development processes fail to produce any marketable outcome (e.g., Fried and Slowik 2004). In support of this argument, Andreou and Boone (2002) indicated that computer users in organizations that are using systems that support routine activities on a regular basis will have relatively high task identity because they can clearly identify their tasks as being completed by one person, and as having a clear beginning and end. On the other hand, users of higher-level systems will report a lower level of task identity, because they tend to be involved with abstract areas which often require interaction with others and experimentation over longer time periods with no immediate and identifiable outcomes.

However, while knowledge-based employees who are involved in complex, long-term projects may report lower task identity based on the current JCM definition and measurement of this construct, they may still experience a different type of identity and related meaningfulness. In such cases, task identity involves the experienced challenge of pursuing stimulating tasks and goals over longer time periods, with a degree of uncertainty about the outcomes. Successful knowledge-based organizations often encourage employees to experiment with innovation, and take risks even at the cost of failure, on the basis of the slogan "fail early to be successful sooner" (e.g., Fried and Slowik 2004; Sitkin 1992). In such a supportive environment and culture that encourages experimentation and failure as the basis for long-term success, employees are likely to feel high task identity, even if the process is "messy" (involving periodic feelings of loss of control due to reliance on other individuals and on trial and error effort), and successful outcomes are probabilistic (uncertain) rather than visible and definite in nature. The growth in importance and size of the knowledge-based industry and its need for knowledge-based employees suggests the need to adjust the definition and measurement of task identity to the specific industry and type of individual it employs. Such an adjustment in definition and measurement will improve our ability to validly assess and understand how the work-related context affects the experience and effects of task identity (cf. Rousseau and Fried 2001).

The third dimension in the JCM is *task significance*, defined as "the degree to which the job has a substantial impact on the lives of other people" (Hackman and Oldham 1980, 79). Employees' experience of high task significance is often related to their ability to observe their effects on others (Grant 2007). Advances in technology enable more employees, particularly in knowledge-based industries, to work away from their offices (e.g., Harrison, Johns, and Martocchio 2000; Shamir and Salomon 1985). This in turn potentially creates a situation in which the remoteness from work and the reduced opportunities to observe and interact with other people at work may reduce employees' experience of task significance (see Grant 2007; Shamir and Salomon 1985). It is thus becoming more important for the organization, especially the immediate supervisors, to actively communicate and demonstrate to their employees the valuable contribution their work efforts make (cf. Grant 2007; Grant et al. 2007; Fried, Levi, and Laurence 2007).

Task significance has become an important job facet in the service industry, where employees are required to have face-to-face or voice contact with customers (e.g., Hochschild 1983; Pough 2001). As technology improves, we can expect an increased level of visual interaction between employees and customers, regardless of the geographical distance. This will increase the importance of task significance as a contributor to the employee psychological experience and work outcomes. While pursuing work successfully is expected to enhance the experience of task significance and meaningfulness, it may also increase the negative experience of emotional labor associated with contact with the public (cf. Pough 2001).

The fourth dimension is work *autonomy*, defined by the JCM as "the degree to which the job provides substantial independence and discretion to the individual in scheduling the work and in determining the procedures to be used in carrying it out" (Hackman and Oldham 1980, 79). This definition refers explicitly to the autonomy dimensions of "when to do" and "how to do." However, it neglects other important dimensions of autonomy, such as "what to do" or "from where to do" (cf. Breaugh 1985; Breaugh and Becker 1987; Latham and Pinder 2005; Morgeson and Humphrey 2006). The autonomy dimension of "what to do" may be more relevant in some contexts and less relevant in others. For example, in knowledge-based organizations (e.g., high-tech start-ups), where the goal is to innovate, this third autonomy dimension concerning "what to do" is highly relevant to the ability of employees to pursue their goals (cf. Breaugh 1985; Breaugh and Becker 1987). In such innovative settings, specific goals and procedures are often left to the discretion of employees, which means that in order to assure successful performance, all three elements of autonomy should be present (cf. Breaugh 1985; Breaugh and Becker 1987). The three autonomy dimensions (when, how, and what) are also relevant to individuals involved in strategic decision making, such as executives or entrepreneurs. On the other hand, in traditional, more mechanistic jobs, where goals and work procedures are formally established, autonomy over "what to do" may be a weaker contributor to employees' ability to perform.

Moreover, the ability of employees to perform outside of work (e.g., from home) on a constant basis, promotes the importance of another facet of autonomy, which refers to "from where to do." This flexibility over where the work will be pursued (home, work, or a combination of the two) and at what time (e.g., working from home during unconventional hours) adds a key dimension to the construct of autonomy which is increasingly significant in the changing world of work. Interestingly, "from where to do" may contribute to both positive and negative effects. On the one hand, it may increase employees' control over their job performance, and consequently their experienced meaningfulness. On the other hand, the ability to engage in job tasks at work and at home can contribute to increased role overload and burnout. Clearly, we need more research on the contributions of these dimensions of autonomy on employee reactions.

The final core dimension is *job feedback*, defined as "the degree to which carrying out the work activities required by the job provides the individual with direct and clear information about the effectiveness of his or her performance" (Hackman and Oldham 1980, 80). The growing use of electronic job feedback (electronic performance monitoring) may create a situation where there is too much feedback. Rather than improving performance, excessive feedback may contribute to cognitive overload and the experience of stress, with a resulting reduction in job performance (e.g., Aiello and Kolb 1995; Kluger and DeNisi 1996; Parker, Wall, and Cordery 2001). Moreover, it may reduce people's experience of control at work by increasing the salience of external, mechanistic aspects of their work. Thus, a growing challenge for organizations in the current advanced technological environment is how to create effective job feedback processes that balance the need for timely job feedback with an appropriate level of detail.

Hackman and Oldham (1980) also discuss the importance of feedback from *supervisors and co-workers*. Here one may expect a challenge for supervisors concerning how to effectively provide useful feedback to their employees who work outside the office, and do not interact regularly with their supervisors or co-workers (Harrison, Johns, and Martocchio 2000; Shamir and Salomon 1985). Similarly, employees can expect reduced feedback from co-workers who do not interact with each other on a regular basis (Harrison, Johns, and Martocchio 2000; Shamir and Salomon 1985).

3.2 The Increased Importance of Additional Job Characteristics

The modern form of work as discussed above suggests that additional job characteristics should be taken into account in analyzing jobs in the new environment. Several scholars (Humphrey, Nahrgang, and Morgeson 2007; Morgeson and Humphrey 2006; Parker, Wall, and Cordery 2001) have proposed a number of such expanded work characteristics. These include, for example, *problem solving*, which refers to the extent to which a job requires creative ideas or solutions, *interaction outside the organization*, which refers to the extent to which employees interact and communicate with individuals external to the organization (e.g., suppliers, customers), and *opportunity for skill acquisition*, which has grown in importance because of the increased requirement of many employees to move to new jobs and organizations (Lawler and Finegold 2000). Yet another dimension that warrants further discussion is *opportunity for social interaction* (i.e., opportunity to interact with superiors and co-workers). The increased flexibility to choose where and when to work can increase employees' ability to perform better, but at the same time may adversely affect the opportunity for social interaction and the development of interpersonal relations (Shamir and Salomon 1985). That is, employees who are working from home or who visit the office irregularly will find it difficult to maintain good social relationships with other employees (Shamir and Salomon 1985). Moreover, because social relations have been identified as a major reason for many individuals to go to work (e.g., Albertson 1977; Jahoda 1979; Shamir and Salomon 1985), the inability to satisfy this social desire is likely to contribute to low satisfaction and quality of work life (Shamir and Salomon 1985).

The issue of social relations as a motivator may play an even bigger role in the twenty-first century, given the global economy and its associated tendency for labor to move from developed, but less affluent countries to more developed countries that offer more job opportunities. People often leave their homes for years for the purpose of supporting their relatives at home and assuring them a better life (Fried, Levi, and Laurence 2007). For such individuals, the issues of social belongingness and social relations may be particularly important in their adjustment to their foreign work environment away from their families and close friends.

3.3 Compensatory Relationships among Job Characteristics

In this context we should note that organizations' decisions concerning which of the job characteristics to focus on and promote may be based on the unique characteristics of the organization or the industry. For example, high reliability organizations (HROs) are characterized by "systemic or technological complexities where actions must be performed in an error-free manner because of the potentially disastrous consequences of errors" (Zohar and Luria 2003, 837). Examples of HROs are nuclear power plants or air traffic control systems (e.g., Vogus and Welbourne 2003). HROs may be high on some job dimensions and low on others. To illustrate, air traffic controllers' work is characterized by many rules and procedures that reduce individual autonomy significantly (Langfred 2007). However, management may increase employees' experience of meaningfulness by emphasizing the importance of their work for the safety and well-being of the public (high task significance; cf. Grant in press; 2007). The important point here is that specific cultural or contextual variables may dictate the relative importance of various job characteristics, and the compensatory relations among them, in affecting employee reactions. It is conceivable that as technology advances, becomes more complex, and has an increasingly strong impact on society, the number of HROs will grow, and with them the challenge of effective job design.

3.4 Balancing Team and Individual Job Design

As indicated, the use of self-managing teams has become increasingly prevalent as a mechanism to enhance employees' ability to function in an increasingly global environment characterized by uncertainty and change (Batt 1999; Cohen and Bailey 1997; Hackman 2002; Macy and Izumi 1993; Parker, Wall, and Cordery 2001; Wall and Jackson 1995). Principally, the job characteristics relevant to the design of individual jobs are also relevant to the design of team jobs (Hackman 1990; 2002). Many of the basic ideas and concepts underlying self-directed teams were originally developed by researchers focusing on the sociotechnical systems theory, an approach aiming to optimize the relation between the social and technical aspects of the organization (Trist et al. 1963; Trist, Susman, and Brown 1977). Self-managing teams are typically responsible for the completion of a large product or work process, and enjoy a high level of freedom and discretion (autonomy), enabling them to organize their work in the most efficient way to maximize their performance (Langfred 2007). This means, for example, that these teams schedule their own work, make decisions about who in the team will do what during the workday, decide on the schedule for equipment maintenance, and determine the necessary methods and frequency for checking product quality. Moreover, the teams regularly receive feedback about their performance and effectiveness (Hackman 1990). This suggests that similar to the individual job design characteristics, the design of self-managing teams also involves the characteristics of high skill variety, task identity, task significance, autonomy, and job feedback (Hackman 1990).

Nevertheless, organizations, managers, and employees increasingly face the dilemma of establishing and maintaining an appropriate balance between team job design and individual job design (e.g., Drach-Zahavy 2004; Langfred 2007). For example, team support and mutual feedback are essential to assure group performance (e.g., Hackman 1990). Yet, as Drach-Zahavy (2004) has suggested, if job characteristics are high at the individual level, the focus of these employees will be primarily on their autonomous, individually defined job, resulting in lower team support and feedback to other team members, and consequently lower team performance. Lending support to this suggestion, Uhl-Bien and Graen (1998) reported that individual self-management (autonomy) was positively related to work-unit effectiveness in functional teams, but negatively related to effectiveness in cross-functional teams, where work team and integrated efforts are required. In a similar vein, Janz, Colquitt, and Noe (1997) found among knowledge-workers that as the levels of task interdependence increased, the positive effect of team autonomy (over planning and work processes) on team motivation was reduced. To add to this potential imbalance between individual- and team-level job design, Langfred (2007) has suggested that when team conflict is high, trust among team members goes down, and this, in turn, reduces team members' willingness to grant other team members work autonomy. The reason for this is that trust is defined as the willingness to incur risk (Mayer, Davis, and Schoorman 1995), and consequently, team members will show less willingness to incur that risk by granting one another autonomy, resulting in lower individual autonomy in the team.

Moreover, Drach-Zahavy's results (2004) also support the idea that leader support may be an important mechanism to help bridge the gap between individual job enrichment and team support. The leader can help enhance team members' mutual support, regardless of the level of individual autonomy, through modeling behavior, and by clarifying and incentivizing the expectations and rules for support. As Anderson and Williams (1996) suggested, leaders who engage in helping behaviors help develop group norms for the acceptability of seeking and providing support at work. There is indeed growing evidence of the importance of a contingency approach to leadership, in which the effectiveness of the leader's behavior is contingent on the needs of his or her followers (see literature on Leader–Member Exchange (LMX) approach; Graen and Scandura 1987; Uhl-Bien, Graen, and Scandura 2000).

In addition, team culture may also offset the negative effect of job enrichment design on team support (see Drach-Zahavy 2004). Drach-Zahavy (2004) showed that when job enrichment was accompanied by a team culture of high power distance, team support was significantly lower in teams performing highly enriched jobs than in teams performing simpler (unenriched) jobs. In contrast, when job enrichment was accompanied by a team culture of low power distance, team support was maintained regardless of the level of job enrichment. Apparently, employees of such teams perceive their team members as equal in knowledge and professional background, and thus also perceive them as a legitimate source of support.

Similarly, a team culture of high collectivism may reduce the negative impact of individual job enrichment on team support, because in a collectivistic team there is high concern for the interest and well-being of all team members (Triandis 1993). In contrast, high individualism can be expected to intensify the adverse effect of individual job enrichment on team support (e.g., Triandis 1993). However, Drach-Zahavy (2004) failed to find support for the moderating effect of individualism/collectivism. Nevertheless, her rationale for the expected moderating effect of this cultural dimension, as discussed above, seems viable, and is worth investigating in additional samples and settings. Overall, we need more research on the processes that help reduce the inherent conflict between individual job enrichment and self-managing teams.

3.5 The Contribution of Additional Moderators

While the JCM offers some potentially important moderators (e.g., Fried and Ferris 1987), the increase in global operations and the rapid changes in the work environment suggest that additional moderators be considered (e.g., Parker, Wall, and Cordery 2001). Parker et al. (2001) offered a number of variables at different levels (organizational, group, and individual) that can serve as additional moderators. Here, we will focus on three additional moderators that can also be expected to play an important role in future job design in the global environment: societal culture, diversity, and the physical work environment. We will discuss the role of each of these three moderators.

3.5.1 *Moderating role of culture*

Multinational organizations with multiple branches in different societies and cultures, and organizations with heterogeneous workforces from different cultural backgrounds, would benefit if they were to take culture into account when designing and implementing job design policies and practices (e.g., Gelfand, Erez, and Aycan 2007; Kirkman and Shapiro 1997; Tsui, Nifadkar, and Ou 2007). For example, based on 107,292 employees from 49 countries, Huang and Van De Vlert (2003) found that the relationship between job characteristics and job satisfaction was stronger in more individualistic countries, richer countries, countries with better governmental and social welfare programs, and countries characterized by smaller power distance. Extrinsic job characteristics were positively linked to job satisfaction in all countries. Roe et al. (2000) also reported a stronger relationship between autonomy and psychological states in the Netherlands, which is characterized by an individualistic culture, than in Bulgaria or Hungary (see also, Gelfand, Erez, and Aycan 2007). Consistent with these results, Eylon and Au 1999 found that empowerment produced lower individual performance in a culture of high power distance (i.e., Asians) than in a culture of low power distance (Canada).

In addition, Robert et al. (2000) found that empowerment (high autonomy and discretion) in India was related to lower job satisfaction because of the lack of fit between the concept of empowerment and a culture that emphasizes hierarchy and status.

At the group level, Man and Lam (2003) reported in a study of teams from Hong Kong and the US branches of an international bank that an increase in job complexity and/or task autonomy increases group cohesiveness, which in turn, contributes to higher performance. However, the results also indicated that among individualistic groups the positive relation between skill variety and autonomy was more prominent than among collectivistic groups (see also Gelfand, Erez, and Aycan 2007).

Overall, these results suggest that job characteristics associated with empowerment (e.g., high variety and autonomy) tend to have a more positive effect in individualistic, low power distance cultures than in collectivistic or high power distance cultures. Therefore, multinational companies, in particular, should adopt policies of implementing differential job design programs, with an emphasis on different job dimensions, contingent on the specific cultural values prevailing in the society. Thus, for example, in collectivistic societies organizations may put more emphasis on the element of task significance (i.e., emphasizing the importance of employees' jobs to the well-being of others), while in individualistic societies a higher emphasis should be placed on autonomy.

Interestingly, though, over time, the culture in these multinational companies may evolve to a new entity that all employees of the company adhere to (Erez and Gati 2004; Gelfand, Erez, and Aycan 2007; Shokef and Erez 2006). In this situation, when employees feel an integral part of the company and adhere to the same value system, they would also compare how similar they are to each other in terms of inputs and outcomes, including the level of job characteristics (cf. Oldham et al. 1986; Oldham, Kulik, and Stepina 1991). When this occurs, management will then face the challenge of equalizing the level of job characteristics for employees in different geographical locations, in order to promote and maintain a perception of fairness, which has been shown to be an important contributor to employee motivation and performance (cf. Oldham et al. 1986; Oldham, Kulick, and Stepina 1991).

3.5.2 *The moderating role of workplace diversity*

3.5.2.1   *Gender diversity and work–family conflict*

The past few decades have witnessed a significant increase in the number and percentage of women at work (Parker, Wall, and Cordery 2001). This, coupled with increased demands and pressures on employees to perform in the competitive work environment, has increased the potential for work–family conflict (Greenhouse and

Beutell 1985; Oldham 1996; Parker, Wall, and Cordery 2001). In terms of its effect, work–family conflict may adversely affect work performance, especially when the work is complex and demanding, and thus requires consistent levels of focus and concentration (Fried, Levi, and Laurence 2007). Therefore, unless organizations take active steps to reduce work–family conflict (e.g., by implementing flexible work hours, work from home, or by offering day care centers in the work facility), the ability of working couples to successfully manage enriched and demanding jobs will be adversely affected. Responding to family needs will continue to be an important issue for organizations in the US and the western world. Moreover, this issue will also increase in importance in the developing countries, as more women join the labor force.

3.5.2.2 *Career diversity*

Different career levels dictate different interests in job characteristics. As more people are living and working for a longer time period, we are likely to see increased diversity in the workforce, such that individuals at different ages and career stages will express different interests in job design. For example, employees at later career stages are likely to express less interest and respond less favorably to demanding tasks, relative to their counterparts at earlier career stages (Fried et al. 2007; Katz 1978a; 1978b; 1980; Hambrick and Fukutomi 1991). On the other hand, employees' interests during mid-life stages tend to shift to opportunities to have a positive effect on other people, as a basis for making meaningful and lasting contributions that are appreciated and valued by others (Fried et al. 2007). These examples suggest the importance of contingencies when analyzing the role of job design in individuals' lives.

3.5.2.3 *Employment diversity*

A growing phenomenon in today's labor market, and one that is likely to continue, is the use of temporary employees on a contract basis (e.g., Boyce et al. 2007; Parker et al. 2002). More than 15,000 temporary-employment agencies in the US hire more than 11 million part-time employees each year (Berchem 2005; Boyce et al. 2007). Temporary employees are employed both in hazardous jobs or in jobs with low complexity, and in professional jobs such as law, teaching, and computing (Boyce et al. 2007). The reasons for the growing use of temporary employees is to increase flexibility in dealing with fluctuations in demand, enable the organization to reduce costs, and add expertise or knowledge to the organization to enhance competitive standing (Boyce et al. 2007). Evidence suggests that temporary employees tend to be stigmatized and to have lower status, which is associated with lower income and benefits, lower involvement in decision making, and lower job security (Boyce et al. 2007; Parker et al. 2002). The devaluation and exclusion of temporary employees is based on the tendency of regular full-time employees to perceive them as a threat, resulting in increased tension between the two groups. In this situation it is conceivable that regular full-time employees will be distracted by the perceived threat of the part-time employees to take their place, and as a result, may have motivational and cognitive difficulties that reduce their performance in demanding and challenging tasks. It is also conceivable that the ability of part-time employees to focus and function in a demanding work environment may be also reduced because of their preoccupation with job insecurity and inequality in work conditions relative to the full-time employees. Clearly, as the number of temporary employees is on the rise, organizations are facing a growing challenge concerning how to successfully manage the two groups of employees for the benefit of the organization.

3.5.3 The moderating role of the surrounding physical work environment

There is growing evidence that characteristics of the physical work environment such as health hazards, temperature, and noise adversely affect employee reactions, by contributing to higher levels of experienced stress (e.g., Humphrey, Nahrgang, and Morgeson 2007; Melamed, Fried, and Froom 2001). In addition, evidence also indicates that the physical work environment significantly affects the relative effectiveness of performance in demanding (i.e., complex) jobs in both industrial and office settings (e.g., Fried, Melamed, and Ben-David 2002; Oldham, Cummings, and Zhou 1995; Melamed, Fried, and Froom 2001). This is because these characteristics may either facilitate or hinder employees' ability to successfully pursue their jobs (Melamed, Fried, and Froom 2004). Moreover, the interaction between these variables and job complexity may contribute to additional outcomes that the JCM fails to address, such as stress and health-related outcomes (Humphrey, Nahrgang, and Morgeson 2007; Oldham 1996). In particular, research has supported the moderating effect of noise and workspace characteristics (e.g., spatial density) on the relation between job characteristics and work-related outcomes (e.g., Oldham, Cummings, and Zhou 1995; Fried, Melamed, and Ben-David 2002; Melamed, Fried, and Froom 2001; 2004). Moreover, in the context of increased global operations, it is important to note that different countries differ in their operations, including the degree to which they focus on the physical work environment as an important facet at work. There are also important changes in the physical work environment which affect employees' reactions to their job environment. Therefore, it is important to analyze the moderating role of the physical work environment. We will discuss the moderating role of two central factors of the physical work environment with potentially significant effects on individual reactions to their jobs: workspace characteristics and noise.

3.5.3.1   *The effect of workspace characteristics*

Evidence suggests that characteristics of the physical work environment (e.g., spatial density, number of enclosures surrounding a work area) have an important effect on employees' ability to benefit from enriched and empowered job characteristics (Fried 1990; Fried, Levi, and Laurence 2007; Oldham, Cummings, and Zhou 1995; Oldham, Kulik, and Stepina 1991). This is because these characteristics may either reduce or facilitate employees' ability to focus on their jobs (Oldham, Cummings, and Zhou 1995).

In the current work environment most employees work in an office environment, which raises the issue of the effect of this environment on employees' ability to perform (e.g., Oldham, Cummings, and Zhou 1995; Oldham, Kulik, and Stepina 1991). Specifically, employees may respond negatively to potentially debilitating social interferences caused by workspace characteristics, such as high spatial density (little space available to an individual in a given area), high social density, close interpersonal distance, or few work station physical boundaries such as walls or partitions. Working in such environments may have a negative effect on employees' ability to concentrate and perform their jobs effectively (e.g., Oldham, Cummings, and Zhou 1995). Moreover, these workspace-related interferences are expected to have the most detrimental effect on performance when job complexity is high, because the ability to concentrate and focus is then particularly important (see review by Oldham, Cummings, and Zhou 1995).

However, as discussed above, today technology enables a growing segment of the workforce to work away from traditional work sites, or to determine more generally how much to work and from where (e.g., Shamir and Salomon 1985). In fact, an increasing number of organizations adopt work structures that promote teleworking, which increases employees' control over their work environment (e.g., two of every three Fortune 500 companies employ teleworkers; Cascio 2000). Teleworking consists of several options, all of which provide employees more flexibility about where to work, and thus reduces the potential adverse effect of the work environment (Apgar 1998; Cascio 2000). One popular form for teleworking is "hoteling," which involves shared offices. In "hotel" work, spaces are reserved by the hour, day, or week. For example, at IBM, about 20,000 of its employees share offices (Cascio 2000). In its most advanced form, "hotel" work space is customized, based on individuals' personal photos and memorabilia, which are stored and retrieved electronically, based on need (Apgar 1998). Teleworking centers (or satellite offices) replace the traditional centralized facilities by a network of smaller offices that are often located near employees' or customers' homes. This relocation of offices helps to minimize commuting time and maximize productivity (Apgar 1998; Cascio 2000).

The increase in employees' control over the location of their work, may, in turn, reduce the expected negative effect of potentially adverse work space characteristics on performance on stimulating jobs. In support of this notion, May, Oldham, and

Rathert (2005) found that under high workloads, spatial density was related more weakly to crowding perceptions and area satisfaction, when the job required physical movement in the work area (i.e., employees were able to move away and thus reduce their length of stay in a potentially negative work environment).

It can be expected that the number of employees who are working outside of traditional work sites, either partially or fully, will grow in the twenty-first century. However, most employees still work at traditional sites such as offices, and we can expect that this form of work will remain commonplace for a significant portion of the workforce into the foreseeable future. We can further expect that the traditional work place will remain the norm in developing countries. Therefore, when employees are working in traditional office settings, with a limited ability to control interferences associated with workspace characteristics, organizations should consider adopting policies and practices aimed at reducing these interferences. For example, managers might develop and promote social behavior norms at work that emphasize consideration and respect toward others (Fried, Levi, and Laurence 2007).

However, in attempting to reduce the effect of work space-related interferences in the global arena, managers should take the norms of the local countries into account to ensure an accurate understanding of the prevailing definitions of concepts such as crowding, privacy, and interference. In many countries, particularly, developing ones, high levels of crowding and contact with other people, and low privacy norms, are prevalent. Moreover, people who grew up with this kind of a background may not consider this environment as debilitating, in contrast to people in more developed societies whose norms and expectations about these issues are different. In support of this argument, Zhou, Oldham, and Cummings (1998) found that employees from high-density childhood residences and urban communities showed higher performance and lower perception of crowding when in high-contact work environments (associated with few enclosures, high spatial density, and close interpersonal distance), in comparison to employees from other combinations of childhood residential density and type of community. This study suggests that the physical environment people are raised in may help determine their perceptions and experience of the physical environment at work. One can extrapolate this conclusion to suggest that when density and crowdedness are prevalent in a society, or segment of a society, it will affect peoples' standards for what they consider to be desirable versus undesirable levels of density, privacy, and interference. In societies characterized by high density and crowdedness, the issue of work space characteristics and related social interference may have a smaller effect on job performance.

3.5.3.2 *The moderating role of noise in the industrial work settings*
Ambient noise has been shown to be one of the most prevalent environmental stressors for the industrial workforce in the US and Europe (Fried, Melamed, and

Ben-David 2002; Kjelberg 1990; Tempest 1985). Evidence indicates that even moderate levels of noise contribute adversely to psychological and health-related outcomes (e.g., Kryter 1994; Sawada 1993). Moreover, noise has shown to moderate the relationship between job characteristics and work outcomes. Research on a large and representative sample of industrial employees in Israel has revealed that chronic noise, even at a moderate level, tends to have an adverse effect on the contribution of job complexity to attitudinal, behavioral, and health-related outcomes (e.g., job satisfaction, absenteeism, blood pressure, injuries) (see, e.g., Fried, Melamed, and Ben-David 2002; Melamed, Fried, and Froom 2001; 2004). These results revealed that high job complexity was detrimental to all these outcomes when noise was high. Moreover, Fried, Melamed, and Ben-David (2002) found that the interactive effect of job complexity and noise had stronger adverse effects on absenteeism among women than among men. These results support the notion that adverse physical conditions such as high noise become a source of stress to employees (Parker, Wall, and Cordery 2001), and therefore also become detrimental to employee reactions (e.g., Fried, Melamed, and Ben-David 2002; Melamed, Fried, and Froom 2001). Moreover, noise may be even more important in developing countries with fewer regulations and higher levels of exposure to noise. Therefore, multinational companies that operate in these countries should recognize the potential detrimental effect of a noisy environment on employees' ability to pursue demanding tasks, and should take steps to reduce the hazardous environment.

4. IMPLEMENTATION OF JOB DESIGN

According to the JCM, levels of job characteristics are determined by the organization, and they are expected to remain stable over time, unless the organization changes them (Hackman and Oldham 1980). Thus, the JCM, which has been the most dominant model in the job design literature, does not explicitly consider the notion that job characteristics may change as a result of the incumbents' initiative to change them (e.g., Ilgen and Hollenbeck 1992).

However, more recent theoretical frameworks and related research strongly support the notion that employees may actively change their job characteristics. For example, Rousseau (2006) introduced the concept of I-deals, which refers to idiosyncratic employment arrangements negotiated by the individual employee and his/her current or prospective employer (see also Rousseau, Ho, and Greenberg 2006). One of the important issues that an individual employee may negotiate about is changes in his/her job characteristics to satisfy personal and career-related aspirations. Other scholars have also suggested that employees may actively engage in changing their work environment, thereby contributing to changes in work outcomes (e.g., Clegg and Spencer 2007; Fried, Levi, and Laurence 2007b; Fried and Slowik 2004; Fried et al. 1999; Ilgen and Hollenbeck 1992; Wrzesniewski and Dutton 2001). For example, Wrzesniewski and Dutton (2001) argued that employees tend to craft their jobs by psychologically redefining and behaviorally changing the characteristics of their jobs. Similarly, Dawis and Lofquist (1984) discuss in their theory of work adjustment the role of "activeness," which focuses on the involvement of employees in the process of changing their environment to achieve better fit. Similarly, in their job-role differentiation theory, Ilgen and Hollenbeck (1992) also discuss how employees negotiate changes in their "emergent task elements." Finally, on the basis of their Leader-Member Exchange theory, Graen and Scandura (1987) discuss how employees help produce changes in their job responsibilities through negotiations with their superiors. Research has supported this notion by showing that employees often respond to personal and contextual expectations by altering their jobs and roles to enhance fit with these expectations (Ashford and Black 1996; Black and Ashford 1995; Fried, Levi, and Laurence 2007).

It is conceivable that the increased pressure on employees to adjust to the growing changes in the global work environment will produce higher job crafting initiated and pursued by the employees, as a mechanism to enhance their ability to manage the uncertain environment and its effect on work-related demands (cf. Fried, Levi, and Laurence 2007). It is also conceivable that supervisors and peers will encourage these initiatives for job crafting by employees, and will support the implementation process. This will be likely to the extent that they recognize the importance of these changes to employees' ability to function and contribute in a global environment characterized by uncertainty and change (Fried, Levi, and Laurence 2007).

5. CONCLUSION AND FUTURE DIRECTIONS

In the present chapter we have analyzed the potential development of the job design area in the twenty-first century. The premise underlying our analysis is that the growing contingencies in the work environment associated, for example, with global and cross-cultural operations, and the increased diversity in the workforce, will require greater sophistication in integrating the different conceptual frameworks and empirical findings, for the purpose of investigating and analyzing the role and effect of job design.

For example, in addition to the JCM, the interdisciplinary job design approach developed by Campion and his colleagues (e.g., Campion 1988; Campion and

Thayer 1985; 1987) is another major theory in the area of job design. This theory identifies four approaches to job design: motivational, mechanical, biological, and perceptual/motor. Consistent with the framework of contexts discussed in this chapter, the job design features of three of the approaches (biological, mechanistic, and perceptual/motor) can potentially be applied as context factor contingencies to the relationships between the core job characteristics of the JCM (which corresponds to the motivational approach in the interdisciplinary model) and employee reactions. For example, noise at work, a factor associated with the biological approach, or characteristics of the architectural design (work space characteristics), associated with the biological and perceptual/motor approach, can be conceptualized as contextual moderators of the relation between job complexity and employee reactions.

Related to the above, the growing contingencies and their importance in the work environment appear to support the development of a "meso theory," which would attempt to systematically specify the relative importance of different job characteristics in predicting outcomes in different contexts and circumstances. For example, as indicated, in high reliability organizations autonomy typically is low and does not play an important role in affecting employee performance. On the other hand, the experience of task significance (the experience of positively affecting others' life) is likely to play an important role in these organizations, in contributing to employees' motivation and performance (e.g., Grant 2007; Grant et al. 2007). In addition, autonomy is expected to be an important contributor in low power distance cultures, but may play a relatively minor and possibly even a negative role in high power distance cultures (e.g., Robert et al. 2000). In yet another example, the literature suggests that the contribution of autonomy to employees' motivation and performance tends to be contingent on the complexity of the tasks for which the employee is responsible. Research conducted by Mullarkey et al. (1997), and Wright and Cordery (1999) demonstrate that having a high level of control (which corresponds to a high level of autonomy) over their work does not necessarily mean employees experience a high level of motivation and satisfaction at work. Instead, high control over the work environment contributes to positive reactions only when the employees are involved in challenging, non-routine operations associated with production uncertainty (as is the case, for example, in knowledge-based units). On the other hand, a high level of control over one's work tends to lead to low motivation and satisfaction when the work is routine and predictable (e.g., Parker, Wall, and Cordery 2001; Wright and Cordery 1999). This is because the lack of challenge contributes to frustration and boredom (cf. Pearce and Ravlin 1987). Thus, when high autonomy is applied to a simple job, often characterized by low skill variety, task identity, and task significance, the high experience of control associated with high autonomy may actually contribute to negative consequences.

In the present chapter we have attempted to analyze the role and contribution of job design in the twenty-first century. We hope that the ideas presented here will guide future theoretical development and research directions.

References

AIELLO, J. R. and KOLB, K. J. 1995. Electronic performance monitoring and social context: impact on productivity and stress. *Journal of Applied Psychology*, 80 (3): 339–64.

ALBERTSON, L. A. 1977. Telecommunications as a travel substitute: some psychological, organizational, and social aspects. *Journal of Communications*, 27 (2): 32–42.

ANDERSON, S. E. and WILLIAMS, L. J. 1996. Interpersonal, job, and individual factors related to helping processes at work. *Journal of Applied Psychology*, 81 (3): 282–96.

ANDREOU, A. N. and BOONE, L. W. 2002. The impact of information technology and cultural differences on organizational behavior in the financial services industry. *Journal of Intellectual Capital*, 3: 248–61.

APGAR, M., IV. 1998. The alternative workplace: changing where and how people work. *Harvard Business Review*, 76 (3): 121–35.

ASHFORD, S. J., and BLACK, J. S. 1996. Proactivity during organizational entry: the role of desire for control. *Journal of Applied Psychology*, 81 (2): 199–215.

BATT, R. 1999. Work organization, technology, and performance in customer service and sales. *Industrial and Labor Relations Review*, 52 (4): 539–65.

BERCHEM, S. P. 2005. Rebound: ASA's Annual Economic Analysis of the Staffing Industry. American Staffing Association. Alexandria, VA.

BLACK, J. S., and ASHFORD, S. J. 1995. Fitting in or making jobs fit: factors affecting mode of adjustment for new hires. *Human Relations*, 48 (4): 421–37.

BOYCE, A. S., RYAN, A. M., IMUS, A. L., and MORGESON, F. P. 2007. Temporary worker, permanent loser? A model of the stigmatization of temporary workers. *Journal of Management*, 33 (1): 5–29.

BREAUGH, J. A. 1985. The measurement of work autonomy. *Human Relations*, 38 (6): 551–70.

—— and BECKER, A. S. 1987. Further examination of the work autonomy scales: three studies. *Human Relations*, 40 (6): 381–99.

CAMPION, M. A. 1988. Interdisciplinary approaches to job design: a constructive replication with extensions. *Journal of Applied Psychology*, 73: 467–81.

—— and THAYER, P. W. 1985. Development and field evaluation of an interdisciplinary measure of job design. *Journal of Applied Psychology*, 70 (1): 29–44.

—— —— (1987). Job design: approaches, outcomes, and trade-offs. *Organizational Dynamics*, 15 (3): 66–79.

CASCIO, W. F. 2000. Managing a virtual workplace. *Academy of Management Executive*, 14 (3): 81–90.

CLEGG, C., and SPENCER, C. 2007. A circular and dynamic model to the process of job design. *Journal of Occupational and Organizational Psychology*, 80: 321–39.

COHEN, S. G., and BAILEY, D. E. 1997. What makes teams work: group effectiveness from the shop floor to the executive suite. *Journal of Management*, 23 (3): 239–90.

DAWIS, R. V., and LOFQUIST, L. H. 1984. *A Psychological Theory of Work Adjustment.* Minneapolis: University of Minnesota Press.

DE VARO, J., LI, R., and BROOKSHIRE, D. 2007. Analysing the job characteristics model: new support from a cross-section of establishments. *International Journal of Human Resource Management,* 18 (6): 986–1003.

DRACH-ZAHAVY, A. 2004. The proficiency trap: how to balance enriched job designs and the team's need for support. *Journal of Organizational Behavior,* 25 (8): 979–96.

EREZ, M., and GATI, E. 2004. A dynamic, multi-level model of culture: from the micro-level to the individual to the macro-level of global culture. *Applied Psychology: An International Review,* 53 (4): 583–98.

EYLON, D., and AU, K. Y. 1999. Exploring empowerment cross-cultural differences among the power distance dimension. *International Journal of Intercultural Relations,* 23: 373–85.

FELDMAN, D. C., and BOLINO, M. C. 1996. Careers within careers: reconceptualizing the nature of career anchors and their consequences. *Human Resource Management Review,* 6 (2): 89–112.

FRIED, Y. 1990. Workspace characteristics, behavioral interferences, and screening ability as joint predictors of employee reactions: an examination of the intensification approach. *Journal of Organizational Behavior,* 11: 267–80.

—— and FERRIS, G. R. 1987. The validity of the job characteristics model: a review and meta-analysis. *Personnel Psychology,* 40 (2): 287–322.

—— and SLOWIK, L. H. 2004. Enriching goal-setting theory with time: an integrated approach. *Academy of Management Review,* 29 (3): 404–22.

—— LEVI, A. S., and LAURENCE, G. 2007. The Job Characteristics Model and LMX-MMX leadership. Pp. 157–97 in *LMX Leadership: The Series,* vol. v, ed. J. B. Graen. Charlotte, NC: Information Age Publishing

—— MELAMED, S., and BEN-DAVID, H. A. 2002. The joint effects of noise, job complexity, and gender on employee sickness absence: an exploratory study across 21 organizations— the CORDIS study. *Journal of Occupational and Organizational Psychology,* 75: 131–44.

—— OLDHAM, G. R., and CUMMINGS, L. A. 1998. Job design. Pp. 532–43 in *International Encyclopedia of Business and Management,* ed. M. Poole and M. Warener. London: International Thomson Business Press.

—— HOLLENBECK J. R., SLOWIK, L. H., TIEGS, R. B., and BEN-DAVID, H. A. (1999). Changes in job decision latitude: the influence of personality and interpersonal satisfaction. *Journal of Vocational Behavior,* 54: 233–43.

—— SNIDER, C., HADANI, M., and LEVI, A. S. 2006. Job design. Pp. 392–6 in *The Encyclopedia of Industrial and Organizational Psychology,* vol. i, ed. S. G. Rogelberg. Thousand Oaks, CA: Sage Publishing.

—— GRANT, A., LEVI, A., HADANI, M. SLOWIK, L. H. 2007. Placing the job characteristics model in context: the contributing role of time. *Journal of Organizational Behavior,* 28: 911–27.

GELFAND, M. J., EREZ, M., and AYCAN, Z. 2007. Cross-cultural organizational behavior. *Annual Review of Psychology,* 58: 479–514.

GRAEN, G. B., and SCANDURA T. A. 1987. Toward a psychology of dyadic organizing. *Research in Organizational Behavior,* 9: 175–208.

GRANT, A. M. 2007. Relational job design and the motivation to make a prosocial difference. *Academy of Management Review,* 32 (2): 393–417.

—— In press. The significance of task significance: job performance effects, relational mechanisms, and boundary conditions. *Journal of Applied Psychology.*

GRANT, A. M., CAMPBELL, E. M., CHEN, G., COTTONE, K., LAPEDIS, D., and LEE, K. 2007. Impact and the art of motivation maintenance: the effects of contact with beneficiaries on persistence behavior. *Organizational Behavior and Human Decision Processes*, 103 (1): 53–67.

GREENHOUSE, J. H., and BEUTELL, N. J. 1985. Sources of conflict between work and family roles. *Academy of Management Review*, 10: 76–88.

GRIFFIN, R. W. 1983. Objective and social sources of information in task redesign: a field experiment. *Administrative Science Quarterly*, 28 (2): 184–200.

—— 1991. Effects of work redesign on employee perceptions, attitudes, and behaviors: a long-term investigation. *Academy of Management Journal*, 34 (2): 425–35.

HACKMAN, J. R. 1990. Groups that work (and those that don't). San Francisco: Jossey-Bass.

—— 2002. Leading teams: setting the stage for great performances. Boston: Harvard Business School Press.

—— and LAWLER, E. E. 1971. Corporate profits and employee satisfaction: must they be in conflict? *California Management Review*, 14 (1): 46–55.

—— and OLDHAM, G. R. 1976. Motivation through the design of work: test of a theory. *Organizational Behavior and Human Performance*, 16: 250–79.

—— —— 1980. Work Redesign. Reading, MA: Addison-Wesley.

HALL, D. T. 1996. Protean careers of the 21st century. *Academy of Management Executive*, 10 (4): 8–16.

HAMBRICK, D. C., and FUKUTOMI, G. D. S. 1991. The seasons of a CEO's tenure. *Academy of Management Review*, 16: 719–42.

HARRISON, D. A., JOHNS, G., and MARTOCCHIO, J. J. 2000. Changes in technology, teamwork, and diversity: new directions for a new century of absenteeism research. *Research in Personnel and Human Resources Management*, 18: 43–91.

HOCHSCHILD, A. R. 1983. *The Managed Heart*. Berkeley and Los Angeles: University of California Press.

HUANG, X., and VAN DE VLIERT, E. 2003. Where intrinsic job satisfaction fails to work: national moderators of intrinsic motivation. *Journal of Organizational Behavior*, 24 (2): 159–79.

HUMPHREY, S. E., NAHRGANG, J. D. and MORGESON, F. P. 2007. Integrating motivational, social, and contextual work design futures: a meta-analytic summary and theoretical extension of the work design literature. *Journal of Applied Psychology*, 92 (5): 1332–56.

ILGEN, D. R. and HOLLENBECK, J. R. 1992. The structure of work: job design and roles. Pp. 165–208 in *Handbook of Industrial and Organizational Psychology*, vol. ii, ed. M. D. Dunette and L. M. Hough. Palo Alto, CA: Consulting Psychologists Press.

JAHODA, M. 1979. The Impact on unemployment in the 1930s and the 1970s. *Bulletin of the British Psychological Society*, 32: 309–14.

JANZ, B. D., COLQUITT, J. A., and NOE, R. A. 1997. Knowledge worker team effectiveness: the role of autonomy, interdependence, team development, and contextual support variables. *Personnel Psychology*, 50: 877–904.

KATZ, R. 1978a. The influence of job longevity on employee reactions to task characteristics. *Human Relations*, 31 (8): 703–25.

—— 1978b. Job longevity as a situational factor in job satisfaction. *Administrative Science Quarterly*, 23 (2): 204–23.

—— 1980. Time and work: toward an integrative perspective. Pp. 81–127 in *Research in Organizational Behavior*, ii, ed. B. M. Staw and L. L. Cummings. Greenwich, CT: JAI Press.

KIRKMAN, B. L. and SHAPIRO, D. L. 1997. The impact of cultural values on employee resistance to teams: toward a model of globalized self-managing work team effectiveness. *Academy of Management Review*, 22 (3): 730–57.

KJELBERG, A. 1990. Subjective, behavioral and psychophysiological effects of noise. *Scandinavian Journal of Work, Environment and Health*, 16: 29–38.

KLUGER, A. N., and DENISI, A. 1996. Effects of feedback intervention on performance: a historical review, a meta-analysis, and a preliminary feedback intervention theory. *Psychological Bulletin*, 119: 254–84.

KOPELMAN, R. E. 1985. Job redesign and productivity: a review of the evidence. *National Productivity Review*, 4 (2): 237–55.

KRYTER, K. D. 1994. *The Handbook of Hearing and the Effects of Noise: Physiology, Psychology, and Public Health*. New York: Academic Press.

LANGFRED, C. W. 2007. The downside of self-management: a longitudinal study of the effects of conflict on trust, autonomy, and task interdependence in self-managing teams. *Academy of Management Journal*, 50 (4): 885–900.

LATHAM, G. P., and PINDER, C. C. 2005. Work motivation theory and research at the dawn of the twenty-first century. *Annual Review of Psychology*, 56: 485–516.

LAWLER, E. E. 1994. From job-based to competency-based organizations. *Journal of Organizational Behavior*, 15 (1): 3–15.

—— and FINEGOLD, D. 2000. Individualizing the organization: past, present, and future. *Organizational Dynamics*, 29 (1): 1–15.

LOHER, B. T., NOE, R. A., MOELLER, N. L., and FITZGERALD, M. P. 1985. A meta-analysis of the relation of job characteristics to job satisfaction. *Journal of Applied Psychology*, 70 (2): 280–9.

MACY, B. A., and IZUMI, H. 1993. Organizational change, design, and work innovation: a meta-analysis of 131 North American field studies—1961–1991. Pp. 235–313 in *Research in Organizational Change and Development*, vol. vii, ed. W. Pasmore and R. Woodman. Greenwich, CT: JAI Press.

MAN, D. C., and LAM, S. S. K. 2003. The effects of job complexity and autonomy on cohesiveness in collectivistic and individualistic work groups: a cross-cultural analysis. *Journal of Organizational Behavior*, 24 (8): 979–1001.

MAY, D. R., OLDHAM, G. R., and RATHERT, C. 2005. Employee affective and behavioral reactions to the spatial density of physical work environments. *Human Resource Management*, 44 (1): 21–33.

MAYER, R. C., DAVIS, J. H., and SCHOORMAN, F. D. 1995. An integration model of organizational trust. *Academy of Management Review*, 20 (3): 709–34.

MELAMED, S., FRIED, Y., and FROOM, P. 2001. The interactive effect of chronic exposure to noise and job complexity on changes in blood pressure and job satisfaction: a longitudinal study of industrial employees. *Journal of Occupational Health Psychology*, 6: 182–95.

—— —— —— 2004. The joint effect of noise exposure and job complexity on distress and injury risk among men and women: the cardiovascular occupational risk factors determination in Israel study. *Journal of Occupational and Environmental Medicine*, 46 (10): 1023–32.

MORGESON, F. P., and CAMPION, M. A. 2003. Work design. Pp. 423–52 in *Handbook of Psychology*, xii: *Industrial and Organizational Psychology*, ed. W. Borman, R. Klimoski, and D. Ilgen. New York: John Wiley.

—— and HUMPHREY, S. E. 2006. The work design questionnaire (WDQ): developing and validating a comprehensive measure for assessing job design and the nature of work. *Journal of Applied Psychology*, 91 (6): 1321–39.

MULLARKEY, S., JACKSON, P. R., WALL, T. D., WILSON, J. R., and GREY-TAYLOR, S. M. 1997. The impact of technology characteristics and job control on worker mental health. *Journal of Organizational Behavior*, 18 (5): 471–90.

OLDHAM, G. R. 1996. Job design. Pp. 33–60 in *International Review of Industrial and Organizational Psychology*, ed. C. L. Cooper and I. T. Robertson. Chichester: Wiley.

—— CUMMINGS, A., and ZHOU, J. 1995. The spatial configuration of organizations: a review of the literature and some new research directions. Pp. 1–37 in *Research in Personnel and Human Resources Management*, vol. xiii, ed. G. Ferris Greenwich, CT: JAI Press.

—— KULIK, C. T., and STEPINA, L. P. 1991. Physical environments and employee reactions: effects of stimulus-screening skills and job complexity. *Academy of Management Journal*, 34: 929–38.

—— —— AMBROSE, M. L., STEPINA, L. P., and Brand, J. F. 1986. Relations between job facet comparisons and employee reactions. *Organizational Behavior and Human Decision Processes*, 38 (1): 28–48.

ORPEN, C. 1979. The effects of job enrichment on employee satisfaction, motivation, involvement, and performance: a field experiment. *Human Relations*, 32 (3): 189–217.

PARKER, S. K. 1998. Enhancing role breadth self-efficacy: the roles of job enrichment and other organizational interventions. *Journal of Applied Psychology*, 83: 835–52.

—— WALL, T. D., and CORDERY J. L. 2001. Future work design research and practice: towards an elaborated model of work design. *Journal of Occupational and Organizational Psychology*, 74: 413–40.

—— GRIFFIN, M. A., SPRIGG, C. A., and WALL, T. D. 2002. Effect of temporary contracts on perceived work characteristics and job strain: a longitudinal study. *Personnel Psychology*, 55 (3): 689–719.

PEARCE, J. A., II, and RAVLIN, E. C. 1987. The design and activation of self-regulating work groups. *Human Relations*, 40 (11): 751–83.

POUGH, S. D. 2001. Service with smile: emotional contagion in the service encounter. *Academy of Management Journal*, 44: 1018–27.

ROBERT, C., PROBST, T. M., MARTOCCHIO, J. J., DRASGOW, F., and LAWLER, E. E. 2000. Empowerment and continuous improvement in the United States, Mexico, Poland, and India: predicting fit on the basis of the dimensions of power distance and individualism. *Journal of Applied Psychology*, 85 (5): 643–58.

ROE, R. A., ZINOVIEVA, I. L., DIENES, E., and TEN HORN, L. A. 2000. Test of a model of work motivation in Bulgaria, Hungary and the Netherlands. *Applied Psychology—An International Review*, 49 (4): 658–87.

ROUSSEAU, D. M. 2006. Is there such a thing as "evidence based management"? *Academy of Management Review*, 31 (2): 256–69.

—— and FRIED, Y. 2001. LOCATION, location, location: contextualizing organizational research. *Journal of Organizational Behavior*, 22 (1): 1–13.

—— HO, V. T., and GREENBURG, J. 2006. I-Deals: idiosyncratic terms in employment relationships. *Academy of Management Review*, 31 (4): 977–94.

SAWADA, Y. 1993. Reprodycibal increases in blood pressure during intermittent noise exposure: underlying haemodynamic mechanisms specific to passive coping. *European Journal of Applied Physiology*, 67: 367–74.

SHAMIR, B., and SALOMON, I. 1985. Work-at-home and the quality of working life. *Academy of Management Review*, 10 (3): 455–64.

SHOKEF, E., and EREZ, M. 2006. Shared meaning systems in multinational teams. Pp. 325–52 in *National Culture and Groups: Research on Managing Groups and Teams*, vol. ix, ed. B. Mannix, M. Neal, and Y.-R. Chen. San-Diego: Elsevier JAI Press.

SITKIN, S. 1992. Learning through failure: the strategy of small losses. *Research in Organizational Behavior*, 14: 231–66.

SPECTOR, P. E. 1985. Higher-order need strength as a moderator of the job scope–employee outcome relationship: a meta-analysis. *Journal of Occupational Psychology*, 58 (2): 119–27.

TAYLOR, F. 1911. *The Principles of Scientific Management*, New York: Norton.

TEMPEST, W. 1985. Noise in industry. Pp. 179–94 in *The Noise Handbook*, ed. W. Tempest. London: Academic Press.

TIEGS, R. B., TETRICK, L. E., and FRIED, Y. 1992. Growth need strength and context satisfactions as moderators of the relations of the job characteristics model. *Journal of Management*, 18 (3): 575–93.

TRIANDIS, H. C. 1993. Collectivism and individualism as cultural syndromes. *Journal of Comparative Social Sciences*, 27 (3–4): 155–80.

TRIST, E. L., SUSMAN, G. I., and BROWN, G. R. 1977. An experiment in autonomous working in an American underground coal mine. *Human Relations*, 30: 201–36.

—— HIGGIN, G. W., MURRAY, H., and POLLOCK, A. B. 1963. *Organizational Choice*. London: Tavistock Publications.

TSUI, A. S., NIFADKAR, S. S., and OU, A. Y. 2007. Cross-national, cross-cultural organizational behavior research: advances, gaps, and recommendations. *Journal of Management*, 33 (3): 426–78.

TURNER, A. N., and LAWRENCE, P. R. 1965. *Individual Jobs and the Worker*. Boston: Harvard UNIVERSITY, Graduate School of Business Administration.

UHL-BIEN, M., and GRAEN, G. 1998. Individual self-management: analysis of professionals' self-managing activities in functional and cross-functional work teams. *Academy of Management Journal*, 41: 340–50.

—— —— and SCANDURA, T. A. 2000. Implications of leader-member exchange (LMX) for strategic human resource management systems: relationships as social capital for competitive advantage. *Research in Personnel and Human Resource Management*, 18: 137–85.

VOGUS, T. J., and WELBOURNE, T. M. 2003. Structuring for high reliability: HR practices and mindful processes in reliability-seeking organizations. *Journal of Organizational Behavior*, 24 (7).

WALL, T. D., and JACKSON, P. R. 1995. New manufacture initiatives and shop floor work design. Pp. 139–74 in *The Changing Nature of Work*, ed. A. Howard. San Francisco: Jossey-Bass.

WRIGHT, B. M., and CORDERY, J. L. 1999. Production uncertainty as a contextual moderator of employee reactions to job design. *Journal of Applied Psychology*, 84 (3): 456–62.

WRZESNIEWSKI, A., and DUTTON, J. E. 2001. Crafting a job: revisioning employees as active crafters of their work. *Academy of Management Review*, 26 (2): 179–202.

ZHOU, J., OLDHAM, G. R., and CUMMINGS, A. 1998. Employee reactions to the physical work environment: effects of childhood residential attributes. *Journal of Applied Social Psychology*, 28 (24): 2213–38.

ZOHAR, D., and LURIA, G. 2003. Organizational meta-scripts as a source of high reliability: the case of an army armored brigade. *Journal of Organizational Behavior*, 24 (7): 837–59.

Name Index

SUBJECT INDEX

and well-being and health 374–6
360-degree feedback 228–9
  and job performance 297
  and on-line testing 241
  and organizational politics 401
  and performance appraisal 329
Threshold Trait Analysis (TTA), and job
      analysis 146
tokenism 529
trade unions, *see* labor relations
training:
  and adaptability 379–81
    active learning 380
    active processing 379
    error training 379
    problem-based learning 380
    technological aids 381
    transfer of training 379
    variety of experiences 380
  and remote working 579–80
training evaluation:
  and changing nature of work 292–3
  and conceptual frameworks 303–4
    attitudes 304
    change models 305–6
    multilevel effects 304–5
  and criteria for 293–4
    four level framework 293–4
    interrelationships among 300–1
    learning outcomes 294–6
    nomological network connecting 300–1
    organizational impact 298–300
    performance constructs 296–7
    trainee perceptions 294
  and definition of 291
  and experimental design and
      methodology 301–3
    computer programs 307
    expanding methodologies 306–8
    formative evaluation 309
    mixed methods 307
    qualitative methods 307–8
    rapid evaluation and assessment method
      (REAM) 309–10
    summative evaluation 309
  and feedback 291
  and formative evaluation 309
  and influence on decision-makers 308–10
  and return on investment (ROI) analysis 298
  and utility analysis 298–300
trait activation theory 76–7, 83
  and assessment center research 231
    construct validity 231
    convergent validity 224–6, 231

correlations with other assessment
    methods 227–9
  criterion-related validity 229–30
  discriminant validity 226–7, 231
  external validation 227–9, 231
  predictor validity 229–30, 231
and assessment centers 215–16, 220–1
  assessor training 223
  development of exercises 222
  dimensions 222–3
  feedback reports 223–4
  implications for practice 221–4, 230
  role-player instructions 223
  scoring methods 223
  trait activation potential 230
and Big Five personality model 219
and main ideas of:
  situation strength 218–20
  situation trait relevance 217–18
  trait-related work behavior 220
and person-situation interactions 217
trait complexes 15
traits:
  and definition of 123
  and entrepreneurship 123
    Big Five trait taxonomy 123–5
    need for achievement 126
    process view of 130–1, 132
    processes affecting role of 129–30
    processes mediating role of 128–9
    risk-taking 126
    situational conditions 129–30
    specific traits 125–6
  and leadership 101–3
  and personality 59–60
  see also personality
transactional leadership 108, 109
transformational leadership 108–9
true scores, and reliability 264–7
trust:
  and remote working 573, 577
  and self-managed teams 596
turnover 371
  and bullying 486, 487
  and organizational politics 391
  and remote working 567

United States Army, and job performance
    appraisal 319–20
utility analysis, and training evaluation 298–300

validity of tests and assessments 163–4, 187–8,
    263–4
  and assessment centers: